R. Selig.
-1958-

Developments in the

VOLUME I

Technique and Theory

Rorschach Technique

BRUNO KLOPFER

Clinical Professor of Psychology,
University of California at Los Angeles

MARY D. AINSWORTH

Department of Psychology, Johns Hopkins University.
Psychologist, Sheppard and Enoch Pratt Hospital, Baltimore

WALTER G. KLOPFER

Chief, Psychological Services, Norfolk (Nebraska) State Hospital.
Assistant Professor of Medical Psychology, University of
Nebraska College of Medicine

ROBERT R. HOLT

Director, Research Center for Mental Health,
Graduate School of Arts and Science,
New York University

World Book Company · *Yonkers-on-Hudson, New York*

Preface

Since the publication of *The Rorschach Technique** in 1942 a great deal of new research and experience with the methods then advocated has been accumulating. The *1946 Supplement* gave a brief survey of the main trends of development up to that date. However, most of these developments have not been brought together in book form; they have been passed on orally in the ever-expanding teaching programs or—at best—have been circulated in mimeographed form. It is true that a voluminous literature on the research and clinical aspects of the Rorschach has been published, but there remains a need for a discussion of the present status of procedures outlined in the 1942 and 1946 publications.

The actual use of *The Rorschach Technique* in teaching has brought to light another need—an urgent need for clarification and amplification of many points that were treated only sketchily in their first formulation. This need has been further reinforced by a process of fusion through the interchange of experiences within the increasing group of competent psychologists using the Rorschach method in clinical practice, teaching, and research.

When the present authors undertook a new treatment of the Rorschach field, this question arose: whether it would be preferable to write a supplementary book, summarizing all the recent developments, or a book of collected papers giving as many competent people as possible an opportunity to contribute their experiences and points of view (as has been done on several occasions recently in the field of projective techniques).

* Bruno Klopfer and Douglas McGlashan Kelley, *The Rorschach Technique*. World Book Company, 1942. New edition with *1946 Supplement* by Bruno Klopfer and Helen H. Davidson, 1946.

The actual procedure followed in these two volumes attempts a synthesis of the two methods, emphasizing the first procedure in Volume I (*Technique and Theory*) and the second procedure in Volume II (*Fields of Application*). The contributors—in addition to being thoroughly experienced in the use of the Rorschach technique—command positions in their fields of application that afford them a broad overview of the field and the necessary perspective to see the application of the Rorschach technique within an appropriate frame of reference.

In this way these two volumes attempt to combine the best features of a technical monograph, a manual, and a handbook. Parts One, Two, and Four of Volume I (Chapters 1 through 13, and 17 through 19) would best be classified as a manual that attempts to be helpful to the practicing clinician but is meant to serve chiefly as a teaching device. It is this portion that is primarily designed to make more explicit and more complete the methods of administration, scoring, and interpretation proposed in *The Rorschach Technique*. The rest of the material in the two volumes is less specifically concerned with these methods, drawing freely upon the findings of those who have used other systems of administration and scoring and somewhat differing interpretative hypotheses. The third part of Volume I ("Theory," Chapters 14, 15, and 16) aims more at the function of a technical monograph on theoretical problems, attempting—with the help of a critical overview of the literature—to relate technical and clinical experience to a theoretical frame of reference. The lack of such a frame of reference was the most pertinent criticism directed against previous publications. The special role of Chapter 16 and the Appendix is discussed in detail at the beginning of the second section of Chapter 16.

The second volume covers the main fields of application after the style of a handbook. It discusses the use of the Rorschach method in the clinical field, in the fields of anthropology and sociology, and in the field of developmental psychology, especially child guidance. It also provides as complete a bibliography as can be assembled at this point and as many more sample case studies beyond the one illustrative case study included in Volume I as space permits.

The bracketed numbers in the text refer to lists of references at the ends of chapters. The Index of Names contains names of all authors appearing in these references, in the text, or in footnotes. An Index of Subject Matter follows the name index. Volume I has its own indexes, while Volume II has cumulative indexes.

As a conclusion to this preface to Volume I, the authors want to extend their thanks to many friends and colleagues who patiently read drafts of various chapters and made helpful comments. Unfortunately, the list of these friendly critics is too long to be given here. The authors' gratitude is none the less sincere for having to be expressed in this general way.

BRUNO KLOPFER

MARY D. AINSWORTH

WALTER G. KLOPFER

ROBERT R. HOLT

Acknowledgments

For permission to reprint extracts from copyrighted material, grateful acknowledgment is made to the following publishers, publications, and authors:

The American Psychological Association for excerpts from the *Journal of Abnormal and Social Psychology* and *Psychological Monographs.*

The British Journal of Medical Psychology for portions of an article by Mary D. Ainsworth.

The Bulletin of the Menninger Clinic for an excerpt from an article by David Rapaport.

Educational and Psychological Measurement for an excerpt from an article by L. J. Cronbach.

Harvard University Press for an excerpt from E. Mayo, *Some Notes on the Psychology of Pierre Janet.*

The Hogarth Press, Ltd., for excerpts from Sigmund Freud, *The Ego and the Id, Civilization and Its Discontents,* and "Analysis Terminable and Interminable" (in Volume V of *The Collected Papers of Sigmund Freud*) .

International Universities Press for an excerpt from *The Psychoanalytic Study of the Child.*

Journal of Nervous and Mental Disease for an excerpt from H. Nunberg, *Practice and Theory of Psychoanalysis.*

Journal of Projective Techniques for excerpts from articles by W. D. Ross and S. L. Block and by P. G. Vorhaus.

Journal of Social Psychology for excerpts from an article by Henry A. Murray.

Modern Library, Inc., for an excerpt from *The Basic Writings of Sigmund Freud,* translated and edited by A. A. Brill.

W. W. Norton & Company, Inc., for excerpts from O. Fenichel, *The Psychoanalytic Theory of Neurosis.*

Oxford University Press, Inc., for excerpts from Henry A. Murray et al., *Explorations in Personality.*

G. P. Putnam's Sons for an excerpt from Pierre Janet, *The Mental State of Hystericals.*

The Rorschach Institute, Inc., and World Book Company for reproductions of pages from the *Rorschach Individual Record Blank,* by Bruno Klopfer and Helen H. Davidson.

Dr. P. G. Vorhaus for excerpts from an unpublished paper.

World Book Company for excerpts from *The Rorschach Technique,* by Bruno Klopfer and Douglas M. Kelley.

Year Book Publishers, Inc., for excerpts from David Rapaport, Merton M. Gill, and Roy Schafer, *Diagnostic Psychological Testing.*

Contents

Part Three: Theory

Part Four: Reporting of Findings

Part One

Administration and Scoring

CHAPTER **1**

Administration

The purpose of the Rorschach technique, like that of any other clinical instrument, is to provide a relatively standardized situation in which behavior can be observed. The assumption is that, on the basis of this limited sample of behavior, it will be possible to predict other kinds of behavior on the part of the subject in other situations. As a projective technique, the Rorschach has the further characteristic of providing a relatively ambiguous stimulus situation which will enable the subject to optimally reveal his individuality of functioning. This point is taken up in greater detail in Part Three.

Preparation of the Subject for the Examination

The Relationship between the Subject and the Examiner

One of the important sources of information that we have in the Rorschach examination is the relationship that exists between the subject taking the test and the clinician administering it. The fact that this information is often used is indicated by the frequently found "behavior note" in the psychological test report. Although it is desirable to have "good" rapport, it is unnecessary to assume that this is essential in order for the test report to be valid. It seems more important that the relationship, whatever it is, should be clearly perceived and understood by the examiner. If the subject is able to relate to the examiner only with some difficulty, if characteristics like negativism and flights from reality occur, they may indeed influence the interpretation of the test results. However, there is no reason to assume that test results obtained under these conditions are "invalid" in the sense of being unusable as a source of important data relevant to personality diagnosis. The kind of role-playing activity engaged in by the subject will be an important source of information for the final evaluation. The interpretation of unusual responses, especially those characterized by unwarranted generalizations or peculiar additions, would be considerably modified if the subject were found to have a facetious attitude.

The examiner should be careful to remember that his particular personality and approach will have a general effect on his relationships with subjects. On the other hand, the particular predilections of the subject may lead him to cast the examiner in a role quite regardless of the reality facts of the examiner's personality. Thus, for example, some subjects may view all older males as authoritarian figures, and react to the examiner as they are accustomed to act towards such figures. On the other hand, the subject may be inclined to interpret any permissiveness on the part of the examiner as an attempt at seduction.

The methods by which an individual examiner becomes aware of his personal stimulus value in the Rorschach situation are similar to those usually employed in acquiring increased understanding and insight into one's own personality. A discussion of this point is obviously beyond the scope of this book.

Assessing the Present Condition of the Subject

In order to place the test behavior in its proper frame of reference, it is extremely important to know something about the condition of the subject at the time the test is administered. First, the examiner would need to know the physical condition of the subject, since factors like malnutrition, fatigue, a recent exposure to somatic therapy, may have a strong influence on the subject's current behavior. Secondly, it is important to have data on the current psychological condition of the subject. If something has recently occurred to upset him, if there has been a recent visit on the part of his relatives, if he has just left a psychotherapeutic session, there may be repercussions which can become manifest in the formal and content characteristics of his Rorschach responses. An example of this is the patient who gave a number of "cloud" and "smoke" responses on his protocol and subsequently opened his hand and handed the examiner a crumpled referral sheet, which stated: "This patient is to be examined in order to determine the severity of his psychosis."

The Set of the Subject

Naturally, it is of considerable importance to give the subject the correct instructions immediately prior to the performance proper phase of the examination. The kinds of instructions that seem most productive are those suggested in an earlier publication [5] to the effect that the subject should say something about what the blots remind him of, what they might represent, or what they could be. It is sometimes important to point out that there are no right or wrong answers; with some subjects, it is necessary to reiterate this point throughout the examination. If the subject feels that there is some doubt as to the purpose of the examination, this question should be taken up by the examiner. It is usually best to say that the test is part of an over-all attempt to evaluate the subject's physical and mental assets and liabilities. The point can be made that, in order to best help the patient, his physician feels that a thorough checkup in various aspects of his functioning is indicated. If the patient continues to be anxious, as much time as is necessary must be spent to make him as comfortable as possible. If it is still felt that the examination would produce more anxiety in the patient, it had better be postponed or eliminated.

An important aspect of the subject's set is the kind of statement made about the test by the referring individual. Very often, the referrent imbues the subject with certain doubtful or negative feelings of his own about psychological testing. In this case, the examiner has the doubly difficult task of dealing with the subject's concern without unduly disturbing the relationship between the subject and the referring professional person.

In summary, it might be stated that the purpose of the Rorschach technique, which is to provide an opportunity for the expression of individuality in a standardized situation, can best be served by relieving the testing situation of any unnecessary stresses and strains. Obviously, a severely disturbed patient will continue to be so in spite of attempts to establish rapport. Any unusual features of the examiner-subject relationship should not be glossed over, but used as one of the sources of information in arriving at conclusions about test performance. The examiner should familiarize himself in advance with the current environmental stimuli impinging upon the patient's psychological life space and should make sure that the subject has a clear-cut and nonconflicting set towards the test.

The Examination

As described fully in a previous publication [5] the examination consists of four parts:

1. PERFORMANCE PROPER. This initial procedure is designed to obtain the responses of the subject to the stimulus material in a highly permissive and unstructured situation, with an absolute minimum of limiting or stimulating the subject to something other than his spontaneous inclination. The role of the examiner is chiefly that of recorder.

2. INQUIRY. This phase is designed to obtain the information required for scoring the record. It is necessary to refrain from suggestions that might prejudice the subject. There is more interaction between subject and examiner.

3. ANALOGY PERIOD. A supplementary period utilized where a nondirective inquiry does not fully clarify the scoring problems. The questioning remains, however, within the framework of the subject's own concepts.

4. TESTING THE LIMITS. This phase consists of more directive questions, tailor-made to suit the particular subject and his record. The relationship can be altered in any way thought to be suitable to the situation. Concepts are deliberately introduced which were not formed by the subject.

The Performance Proper Phase of the Administration

The performance proper or free-association procedure, as it has been called, is the oldest and most widely employed part of the Rorschach procedure. Most writers have agreed that the essential characteristic of this phase should be a lack of structure, which forces the individual being examined to assume responsibility for dealing with the situation. Direct questions as to procedure on the part of the subject are usually evaded. Questions that a subject might raise include: "May I turn the card?" "Should I just tell you what I see or use my imagination?" "Should I tell you what comes to my mind immediately or think it through?" and the like. All such questions should be answered as noncommittally as possible, throwing the responsibility for making the decision right back upon the subject. Such statements as, "That is entirely up to you," "You may do it in any way you like," are usually adequate. With some particularly anxious subjects, it may be necessary to stop the procedure somewhere along the line and reassure him. A note should be made of the particular place during the examination at which anxiety becomes manifest. It may be related to the particular stimulus value of the card the subject has before him, a particularly significant response he has just given, or some environmental stimulus tangential to the testing situation *per se*. It may be necessary at these times to re-establish rapport by the methods described in the preceding section.

A question that deserves special mention is the one sometimes raised by subjects as to whether the response they have given is "correct." This question may arise in spite of the fact that the examiner has previously made quite explicit the fact that there are no right and wrong answers. If the subject refuses to be reassured by a repetition of this point, it may be necessary to encourage him by expressing some approval of his efforts without committing oneself on the question of correctness.

In general, every effort should be made to discourage a conversation between the examiner and the subject during this phase of the examination. The more the examiner is able to retreat into the background of the subject's psychological field, the more likely are the subject's responses to be spontaneous. The more spontaneous the responses are, the more are they apt to reflect basic conflictual patterns and personality characteristics—as opposed to the kind of blocking and defensive measures employed by self-conscious subjects.

A rather different problem which occasionally arises is the case of the subject who feels compelled to continue indefinitely with the production of responses. For the busy clinician, the Rorschach test reaches a point of diminishing returns after so many responses. It may be necessary, under these circumstances, to point out to the subject that we are not particularly interested in seeing how many responses he can give, but more in the first few impressions that he gets. In extreme cases, it may even be necessary to limit the subject to a certain number of responses per card. These procedures should be employed only in extreme cases and after the first card or two have been responded to. When they are employed, many of the usual ratios and percentages, obviously, become inapplicable. Such records must be eliminated from research samples. Whereas such a restriction of the subject's activities is regrettable, spending ten to twenty hours on a Rorschach examination is usually not consistent with the over-all demands of a clinical situation.

The Inquiry

The inquiry is a part of the administration devised in order to make possible the use of scores. Scoring provides a means of classifying the highly qualitative data of the Rorschach protocol, so that the material may be dealt with more readily. It would be a great mistake, however, to assume that scoring the Rorschach is a simple and mechanical procedure equivalent to the scoring of psychometric tests. In order to be able to inquire properly, the examiner must know not only what scoring symbols he is evaluating the presence or absence of; he must also be thoroughly acquainted with their interpretative significance. In effect, each question put to a subject during the inquiry must have behind it an interpretative hypothesis that is explicit in the examiner's mind.*

Much use of scores has been made in research with the Rorschach.

---

* This statement becomes necessary owing to the practice of having the test administered (though not interpreted) by untrained personnel.

It is distressing to note that those examiners who tend to make the greatest use of scores as a basis for interpretation (for example, Buhler, Buhler, and Lefever [1], Harrower and Steiner [2]) very frequently have the least basis for arriving at these scores. The very procedure of group testing obviously makes the inquiry rather sketchy and undependable as a basis for scoring. Perusal of the sample records in Buhler's monograph demonstrates very brief inquiries in most instances, with the inquiry completely lacking in others.

Scores may thus be thought of essentially as shorthand pointers to interpretative hypotheses. Viewed in this light, our methods of arriving at these scores by means of the inquiry must be carefully scrutinized. We must be careful not to put words into the subject's mouth or suggest anything to him. A rather extreme example of caution in this respect is the suggestion made by Rapaport, Gill, and Schafer [6] that the cards be held face down during the inquiry period, so that no extra cues can be obtained by the subject on the basis of further perusal of the card. Most people are content with merely phrasing their questions in general terms, relying on the words used by the subject to phrase questions.

Inquiring for Location

In order to evaluate the accuracy of the responses and the manner of approach used by the subject, it is essential to know exactly what part of the blot is being employed. A rather inadequate method sometimes used for this purpose is to have the subject outline his response on a location chart. This makes the unwarranted assumption that the subject is as keenly aware of our methods of evaluating Rorschach protocols as we ourselves. A better method is to question the subject carefully, asking him to describe parts of the concept perceived and to account for various areas of the blot whose use by him seems questionable to the examiner. If this method fails, the subject may be asked to trace his responses by means of a piece of onionskin paper. If the issue is still in doubt, he might be asked to draw his response free-hand, so that we may compare the drawing with the original ink blot. If we are unable to discover by any of these means where the concept is perceived, we are left in doubt as to the accuracy or appropriateness of the perception.

Inquiring for Determinants

A frequent error is to score the presence or absence of determinants on an empirical basis. Thus, whenever the concept "bow" appears for the center D in Card III, it is a mistake to assume automatically that, since color is employed in the majority of cases, color has been employed in this case. If such an assumption is made, the necessity for inquiring further has been obviated. However, this procedure fails to take into account the essential purpose of the test as an instrument for the assessment of individual personality. Whether or not most people would employ color under those circumstances is not as significant as whether our particular subject admits to doing so or not.

Our essential purpose in inquiring for determinants is to determine accurately the absence or presence of every potential determinant. The use of form is a hypothesis in every case. Wherever animate objects are seen, movement becomes a possibility. If the area employed is colored or shaded, we must determine the influence of these factors upon the perceived concept. The inquiry consists essentially of setting all these up as hypotheses and verifying or eliminating them by means of skillful probing. An adequate inquiry of this sort eliminates any subsequent squabbles over scoring, since it makes clear what the subject's projections are, allowing little room for the projections of the examiner to have any undue influence.

It is usually best to phrase the questions as generally as possible and to employ the terminology suggested by the subject himself. Thus, if a subject sees a pretty butterfly, one could inquire what makes it look like a butterfly and what makes it look pretty. The formulation of subsequent questions should depend upon the answers to these. A method sometimes employed to determine the presence of color as a determinant is a comparison of the Rorschach plates with the small achromatic diagrams on the location chart. The idea is that if the subject can perceive the concept equally well in black, then color is not an important determinant. The hazard in this procedure is the dissimilarity between the small diagrams and the original blots in various unknown ways. Before such a procedure is routinely employed, it must be demonstrated that the stimulus value of the blots on the location chart is equivalent to that of the blots on the cards, except for color. When inquiring for movement, the examiner might ask the subject how the concept is seen. If this fails to produce sufficient information, he might go on to question the subject about the position of the perceived concept. Questions such as "Is it alive or dead?" are generally rather unproductive and possibly too structured. The rules for scoring the various determinants are quite explicitly stated in other sections of this book. When inquiring for the presence or absence of various determinants, these rules should be clearly kept in mind, and sufficient information should be gathered to enable the examiner to state clearly that a given determinant is either present or absent.

The inquiry period can thus be seen as a process of attempting to ascertain the implicit thinking of the subject during the prior, or performance proper, phase. Caution should be exercised to avoid suggesting, in a leading way, any particular determinant. This can best be accomplished by sticking rather closely to terms employed by the subject himself. On the other hand, care should be taken not to leave the presence or absence of any given variable in unnecessary doubt.

The Analogy Period

The analogy period is optional, used only where the inquiry has not fully clarified the scoring problems. It consists of asking the subject whether a determinant admittedly employed in connection with one response is applicable to others. This makes the question less structured than if asked out of context during the subsequent, or testing the limits, phase. Determinants brought into the picture as the result of this procedure can be included in the scoring as additionals.

This procedure is very helpful in that it lightens considerably the load of routine inquiry. It makes it unnecessary to continually ask prodding questions when the use of a given determinant is not clear.

The subject's attitude toward the use of the determinant should be further investigated during this part of the procedure. The subject may be reluctant to utilize the determinant, he may be completely insensitive to it, or may not have the language necessary to be articulate about it. However, the presence or absence of these elements in the subject's responses should definitely be determined before the testing is over.

The attitude of the subject, if it has not become clarified during the analogy period, can be further investigated in a more structured way during the subsequent testing-the-limits procedure. During this more structured part of the test, a definite clarification of the response patterns to determine the areas is possible. This information is indispensable for interpretation, especially in the case of otherwise barren records.

The Testing-the-Limits Procedure

Testing the limits is a procedure that has been suggested in a previous publication [5]. Its basic philosophy is to establish a situation that is more highly structured for the subject and less highly restricted for the examiner. This procedure is helpful to those whose emphasis in giving the test is primarily on individual assessment. It constitutes their opportunity to restructure the situation as they please, and in any way that they think might throw further light upon the patient's functioning. Thus, for example, if the examiner believes that the performance has been influenced by a misconception of the role of the examiner by the patient, by a free association technique, or by some particular flavor that has crept into the relationship, the examiner might use the testing-the-limits phase to test out this hypothesis and to see whether the patient could perform differently after having been reoriented. It is especially useful in the case of subjects who are made to feel anxious by the ambiguous nature of the previous parts of the administration, resulting in a meager record, but who could give some information in this more highly structured setting.

As a rule, questions raised during this part of the administration should proceed from the general to the specific. Thus, the examiner might start out by saying, "Sometimes, people use just a part of the blot in order to see something and not all of it. Can you do that?" If this produces no results, he could go on to point out specific areas that are commonly used as *D*'s. This failing, he could suggest specific concepts to the subject that are popularly seen in parts of the blot, such as the animals in Card VIII, the crabs in Card X.

The refusal by or inability of the subjects to see suggested popular concepts—even after the details of the concept have been pointed out—should always be followed by a question: "What do you think is wrong, if other people see a . . .?" The answers to such a question are often surprisingly clarifying. The fact that responses can thus be produced by questions of increasing specificity has caused Hutt [3] to coin the expression "levels of response." Thus, a spontaneously given response during the testing of the limits would be a level 1 response, whereas a directly suggested response accepted by the subject would be a level 3 response. A level 2 response is one given in response to a more general kind of prompting.

Among procedures that may be employed in testing the limits, there are some that should be used only in case of need. This means that they should be used if there is insufficient evidence in the record itself on which to base conclusions in the given area. These procedures would include the following:

1. Testing the limits of the manner of approach. If the individual has given only *W*'s, we would investigate his ability to use details. On the other hand, if an individual has used only details, his ability to integrate them into wholes would be of interest.

2. Testing the limits for the individual's ability to perceive human content and to project movement into it. If necessary, some of the more common responses of this kind might be suggested to the subject in order to see how much difficulty he would have in accepting them.

3. Testing the limits for the individual's ability to integrate form and color in a stable flexible manner (*FC*). Other techniques failing, some of the common *FC* responses (bow on Card III, green caterpillars on Card X) could be suggested.

4.   Testing the limits for the individual's ability to respond to the shading nuances of the blot. If necessary, Cards IV and VI could be employed in terms of their common interpretation as animal skins.

5.   Testing the limits of the individual's ability to perceive and think along conventional lines. If the individual has not given many popular responses during the test proper, it is very important to know whether he failed to do this because he chose not to give such responses or because he is unable to give them. The interpretative importance of this point is discussed elsewhere (pages 312, 400).

In addition to these more routine procedures, certain special procedures have been suggested by various investigators. These include:

1.   The free association procedure suggested by Janis and Janis [4]. This consists of asking people to give free associations to certain Rorschach responses. Janis and Janis have suggested that it be used with all Rorschach responses, but it is possible to modify the procedure and ask for free associations only to certain commonly occurring contents within a protocol which seem to have a special personal significance to the subject.

2.   The concept formation technique. A variation of this technique was suggested by Hutt [3]. It consists of asking the subject to put the cards into various piles on the basis of some principle of his own device. He may do this on the basis of content, affective attitudes, color or form differences, and the like. The meaning of these various kinds of behavior is discussed in the chapters on interpretation (see Part Two).

3.   The like-dislike procedure. By asking the subject to pick out the card he likes the best and the one he likes the least and give his reasons for these choices, valuable information can sometimes be obtained which will enhance the interpretative significance of the responses previously given to these cards.

The testing-the-limits procedure can thus be an extremely useful adjunct to the test itself. The richer the original protocol, the less urgent the testing-the-limits procedure becomes. However, there are always some questions still in the mind of the clinician which he can answer in this way. The reader should consider the above section as merely illustrative of the kinds of things that might be done during the testing of the limits. It is by no means designed to limit the clinician in any way.

Terminating the Examination

Equal in importance to an adequate preparation for the test is the technique of ending it. Examiners frequently find it desirable to spend some time with a subject after completing the administration proper. The test may have aroused anxiety, which can be alleviated by a repetition of some of the statements made at the outset. The subject may want to be reassured concerning the confidential nature of the material and the use to which it will be put.

The clinician, when functioning in a purely diagnostic role, must strike a fine balance between treating the subject in a warm and accepting manner, and avoiding any involvement that would be difficult to handle in such a brief contact. It is sometimes necessary to set limits since some topics might better be discussed with the professional person who has treatment responsibilities.

Optimally, a subject should leave the examination pleased and satisfied. However, a generally suspicious and hostile person is apt to maintain this same attitude in regard to the Rorschach examination.

Any questions about the meaning of test performance should be referred to the therapist whenever possible. If the subject insists upon a statement on the part of the examiner, it might be pointed out that this is an example of how people behave in a situation with which they have no previous experience. Performance, therefore, reveals individual ways of behaving. It is often more important to find out why the subject feels anxious about the tests than to be concerned about answering his questions.

Anything told the subject about his performance should stress positive and superficial kinds of interpretations. The examiner should be keenly aware of the fact that he is stepping into a treatment role as soon as he departs from the standard test administration. Everything he says should be thought through carefully in terms of the patient's needs and relationships. Needless to say, written reports should never be presented to patients.

Special Problems in Administration

Children

Many of the suggestions made above are inapplicable to the use of the Rorschach with young children. It would be foolish, indeed, to attempt to maintain any rigid standard procedure in dealing with children below school age. These questions are discussed in detail in the chapter on children's Rorschach records in Volume II.

Psychosomatic Patients

Some patients are referred for psychological examination although they have not come to a physician for any sort of psychiatric disorder. They may, indeed, conceive of their disorder as purely medical in nature and be very much surprised at being asked to take a psychological test. Obviously, the major responsibility for overcoming this difficulty rests in the hands of the referring physician. The examiner can usually explain the test as part of a comprehensive evaluation of the subject's physical and mental state, designed to permit the medical team to assist optimally in the subject's rehabilitation. The Rorschach technique can be described as a procedure designed to demonstrate the subject's way of handling a novel situation. Once the subject has agreed to take the test, the examiner can usually proceed in the customary manner.

Acutely Ill Patients

Severely sick patients present special problems to the examiner. If the illness is of a physical sort, it may be necessary to examine the patient in bed, hold the cards for him, try to cut down the length of the procedure, and so on. If the illness is of a mental sort, other problems arise. A severely depressed or withdrawn individual might have little reason to become interested in the production of responses on the Rorschach test. Occasionally, the use of drugs to elicit a state of greater verbal fluency may be indicated. For unresponsive subjects, the testing-the-limits procedure sometimes assumes a special role. Subjects who are actively hallucinating during the examination will produce records capable of interpretation. An attempt should be made to assess which of the responses are subjectively felt to come from the subject and which comments are the result of the subject's "voices," and the like.

Examinations under Objective Stress

Sometimes we are asked to examine people under conditions of considerable stress. The problem may be a legal one, and the clinician might have been asked to offer an opinion as to responsibility. The subject may be facing commitment. Personnel selection or promotion may be involved. Under conditions such as these, it is rather ludicrous to proceed as though there were no serious purpose in giving the test. Anxiety demonstrated by the subject should not be made light of, but should be handled in the same way that such anxiety is handled in any other type of clinical situation.

Summary

The purpose of the Rorschach technique, as of other clinical tests, has been defined as the prediction of individual behavior patterns from a standardized sample situation. This purpose is best served by a test which consists, as the Rorschach does, of ambiguous stimulus materials, but which is administered in a relatively structured and standardized manner.

There is good reason why the Rorschach is individually administered by human beings rather than being ordinarily given in group form or by machine. This reason consists of the value of the interpersonal relationship between the subject and the examiner as a source of information. In doing justice to the interpretation of the test protocol, it would be foolish, indeed, to consider all examiners as equipotential. Although it is desirable for the contact to be as smooth and unruffled as possible, difficulties in the relationship should not be considered as invalidating the test results, but rather as modifying their meaning.

In order to provide some degree of structure, some suggestions have been made in this chapter as to how the purposes of the Rorschach technique may best be served in the administration of the test.

The Rorschach offers the dual advantage of a sample of behavior taken under standardized conditions, and a clinically flexible instrument (see "testing the limits"). The clinician must be flexible enough to adapt the technique to the immediate needs of the situation.

References

1. Buhler, C.; Buhler, K.; and Lefever, D. W. *Development of the Basic Rorschach Score with Manual of Directions.* Los Angeles; Rorschach Standardization Studies, No. 1, 1948 (mimeographed).

2. Harrower, M. R., and Steiner, M. E. *Large Scale Rorschach Techniques: A Manual for the Group Rorschach and Multiple Choice Test.* Springfield, Illinois: Charles C. Thomas, Publisher; 1945.

3. Hutt, M. L., and Shor, J. "Rationale for Routine Rorschach 'Testing the Limits,'" *Rorschach Res. Exch.*, 1946, 10, 70–76.

4. Janis, M. G., and Janis, I. L. "A Supplementary Test Based on Free Associations to Rorschach Responses," *Rorschach Res. Exch.*, 1946, 10, 1–19.

5. Klopfer, B., and Kelley, D. M. *The Rorschach Technique.* Yonkers, New York: World Book Company; 1942.

6. Rapaport, D.; Gill, M.; and Schafer, R. *Diagnostic Psychological Testing: The Theory, Statistical Evaluation, and Diagnostic Application of a Battery of Tests*, Vol. II. Chicago: Year Book Publishers; 1946.

CHAPTER 2

Scoring: Defining the Response

In the Rorschach technique scoring is a process of classification. Responses that are similar with respect to some significant characteristic are classified together and assigned the same scoring symbol. Quantification enters in only when a frequency count is made of the responses in each scoring category, and when these frequencies are compared in terms of absolute number, percentage, or ratio. The only score that is directly quantitative is form-level rating, which involves rating on a scale ranging from -2.0 to $+5.0$ with intervals of 0.5.

In the application of any system of classification, differences of opinion are likely to arise when responses fall on the borderline between one class and another. Such difficulties are not an indication of particular weakness in the Rorschach technique, since such problems are inevitable in any system of classification of qualitative material. Nevertheless, differences of opinion raise the problem of reliability. It is desirable to make the system of classification as reliable as possible, so that different examiners will arrive at essentially similar classifications of the same sets of responses.

There are two chief ways of achieving reliability in classification. The first is to make the rules of classification as explicit as possible so that different examiners will be able to classify on exactly the same basis. It is the purpose of these chapters to make more explicit the basis of classification set forward by Klopfer in *The Rorschach Technique*. The second safeguard is to train psychologists to use the same basis of classification in the same way. This second need can be met only indirectly in these pages, in that an explicit basis of classification is the first essential for training towards reliable scoring.

Important though reliability may be, it is secondary to interpretation. Scoring is only an intermediate step in the process of rendering down the qualitative material of a Rorschach protocol into a meaningful, dynamic picture of a functioning personality. The responses are classified in certain ways to make the material more manipulable, but all methods of classification are not equally satisfactory. The particular scoring categories used in the Rorschach technique have emerged because interpretative hypotheses are attached to them. As new interpretative hypotheses have been formed through experience with the technique, new scoring classifications have been included. This may be seen in the elaboration of scoring from the relatively simple classificatory system used by Rorschach himself to the more complex system presented here. Presumably, as research continues and the interpretative hypotheses are refined, modified, or added to—or indeed dropped out as invalid—the scoring system will be subject to corresponding changes.

There must be a lag, however, between the refinement of hypotheses and the modification of a scoring system. It is entirely likely that individual clinicians, particularly those more gifted in clinical and scientific insight, will develop new interpretative hypotheses which can but gradually be communicated to others using the technique. Should they and their pupils immediately proceed to modify the system of classification of responses, their work would not be comparable with the work of other Rorschach examiners; and such chaos would soon reign in the field that communication of findings would be well-nigh impossible. Some difficulties in communication have already arisen. Conscientious adherence to a recognized, explicit system of classification of responses seems the chief solution. To the extent that the examiner finds it necessary to introduce modifications to meet refinements of interpretative hypotheses required for adequate handling of his findings, he should be quite clear in describing such modifications.

Finally, clinicians focussing on a particular clinical category such as organic brain disease or schizophrenia may find it necessary to introduce some modifications of classification because of the particular interpretative hypotheses relevant to the patients with whom they deal. These refinements of classification have become common, communicable knowledge within the literature of the diagnostic use of the Rorschach technique. Nevertheless, many of them are omitted from this general scoring system designed to be applicable to the population-in-general, because their inclusion would unduly complicate the general system of classification of responses and because they would apply to such a small number of subjects as to make the additional precision undesirable.

Thus, in summary, the purpose of Chapters 2–8 is to present a system of classification of responses which is as explicit as possible in the interests of reliability, but which is simple in being limited to classifications relating to significant interpretative hypotheses with enough relevance to the population-in-general to warrant inclusion.

The experienced Rorschach examiner may feel a certain sense of restriction in being limited to a relatively fixed system of classification of responses. He may feel that many of the subtleties of the protocol are lost and be tempted to modify his scoring to suit the peculiarities of the individual record. It is true that the uniqueness of the individual record is lost in any system of classification; this is an inevitable sacrifice to generalization but does not justify capricious modification of scoring. The Rorschach technique makes provision for interpretation of the unique and subtle aspects of the individual record in the qualitative aspects of interpretation, and through the analysis of the sequence and content of responses. Since this second line of interpretation is available, it seems justifiable to urge adherence to a standard and communicable system for the quantitative aspects of the analysis, both in the interests of reliability in the communication of findings, and so that interpretative hypotheses derived from the relatively stable central core of literature may be applied to the individual record as a check on the more flexible, "intuitive," qualitative interpretation.

The Five Steps in Scoring

Scoring a Rorschach protocol consists of the following five steps for each response. (These steps are discussed in Chapters 3 through 8.)

1. LOCATION SCORE: Classification of the response according to the area of the blot used for the concept: that is, the whole blot or part of it, and if a part, whether large or small, usual or unusual.

2. DETERMINANT SCORE: Classification of the response according to those aspects of the blot material (or attributed to the material by the subject) that determine the concept. The form, color, or shading of the blot area may make it seem like the object conceptualized; movement or three-dimensional space may be contributed by the subject although not present in the blot material itself.

3. CONTENT SCORE: Classification of the response according to the kind of concept given—for example, human, animal, man-made object, clouds.

4. POPULARITY OR ORIGINALITY: Classifying as *popular* responses those that tally with a list of the ten responses* that have been found to be the most frequent, and as *original* responses those that occur as rarely as once in one hundred records in the experience of the individual examiner. Many responses are neither popular nor original according to these definitions.

5. FORM-LEVEL RATING: Rating each response on a scale ranging from —2.0 to +5.0 according to the extent to which the concept matches or fits the blot area used and, within the range of good match, the degree of elaboration of the concept.

Defining the Response

Before embarking on the five steps of scoring it is first necessary to distinguish each separate response, since the response is the basic unit of scoring and quantitative analysis. For most subjects this is easy, discrete responses being readily distinguishable. Other sub-

---

* Klopfer and Kelley, *The Rorschach Technique,* pages 177–181.

jects present such difficulty as to require the elucidation of rules to guide the division of the protocol into response units. These problems resolve themselves into three chief questions:

1. Is the verbalization a response or a mere remark?
2. Is the verbalization a response which the subject accepts and is hence to be scored, or is it rejected, or discarded in favor of another concept?
3. Is the verbalization a response in its own right which can serve as a unit of scoring, or is it merely part of another response?

A compromise between scoring and not scoring a response is provided in the distinctions between main and additional responses and between main and additional scores within a response. These distinctions are difficult to discuss independently of a detailed consideration of the scoring process; they will be given particular attention in the chapters on scoring of locations and determinants. The general scoring problems which constitute a necessary introduction to scoring are subsumed in the three questions above and will be dealt with in the following three sections of this chapter.

Remark vs. Response

In the inquiry, the examiner should investigate each comment or remark that could possibly be construed as a response to ascertain whether the subject was indeed merely commenting or whether he meant to imply an interpretation ("This is what it looks like to me") .

There may well be semantic difficulties between subject and examiner. Young children cannot be expected to clarify the distinction between remarks and responses. Even with older and more intelligent subjects it is sometimes difficult to establish a distinction, some subjects insisting that all comments are meant as responses, others insisting that extensive and repeated comments are merely remarks. Tendencies to describe the card sometimes offer particular difficulties in the task of identifying scorable responses.

To assist the examiner in identifying scorable responses the three following rules-of-thumb are offered:

1.　As a general rule, the verbalization is scored as a response if in the inquiry the subject says he meant it as a response and goes on to elaborate or explain it further. It would not be scored as a response if the subject indicated that he meant it merely as a comment or remark: For example:

Card X (after subject had given 8 obviously scorable responses)

PERFORMANCE	INQUIRY
This card is nicely designed.	E: Did you mean that just as a remark, or as a response, like the spiders and the man you saw here?
	S: I meant it as a remark, a comment. The blot is symmetrical and the parts are nicely distributed.

COMMENT:　The inquiry clarifies that this is a descriptive remark, not a scorable response.

Card X (another subject, 4th response)

PERFORMANCE	INQUIRY
It's a feeling of balance here.	E: Did you mean that as a remark or as a response (explaining the distinction)?
	S: I meant it as a response. This balances this, this balances this, etc. etc. They are all in balance.

Score:　W　　mF　　Abs　　0.5

COMMENT:　The subject not only indicates that this was intended as a response, but goes on to give some elaboration of his original verbalization.

2.　When the verbalization involves the naming of colors special stringency is observed in distinguishing between a response and a remark. Since the interpretative hypothesis attached to the score C_n, or color naming, involves possibly a pathognomic cue, in general a response is not assigned to this scoring category unless it constitutes the only mode of handling the card, even though the subject may insist that he meant the enumeration of colors as a response. For further discussion and examples see pages 191–195.

3. Descriptive tendencies are generally not scored, although the subject may insist that these are meant as responses. However, if five or more such descriptive remarks are offered for any given card, they are lumped together to form one response scorable as a form description, shading description, or color description. Sometimes these descriptive tendencies merge with a more interpretative attitude. This is most likely with color description and may be scored C_{des}, although it sometimes occurs with achromatic color or shading. (For fuller discussion of C_{des} and an example, see page 196.) Three examples of handling descriptive remarks follow:

Card VII

PERFORMANCE

I like this one.

Two old ladies, pleasant old girls. Wearing little hats with high feathers. They have a ridiculous and rather appealing look.

This card gives a general impression of furriness.

The shapes in this one are nice.

Upside down it looks rather like a Mayan arch. It is rather heavy at the top. There is not much support at the bottom, but it is neatly balanced and will probably stand.

INQUIRY

S: The ladies are wearing long skirts. They have wasp waists and are facing each other. They look as though they were startled and had just whirled around.

E: What about the blot gave you the impression of feathers on their hats?

S: This piece sticking up. And it is soft and fluffy like a feather.

E: What about the blot gave the impression of Mayan arches?

S: Just the shape.

E: When you mentioned "general furriness" did you mean that as a response like the "old ladies" or the "arches" or just as a remark as when you said "The shapes in this one are nice."

S: It was just a remark. The blot gives a furry impression, characteristic of the blot as a blot. The way the ink is on the card.

E: Could it be a piece of fur?

S: No, it isn't anything. I just mentioned it descriptively in passing.

Score: 1. W   M,Fc   H   3.0
          2. W   Fm   Arch   1.0

COMMENT: Here the subject makes two clear-cut remarks
which are not scorable: "I like this one" and "The shapes in
this one are nice." The comment "This card gives a general
impression of furriness" is more difficult to distinguish from a
response, since it approaches an interpretative attitude. However, since the subject insists that it was just a remark and implies that he was merely describing the card and not interpreting
it, no score was assigned. Had he acknowledged it as a response
the scoring would have been c_{des}.

Card X

PERFORMANCE

Here is a cervix.

And another cervix.

I get two rather stupid looking small animals.

Two islands, with a forest in the peninsula.

Two birds again, with their heads together.

These are true and very attractive colors. The blue is particularly good and there is lovely blending between the green and the blue. I like the pink too.

A turkey wishbone.

INQUIRY

S: Here in the top gray bit. It was just the shape.

S: (Pointed to bottom green detail.)

S: (Pointed to side gray details.) It is the eye being so large that gives them the stupid look.

S: These blue things are the islands and the attached green part is a peninsula with the green indicating a forest.

S: (Blue center details.) Here are their long skinny necks and heads.
E: You said their heads were together?
S: That's just the way they are on the card. They couldn't really be like that in the air. They would have to be on something.

E: Did you mean that as a remark, or as a response like the animals and the islands, for example?
S: It was just a comment, a remark. I didn't mean it to be like the others, which *are* something.

S: It was the shape (indicating the center orange detail).

Score:				
1.	D	F	Sex	1.0
2.	D	F	Sex	1.0
3.	D,S	F	A	1.5
4.	D	F,CF	Geo	0.5
5.	D	F	A	1.5
6.	D	F	A_{obj}	1.0

COMMENT: Here six responses are scored. The verbalization about the "attractive colors" is not scored since the subject states that "it was just a comment." Had the subject acknowledged it as a response the scoring would have been C_{des}.

Card VIII

PERFORMANCE

The color strikes me right off the bat.

Two beaver-like animals on each side in red.

INQUIRY

S: They are beavers, only the tail isn't flat enough. A squirrel possibly. A small animal.
E: Did you mean they were red animals, or that you used the red parts?
S: They would be brown animals. It could be a drawing.
E: How do you see them?
S: Sort of balanced on each side. They seem real because of the texture, but they couldn't stand like that. They could be stuffed.

(inverted card)

The shades of colors are pretty the way they are worked in together.

E: Did you mean that as a response like the animals, or as a remark as when you said: "The color strikes me right off the bat"?
S: I meant it as a response. The color is light and I appreciate color. Mild color, pastel, not harsh. It is pleasant.

The top part is sort of like stalactites.

S: A cavern in the States somewhere is colored like this. Multicolored. It is the roof of a cave looking up at it. (Pointed to pink and orange detail.)

A fish's backbone

S: This center part. Just the shape.

PERFORMANCE (*continued*)

I notice these in the center. Two elongated blobs, but they don't signify anything. They are out of tune with the rest of the picture. The brown blob in the middle is out of place too. The lines drawn around the elongated blobs are not finely shaded like the rest of the picture.

Score:	1. D	Fc	(A) →P	2.0
	2. W	C_{des}	des	0.0
	3. D	CF	N	0.5
	4. D	F	A.At	1.0

COMMENT: The subject first makes a clear-cut color remark, then gives an "animal" response. He then comments again about the colors; this is scored as color description since he states he intended it as a response. He ends with typical non-scorable descriptive remarks.

Alternative and Rejected Responses

Some subjects seem to feel that each location can only "be" one thing, and they tend to reject one response if later they see something that seems better. Other subjects may use the same blot or blot area over and over again for different responses, with no apparent implication that earlier responses are rejected in favor of later ones. Still other subjects give alternatives for the same blot area with varying indications of rejection or correction. The four rules and the illustrative examples that follow will serve as guides to identification of scorable responses where alternatives, corrections, and/or rejections are involved.

1. Two or more responses to the same blot area are to be scored separately, unless the subject clearly implies that they are merely different names for or descriptions of essentially the same concept. Sometimes the subject uses two names for a concept which to him are synonymous, but which to the examiner denote different concepts; this confusion should be cleared up in the in-

quiry. (At other times there is a question of alternative concepts, which will be dealt with more fully in another subsection.) Note the following examples:

Card I

PERFORMANCE	INQUIRY
It could be a wolf, like a wolf's face, with features.	S: The whole thing. Here are the eyes, nose, mouth, ears, chin. E: What about the blot gave you the impression of the wolf's face? S: The outline and the shadows in it. E: How did the shadows help? S: This part has more shadows where the nose protrudes. The eyes are slanting and leering. It is a frightening face.
It could be a bat.	S: The whole thing again. Head, wings.
It could also be a map of a continent.	S: The whole. E: Did you have any particular continent in mind? S: No, it doesn't look like any known one. Perhaps a little like North America with the bay at the top.

Score:					
1.	W,S	Fc, Fm	Ad		3.0
2.	W	F	A	P	1.0
3.	W	F	geo		1.0

COMMENT: Here the subject has given three responses using the whole blot with no implication that they are alternatives. Three separate responses are therefore scored.

Card IV

PERFORMANCE	INQUIRY
This lower part might be a crab or some sort of insect.	S: It was these things sticking out (pointing to projections from lower center *D*). E: And what about it made it seem like an insect? S: Well! these things sticking out might be claws and legs, like insects have.

INQUIRY (*continued*)

It's my idea of a crab, but I've never seen one, so it might be some other insect something like a crab. It was just that it had a lot of things sticking out.

Score: D   F   A   1.0

COMMENT: Although one first has the impression of two possibly alternative concepts, the inquiry brings to light the fact that the subject thinks of a "crab" as an insect and the two names are applied to the same concept. Hence only one response is scored.

2. When the subject corrects his response spontaneously, substituting a new concept which seems more appropriate to him than the one originally formulated, this is to be considered an elaboration of the original response even though the correction may take place in the inquiry. In such a case one main response is scored. If, however, the substitution of the new response involves a change in determinants, the rejected response is accounted for by an additional determinant score. Three examples follow:

Card V

PERFORMANCE	INQUIRY
Well! it looks like a pretty good butterfly, except that the wing tips are split and it has gigantic wings for the size of its body. The body is like that of a small fox. It is like a bat. A bat is better.	E: Do you mean this as a bat or a butterfly or could it be both? S: It is a better bat. Here are the wings, the narrow body down the center. The ears like bat's ears, and the feet bent back in flight. Just skip the butterfly. It's the wrong shape for a butterfly.

Score: W   FM   A   P   2.0

COMMENT: Here we have a spontaneous correction, with no change in determinants. One response only is scored and the original "butterfly" is ignored for scoring purposes.

Card VIII

PERFORMANCE

INQUIRY

There seem to be two animals here on the sides, in the act of taking a step. It's practically like a heraldic motif.

E: Where did you see the animals?
S: (Pointing to side *D*'s) Here, but I went from the animals to the whole thing. They look like boars. The kind you see in a heraldic motif.
E: Tell me more about the animals.
S: They have definite heads, eye is clearly discerned, rather Roman noses, heavy bodies, bristly hair, powerful hind quarters and very spindly forelegs.
E: What about it makes it seem like bristly hair?
S: The outline. The face is very distinct. Not pugnacious like a boar usually is . . . stylized.
E: You said they were in the act of taking a step?
S: That was when I thought of them just as animals. But as a heraldic motif they wouldn't be alive.

Score: D→W   F→FM   (A), Embl   P   3.5

COMMENT: Here the concept of "animals" is enlarged to "heraldic motif," presumably to take into account the whole blot. Only one response is scored. The change from animal to the "heraldic motif" makes the subject ambivalent about the movement and therefore only a tendency to *FM* is scored as determinant.

Card IV

PERFORMANCE

INQUIRY

Like a bear with huge feet seen out of focus. Has a beak instead of a proper head . . . or like a great sprawling human shape with feet towards you and hands hanging loose . . . down here is the face of an animal . . . (long pause) Could be a tiger perhaps, with fangs . . . this bit could be a vulture's head, side-

E: Where did you see the bear?
S: I used the whole thing. It is disappearing. Here the beak is coming towards you.
E: What about the blot made it seem shaggy?
S: It is rough, shaggy and unkempt. It is a great, sprawling, drunken troll-

PERFORMANCE (*continued*)

ways. . . . Another face at the top, rather debauched . . . mediaeval . . . Norse look about it. A bush of hair and beard . . . headdress . . . looks as if he's had a night out . . . The chief thing is that it's shaggy . . . whether man or animal . . . relaxed and slightly drunk.

INQUIRY (*continued*)

king. A Norse head. Hands over the arm of the chair, hanging.

E: Did you use this (pointing to lower, center *D*)?

S: It is something he's sitting on.

E: Where is the face of an animal?

S: Here (pointing to lower center detail). Eyes, heavy lids, highlight on eye, square muzzle, fangs and whiskers. A cat-like stripe.

E: Is this one shaggy too?

S: No, it is a sleek tailored animal. The head is lowering towards you. It's looking up under its eyelids.

E: And the vulture?

S: (Pointed to side extension.) It is bald, a cruel beak, featherless head and ruffled feathers behind the skull.

E: Did you include the white?

S: Yes, it hasn't any eyes.

E: Can you tell me about the face at the top?

S: The eyes are half shut . . . eyebrows, long nose, moustache, formally shaped beard. Also a crown on top. That's why he's a king.

E: Oh! It's the same as the drunken man?

S: Yes. I thought it was an animal at first because it was shaggy, but it is a better man. Could be a Viking dressed in furs. A troll-king.

Score:				
1.	W	M, Fc	(H)←A	5.0
2.	D	Fc→FM	Ad	3.5
3.	d,S	F, Fc	Ad	2.5

COMMENT: Here there are three responses: (1) the sprawling troll-king, (2) the tiger's head and (3) the vulture's head. The "bear" is corrected making it a human figure, involving no change of determinant since the "shagginess" is accounted for by making the human figure dressed in furs, and the posture is a human-like posture described variously as "sprawling," "relaxed, and slightly drunk." The inquiry clarifies also that the face, which is described variously as "mediaeval," "Norse," "debauched," "Viking," and "troll-king," is the face of the figure that constitutes the first main response. The "beak" seems to be subsumed in the "crown" of the king. Thus much of the verbalization shows the gradual growth and elaboration of the main concept, involving spontaneous corrections which are in no way intended to be alternative concepts, but rather all refer to the same main concept. The fact that references to the two other concepts are interspersed makes the performance more difficult to sort out.

3. When the subject gives two concepts for the same area, and one is not corrected or rejected in favor of the other, there is a question as to whether one or two responses should be scored. If the inquiry makes it clear that the attitude of the subject is that the responses could be interchangeable (that it could be either and it doesn't matter which) it seems that one response only should be scored. However, if the subject insists that both responses are intended and they are not to be considered interchangeable, two responses are scored. Both responses are scored as main responses if both are given in the performance proper, while one may be scored as additional if it is not given until the inquiry. The issue is clearer if different scoring elements are involved, or if the subject gives different specifications for the two separate responses; but, even if the responses seem interchangeable to the examiner, they are to be scored separately if the subject insists that they are not the same. Three examples follow:

Card V

PERFORMANCE

This also looks like a bat seen from above. The ears are big for a bat, and the feet are like bats' feet.

INQUIRY

E: What about it made it seem like a bat?

S: The body with the exception of the ears is like a bat, and the wings are rather irregular like bats. Also it is soaring, trailing his feet along behind.

PERFORMANCE (*continued*)

It might also be an insect like a butterfly or a grasshopper. The wings are very irregular for a grasshopper.

INQUIRY (*continued*)

E: It seemed also like a butterfly?
S: Or a grasshopper. An effort to try to get the ears into something more consistent. They are like a grasshopper's whiskers, but even these are too big. This effort failed . . . to get something typical all over. It's just like the bat, also soaring, but the wings are too irregular.
E: Which is it then, or could it be any one of them?
S: It is a bat if you look at the wings and feet. Otherwise if you look at these things at the top, it could be an insect of some sort.

Score: 1. W FM A P 2.0
2. W FM A P 1.5

COMMENT: Here two responses are scored, the bat and the insect (butterfly or grasshopper). The subject does not consider the bat and the insect interchangeable, although the scoring differs only in the degree of specification which is reflected in the form-level rating. On the other hand, the butterfly and the insect are apparently considered interchangeable and hence are not scored separately.

Card V

PERFORMANCE

This looks like a bat . . . or a butterfly.

INQUIRY

E: Where did you see the bat?
S: Here (indicating the whole). Here are the wings, head, tail. The head is thicker than the tail.
E: How did you see it?
S: Flying . . . gliding.
E: You said it could be a butterfly too.
S: It looks like either a bat or a butterfly.
E: Did you mean it as the same thing, then?
S: No, I meant it as two different things. Here are the two feelers. I think

butterflies have feelers. The wings
. . . they are heavy colored in some
spots and light colored in others.
It's a gray and black butterfly. It's
flying too.

Score:	1.	W	F→FM	A	P	1.5
	2.	W	FC′, FM	A	P	2.0

COMMENT: Here the subject insists that the responses are not interchangeable, and goes on to make it clear that achromatic color entered in as a factor in one concept, the butterfly, but not in the other. Two responses are scored.

Card V

PERFORMANCE

This is a moth or bat with oversize wings. These are antennae. There is a note of incongruity. The wings are heavy in relationship to the central body. Makes the whole thing ridiculous if you think of an insect or bat. Immense wings.

INQUIRY

E: Did you use the whole thing?
S: Yes.
E: What about it made it seem like a moth or bat?
S: The shape only.
E: Does it seem more a moth than a bat, or could it be either?
S: It is a better moth because of the antennae.
E: Where would you be likely to see such a moth?
S: Spreadeagled in a museum, because of the shape.

Score: W   F   A   P   1.5

COMMENT: The performance proper implies alternative responses, but the inquiry brings out a preference for the "moth" and presumably a correction with rejection of the "bat." No difference in the scoring elements is involved, so in scoring one response no account is taken of the "bat."

4.   A response may be rejected without implication of correcting it for a better one. In such a case it is scored as an additional response, with an arrow pointing to the main from the additional column of the scoring list to indicate the rejection. Since, usu-

ally, the subject cannot be induced to elaborate upon a rejected response, the scoring often must be based on guesswork. Sometimes the subject cannot even locate a response previously given in the performance proper. When not even the location can be scored it seems best simply to omit that response from scoring altogether. One example of a rejected response follows:

Card VI

PERFORMANCE

Oh! this doesn't mean anything . . . It could be an animal skin . . . I really can't think of anything.

INQUIRY

E: What part of the blot did you use for the animal skin?

S: I meant the whole, but it doesn't seem like an animal skin now. I don't know why I said it. This one doesn't mean anything.

E: (In analogy period) Some people do call this an animal skin because the shading makes it seem furry. I wondered if that was what made it seem like an animal skin.

S: No. That wasn't it. It doesn't seem like an animal skin at all.

Score: $(\leftarrow W \quad \leftarrow F \quad \leftarrow A_{obj} \quad \leftarrow P \quad 0.5)$ * †

COMMENT: Here is a clear case of a rejected response, important to record since it is a rejection of a popular response. It would have been difficult to guess whether a texture determinant was implied without the analogy period, where there was clear denial of texture. (A question such as the second one asked by the examiner ordinarily belongs to the testing of the limits, but since the resistance of the subject was so acutely verbalized at this point, it seemed appropriate to follow up with such a question instead of waiting in the usual manner.) This is a classic example of rejection due to denial of shading.

---

* Arrow to the right indicates reluctance, but giving in and ending with acceptance. Double arrow means ambivalence ending in special effort. Arrow to the left means reluctance ending in rejection.

† Here and subsequently in the text when the score of a response is placed in parentheses it indicates that all elements (i.e. location, determinant, content and popular or original scores) are to be placed in the additional columns of the scoring list.

Independent Concepts vs. Specifications

One important aspect of the problem of identifying the independent responses that are to serve as scoring units is that of distinguishing between an independent response that stands in its own right and a specification that is merely part of that response.

It is difficult to discuss this problem without anticipating the later discussions of main and additional location and determinant scores. For the purpose of this present discussion suffice it to say that each independent concept is assigned a main location score together with main scores for each of the other scoring classifications (determinant, content, popular vs. original, and form-level rating). However, specifications are not reflected in separate location scores, either main or additional. They contribute to raising the form level. If they introduce new determinants these may be taken into account in scoring, for each response may have additional determinants as well as a main determinant. But they do not appear as separate responses in the scoring list, and they in no way serve to increase the number of response units for the purposes of quantitative analysis and interpretation.

Although the problems of assigning main and additional scores must be discussed later with respect to the various location and determinant classifications, the general scoring problem of identification of independent concepts transcends the artificial boundaries between classifications and must be introduced here. The following four points seem to cover the main problems encountered.

1. Elements that form essential parts of a larger concept—such as feet, head, and arms all belonging to the same man—are considered to be specifications and are not scored as separate responses even though they are mentioned separately. This is a difficulty only with the records of young children, feeble-minded subjects, and occasionally with subjects with pathological diagnoses. Note this example from a child's performance:

Card IV (subject is six years old)

PERFORMANCE	INQUIRY
Here is a father bear . . . here are some great big feet.	E: What about it makes it seem like a bear? S: He's sitting up, here are his paws, and here is the tail. E: Where are the feet you saw? S: (Pointed to lower, side details.) E: What kind of feet are they? S: They're the daddy bear's feet.

Score: W   FM   A   2.0

COMMENT: Here the performance proper implies two concepts, but the inquiry confirms that the "feet" belong to the "bear"; hence only one response is scored, and the feet are considered an essential part of the main concept.

2.   Elements that are specifications within a larger concept are not scored as separate responses. The criterion of a semi-independent detail as contrasted with a specification is generally whether the element could be, and indeed ordinarily is, seen as a separate response. Thus "noses" are specifications of faces and could scarcely be seen separately. Similarly, "hats" may be thought of as a specification of "heads." Although they are occasionally seen separately (as for the top red detail of Card II) they are much more frequently seen as accessories to a human figure. Similarly "rivers" and "forests" are specifications of landscapes. On Card X the green detail attached to the outer blue detail is often seen as a "claw" belonging to a "crab," and as such is obviously a specification. It seems reasonable that when the blue detail is seen as a Walt Disney "spider with a stick in its hand," the "stick" still constitutes a specification and is seen as such by virtue of the main concept. Similarly, for the top gray detail, when two animals are seen gnawing at a tree, it seems that the "tree" is so tightly organized into the concept that it should be considered a specification, even though some subjects isolate the center gray bit to treat as an obviously separate response. On the other hand, certain concepts such as the "butterfly" or

"bow" on Card III, the "crab" on Card III, the "animals" on Card VIII, the "crabs," the "rabbit," and the "caterpillars" on Card X, are so usually seen separately that they seem to deserve separate scoring even when they are woven into a complex whole response as seeming specifications. Card III examples are:

Card III

PERFORMANCE

Here are a couple of guys at a party hanging onto something and whirling around. They might be having a tug of war over a punch bowl.

INQUIRY

(Relevant parts only)

E: What about it makes it seem like a punch bowl?

S: What else would two guys at a party be fighting over?

Score: W   M   H   P

COMMENT: Here only one response is scored since it is clear that the "punch bowl" is seen as such by reason of the context of the larger concept and not by reason of the character of the blot area itself.

Card III

PERFORMANCE

Here are two African natives . . . rather skinny females . . . and here is a crab . . . they seem to be fighting over the crab.

INQUIRY

(Relevant parts only)

E: What about it made it seem like a crab?

S: The shape. This center part and then all the legs.

Score: 1. W⎫ M H P
       2. D⎭ F A

COMMENT: Here the "crab" seems to be an independent concept, which though brought into organization with the human figures could have been seen quite separately. This is indicated both by the fact that the subject justifies the concept by the blot features rather than by relationship to the main concept, and by the fact that in the performance proper the crab was first seen separately and then built into the larger concept. Score two main responses, and indicate the linkage by bracketing.

Card III

PERFORMANCE	INQUIRY
This is a scene from an Oscar Wilde comedy. There are two English butlers bowing out of the room. Each is precise and correct, saying, "After you, my dear Alphonse". Both figures indicate slimness and officiousness. . . . The red is the satirical comment of the dramatist suggesting the foolishness or irony of the situation. The red here is a butterfly. What has it to do with the polite butlers? It is light and insubstantial . . . The butlers are opening doors or lifting up similar objects. They have high-heeled shoes, indicating the ornate, aristocratic, old-fashioned nature of the picture.	S: I used all the blot. The side bits of red don't fit in. The red butterfly is an ironic comment. It has form, beauty and pattern. An orthodoxy, yet it is insubstantial and fluttery like the butlers. E: You said they were lifting something. S: Yes, it looks like a menial task, lifting bed warmers or something. They have high white collars, white sideburns, indicating gentility. E: What about this made it seem a butterfly? S: The shape of the wings, central body, and the pronounced color.

$$\textit{Score:} \quad \begin{array}{l} 1. \\ 2. \end{array} \left. \begin{array}{l} \text{W} \\ \text{D} \end{array} \right\} \quad \begin{array}{l} \text{M,Fc,FC}' \\ \text{FC}_{\text{sym}}\text{,FM} \end{array} \quad \begin{array}{l} \text{H} \\ \text{A} \end{array} \quad \left. \begin{array}{l} \text{P} \\ \text{P} \end{array} \right\} {\rightarrow} \text{O} \quad \begin{array}{l} 3.0 \\ 1.5 \end{array}$$

COMMENT: The comment "the red is the satirical comment of the dramatist" at first gives the impression that the center red *D* is used in a way completely subordinate to the main concept, and hence not to be scored separately. However, when it emerges as a "butterfly" which is popularly seen as a separate concept, it is given a separate location score, and the linkage is shown by bracketing it with the main *W* for the "butlers." The "bed-warmers or something" are not given a separate location score since they are clearly accessory to the concept of "butlers" and could not have been seen separately.

3. Apart from the criterion of whether or not the response could have been seen separately, the tightness or looseness of the organization plays a part in determining whether separate main responses should be scored, or whether all elaborations are subsumed under one main concept.

a. Where the organization is very tight, the parts should not be given separate location scores, either main or additional, unless a popular concept is involved in the elaboration such as the "animals" in Card VIII, the "butterfly" or "bow" on Card III, or the populars on X. In this latter instance the subsidiary semi-independent concept should be scored as a separate main response. Some cards lend themselves to much more tightly organized concepts than do others, for example, Cards I, IV, V, VII and to a lesser extent II, VIII, and IX. Examples using Card I and Card VIII follow:

Card I

PERFORMANCE

Three dancers. The two on the side are men dressed in hoods and capes and they are whirling around the one in the center. The one in the center is a woman with her arms raised and her head back. The men are making as if to fight over her and the winner carry her off.

INQUIRY

S: I used the whole thing. It is a ballet. The woman has a transparent skirt on, too.

Score: W   M,Fc   H   4.5

COMMENT: Here we are dealing with a very tightly organized concept. Despite the fact that the center "woman" is often seen separately, this is not at the "popular" level and does not seem to justify breaking down this tight organization into its component parts.

Card VIII

PERFORMANCE

This is a coat of arms. There are heraldic animals on the sides, rampant, as they say. The color, I think, suggests this, since coats-of-arms are multicolored.

INQUIRY

E: Can you tell me about the rest of it?
S: Well! there are these rampant animals, and then the suggestion of a shield or something. The center part is rather vague, but it is the right general shape.
E: What do you mean "rampant"?
S: Of course, if it weren't for the coat-of-arms idea I would say the animals are climbing up something. But on coats-of-arms they are usually standing on their hind legs in stylized, frozen action. That's what I meant by "rampant."

Score: 1. W ⎫   FC   Embl   2.0
          2. D ⎭   FM   (A)   P   1.5

COMMENT: This is a tightly organized concept; but though the animals are built in as an integral part, as populars they must be given separate treatment in the scoring. Two main location scores are given and bracketed to indicate linkage into a whole.

b. When an organization is loose, those parts that have been, or could well have been, seen separately are given main location scores (or additional location scores if the semi-independent concepts are not mentioned until the inquiry). In some cases there is a whole concept built up with a main determinant score that seems to subsume all the independent concepts and tie them together. Then the whole concept is given a main *W,* the separate details main scores also, and the organization indicated by bracketing them together. In other instances there is no subsuming whole given, and the only *W* that can be scored is an additional one, bracketing the component responses together to indicate the intention of the subject. Certain cards, especially III and X, lend themselves to a loose organization if an integrated whole is to be built up at all. Here are three instances:

Card VIII

PERFORMANCE

Brings to mind immediately a book I read as a kid on the South Seas. These are under-water creatures and coral. What fascinated me most was the account of how coral organisms generate quickly producing a honeycomb. The green and the pink are water and flowers. These two side things are sea lizards with a sense of climbing up. But the whole, the colors most of all, they're under water, a covering of green water.

Kaleidoscopic patterns. There is still something wrong. The colors are not

INQUIRY

S: Oh yes! The South Seas. It was the whole thing. The colors chiefly. Coral is pink. The whole pink or part of it. This is the green sea (pointing to center blue).

E: Did you use this part? (pointing to the side pink detail).

S: No, except that it reinforces the idea of water.

E: You mentioned sea lizards.

S: Here (pointing to side pink details and elaborating the parts and movement).

E: You mentioned a kaleidoscope?

S: I rejected the kaleidoscopic pattern

right. The green should be below and the pink above, but this is an afterthought.

partially. It was only the different colors giving an impression of weirdness. Weird shapes in a symmetrical pattern. You know how it is in a kaleidoscope. One gets symmetrical patterns of colors, accidentally, and you can't explain all of the pattern. And that's what made me think of an under-the-sea scene.

Score:
1.	W ⎫	CF	N		0.5
2.	D ⎭	FM	A	P	1.5

COMMENT: The "under-the-sea" concept subsumes the whole and is essentially color-determined. The popular animals are losely organized into this whole, the chief concession to the "under-the-sea" concept being to call them "sea-lizards." Although the animals must be scored separately, neither the "flowers" nor the "sea water" achieve the status of semi-independent concepts, being part of the vaguely specified "kaleidoscopic patterns . . . different colors giving an impression of weirdness."

Card IX

PERFORMANCE

This one is jolly . . . It is a marine extravaganza.

INQUIRY

E: What about the blot made it seem like a marine extravaganza?

S: The little orange bits at the top center are lobster claws and the right color. The whole blot is something like what you would see through the glass bottom of a boat. The orange are fish with their tails up, swimming down. They might be goldfish. Here are some white oyster-shells (bottom *D*'s of "violin"). There is some coral at the bottom, the pink. That is both shape and color, a mass and details in the branching center part. Finally the green growth is seaweed.

E: Was it just the parts that made you think of the marine extravaganza?

S: It was chiefly the color, the parts fitted in.

Score: 1.   W   CF   N   0.5

      add.1.   (d   FC   Ad   1.0)

      add.2.   (D   FM,FC   A   2.0)

      add.3.   (D   FC′ A_{obj} 1.0)

COMMENT: The concept "marine extravaganza" is given in the performance proper, while the subordinate parts are not mentioned until the inquiry. Some of these have the status of semi-independent details—that is, the "lobster claws," the "gold-fish," and the "oyster shells"—since each of these involves a combination of form and determinant applicable only to a part of the total blot area, and each, though "woven into" the main concept, has no essential functional dependence upon it. Additional location scores are given for semi-independent details which do not emerge until the inquiry.

Card X

PERFORMANCE

Nothing but claws.

At the top, the root of a tree, gnarled.

At each side a sea crab.

Two green caterpillars at the bottom devouring a leaf, a mulberry leaf.

Above that, two quarters of beef, hanging upside down from a butcher's hook.

A pawn shop symbol—only two though.

INQUIRY

S: These green claws (1) and these blue ones (2) and these other blue ones (3) and these gray ones at the top (4).

S: You can see part of the trunk (pointing to top center gray). The bottom part is the root (5).

S: The blue blots (6).
E: How do you see them?
S: As if swimming up through the water like this (motioning).

E: This whole green part. It was the shape and the color. The dark part at the top is the head (7).

S: (Pointed to the blue center.) Part of the pink is the hook. They still have their hide on. I think they're Holsteins (8).
E: You said they were hanging?
S: Yes, they look heavy.

S: (Pointed to upper center orange.) The shape and the color (9).

On each side of the red there seems the carcass of a mouse stretched out. A prehistoric form of some sort.

S: (Pointed to outer gray-brown details.) I think it is a prehistoric form. Long head, legs, short front ones, long body. It is not alive (10).
E: What made it seem like a mouse?
S: The gray color.

Seems to be a face where I saw the butcher's hook. A mask of jesters in the theatre, seen sideways. Both laughing.

S: (Indicated inside edge of pink detail.) Just the outline. They might be clowns (11).

On each side the orange seems to be an old and partly consumed carrot.

S: The shape and the color (12).
E: What makes it seem old?
S: The shading. No firmness.

The whole thing has an atmosphere of death and decay, except for the laughing faces.

E: What made it seem like death and decay?
S: The tree is dead, the monster is dead, the carrot is decayed, the lobster claws are detached, the beef is dead, and there is something sinister about the crabs. Things are being consumed. It is a cumulative impression. It was built up.
E: Did you mean that as a comment or a response?
S: As a response.

Two yellow things which are poodles sitting back on their haunches and barking. Seem to be laughing too.

E: Do you think of their laughter as being dog-like or human-like?
S: Dog-like (13).

Score:							
1.	D		F		Ad		1.0
2.	dd		F		Ad		1.0
3.	dd		F		Ad		1.0
4.	dd		F		Ad		1.0
5.	D		F		Pl		1.0
6.	D		F→FM		A	P	1.0
7.	D	W	FC,FM	m	A	P →O	2.0
8.	D		Fm		Food		2.0
9.	D		FC		obj		1.5
10.	D		FC'		A		1.5
12.	D		FC,Fc		Pl		2.0
11.	dr		F→M		(Hd)		1.5
13.	D		FM		A		2.0

COMMENT: Here the whole concept is built up, as the subject says, by a cumulative impression. All the component responses are considered as independent and given main location scores. The wholeness is shown by bracketing the main details together with an additional *W* score, and the concept of "death and decay" which provides the linkage is shown by bracketing all the determinants together with an additional *m* determinant. An additional *O* score is also given to the whole. Responses 11 and 13 are not included in the bracketed whole.

4.   As an additional consideration, the subject's apparent intention with respect to determinants must be taken into account. Where the subject uses concepts involving relatively "formless" determinants as part of a larger organization characterized by well-controlled form, these "formless" components should not be represented by main location scores. Although, for example, some subjects might give as an independent response "blood," "paint," or "fire" to the red spots on Cards II and III, the subject who carefully includes such concepts in a highly elaborated whole response probably would never be satisfied to give them as independent responses since not enough "control" in terms of form elaboration would be involved. The same consideration applies to undifferentiated shading responses built into a landscape concept. For example:

Card II

PERFORMANCE

INQUIRY

Two comical witches bowing to each other as they dance. They are laughing. Their faces are red, and they have red paint on their boots. And they clap one hand.

S: Their knees are stuck in red paint and they're laughing about it.
E: Did you use this part (top red)?
S: The bottom part of it is their red faces, and the top part is their red hats.

Score: W   M,FC,CF   (H),paint   →O   3.5

COMMENT: Here the "red paint" is built into the concept in an ingenious way. The whole thing is so tightly organized that it would be an abuse of the subject's intention to break it down into separate responses.

Card III

PERFORMANCE	INQUIRY
Two natives pounding drums while embers fly from the ashes of the fire.	S: The center bottom parts are the drums. Here are the heads and the figures. The sparks are red, so there must be fire near the drums, although I don't see red down there, so I said ashes. (Went on to detail the black natives with brass rings round their necks, etc.)

Score: W   M,CF,Fc,FC', mF   H,fire   P→O   4.5

COMMENT: Here again the subject obviously intends a whole response, and probably would never give "fire" to the red details on this card unless subordinated to a whole. The use of color, therefore, must be acknowledged through an additional determinant score without a separate location score.

In summary, there are four chief patterns of scoring more or less tightly organized concepts, usually wholes:

1.   One main location score only.

W   M,Fc   H   4.5

This is the pattern for tightly organized responses with specifications but no separate independent or semi-independent details.

2.   One main whole bracketed with independent main details.

1.   W ⎫   CF   N   0.5
2.   D ⎬   FM   A   P   1.5
       ⎭

This pattern is applicable to a more loosely built-up response where there is one determinant that subsumes the whole, but the details are semi-independent and scored as separate main responses.

3. Separate main detail responses bracketed together with an additional whole:

1.	D		F		Ad			1.0
2.	D		F		Pl			1.0
3.	D	W	F→FM	m	A	P	→O	1.0
4.	D		Fm		Food			2.0
5.	D		FC		obj			1.5

This pattern is for loosely built-up responses where the subject indicates linkage but provides no determinant that can cover the whole concept as a main determinant.

4. One main location score and additional location scores for semi-independent details not mentioned until the inquiry.

1.	W	CF	N	0.5
add.1.	(d	FC	Ad	1.0)
add.2.	(D	FM,FC	A	2.0)
add.3.	(D	FC′	A$_{obj}$	1.0)

CHAPTER 3

Scoring: Locations

Scoring for location of responses consists of classifying each response according to the area of the blot used. There are five main categories of location, with sub-categories which will be described later. These five main categories are:

1. *W*, or whole responses: all or nearly all of the blot is used.
2. *D*, or large usual detail responses: using large parts of the blot which are marked off by the Gestalt qualities of the blot itself, either by space (that is, insular), by shading, or by color.
3. *d*, or small usual detail responses: using smaller parts of the blot marked off by the Gestalt qualities of the blot itself, either by space (that is, insular or peninsular), by shading, or by color.
4. *Dd*, or unusual details: the part of the blot used is not classifiable as either a large or a small usual detail.
5. *S*, or white space responses: the white background becomes the figure and the chromatic or shaded area the background.

Main Location Scores

Main location scores are assigned to all the independent or semi-independent concepts formed by the subject during the performance proper, the location symbol being placed in the left-hand or main column of the scoring list. The chief provisions for assigning main location scores are:

1. That there be a scorable response rather than a remark (see pages 23–28) .

2. That the concept be not subsequently rejected in the inquiry (see pages 34–35) .

3. That the concept be not subsequently corrected in favor of another concept which replaces the first (see pages 28–35) .

4. That the concept be not a subordinate detail or mere specification (see pages 37–48) .

Additional Location Scores

Additional location scores are assigned under the four following conditions:

1. An additional location score is assigned for a new scorable response given spontaneously in the inquiry but not mentioned in the performance proper. Additional scores are then also assigned for determinants, content, and form level. Here are two examples:

Card IX

PERFORMANCE

Gosh, we're getting worse. . . . This is what happens when you blow on Aladdin's lamp and all the colors come out the top. Just an explosion of color. Fireworks.

INQUIRY

S: It's the whole thing. There is a profusion of color with no pattern. Like kids' fireworks or a chemical experiment.

E: When you said an explosion, did you mean it is happening right now? Or that it has happened?

S: It's happening right now. It is right in motion. It will be gone in thirty seconds. . . . And here are some clowns at the top. They have clowns' hats on. They are throwing things into the center. Here are their hands. . . . And here are some animals (pointing to the green part) with heads and snouts. They seem part of somebody's decoration.

E: What makes them like a decoration?
S: They're not doing anything . . . just the shape.

Score:	1.	W	CF,m	explosion		0.5
	add.1.	(D	M		H	2.5)
	add.2.	(D	F		(Ad)	1.0)

COMMENT: Here the "clowns" and "animals" are given additional location scores as spontaneous new concepts in the inquiry period.

Card VIII (Subject is 4 years of age)

PERFORMANCE

INQUIRY

A flower.

E: Show me the flower.
S: (Gestured to the whole blot.) I can see those climbing up now.
E: What are they?
S: They are lambs because of their legs. There's a house too.
E: Can you show me the house?
S: (Vaguely circled the whole blot.)
E: Can you tell me more about the house?
S: Don't know.

Score:	1.	W	CF	Pl		0.5
	add.1.	(D	FM	A	P	1.0)
	add.2.	(W	F—	Arch		—2.0)

COMMENT: The "flower" is given the main location score, and additional location scores for the "lambs" and the "house" which are not mentioned till the inquiry. (For an explanation of the CF scoring, see the example following item 2.)

2. An additional location score is assigned for a response given in the performance proper but later rejected in the inquiry, remembered by the subject but found unacceptable. Additional determinant, content and form-level scores are given too, even though guess-work may be necessary to assign them. An arrow pointing to the main from the additional location column indicates the rejection. For instance:

Card IX (Same 4-year-old as above)

PERFORMANCE

Another flower. (She looked away and then shook her head.) Nothing else.

INQUIRY

S: I don't want that one 'cos that's nasty.
E: Where is the flower you saw before?
S: Don't know.

Score: (←W   ←CF   ←Pl   0.5)

COMMENT: This appears to be a rejected response, and hence all scores are moved to the additional columns of the scoring list. (A *CF* determinant is assumed because this subject gives the concept "flower" to each of the last three cards, which are all colored, and to the center red detail on Card III.)

3. Additional location scores are assigned for semi-independent details in a more or less loosely organized whole when these details are not mentioned until the inquiry and hence cannot be given main location scores. (See pages 42–46.)
4. Additional location scores without additional determinant and content scores are assigned in the following instances, which are discussed more fully elsewhere:
   a.   For whole tendencies. (See pages 57–58.)
   b.   For the supplementary use of white space. (See pages 90–94.)

Wholes

There are four sub-classifications of *W* responses: (1) *W*, or whole, where the entire blot is used. (2) *W̶*, or cut-off whole, where almost all the blot is used (at least two-thirds). (3) *DW*, or confabulatory whole, where a detail is interpreted and then its meaning is generalized to the whole blot without justification in terms of matching the concept accurately to the blot material. (4) *W,S* where the entire blot plus the white spaces are used, the *S* being scored as additional.

1. W, or Whole: Score a Main W

a. *Score a main W* where the entire blot is used for the concept. For example:

Card VI

PERFORMANCE

The only thing I make out of this is the skin of an animal stretched to dry. A fur-bearing animal with very luxuriant fur. It could be a fox with the "brush" left on.

INQUIRY

S: Here's the tail (pointing to top part) and this would be the wide fur on the end.

E: What about the blot made it seem like fur?

S: The shading. Just as if the sunlight caught on it and gave the highlights and shadows.

E: What about it made it seem stretched?

S: Its shape. It has no head and both forefeet have been taken off. Just the hide itself.

E: Could it be laid on the floor?

S: No, it is tacked against the side of a wall. It is being stretched very tightly.

Score: W   Fc,m A_{obj} P   1.0

COMMENT: Here a *W* is scored, as the subject uses the entire blot for his concept.

b. *Score a main W* where the *W* is inadvertently incomplete, the intention having been to use the whole blot with no spontaneous mention of any parts of the blot to be disregarded. Specific questioning may establish that a certain part did not contribute, but since it was not the subject's intention to draw specific attention to this part to be omitted, the location is nevertheless scored as a *W*. An example, from a response to Card II, is given on the next page.

Card II

PERFORMANCE

Two clowns, hats here, and stripes painted on their faces. They're playing patty-cake.

INQUIRY

S: Their knees come up here, and they are squatting down. They have tall, soft hats, like toques kids wear to school. They have red stripes painted on their faces. They are wearing stiff white collars.

E: What about the blot made the hats look soft?

S: The shading and the irregular shape.

E: Did you include this part (bottom red *D*)?

S: No.

Score: W   M,FC,Fc   H   O   4.0

COMMENT: This is an instance of an inadvertently incomplete whole. The subject did not use the bottom center red detail but did not draw attention to this fact except in response to a direct question.

c. *Score a main W* where the subject focusses his response on one symmetrical half of the card, but makes his answer cover the whole card by bringing in the other half. This may be accomplished by relating the two halves together by action, by a concept involving "reflection," or even by saying: "It is the same on the other side."

Card VII

PERFORMANCE

A woman. She is looking at herself in the mirror. She is all dressed up before going out in the evening.

INQUIRY

S: She has a feather plume in her hair. She is sticking her lips out at herself, making sure her lipstick is just right. (The inquiry was then continued to establish determinants.)

Score: W   M,Fc   H   O

COMMENT: The two sides are related here by both action and reflection.

Card VII (subject is 7 years of age)

PERFORMANCE

Here are two puppies.

INQUIRY

E: Where are the puppies?
S: (Indicating upper two-thirds on each side) One is here and one is here.
E: Can you tell me about them?
S: Ears, head, and here is the tail.
E: Did you use this part (pointing to lower *D*)?
S: They're standing on it.

Score: W   F→FM   A   1.0

COMMENT: Here the subject intends to use the whole blot, even though no special device such as action or reflection was used to bring the two sides into relationship.

d. *Score a main W* for the main concept in an organized whole with independent or semi-independent details, provided of course that the main concept covers the whole blot. Two examples are given below; for other examples see pages 38–43.

Card X

PERFORMANCE

Two otters eating away at a branch.

INQUIRY

S: It has the general appearance of an otter (pointing to top gray). They are eating into a tree. Here is the bark eaten away.

Two circus performers with helmets, hanging on to two chickens and running square into a pole.

S: (Indicated the pink *D*'s for the performers with the gray *D*'s for helmets, and the center blue for the chickens.) They look like performers. They are carrying something or dashing about. The colors are wrong for chickens but they are the shape of chickens.

This is the grand finale of a musical comedy.

E: Tell me about the grand finale.
S: The whole is the grand finale. People are dancing. The perspective is wrong because of the side. These are decorations (pointing to the yellows and brown). They blend into the whole picture. It is a colorful pageant.

PERFORMANCE (*continued*)

INQUIRY (*continued*)

E: What could the decorations be?
S: They might be leaves or any damn thing.
E: What could these be (blue side *D*'s)?
S: They are gargoyles dancing. Everything is in motion.
E: (Pointing to top gray *D*'s) What could these be in the pageant?
S: Those are the otters.

Two trained worms.

S: (Indicating bottom green) The worms are eating something like a leaf.
E: What about the blot makes them look like worms?
S: They just look like worms.
E: Could they be caterpillars?
S: They are the right shape for caterpillars.
E: (Analogy period) Did you use the color here?
S: The leaf is green, therefore I thought it might be a leaf. Besides what else would worms eat?

Score:	1.	D ⎫	FM	A		1.5
	2.	W ⎬	M,CF	H		3.5
	3.	D ⎭	FM,CF	A	→P	1.5

COMMENT: Here the "grand finale of a musical comedy" emerges as the main concept and certainly includes the "circus performers" and the "chickens" they are carrying, as well as the "decorations" and the "gargoyles" mentioned in the inquiry. The subject obviously intends the concept to cover the whole blot. The usual "worms" are called "trained" for them to fit into the concept, although the elaboration shows them in typical animal-like action without showing how they fit into the "pageant." Similarly the "otters" are said to be there, although just how they fit in is not elaborated. It seems best to give one main *W* for the "finale," and score the "otters" and "worms" as independent concepts, though bracketing the locations in the scoring list to show the subject's intention.

Score an Additional W

a. For a whole response given in the performance proper but subsequently rejected. (See pages 35–36.)

b. For a new response, involving the whole blot, which is not mentioned until the inquiry.

c. In a loosely organized whole score an additional *W* to bracket together independent main details, thus indicating a loose linkage, there being no main determinant which covers the entire larger concept. An additional *W* is not scored when one of the semi-independent concepts is itself a *W*. (See pages 42–46.)

d. Where the whole blot serves as "ground" and the white space as "figure." (See pages 88–90.)

e. For *whole tendencies* $(\rightarrow W)$. These are scored with a *D* (or *d*, *dr*, and so on) in the main column with an arrow pointing to a *W* in the additional column. This is done where only part of the blot is used for a clear concept but the subject intends to use the whole blot. The most frequent examples of whole tendencies occur on Card VIII where the "animals" are the focus of the concept, but the subject brings in the whole blot in an unspecified or very vaguely specified way. These must be distinguished from confabulations *(DW)*, for the very vagueness of the specification prevents violence being done to the form qualities of the blot reality. Score $\rightarrow W$ also where a detail is interpreted in the performance proper but is generalized to the whole blot in the inquiry. Two examples of whole tendencies follow:

Card VIII

PERFORMANCE   INQUIRY

A couple of mice climbing the side of a wall or something.

E: Where is the wall?
S: Here (gesturing to the center part)!
E: What about it made it seem like a wall?
S: It's just where they are climbing to.

Score: D→W   FM   A   P   1.0

COMMENT: Here the intention is to use the whole blot; but only part of it, the animals in the side pink details, are seen clearly. This is not a confabulation, for violence is not done to the reality structure of the blot. It has in common with a confabulatory whole a tendency to over-generalize, though to a lesser degree and with more regard for reality.

Card I

PERFORMANCE	INQUIRY
The wings of a bat.	S: I originally saw only these (pointing to side projections) but now I look at it the whole thing seems like a bat.

Score: d→W   F   A   P   1.0

COMMENT: Here only part of the blot is used in the performance for part of the usual bat, but the whole bat is seen in the whole blot in the inquiry.

2.   W̶, or Cut-Off Whole: Score a Main W̶

a.   *Score a main* W̶ where the subject uses almost all the blot (at least two-thirds) but makes a point of omitting or disregarding certain portions which do not fit with the concept. Very frequently, the cut-off whole is a superior concept in which the match of the concept to the blot is improved by the omission of certain parts of the blot. In other instances, this effort for form-accuracy may be carried to an overcritical extreme. In instances where greater accuracy is not involved, a cut-off whole is the result of not being able to work certain parts of the blot into the concept. For example, the red details in Cards II and III are commonly omitted, if not specifically in the performance proper, at least in the inquiry when the subject is asked to indicate the location used. To score a cut-off whole on cards other than II or III, the subject must make *spontaneous* mention of any parts of the blot to be disregarded; if the fact that certain portions are not used emerges only in response to questions in the inquiry such as "Did you use this part?," an incomplete whole is involved which should be scored W (see page 53). However, on

Card II and Card III the examiner can usually assume a W̶ unless specific mention is made of the use of the red details. Three examples of W̶ scores follow:

Card II

PERFORMANCE

Looks like two little lambs with noses together and paws down. Ears and head.

INQUIRY

S: (Indicating the whole black area) Here they are. Eyes, ears, part of front paw, neck. Just the neck and paw showing.

E: What about the blot makes them seem like lambs?

S: They are woolly. Lambs' wool is in ridges like this. That's why I called them lambs.

E: How do you see them?

S: (Long pause) This is kinda foolish. It looks as though they were jumping at each other, or standing up towards each other.

Score: W̶   Fc,FM   A   P   3.0

COMMENT: This is a W̶ rather than a W because the subject used only the black parts.

Card I

PERFORMANCE

A woman's pelvis.

INQUIRY

S: I used it all except for these (pointing to side ear-like projections), which didn't fit. It is three-dimensional. When I first picked it out it seemed like something you might see in a medical book, or an X-ray. Vertebrae and bones around the pelvis.

Score: W̶   Fk   Sex   1.0

COMMENT: This is clearly a W̶, where the subject specifically states that certain parts were not used because they did not fit.

Card VIII

PERFORMANCE

INQUIRY

It suggests a coat-of-arms. There is the crown motif, with supporting figures. Then there are lions or stags. These are important in heraldry.

E: Can you show me the crown?
S: Here it is in the center part of the gray, and the rest of the gray is the lions. Then of course these animals on the side. I was really only thinking of the pink and the gray. The rest doesn't contribute particularly.

Score: 1.   W̶   F   Embl   2.0
add.1.   (D   F   A   →P   1.0)

COMMENT: The main location score is a W̶, to exclude the popular animals which were not mentioned until the inquiry. Had they been mentioned in the performance proper two main location scores would have been given, a W̶ and a *D,* with a bracket to show the linkage. Here, however, the animals are given an additional location score.

b.   *Score a main* W̶ where the subject uses the two sides of the blot but ignores the connecting middle portion, as where there are two human or animal figures, one on each side, as for example in Card I. Here the rule is to score a W̶ if the two figures are seen in relationship and the subject specifically states that he is not using the center part; otherwise a *W* would be scored, since his intention clearly would be to use the whole blot.

Card I

PERFORMANCE

INQUIRY

Two very charming goblins dancing in the moonlight, holding hands and swirling around at a great rate. That is what I saw immediately but that can't explain it all. They have Rip Van Winkle hats on, their hands are extended. Short dwarfish bodies. It is macabre. It doesn't explain this (pointing to the center).

E: Where are the goblins?
S: (Pointed to the two side portions.) I intended to use the whole thing, but can't work in the center part. Here are their hands, and feet. Brim and crown of their hats. Can't see their faces. Squat, humped body.
E: What about it made it like moonlight?
S: That's when goblins dance.

Score: W   M   (H)   3.5

COMMENT: This is a W̶ rather than a *D* because the two figures are seen in relationship. It is not a *W* because the subject
did not use the center part of the blot for the concept.

c. Card VI presents certain difficulties in applying the general
rules that govern scoring W̶ as distinct from *D,* since the lower
part of the card (more than two-thirds of the area) is scored *D*
if used separately. A W̶ is scored if the subject seems to consider
the lower part of the card to be *the main part* of the card (excluding the upper detail). If, on the other hand, he considers
the lower part to be merely *a part* of the card, a *D* would be
scored. A W̶ scoring would usually be indicated by such wording as: "This card is a . . . but this (pointing to upper detail)
does not fit," or "This is a . . . without that (upper detail)."
A *D* scoring would usually be indicated if the subject says:
"This part is a . . ., and this part is a . . . ." Where the attitude
of the subject is not clear from his original formulation, it
should be clarified in the inquiry; otherwise his attitude can
only be assumed to be that which he demonstrates in the rest
of the record. Note these cases:

Card VI

PERFORMANCE

INQUIRY

An animal skin, perhaps of a bear.

S: It was the whole thing only I sort of
ignored this part up here. The general
impression was of an animal skin.
The sort of furry impression. And
then it is the right shape. The head
is not there but here are the parts for
the feet.

Score: W̶   Fc   A$_{obj}$ P   1.0

COMMENT: The W̶ intention is clear from the spontaneous
formulation in the inquiry. The lower part of the blot is considered the main part of the card, and the upper detail is excluded by being "ignored."

Card VI

PERFORMANCE	INQUIRY
1. This part here is a polar bear instead of an ordinary bear. A bear rug, at least.	1. S: It was the grayish white color that made it seem a polar bear. It is furry. It is no particular shape, which is why I said it was a rug.
2. This part here could be a butterfly.	2. S: This top part. It is the shape of a butterfly.

Score:
1.	D	cF, C'F	A_{obj}	0.5
2.	D	F	A	1.0

COMMENT: Here a D is scored for the lower part since the subject calls it "this part here" and goes on to use the top part for another concept.

d. Card VII presents similar difficulties in applying the general rules that govern scoring W as distinct from D. A W is scored if the subject seems to consider the upper two-thirds of the blot *the main part* of the card (excluding the lower detail), provided that both sides of the card are used in some sort of relationship. This would not necessarily be a relationship of movement, as long as the position of the pair of figures or objects has some significance. However, if he considers the upper part to be merely *a part* of the card, a D would be scored. In any case a D would be scored if either side of the upper two-thirds is used alone, or if the subject merely indicates that there is one object or figure on each side, and does not see the pair of objects as related in any way. Two examples follow:

Card VII

PERFORMANCE	INQUIRY
It could be a couple of dogs. They might be book ends, the way they are with their tails out.	S: (Indicating upper two-thirds of the blot) Here are the dogs. Head, body, tail. Their ears are standing straight up. They are facing each other with their tails extended. E: What made them seem like book ends?

S: They're not really the right kind of dogs. They usually have pointers with their tails out like that. It is a terrier in a pointer pose. Sort of a silly dog. Their ears are too long for terriers. And then you could put the books in between them. They are apart like book ends.

Score: W   FM   (A)   2.0

COMMENT: The pair of dogs are seen in relationship, and the concept is presented as though it referred to the card as a whole, rather than to a part of it, although the subject clearly pointed to only the upper part and did not bring in the lower portion. *W* seems the best scoring. Indeed, *W* could be scored even though later the subject might have used the lower part for some other concept.

Card VII

PERFORMANCE

This part could be a dog (pointing to upper two-thirds of the left side). And this could be a butterfly (pointing to lower centre portion). There's another dog on this side (pointing to right side).

INQUIRY

S: Here is the head, tail, and this might be its ear. It's the same on the other side.
E: Anything else?
S: The butterfly. Wings, body.

Score: 1.   D   F   A   1.5
          2.   D   F   A   1.0

COMMENT: Here the subject uses the top portion as only part of the card, and immediately points to the lower portion, suggesting a second concept. Moreover, the upper details are not seen in relationship to each other but are simply duplicated, one on each side. In such a case *D* rather than *W* is scored.

Score an Additional W

a. For a *W* response given in the performance proper but subsequently rejected. (See pages 35–36.)
b. For a new response, involving a *W*, which is not mentioned until the inquiry.

c. In a loosely organized response where two-thirds or more (but not all) of the blot is used, a W^x may be scored as an additional, bracketing together independent main details to indicate the loose linkage. (See page 42.)

d. Where two-thirds or more (but not all) of the blot serves as "ground" and the white space as "figure."

3.   DW, or Confabulatory Whole: Score a Main DW

Score a main DW where the subject generalizes from one detail to the whole card, but he is able to justify his response only in terms of the one clearly seen detail, and insists that the whole card is used when it is impossible to reconcile the concept with the shape of the whole blot. A *DW* always involves minus form level—that is, the concept is a poor match for the blot. Thus a *DW* always implies a concept with a definite form; a vague concept could not be a *DW*. Genuine *DW* are practically limited to preschool children and subjects with marked deficiencies in intellectual function. Three samples follow:

Card IV

PERFORMANCE

A snake.

INQUIRY

E: Where is the snake?
S: (Indicated the whole blot vaguely.)
E: What about it made it seem like a snake?
S: (Pointing to left side projection) Here is the head and neck.
E: Did you use this (pointing to the main part of the blot)?
S: That's the rest of the snake.

Score: DW   F—   A   —1.5   O—

COMMENT: Here the subject overgeneralizes from the side *d* which resembles part of the snake, using the whole blot for the "rest of the snake" although the shape of the blot as a whole cannot be reconciled with the shape of a snake.

Card VI (subject aged 4)

PERFORMANCE

Kitty.

INQUIRY

E: Where is the kitty?
S: (Pointing to the top part) Whiskers.
E: What could this be (pointing to lower portion)?
S: Kitty.

Score: DW   F—   A   —1.5   O—

COMMENT: The subject indicates his intention to use the whole blot (indeed, this was compatible with his general approach, for he used whole locations throughout the record) yet the only justification offered for the concept is the top part. It is not clear whether he confabulated from the tiny details or from the "usual wings"; but this does not matter in this instance, for the *DW* would be scored in either case.

Card VI

PERFORMANCE

An X-ray plate of a cat. A poor one.

INQUIRY

S: Here is the straight backbone, and the light and dark shading of an X-ray plate.
E: Why a poor one?
S: The lines are not clearly defined.
E: What about it makes it seem the X-ray of a cat particularly?
S: Here are the whiskers, and the general contours. It is exactly what X-ray plates look like with light and dark shading.

Score: DW   Fk—   A.At   —1.5

COMMENT: This is a mixture of confabulation and "contamination." The confabulated aspect is an overgeneralization from the "whiskers" to the whole blot to give the concept "cat." The shading is interpreted as an X ray. The two concepts are telescoped giving "an X-ray plate of a cat"; this is known as "contamination."

Score an Additional DW

a. Where the *DW* is given in the performance but rejected in the inquiry;

b. Where the *DW* is not given as a response until the inquiry.

Do Not Score DW

a. *Do not score DW* where one detail is clearly seen, and the intention is to use the whole blot, but the remainder of the blot is vaguely specified in such a way that it does not do violence to the shape of the blot area. In such a case score $D{\rightarrow}W$ (or $d{\rightarrow}W$, and the like). Minus form level is an essential aspect of a *DW;* vague specifications could fit almost any part of the blot area, and hence do not bring the response into the minus form-level range. Note the examples below. (For discussion and further examples, see pages 57–58.)

Card V

PERFORMANCE

A sort of person, perhaps an animal, dressed in human clothes, gaining human attributes, standing upright. Perhaps a rabbit standing in back of something. Rather a long way away.

INQUIRY

S: It was this center part for the rabbit, but I used the whole thing.

E: You said the rabbit was standing behind something.

S: They might be bushes and trees.

E: What about them made them seem like bushes and trees.

S: Just the outline. Something he is standing behind.

Score: D→W   M,FK   (A)   2.0

COMMENT: Here the subject's intention was to use the whole, although only the central detail is clearly visualized. The rest of the blot is explained but remains sufficiently vague that a tendency to a whole seems best to represent the performance.

Card II (19-year-old male)

PERFORMANCE

Really conveys hardly anything at all. Slight thought of a woman's sex organ.

INQUIRY

E: What part of the blot did you use?

S: The whole thing.

A vague idea.

E: What about it made it seem like a woman's sex organ?

S: It was suggested by the redness, indicating the breaking of the membrane. It was only a vague impression; something like you might see in medical books.

Score: D→W   CF   Sex   0.5

COMMENT: Here the subject generalizes from the lower red *D* to the whole blot, but the resulting concept is vague and indefinite rather than inaccurate; hence a *DW* score is inappropriate.

b. *Do not score DW* where the subject generalizes from a small, clearly seen detail to the whole blot, but manages to reconcile the rest of the concept with the rest of the blot sufficiently well to avoid minus form level. Here score *W*, not *DW*.

Card VI

PERFORMANCE

A cat that has been run over by a steam roller. Its whiskers are up at the top.

INQUIRY

S: It is a cat because of the whiskers (pointing to the light shaded parts of the top detail).

E: What about the blot made it look as though it had been run over by a steam roller?

S: Look how flat it is!

E: Can you tell me more about the cat?

S: The shading makes it look furry. That's part of the reason it looked like a cat. It is very furry but very flat.

Score: W   Fc   A   P→O   1.5

COMMENT: This is a *W*, not a *DW* (nor even a *D→W*) since the whole blot is used, and in a way that does justice to the shape of the whole. Even though the top part is the clearest, the way the bottom part is used, especially with an *Fc* determinant, takes it out of the range of a "vague something" which characterizes the whole tendency. However, had the subject said, "This is a cat because of the whiskers at the top," giving nothing further to justify the fit of the concept of "cat" to the rest of the blot, it would be a *DW*.

Card I (subject is 6½ years old)

PERFORMANCE	INQUIRY
I don't know . . . there's black stuff . . . it looks funny . . . there is a big crab . . . these two things here (pointing to small center top projections).	E: Show me the crab. S: (Indicated whole blot.) E: What about it made it seem like a crab? S: These (pointing to projections again). E: What could those be? S: Its claws. E: Can you tell me more about the crab? S: Don't know.

Score: W   F   A   1.0

COMMENT: Although the main justification of the crab is the "claws," this does not meet the requirements of a *DW* since the shape of the whole blot is not incompatible with the shape of a crab.

c.   *Do not score DW* where the inaccuracy is not a matter of over-generalization from one detail, but a combination of a number of different details or specifications together in a bizarre way. The resulting concept matches the blot but is an illogical concept and belongs in the category of confabulatory combinations. Score a *W* if the whole blot is used, otherwise assign the appropriate detail score. For example:

Card V (inverted—subject is 4½)

PERFORMANCE	INQUIRY
Buttercups . . . that is how they are. There was once one in my house.	S: (Indicated whole.) There is its mouth. Here are its legs. Here are some more legs. It flies. (Mouth was where the bottom *d* would be with the card in an upright position. One set of legs was the top *d*, the other set the side projections.)

Score: W   F—   A   P   —0.5

COMMENT: Here the "mouth" is a minus element, and the extra pair of legs also. Yet the concept is related to the blot, detail by detail, in a way much too specific to leave any possibility of a *DW*. (It is assumed that the subject meant "butterfly" when she said "buttercup.")

4. W,S or Whole with Supplementary Use of White Space: Score W,S

Score W,S (a main whole with an additional *S*) where the white spaces more or less surrounded by the blot area are used as part of the whole concept. Thus on Card I the four white spaces may be used as "lakes" in a "landscape" concept, or as "eyes and mouth" in a concept of "mask" or "cat's face." This constitutes an exception to the general rule that no additional location is scored for details that are parts of a tightly-organized whole. (For further discussion of the supplementary use of white space, see pages 90–94.)

Usual Details

Usual details are those listed on pages 95–99 in *The Rorschach Technique*. This list is based on those details most frequently used by subjects who break the whole up into parts, and as such represent obvious subdivisions of the blot, presumably facilitated by the structure of the blot material itself. Large and small usual details are differentiated:

1. *D, or large usual detail,* usually insular in location, marked off by space, shading or color from the rest of the blot.
2. *d, or small usual detail,* usually insular or peninsular, similarly marked off by space, shading or color from the rest of the blot.

For assistance in scoring usual details, the Klopfer and Kelley lists are reproduced on pages 70 to 79, where the blot areas to which they refer are marked off on achromatic reproductions of the blots.

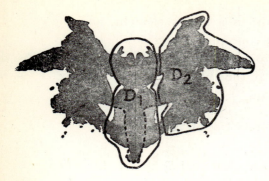

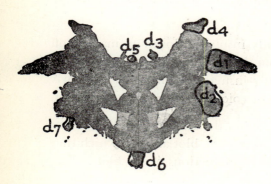

Card I

Large Usual Details

D_1 Entire center with or without lighter gray in lower portion.

D_2 Entire side.

D_3 Lower center without lighter gray.

D_4 Entire lower center.

D_5 Upper side.

D_6 Upper third of center.

Small Usual Details

d_1 Upper outer projections.

d_2 Lower side.

d_3 Upper, inner, claw-like extensions.

d_4 Uppermost projections.

d_5 Upper innermost details.

d_6 Bottom projection.

d_7 Small knob-like extension at lower side.

Popular Response

W or Cut-off *W:* Any creature with the body in the center *D* and wings at the sides.

Card II

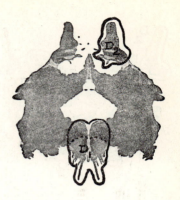

Large Usual Details

D₁ Lower red with or without black-red mixture.

D₂ Upper red.

D₃ Entire side black.

D₄ Upper portion of black.

Small Usual Details

d₁ Upper center.

d₂ Bottom outer projection.

d₃ Bottom projection adjacent to preceding *d.*

d₄ Upper side projection.

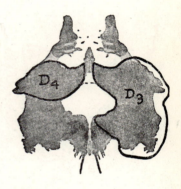

Popular Response

Black area, either as an organized cut-off whole with or without top center *d,* or as a *D:* Any animal or part of an animal of the dog, bear, rabbit, bull or rhinoceros variety.

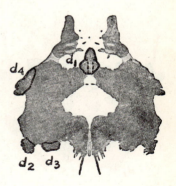

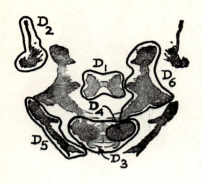

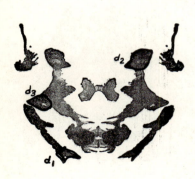

Card III

Large Usual Details

D₁ Inner red.

D₂ Outer red with or without tail-like extension.

D₃ Entire lower center.

D₄ Lower center black.

D₅ Lower side black.

D₆ Upper side black, head and upper part of body of usual figure.

D₇ Middle side black.

D₈ One of the two human figures.

D₉ Lower center light gray.

Small Usual Details

d₁ Bottom side portion, with or without lower part of "leg."

d₂ Top side black.

d₃ Side black lateral protrusion, usually upside down.

Popular Responses

1. Entire black area: Two human figures in a bending position. Legs must be seen in side bottom *D* and figures in action. Includes dressed up animals. If legs seen where arms usually are, or non-dressed up animals with two pairs of legs, at most the score is an additional *P*.

2. Center red *D:* As "bow tie," "hair ribbon," or "butterfly." The shape alone or shape combined with color.

Card IV

Large Usual Details

D₁ Lower center.

D₂ Lower side black and gray, sometimes including upper side portion.

D₃ Lower side light gray.

D₄ Entire vertical dark center.

D₅ Inner dark side detail.

Small Usual Details

d₁ Upper side extensions, sometimes with small adjacent portion.

d₂ Uppermost portion, sometimes including adjacent shaded portion.

d₃ Outermost lower side extension.

d₄ Lowermost portion of lower center detail.

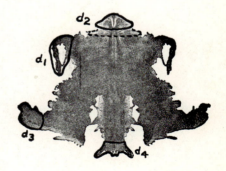

Card V

Large Usual Details

D_1 Entire side with or without light gray extensions.

D_2 Center vertical portion.

Small Usual Details

d_1 Bottom center.

d_2 Side extension sometimes with adjacent thin extension.

d_3 Top center, with or without uppermost protrusions.

d_4 Contour of lower side detail.

Popular Response

W or cut-off *W:* Any winged creature with the body in the center *D* and the wings at the sides. Same concept with card upside down.

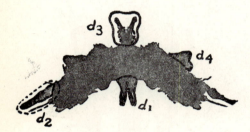

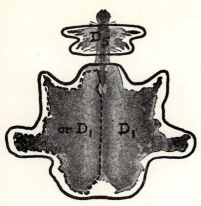 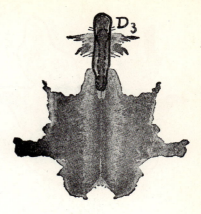

Large Usual Details

D₁   Entire lower portion or half of lower portion.

D₂   Entire upper portion, sometimes including light gray uppermost portion of lower detail.

D₃   Upper black portion only of center column, sometimes without slightly shaded outer portion.

D₄   Entire dark vertical center.

D₅   Lighter part only of upper portion.

Small Usual Details

d₁   Uppermost detail with or without "whiskers."

d₂   Lower lateral extensions.

d₃   Two inner light gray ovals.

d₄   Bottom inner projections.

Popular Response   With or without the top *D:*   The skin of an animal. The use of shading for furriness or markings on the inside of the skin is essential.

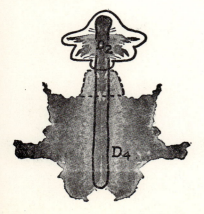 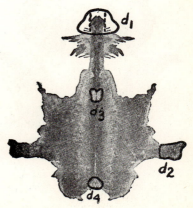

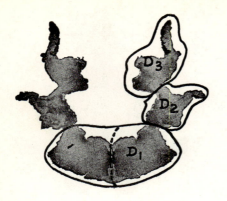

Card VII

Large Usual Details

D_1 Entire bottom portion, sometimes each half separately.

D_2 Middle third.

D^3 Upper third, with or without uppermost projection.

D_4 Upper two-thirds.

Small Usual Details

d_1 Dark center bottom detail.

d_2 Top projections.

d_3 Light gray projections on upper inner corner of top third.

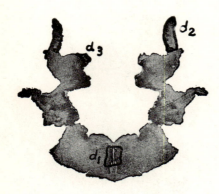

Card VIII

Large Usual Details

D₁   Side pink.

D₂   Lower pink and orange.

D₃   Top gray portion with or without center line, sometimes including rib-like figure and/or blue portion.

D₄   Middle blue portion.

D₅   Rib-like figure in upper center.

D₆   Bottom pink alone.

D₇   Bottom orange alone.

Small Usual Details

d₁   Lateral extensions of bottom orange.

Popular Response

Side *D:* Any kind of four-legged animal in any kind of motion. If not seen in action or inaccurately called birds or fish, only a tendency toward *P* can be scored. If color is used, an additional original score is given.

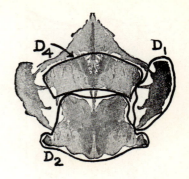

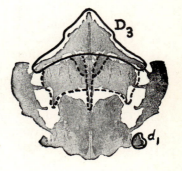

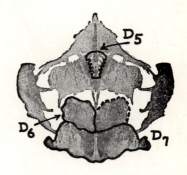

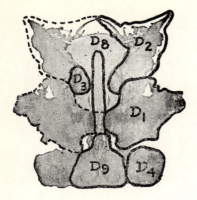

Card IX

Large Usual Details

D_1 Green portion.
D_2 Orange portion.
D_3 Small inner portion at junction of green and orange.
D_4 Lateral pink.
D_5 Entire pink portion plus center line, card inverted.
D_6 Entire pink or either half.
D_7 Center portion between lateral greens.
D_8 Center gray portion, with or without D_7.
D_9 Inner pink portion.

Small Usual Details

d_1 All or most of upper inner orange projections.
d_2 Eye-like portion in middle including green and white slits.
d_3 Arch-like light orange at top center.

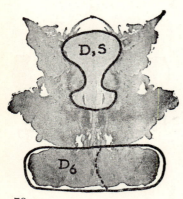

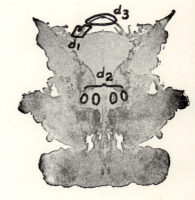

Card X

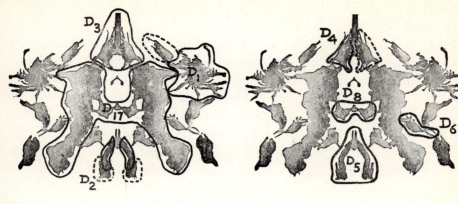

Large Usual Details

D₁ Outer blue, sometimes with outer green.
D₂ Inner green, dark portions only.
D₃ Entire gray portion at top.
D₄ Gray "animals" at top without inner gray column.
D₅ Entire inner green.
D₆ Outer gray-brown figures.
D₇ Light portion between inner greens.
D₈ Inner blue.
D₉ Pink portion separately.

D₁₀ Inner yellow.
D₁₁ Outer orange.
D₁₂ Inner orange.
D₁₃ Outer upper green.
D₁₄ Gray column at top without gray "animals" beside it.
D₁₅ Outer yellow.
D₁₆ Pink with entire top gray, card inverted.
D₁₇ Pink with inner blue.

Popular Responses

1. Outer blue D: Any many-legged animal, such as a spider, crab or octopus. Use of color gives an additional original score.
2. To center green D (D₂): Any elongated greenish animal, such as caterpillar, garden snake, tobacco worm.

Color must be used, otherwise only additional P is scored.
3. Light green D (D₇): The head of an animal with long ears or horns, such as a rabbit, donkey, or goat. Any addition (e.g. D₂ or S) adds an original element scored as an additional O.

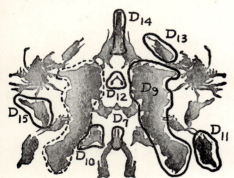

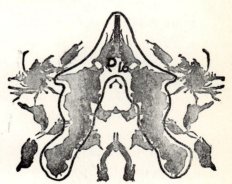

Score D or d

a.   *Score D or d* where the intention of the subject seems to be to use the entire area delimited by the Klopfer and Kelley definition (as marked on pages 70–79). Sometimes there are omissions or additions, most of which are themselves allowed within the definition. For example, on Card III, *D* is scored for the outer red portion of the blot, even though the tail-like extension is omitted. Again on Card IV, *d* is scored for the upper side extensions even though a small adjacent portion of the blot may be included. Sometimes the subject may add or omit bits that are not allowed for in the Klopfer and Kelley list. These may still be scored *D* (or *d*) when they constitute an unimportant part of the concept, and indeed seem to be more or less inadvertently omitted or added. This is similar to the case of the inadvertently incomplete whole, where a *W* is scored despite the fact that certain parts of the blot may not actually be used for the concept. (See page 53.)

b.   *Score D* where there is a combination of usual details which itself is listed as a usual detail. For example, in Card X the pink *D* is so frequently used in combination with the center gray *D* and/or the center blue *D* that the resulting combination itself is listed as a *D*.

c.   *Score D* rather than *W* for the lower portion of Card VI, when the subject uses it as *a part* rather than as *the main part* of the blot. (See pages 61–62 for discussion and examples.)

Score Additional D or d

a.   For a new response not given until the inquiry.

b.   For a response given in the performance proper but later rejected in the inquiry. (See pages 35–36.)

c.   For semi-independent details in a more or less loosely organized whole when the details are not mentioned until the inquiry. (See pages 42–44.)

d.   For usual details used as supplementary to a white space response. (See page 88.)

Do Not Score D or d

a. *Score dr* where additions or omissions are made to or from the defined areas which are not themselves accounted for in the definitions, and which make a material difference in the concept. Usually these additions and omissions are carefully specified by the subject, as in the case of *W*. Examples are given on pages 86–88.

b. A *dr* is scored where the combination of usual details is itself not frequent enough to be listed as a *D*. For example, in Card X a combination of the outer yellow, gray-brown and orange *D*'s constitutes an unusual combination and would be scored *dr*.

Unusual Details, or Dd

If the response is not a whole, not listed among usual details, and not a space response, it must be scored as an unusual detail. There are four sub-divisions of *Dd:* (1) *dd,* or tiny details, (2) *de,* or edge details, (3) *di,* or inside details, (4) *dr,* or rare details.

1. dd, or Tiny Details: Score dd

Score dd for small or tiny details, which like *d* are insular or peninsular, marked off by space, shading or color from the rest of the blot, but which are less frequent than usual details and hence are not listed as *d*. For instance:

Card VI: upper outer projection. "A statue of Venus sitting on a rock."

Card VI: narrow light gray center strip. "A highway looked at from an aeroplane. Just the straight, narrow, white strip. A white cement highway."

Card VI: black tips of upper *D*. "Disney birds of prey. Vultures."

For these and further examples, see page 82.

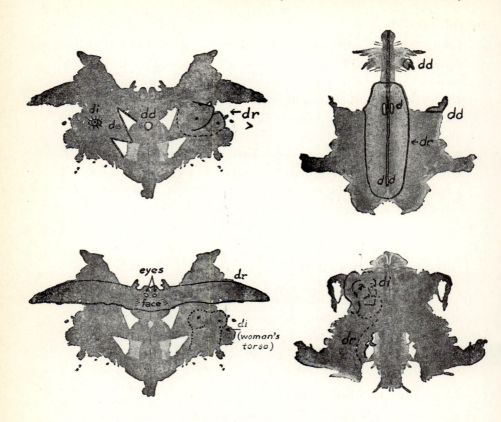

Some Examples of Unusual Detail Locations. Card I (left) , Card VI (upper right) , Card IV (lower right) .

Do Not Score dd

a. *Score d* for small usual details, even though approaching "tiny" in size.

b. *Do not score dd* for details, however tiny, which are not clearly marked off by the Gestalt qualities of the blot. Score *di* if these are carved out of the shading; score *de* if they constitute a bit of the edge; score *dr* if they are arbitrarily delimited to suit the needs of the concept.

2. de, or Edge Details: Score de

Score de for locations using *only* the edge of the blot. The facts that none of the shaded portion was used and that it is the contour of the edge itself that was the location for the response must be determined in the inquiry. The two most frequent types of edge detail are:

a. Profiles, with denial of the use of the shaded portion, even when described as a silhouette, and with no specifications from the shaded area, such as eye, check, or the like.

b. Coastlines, if again only the irregular outline was used. Other examples are as follows:

Card II: lower edge of center *S.* "Steps descending towards each other. Just the edge. A wide step, sort of rounded, like those you might see in fun houses, rolling, although I don't see them in motion now."

Card I: zig-zag lines marking off white spaces from the dark gray side detail. "Lightning. Just the zig-zag line." (Page 82.)

Do Not Score de

a. *Do not score de* where the blot itself or any part of it except the very edge is used for the concept. Thus a concept involving tiny human or animal figures or objects seen in small projections along the edge would be scored *dd* rather than *de*. Similarly, profiles would not be scored *de* if the shaded area is used for elaborations, such as eye or cheek.

b. *Score D* for the upper edge of the side *D* on Card V. This is so frequently used as the profile of a man that it is listed as a usual detail.

c. *Do not score de* where a coastline response is given, but when the subject elaborates the interior as geography, or gives a vista response or a topographical map response indicating the use of shading.

3. di, or Inside Details: Score di

Score di when the inside shaded portion of the blot is used without involving the edges at all (or only quite coincidentally) and where any minute shading differences used to delimit and specify the concept are not obvious ones. It is frequently necessary to have the subject trace the concept in order for the examiner to ascertain whether or not there is a match between concept and blot area. The essential factor is that *di*'s are seen inside a blot area which to the overwhelming majority of subjects is an unbroken surface. Therefore, shaded areas that are conspicuous enough to be taken not uncommonly out of surrounding areas by other subjects should be considered rare details rather than *di* (unless they are usual *D*'s like the "deer's head" on Card IX). Below are three examples (illustrated on page 82).

Card IV

PERFORMANCE	INQUIRY
This is a Cavalier from the time of Charles I.	S: (Indicating upper shaded section in left side) Here are his eyes; eyebrows; long, curling hair; nose; moustache; beard; and the suggestion of a ruff here. He's looking out of the corner of his eye in rather a distrustful way.

Score: di   Fc→M   Hd   O   4.0

COMMENT: This is scored *di* despite the fact that the location reaches the edge of the blot in two places, because the location is carved out of the shaded area, using differentiations in shading for delimitation and specification which are not usually used for such purposes.

Card I

PERFORMANCE	INQUIRY
A pair of breasts, with nipples and part of the rest of the torso.	S: (Indicating shaded section in right, lower side portion) The breasts are beautifully modelled and firm.

Score: di   Fc   Hd   O   2.0

COMMENT: This again coincidentally reaches the edge in one portion, but is essentially carved out of the shaded portion. The "nipples" are clearly enough marked off to be *dd* themselves, but the best scoring for the whole location used is *di*.

Card I

PERFORMANCE	INQUIRY
This is an eye staring at you.	S: (Indicated shaded section in left, middle portion of the blot.)
	E: Can you tell me more about the eye?
	S: It is like the ever-watching eye of God.
	E: Can you show me exactly where you see it? Here, trace it for me.
	S: (Traced a stylized eye with eyelashes.)

Score: di   Fm—   (Hd)   O—   —2.0

COMMENT: In this case there is no apparent justification in the blot material for the delimitation of this concept. This is reflected in the minus form-level rating; the location, however, is *di*.

Do Not Score a di

a. *Score D, d, or dd* where the distinctions in shading or color serve clearly to delimit the blot area from the surrounding shaded area. For example: the light gray details near the center line in Card VI, which are listed as *d,* or the light gray center detail in Card I, which should be *dd,* or the usual deer's head in Card IX, which is scored *D*.

b. *Do not score a di* where the edge of the blot is used for some part of the concept, even though the rest of the location meets the requirements of a *di* (see page 82) .

Card I

PERFORMANCE

A rodent of some sort. Paw and eyes.

INQUIRY

S: (Pointed to shaded section in right middle portion of the blot, towards the edge.) It is a mother mouse, peeking out of a hole. A little one is snuggled up next to her. Two little feet. It is soft and gray. Furry and mouse colored.

Score: dr   Fc,FC′,FM   Ad   3.0

COMMENT: This comes very close to a *di,* but seems better scored as a *dr* since the edge is definitely used to help delimit the concept, and the tiny peninsular portions are used for the "feet."

4.   dr, or Rare Details: Score dr

Score dr where an unusual location is used which cannot be classified as *dd, de,* or *di,* and which departs sufficiently from *D* or *d* or *W* that it cannot be scored as such. These rare details may be large or small, approaching *W* at one extreme and *dd* at the other. There are two main kinds of *dr:*

a. *Score dr* for an unusual area involving less than two-thirds of the blot, neither *de* nor *di,* which is not delimited by the structural qualities of the blot (that is, not marked off by space, color or shading) but rather is delimited by the needs of the concept given. As with a *W*, parts are cut off (or added) to improve the match of concept to blot. For example (see page 82) :

Card I

PERFORMANCE

A bat.

INQUIRY

S: Here are the hooks on the wings, and a kind of face formed by the dark

part all squashed up with the eyes
close together. That's my impression
of a bat.

E: Show me what part of the blot you
used, or did you mean the whole
thing?

S: (Indicated the upper half of upper
center D, plus horizontal area ter-
minating in the outermost side *d*'s.)

Score: dr   F   A   O—   1.0

COMMENT: In terms of general contour, especially wings, this
is a better match to the blot than the popular whole often called
a "bat." The subject tends to spoil the concept, however, with
the "squashed up face" and the "eyes" out of proportion to the
"bat" itself.

Card IV

PERFORMANCE   INQUIRY

Half of a ballet dancer peeking out from   S: (Indicating the inside edge portion of
behind a dark curtain.   side D) A short frilly skirt, arm, head,
                                                 shoulder, leg. She is just dancing out
                                                 on the stage. There is a dark curtain
                                                 here hiding her, and she is silhouetted
                                                 against the bright light.

Score: dr,S   M,FK   Hd   O   3.0

COMMENT: This is a *dr* rather than a *de* because it is more
than the edge; the black is used as "silhouette" and "curtain."
The additional S is scored since the space is used for "bright
light."

Card VI

PERFORMANCE   INQUIRY

A wide highway with snow thrown up   S: (Indicating entire center light por-
on either side.   tion.)

                                         E: What about the blot gives the im-
                                            pression of snow?

S: The lightness on either side is snow, white fluffy snow. The snow is high above the ground and I am looking down on it. The tiny white strip is the painted strip to mark off the driving lanes.

Score: dr   FK, FC′   N   →O   2.0

COMMENT: This goes beyond the *D* defined as the "entire dark vertical center," with the "snow" an important part of this concept beyond the *D* limits. Hence it is scored *dr*.

b   *Score dr* for an unusual combination of *D* or *d* areas, not including the combinations which themselves are scored *D* or *d*. Thus:

Card II: Upper red *D*'s plus upper, center *d*. "Two women talking over a fence."

Card X: Outer gray, orange, and yellow. "A deer leaping across a hedge into the sunset."

S, or White Space Responses

Score a Main S

1.   *Score a main S* where there is complete reversal of figure and ground and the white space is the location for the concept itself. Additional locations may be scored (*W, D, d, dr,* etc.) if all or part of the shaded or colored background is used in an accessory manner. Note these examples:

Card VII

PERFORMANCE   INQUIRY

The outline for a lamp or a lampstand.   S: (Pointed to the center *S*.)

                                          E: What kind of a lamp could it be?

                                          S: The kind you see on a living-room table.

Score: S   F   obj   1.5

COMMENT: The white space alone was used here, and the outline only.

Card III

PERFORMANCE

INQUIRY

A chalice with a stem and a wide-mouthed bowl.

S: It is a goblet actually (indicating the center *S*). It is cut-glass with a suggestion of incising here around the stem and base (pointing to light gray streaks).

Score: S,D   F,Fc   obj   O   2.0

COMMENT: An additional *D* is scored for the light gray shaded portion used as part of the location.

Card III

PERFORMANCE

INQUIRY

The white part in between the figures is a frowsy-headed girl with a big red bow in her hair.

S: She has her head bent; here are her eyes (second set of light gray streaks from the top) which are shadowed; pug nose; mouth. The irregular outline made it seem frowsy.

Score: 1.   S,dr ⎫   M   Hd   O   3.0
           2.   D   ⎭   FC   obj   P   1.0

COMMENT: Here two responses are scored, even though the organization is tight; the *D* is popularly seen as a "bow" and hence is given a separate main location score as a semi-independent detail. The *S* also must be given a main location score as the central location for the concept; an additional *dr* is given for the light gray parts used, which are only part of the lower center *D* area.

2.   *Score a main S* even where there is not complete reversal of figure and ground, when the total white space on the card is used for sky, ocean, and the like, and the blot for clouds, islands, and so on, in it. For instance:

Card VII

PERFORMANCE	INQUIRY
This is the ocean, with an island in it. The island has a lagoon.	S: I used the whole card. All the white is the ocean, and the gray part is the island. This part at the top made me think of the lagoon, the way the white extends into the gray part. E: How did you see the island? S: Well! it's kinda like a map. It was just the outline.

Score: S,W   F   geo   1.0

COMMENT: The fact that the subject focusses so much attention on the "ocean" and the "lagoon," and draws specific attention to his use of the white space, justifies a main *S* response with an additional *W* for the "island."

Score an Additional S

1. *Score an additional S* where the accessory white space has a rather solid quality, for example, where it is used for a "lake" or a "road" or a "plaza" to fill in a landscape, or where it is used for a specification such as the "eye" of an animal or human face.

Card III (inverted)

PERFORMANCE	INQUIRY
A wolf's head.	S: (Indicated side black lateral protrusions.) The shape of the head here, and here is the eye.

Score: d,S   F   Ad   1.5

COMMENT: Even this tiny *S* is given an additional scoring since it is used to specify the concept.

Card II

PERFORMANCE	INQUIRY
Gums shown, minus a tooth.	S: Here at the top. The red color made it look like gums. Now it seems that the white part might be a tooth after all. It's the right color.

Score: D,S   FC, FC′   Hd   1.5

COMMENT: Had the concept remained "minus a tooth" the solid quality would be lacking; however, when the subject makes the *S* a tooth it must be scored. It is scored additionally because it does not appear until the inquiry, whereas the "gums" are mentioned in the performance proper.

2.   *Score an additional S* where the white space is used as a background for the "figure" of the blot or part of it, but where it has a reality or solidity about it in the subject's concept, and he draws specific attention to it.

Card III (inverted)

PERFORMANCE	INQUIRY
Looks like a desert scene (edged card). Just a picture, that's all. Trees, grounds, and a little lake on the edge.	S: These (red side *D*'s) are palm trees. The center part is an oasis. The shaded part at the top could be water, a small pool. I'm looking at it from the air, from a great height. E: What makes it seem as though you were at a great height? S: The shading here, and here. E: What suggested a desert to you? S: The white part is the desert. White sand.

Score: W,S   FK, C′F   N   O   1.0

COMMENT: The white space is used as a definite part of the concept ("desert, white sand") not as mere background to be taken for granted.

3.   *Score an additional S* where the white space is used as cut-outs, for example, for eyes and mouth in a mask or pumpkin's face, or as an entrance or exit to a cave. As an example, a response to Card I is quoted on the following page.

Card I

PERFORMANCE

This is a mask, with holes for the eyes, and a hole for the mouth, with some teeth left in. The kind of false face kids wear at Hallowe'en.

INQUIRY

E: Do you think of someone wearing it?
S: No, it is just there. If someone was wearing it you would see their eyes. These are just holes so that *if* someone put it on they could see through them.

Score: W,S   F   mask   1.5

COMMENT: Here the white space has no solidity and is just a hole or empty space; but it is still an important part of the concept and hence is scored as an additional location.

4. *Score an additional S* where the white spaces are holes even in a fabric or skin rug, as long as they are particularly commented upon by the subject without any special prodding.

Card I

PERFORMANCE

A raggedy animal skin.

INQUIRY

S: I used the whole blot.
E: What about it made it seem like an animal skin?
S: Well! It looks kinda furry. It was because of the white spaces. I thought of a skin first, but then these spaces didn't fit in and then I thought they must be holes. And then the jagged outline makes it seem raggedy too.

Score: W,S   cF   A$_{obj}$ 0.5

COMMENT: The subject spontaneously mentions his use of the white space in the inquiry, justifying an additional S for "holes."

5. *Score an additional S* on Card IX if the total inside area between the lateral orange and green details is used. A main S is never given for this area, because the faint colorings and shadings make it unlikely that a complete reversal of figure and ground

takes place. The conventional scoring for this area used by itself is a main *D* and an additional *S*. The most usual concepts given here are a "violin" or "vase." Of course, if the area is used in conjunction with the whole blot, as for a "lake" as part of a landscape, the scoring would be a main *W* with an additional *S*.

Do Not Score S

1. *Do not score S* where the white spaces are simply vacant spots or "holes" in the blot, which have no essential significance as part of the concept and are given no emphasis by the subject. For example:

Card I

PERFORMANCE

This is an animal skin. Sort of a poor shape.

INQUIRY

S: It was the whole thing. The shading gave the impression of an animal skin.
E: Can you tell me more about it?
S: Well! it has no legs or head like animal skins usually do. It is sort of tattered, and worn out.
E: What makes it seem tattered and worn out?
S: It's the outline. And then you might say there are holes in it.

Score: W   cF   A$_{obj}$ 0.5

COMMENT: Here the subject only mentioned the "holes" after a fair amount of non-directive questioning. The white spaces seem to play a minor role in his concept, and hence are not scored.

2. *Do not score S* where a background for the details mentioned in the concept is implied in the sense that all the details are spread out, but the white space is in no way mentioned as a background. Note the example, from a response to Card X, given on the following page.

Card X (inverted)

PERFORMANCE

This looks like a display of botanical specimens.

INQUIRY

S: Here is a pink lily-like flower cut open, with the stamens inside, the yellow. And this green one at the bottom might be a rare kind of lily. The blue part is like pansy petals, even the right color, a purply blue with part of the "face" showing. Here is a brown and yellow orchid on the side. They could all be flowers, spread out in a stylized display.

Score:	1.	W		CF	Pl.	0.5
	add.1.	(D		FC	Pl.	2.0)
	add.2.	(D		FC	Pl.	1.5)
	add.3.	(D		FC	Pl.	2.0)
	add.4.	(D		FC	Pl.	2.0)

COMMENT: The "spread out" nature of the botanical display may imply that the flowers must be spread out on something. However, the white space is unspecified as background, not mentioned by the subject, and hence not scored.

3. *Do not score an additional S* for accessory use of space when the accessory area is light gray, even though the subject may designate it as "white." For example, the usual men in Card III may be seen as having "white collars." Since the "collar" area is gray rather than white, an additional S would not be scored. However, an additional S would be scored on the same card for "white aprons" or a "white handkerchief peeping out of the pocket," since these refer to areas that actually are white space.

CHAPTER 4

Scoring: Determinants—
Form and Movement Responses

Scoring for determinants consists of classifying every response according to those aspects of the subject's experience which determine the particular concept described in the response. Answered properly, the question: "What about the blot gives you the impression of a ...?" will suggest the determinant or determinants to be scored. Was it just the shape? Or was it primarily some other aspect of the blot material such as color or shading? Or was it a combination of the form and the color or the form and the shading? Or was it not so much the shape and character of the blot material itself that determined the response as something the subject read into the material, a subjective contribution to the perception?

There are four main classes of determinants, with sub-categories that will be described later. These four main classes are:

1. FORM RESPONSES: The concept is determined by the shape of the blot only; neither color nor shading contributes, nor is kinesthesia attributed to the blot material.

2. MOVEMENT RESPONSES: Concepts into which the subject has projected some action, movement, or life. Such movement may be attributed to human and animal figures, to inanimate objects, or even projected in terms of abstract forces. In most instances movement responses imply the use of form,—that is, that the concept was at least in part a function of the shape of the blot. The sub-classifica-

tions make clear to what extent form was combined with movement or omitted from consideration.

3. SHADING RESPONSES: Concepts in which the nuances of achromatic shading are determinants, either contributing to a feeling of surface texture, or to depth impressions, or to achromatic color. Again the concept may also be in part a function of the shape of the blot, or the form, and sub-classifications make clear to what extent the form and shading are integrated or to what extent shading dominates over form.

4. COLOR RESPONSES: Concepts in which the chromatic aspects of the blot material determine the response, either as integrated with the form elements or over-riding them.

Before considering these classes of determinants in detail, the more general differentiation between main and additional determinant scores will be discussed.

Main and Additional Determinants

Main Determinants

A main determinant score is given for each response to which a main location score has been assigned. In the absence of movement, shading, or color determinants, the main determinant is automatically scored as a form response, or *F*. However, if the subject spontaneously indicates the use of shading, color, or movement, the main determinant is assigned accordingly. Thus, if the determinant is *spontaneously* mentioned or implied, either in the performance proper or in the inquiry, a main determinant score is given. It is considered a spontaneous mention after non-directive questions such as "What about the blot made you think it was a . . .?" or "Describe the . . ." or "Tell me more about it."

Additional Determinants

An additional determinant is given where the individual makes use of movement, color or shading in a way that is too reserved to permit a judgment that this was the chief factor in determining that the concept was seen as it was seen. As a guide to scoring additionals the following rules are given:

1. An additional rather than a main determinant score is given where the determinant is applicable to part of the location only. Thus, for example, in Card II, color is scored additionally for "bears with red hats on," while the main determinant is form (or shading or movement as the case may be).

2. Where the use of the determinant is elicited only through prodding in the inquiry, and does not emerge spontaneously, an additional determinant score is assigned. Thus, an additional determinant would be scored for movement in Card VIII for "animals" which were not described as "climbing" or "stepping" until some relatively directive question was used, such as "How did you see them?"

3. Where the determinant is used very reluctantly or doubtfully an additional rather than a main score is given. Reluctance may be indicated as above by acknowledging the determinant only under prodding. Or there may be considerable doubt expressed either in the performance proper or in the inquiry when the subject is given an opportunity to elaborate his concept. Or the subject may reveal the use of the determinant very indirectly and imply it only, without fully acknowledging it. Examples will be given in discussing the scoring of the separate determinants.

Choice between Main and Additional Determinants

It is acknowledged that in many instances more than one determinant contributes to the production of the concept. Thus it is by no means rare to encounter a response that is determined by two or more of the movement, shading, color, or form factors. Although only one main determinant score may be assigned, the other determinants should be scored as additionals in order to give as complete a picture as possible of all the various aspects of the subject's experience in interaction with the blot material that played a part in forming the concept. It is necessary to decide which determinant should be assigned the main scoring. The following rules apply:

1. Score as the main determinant that which is clearly given most emphasis by the subject in his description and elaboration of the response. This is sometimes quite difficult to ascertain; the other rules are intended to supplement this first rule in doubtful cases.

2. It is assumed that a determinant mentioned or clearly implied in the performance proper is more important than a determinant which does not emerge until the inquiry, and therefore the main score should be given to it.

3. If two or more determinants are mentioned in the performance proper, and both or all seem of equal importance, the following rules of precedence serve in selecting the main determinant score:

a. Precedence is given to human movement (M) unless it is very reluctant, repressed, or minor, in which case it would in any event be given an additional rather than a main determinant score.

b. Precedence is given to color responses (FC, CF, or C) over every determinant save human movement (M).

c. Precedence is given to differentiated texture responses (Fc) over every determinant except M and color.

Instances in Which an Additional Determinant Is Not Scored

1. Where the subject denies the use of a determinant it cannot be scored even as additional. Thus, for example, on Card VI the subject may deny that shading has anything to do with his "animal skin." Hence texture cannot be scored as a determinant at all, even though the vigorous denial would be interpreted in the course of the sequence analysis.

2. Since the use of form is taken care of in the movement, shading, and color determinant scores, form (F) is never scored as an additional determinant, unless a separate additional location score is also involved.

Form Responses, or F

Score F

Score as form responses all responses where there is no other main determinant (movement, shading, or color). This applies even when the form is vague, indefinite or abstract. The vagueness is taken care of in form-level rating and does not counterindicate an *F* score. Note, for example:

Card I

PERFORMANCE

It looks like a mask.

INQUIRY

S: Here are the eyes, nose and cheek-bones. It is a primitive mask of some sort.
E: Is it the mask alone or do you think of someone wearing it?
S: No one is wearing it. It is not that sort of mask. It is larger than life size. It would be used in primitive religious ceremonies.

Score: W F Mask 2.0

COMMENT: Despite the specifications there is no determinant present except form, even with a fairly directive inquiry to ascertain whether *M* was implied.

Card III

PERFORMANCE

This lower part reminds me faintly of some internal organ. A liver is what I thought of.

INQUIRY

S: You know, like medical charts. The lines are vague. It just reminds me of . . . well, it might be the stomach of someone who has drunk too much.

Score: D F At 0.5

COMMENT: This is a vague concept with no determinant except form, hence it is scored *F*. The vagueness, indicated by the interchangeability of "liver" and "stomach," is indicated by a form-level rating of 0.5.

Card IX

PERFORMANCE

INQUIRY

I can't get anything out of the thing as a whole except an abstract pattern. It is symmetrical, with this balancing this.

E: Did you mean that as a response or as a comment?

S: It was a response.

Score: W   F   Abs   0.5

COMMENT: This is an indefinite concept, and yet it is scored *F* because no other determinant entered in.

Movement Responses

Movement responses include those where the subject has read into the static ink blots some kind of action, movement, expression, posture or life. There are three main classifications of movement response: (1) Human movement responses—or *M*. (2) Animal movement responses—or *FM*. (3) Minor or inanimate movement responses—or *m*, *mF*, or *Fm*.

1.   M, or Human Movement: Score a Main M

Score a main *M* for the inclusion of a kinesthetic quality in human concepts. The following are instances where *M* is scored:

a.   *Score a main M* for human beings seen in action, even if the reality of the human figures is qualified by describing them as caricatures, drawings, "petit point," statues, or the like.

Card II

PERFORMANCE

INQUIRY

A couple of clowns clapping hands.

S: They are having a good time being clownish.

E: What about them made them seem like clowns?

S: The red hats and the funny expressions and the movement of the blot.

E: Did you include this part? (Pointing to lower red detail)

S: There is one foot here and the other foot here, and here their knees are touching as their hands touch.

Score: W   M,FC   H   3.0

COMMENT: This is an example of vigorous, clear-cut *M*.

Card III

PERFORMANCE

The little red blots on the side are like cartoons of Powerful Katrinka in hell, smoking a cigar.

INQUIRY

S: Here is the cigar.
E: What about it made it seem like Powerful Katrinka?
S: It's the profile, that of an Irish washerwoman type. Comic, no refinement, cheerful. I didn't use this part at the top.
E: What about it made it seem like hell?
S: It's red.

Score: D   M,FC$_{sym}$ (H)   →O   3.0

COMMENT: This is an *M* even though the human figure is qualified as a "cartoon" and the movement is less vigorous than in the example above. The lack of reality is indicated by scoring *(H)*. *M* is given precedence even though *FC*$_{sym}$ is also implied in the performance proper.

b.   *Score a main M for human beings seen in any live posture*, unless the reality of the human figure is qualified as a drawing, statue, and so on. For example:

Card V

PERFORMANCE

Two women asleep. Long black hair which covers their backs.

INQUIRY

S: (Pointed to side *D*'s) Here is the face, eyelash, hair, arms folded. This dark shading is her dark hair. It looks soft. Here are her legs.

Score: D   M,FC′,Fc   H   3.5

COMMENT: This is an *M* by reason of the live posture, despite the fact that there is no active movement. The posture would have been indicated by saying that the "women are asleep"; indicating the folded arms merely emphasizes the postural aspects. *M* is given precedence over achromatic color and texture, which are scored as additional determinants.

c. *Score a main M* for human-like movement in animals such as fairy-tale creatures or Walt Disney animals. However, do not score *M* for movement in trained animals, such as a trained dog, ape, or seal. Two illustrations follow:

Card X

PERFORMANCE

(Pointing to upper gray detail) Here are two little symbolical animals angrily having a fight or remonstrating with each other around the trunk of a tree. They're two little gnats seeing who can climb the tree first.

INQUIRY

S: They look like personified insects in a fairy tale. They are bigger than life, because here is the tree. The whole insect is there . . . tails here and legs here.

Score: D   M   (A)   2.0

COMMENT: Both the description of them as "personified insects" and the action "remonstrating with each other" lifts the response into the *M* classification; the fact that animal figures are in human-like action is indicated in the (*A*).

Card X

PERFORMANCE

(Blue side *D*'s) Two drunken spiders, leg in leg, singing. One is waving something I take to be a bottle.

INQUIRY

S: I see the side view of one and the front view of the other, mouth open, and eyes.
E: What about it made it seem like a bottle?
S: What else would they be waving?

Score: D   M   (A)   O→P   3.0

COMMENT: This response was well seen in one side blue detail. The human-like action is obvious; the fact that the figures are animal-like is shown by scoring (*A*).

d. *Score a main M* for movement controlled by an individual (for instance, person whirling with skirts blowing) even though the subject's statement includes reference to "wind"—which on the face of it implies inanimate movement.

Card I

PERFORMANCE

INQUIRY

Two ballet dancers whirling around in centrifugal whirls with their capes flying out in the wind.

S: I used the whole thing more or less ignoring the middle part.

E: What did you mean when you said their capes were flying out in the wind?

S: It is just that they are whirling so fast that they make a real breeze.

Score: W   M   H   3.0

COMMENT: Here the "wind" is subsumed under the *M* scored for the whirling dance and does not justify an additional inanimate movement score.

e. *Score a main M* for parts of human beings seen in action. Note the two examples that are given below—one from a response to Card IV and the other from Card I.

Card IV

PERFORMANCE

INQUIRY

A great boot kicking somebody.

S: It was the shape.

E: You said it was kicking?

S: Yes, like this. (Demonstrated.) It is a big boot, a man's boot. This is the trouser part of the leg and this is the foot part.

Score: D   M   Hd   1.5

COMMENT: This illustrates that vigorous kinesthesia can be referred to mere parts; the vigor is underlined by the subject's demonstration.

Card I

PERFORMANCE   INQUIRY

Two hands with index fingers pointing   S: (Indicated side *D*). The projections
and the thumbs are on too.   look like fingers pointing. The
                                             thumbs are clenched. Almost as
                                             though shooting. Like this. (Demon-
                                             strated.)

Score: D   M   Hd   2.0

COMMENT: This is human movement, though applied only to
a part; the demonstration adds to this conviction but was not
necessary for a score of *M*.

f.   *Score a main M* for a human face with an expression, provided
     it is distinctly lifelike and is not considered a symbol of some
     abstract force.

Card VII

PERFORMANCE   INQUIRY

Two females with their hair piled on top   S: It was their exaggerated profiles,
of their heads, scowling at each other.   their mouths. They are grimacing,
                                              not cross, comic. Making comic
                                              "moues" at each other. Just the top
                                              of them.

Score: D   M   Hd   2.5

COMMENT: This is a good example of a lifelike expression
scored as *M*.

Score an Additional M or Tendency to M (→M)

a.   *Score a tendency to M* where movement or posture is only con-
     ceded under fairly directive questioning in the inquiry—that
     is, in response to questions such as "How do you see it?" or
     "What is this part?" For example:

Card I

PERFORMANCE   INQUIRY

Like witches, that's all.   E: Where do you see them?
                                            S: Here (pointing to side *D*'s).

E: What about the blot makes them
   seem like witches?
S: Just the shape.
E: Describe them.
S: The head is here.
E: What could this be (center *D*)?
S: That is the broomstick. They are
   riding on it.

Score: W   F→M   (H)   1.5

COMMENT: So much questioning was necessary to elicit any suggestion of posture or movement that only a tendency to *M* seems justified.

b. *Score a tendency to M* where live posture is attributed to a human figure, the reality of which is qualified by making it a drawing, caricature, statue, or the like. It is felt that the inhibition of kinesthetic quality implied by the expression of two kinds of reluctance (reluctance to project action and reluctance to concede reality to the figure) precludes a main *M* score.

Card II

PERFORMANCE

These two pieces (indicating the side halves of the gray portions of the blot) are like ships' figureheads seen sideways. A thrust-out look of the chest and chin.

INQUIRY

S: A splendid woman carved in wood.
E: What about it makes it seem like
   carving?
S: The three-dimensional effect, darker
   and lighter. Also there is a suggestion
   of grain in the wood.

Score: dr   Fc→M   (Hd)   →0   3.0

COMMENT: Here the main score is *Fc* for the use of shading. The kinesthetic element is reduced to a →*M* by the combination of posture (rather than movement) and a carved figure (rather than a real human figure).

c. *Score a tendency to M* where only the expression is left on a human figure that is usually seen by other subjects in definite posture or action. This scoring is reserved for responses where the kinesthetic element is very reluctant. For instance:

Card VII

PERFORMANCE

INQUIRY

I immediately see there two heads facing each other. It's a bust, not a head (indicating upper two-thirds of the blot). Two female busts with identical protruding jaws and high up-swept hair-do.

S: They are two old spinsters from the late Victorian era.
E: Can you tell me more about them?
S: They are sorry for themselves. They have mournful eyes, with hair forming heavy brows. Here are their brows, or they might be bangs.
E: How do you see them?
S: Here is the top of the head, eyes, nose, jaw, scrawny neck.

Score: W   F→M   Hd   2.5

COMMENT: The "mournful eyes" are the only vestiges of human movement here, despite prodding questioning. Compare with the example on page 104 where the faces were making "moues" at each other, and were scored *M* since the much more lively expression implied more kinesthetic projection.

d. *Score a tendency to M* for human-like expression on the face of an animal, the animal not otherwise being in human-like action.

Card II (sideways)

PERFORMANCE

INQUIRY

This is a small dog, skidding suddenly to a stop. It looks surprised and disconcerted.

E: What about it makes him seem surprised?
S: He is rather like a dignified old gentleman who suddenly finds something unexpected waved in his face. (Demonstrated the expression).

Score: D   FM→M   A   2.5

COMMENT: A main *FM* is scored for the definitely animal-like action, implied in "skidding suddenly to a stop." However, the expression and feeling attributed to the dog are distinctly human-like (as emphasized by the demonstration); hence a tendency to *M* is also scored.

e.   *Score a tendency to M* for doubtful human action in an animal.

Card I

PERFORMANCE	INQUIRY

There were three crows sat on a tree. Here is the nest. They might be eagles, on top of the tree. The tree is cut off at the top. The nest has two little ones in it. The male is on the left. . . . I don't know why.

S: There were only two of course. I used the whole thing. Here is the trunk, gnarled branches, no leaves. The nest is here with two little ones in it in the center, and two more with their mouths open. The left one is more blasé, and the right one is worried. That's why I said male and female.

E: Can you tell me more about the crows?

S: Here is the head and the wing and the other wing is behind the nest. I feel that the left one is about to take off and the right one has just landed. The wing is a little lower down on the right one.

Score: W   FM→M   A   O   3.5

COMMENT: Here the chief action component seems to be animal-like—the birds in typically bird-like action, flying and caring for their young. However, the feelings attributed to them are human-like; it seems best to take this into account by a tendency to *M*, although a main *M* could not be scored.

f.   *Score a tendency to M* for human beings in some posture but at the mercy of inanimate forces.

Card III

PERFORMANCE	INQUIRY

Two little cherubs falling through space.

S: Here they are (side red *D*'s). Their hands, rears up, maintaining themselves upright with some difficulty. They are all braced in falling.

Score: D   Fm→M   (H)   2.0

COMMENT: Here the "falling" is major; hence *Fm* is given the main determinant score, but the active posture on the part of the cherubs necessitates a tendency to an *M* as well.

g. *Score an additional M* for tiny human beings, unimportant in a landscape. For example:

Card VI

PERFORMANCE

A crevasse in the ice. A deep crevasse with water at the bottom, and there is someone peering over the edge, a girl I think.

INQUIRY

S: (Indicated the entire light center surrounding the dark vertical center line, with the card inverted.) The crevasse is down the middle. At first I thought I was looking down from the top and this faint gleam was water, and then I switched and was looking up, and here was a person peering down.

Score: dr   FK, M   N,H   →O   2.0

COMMENT: In both location used and in concept the crevasse is the major emphasis, and the human figure is quite minor in comparison. Therefore, an additional *M* is scored.

Do Not Score M

a. *Score FM* for monkeys or apes or trained animals in action that is quite possible for the species even though it has a human-like quality—for instance, trained bears dancing, trained seals juggling.

Card III

PERFORMANCE

These are two monkeys throwing sausages at each other.

INQUIRY

E: Where did you see them?
S: (Pointed to the usual human figures for the monkeys and the center red detail for the sausages.)
E: What about the blot makes them seem like monkeys?

> S: The head here. Hands here. Legs here.
> E: What makes it seem like sausages?
> S: They are round-shaped like sausages. Two are stuck together.

Score: W   FM   A   2.0

COMMENT: These monkeys are in quite monkey-like action; hence the score is *FM*, even though "throwing things" is also human-like.

b.   *Score Fm (or F→Fm)* if a part of the human being is thought of as an abstract symbol rather than as part of a living person in action. (See page 122.)

c.   *Score Fm (or F→Fm)* for an expressive description where the expression on a human face is taken as symbolic of some abstract force. (See page 121.)

d.   *Score F* only if the expressive description involves neither action nor emotion on the part of the person or creature perceived, nor an emotional effect on the subject or others who witness it. Thus, faces may be described as "funny," "grotesque"—or even "grinning" or "amusing"—apparently implying that the face is odd, or the mouth is wide, or that there is some other similar qualification or elaboration. Note this example:

Card II

PERFORMANCE

This is a man with a funny face.

INQUIRY

> E: Tell me about the man.
> S: Here is his head, and here are his feet.
> E: What made his face seem funny?
> S: It looks funny. All streaky.

Score: dr   F   H   1.5

COMMENT: Here the term "funny" seems to imply odd or peculiar, rather than any expression or emotion; hence no movement score is assigned.

2. FM, or Animal Movement: Score a Main FM

a. *Score a main FM* for animals in movement of an animal-like nature, even if qualified as caricatures, drawings, ornaments, and so on.

Card IV

PERFORMANCE

A gorilla taking a flying leap down from a perch.

INQUIRY

S: The whole thing. The size of the feet, and the bend of the knees, and the hands out as though he just had sprung off. Looks like a gorilla because of the white inside of the palms, broad shoulders, hunched up, and the feet. Here are his great chest muscles, the shading here. The center business is part of what he is leaping off.

Score: W,S   FM,FC′, Fc   A   4.5

COMMENT: This is vigorous movement attributed to an animal, the movement being appropriately animal-like.

b. *Score a main FM* for animals in a lifelike posture, provided that there is not further qualification of the animals as caricatures, drawings, statues, ornaments, and the like. There should be some dynamic aspect to the animal; if still, it should be sleeping, resting, about to pounce, or in some lifelike posture.

Card X

PERFORMANCE

A fine collie dog.

INQUIRY

S: He's in a dog show, proudly showing off, standing up stiff and proud the way they do, with the hind quarters extended back and the tail out. Here is his muzzle, ruff standing out, feet and tail.

Score: D   FM   A   2.5

COMMENT: There is no actual movement here, but *FM* is scored for the definite animal-like posture.

c.   *Score a main FM* for parts of animals in animal-like action.

Card VIII

PERFORMANCE

A bullfrog croaking.

INQUIRY

S: (Indicated lower pink *D*.) His head is up in the air. He is croaking. Here is his mouth. Just the upper part of body.

Score: D   FM   Ad   1.5

COMMENT: This is still *FM* though only part of the animal is there.

Score an Additional FM or Tendency to FM (→FM)

a.   *Score a tendency to FM* if the animal movement is acknowledged reluctantly, either with considerable doubt expressed, or only after prodding in the inquiry.

Card I

PERFORMANCE

Could almost be a horned toad.

INQUIRY

S: (Indicated upper center *D* with claw-like projections.) These bumpy parts in the top center part, and the squat effect here. I can't pick out parts. It's a whole impression of this part. The projections might be its front paws.
E: What did you mean squat?
S: A squat shape.
E: How did you see it?
S: It's just squatting on a rock. Not moving. He's just a-settin there.

Score: D   F→FM   A   1.5

COMMENT: Here *FM* is minimal and acknowledged only after prodding in the inquiry. Indeed, the inquiry was probably carried too far for a concept neither popularly *FM* nor suggesting *FM*.

b. *Score a tendency to FM* where the movement is reduced to posture at the same time that the reality of the animal figure is qualified by making it a drawing, statue, caricature, silhouette, ornament. Note this illustration:

Card II

PERFORMANCE

INQUIRY

Two dogs supporting a pointed object.

S: The ears are lying back, the front paws raised, and their noses touch this object.

E: What about the blot makes them seem like dogs?

S: The shape and the color too. They are black. They are sort of silhouettes and poor ones at that. They're book-ends, but that wouldn't account for this center thing they're supporting. No, it's more of a drawing. The paint is smeared, you can see the brush marks.

Score: W   FC′→FM,Fc   (A)   P   3.0

COMMENT: Here only a tendency to *FM* may be scored because movement is reduced to posture at the same time that the reality of the animal figure is qualified by making it first a silhouette, then a book-end and finally a drawing. The unreality of the figure is further shown in the (*A*) score. The main determinant is *FC′* for the blackness, and an additional *Fc* is given for the "brush-marks."

c. *Score a tendency to FM* if there is an animal-like expression and no other movement.

Card I

PERFORMANCE	INQUIRY
Looks like a cat's face, looking straight at you and kinda mad.	S: The whole thing. Ears, eyes, mouth, and the side of the face bulged out.
	E: What about it made it look like a cat?
	S: The shape. It could be a black Persian cat. That's what I had in mind.
	E: What made it seem like a Persian cat particularly?
	S: Persian cats' heads are bigger and heavier than the ordinary cat.
	E: What made it seem mad?
	S: It had an angry look on its face, like cats sometimes do.

Score: W   FC′→FM   Ad   2.5

COMMENT: This is seen to be an animal-like expression, rather than a human-like or frightening, symbolic expression. Since no movement other than expression is implied the scoring is a tendency to *FM*. The main determinant is given for the "blackness," which comes out spontaneously in the inquiry.

d. *Score a tendency to FM* if the movement or posture is very weak or if the animal in action (or posture) is at the mercy of inanimate forces, or both.

Card IV

PERFORMANCE	INQUIRY
This side bit looks like a duck. It has been shot at and is dying slowly, but is not dead yet.	E: What about it makes it look like a duck?
	S: The long neck and the bill. The head is hanging limp. That's what made me think it was dying.

Score: d   Fm→FM   Ad   2.0

COMMENT: Only a tendency to *FM* can be scored for this very weak posture. A main *Fm* is scored for the action of forces upon the animal in the face of which he is powerless.

Do Not Score FM

a. *Score M* if the animal is in human-like action. (See page 102.)
b. *Score Fm* if the expression on the animal is taken as symbolic of some abstract force. (See pages 121–122.)
c. *Score F* if there is indeed no kinesthetic element involved in the animal figure; this is sometimes the case even when the subject's verbalization seems to imply movement or posture but where inquiry elicits the fact that positional or logical considerations were foremost. For example:

Card VII

PERFORMANCE   INQUIRY

Two bunny rabbits facing each other.

S: It was chiefly their ears that made them seem bunny rabbits. These things sticking up.
E: Can you tell me more about them?
S: Here is the nose, the head and the body.
E: How did you mean "facing each other"?
S: There is one on each side. One is facing this way and one is facing that way.

Score: W   F   A   2.0

COMMENT: There seems to be no movement implied in "facing"; *FM* is not scored for purely positional considerations.

3.   m, or Inanimate Movement: Differentiation between Fm, mF, and m

There are three scoring categories included under *m*, representing three degrees of differentiation in form perception.

a. *Score Fm* if the object that is moving or being moved has definite form, such as a spinning top, an aircraft flying. An instance of a "top" response follows:

Card II

PERFORMANCE

A beautiful spinning top.

INQUIRY

S: The white part. It stands upright; therefore it is spinning. It's just a drawing of one. These little lines indicate the movement.

Score: S,dd   Fm   obj   1.5

COMMENT: A "top" has a definite form, therefore the movement is scored *Fm*. The fact that it is qualified as a "drawing" does not detract from the movement score.

b. *Score mF* if the object that is moving or being moved is of indefinite or semi-definite shape, such as tongues of flame leaping, clouds swirling. For example:

Card IX (card inverted)

PERFORMANCE

There is a billowing of red cloud at the top and darker clouds underneath.

INQUIRY

S: The whole thing. This is the atomic explosion at Bikini. The whole business is like moving pictures of that with the mushroom-shaped cloud at the top.

E: Was it just the shape of the cloud that suggested it to you?

S: No, although the shape is the typical mushroom effect. But it is red and that is an explosion.

E: (Later, in the Analogy Period) In this card (Card II) you said it was the shading that made it seem like a cloud. How was it on this one?

S: It was the shape and the color, not the shading.

Score: W   mF, CF   explosion   0.5

COMMENT: Here an *mF* is scored for moving clouds of semi-definite shape. Even though "mushroom-shaped" seems to imply definite shape, occurring as it does within the concept "explosion" which precludes organized structure of any permanent shape, *mF* is a better scoring than *Fm*. The word "billowing" in this example emphasizes the essential indefiniteness of the "cloud" concept; it implies that any definite shape is evanescent and subject to immediate change. Movement is given precedence because the movement determinant applies to the whole blot, and because it seems more important in an "explosion" concept, whereas the "red" can apply to only part of the location. It was established that shading was not involved in the concept.

c. *Score m* if there is no form, only movement (kaleidoscopic movement, abstract force, and the like) .

Card VII

PERFORMANCE

All I get here is a feeling of disintegration, of things falling apart.

INQUIRY

S: It's just a feeling this card gives me.
E: Can you tell me more about the things that are falling apart?
S: There isn't any *thing*. Or it could be *any*thing. Just an impression of instability.

Score: W   m   abs   0.0

COMMENT: It is quite rare to find *m* rather than *Fm* or *mF* as the main determinant; usually some form is implied, or else the formless movement or force is secondary to some other concept. Here, however, is an example of inanimate movement where no form seems to be implied.

Types of Concept Scored m or mF or Fm

The following are the types of concept to which an *m* score is assigned. Very frequently the inanimate movement is an additional determinant, and in this case it is customary to assign merely an *m*, leaving the distinction between *Fm, mF,* and *m* for the main determinant. However it would be sounder practice to retain the distinctions with additional determinants in the interests of sequence analysis, even though *Fm, mF,* and *m* are grouped together in the psychogram. The following discussion and examples include both main and additional scorings.

a. *Score Fm,* occasionally *mF,* for a moving inanimate object. (See example on page 115.)

b. *Score mF* for inanimate movement such as falling water, swirling smoke, leaping flames, dripping blood. It is not necessary for the subject to specify that the movement be going on at the time, as long as he clearly implies an inanimate movement or force and does not merely refer to formal qualities. Score a main *mF* if the natural forces dominate clearly; frequently the *mF* score is additional to color or shading. Examples follow:

Card VI

PERFORMANCE

Looks like a photograph taken from the air, from a plane strafing a railway.

INQUIRY

S: It reminds me of pictures I've seen. I left out this top bit. It has been cut off to put in the paper, the jagged edge. The strip down the center is the railway, and the lighter coloring looks like puffs of ground and smoke going when bullets hit it. This dark spot here is part of an object like an oil tank, and this light spot is the small burst of flame. It has just been hit.

Score: W   FK, KF, mF   N,smoke   2.0

COMMENT: The *FK* for the aerial view is given as the main determinant, and *mF* is additional.

Card IX

PERFORMANCE

Looking down on a scene. A small lake. It is autumn, with colored trees. A stream is running through.

INQUIRY

S: Here is the lake (pointing to the center violin-shaped space). The stream is coming into it and petering out. It is flowing straight forward pretty fast, hitting the large body of water, then petering out.

E: You said you were looking down?

INQUIRY (*continued*)

S: Yes, I get some sense of depth too
from the coloring around the edges of
the lake. But the autumn colors of
the trees are the most striking thing.

Score: W,S   CF,mF,FK   N   O   1.5

COMMENT: Although the color should be given precedence,
both because it applies to all the blot, and because the subject
states that it was more important, the movement attributed to
the "stream running" is scored as an additional *mF*.

Card II

PERFORMANCE   INQUIRY

There has been an explosion here.   S: It was the whole thing. It reminded
                                         me of a wall with a hole blasted in it.
                                         A bomb fell and smashed it up. The
                                         color probably contributed to the
                                         impression. It looks like blood. Some-
                                         one was hurt in the explosion.

Score: W,S   mF, CF   explosion   0.5

COMMENT: Here the fact that the explosion is not actually
seen does not detract from the strong implication of inanimate
force. The scoring is *mF* rather than *Fm* because the "wall with
a hole blasted in it" could apply to any blot area in which the
blot surrounds white space, and hence is classed as a semi-
definite concept.

c.   *Score a main Fm* for abstract forces outside a human or animal
figure which are acting upon him in some way so that he is powerless. For example, if marionettes are bowing, being manipu-
lated, score a main *Fm* and additional *M*. If the figure itself is
moving, and in addition there is an abstract force acting, then
the scoring would be main *M* (or *FM*) and an additional *m*. For
instance:

Card I

PERFORMANCE

INQUIRY

Two Teddy Bears clinging to a tree. The real kind they have in Australia.

S: Ears, eyes, feet. The right one has no eye, but here is a suggestion of its nose. They are peering out to look at something. There is a feeling of wind blowing the ears of the two bears. A feeling of wind behind them.

Score: W   FM,m   A   2.5

COMMENT: Here the wind is acting upon the animal figures, and is in no way a product of their own movement. Hence *m* is scored, although additionally to the main *FM*.

d.   *Score Fm or mF or an additional m* for tension or gravity clearly expressed. The most common concepts are "an animal skin stretched out to dry," "an animal or person falling," and "precarious balance." A main score is given when the inanimate movement is the most important determinant. An additional *m* is given when animal or human movement, shading, or the like, is more important. Note these three sample cases:

Card VI

PERFORMANCE

INQUIRY

The skin of some animal stretched out to dry. That doesn't account for this dingus at the top.

S: The protuberances are paws, the forepaws being thinner.

E: What about it makes it like an animal skin?

S: The hairiness. It is a coon skin or a lynx skin tacked on a wall.

E: What about it makes it seem tacked on a wall?

S: I get a sense of pull to it. It is fairly tight.

Score: W   Fc,m   A$_{obj}$ P   1.5

COMMENT: *Fc* takes precedence for this concept, but *m* is clearly indicated in the inquiry and given an additional score. If the subject had merely stated "stretched out to dry" and not verbalized any sense of "pull," the *m* could not have been scored.

Card III

PERFORMANCE

The red things on the side are flowers. Flowers with a sac.

INQUIRY

S: This is the heavy weighted sac. They are lush, exotic things. Sundew flowers.

E: You said "these red things are flowers." Did you mean they were red flowers?

S: No. But it is a fleshy, hothouse flower. A fat-bodied look.

E: How do you mean a fat-bodied look?

S: It is both the shape, and the shading that makes it seem lush and fat.

Score: D   Fc,m   Pl   O   1.0

COMMENT: The "heavy weighted" description is the justification for the additional *m,* although *Fc* is given the main score.

Card VIII

PERFORMANCE

Two tree animals upright.

INQUIRY

S: Four paws, fur, general shape of the body. They are standing upright, yet almost falling backwards. They do not have a very good grip on the structure. They're a type of rodent. A fur-bearing animal.

E: What about it makes it seem like fur?

S: The texture.

Score: D→W   FM,m,Fc   A   P   2.0

COMMENT: Here is an example where *m* is scored for precarious balance, although here the *FM* for "standing upright" takes precedence.

e. *Score Fm* for a phallic force accompanying a phallic symbol.

Card VI

PERFORMANCE

Here is the male sexual organ. Like a symbol of potency.

INQUIRY

S: I used this top part.

E: What makes it seem the symbol of potency?

S: I suppose it is the erect, distended look.

Score: D   Fm   Sex   1.0

COMMENT: This is a special case where a human detail is scored *Fm* rather than *M*. The rationale rests on the argument that sexual forces may be felt as something outside the control of the person and acting on him, rather than as a voluntary movement or posture.

f.   *Score Fm or F→Fm* for human or animal faces or figures or masks that are horrible, frightening, sinister, or gruesome, even when the wording of the response suggests that the facial expression is the basis for this effect. In these cases the expression seems to symbolize an abstract or evil force which is threatening to the beholder. Below are three examples:

Card VI

PERFORMANCE

This is Adolf Hitler. Just the face. He has a very sinister look.

INQUIRY

S: This side part. It is sort of a caricature, for the nose is too big. It was the little moustache that made me think of Hitler.

E: What about the blot made it seem sinister?

S: Well, Hitler is a sinister figure. The personification of evil brutality to many people.

Score: D   Fm   (Hd)   1.5

COMMENT: Here the subject makes it clear that the face is symbolic of an evil force. Even had this not been made explicit in the inquiry the score would be *Fm*.

Card I

PERFORMANCE

This is a charming cat's face. Eyes and grinning mouth.

INQUIRY

S: The whole thing. It is the kind of cat that you see in a Hallowe'en mask. It is frightening, grinning at you in the night (laughed).

Score: W,S   Fm   Ad   1.5

COMMENT: Despite the expression implied in "grinning" the remarks offered in the inquiry make it clear that the face is threatening, implying that it symbolizes an evil or abstract force.

Card IV

PERFORMANCE

This is a curious abstraction as if someone had pictured a childhood idea of night. There is a horror about the whole business. Blackness, darkness, places light comes in like streaks under the door. The whole picture is of a horrible monster approaching to envelop you. As a child who is desperately afraid would picture night. Something with arms and great clumping feet and a general appearance of going at you.

INQUIRY

S: His eyes are glaring, hands outstretched and hanging down. The horror comes in the shading in the center. Here are his feet. You know how a noise in the night scares you. His feet are so huge as if clumping closer and closer towards you.

E: What did you mean by the horror being in the shading in the center?

S: Something soft and dark and enveloping, coming down to smother you. The texture.

E: The light streaks?

S: Just that here and here (near arms and legs) you can see through. If it had been absolutely dark you couldn't have drawn the monster. It would have got you, but now you have time to get away.

Score: W,S   M, m, K, cF_{sym} (H)   →O   2.5

COMMENT: There is too much elaboration of the movement of the monster to avoid giving M as the main determinant, but the additional m is well-justified in that such stress is given to fear which the monster inspires. In this case an additional m is scored rather than →Fm because the fear-inspiring quality is not only embodied in something well-structured but also in something "soft and enveloping" (cF_{sym}) and in space-filling "darkness" (K).

g. *Score Fm* for a human detail used abstractly or symbolically, rather than as part of a human being in action.

Card I

PERFORMANCE

Here is the finger of scorn.

INQUIRY

S: (Pointed to the top portion of side detail.)

E: Did you think of it as belonging to anyone?

S: No, it is just a finger, kind of a symbol. The finger of scorn pointing at you.

Score: D   Fm   (Hd)   1.0

COMMENT: Compare this with the example on page 104, where the fingers were thought of as part of a living person in action, real kinesthetic projection being involved. Here, as with the descriptive expression scored *Fm,* the symbolic significance attached to the human part is the basis for *Fm* rather than *M.*

h.   *Score m,* main or additional, for spiritual, psychic or abstract forces, such as "evil moving through the land," "invisible power drawing things together," "death," "decay," "disintegration."

Card IX

PERFORMANCE

A magician, Merlin or Moses. Moses performing miracles before King Pharaoh. One arm outstretched to the king and the other pointing to the miracle.

INQUIRY

S: Here in the orange. The rays leaving his arm indicate magic power.

Score: D   M,m   H   →O   2.5

COMMENT: An additional *m* for spiritual or magic force.

Card X

PERFORMANCE

At the bottom is a grasshopper with green clouds coming out of his eyes. No, it is a rabbit.

INQUIRY

E: What about them made them seem like clouds?

S: The outline and the shading, no harsh lines.

E: You said they were green clouds?

S: Yes, as a symbolic notion of mystery and hypnotic power.

Score: D   F,m,KF,CF$_{sym}$ Ad,clouds   P→O—   —0.5

COMMENT: An additional score of *m* is given both for the "symbolic notion of mystery and hypnotic power" and for "coming out." Note the minus form-level rating achieved by subtracting 0.5 from the basal 1.0 assigned to the popular "rabbit's head." (See pages 223–225.)

Do Not Score m

a.   *Score M or FM* where the movement of an object or the "force" mentioned is clearly the result of the movement of a human or animal figure. Thus, no *m* is scored for "wind" created by the rapid movement of figures on Cards I or III (see example on page 103). Here is an example from Card IV:

Card IV

PERFORMANCE	INQUIRY
Two drunk men leaning against a lamp post.	S: They're all scruffy. Their clothes, I mean. Their trousers are falling down. Dishevelled. Half against the lamp post and half on the ground. Here is the head (indicating side projection including S). The tail coat comes down here. It's blacker than the rest. It is the slumped appearance chiefly that made me think of a drunk.

Score: W,S   M,FC'   H   O   3.0

COMMENT: Here the "slumped" posture is covered by *M*, rather than requiring an *m* score for the pull of gravity.

b.   *Score F* (or *Fc* or *cF*, etc.) rather than *Fm* or *mF* if the "hanging" or "stretched" concept seems to be purely logical or positional, and does not evoke any kinesthetic feeling of tension.

Card VI

PERFORMANCE	INQUIRY
Nasty kids put pins in the wings of flies and spread them out.	S: The whole thing. It is spread out flat.

E: What about it made you think of pins?

S: You could justify it in terms of saying some dark spots were pins, but frankly I don't see them.

E: What about it made it seem spread out?

S: It is obviously flat, flattened out.

Score: W F A 1.0

COMMENT: The inquiry fails to elicit any notion of tension; therefore, no *m* is scored. The same would be the case for "a skin hanging on the wall" when it emerges in the inquiry that that is where one sees such skins, with no implication of tension and no specification of tension lines where the skin is stretched out.

c. *Score M or tendencies to M or FM* for expressions that pertain to the human or animal figure without being threatening symbols of some abstract or evil force. For examples, see pages 104, 106, 113.

d. *Score F only* (or *FC, CF,* and so on) when the subject clearly refers to form rather than to movement, even though his language might at first glance suggest that movement might have been implied.

Card IX

PERFORMANCE

Here is a candle with the wax dripping.

INQUIRY

E: I am not sure what you meant when you said "a candle with the wax dripping."

S: It was the irregular outlines that look like a candle with the wax on the sides. You know how they look when you have burned them for a while. It's sort of a green candle, with a little yellow pointed flame at the top.

Score: D FC obj 1.0

COMMENT: Here no movement is seen, although the use of words in the performance implied movement. No *m* is scored.

CHAPTER 5

Scoring: Determinants—Shading Responses

Shading responses include those where the subject uses the darker and lighter shading of the gray areas, and occasionally also that of the chromatic areas, to contribute to one of the following three major effects:

c: Shading gives the impression of surface or texture.

K: Shading gives the impression of three-dimensions or depth, either in the sense of diffusion (*K* or *KF*) or vista (*FK*).

k: Shading gives the impression of a three-dimensional expanse projected on a two-dimensional plane.

Cutting across this three-fold classification is the important distinction between differentiated and undifferentiated use of shading.

Differentiated Shading Responses

These include:

Fc: Where the surface or texture effect is either itself highly differentiated or, more usually, where the object possessing surface or texture qualities has definite form.

FK: Where the three-dimensional or depth impression is combined with definite form perception, giving vista or perspective to a landscape, for example.

Fk: Where the shading gives the impression of a three-dimensional expanse projected on a two-dimensional plane involving definite shape. Although the shading is used within the context of a definite object (for instance, an X ray of the chest with ribs showing, or the topographical map of a definite country) it is characteristic of the *Fk* response that the shading effect itself is used in a relatively undifferentiated way.

Undifferentiated Shading Responses

These include:

cF: Where the object has a vague or indefinite form, and the attention of the subject is focussed on the surface.

c: Where the subject demonstrates that he quite disregards any form element, and focusses interest only on the surface or texture effect. This demonstration can only be assumed if the subject uses the shading in this way mechanically, repeating this type of response more than twice in the series of blots.

KF: Where some form enters into the depth or diffusion impression, but with formlessness and flux implicit in the concept.

K: Where the response implies depth or diffusion with no form.

kF: Where the three-dimensional expanse is projected in a two-dimensional plane on an object of indefinite shape.

k: Where the three-dimensional expanse is projected on a two-dimensional plane in a way that implies no form at all; this is extremely rare.

Thus there are nine scoring categories to be distinguished for shading responses. For convenience, however, the discussion will be organized in five parts, as follows: (1) Differentiated texture (or surface) responses. (2) Undifferentiated texture (or surface) responses. (3) Differentiated depth or vista responses. (4) Undifferentiated depth or diffusion responses. (5) Responses in which a three-dimensional expanse is projected on a two-dimensional plane.

1. Differentiated Texture or Surface Responses: Fc

Score Fc

a. *Score Fc* for any texture effect in an object with definite form
(such as a furry animal, a silk or satin dress, a woollen glove, a
marble statue, steel pliers) provided that it is established that
the shading determined the texture effect. The texture effect may
be soft or hard, rough or smooth. Three examples follow:

Card VII

PERFORMANCE	INQUIRY
A Teddy Bear.	S: (Pointing to middle D) Here are the eyes, nose, mouth, and the ears, which are rather out of place.
	E: What about the blot suggested a Teddy Bear?
	S: The shape, and it is fuzzy, like a Teddy Bear. It looks soft and downy throughout. A toy of course. Just the head.

Score: D   Fc   (Ad)   2.5

COMMENT: A Teddy Bear has definite form, therefore *Fc* is
scored.

Card II

PERFORMANCE	INQUIRY
A Christmas stocking.	S: (Indicating top red portion) It was the red that suggested the Christmas stocking. It is a red sock, I guess, from the shape. It is a wool sock.
	E: What about the blot gave the impression that it might be wool?
	S: It looks soft like wool. It was the shading I guess.

Score: D   FC,Fc   obj   2.0

COMMENT: Color takes precedence here, being implied in the
performance proper, while the use of texture does not emerge

until the inquiry, and hence is scored additionally. This is a differentiated concept since the object has a definite shape.

Card VI

PERFORMANCE

A bearskin rug spread out in front of the fireplace.

INQUIRY

S: I think of it as not having a head, but here are the fore feet and hind feet, rather chopped off and flattened out as they often are. I didn't use this top part.

E: What made it seem like a bearskin?

S: It looks thick, like thick fur. It has a pile—a feeling that it would change form under your hand.

Score: W Fc A_{obj} 1.0

COMMENT: Here the animal skin with feet specified is an object of definite shape, hence the texture is scored *Fc*.

b. *Score Fc* for a finely differentiated texture effect in an object with indeterminate form. Here the differentiation applies to the texture effect itself, even though the outline of the object is vague or indefinite. Such finely differentiated textures include the weave or fine surface of fabrics (such as silk or satin), marble effects, and the like. Three examples follow:

Card VI

PERFORMANCE

A fur rug

INQUIRY

S: I used the whole thing.

E: What about it made it seem like a fur rug?

S: The fine shades of dark and light here.

E: Can you tell me more about the rug?

S: It could be a lynx skin, although I have never seen them used for a rug. It's the long hair, and the fine mottling makes it look just the way a lynx skin looks.

E: Did you use this part (upper *D*)?

INQUIRY (*continued*)

S: No, I suppose I didn't. The shape isn't important though. Not like a bear rug with the head and feet left on.

Score: W   Fc A_{obj} 1.0

COMMENT: Here, even though the outline of the skin itself is of indefinite shape, the description of the fur effect is sufficiently differentiated to justify a score of *Fc*.

Card VI

PERFORMANCE

An Indian rug

INQUIRY

S: It was this bottom part. You know the definite woven look of a Navajo rug. With the warp and woof very evident.

Score: D   Fc   obj   1.0

COMMENT: Emphasis on weave is one kind of response scored *Fc* for differentiated texture effect in an object of indefinite form.

Card VIII

PERFORMANCE

It looks like little snakeskins (pointing to blue *D*'s). This is the design on the back.

INQUIRY

S: All the blue part. It was the design in the shading and the frayed edge that made me think of a snakeskin. Not the color. It is opened out, flat, ready for use.

Score: D   Fc A_{obj} →O   1.0

COMMENT: Here again there is differentiated texture, even though the object has a vague shape.

c. *Score Fc* for emphasis on a rounded effect given by the shading. This is a reduced three-dimensional effect, like bas-relief; but it is considered a surface phenomenon and scored *Fc,* rather than a vista effect with emphasis on several surfaces with distance between them, for which the *FK* score is reserved. Sometimes a concept is encountered which seems to combine elements of a rounded surface *(Fc)* in which one part is considerably closer than another part *(FK)*. In such cases the scoring is *Fc→FK,* provided that definite emphasis is given to the surface effect. In cases where emphasis is not given to the surface effect but rather rests on the differences between surfaces, a main *FK* is given and *Fc* is not scored at all.

Card VII

PERFORMANCE

Oh! two delicately carved busts of women facing each other, poised. They have Regency headdresses with a feather on top.

INQUIRY

S: Head, neck, thrust out as in a conventional bust—tilted forward. Hair-do piled up, and the feather.

E: What did you mean "thrust out"?

S: Just the conventional way a bust is shown. Artificial. The women are putting on an act of being delicate and fragile for the sculptor who sculped them. Actually I think they must be porcelain.

E: Do you think of them as carved simply because they are not real?

S: Oh no! There is a very distinct three-dimensional effect.

Score: W   Fc→M   (Hd)   3.0

COMMENT: This is the "carved" effect regularly scored *Fc.*

Card V

PERFORMANCE

A piece of clay crumpled in the hand so it gives a series of corrugations around it.

INQUIRY

S: The whole thing, except for these projections. I'm looking at it sideways.

E: What gave the impression of a crumpled piece of clay.

S: The outline chiefly, and also the variation in intensity gives a three-dimensional roundness.

Score: W   Fc   clay   O   1.0

COMMENT: A "piece of clay" with a mere texture effect would be *cF*. However, here the form element is given emphasis both because of the rounded effect, which is always scored *Fc,* and by the distinct form of the concept, which corresponds very well to the shape of the blot.

Card III

PERFORMANCE

A vertebra (pointing to red center portion).

INQUIRY

S: It just looked like a vertebra bone, symmetrical.
E: The shape?
S: Yes, and the darker part seems like depth in it. It is bent in like this (gesturing to indicate concavity) rounded and smooth, and this light bit in the center is jutting forward.

Score: D   Fc→FK   At   1.0

COMMENT: This is an example of the *Fc→FK* scoring for an emphasis on surface combined with a specification of distances between surfaces.

Card I

PERFORMANCE

Here in the center is a dressmaker's form.

INQUIRY

E: What about the blot made it seem like a dressmaker's form?
S: It is in the form of a female figure — bust, waist and hips, and there is no head. Then there is the three-dimensional effect.
E: What about it made it seem three-dimensional?
S: Well! you know how they're solid at the top down to the hips and then it stops. That's like this. Through the dress that is on the form you can see the wooden structure that holds the form together. The effect of one thing behind another. This wooden thing standing behind the skirt.

Score: D   FK   (Hd)   2.0

COMMENT: Here the emphasis is on the distance between surfaces of separate objects—the transparent dress and the wooden structure behind it—not on rounded surfaces. *FK* is scored in this case. Note also the difference between this kind of three-dimensional transparency, which is scored *FK,* and "cellophane" transparency, which is scored *Fc* since it implies interest in a surface effect.

d. Score *Fc* for "cellophane transparency," with no particular distance effect.

Card I

PERFORMANCE

INQUIRY

A woman wearing a transparent skirt. She might be a dancer from the way her feet are placed.

S: You can see her just from the waist down, here in the center. You can see her hips and thighs through the skirt.

Score: D   M,Fc   Hd   2.5

COMMENT: This is the most frequent concept and location for a transparency effect. Here there is no mention of distance between surfaces. Although not explicit in the subject's statement, the usual implication of a transparent skirt is that the surface of the woman's body is seen through it, made more alluring by the transparent covering. This is in interesting contrast to the immediately preceding example, scored *FK,* in which the emphasis had shifted to the distance between the surfaces of separate objects which had no interesting contact with each other. A transparency concept for this location in Card I is scored *Fc,* unless the subject makes a special point of a distance effect. In other locations it is usually necessary to undertake an inquiry to establish whether transparency implies surface (*Fc*) or distance between surfaces (*FK*).

Card III

PERFORMANCE

INQUIRY

Icicles (indicating tiny light projections in lower center portion).

S: The transparent effect makes them icicles.

Score: dd   Fc   icicle   1.5

COMMENT: Even though an icicle is three-dimensional this transparency concept does not imply any marked "distance" effect, and hence is scored *Fc.*

e. *Score Fc* for highlights on a highly polished surface or a smooth glossy impression, as in the following case:

Card VI

PERFORMANCE   INQUIRY

The thing at the top looks like the post of   S: This (dark portion of top section,
a four-poster bed.   extending down into the middle sec-
                                                  tion). It is an elaborate post with a
                                                  carved knob. Large spools, tapering
                                                  down to a smaller spindle.
                                               E: Was there anything else about it?
                                               S: There is a sheen to it, which is the
                                                  thing that makes it so real.

Score: D   Fc   obj   2.0

COMMENT: This is the most frequent concept and location for this kind of *Fc.*

f. *Score Fc* for the achromatic representation of bright colors, as in a photograph.

Card VI

PERFORMANCE   INQUIRY

The bottom part makes me think of a   S: The whole central band, taking in
spectrum with one color shading into   this shaded part. You see the blend-
another. This is not quite right for there   ing. Light, dark, light. Yellow to
is no central line for a spectrum.   green to blue.

Score: dr   Fc   spectrum   O   1.0

COMMENT: Here it is definitely the shading that is interpreted as a chromatic color effect; hence the scoring is *Fc.*

g.   *Score Fc* where fine differentiations in the shading are used to specify parts of objects, such as facial features, even though a modelled or bas-relief effect is not specified. This must not be pushed to cover all delimitation of parts assisted by clear demarcations in the shading. Thus, for example, an *Fc* would not be scored for identifying an "eye" in the "moose's head" on Card IX, any more than a *di* rather than a *D* would be scored for the location of the "moose's head" itself. Nor would an *Fc* be scored for an "eye" in the "animal's head" in the lower *D* on Card IV, nor for the "nose" of the popular "dog" on Card II, nor for the "shoes" of the usual men on Card III. In these cases the Gestalt qualities of the blot delimit the parts so clearly that they are commonly seen even by individuals who have little interest in the shading. It is only when the subject uses fine shading differences that are usually ignored to carve out a differentiated concept that *Fc* would be scored. This would be the case with well-seen *di*'s; an excellent example appears on page 84. Two other examples are presented below:

Card VII

PERFORMANCE	INQUIRY
Here is the court jester. He is about to say something funny. Perhaps malicious.	S: Here he is (left middle *D*). He has on a jester's cap. His mouth is open slightly, and you can see his lower lip and lower teeth. As if he had drawn his lip back before saying something in malicious jest. There is sort of a half-humorous, half-malicious gleam in his eye, too.

Score: D   M, Fc   Hd   3.5

COMMENT: Here the fine differences in shading are used not only for the eye but for the lower lip and teeth as well. The interest in shading justifies an *Fc* score, additional to main *M*.

Card VI

PERFORMANCE	INQUIRY
A totem pole at the top. Face and wings.	E: What about the blot made it seem like a totem pole.
	S: The shape, and here is the suggestion of eyes, nose and whiskers, and here the wings. They are brightly painted, as totem poles are—and that is shown by the differences in the shading here.

Score: D   Fc   obj   3.0

COMMENT: This *Fc* score is doubly determined, both by the use of fine differentiations in the shading to give facial features and by the use of shading for achromatic representation of bright color.

Score Additional Fc

a. In the many instances where some surface or texture effect of a differentiated sort is secondary to some other determinant such as *M, FM, FK, FC,* an additional *Fc* is scored.

b. *Score an additional Fc* where the use of shading for texture or surface is reluctantly conceded. This would rarely occur except in Card VI; for a prodding inquiry would not be pursued for *Fc* on other cards, unless the concept or the spontaneous verbalization makes it seem very likely that shading was involved. Examples follow:

Card VI

PERFORMANCE	INQUIRY
An animal skin.	S: The head is not there; but here are fore paws, hind paws, and I think this might be the tail.
	E: What about the blot makes it seem like an animal skin?
	S: It is the right sort of shape for an animal skin. The kind of thing you see in front of a fire.
	E: What kind of a skin might it be?
	S: It is a bear rug.

E: What about it made it seem like a bear rug?

S: That is the usual kind you see in front of a fire.

E: Which side could be up?

S: The furry side, I guess. That is the side that is usually up, and this coloring perhaps suggests fur.

Score: W   F→Fc   A$_{obj}$ P   1.5

COMMENT: Prodding such as this would not be undertaken unless the concept seemed clearly to imply texture, and even then would not be carried to this extent except on Card VI where the use of texture for this concept is a popular response. However, the "furriness" takes so much questioning to elicit, and then is so reluctantly conceded, that a tendency to *Fc* seems a better scoring than a main *Fc*.

Do Not Score Fc

a. *Score cF* where the shading effect is undifferentiated and the outline of the object is vague or indefinite. (See pages 141–143.)

b. *Score FK* where the transparency involves a distance or depth effect. (See pages 145–150.)

c. *Omit Fc* where the texture effect is given only by the outline, or where the use of shading is clearly denied even with a concept that seems to imply it.

Card VI

PERFORMANCE

This is an animal skin stretched out to dry.

INQUIRY

S: I just used the lower part. Here are the paws which have been left on but there is no head.

E: What about the blot made it seem like an animal skin?

S: It just looks like the kind of skin that trappers tack up on the walls of their cabins to dry. I used to do this kind of thing with rabbits.

E: Which side of the skin is out?

S: It could be either side.

INQUIRY (*continued*)

E: What made it seem stretched?

S: You have to stretch them (gestured). They tend to shrink and pull against the nails you put them up with.

E: (Testing the limits) Some people see this as an animal skin because the light and dark shading makes it seem furry.

S: It doesn't look that way to me.

Score: D   Fm A_{obj} P   1.5

COMMENT: Here the subject denies the use of shading even when it is directly put up to him in the testing-the-limits period. There is no alternative but to omit *Fc*.

Card VIII

PERFORMANCE

Two fur-bearing animals climbing over something.

INQUIRY

S: Here they are. They have long, slim bodies, four legs. Here is an eye. Short muzzles. They seem to be climbing over rocks or something.

E: What about the animals made them seem furry?

S: You can see the irregularity of the edge. Little hairs standing up. It looks like fur.

Score: D→W   FM   A   P   2.5

COMMENT: Here the outline is used rather than the shading; texture, therefore, is not implied, despite the concept used. The inquiry is not pushed; it would only be pushed on Card VI, or possibly Card IV.

d.   *Score FC′* where the shading is used for achromatic color rather than for surface or texture, even though the words the subject uses seem at first to imply texture. For example:

Card VI

PERFORMANCE   INQUIRY

This top part is a British Columbia totem pole. The head and wings.

E: What about the blot made it like a totem pole?

S: The shape. Here is the head and here are the wings, eagle wings.

E: What made them seem like wings?

S: The shading here made it seem like feathers.

E: I'm not sure what you mean by shading.

S: The different shades suggest the different colors of eagle wings, black, dark gray and lighter gray.

Score: D   FC′   obj   2.0

COMMENT: Here the shading is used to give an achromatic color effect and does not imply textural quality.

e. *Do not score Fc* just because some minor surface effect can be discovered within a vista response. This could almost always be done, especially if an inquiry were to be pursued into the components of the landscape. Score an additional *Fc* only where the subject deliberately emphasizes the differences in the use of shading to indicate an interest in the touch-textural effect in a large portion of the shading surrounding the vista. Two examples from Card VI follow:

Card VI

PERFORMANCE   INQUIRY

That looks like some survey from the air, of some excavation. They are digging a canal or something.

S: The whole thing. This part down the middle is a big canal or trench. It looks earthy around it. The darker color shows it has been dug. Down in the trench you get a gleam of water. The rest of the soil seems lighter.

E: Did you use this part (top portion)?

S: No, it doesn't really belong.

E: What about it made it seem earthy?

INQUIRY (*continued*)

S: It was the lighter and darker color around the deep trench. It seemed logical that it should be the earth thrown up which was a different color than the rest around it.

Score: W   FK   N   2.0

COMMENT: The deep ditch and the aerial view clearly make a main *FK* the appropriate main determinant score. This seems to cover the use of shading quite adequately. An additional *Fc* is not given for the highlight effect implied in "a gleam of water" since it is a minor surface effect in the total landscape and does not imply any direct interest in touch. Similarly, the "lighter and darker color around the deep trench" seems to be a logical contribution to the total three-dimensional effect rather than an emphasis on any textural effect implied in "earthy."

Card VI

PERFORMANCE

This is looking down into the Grand Canyon. You can sit here and look down. Sit on the rocks.

INQUIRY

S: (Indicated omission of top *D*.) This part is the Canyon. And here on each side are the rocks where you sit. The lighter and darker color makes it seem rough like rocks, and this center part is the deep Canyon, dark with the light part the river at the bottom.

Score: W   FK,Fc   N   1.5

COMMENT: The main *FK* is supported here by a definite interest in texture implied in the use of the word "rough." This textural effect is scored *Fc* rather than *cF* because its organization within the context of a structured landscape constitutes a differentiated use of shading to give texture.

f.   *Fc cannot be scored* where color is projected upon an area, unless it is established that the nuances of shading are interpreted as differences in color, as in a photograph.

Card IX

PERFORMANCE

A red-headed man walking quickly, bending over to walk against a wind.

INQUIRY

S: It is this green part (card held sideways). Here is his head, with a shock of hair. His hand extended, perhaps with a walking stick. He is bent over, and his hair is blown back in the wind.

E: What gave you the impression of red hair?

S: Well! of course the blot is green, but I think of him as having red hair. He is definitely red-headed.

Score: D   M,m   H   3.5

COMMENT: Here the "red hair" seems a purely capricious projection, and not similar to the use of shading for photographic representation of color, which is scored *Fc*.

2. Undifferentiated Surface or Texture Responses: cF and c

Score a Main cF

Score cF for responses where the object has vague form, and interest is focussed on the surface, but where the surface effect itself is not highly differentiated. It must be established that the shading contributed to the surface emphasis. Examples include indefinitely shaped pieces of fur, rocks, grass, coral, snow. The texture effect may be soft or hard, rough or smooth. Two examples follow:

Card II

PERFORMANCE

A bear rug in front of a fireplace with a hole worn in it.

INQUIRY

S: The black part only.

E: What about it made it seem like a bear rug?

S: The black color and shape, and it is furry. (Rubbed the card.)

E: Can you describe the shape?

S: Well, it hasn't any particular shape, it's not the kind that has head and legs left on.

Score: W   cF,C′F   A$_{obj}$ 0.5

COMMENT: Here is a texture effect, itself undifferentiated, in an object with indefinite shape. The emphasis given to the surface by the subject's rubbing the card is justification for giving *cF* as the main score and achromatic color as additional.

Card VI

PERFORMANCE   INQUIRY

The whole formation reminds me of rock.   S: It was the way it was shaded.
                                          E: How did the shading make it seem
                                              like rock?
                                          S: It made it look rough, and it is the
                                              color of rocks, some rocks . . . a kind
                                              of gray.

Score: W   cF, C′F   rock   0.5

COMMENT: Here the object is of indefinite form and the shading contributed to a surface or texture effect. Since the texture effect is not itself differentiated, a *cF* would be scored.

Score an Additional cF

a.   *Score an additional cF* where the undifferentiated surface effect is used as secondary to another determinant (for instance, *CF, cF* where an object with vague form has both color and undifferentiated texture) .

Card VIII

PERFORMANCE   INQUIRY

This orange part looks like orange water-   S: It was the color, of course, which is
ice   exactly right; and it looks as if it
                                                would be mushy like water-ice.
                                            E: What makes it seem mushy?
                                            S: The unevenness of the color.

Score: D   CF,cF   food   0.5

b. *Score an additional cF* where the undifferentiated surface effect is loosely integrated into a composite concept in which definite form predominates. If the definite form also implies a differentiated use of shading, *cF* need not be scored, since the *Fc* would cover the textural interest. This would be the case where minor undifferentiated texture effects are found within a context of differentiated use of shading. However, if the undifferentiated shaded area exceeds the differentiated shaded area in size (a smaller differentiated concept in a larger undifferentiated surrounding) a main *Fc* and additional *cF* should be scored. For example:

Card VI

PERFORMANCE

INQUIRY

A chess piece twirling down into the soft part lower down. It's shiny black wood.

S: This dark part at the top. Looks like highly polished wood with a cross piece on top. The soft part looks like putty.

Score: W   Fm, Fc,FC′,cF   obj, putty   2.0

COMMENT: This is an interesting combination of use of shading to give texture in both a differentiated and undifferentiated way. *Fc* is scored for the "highly polished wood." An additional *cF* is scored for the soft putty, since the undifferentiated area is so large in extent that it cannot be subsumed under an overriding *Fc*. In such a complex concept it seems desirable to give precedence to the differentiated elements, so the main determinant was drawn from the "twirling chess piece" rather than from the putty. *Fm* was scored as main determinant both because it seemed the more important and because it is the movement that serves as the link between the two parts of the concept. *FC′* was added for the "blackness" of the wood. Had texture not been used in a differentiated way (if the wood had not been described as highly polished) the scoring would have been *Fm, FC′, cF*. Had movement not been projected (if the highly polished dark chess-piece had been described as buried in the putty) the scoring would have been *Fc, FC′,cF*.

Do Not Score cF

a.   *Score Fc* where the texture effect is differentiated even though
     the object has indefinite shape (see pages 129–130).

b.   *Score Fc* where the texture effect is very marked (great emphasis
     on softness or furriness) and the object has definite shape.
     Sometimes the error is made of scoring *cF* to indicate the very
     marked textural qualities despite the fact that the texture effect
     is integrated with definite form. *cF* is reserved for undifferenti-
     ated concepts and does not indicate degree of emphasis. Thus
     the soft Teddy Bear on page 128 and the thick pile of the
     bearskin rug on page 129 are scored *Fc*. It is only where the
     textural element is loosely integrated with an object of definite
     form that *cF* can be scored as additional to the form. Thus, in
     the example of the chessman twirling into the soft putty given
     above, the integration is loose enough (and the undifferentiated
     area large enough) for *cF* to be scored in addition to the *Fc*
     scored for the chess piece.

c.   *Score Fc* rather than *cF* for all instances of highlight, photo-
     graphic use of color, modelled effects, even though the outline
     of the object is indefinite. These ways of using shading to give
     surface or texture are themselves considered as differentiated.

d.   *Omit cF* for a minor undifferentiated texture effect in a complex
     concept in which the differentiated use of shading is already ac-
     knowledged by an *Fc* or *FK* score. (Compare a similar omission
     of *Fc* discussed on pages 139–140.)

Score c

A *c* score is given only where the subject shows a complete disregard for form and mechanically uses shading in an undifferentiated
way in several cards. This is very rarely to be encountered and then
only in cases of severe pathology. A classic example is that of a patient with very extensive damage to his frontal lobes who responded
to five heavily shaded cards with the concept "animal skin," making
it quite clear that the skin had no definite shape and that it was the
textural qualities that determined the concept. (See discussion on
page 590.)

Do Not Score c

a. *Score cF* for an undifferentiated texture response in an object of indefinite form if only one or two such responses are given in any one protocol.

b. *Score cF* for such a concept even though repeated if the subject integrates the undifferentiated texture response within a larger concept with elements of differentiated form and organization. An example of such organization is given on page 143 in the response of the chess-piece twirling into soft putty.

3. Differentiated Depth or Vista Responses

Score FK

a. *Score FK* for vista viewed horizontally, where the shading contributes to the depth effect. This can rarely, if ever, be scored unless there are three adjacent areas, the shading differences of which are used for the formation of the concept. If the concept of a three-dimensional landscape or architectural vista is given to a blot area meeting this criterion, it may be scored *FK,* even though the subject cannot verbalize the use of shading. Indeed, it is the concept itself that usually gives the clue to the use of shading, rather than the explicit statement of the subject. For example:

Card VII

PERFORMANCE

This is a chunk of the Grand Canyon. The sun is setting at the far end of the narrow chasm, at the bottom in the far distance. There is a little rim of cloud around the sun.

INQUIRY

S: The whole thing is the canyon, and you are at the entrance of it. The sun is at the end (pointing to the top portion of the bottom *D*) and there are clouds around the sun.

Score: W   FK, KF   N   1.5

COMMENT: Here, although shading is not mentioned, the blot material, and the concept, distinctly implying distance and vista, make an *FK* score quite clear. An additional *KF* covers both the cloud and the light effect of the sun.

Card II

PERFORMANCE

A circular staircase

INQUIRY

S: (Pointed to top red portion.) It is a balustrade on a staircase winding upwards. The shading gives the impression of winding.

Score: D   FK   Arch   O   1.5

COMMENT: Here shading is mentioned as the basis for the architectural vista, occurring in an area that has sufficient differentiation of shading to make this plausible, even though it is a chromatic area.

b. *Score FK* for reflections where the water or waterline is specified in the shading and is not merely a device to explain the symmetrical character of the blots.

Card IV

PERFORMANCE

Sideways, a tangled bush reflected in a lake, with gnarled trees.

INQUIRY

S: These twisted projections, and heavy masses.
E: What about the blot gives the impression of a reflection?
S: It is bilaterally symmetrical.
E: Are both sides the same?
S: No, the reflection is a bit different. The water seems dirty, with little bits floating in it. Also it seems glossier on the water side, although that may be just because I thought of a reflection.

Score: W   FK   N   2.0

COMMENT: This is a clear example of a reflected vista where the shading contributes to the three-dimensional effect.

c. *Score FK* for a vista viewed horizontally, even though the form of the blot is unimportant and the concept is rather shapeless, provided that the shading contributes to the three-dimensional effect.

Card VI

PERFORMANCE

I get the impression of a murky landscape, reflected in a lake, the sort of thing that one would see at twilight in the north country. (The card was held sideways.)

INQUIRY

S: I used the whole thing, except this top bit.

E: Can you tell me more about the landscape?

S: No it is very indefinite. You can't distinguish any parts.

E: What made it seem reflected?

S: There is a quality of distance to it, to which I suppose the misty quality contributes. That's why I said twilight.

Score: D   FK,K   N   1.0

COMMENT: Here *FK* must be scored for the three-dimensional vista effect, plus the reflection, even though the concept is indefinite. An additional *K* is given for the "misty quality." (A basic 0.5 form-level rating is assigned to this semi-definite concept, and 0.5 is added for the organization implied in "reflected in a lake.")

d. *Score FK* for a vertical vista, such as a vista seen from above or an aerial view or aerial photograph, where shading contributes to the three-dimensional effect. Note the following examples:

Card IV

PERFORMANCE

Could be an island with water around it, bays and mountains.

INQUIRY

S: The heavy shaded parts would be the mountains, the lighter parts are lower and flat like, and the white parts would be the water and bays. I'm looking at it from the air.

Score: W,S   FK   N   1.0

COMMENT: The inquiry establishes that the shading contributed to a depth or distance effect in an aerial view. Hence *FK* is scored.

Card VIII

PERFORMANCE

A piece of coral rock of different colors. You are looking straight down through the water at it.

INQUIRY

S: The whole.
E: What about it seemed like coral rock?
S: The pastel colors.
E: What about it gave the impression of looking down through water?
S: It is hazy, and therefore you are looking straight down at it through water.

Score: W   CF, FK   coral   0.5

COMMENT: Although *CF* is clearly the main determinant, the shading on this chromatic card is used to give a vertical depth effect, which differs from the cellophane transparency effect, scored *Fc*. Here is another example of an *FK* score given to a concept of indefinite shape.

e.   *Score FK* for an entrance to or from a cave, or a vista through holes or archways, where the three-dimensional effect is specified, and can be attributed to shading.

Card IV

PERFORMANCE

This is the entrance to a cave, with something hanging over the entrance. I think it might be an animal skin. Yes, the cave of a cave man with the skin hung there to keep the draught out.

INQUIRY

S: Here is the entrance (pointing to the lower part of the card) and here is the skin (indicating lower center *D*).
E: What about the blot made it seem like the entrance to a cave?
S: Well! it's the way these dark shadows extend inwards that gives you the feeling of recession and depth.
E: And the animal skin? What made you think of that?
S: Well! it looks thick and furry, and then it seemed a logical thing to have too.

Score: W   FK,cF   N,A$_{obj}$ 1.5

COMMENT: Here the main determinant is *FK* for a three-dimensional effect clearly resting upon shading. An additional *cF* is given for the additional undifferentiated textural use of shading where the touch emphasis is so great that it cannot be considered a minor elaboration in the total structure of the concept.

f. *Score FK* generally for any three-dimensional effect where it is the one-object-in-front-of-another that is stressed rather than a rounded effect. The same applies to one object being distinctly closer than another object or part of the same object. The distinction between *FK* and *Fc* is that the *FK* concept stresses distances between surfaces rather than the surface itself *(Fc)*. Again it must be emphasized that the examiner is rarely justified in scoring *FK* unless such a concept is applied to an area with three adjacent areas, the shading differences of which are used for the formation of the concept. Mere linear perspective, or logical position, is not enough to justify *FK*. A sample case follows:

Card II

PERFORMANCE	INQUIRY
Like a face seen from below.	S: Nose, forehead, narrowing in perspective. Cheekbones seen in section. Mouth. There is perspective about it.
	E: What about the blot gives the impression of perspective?
	S: The paling of the color suggesting recession. It is a fantastic face like a mask.

Score: W   FK   (Hd)   0   2.0

COMMENT: A three-dimensional effect to a face is usually of a rounded, bas-relief variety, scored *Fc*. Here, however, the emphasis on perspective and recession seems to bring it into the *FK* classification.

Score Additional FK

a. Where the vista is of secondary importance in the concept, and
   M, FM, Fc, CF, etc. is the main determinant, score an additional *FK.* For example:

Card IX

PERFORMANCE

Here are two old Roman bridges. You
can see them made of heavy stone. Here
the light reflects through the arch and
here is deep shadow on the side.

INQUIRY

S: It has that rock look, granite, gritty,
   carved. Heavy shading. Here is clear
   light showing through.
E: Do you get a depth effect?
S: Yes, very definitely. That is what I
   was trying to explain.

Score: D,S   Fc, FK   Arch   2.0

COMMENT: The texture effect of the stone bridges takes precedence. The shading is used to give depth also, hence there is
an additional *FK. K* cannot be scored for the "clear light" since
it applies to a white rather than a shaded area. It seems part of
the *FK* concept.

b. In the special case previously mentioned on page 131, where a
   surface or texture effect is emphasized as well as the distance between surfaces, the scoring is *Fc→FK.*

Card IV

PERFORMANCE

A huge insect. It seems to be crawling
out from behind a split leaf.

INQUIRY

S: The insect is here (pointing to bottom *D*). It has two antennae. It
   reminds me of a bee. The thick part
   is the thorax. The rest is the leaf, the
   curled wide sides. It is a dried leaf
   with crisp edges. I see three dimensions in this. It is like a fall leaf, and
   this is the other side.

Score: 1. D ⎫   FM   Ad ⎫   1.5
          2. W ⎭   Fc→FK   Pl ⎭ →O   1.0

COMMENT: This seems loosely enough organized to justify two main responses being scored. The leaf response is an excellent example of *Fc→FK*. The interest in surface and texture is evinced by the mention of "the other side" and by the "dried," "crisp" adjectives. The three-dimensional effect is clearly stated in the emphasis on several surfaces with distance between them and in the overlapping of the "leaf" and "insect" and of the edges of the leaf itself.

Do Not Score FK

a. *Score F* (or other main determinant) where perspective is merely linear, and the shading is not used to give the three-dimensional effect.

Card IV (inverted)

PERFORMANCE	INQUIRY
Here this dark part reminds me of a grand piano, set at sort of an angle to me.	S: (Indicated lower dark gray *D*.) It is the curving line of this dark part that reminds me of a grand piano, and the dark color of course. E: What made it seem at an angle? S: With the curved line of that shape it would have to be at an angle. It's the perspective of the thing.

Score: D   FC′   obj   O   1.5

COMMENT: Although "set at an angle" might imply a depth effect, and the area is shaded in such a way as to contribute to this, the inquiry establishes that the depth effect was purely a matter of linear perspective and the shading was not used to give a three-dimensional object.

b. *Score F* where a reflection is merely a matter of symmetry, and there is no evidence that shading was used to give a three-dimensional effect. An example, from a response to Card VIII, follows on the next page:

Card VIII

PERFORMANCE

Here is an animal looking at itself in the water (card held sideways).

INQUIRY

S: He has his head down, looking at his image. He is standing on a rock. All of this rest could be rocks.

E: What about it made it seem like rocks?

S: Well! the shape, and it seems reasonable that rocks might be around water.

E: What gave the impression of a reflection.

S: It is the same on both sides.

E: There is no difference on the water side?

S: No, the water is perfectly still, so the reflection is not disturbed.

Score: W   FM   A   P   1.5

COMMENT: The reflection was brought in to satisfy the need of the subject to use the whole card, and seems based on bilateral symmetry with no suggestion of use of shading and no mention of a three-dimensional effect.

c. *Score F* (or other main determinant) where the aerial view is dictated by a positional need, and shading is not used to give vertical vista (for example, a coastline seen from the air).

Card VII

PERFORMANCE

Here is James Bay seen from the air.

INQUIRY

S: The white space. It has no outlet. There is a little inlet at the bottom.

E: What about it made it seem as though you viewed it from the air?

S: Otherwise you couldn't see it like this.

E: Could it be an outline map?

S: Yes.

Score: S   F   Geo   1.0

COMMENT: The inquiry makes it clear that the emphasis was on the shape of the white space, and shading did not enter in to give aerial perspective.

d. *Score Fk* (or *kF*) where the concept develops to be a topographical map rather than an aerial view (see pages 162–164).

e. *Score Fc* where the effect is one of a rounded surface rather than several surfaces with space in between.

Card I

PERFORMANCE	INQUIRY
Some sort of bones.	S: Looking at the whole thing as a mass, instead of flat. Trying to put volume into it. It is a hard substance, reminiscent of a pelvis. Rounded and three-dimensional. The effect of difference in densities gives it a modelling.
	E: What part is closer to you?
	S: This center part. It is rounded.

Score: W   Fc   At   1.0

COMMENT: Although at first it would seem that there is an additional *FK* implied for a three-dimensional effect, it emerges that the whole thing is covered by *Fc* for a rounded surface effect. Frequently, however, the light gray is seen as the more distant surface of the pelvic girdle overlapped by the rounded darker areas; in this instance the scoring would be *Fc→FK* for a rounded effect with partial use of vista. (See page 132.)

f. *Score Fc* where there is transparency without three-dimensional space. (See page 133.)

g. *Score F* (or other determinant) where the entrance to a cave or archway does not imply three-dimensional perspective. For example:

Card IX (inverted)

Here is a wall with an archway here and   S: It was the shape. The archway here
peepholes above it. It might be a fortifi-   below, and these little slit-like spaces.
cation, with slits to fire through.   (Placed his hand over the pink detail
                                                                     to indicate the area he used.)

Score: W,S   F   Arch   1.5

COMMENT: There is no evidence here that shading was used
to give an impression of three dimensions, hence *FK* is not
scored.

h. *Do not score FK* for diffusion combined with an object of defi-
    nite form unless diffusion is emphasized as an element in a land-
    scape in which case a scoring of *FK,KF* may be given. Mush-
    room-shaped clouds of an atomic explosion would be scored *KF*.
    Clouds in a more definite shape such as Hamlet's "cloud in the
    shape of a camel" would be scored *F* with an additional *KF*.
    FK must be reserved for the organized use of shading to sug-
    gest several areas at various distances from the observer.

4. Undifferentiated Depth or Diffusion Responses: K and KF

Score K

a. *Score K* for diffusion responses, implying depth with no form.
    Implicit is the feeling of formlessness and flux. The criterion
    of diffusion is that "one could put a knife through it without
    separating it." This is a three-dimensional response in that the
    diffuse substance is space-filling. Examples are fog, mist, smoke,
    clouds that are quite undifferentiated, and water with no form.
    When such concepts are given to shaded areas *K* may be scored
    (in the absence of contrary evidence) even though the subject
    does not verbalize that the shading contributed to the effect.
    If, however, the concepts are given to areas where the shading
    gives little reality basis for the concept, it is possible that the

subject merely refers to something of indeterminate outline, or that the logic of the concept dictates such a response. Therefore, in such instances, particularly on the colored cards, it is necessary to obtain evidence that shading was used before K can be scored.

Card IV

PERFORMANCE

INQUIRY

If you just look at this center part it looks like the swirling of water in a stream running fast. (Indicated shaded area in upper portion, extending nearly to edges, but not including them.)

E: What about the blot gives you that impression?

S: The ripple of this light and dark shading. It has depths to it as if you were looking through water. Only it is so deep you can't see the bottom.

Score: di   K,m   water   O   0.0

COMMENT: The shading here is used for a diffusion response with no form, and hence is scored K.

b.   *Score K* for light that has a space-filling quality or represents "streaming" from a light source, provided of course that the shading of the card is used to give this effect. It must be emphasized that there must be a depth effect or diffusion effect of some kind; mere use of the surface in an achromatic color sense is scored otherwise (C'). For example:

Card VI

PERFORMANCE

INQUIRY

Here we have a summer's night with northern lights flickering in the sky. And low-lying land on the horizon. The whole thing is reflected.

E: What about the card gave the impression of northern lights?

S: The dark sky here, and this irregular band of lighter shading.

E: What about the blot made it seem reflected?

S: That was just to bring in this part. I don't see the water.

E: Did you use this part (top D)?

S: No, it doesn't enter in.

Score: W   FK,K,m   N, light   1.0

COMMENT: It is clear that there is a *K* element for the "northern lights." Although *FK* cannot be scored for the reflection, a main *K* does not seem appropriate, since within the structure of a landscape, with "low-lying land" and sky above it, there is too much form differentiation to be properly represented by a determinant implying pure formlessness. Therefore, a main *FK* is scored with an additional *K*, and an additional *m* for the "flickering" movement.

c. *Score K* for darkness that has space-filling qualities, as distinct from mere dark color.

Card V

PERFORMANCE	INQUIRY
Two animals diving into what I can only describe as darkness.	S: These side things are the animals diving in. You can see only part of them. E: Can you tell me more about the thing they are diving into? S: It's sort of diffuse, three-dimensional. Like a cloud of darkness. It isn't a cloud though. I suppose it is symbolic, somehow. Symbolizing cover, concealment, where they can't be seen. Like night.

Score: W   FM,K$_{sym}$ Ad,darkness   →O   1.5

COMMENT: Here the "darkness" has diffusion and space-filling qualities. Note that *C′* cannot be scored also, since there is no question of surface color.

Do Not Score K

a. *K* cannot be scored where the concept implying diffusion is suggested by position or logic rather than shading. An example is given on the next page.

Card IX

PERFORMANCE	INQUIRY
Fire, hell, brimstone and fire. The red underneath is the fire of hell. It suggests something threatening.	S: It was the whole thing. The fire is at the top and bottom. At the top there are flames, and at the bottom smouldering coals. The middle part is smoke. E: What about it makes it seem like fire? S: The color, the orange for flames and the red for smouldering coals. E: How about the smoke? S: It was the only way I could bring in this part (indicating green). One could see smoke rising from the coals then flames leaping above.

Score: W CF_{sym}, m   fire   →O   0.5

COMMENT: The "smoke" here seems to be positional and logical, implying no use of shading, and hence is not scored *K*.

b. *Do not score K* for "water" concepts where reflection is involved and either *FK* or *F* should be scored (see page 146) ; or where water is part of vertical vista (another *FK* scoring, see page 147) ; or where there is a "highlight" or "cellophane transparency" concept, in which case the scoring is *Fc* (see page 133) .

c. *K* cannot be scored for "light" attributed to a white space, since there is no shading which can possibly be used for a diffusion effect. Score *F*, or *C'* if "whiteness" is attributed to the area.

d. *K* cannot be scored for "dark" unless a space-filling effect is involved. For dark, black, or gray in the sense of surface color, score *C'*.

e. *Score KF* rather than *K* where there is vague or indefinite form rather than pure formlessness. This is very likely to be the case where the diffusion element is emphasized within the structure of an organized landscape.

Score KF

a.   Score *KF* where some form is involved in the diffusion concept
—clouds, smoke spiralling, and the like.

Card VII

PERFORMANCE   INQUIRY

Clouds in the sky.   S: The whole thing.
                                     E: What about it made them seem like
                                         clouds?
                                     S: The outline is not distinct. There
                                         is depth and thickness and light.

   Score: W   KF   clouds   0.5

COMMENT: Even clouds this vaguely shaped would be scored
KF rather than *K*. To be scored *K* a cloud concept would have
to be as formless as "a cloud of mist, no shape at all." Here the
use of shading to give **an** effect of diffusion is clearly formulated.

Card II

PERFORMANCE   INQUIRY

Upside down the dark part could be two   S: I include all the black part. It was
tornado clouds.   the shape that made me say tornado
                                               clouds. Ending in this narrow neck
                                               at the bottom. That is the part that
                                               does the damage. It might be moving
                                               now. I now notice these lines in it
                                               which suggest the whirling move-
                                               ment.

   Score: W   KF,mF   clouds   0.5

COMMENT: Although of semi-definite shape (rather than
vaguely shaped as in the preceding example) these clouds are
also scored *KF*. Although the subject does not actually verbalize the use of shading to give a diffusion effect, this may be
assumed with a "cloud" concept in a shaded area unless there
is some indication to the contrary. An additional *mF* is scored

for the inanimate movement, which did not emerge until the inquiry. Had the movement been emphasized in the performance proper it would have been given precedence since the "whirling" movment of a tornado cloud is so violent.

Card VII

PERFORMANCE   INQUIRY

Smoke rising in spirals.   S: I used the whole thing. This might be the chimney at the bottom. It's the shading and indefiniteness of it that makes it seem like smoke.

Score: W   KF,mF   smoke   0.5

COMMENT: The "spiral" concept suggests *KF* rather than *K*. The "chimney" is an object of definite form but is not scored. It is clearly subordinate to the smoke, and additional *F* scores are never given (unless they are sufficiently independent to be given a separate location score for a semi-independent concept mentioned in the inquiry) .

b. *Score KF* rather than *FK* for diffusion concepts such as clouds that approach definite form. An example is the mushroom-shaped cloud of an atomic explosion, frequently seen in Card IX inverted; this should be scored *KF* if the diffusion is emphasized at all. Score *KF,mF* or *mF,KF* depending upon whether the explosion or the diffusion seems to have priority in the formation of the concept; if no diffusion is implied, score *mF* (as in the case cited on page 115) . Do not score *FK,* since this scoring is reserved for an organized use of shading in which the differences in shading indicate surfaces at different distances from the observer.

Score an Additional KF

a. *Score an additional KF* where some other determinant such as color takes precedence over diffusion. For example, note the following response to Card II:

Card II

PERFORMANCE	INQUIRY
I get a feeling of illumination above clouds. Flames behind clouds.	S: The red. The flames and red behind the clouds here (pointing to the red-black mixture at bottom center). E: What about them makes them seem like clouds? S: The diffuse mass of them.

Score: D   CF,KF   flames, clouds   →O   0.5

COMMENT: The shading is used to give diffusion here, in conjunction with a main color determinant.

b. *Score additional KF* if diffusion is emphasized in the context of a landscape or other three-dimensional concept. Here the diffusion must be emphasized beyond the point necessary to give a distance effect in a landscape, because this use of shading would be covered adequately by the main *FK* score. However, if the landscape concept includes elements described as vapor, smoke, or mist, a *KF* may be scored as additional to *FK*.

Card VI

PERFORMANCE	INQUIRY
Sideways, a forest fire raging, and reflected in dirty water.	S: The dark part is heavy smoke. In the reflection it is dirty water. The lighter part near the center is fire. The smoke is rising up. The dark bits in the smoke are soot. This dark part is the muddy bank near the center. The same thing is reflected in the water, only the water looks dirty.

Score: W   FK,KF,C'F,mF   N,smoke   O   2.5

COMMENT: This complex response deserves a main *FK* for the reflection concept. It is interesting how undifferentiated shading is subordinated to the organized structure of a landscape. The emphasis on diffusion implied in the "smoke rising up" is such that a *KF* score must be given in addition to the *FK*. There is indefinite form rather than formlessness by virtue of building the "smoke" into the landscape, hence the score is *KF* rather than *K*. Achromatic color for the dark sooty bits and inanimate movement implied in rising are reflected in additional *C'F* and *mF* respectively. The "muddy bank" implies a possible additional use of undifferentiated texture; but since this is a minor element in the total concept and has not been elaborated to emphasize a touch effect, it is believed that the use of shading is adequately covered by the *FK,KF* scoring.

c. Very occasionally subjects may use diffusion in the context of an object or figure of quite definite form. Thus, for example, on Card VII they may see "a cloud in the shape of a camel" or "a cloud in the shape of a face." In such instances the main determinant must be *F* (or *M* or *FM* or *Fm* if movement is involved) and the diffusion in the cloud concept is represented by an additional *KF*. *FK* cannot be used in such instances for a combination of diffusion and definite form since the *FK* score is reserved for concepts involving the inner organization of shading.

Do Not Score KF

a. *Do not score KF* where clouds and the like are determined merely by the vague outline, and the shading is not used to give a diffuse effect. For example:

Card X

PERFORMANCE

Here are some little orange sunset clouds.

INQUIRY

E: What about them made them seem like clouds?

S: The color reminded me of sunset, and the shape doesn't detract, in that it isn't anything in particular, and therefore shaped like a cloud.

Score: D   CF   cloud   0.5

COMMENT: Here there is no suggestion that shading is used in addition to color and vague outline, therefore *KF* is not scored.

b. *Do not score KF* where clouds are described as solid bodies with a surface color.

Card IV

PERFORMANCE

Definitely clouds lit from behind. This edge here.

INQUIRY

S: (Indicated light portion of lower part of "boots.") It is more like a negative for a film taken of clouds. You get a goldy sort of effect on the edge of the cloud and the rest looks dark in comparison. Only in a photograph the goldy part just comes out light. The unusualness of the apparent solidification of a hard edge.

Score: D   Fc   clouds   1.0

COMMENT: Here the clouds are solid rather than diffuse, hence *KF* cannot be scored. The emphasis is upon the surface color, which is scored *Fc* for photographic representation of color.

5. Responses in Which a Three-Dimensional Expanse Is Projected on a Two-Dimensional Plane: Fk, kF, and k

Fk: Shape definite, but shading undifferentiated.
kF: Shape indefinite and shading undifferentiated.
 k: No form at all (very rare).

There are two chief kinds of responses for which *Fk* or *kF* (or *k*) scoring may be given. These two kinds, which include all or nearly all such concepts, are topographical maps and X-ray pictures.

Topographical Maps: Score Fk or kF

We are concerned here with topographical maps in which a three-dimensional effect is represented on a two-dimensional plane, the existence of shading representing differences in the height of the land without specification of these differences.

Score Fk where the map is of some particular country of definite geographical shape and the shading is used in the undifferentiated manner described above. For example:

Card I

PERFORMANCE	INQUIRY
A relief map of the world.	S: It suggested a map we had in geography of the peeling of the skin of the earth outwards in several directions, out flat so you can see all parts of the sphere flattened out or plane. It gives a strange relationship between Africa and India pulled apart (pointing to side *d*'s).
	E: I'm not sure what you mean by a relief map; different people sometimes mean different things.
	S: It is the varying darknesses which counterfeit three dimensions. I should have referred to topography.

Score: W   Fk   geo   1.0

COMMENT: The degree of specification here, making it a relief map of the world and indicating two continents, gives reason for *Fk* rather than *kF*.

Score *kF* where the map is of no particular country, and the shading is used to indicate unspecified differences in the height of land.

Card I

PERFORMANCE	INQUIRY
The coast of a big piece of land.	S: (Indicated lower third of side *D*.) It is an irregular coast, with jagged edges and little inlets.
	E: How do you see it?
	S: It is a relief map as in the geography books. The dark indicates the higher area. There is the sense of elevation and depression.
	E: Do you think of it as having three dimensions then?

INQUIRY (*continued*)

S: It is definitely a picture, two-dimensional, but which demonstrates a
three-dimensional depth.

Score:　dr　　　kF　　　geo　　　0.5

COMMENT:　The subject here verbalizes the basis of *kF* scoring
very well; it is *kF* rather than *Fk* because no particular country is mentioned.

Omit Fk or kF

a.　*Score F* for an outline map. (See example on page 152.)
b.　*Score FK* for an actual landscape seen from the air. (See pages
147–148.)
c.　*Score Fc* for a clay model or actual relief map. An example
follows:

Card I

PERFORMANCE

The Rocky Mountains.

INQUIRY

S: The whole thing. It is the shading that
gave the impression of high mountains and valleys. A relief map.
E: I'm not sure what you mean by a
relief map.
S: I used to make them in school as a
child, out of cornstarch and salt and
stuff. You model the country. I remember doing Australia, particularly.
E: What about this suggested the Rocky
Mountains particularly?
S: Nothing specific—it could be any
very mountainous area.

Score:　W　　　Fc　　　geo　　　1.0

COMMENT:　This must be scored *Fc* for surface modelling; had
it been such a map in pictorial form, the scoring would have
been *kF*.

X-ray Pictures: Score kF (or Fk or k)

A second problem concerns X-ray pictures in which a three-dimensional expanse is presented in two dimensions, although relatively few subjects can verbalize this. If the concept of X ray is used (or occasionally pictures in medical books) and it can be established that shading is used (or assumed because the concept is applied to a heavily shaded area) a *k* scoring is given. Usually the scoring is *kF*, but if the subject can distinguish definite anatomical parts, *Fk* is scored; *k* would only be scored if the concept of X ray was given, unspecified, to three shaded cards.

Card I

PERFORMANCE

This is faintly reminiscent of an X ray. Dark seen through a lighter surface.

INQUIRY

S: (Indicated lower center portion.) The bones are showing through.

Score: D   kF   At   0.5

COMMENT: This subject verbalizes the concept better than is usually the case. No particular anatomical part is mentioned; therefore a *kF* is scored.

Card III

PERFORMANCE

This bottom part is an anatomical diagram. The bones are light and the rest is darker. It might be an anatomical diagram of the chest.

INQUIRY

S: It is an X ray of course. I saw a lot in the Army. Here are the ribs (pointing to light portions) and the lungs (the darker parts).

Score: D   Fk   At.   1.0

COMMENT: The ribs and lungs are accurately enough specified to score *Fk* rather than *kF*.

Do Not Score kF (or Fk or k)

a. *Score F* for a skeleton, where there is no implication of use of shading.

b. *Score F* for a medical picture in which the shading simply differentiates the parts, without implication of three-dimensional representation.

c. *Score C/F or F/C* for an anatomical chart using color. (See pages 178–179, 186–187.)

d. *Score Fc or Fc→FK* for an anatomical concept seen actually in three-dimensions. (See pages 130–131.)

CHAPTER **6**

Scoring: Determinants—Color Responses

Color responses are those in which the subject utilizes the color of the blot material in the formation of his concept. There are two obvious types of color response, achromatic and chromatic.

Achromatic Color Responses, or C′

These are the only color responses possible in the achromatic cards; they are possible also in the chromatic cards, either in the areas of white space or in areas of low saturation where brown, green, or blue may be seen as gray by some subjects. C' is scored where the subject is interested in black, white, or gray as color, not in terms of texture or diffusion. For example, a black moth, a white dress, gray hair, black symbolizing dreariness.

Three subdivisions of C' responses are made, according to the now familiar principle of the degree of definiteness of the form of the concept in question.

Score FC′

Score FC′ where an object of definite form is designated as black, white, or gray. For instance, note the following responses to Card V and Card VI:

Card V

PERFORMANCE

A bat, with feet, head and wings.

INQUIRY

E: What about it made it seem like a bat?

S: The shape and the color. It is the right dark gray, nearly black, for a bat. Also these things on the wings suggest ribs that keep the wings extended, like the ribs in an umbrella.

E: How do you see it?

S: At rest, or one couldn't see it so clearly. There is no movement.

Score: W   FC′   A   P   2.0

COMMENT: Achromatic color is here the sole determinant, integrated with definite form.

Card VI

PERFORMANCE

This top part makes me think of a bird in flight. A Canada goose migrating.

INQUIRY

S: A Canada goose is the type of bird with wings like that. The way they fly. It has coloring like a goose. Black, white, and gray.

Score: D   FM, FC′   A   2.0

COMMENT: Achromatic color is integrated with a figure of definite form, but is scored as an additional since the color is not elaborated until the inquiry whilst the movement is stressed in the performance proper.

Score C′F

Score C′F where an object of vague form is designated as black, white, or gray. For example:

Card VI

PERFORMANCE

A fur rug.

INQUIRY

S: Just this lower part. It's not the shape, because that is indefinite. But it looks like heavy fur. I think of it as skin from a polar bear.

> E: What about the blot makes it seem like skin from a polar bear particularly?
> S: The dirty, light gray. Should be white, but isn't. They never are.

Score: D   Fc, C′F A_{obj} P   1.0

COMMENT: Texture takes precedence, and achromatic color is scored as additional C′F since the object has indefinite form. Despite the fact that the object has indefinite form, the texture score is Fc because "heavy fur" implies a differentiated use of shading. (See pages 129–130.)

Score C′

Score C′ where something with no form is designated as black, white, or gray. Note this example:

Card VII

PERFORMANCE

Black smoke.

INQUIRY

> S: The whole thing.
> E: What about the blot gave the impression of smoke?
> S: The differences in the coloring make it seem like smoke. It's black smoke like you get from a smudge.

Score: W   K,C′   smoke   0.0

COMMENT: The concept "smoke" implies K as the main determinant. Although C′ is scored additionally for "blackness" attributed to something with no form, the references to "differences in coloring" may be taken as referring to shading and would not themselves be justification for scoring C′.

Do Not Score C′

1. *Do not score C′* where the subject simply designates "this white part is ..." without later specifying that it is a white object. Similarly for black or gray. As an example of this situation, consider the following response to Card II:

Card II

PERFORMANCE	INQUIRY
This white part is a spinning top.	E: When you said "this white part" did you mean the top was white, or did you merely mean that you were using the white part?
	S: I meant that I was using this part (pointing). Tops would more likely be some other color.

Score: S   Fm   obj   1.5

COMMENT: *FC'* is not justified here. Even had this not been demonstrated in the inquiry, it could not be scored from the verbalization in the performance proper. The subject would have to state in explanation that "this top is white," before achromatic color could be scored.

b.   *Score FC or CF* when the subject sees chromatic color of low saturation such as brown, green, blue, even though this occurs in an area where gray is seen by many subjects. The areas in which this most commonly occurs are the top gray detail of Card VIII and the upper and outer grays in Card X.

Card X

PERFORMANCE	INQUIRY
A mouse.	S: (Pointed to outer gray-brown portion.) The shape and color.
	E: I'm not sure what you mean by the color. What color of mouse is it?
	S: Brown.

Score: D   FC   A   1.5

COMMENT: Had the subject said "gray," *FC'* would have been scored; for "brown" the scoring is *FC*.

c.   *C'* may not be scored where the reference is to highlights *(Fc)* or to light streaming *(K)*, or to lightness or darkness with space filling qualities *(K)*. The achromatic color score is limited to surface color.

d.   *C'* may not be scored where color is photographically reproduced as black and white *(Fc)*, or where the subject refers to the shades of gray in an X ray or topographical map *(k)*.

Chromatic Color Responses, or C

These are responses in which the subject utilizes the chromatic elements of the colored cards in the formation of his concept. There are three chief divisions of scoring classification for color responses:

FC: For colored objects of definite form.
CF: For colored objects of vague or indefinite form.
C: Special categories for responses where color is used and the form is non-existent in the concept.

Within each of these main divisions there are further subdivisions, the accurate use of which is highly important since different interpretative hypotheses are attached to each.

1. FC, or Form-Color Responses

There are several different ways in which color can be used in a concept referring to an object of definite form:

a. *FC,* or natural form-color response, where the color used is that of the object in its natural state.

b. *F↔C,* or forced form-color response, where the color used is not that of the object in its natural state, and yet the subject "forces" the use of color. The color of the blot area must be "used" in formation of the concept.

c. *F/C,* or arbitrary form-color response, where the color is used in a colorless manner, merely to mark off subdivisions.

d. *FC_{sym},* or symbolic form-color response, where the color attributed to the object has a symbolic significance.

e. *FC—,* or a form-color response with minus form-level rating, where the concept is of a colored object of definite form, but where the match to the blot area used is inaccurate with respect to form.

Score FC, a Natural FC

The following criteria must be met before *FC* can be scored: (1) The object (for example, person, animal, plant, article of clothing) must be of definite form. (2) The color must be "used" in the concept. (3) The color used must be the natural color of the creature or object (that is, an object of that kind could be found in that color in its natural state). Note these examples:

Card III

PERFORMANCE	INQUIRY
A butterfly in the center.	E: What about it made it look like a butterfly? S: The shape and the color. It is flying and the wings are outspread.

Score: D   FC,FM   A   P   1.5

COMMENT: A butterfly is of definite shape; the subject "uses" the color, implying that he thinks of it as a red butterfly; there are red butterflies (even though perhaps they may not be exactly the same color of red as this blot area); therefore, scoring is *FC*. Color takes precedence over animal movement when they seem equally stressed by the subject, as is the case here.

Card IX

PERFORMANCE	INQUIRY
The green blots give me a feeling of horses, china ones.	S: They are jade green china. Here is the eye and here are the ears and the nose (included "moose's head"). Here is the rest of the body. They are rocking forward. Happy and playing.

Score: dr   FC,FM   (A)   3.0

COMMENT: A horse is of definite shape; the subject thinks of them as green horses, thus using the color; china horses could well be green in their natural state; therefore *FC* is scored. If the dodge of making them china horses or ornaments had not occurred to the subject, and they were thought of as real horses, albeit green, this would be an example of forced use of color.

Card VIII

PERFORMANCE

INQUIRY

Reminds me of one of "The Two Grenadiers," a skeleton-faced remnant of Napoleon's army, who keeps on marching forever.

S: Here is his gray tricorne hat, and his faded blue greatcoat, and his white emaciated face. Just the top of him. He is all hunched up marching into the cold.

Score: D   M,FC,FC′   Hd   O   3.0

COMMENT: *M* takes precedence, but *FC* is scored for the blue greatcoat, and *FC′* for the gray hat. The criteria for *FC* are met as follows: a coat is of definite shape, the color is used, and greatcoats can be blue in their natural state. Clothing, indeed, can be almost any color and meet the criterion of "natural state," unless the subject definitely stresses the artificiality of the color.

Score an Additional FC

a. Where some other determinant has precedence, as is usually the case with *M*, and less frequently so with other determinants. (See rules for determining precedence, on pages 97–98.)

b. Where the form-color response applies to only part of a concept, although the whole concept is of definite form. For example, the colored hats on human or animal figures in Card II could not be scored with *FC* for the main determinant, since only a portion of the total area used is red.

c. Where the form-color response applies to only part of a colored concept. For example, if the whole concept for Card X is an underwater scene because it is colored *(CF)*, and one or two of the component details are elaborated as of definite form, an additional *FC* would be scored.

d. Where the whole area is colored, but the color is used for only part of the concept. An example follows:

Card III

PERFORMANCE	INQUIRY
Two roosters, they're falling downwards.	S: These red things on the side.
	E: What about the blot made them seem like roosters?
	S: They are roosters because of the color.
	E: You mean them as red roosters?
	S: Yes. The animal isn't red, but roosters' combs are red. I'm applying the redness of the comb of the rooster to the whole animal. It is only the comb that is red, really.

Score: D   Fm,FC   A   O   2.0

COMMENT: Even though the color is emphasized it can be scored only as additional, since the color is used for only part of the concept—namely, the comb.

Do Not Score FC

a. *Do not score FC* where the subject merely designates the location used in mentioning the color, and does not "use" the color in his concept.

Card X

PERFORMANCE	INQUIRY
Here are some blue spiders.	E: Did you think of them as blue spiders, or did you just mean that these blue blots were spiders?
	S: I just meant that I used those blue parts for the spiders.

Score: D   F   A   P   1.0

COMMENT: The verbalization of the performance proper seems to imply the use of color, but it is established in the inquiry that the color was not used except to designate the location. It can never be taken for granted that color is or is not used; inquiry is essential.

b. *Score CF* where the object is of indefinite form. (See pages 182 and following.)
c. *Score C'* where color of low saturation is seen as gray. (See pages 169–171.)
d. Where the object is of definite form and color is used, but the criterion of the object being so in its natural state is not met, score $F \leftrightarrow C$, F/C, or FC_{sym}. (See pages 167–169.)
e. Where the object is of definite form, color is used, and the object is of that color in the natural state, *but* the concept does not match the blot area, FC is still the scoring but with minus form-level $(FC-)$.
f. Where a chromatic response is given to an achromatic area, score Fc if there is photographic use of color. It is unscorable if color is simply attributed arbitrarily to an achromatic area (or a chromatic area of different color).

Score Forced FC, or F↔C

Score $F \leftrightarrow C$ where the object is of definite form and the color is used in the concept but in a forced way. The specific color in the blot is not the natural color of the object, although it may be natural for the object to be colored. The subject goes through some effort or rationalization to reconcile the color of the blot area with the object seen. Although he seems to have difficulty in integrating form and color, color is apparently too important to abandon, and it is insisted upon even though the result may be a far-fetched concept or one requiring much ingenuity to rationalize. Four examples follow:

Card II

PERFORMANCE	INQUIRY
Two red seals.	S: (Pointed to the upper red.) They are tumbling on two balls. The lower part of the red is the ball, and the upper part is the seal. It is just an impression.
	E: Did you mean them as red seals or did you just mean that you were using the red part of the blot?

S: I meant red seals. They are artificially colored. They are red and they are seals.

Score: D   F↔C, FM   A   O   1.5

COMMENT: "They are red, and they are seals" verbalizes the essential criterion of a forced *FC*—assuming, of course, that seals naturally are not red but these happen to be somehow. Color is given precedence in this instance, being mentioned in the performance proper, while the movement does not emerge until the inquiry.

Card VIII

PERFORMANCE

Like coat of arms with supporters, like red chameleons on their tails. No, like salamanders coming out of a fire.

INQUIRY

S: Salamanders rampant.
E: What suggested the fire?
S: The color and shape of this bottom part.
E: What made the animals seem like salamanders?
S: Because salamanders are associated with fire. These are pink, being colored by the reflection from the fire. I think of it as a colored coat of arms. Vivid and heraldic.

Score: 1. W ⎫   FC,CF   embl,fire   ⎫   2.0
          2. D ⎭   FM,F↔C   A   P ⎭ →O   1.0

COMMENT: This rather complex response is best scored by giving a main *FC* for the "colored coat of arms," since coats of arms in their natural state are colored. A semi-independent location score is given for the salamanders, with a *F↔C* as an additional determinant, since any attempt to explain the color of the pink animals is considered to be forced, even one as ingenious as this. In the first response an additional *CF* is given for the fire.

Card VIII

PERFORMANCE

A fur cape.

INQUIRY

S: The pink and orange part (card inverted). Here is the neck, shoulders, front, collar. It is not a long cape. I said fur because of the texture; that is the main thing. The color is wrong. The top is O.K. but the bottom is not. It is as though someone had said "dye the damn thing"—the latest style for a party.

Score: D   Fc,F↔C   obj   O   2.0

COMMENT: Clothes usually must be scored natural *FC,* for they can and do occur in almost any color. This is an exception, for fur capes do not ordinarily occur in pink and orange. It might be argued that they *are* occasionally dyed such colors, but this seems a quibble. The subject's own attitude would justify the forced *FC* scoring, in which he acknowledges the color is wrong and then finds an explanation that he himself implies is artificial.

Card VIII

PERFORMANCE

There seems a red rat on each side.

INQUIRY

S: It has a head like a rat. No tail or whiskers but the shape of the body and legs. Ears and pointed noses like rats.

E: Was the color part of it?

S: No, they are just red rats.

E: Where would you be likely to see such rats?

S: I have only seen two rats in my life. I have a feeling that they are climbing up and trying to get at something. It is a wasteland or dump with rubble at the bottom.

E: When you said they were red rats did you mean just that, or did you mean that you were using the red areas for the rats?

S: They are rats, and they are red. It's like the purple cow. You never hope to see one.

Score: D→W   F↔C,FM   A   P→O   2.0

COMMENT: The inquiry is not skillful here. The last question should have been asked first. However, the subject's verbalization clearly shows the feeling behind a forced *FC*.

Do Not Score F↔C

Score FC if the object could occur in the specified color in its natural state. Sometimes what seems a forced and unnatural use of color can be justified in terms of the subject's knowledge. For example, on Card IX a green and orange butterfly would be scored a forced *FC*, except where the subject can point out that he has read (or seen) that there are indeed butterflies that color in tropical South America. Similarly, on Card X the concept of blue crabs at first seems forced, and would be so scored if the subject tried to justify it by saying that they are painted that way, or that they look that way through the water. If, on the other hand, he says that he has seen crabs in their natural state and they are a greenish-blue, and that is what these remind him of, then a natural *FC* is indicated. Another example from Card X is of the lower green detail (card inverted) as a parachute jumper with parachute all in green because he is jumping in the tropics. This would have to be scored as a natural *FC* because, in fact, green is used for paratroopers and their equipment in tropic warfare. There are certain other less unusual responses that should be scored *FC* even though the form-color integration is rather loose: namely, flowers, painted furniture, colored ornaments, clothing, and the like, which might well appear in that color in the "natural state."

Score an Arbitrary FC, or F/C

Score F/C where the subject uses color in a colorless way, to mark off subdivisions in an object of definite form. Here it is of little importance that the particular color or colors are used; any other colors would serve equally well to subdivide the parts. There are two chief concepts for which arbitrary use of color enters in: (1) colored maps, (2) medical charts. It may be noted that F/C is not a common scoring classification, for it is unusual to find this arbitrary use of color for an object of definite form; C/F is a more common response. An example of F/C scoring follows:

Card X

PERFORMANCE	INQUIRY
This in the center looks like the perfect map drawing of two shore lines of two countries with what looks like a bridge between them.	S: (Pointed to the red portions with center blue.) Looks like the west shore of South America. Here is Peru and Chile. The bridge is an underwater bridge, a land bridge to another country. E: What about the blot gave you this impression? S: The color. It is the color they put on maps for contrast. The whole thing is a cartographer's fancy.

Score: D   F/C   geo   1.5

COMMENT: Both the "underwater bridge" and the mention of definite countries makes this "of definite form"; hence the arbitrary use of color is scored F/C.

Do Not Score F/C

a. *Score C/F* where the object is of indefinite form and the use of color is arbitrary.

b. *Score forced FC ($F \leftrightarrow C$)* where the subject makes the point that the object *is* the same color as the blot. The flavor of an F/C response is that it was the variety of colors that suggested the concept, but the particular color or combination of colors does not matter at all.

c. *Score FC* for the occasional medical or geographical concept where the object in its natural state is the same color as that of the blot. For example, in Card III an FC would be scored if the subject gave the concept "medical drawing" for the outer red detail, and then further specified that it was "the heart with the aorta leading to it" and it was red as it would be in its natural state. Similarly, on Card X if the left-hand red portion is called "a map of England and Scotland" because of the shape and because it is red as it always is on the map, this would be a natural *FC*.

d. Some examiners fall into the error of scoring *F/C* for clothing, flowers, painted furniture, and the like, on the assumption that these objects need not be these particular colors and hence the use of color is arbitrary. On the contrary, such use of color is classed as natural and deserves an *FC* scoring. As a safe rule, do not score *F/C* except for medical charts or maps.

Score FC$_{sym}$

Score FC$_{sym}$ where the color is used symbolically for an object with a definite form. This must apply to the whole object if it is to be a main determinant, otherwise it would be scored as an additional determinant. For example:

Card II

PERFORMANCE   INQUIRY

Two old ladies saying, "Oh my dear!"   S: It was the red and the mouth being open that made me think of two old ladies.
                                              E: How did the red help?
                                              S: I didn't use it much, but being red made me think of old ladies.
                                              E: How was that?
                                              S: Because red means anger, cross and gossipy.

Score: W   M,FC$_{sym}$ H   →O   2.0

COMMENT: Here the red is used symbolically; and since applied to a part of the concept (head and face) that has definite form, it is scored *FC$_{sym}$*.

Card III

PERFORMANCE

Here are two rejected suitors bowing to each other as they meet outside the door of the house where their lady lives. They each have bouquets of flowers in their hands. This red part (center) symbolizes heartbreak.

INQUIRY

E: How does the red symbolize heartbreak?

S: Each side has a little red heart and there is a bond between them, symbolizing that they are united in both being rejected.

Score: W   M, FC_{sym} H   P→O   2.5

COMMENT: Red hearts alone would have been *FC*, but to use the colored objects of definite form in a symbolic way makes the scoring FC_{sym}.

Score FC minus

Score FC— where a color concept with definite form is applied inaccurately to a blot area, even though the color be appropriate. Below are two instances.

Card IX

PERFORMANCE

Here are four apples.

INQUIRY

S: Here at the bottom.

E: What about them made them seem like apples?

S: The color and the shape.

E: Can you describe them further?

S: It was the color. They are red apples and they are round like apples.

Score: D   FC—   Pl   O—   —0.5

COMMENT: The thinking of the subject seems to go as follows: "This part of the blot is red; apples are red; therefore, this part of the blot is like apples." It is true that the outside portions of the red blot are round like apples. Had the subject used only that part the form level would be at a 1.0 level. Or if he had gone on to explain that the inside two apples were overlapped by the outer pair, the form level would be accurate. However, since neither of these safeguards of accuracy was used the form level must be scored minus.

Card VIII

A colored butterfly.

S: All of it.
E: Can you describe it to me?
S: Here is the body (gesturing to the central portion) and the rest is the wings. A bright colored butterfly.

Score: D   FC—   A   —0.5

COMMENT: Here again it seems to be the color that suggested the concept. This blot is brightly colored, butterflies are brightly colored, therefore this is a butterfly. With Card IX this concept would not be an abuse of the shape of the blot. However, in Card VIII the concept "butterfly" is too much at variance with the shape of the blot, particularly when the subject does not differentiate the popularly seen animals.

2.   CF, or Color-Form Responses

There are several different ways in which color can be used in a concept referring to an object of indefinite or vague form:

a.   *CF* or natural color-form response, where the color used is that of the object in its natural state.

b. $C \leftrightarrow F$ or forced color-form response, where the color used is not that of the object in its natural state, and yet the subject forces the use of color.

c. C/F or arbitrary color-form response, where the color is used in a colorless manner, merely to mark off subdivisions.

d. CF_{sym} or symbolic color-form response, where the color attributed to the vaguely-shaped object has a symbolic significance.

e.   *CF—* or color-form response with minus form-level rating, where the concept is of a colored object of indefinite form but is applied to a blot area of such definite, popularly-seen form that the concept represents an abuse of the form qualities of the blot.

Score CF

The following criteria must be met before *CF* may be scored: (1) The object (such as clouds, explosions, fire, flames, blood, ice cream, flowers, rocks, grass) must be of indefinite form. (2) The color must be "used" in the concept. (3) The color used must be the natural color of the "object" (that is, the object could be found in that color in its natural state). Five examples are cited.

Card VIII

PERFORMANCE

The whole thing is reminiscent of a marine scene, the bottom of the sea.

INQUIRY

S: It was the colors. Made me think of coral, odd shapes and colored. The whole thing could be a coral and rock combination.

Score: W CF N 0.5

COMMENT: The color is definitely used, and the concept is of indefinite form but with the colors reasonably appropriate to the concept. That is, coral and rock could appear in these colors in their natural state.

Card IX

PERFORMANCE

Just paint here.

INQUIRY

S: The whole thing. I thought there was some virtue in getting a whole. Just paint spattered.

Score: W CF paint 0.5

COMMENT: The obvious assumption is that color is used, and in a concept of indefinite form. "Just paint" certainly could come in the colors presented in the blot. The criteria of a *CF* score are satisfied.

Card VIII

PERFORMANCE

Some beautiful strawberry ice-cream, with orange water-ice and apricot down below that.

INQUIRY

S: The pink is the strawberry. The center orange is the water-ice, and the rest of the orange is apricot ice-cream.

Score: D CF food 0.5

COMMENT: The subject here is differentiating finely with respect to the shades of the colors and matching them carefully to the concept. However, the shape is indefinite and *CF* is scored despite all the elaboration.

Card X

PERFORMANCE   INQUIRY

A design in pastels.   S: Fresh and gay. The sort of thing you find in chintz made to freshen up a room.

Score: W   CF   art   0.5

COMMENT: Design implies form semantically, but in fact the form is indefinite; therefore, a *CF* is scored.

Card IX

PERFORMANCE   INQUIRY

A flower. The whole thing.   E: What about it made it seem a flower?
                                               S: The color and shape.
                                               E: What kind of flower does it make you think of?
                                               S: I don't know their names.

Score: W   CF   Pl   0.5

COMMENT: The fact that the subject says "the color and the shape" does not imply *FC*. A flower is scored *CF* unless the subject can specify a species of flower with characteristic shape that matches the blot area in both color and shape.

Score Additional CF

a.   *Score an additional CF* where some other determinant has precedence. For example:

Card X

PERFORMANCE   INQUIRY

A tar torch. This is the cup holding the   S: (Indicated outer yellow with adjoining gray-brown portion.) The gray part is the fixture to which it is
tar, and they light it.

> attached. It might be outside an inn.
> The yellow is the flame. It is burning.
> E: How do you mean it is burning?
> S: It is flaming, blowing in the wind.

Score: dr Fm,CF flame, obj O 2.0

COMMENT: This presents a problem in scoring, since the "fixture" gives an element of good form to the concept, yet undeniably the flame itself is a *CF*. The main determinant score is *Fm* for an inanimate object in motion, which is emphasized most in the spontaneous inquiry.

b. *Score an additional CF* where the *CF* response applies only to part of the concept, as in part of a landscape or background. However, where it applies to a large part, nearly all, of a colorful scene it may be given the chief determinant score.

Card II

PERFORMANCE	INQUIRY
Two little bears with their claws dipped in blood. They are sniffing at something.	S: The red part made me think of blood and the dark red the claws. E: What about it made them seem like bears? S: Their snouts. They are dark, tame and gentle.

Score: W FM,CF,FC' A P 2.5

COMMENT: An additional *CF* is given for the blood.

Do Not Score CF

a. *Do not score CF* where the subject merely designates the part used in mentioning the color, and does not "use" the color in his concept. This is rare in the case of *CF;* usually the concept either clearly implies color or it does not. However, occasionally the subject denies color even when his concept seems to imply it clearly.

b. *Score FC* where the concept is of definite form. For example, if the subject can specify a kind of flower that is of distinctive form (such as an iris, pansy, snapdragon) and show its match to the blot with respect to form and color.

c.   Where the object is of indefinite form and color is used but the criterion of the object being so in its natural state is not met, score $C{\leftrightarrow}F$, C/F, or CF_{sym}. (See below.)

Score C↔F, or Forced CF

Score $C{\leftrightarrow}F$ where there is forced and unnatural use of color with objects of indefinite form. This is very rare indeed.

Card VIII

PERFORMANCE	INQUIRY
Colored rock.	S: (Indicated bottom *D*.) It is hard, smooth, slightly bumpy.
	E: What about it made it seem like rock?
	S: The shape, nice smooth rocks.
	E: What did you mean when you said colored rock?
	S: They are pink rocks. They are colored pink on the card. They are rocks and they are colored pink. Not that rocks ever are like that.

Score: D   cF, C↔F   rocks   O   0.5

COMMENT: Texture is given the main score, because it is so emphasized in the inquiry. The criterion for forced use of color seems to be met. It matters not at all that in fact rocks can be pinkish, since this subject thinks it is artificial to have them so. Most subjects seeing colored rocks consider this to be a natural phenomenon.

Score C/F, or Arbitrary CF

Score C/F for arbitrary or colorless use of color to mark off subdivisions in an object of indefinite form. There are two chief classes of such responses: (1) Indefinite political maps, where no particular countries are mentioned. (2) Anatomical charts, microscope slides, and the like, where color is used, and the parts differentiated are vaguely specified.

Here it is of little importance that these particular colors are used; any other colors would serve equally well to subdivide the parts. With either of the above two types of concept it is assumed that color is used thus arbitrarily, even though the subject does not verbalize that the particular colors do not matter. Such a use of color is completely void of emotional overtones.

Card VIII

PERFORMANCE

A slide you can examine under a microscope. I wish I had examined more slides and I would know more what to say it is.

INQUIRY

E: What about it made it seem like a microscope slide?

S: God only knows! The color I think. And the geometric configuration of the whole thing.

Score: W   C/F   At   0.5

COMMENT: Although the subject was not prodded into saying that the different colors mark off different parts, and they could be different colors and still be a microscope slide, *C/F* is justified for this concept.

Card X

PERFORMANCE

Could be a chart, a rather disorganized chart where the color is significant rather than the line.

INQUIRY

E: How do you mean the color is significant?

S: They could represent something. There is some order in it. Blue is here and here, yellow is here and here.

E: What kind of chart is it?

S: A geographical chart.

Score: W   C/F   geo   0.5

COMMENT: Here the subject verbalizes the actual basis of a *C/F* scoring, by implying that the differences in color signify something, although attaching no particular significance to any given color.

Score CF_{sym}

Score CF_{sym} where the color used with an object of indefinite form is given symbolic significance. For example:

Card II

PERFORMANCE	INQUIRY
Here there is opposition, violent opposition. Two Turks. The opposition is symbolized by the opposition of their two hands, and the clashing of fire.	S: The fire is at the bottom, fire and sparks. E: What made them seem Turks? S: The red fez.

Score: W M_{sym}, FC, CF_{sym} H,fire   →O   3.0

COMMENT: Fire is of indefinite shape and is used symbolically, hence scored CF_{sym}. An M_{sym} score is given as the main determinant since the posture is given symbolic significance. An additional *FC* is scored for the red fez.

Card II

PERFORMANCE	INQUIRY
These are two bears because they are furry. They have just murdered someone. Their hands are dripping. Above them is a symbol written in blood of what they have done.	S: They have just finished murdering someone. The symbols at the top are the most important, malignant. The bears are just instruments. The bears look surprised, from the tilt of their heads. E: What made it seem like blood? S: The red. And it is dripping. E: Do you think of the bears as having behaved like animals or people? S: Animals. E: What about the bears made them seem furry? S: The rough outer edge. (And in the testing-the-limits period the subject clearly denied the use of shading.)

Score: W   FM, CF_{sym}, m   A   P→0   2.0

COMMENT: The "symbol written in blood" is given CF_{sym}. Although the lower red *D* could be scored a natural *CF,* it would seem overloading it to score it also.

Score CF Minus

Score CF— where an indefinite color-form concept is applied to an area that popularly has definite form, the color being appropriate. There are two chief areas where the popular form should be used and where a *CF* represents an abuse of the form of the blot: namely, the center red in Card III and the outer pink details in Card VIII.

Card VIII

PERFORMANCE

A sunset.

INQUIRY

S: It was the color. The whole thing but especially these pink clouds. (Pointed to the outer and lower pink portions.)

E: What about the blot made it seem like clouds?

S: The color. Sunset clouds, with the sun reflected on them.

Score: W   CF—   Clouds   —0.5

COMMENT: Here the pink animals are of definite enough form and so popularly seen that to use them for an indefinite concept represents an abuse of the form of the blot.

Card VIII

PERFORMANCE

I don't like any of the colors in this one at all. It looks like the worst end of an operation.

INQUIRY

E: Did you mean that as a remark or a response? (Explaining.)

S: As a response.

E: What about it made it seem like an operation?

S: The colors. (Gestured around whole.)

E: I'm not sure I understand what you mean.

S: I can't tell you any more about it.

Score: W   CF—   At   —1.0

COMMENT: Here the subject does not specifically point out that the side pink details were used in the concept, but she implies it by her gesture.

3.   C, or Pure Color Responses

These responses have in common an emphasis on color without any implication of form, even indefinite form. There are four subdivisions, which it is highly important to distinguish.

a. C, or crude color, for a mechanical use of color with no form.

b. C_n, or color naming.

c. C_{des}, or color description.

d. C_{sym}, or color symbolism.

Score C

Score C where a certain color signifies a given concept in several cards, and there is no attempt to relate the concept to the rest of the blot. The criteria for scoring C are thus: the association between color and concept is (1) repetitive, (2) totally undifferentiated, and (3) without organizational relationship to any other concept in the same card. An example of a C score was obtained a few times from epileptic patients, who gave a response of "water" (or some patients said "sky") to all bluish parts in Cards VIII, IX, and X. One of these subjects caught himself after saying "water" to the center part of Card VIII by saying: "But the animals could not walk on water, so it must be sky"—a feeble attempt to get away from the pure C.

Another example would be if every red or pink portion were called blood, without an attempt to integrate the concept with the rest of the card in question. However, one or two separate responses of "blood" would not be considered a mechanical use of color and would be scored CF, even though the subject did not refer to shape at all. "Blood" could not be scored crude C if the subject introduced some differentiation or form to the concept, as, for example, describing a "splash of blood" on Card II. Moreover, even though blood were given to the red blots several times without such differentiation, C could not be scored if in one or more instances it was worked into a more elaborate concept, such as "bears fighting" on Card II. Holding to these rigid criteria of scoring, a crude C is extremely rare. As such it is a pathognomic clue. Too liberal scoring of C where CF should be scored may lead to awkward errors in diagnostic interpretation.

Score C_n

Score C_n, or color naming, where the response to color is to name the various colors on the card, perhaps going into minute differences in hue and tint. Since the interpretative hypothesis attached to the score C_n involves possibly a pathognomic cue, in general C_n is not scored unless color naming constitutes the only mode of handling the card. Very frequently, naming the various colors is simply a polite way for the subject to reject the card or to indicate that he sees the colors but does not know what to make of them. Two criteria should be met before color naming is scored C_n:

a. It must be quite clear that the subject feels satisfied that color naming constitutes an adequate way of handling the material. The inquiry must establish that this is a response and not a remark. Even though the subject insists it is a response, C_n would still not be scored if it is apparent that he does not consider this to be an adequate response.

b. The subject must fail to "recover"—that is, to give another response of at least 1.0 form level to the same card.

These conditions apply chiefly to an isolated instance of naming colors. They do not apply strictly to cases where the subject tends to give a color naming type of verbalization to all or nearly all the colored cards, even though he may occasionally follow up the color naming by another response.

Below is an example of a C_n score:

Card X (subject is a seven-year-old girl)

PERFORMANCE	INQUIRY
Here are two blue things and two yellow things, and two red things and two green things, and two more green things.	E: Can you tell me more about the things you saw on this card? S: No. E: What could this one be (pointing to the outer blue detail)? S: It's blue. And this one is yellow, and this one is red, and this is green and this is green. I don't know this one (pointing to orange *D*).

Score: W C_n Color   0.0

COMMENT: Here it is apparent that the subject considers color naming an adequate mode of handling the card material. Although it is doubtful that with a seven-year-old child the interpretative hypothesis would be applied without some modification, nevertheless this response is scored as color naming.

The following example quotes the responses one subject gave to all colored cards:

Card II

PERFORMANCE

Red and black blotches. What it looks like I can't describe. I also see bear heads.

INQUIRY

S: The nose wouldn't be made that way. Legs, ears. Of course I told you about the colors.
E: What about it made them seem like bears?
S: They are black bears pushing their noses together. They ain't exactly black. It's got red through it. Red ink.

Score:	1.	W	C_n	color		0.0
	2.	W	FM,FC'	A	P	2.0

Card III

PERFORMANCE

These also are red and black blotches. I don't know what they look like. The inside of the chest. A chest picture. And if I used my imagination this might be a bow.

INQUIRY

S: Oh yes. An X ray. (Indicated lower D.)
E: And the bow?
S: A girl would wear it.
E: Tell me what you mean?
S: If she had a red bow she might wear it with a red dress.
E: Did you want to say more?
S: Just these red and black blotches. How am I doing? I know I'm mentally O.K.

Score:	1.	D	Fk	At		0.5
	2.	D	FC	obj.	P	1.0

Card VIII

PERFORMANCE

Do you want me to give you the colors?
E: Tell me what the cards look like.
S: Some kind of animal. I know all the colors on this one. (Named them all very accurately.) Not a large animal. A rodent or something.

   Score: 1.   D   F   A   P   **1.0**

Card IX

PERFORMANCE

Do you want me to tell you colors on this one?
E: Tell me what you see on the card.
S: (Named the colors.) But the design? I don't know.

   Score: W C_n Color   **0.0**

Card X

PERFORMANCE

Blue, yellow, pink, purplish pink. You see this yellow. It could be a flower, a bud. This is greenish here and blue over here.

INQUIRY

E: Tell me about the flower.
S: It is a yellow snapdragon (described it very well.)

   Score: 1.   W C_n color   0.0
   2.   D   FC   pl   1.0

COMMENT: There is no doubt that the tendency to color naming is clearly established in this record. Indeed, the record is quoted to exemplify the lengths to which some subjects can carry this type of response, even when able to respond otherwise to the cards. It becomes a matter of relatively little importance interpretatively how many of these responses are actually scored C_n, since the tendency is manifestly strong, and clear-cut, though with some recoverability.

Clearly the score is justified in Card IX, where no other response is given. It does not seem justified in Cards III and VIII where other responses are given fairly readily. It seems justified in Card X where the subject gives an *FC* response in the midst of color naming, and then proceeds to name other colors. It is doubtful in Card II, but was scored because he persisted in dwelling upon the colors in the inquiry while describing the animals.

It must be emphasized that these responses in isolation could not be scored C_n with the present evidence. In four of the cards the subject recovers and gives another response of at least popular form level. Card IX in isolation (as the only color naming in the entire record) could not be scored without inquiry. In this case the subject was not asked, "Is this a response or a remark?" for the color-naming tendency seemed clearly established in any case. Such an assumption could not be made for an isolated response.

Do Not Score C_n

Do not score C_n where the subject gives another response to the card of at least 1.0 form level, or where the color naming is clearly a remark, or where the subject does not seem to consider color naming an adequate response to the card. Three examples follow:

Card II (seven-year-old girl; see example on pages 191–192)

PERFORMANCE	INQUIRY
Here are two red things, and two black things . . . and two doggies.	E: Show me the doggies? (Subject pointed to the popular area.) Can you tell me about the doggies? S: They are trying to get at this thing (center d) to eat it.

Score: W   FM   A   P   2.0

COMMENT: Here the subject begins by naming colors, but this is not scored C_n since she goes on to give a response of at least 1.0 form level. Color naming could only have been scored if she had given no other adequate response to the card, as indeed was the case with the same subject on Card X (see example on pages 191–192).

Card II (25-year-old male)

PERFORMANCE

I notice two colors, red and black.

Something like a doughnut, irregular.

Also it could be taken very much as a butterfly.

Also I see the red and black are merged together in the center part.

Also it reminds me of a pelvis. Hipbones. It's not very clear. This one leaves me pretty blank.

INQUIRY (relevant parts only)

E: (Referring to first comment) Was this a remark or did you mean it as a response like the doughnut or the butterfly?

S: I found it hard to make anything of it. I wouldn't have made it if something more definite had occurred in the pattern.

E: (Later referring to the subsequent comment about color) Did you mean that as a remark or a response?

S: A response I think. I was lost on this one. I couldn't get the shape so I started looking for colors and shading as a last resort.

COMMENT: Here the fact that the subject gives other responses to the card, two of which are of 1.0 form level, makes it impossible to score color naming, despite the fact that he states in the case of one color remark that he meant it as a response. Indeed his explanations in the inquiry constitute a very good statement of how such color remarks are likely to arise. The very insight shown in the explanation seems to obviate a color naming score. Had the remarks stood alone without the other responses, they would constitute a polite way of rejecting the card.

Card II (first response)

PERFORMANCE

Two Scotty dogs, nose to nose. The dogs' heads are here, their chests up. It's ridiculous, isn't it? I'm ignoring the red; it is just splotched in to confuse one.

INQUIRY

(In the inquiry the subject went on to elaborate the dogs in some detail, and made no further mention of the red.)

COMMENT: This example is given to illustrate a frequent kind of color remark which is obviously not a scorable response and which indicates inability of the subject to use the color and his intention to eliminate it by mentioning it.

Score C_{des}

Score C_{des} where the response to color is a description of the colors appearing in the card, usually involving statements about the artistic quality of the colors—for example, whether they look like pastels or water colors, or perhaps referring to the surface appearances of the different colors, thus bringing in a *cF* score as well. Two conditions must be met before scoring *C_{des}*. (1) The subject must clearly mean it as a response, not a remark. (2) The subject must not use the description as an elaboration of a *CF* or *FC* concept, for these scores adequately cover the use of color. Note this example:

Card VIII

PERFORMANCE	INQUIRY
These are pastel colors, pretty and soft. This is an especially nice satiny turquoise. A pretty raspberry red, and soft apricot. Very pleasant.	E: Did you mean this as a remark? S: No, I meant it as a response. They are like the pastels that artists use. Lovely soft colors.

Score: W   C_{des}, cF   art   0.0

COMMENT: The subject intends this as a response, and describes the colors in an artistic way without using them as part of a concept implying interpretation—that is an object, thing or figure. The "satiny" specification is grounds for an additional *cF*.

Score C_{sym}

Score C_{sym} where the color stands for an abstract idea, such as evil, youth, gaiety. These must have no form at all, otherwise they are scored *FC_{sym}* or *CF_{sym}*. Examples follow:

Card VIII

PERFORMANCE	INQUIRY
The quality of whatever material is represented here looks like it is alive and could give growth.	E: Did you mean that as a remark? S: No, as a response. It was the colors and the shading of the colors that symbolized life, made it look alive and not barren.

Score: W C_{sym},c_{sym} abs 0.0

COMMENT: This is certainly formless. Color and shading are both used in a symbolic way.

Card IX

PERFORMANCE	INQUIRY
Looks like a child's drawing. I should think his idea of something very nice and happy. Like a party at the top where it is orange—gaiety—people wearing silly hats and throwing things about. Then perhaps an idea of having a meal underneath where it is green. There is a form of something putting something into its mouth. Then down at the bottom something very ordinary and unexciting is happening like going to bed.	S: This is a very labored reaction. I got the impression after a long time; then it seemed something light and playful. I don't mean that these were not two people—that was important. If you turn the card on the side this (green) is like Pooh Bear eating. Here is his head. The idea of a child at a party and after you have food you go to bed. The red part is so shapeless and uninteresting compared to the rest.
	E: (Analogy period: inquired regarding the use of color.)
	S: Oh yes, the color had something to do with it. Both the orange and the red are party colors. Even though the red is shapeless, and uninteresting in that sense, it still symbolizes gaiety, a party color. Going to bed, after a party.

Score:

1.	D ⎫		M, FC_{sym}	H ⎫	2.5
2.	D ⎬ W		FM	(A) ⎬ →O	1.5
3.	D ⎭		C_{sym}	abs ⎭	0.0

COMMENT: This is loosely enough organized to justify three separate location scores, linked together by an additional *W*. The third response has no form whatsoever. A C_{sym} score is justified, but the full impact of use of color is somewhat weakened by the fact that the demands of logic alone might have led to the interpretation attached, that is, to complete the story. Note that the orange is combined with "people throwing things about"—with an object of definite form—and thus is scored FC_{sym}.

Card IX

PERFORMANCE

Horrors! A witches' dance. They are dancing over the remains, the skulls, of four dead men or women. The witches are above rejoicing. But the dance is coming to an end and they are evaporating.

INQUIRY

S: The orange and green part are the witches, and here are their feet. I think the green is something draped around them here.

E: What about it made it seem like skulls?

S: The general outline, forehead, eye-sockets. The pinkish color indicates subterranean or lifeless. Not a virile color like green. They look anaemic or dead.

E: The witches are evaporating?

S: Yes, they are being swallowed up in the green, which is life and fighting against it, being drawn down in. There is a contrast between death and life. The orange which is almost yellow is being swallowed up in the green. The rejoicing will come to an end. The orange makes it sort of Hallowe'en.

Score: W   M, FC$_{sym}$, C$_{sym}$, m   (H), abs.   2.0

COMMENT: This complex response seems too tightly integrated for separate main location scores, but requires additional determinant scores to represent the rather complicated determinants involved. Both the orange and the pink are used symbolically, but in combination with figures or objects of definite form and hence are scored *FC$_{sym}$*. The green is used in a sufficiently formless way ("life fighting against death") to warrant a *C$_{sym}$* score. The symbolic or abstract forces represented in "evaporating," "drawn down in," and so on, are scored with an additional *m*.

CHAPTER **7**

Scoring: Content; Popular and Original Responses

There are so many possible classifications of the content of the responses to the Rorschach blots that scoring for content could be a very complex matter indeed. Yet, since the interpretative hypotheses attached to content scores are relatively few, the number of categories into which content is classified is small. Despite the fact that the literature contains some studies dealing with content, these tend to concern themselves with narrowly delimited diagnostic classifications, and have not yielded interpretative hypotheses that are broadly applicable. On the other hand, interpretation of content is a very important aspect of sequence analysis, but as such has a highly individualized phenomenological or symbolic basis of interpretation. Thus, despite the importance of content for interpretation, the quantitative aspects of analysis of content have not been developed to such a point that a complex and detailed scoring system seems warranted.

Here the discussion will be limited to those scoring categories listed on the Klopfer and Davidson *Individual Record Blank*, together with a few more that are commonly distinguished. Concepts that do not fall within these categories are "scored" by adding such categories as the content itself dictates. Thus, for example, concepts such as "explosion," "death," "slime," may be added to the tabulation in the blank spaces provided on the Record Blank.

Content Categories

The following are the content categories most frequently assigned scoring symbols:

H: Human figures, whole or almost whole.

(H):   Human figures portrayed as drawings, sculpture, caricatures, and the like, or mythological human figures such as ghosts, monsters, witches. The symbol (H) is used to indicate that the human figure is deprived of reality in some manner.

Hd: Parts of human figures which can be thought of as belonging to a living body (that is, not anatomical).

(Hd):   Parts of human figures portrayed in drawings, caricatures, sculpture, or parts of mythological human figures.

ÆH: Figures that are part human and part animal, such as "Pan—half-goat, half-man."

H_{obj}:   Human parts such as false teeth, which though not part of the body are so closely associated with it that to score them as man-made objects would be misleading.

At: Parts of the human body or concepts dealing with the human body in an anatomical sense. These include dissected parts, operations, X rays, anatomical charts, and so forth.

Sex: These include both open references to sexual organs or sexual activity and veiled references to the pelvis or the lower part of the body. If it is not clear whether or not such references have sexual connotations, this can usually be ascertained in tactful inquiry.

A: An animal figure, whole or almost whole.

(A):   A mythological animal; a monster with animal characteristics; a caricature, drawing, or the like, of an animal figure; an ornament in animal form; or a fairy-tale or Walt Disney animal given human attributes. The symbol

> *(A)* is used generally where the animal figure is either deprived of reality or humanized.

Ad: Part of an animal, usually a head or paw.

(Ad): Part of an animal that is deprived of reality or humanized.

A_{obj}: Objects derived from or connected with the body of an animal, such as fur, wishbone, an animal skin, or even a horseshoe. These objects serve some decorative or practical function, or are in a stage of preparation to do so.

A.At: Animal anatomy concepts, including dissections, X ray of an animal, biological charts, and so on.

Food: When an animal part is prepared for eating it is classified as food rather than as animal anatomy (for example, pork chop, plucked chicken, side of beef). Here also would be classified concepts such as ice-cream, lollipop, fried egg. Fruits and vegetables, unless obviously prepared for eating, are classified as plants, however. If there is doubt regarding the food implications of a concept, this usually can be cleared easily in the inquiry.

N: Nature concepts, including landscapes, aerial views, sunsets, and rivers and lakes when they are part of scenery. Concepts including some architectural component are also classified as *N* if the architecture seems subordinate to the total landscape. If a human or animal figure is seen as an important component in a landscape, the scoring is a main *H* or *A* with an additional *N*. This would be reversed if the human or animal figure were a minor part of a landscape—that is, a main *N* with an additional *H* or *A*.

Geo: Geographical concepts, which include maps of all kinds, and such things as islands, gulfs, lakes, rivers, not seen in vista or as part of a landscape.

Pl: Plants of all kinds, including flowers, trees, fruit, vegetables, seaweed, and parts of plants such as leaf, petal, stamen.

Bot: Plants or parts of plants seen as botanical specimens, for instance, as a botanical display (without the individual flowers or plants identified) or as a botanical chart.

Obj: Man-made objects such as aircraft, bedpost, chair, vase, top, pliers. Distinguish from statues which are scored (*H*) or animal-shaped ornaments scored (*A*).

Arch: Architectural concepts such as house, bridge, lighthouse, church, chimney.

Art: Art includes vague concepts like a painter's palette, design, a child's drawing, water-colors, pastels, in which the drawing or painting has no specific content. A drawing of a human figure would be scored (*H*), a painting of a landscape would be scored *N*, and so on.

Abs: Abstract concepts are scored *Abs* when there is no other specific content. For example, a "power" or "force." A specific content symbolizing something abstract would be scored for content according to whether an animal or human figure, fire, smoke, etc. were involved, and the subscript "sym" would be added to the appropriate determinant.

The following concepts are given separate scoring classifications, which are self-explanatory: fire, blood, clouds, smoke, mask, emblem, crown.

Scoring for Popular and Original Responses

Many responses are assigned neither a popular nor an original score, being neither common enough to be "popular" nor unusual enough to be scored "original." Requirements for *P* and *O* scores are given below.

P, or Popular Responses

In this scoring system only ten responses are scored as popular. These are described on pages 179 to 181 of Klopfer and Kelley, *The Rorschach Technique*. (For convenience of the beginner these are listed with the usual detail locations on pages 70 to 79 of the present volume.) The requirements of the popular score are quoted below, with a discussion of points that seem to present difficulty.

1. "To Card I as *W* or *W*: Any creature with the body in the center *D* and wings at the side." The concept "bat" or "butterfly" is usual for this location, but is not scored as a *P* for a *dr* location.

2. "To the black area of Card II (either as an organized incomplete whole, with or without the top center *d,* or as *D*) : Any animal or part of an animal of the dog, bear, rabbit, bull, or rhinoceros variety." The inclusion of the upper red or lower red *D* sometimes presents a problem. However, if the essential animal concept is present a *P* is scored, even though additions may be made—for example, bears wearing red hats, or dogs sniffing pieces of meat, or dogs with bleeding paws. (An additional *O* may be involved for such combinations.) However, if an essential part of the animal is placed in the additional location (for example, the animal's head in the upper red *D*) the response cannot be scored *P*.

P is not scored unless the parts are seen as in the popular response —with the nose in the upper inner region, ears in the upper outer projections, the paws (if any) in the outer lower projections. (This does not imply that this degree of specification is required for the *P* score.) Thus a *P* cannot be scored for dogs or heads of dogs seen with the card turned sideways or upside-down. Sometimes only the upper portion of the black area is used for an animal's head, which seems to justify a tendency to *P* rather than a main *P* score. Care should be exercised in the inquiry to obtain the exact location of the concept, even though the content suggests that the popular area may have been used.

3. "To the entire black area of Card III: Two human figures in a bending position (bowing, lifting, carrying, or dancing) . It seems to matter little what object these figures are holding in their hands; the important thing is that the legs are seen in the side bottom *D* and that the figures are really seen in action. Dressed-up animals instead of people may still represent the popular concept." *P* is not scored for human figures or parts of human figures in the

black area with the card held upside-down—for instance, heads of Negroes, or Negro figures dancing, with one leg kicking high in the air.

4. "To the center red *D* in Card III: 'Bow tie,' 'hair ribbon,' or 'butterfly.' The shape alone and the combination of shape and color are used with about equal frequency." *P* is scored for either *F* or *FC*.

5. "To Card V as *W* or *W^x*: Again any winged creature with the body in the center *D* and wings at the sides. The same concept can be applied with the card held upside down." Elaborations of these basic concepts may add to the form-level rating but do not change the *P* score. *P* is scored for *F*, *FM*, *FC'*, and so on.

6. "To Card VI with or without the top *D*: The skin of an animal. The use of shading for the impression of furriness or for the markings on the inside of the skin is essential. This response may be given as *W* or *W^x* or *D*." This implies that either *Fc* or *cF* is required for a *P*; for an animal skin concept in which shading is denied, at most a tendency to *P* may be scored.

7. "To the side *D* in Card VIII: Any kind of four-legged animal in any kind of motion. If the animals are inaccurately called birds or fish, only a tendency toward *P* can be scored. The same is true of animals not seen in action." The card may be in any position, although it is usually right-side-up or sideways.

8. "To the outer blue *D* in Card X: Any many-legged animal such as a spider, a crab, or an octopus." This seems to present no problem.

9. "To the center green *D* in Card X (without the light green *D* between the darker green areas): Any elongated greenish animal such as a caterpillar, a garden snake, or a tobacco worm. In this case the popular concept includes the use of color. The exclusion of the color by a subject limits the scoring to an additional *P*." The use of the light green *D* as an accessory object compatible with the concept of a worm or snake does not detract from the *P* score (for example, if there are two green worms eating a leaf).

10. "To the light green *D* in the center green area of Card X: The head of an animal with long ears or horns such as a rabbit, a donkey, or a goat. Any addition, such as the darker green *D*'s seen

as 'something coming out of the eyes of the animal,' or the white space as 'the body of a white rabbit,' adds an original element to be scored as an additional original." Nothwithstanding this caution, the use of the light green *D*, not as an animal's head but as an object logically compatible with the concept of worm or snake in the center darker green areas, does not warrant an *O*. (See item 9, above.)

Additional Populars

An additional *P* score is given under the following circumstances:
1. Where a popular response is not given until the inquiry.
2. Where a popular response is given in the performance proper, but later rejected.
3. Where the response does not quite fulfil the requirements for a popular score, either in location, or determinants, or content, but approximates it closely enough that a tendency to *P* seems best to represent the response.

O, or Original Responses

The scoring of originals may not be undertaken by beginners, because by definition an original response is one that does not appear more than once in a hundred records. This definition has obvious shortcomings, since different examiners often deal with different groups of subjects, rather than with a stratified sample of the population in general. Therefore, scoring of originals cannot be undertaken very satisfactorily except by examiners who have broad experience with a wide variety of subjects, or who have supplemented their personal experience with extensive reading of published protocols and lists of sample responses.

Additional Originals

An additional *O* score is given under the following circumstances:
1. Where an original response is not given until the inquiry.
2. Where an original response is given in the performance proper but later rejected.
3. Where the response, though not itself sufficiently uncommon

to be given a main original score, contains some original element or twist that would not be encountered more frequently than once in a hundred cases.

4.   By definition, the following popular responses are given an additional original score:

(a) If color is used with the popular animal response in Card VIII, any use of color here warranting a score of $F \leftrightarrow C$.

(b) If the color is used for the popular crab, spider, and so on, in Card X, either as FC or $F \leftrightarrow C$.

(c) If the darker green D's are seen as "something coming out of the eyes" of the popular animal's head on Card X, or if the white space is used for the body of the animal.

O—, or Original Minus Responses

Although original responses are usually the result of keen differentiation or good organization in form perception, and hence are given high form-level rating, a response may be unusual enough to meet the definition of original by reason of distortion or form perception to produce bizarreness, or downright inaccuracy. Bizarre or inaccurate originals are distinguished by the symbol O—. Similarly, original additions to non-original concepts are scored with an additional O—, if these additions serve to give a bizarre or inaccurate flavor.

CHAPTER **8**

Scoring: Form-Level Rating*

In estimating the form level of a response there are three considerations: accuracy, specification, and organization.

Accuracy

The term *accuracy* applies to the fit or match of concept to blot area in terms of outline, shape or form. There are three chief degrees of accuracy.

1. Accurate Responses

Accurate responses are those in which the concept is of definite form (that is, by definition the concept would refer to a class of objects that have a certain specified shape as a common feature) and is applied to a blot area, the outline of which corresponds to the form implied in the definition of the concept. Here are three examples:

---

* This section is based both on the *1946 Supplement* to Klopfer and Kelley, *The Rorschach Technique*, and on the mimeographed draft "Further Contributions to Form Level," by Klopfer, Baker, Kirkner, and Wisham.

Card III: Center red *D,* "A butterfly."

The concept of "butterfly" involves a relatively narrow, short, center section for the body and a symmetrical spread-out area on each side for the wings. The center red *D* corresponds to this definite shape, hence this is said to be an accurate response.

Card IX: Orange *D,* "A witch."

The concept is of a human figure, hence there should be a large bulk, narrower than it is long, for the body and a smaller portion on top for the head. The human figure also implies arms and legs appropriately attached, if the whole figure is seen. Moreover, the concept "witch" implies a tall conical hat (unless some other feature is invoked, such as an ugly profile). The orange area on this card has formal features which correspond to the head, body, and conical hat. The projections on the inner side may or may not be used by the subject for arms. There are no blot features corresponding to legs, although the subject may cover this by specifying that the figure is seated and not all visible. However, whether or not the arms and legs are included, the requirements for accuracy are met in the match of hat, head, and body.

Card VIII, inverted: Lower outer projection from orange portion, "A hound, just the front part."

The concept matches the blot area in that there is a rough oval for the dog's face, somewhat pointed at the bottom, with darker strips on each side that could be the ears of a brown and white hound, a narrower bit for the neck, and again a widening area corresponding to the front quarter of the dog. This is not a popular concept, nor even one frequently encountered; yet when pointed out by the subject the match of concept to blot can be seen to be an accurate one.

2. Semi-Definite or Indefinite Responses

These are responses in which the concept refers to objects so vague or various in shape that almost any blot or blot area could be said to provide a good fit. (An exception would be where the blot area itself is of such a definite shape that it could not be said to be a good fit to an indefinite concept: for instance, the center red *D* in Card III, or the pink side *D*'s in Card VIII.) Examples of semi-definite or indefinite responses are:

Card VII: Whole blot, "Clouds."

Clouds are characteristically indefinite in shape, and although they are by reason of shading effects particularly appropriate to this card, the excellence of the fit applies to determinant rather than outline. It is the characteristic indefiniteness of shape of the concept that prevents this response from being classified as "accurate."

Card IX: Whole blot, "A flower."

Flowers are various in shape, hence almost any blot or portion of a blot could be said to be flower-shaped without introducing any serious inaccuracy. Yet the concept cannot be said to be an accurate one, unless a flower of definite shape is mentioned, and the correspondence between that shape and the blot area is quite demonstrable.

Card I: Whole blot, "The map of an island with four odd-shaped lakes."

Here again an indefinite concept is involved; an island can be of any shape, and hence can "match" any blot area. Similarly, any space might be said to be a lake, regardless of the shape of the white space actually present in the blot. That these triangular spaces are called "odd-shaped lakes" does not alter the fact that "lake" is an indefinite concept. If on the other hand the subject names a specific lake that corresponds in shape to one of these spaces, that concept would be accurate, since the concept implies a definite shape.

3.   Inaccurate Responses

Inaccurate responses are those in which the concept is of definite form but is referred to a blot area of dissimilar form. Occasionally a response is said to be inaccurate (even though the concept is of indefinite form) when it is referred to a blot area that has an unusual specificity of form, so that the fit is a poor one. Perhaps most frequently the subject makes no attempt to reconcile the concept to the blot outline. Sometimes he makes such an attempt but either does not carry it through or is otherwise unsuccessful. Occasionally, the subject manages to avoid inaccuracy either by "cutting off" bits of the blot that do not fit, or by so defining the concept that a match with the blot area is achieved. Examples follow:

Card VII: Whole blot, "A house."

The concept "house" implies certain basic features, even though houses may be of various shapes. It suggests a square or rectangular shape, perhaps with a projection or projections for the chimney or openings for door and windows. The whole blot on this card seems to have no resemblance to this basic form, and hence this response is inaccurate. On the other hand, minimum requirements of accuracy would be fulfilled by referring the concept "house" to the bottom center light-gray portion, which is roughly square, with two projections on top, and a darker "opening" in the center.

Card IV: Whole blot, "A snake."

Here the subject justified the concept by pointing to the two side projections as head and tail of the snake, but he insisted that the remainder of the blot was the rest of the snake. The concept snake implies an elongated form of fairly regular or undulating shape. The side projection satisfied this requirement, but the whole blot does not. Thus the response is inaccurate despite the fact that some attempt is made to reconcile concept to blot. Had the subject described the whole as "two snakes' heads hanging out of a dark mass" the response would be characterized as accurate, since he so defines the total concept as to achieve a match with the blot area used.

Card VIII: Side pink details, "Sunset clouds."

Here the subject's concept is indefinite but is applied to one of the few areas of such definite shape that the match of concept to blot must be described as inaccurate.

Specification

In addition to the primary consideration of match of concept to blot outline (basic accuracy) the accuracy of the match may be improved or spoiled by the extent to which the elaborations or "specifications" offered by the subject correspond to the detailed structure of the blot area used. Specifications may be classified as (1) those that are constructive, (2) those that are irrelevant, and (3) those that weaken the form level or destroy it.

1. Constructive Specifications

Constructive specifications are elaborations of the concept which themselves match in detail the particular structure of the blot area. The more constructive specifications given, the more demonstrable it is that the subject is capable of highly differentiated perception. It must be remembered, however, that subjects differ not only in the degree of their perceptual differentiation but also in the extent to which they spontaneously verbalize the details of their concepts. When conducting an inquiry the examiner should keep form-level rating in mind as well as location and determinants, and should encourage the subject to expand his specifications by non-directive questions, even though this may not be necessary to clarify other aspects of the scoring.

Constructive specifications are of two chief kinds:

Form specifications, which specify a more detailed match of the concept to the outline of the blot area (whiskers on a cat, ears on a dog, facial features or details of clothing on a human figure) provided, of course, that the formal qualities of the blot outline give a reality basis for these specifications.

Determinant specifications, which specify a more detailed match of the concept to the blot by use of color, shading, or movement. Not all determinants are counted as constructive specifications. The following criteria must be met:

a. CRITERIA FOR MOVEMENT SPECIFICATIONS: The movement must be within the context of definite form—for example, scored *M*,

FM, or *Fm,* not *mF* or *m.* Further, the movement or posture attributed to the figure or object must be justified in terms of the structural qualities of the blot rather than merely projected on the blot without formal justification. Note these examples:

Card II: Whole blot, "People clapping hands."

To specify this action for the human figures acknowledges the particular structure of the blot area and improves the match of concept to blot. Therefore "clapping hands" is counted as a constructive specification.

Card II: White space, card inverted, "A spinning top; these little gray streaks give the impression of movement."

The use of the little gray streaks makes the "spinning" a constructive specification. If, however, the subject had explained that he said the top was spinning because that is what tops do, the verbal specification would be counted as irrelevant, since it does not imply a more detailed match of concept to blot.

Card VII: Upper two-thirds, "Two impudent faces."

If the subject explains that the faces are "impudent" either because the two figures are thrusting their faces forwards towards each other as if they were making faces, or because the features are small and pert, "impudent" would count as a constructive specification. On the other hand an expression or emotion attributed to a human figure which does not seem to be suggested by any formal feature of the blot would be classified as an irrelevant specification.

b.   CRITERIA FOR SHADING AND COLOR SPECIFICATIONS: The shading or color must be combined with definite form (*FC, FC', Fc, FK*) and must be an essential component of the concept named. For example:

Card X: Lower center dark green *D,* "Two tomato worms, they are tomato worms because they are green."

Here the blot is elongated, and thus the match of the concept "worm" with the blot fulfils the requirements of basic accuracy. Color is combined with form to give an *FC* score;

moreover, "tomato worms" are invariably green. Hence this specification improves the match of concept to blot. Thus this is counted as a constructive specification. However, had the subject merely said "two green worms" and explained that they were worms *and* they are green, an *FC* scoring is justified because some worms are indeed green; but the form-level rating would not be raised because worms are not necessarily green, and hence the match of concept to blot is not improved in the statement of the concept itself.

Card III: Lower center dark gray, card inverted, "Heads of Negroes; because of the prognathous jaw and the black color."

Here there are two constructive specifications. The "prognathous jaw" refers to the form. The "black" reconciles form and color. Both could be considered essential components of the concept "Negro," and thus are constructive specifications.

Card VI: Upper center dark *D*, "A polished walnut bedpost. Walnut because it is dark, polished because of the highlight."

Here again there are two constructive specifications, "polished" combining form and shading, and "walnut" combining form and achromatic color, both being essential to the total concept "polished walnut bedpost."

2. Irrelevant Specifications

Irrelevant specifications are verbalizations of the subject which neither improve nor detract from the accuracy of the match of concept to blot. There are several types of irrelevant specifications, some of which are mentioned below:

a. Specifications already covered by an earlier specification. For example:

Card IX: Orange detail, "Witches. Here are their hats. Pointed crown and brim."

The hats count as a constructive specification but the crown and brim do not, being an essential part of the concept of hat. and covered by it.

Card III: Black area, "Two men bowing to each other. Here are their legs and their backs bent over."

The posture is already covered by "bowing"; the rest of the verbalization adds nothing to the accuracy of the match to the blot.

b.   Specifications referring to determinants that are not essential to the definition of the concept.

Card III: Center red D, "A red butterfly."

Butterflies are not necessarily red, therefore the determinant specification is considered irrelevant.

Card IX: Whole blot, "Two Gay Ninety figures, with leg-o-mutton sleeves, pink feather hats, dressed in green jackets and orange hobble skirts narrow at the bottom. They are mincing along, with hips swaying and hands on hips."

All the separate formal portions of the attire and movement would count as constructive specifications as well as the shading, since soft texture is an essential component of a feather. However, pink, orange, and green just happen to be the colors in the blot; clothes could be those colors but are not necessarily so. Hence the use of color would be an irrelevant specification.

c.   Specifications that improve the match to the blot as far as the determinant is concerned, but refer to an indefinite concept and hence do not represent an integration of the determinant with definite form. For example:

Card IX: Bottom pink D, "Strawberry ice cream; because it is pink."

The use of color is considered an irrelevant specification, despite the fact that "pink" is an essential component of "strawberry ice cream," because it refers to a concept of indefinite form.

d.   Specifications that are mere verbiage, or reflections of the thoughts and feelings of the subject, or descriptions of the form, shading or color of the blot, and do not serve to improve the detailed nature of the match of concept to blot. Two examples follow:

Card III

PERFORMANCE	INQUIRY
A crab's shape. Emphasis of coöperation. Posed arms. Feelings of symmetry, even and well-balanced. Pleasant shapes.	S: I used this part (center gray *D*). Here is its head, and rear.
	E: Anything else?
	S: Well, it could be part of the whole ritual (referring to previous response involving the usual human figures). The blur makes it seem full of life.

Score: D   FM   A   1.5

COMMENT: The "arms" are an essential part of the concept "crab," and hence are included in the basic accuracy of the fit of the concept to blot. Most of the rest of the verbalization is considered irrelevant, even though it tends to "dress up" the concept, and make it seem more impressive, and even more definite; carefully viewed it may be seen to contribute in no way to specify a more exact fit with the blot. (However, the comment, "The blur makes it seem full of life" constitutes a constructive determinant specification.)

Card X (after six previous responses all linked into the concept of a party)

PERFORMANCE	INQUIRY
These two yellow bugs are the glamor girls of the party. They are not contributing anything but they are perfectly happy.	S: (Indicated yellow outside *D*'s.)
	E: What about them makes them seem like glamor girls?
	S: They are floating and they are blonde. Blondes are supposed to be glamorous. They are really rather dull.
	E: What makes them seem dull?
	S: They have no shape. They are just blots.

Score: D CF_{sym}, m   (A)   O   0.5

COMMENT: This verbalization is irrelevant as far as form-level rating is concerned. The concept itself lacks definite shape; it is a "bug," and later the subject says, "They have no shape. They are just blots." Therefore, the specifications do not contribute to the match of the concept to the shape of the blot, although they serve to give an intellectual flavor through a symbolic linkage. They represent much "read into" the percept by the subject. (The scoring of the determinant presents a problem here. There is intent to attribute human characteristics to the area and human emotions are ascribed. Yet an M seems unsatisfactory since it should imply a concept of definite form. The scoring of CF_{sym} seems best for the main determinant; m seems better than M to represent the movement, since the floating figures without definite form seem to represent more the abstract idea of a "glamor girl" than concrete human movement.)

3.   Specifications that Weaken or Destroy the Form Level

There are two chief types of specifications that weaken the form level: (a) those that destroy the match of concept to blot, and (b) those that serve to detract from the accuracy of the fit but do not absolutely spoil it.

a.   Specifications that destroy the match of concept to blot are those affecting the focal part of the concept. For example:

Card IX

PERFORMANCE

A face showing the interior of heads. Here is a small body. Only the upper part is shown, clad in a short jacket. And two hands holding weights.

INQUIRY

S: Eyes (indicating oval white spaces). Hands (indicating upper central portion of each side of the lower pink D). It is funny because he is holding up those heavy weights (the outer portion of each pink D). He has a jacket with two little buttons. You can see right into his head. It is transparent. He has a high collar on the jacket. His hands are clenched. These little lines give the outlines of the

fingers (tiny green projections) and
there is even a thumb here.

E: Where is the head?

S: This transparent part (indicating the
whole upper orange, green and inner
shaded space). This is the long nose
here (pointing to midline) extending
right up into the head.

Score: W,S   M—   Hd   O—   —1.0

COMMENT: All the specifications about the hands and the
jacket are constructive. The form-level rating would be high,
were it not for the concept of face and head; the features mentioned (eyes and nose) are not only incompatible with the concept of "interior of heads" but are represented by blot areas of
the wrong proportions. Since the face is the focal part of the
concept (indeed it is the first mentioned) it quite destroys the
match of concept to blot for it to be seen inaccurately.

b. Specifications that detract from the match of concept to blot,
but being peripheral or secondary in importance do not destroy the basic accuracy of the match of concept to blot. The
usual effect of these weakening specifications is to make the
concept crude or sloppy or infantile. An example follows :

Card V (subject is aged 5)

PERFORMANCE

A bat.

INQUIRY

E: Show me the bat.

S: (Indicated the whole.)

E: Tell me about it.

S: Here are the legs (center lower d) the
head (top d) and here are some legs
(outer projections).

Score: W   F—   A   P   —0.5

COMMENT: The extra pair of legs detracts from the concept;
but does not destroy it. Basically the concept of "bat" is an
accurate match for the blot.

Card X (same subject gave the "glamor girl" concept on page 215)

PERFORMANCE   INQUIRY

Here is a green rabbit at the bottom with   S: The rabbit is at the party (referring to
two green caterpillars as eyes which he   the total concept which the subject
waves about.   worked out for the whole blot). It's
                                                   in the nature of a parlor trick.

Score: 1. D⎫   M   Ad   P⎫   —0.5
          2. D⎭   FC   A   P⎭ →O—   1.0

COMMENT: Either the "rabbit" or the "caterpillars" alone
would be accurate; indeed they match the blot so well that they
are popular responses. But to call the caterpillars the eyes of
the rabbit and add that he waves them about detracts from the
accuracy of the concept, even though it does not serve to destroy
the basic accuracy of the match. In concepts with semi-independent components which are given separate location scores,
the —0.5 for a combination that weakens the form level is subtracted from the first of the two form-level ratings.

Organization

Any procedure used by the subject to organize the various parts
of the blot into a meaningful larger concept is recognized by an increase in form-level rating. Such organization may be loose or well-
integrated. It may be by virtue of interaction of figures in movement, functional interdependence, position, or even symbolism.
However, an attempt to organize by means of mere juxtaposition of
two concepts without any genuinely meaningful connection would
not be considered justification for increasing the form-level rating.

Card III: Whole, "Men bowing to each other, with hats in their
hands."

The posture is included in the basic requirements for popular
form level on this card, and the "hats" constitute a constructive
specification. In addition, the organization involved in bringing

the two sides of the blot into relationship further improves the form level.

Card IX: Whole, "Flames at the top; red coals glowing at the bottom, and the green part is smoke."

Although the basic component concepts are indefinite, the organization is meaningful, even though based on mere position.

Card VI: Whole, "A totem pole attached to a fur rug."

Here there are two independent concepts, which the subject tries to organize by having them "attached." The organization is not a meaningful one; indeed it tends to detract from the form level.

The Rating Scale

Form level is rated on a scale ranging from —2.0 through 0.0 to +5.0. There are two essential steps in ascertaining the form-level rating:

1. Assigning a basal rating, or a basal minus rating.
2. Adding a credit of 0.5 for each constructive specification or for a successful organization, and subtracting a credit of 0.5 for a specification or organization that weakens the match of concept to blot.

Basal Ratings

1. *Basal Rating of 1.0*

A basal rating of 1.0 is given for a concept that fulfils minimum requirements for a "definite" concept, and as such has basic accuracy of fit with the blot area. There are three kinds of response that are assigned a basal rating of 1.0.

a. The ten popular responses are given a basal rating of 1.0, to which additions may be made for constructive specifications which exceed the minimum requirements for the popular scoring. Thus a "bat" on Cards I or V would be given a basal rating of 1.0. Similarly, human figures in a bending posture on Card III, or four-legged animals in some sort of action on Card VIII.

b. "Popular level" responses, frequently given to fairly obvious blot areas, and requiring about the same level of organizational ability as popular responses themselves, are also given a basal rating of 1.0. A few examples are:

CRAB: bottom center *D* in Card III.

HANDS: upper center projections in Card I.

BUTTERFLY: lower red *D* in Card II.

BOOTS: lower outer *D*'s in Card IV.

ANIMAL'S HEAD: bottom center *D* in Card IV.

A WOMAN'S LEG: side projection in Card V.

A BUTTERFLY: top *D* in Card VI.

ANIMAL'S HEAD: shaded brown-green *D* in Card IX.

TWO BUGS: upper center gray *D* in Card X.

ANIMAL: outer gray *D* in Card X.

STOMACH: bottom center *D* in Card III.

LUNGS: center red *D* in Card III.

c. Concepts that require little imagination or organizational capacity, regardless of the frequency with which they are seen in given blot areas, are assigned a basal level of 1.0. These concepts imply definite form, but the basic requirements for this form are relatively simple, involving three (not fewer than two) characteristics only. A few examples follow:

BUTTERFLY: for any area with a central narrow smaller "body" and symmetrical "wings" on each side. Indeed the "body" may be ignored and the "wings" fulfil the basic requirements for a definite concept.

TREE: for any area with a narrow projection for a trunk with a larger spread above for the rest of the tree.

SPIDER OR CRAB: for any roundish area with projections which may be termed legs.

ANIMAL: for any area with a reasonable shape for body, head and legs.

FISH: for any long, narrow area.

2. *Basal Rating of 1.5*

A basal rating of 1.5 is given for concepts above the minimum requirements for "definiteness" (that is, implying a distinctive shape) provided that this definite shape is compatible with the shape of the blot area used. The 1.5 concept usually involves four or more essential form characteristics, whereas the 1.0 concept involves only three (sometimes as few as two). For example:

> A HUMAN PROFILE: The concept implies as a minimum a "nose" projecting from a face which has forehead, chin and mouth implied in outline. It is not only the complexity of the shape but also the proportions that imply a very definite shape.
>
> A HUMAN FIGURE: The concept implies a long, relatively narrow body, a head which is rounded, smaller and above, legs appropriately placed, and possibly arms as well. Again it is not merely the number of the parts but also the necessity of matching the concept to a blot area with proper proportions.
>
> A SPECIFIC ANIMAL FIGURE: The concept "Scotch terrier" implies a much more distinctive shape than merely "dog" or four-legged animal. Moreover, it may imply a much better integration of concept and blot material with respect to the determinants essential to the concept. This increased specificity in definition places more rigorous demands regarding basic accuracy, and hence warrants a higher basal rating when these demands are met.

It must be noted that in Card III the popular human figures are given a basal level of 1.0 as populars; the blot material so facilitates perception of a human figure that it requires less capacity for differentiated perception to see it on this card than elsewhere. Similarly, the concept "rabbit's head" receives a basal rating on Card X as a popular; but seen elsewhere it would rate 1.5, provided, of course, that the blot material justified the concept of a long-eared animal.

3. *Basal Rating of 0.0*

This rating is reserved for responses in which the concept is completely indefinite in form, indeed neglecting form altogether, and where this shapelessness is appropriate to the blot area—that is, where the blot itself is not so structured that an indefinite concept does violence to it, as it would if applied to the center red area of Card III or the outer pink details in Card VIII.

Basal ratings of 0.0 would be given to responses in which the determinants similarly imply neglect of form: namely, C, C_{des}, C_n, C_{sym}, c, C', K, k, and m. The 0.0 level is rare, since these completely unstructured concepts are relatively rare.

4. *Basal Rating of 0.5*

The 0.5 rating is reserved for responses that are vague or semidefinite in form, but where form is not completely neglected. The 0.5 concept has one essential form element. Very frequently the 0.5 responses emphasize the determinant rather than form and thus are associated with determinant scores of CF, $C'F$, cF, KF, kF, or mF. Vague F responses are also included. Examples follow:

A LEAF: This may merely imply an insular portion of indefinite shape, or emphasize the "stem" without concern for the shape of the rest of the area spreading out from the center line.

AN ISLAND: If no particular island of definite shape is specified, all that is implied is that the blot area should be surrounded by white space (or lighter shading).

A DESIGN: This concept often is used to refer to a center line with symmetrical shapes on each side, without any concern for the particular shape or arrangement of the elements entering into the design.

VAGUE ANATOMICAL CONCEPTS: These may either mention "internal organs" in a vague way, or may use a specific concept implying definite shape but used in a vague way. Thus it may emerge in inquiry that the subject is quite ignorant of the actual shape of the liver, stomach, lungs, and the like; thus any vague shape will do.

ORGANIZATIONAL CONCEPTS: Where the elements are themselves quite shapeless, and the concept depends on a positional linkage or some other vague organization, such as, "earth, sea, and sky."

Minus Ratings

1. *Rating of —0.5*

This rating may be achieved in one of two ways:

a. A rating of —0.5 may result from a lowering from a basal level of 1.0 (sometimes 1.5) because of a specification that weakens the basic accuracy of the match of concept to blot, but does not destroy it. This rating arises as the result of the problem of what to do about a response that would be reduced from 1.0 or 1.5 to 0.5 or 0.0 by simple subtraction of 0.5 for each specification that weakens the form level. Since 0.0 and 0.5 are reserved for indefinite concepts, the convention is to score such lowered responses —0.5. This does not apply to all lowered responses, for one weakening specification for a response of 1.5 basal rating would merely reduce the form level to 1.0. Rarely can an examiner rate —0.5 for a response with more than one weakening specification, for this usually serves to damage the total concept so completely that a —1.0 seems justified. Some examples of —0.5 resulting from lowered ratings follow:

Card I

PERFORMANCE

Looks like an eagle.

INQUIRY

S: It is a big daddy eagle. Here is the head (upper center rounded *d*'s) the wings (side projections) and the body (vaguely indicating the rest of the blot). It's dead.

E: What makes it seem dead?

S: Because its head and wings are small.

Score: W   F—   A   →P   —0.5

COMMENT: This departs from the popular response in that the wings are limited to the small side projections, rather than covering the whole side portion of the blot. This in itself is not inaccurate, since the projections are a good shape for wings; the specification which weakens the form level is to have the body concept expanded beyond the center *D*. It seems justified to give a basal rating of 1.0 for the popular concept and to subtract 0.5 for the body of inappropriate size. The specification "head" is counted as irrelevant since it seems positionally determined and is not a particularly good shape for the head of an eagle.

Card I

PERFORMANCE

It could be the map of a continent.

INQUIRY

S: It looks . . . what way was I looking at it? . . . Looks like Canada. Hudson's Bay is more in the center here. There's the St. Lawrence River.

E: Can you show me the St. Lawrence River?

S: (Looked somewhat confused and after hesitating, pointed vaguely to an undifferentiated portion on the right side of the blot. He then pointed to an indentation on the side and said with a rather relieved expression): Anyhow here is the Gulf of St. Lawrence. It's rather a far-fetched idea.

Score: W,S   F—   geo   O—   —0.5

COMMENT: The concept "map of a continent" would be a semi-definite concept had the subject not given further specification, and as such would have been rated 0.5. However, the subject makes it definite by saying it looks like Canada. He then tries to justify the definiteness by pointing out the various parts. "Hudson's Bay" may be counted as essential to a basal rating of 1.0, since it is the one specification that seems at all to justify a definite concept here. The specification "St. Lawrence River" is in no way justified by the blot material and is thus a weakening one. It is not considered that the subject's efforts to restore accuracy by pointing to the "gulf" or by saying "it is rather a far-fetched idea" ameliorate this inaccuracy. By subtraction from the basal rating of 1.0 a rating of —0.5 is arrived at.

Card V (see example on page 68)

COMMENT: The specification of the "mouth" in the lower *d* of the "butterfly" is considered inaccurate, not only because it is in the wrong position when the card is viewed upright, but because it is an inappropriate shape for the mouth of any such creature, even with allowances for uncertainty as to what a "butterfly's mouth" looks like. One senses a certain preoccupation with the concept "mouth" for it to be applied to this area.

Card V (see example on page 217). An extra pair of legs for the popular bat would lower the form level to —0.5.

Card X (see example on page 218)

COMMENT: The linking of the popular rabbit and the popular caterpillars is counted an inaccurate specification, which—subtracting from the 1.0 level for the "rabbit's head"—gives a rating of —0.5.

b. A —0.5 rating is also assigned for giving an indefinite concept to an area so definite in structure that the indefinite concept represents an abuse of the structure of the blot. For example, where the center red *D* on Card III is seen as "blood" or "fire," or where the pink *D*'s on Card VIII are seen as "pink clouds" or "blood" instead of as the popular animals.

2. *Rating of —1.0*

A basal rating of —1.0 is given to a concept where the subject makes some effort to reconcile the concept to the shape of the blot area used but fails to meet the minimum requirements for basic accuracy. This may be the case either with a basically inaccurate response where some effort is made to indicate the "parts" on the blot, or where part of the concept is well seen and quite accurate, but the weakening specifications are sufficiently numerous or focal to destroy the basic accuracy of the fit. The confabulatory combination is a classic example of the —1.0 rating, where "the discrepancy . . . is not so much between the shape of the various blot details and the corresponding parts of the concept, but rather between the organization of these parts in the concept and the configuration of the blot material." [1, p. 162] This —1.0 level is perhaps the most frequent minus rating. Six examples follow:

Card I

PERFORMANCE	INQUIRY
In my imagination I picture—I might have seen a queer type of fish. One of the things you read in the Encyclopaedia Britannica.	E: Where did you see the fish? Show me here (indicating location chart).
	S: (Gestured indicating the whole.)
	E: Describe the fish.
	S: Here is the mouth, fins, body.
	E: What about it made it seem like a fish?
	S: Small face, two eyes, body, silhouette, fins and coloring. (Note: the gestures did not enable the examiner to locate the different parts indicated.)

Score: W   F—   A   O—   —1.0

COMMENT: A "fish" concept implies an elongated shape, unless the subject specifies a fish of some other definite shape. Card I does not present an elongated shape. Presumably, the subject meant to indicate the white spaces for mouth and eyes and the side projections for fins. It is impossible to say where the "small face" could be. In any event, if the "mouth and eyes" determined the concept, a mask or face of some other animal would have been more appropriate. Thus despite the effort the subject made to reconcile his concept with the blot, it remains a basically inaccurate fit.

Card IV

PERFORMANCE	INQUIRY
It doesn't look like very much. It's more like the X ray of the lower part of the spine than anything else.	S: (Indicated that he used the whole blot except for the lower side, light gray portions.) Well, the first thing which attracted my attention was the lower part which looked like a vertebra and the after bits. The darker bits looked like the bones of

the pelvic basin. Also the two dark
bits at the top look like ureters leading from the kidney and the top
looks something like a vertebra.

E: What suggests a vertebra?

S: Well, being symmetrical and having
the spikes sticking out. And I said
X ray because in appearance it is like
an X ray, just sort of light and dark.

Score: W   Fk—   At   —1.0

COMMENT: An "X ray" or even an "X ray of the spine" would
be a sufficiently indefinite concept to have been scored *kF* and
rated 0.5. However, the subject makes his concept a definite one
by his specifications, yet fails to achieve a basic accuracy for the
combined concept. It has the flavor of a confabulatory combination, in that the spiky appearance suggests "vertebra" and the
side projections suggest "ureters," and the shading suggests
X ray, and it is all put together to be an "X ray of the lower
part of the spine." There is effort to reconcile concept to blot,
but it is ineffectual.

Card I

PERFORMANCE

INQUIRY

You could say the whole shape might be
someone sitting down with his arms out.

S: These side things are the arms. It is
just an impression.

Score: W   M—   H   O—   —1.0

COMMENT: There is basic inaccuracy in the match of concept
to blot. The subject tries to reconcile the fit by pointing out the
"arms," which are not very accurate in themselves. The fact
that he excuses it by saying "it is just an impression" does not
alter the rating of —1.0. If he had totally rejected the concept,
the rating would still be —1.0, although the whole scoring
would be additional as a rejected concept.

Card I

PERFORMANCE

In some respects it reminds me of a maple leaf.

INQUIRY

S: If it only had that there (drawing in a point in the white space at the top) and had other parts taken away, it would look like a leaf. It is just my imagination of course.

Score: dr,S   F—   Pl   O—   —1.0

COMMENT: The blot is basically not the shape of a "maple leaf"; the subject has to add white space to make it so, and could not indicate what portions he would cut off to improve the concept. As a basically inaccurate concept, with some effort to reconcile the concept to blot, it is scored —1.0.

Card IX

PERFORMANCE

The whole thing seems to be three separate things as though united, dancing, swaying from side to side in the communcal (sic) kinds of dances that one does. The first one is tipping over on the ground. The third is rooted on the ground or sitting firmly on it in some way, and the second is running. It's having difficulty, being pushed forward.

INQUIRY

E: Show me the separate things.
S: Two are people, and the first is the lobster shape (referring to an earlier response).

Score: W   M—,m   (H)   O—   —1.0

COMMENT: This is a very confused response. There is certainly some effort to reconcile concept to blot and one that might have been carried out more successfully, although the organization would still detract from the form level. The subject fails, however, to match concept to blot in any convincing way; hence the score is —1.0.

Card IV

PERFORMANCE

Here is something very, very menacing. Something I remember from a long time

INQUIRY

S: The whole thing is the beetle's head. Just the head.

back when I was three or four. This is a beetle or something from the beetle family. It has antennae, no eyes, but it is looking very, very hard. Here are the upper mandibles. It has no lower ones. The effect is of an open mouth ready to close right away. The whole effect is very menacing.

E: What could these be (pointing to side projections)?
S: Those are the antennae.
E: Did you mention eyes?
S: No, it has no eyes, although it is looking very hard.
E: What is this (lower center *D*)?
S: This lower part is the upper mandibles. It is split up the center when it eats.
E: Is that what you meant by a mouth?
S: There isn't an open mouth actually showing. It is underneath, coming up to snap.

Score: W   FM—, m   Ad   O—   —1.0

COMMENT: If the subject had merely said "beetle" and pointed to head or antennae, the basal rating would have been reasonably accurate, namely, 1.0. However, the specifications of "eyes that aren't there but it is looking very hard," "mandibles that split open in the center when it eats," and especially the "open mouth" that cannot be seen, all give a bizarre inaccuracy; this number of poor specifications serves to weaken the match to such an extent that a basal rating of —1.0 seems justified.

3.   *Rating of —1.5*

The —1.5 rating is reserved for the classical confabulatory response, which is scored *DW* for location. This response is a generalization from one clearly seen detail, the subject insisting that the whole blot is used, when it is impossible to reconcile the concept with the shape of the whole blot. For further discussion and examples, see pages 64–69.

4.   *Rating of —2.0*

The —2.0 rating is given to responses in which the concept does not match the blot area used and there is no effort on the part of the subject to reconcile the shape of the blot with the form elements of the concept. Many of these responses are perseverations, either encountered with very young children or quite irrational clinical cases. Occasionally a rating of —2.0 is given for a non-perseverated response which is obviously inaccurate, and where for some reason or another the subject does not give any specifications or explanations. The prototype of the —2.0 rating with adults is the contaminated response, where two entirely incompatible concepts are merged together. Perhaps either would be a reasonable match for the blot if given separately, but together they constitute a nonsense concept. It is as though the boundaries between concepts were so fluid that if two concepts were suggested by the same blot area they could not be kept separate, but fuse together as one. However, such a fusion of concepts would only be considered to be "contamination" if the subject presents the response seriously; if he himself seems amused by the incongruity it may simply be a case of a flexible subject playfully approaching the task in a permissive situation where the usual rules for "reality testing" may be laid aside. For example:

> PERSEVERATION: A child aged 3 years, 3 months, saw a "doggie" on Card II, indicating the usual popular animals, although giving no specifications. He then proceeded to give the response "doggie" to Cards III, IV, V, VI, VII, VIII, indicating the whole blot in a vague sort of way, and being unresponsive to any inquiry. Although it is quite conceivable that the concept "doggie" could have been justified in the case of Cards III and VIII, the automatic quality of the perseveration seems to require a —2.0 scoring for all these responses except the first popular on Card II.

> **Card VII** as a "house" (see example on page 210) : If the subject gives no justification for the concept whatsoever, there seems little alternative to a —2.0 scoring when this concept is used for the whole blot.

> CONTAMINATION: For examples and discussion see Klopfer and Kelley [1], pages 353–354, and Rapaport [2], Volume II, pages 338–341, 478–479.

Adding Credits

Each constructive specification adds 0.5 credit to the basal rating, except in the case of minus ratings that are minus by definition and not improvable by additional constructive specifications. Usually the credits are added to basal ratings of 1.0 or 1.5. Occasionally a basal rating of 0.0 or 0.5 can be improved by constructive specifications. The upper limit of form-level rating is 5.0; any further constructive specifications receive no additional credit. A credit of 0.5 is also given for a constructive organization, but in this case further organization does not add further credit.

The following conditions must be observed before credits can be added:

1. The specification must be spontaneous, either in the performance proper or in the inquiry. Specifications given in response to prodding questions such as "What is this part?" or "Where is the head?" or "How do you see it?" cannot be included in form-level rating.

2. The specification must exceed the essential formal elements of the concept. Thus the concept "bat" includes at least wings and body as essential elements; legs for the "bat" and "antennae" for the "butterfly" seem also essential to the concept and covered by the basal rating. However, if the subject points out the articulation of the wings of the bat, or points out that the ears are essentially mammalian in nature and therefore the creature could not be a butterfly, these count as constructive specifications. (See also the discussion on pages 211–213.)

3. If the specification involves the use of a determinant, this must be an essential aspect of the concept (for example, blue for a bluebird, black for a bat, long hair for a Persian cat) and exceed the minimum requirements for a popular response in the case of populars. (See discussion of determinant specifications on pages 211–213.) It may be noted that where the determinant in question is instrumental in raising the basal rating from 1.0 to 1.5, the same determinant specification cannot be given added credit. Thus if specifying "bluebird" raises the basal level from 1.0 for a simple "bird" to 1.5, it is not possible to give an additional 0.5 for the color determinant; this is subsumed in the higher basal rating.

4. The specification must be independent. Thus eyes and eyebrows would constitute one constructive specification, rather than two, since these are interdependent. Similarly, 0.5 might be added

for a hat seen on a human figure, but additional credits would not be given for pointing out the crown and brim of the hat.

5.   The organizational procedure must be "meaningful," whether loose or integrated. Credit is not given for mere juxtaposition. Only one organizational credit is permitted for each concept. When the organization is so loose that two or more main location scores are given and bracketed together, the organizational credit should be given to the first form-level rating, but not to both or all. (See page 218 for further discussion of organization.)

Examples of Adding Credits

Card II

PERFORMANCE

Two little dogs, sitting up begging. Their noses are practically touching.

INQUIRY

S: Here are their paws, noses, ears, fore-head. You can't see their hind feet, but they are sitting up begging.
E: What kind of dogs could they be?
S: They are terrier pups.
E: What makes them seem like terrier pups?
S: They have the shape of puppies' heads and the roundness. The shape through the noses and puppy-like thick necks.
E: Was this part of it (center *d*)?
S: It could be a little tidbit that they are both begging for.

Score: W   FM   Ad   P   3.0

COMMENT: The basal rating is 1.0 since this is a popular concept. The following credits are added: 0.5 for the position of "begging" including the "paws"; 0.5 for the "nose" since this is a particularly good match to the blot in this case—"fore-head," however, not being considered independent of "nose"; 0.5 for "ears"; 0.5 for organization (seeing the dogs in relationship). Credit is not added for the "titbit," nor for the description of the shape of the puppies' heads, since these follow prodding questions.

Card II

PERFORMANCE

A big fat white rabbit, and here are its ears.

INQUIRY

S: (Indicated all of the center white space plus the light gray bit above.) This line suggests a heavy fold at its neck because it is so plump. Here is the tail, although it isn't really like a rabbit's tail. It is sitting down, back to us, and the light gray is the ears.

Score: S,dd   FC',FM   A   O   2.5

COMMENT: The basal rating here is 1.5 since the concept "rabbit" implies a distinctive shape involving "long ears," and the concept is applied to a blot area of appropriate shape. The following credits are added: 0.5 for "white" since this may be considered an additional essential aspect of the concept rabbit (the most popular variety being white) ; 0.5 for the "plump" specification and the justification thereof in terms of the "fold" since this makes the concept a more precise match to the blot. No additional credit is given for the "tail" since it does not improve the match, and as the subject points out "it is not really like a rabbit's tail." No credit is given for the "ears" because these are an essential specification for the concept "rabbit"—and, indeed, are responsible themselves for the basal rating of 1.5 rather than 1.0.

Card V

PERFORMANCE

Two cobras just sizing each other up, or courting maybe.

INQUIRY

S: (Indicated upper *d*, card inverted.) The suspended motion that snakes have, swaying.
E: What about them made them seem like cobras especially?
S: That is the way cobras behave.

Score: d   FM   A   2.0

COMMENT: The basal level here is 1.0. "Cobra" is taken to imply no more definite shape than any "snake." All that is required is an elongated shape to satisfy requirements of accuracy. (If the subject had pointed out an area where there was a "hood" for the cobra, then the basal level would be 1.5, because it would be obvious that a particular shape was implied in the concept.) Additional credits were given for each of the elements of movement and organization.

Card I

PERFORMANCE

An insect of some sort.

INQUIRY

S: The whole thing. A hard black type of insect. A winged beetle. It is a stag beetle, and here are the typical "stags" (pointing to claw-like projections).
E: What makes it seem hard?
S: It has the hard modelling effect of a beetle; that's part of why I called it a stag beetle. They are hard and black like this.

Score: W   Fc,FC′   A   2.5

COMMENT: This is a very interesting example illustrating differences between basal ratings. For a "winged beetle" without further specifications, the basal level would have been 1.0 for a "popular." However, a basal level of 1.5 is given for the "stag beetle," implying certain definite form requirements over the 1.0 level. Since the "stags" are an essential part of this requirement, no additional credit is given for them, nor for the wings, which are part of the basic requirement. However, additional credits are given both for the color and the "hardness," which are integral aspects of the concept of "stag beetle."

Card VI

PERFORMANCE

Looks like an incision being made in flesh in the middle. Poor-looking flesh. The knife is still pulling along.

INQUIRY

S: The flesh looks soft in comparison to the hard instrument. It looks light, as when you just make an incision. It is still going on.

Score: W   Fm,cF, Fc   obj.At   1.5

COMMENT: This is an example of constructive specifications changing an indefinite concept to a definite one. Indeed the emphasis changes sufficiently to definiteness that the main determinant is chosen to reflect this. The focal concept seems to be "flesh," which is scored *cF* and justifies a basal rating of 0.5. Additional credit is given for the "instrument" and further for the motion attributed to the instrument. The final form-level rating of 1.5, and the main determinant of *Fm,* mask the fact that the underlying concept is fairly undifferentiated. That the scoring should so mask this seems an accurate representation of the effort at control implied in this concept.

Card X

PERFORMANCE

Two parakeets.

INQUIRY

S: (Indicating upper green *D*'s) Because they are green. Parrots aren't always green.

Score: D   FC   A   1.5

COMMENT: Here "parakeet" is a definite concept, but for color rather than form. The basal rating is 1.0 for "bird"; 0.5 is added for the use of color, which is an essential characteristic of the particular bird named.

Subtracting Credits

Each weakening specification (including a bizarre organizational element) subtracts 0.5 from the basal rating, provided that the basal rating is 1.0 or 1.5. Indefinite concepts are not inaccurate, except in the few instances where they are inappropriately applied to a particularly well-structured blot area and the form level is scored —0.5. Further subtractions cannot be made from ratings assigned basal minus ratings. Subtractions that lower the form level below 1.0 take it to the level —0.5 by definition (unless they serve completely to destroy the match of blot to concept). However, quite frequently weakening specifications are mingled with constructive specifications so that, although subtractions are made for the weaknesses, the form-level rating remains in the range of accurate perception—that is, 1.0 or better.

Examples of Subtracting Credits

Card I

PERFORMANCE	INQUIRY
Two ballet dancers whirling around a central figure. Their feet are together. They have broken ankles, Superman capes, pointed heads and beetle brows. The figure in the middle is a ballet dancer with middle-aged spread. A girl.	S: It was the whole thing. Here are the hands joined, their heads, their capes. Their feet couldn't be like this. Their heels should be out, therefore obviously they have broken ankles. The middle one has no head.
	E: What about the blot made her seem like a ballet dancer?
	S: Her feet are like a ballet dancer. In the fifth position (demonstrating). She is raised on her points. Size 40 bust. She has a girdle on and she is popping out over it. She has large calves. You can see through her skirt.

Score: W   M,Fc   H   O—   3.0

COMMENT: The basal rating here is 1.5. Additional credits are given as follows: 0.5 for the dancing; 0.5 for the organization; 0.5 for introducing the human figure in the center portion; 0.5 for "capes"; 0.5 for "feet in the fifth position"; 0.5 for the transparent skirt (total now is 4.5). Irrelevant specifications are as follows: (1) "Pointed heads" which are descriptive of the blot structure but do not represent the constructive specification that pointed hats would have made. (2) Similarly, the "beetle brows." (3) Specifying that the capes are "Superman capes," which adds nothing to the precision of the concept. (4) It is also considered irrelevant to point out that the central figure is headless, although it would have been inaccurate to describe a head that is not there (unless some meaningful explanation could have been given of why one could not see the head). The following subtractions are made for weakening specifications: —0.5 for "broken ankles," which strain the logic of the concept of "ballet dancers whirling"; —0.5 for "raised on her points," which is incompatible with the immediately preceding description of the feet "in the fifth position" (which itself is quite a good match to the blot) ; —0.5 for "she has size 40 bust, she has a girdle on and is popping out over it," for one can either see a full figure with a skirt, waist and bust, or one can see in the lower half of the center portion the outline of a figure from the waist down with or without a surrounding skirt. These two concepts are essentially incompatible, which is reflected by the bizarre explanation of this subject who tries to integrate them into one concept. With these three subtractions the form level is lowered from 4.5 to 3.0.

Card III (inverted)

PERFORMANCE	INQUIRY
Strikes me as a person holding his hands up. The red doojiggy in the middle symbolizes his lungs. . . . X rays.	S: It is a grotesque sort of creature, a medicine man of Africa. Hands (pointed to legs of usual men), eyes, (lower center *d*, dark portions), upper part of body, broken off at the waist. I was trying to make something of the whole. Here is someone greeting welcome or salutation. E: Tell me about the lungs. S: These are the lungs (red center *D*). E: What makes them seem like lungs? S: The position in relation to the man. Right in the chest. They fitted into the picture. E: What makes them seem an X ray? S: Either the lungs would have to be painted on the costume, or an X ray. But if an X ray the red color wouldn't show up. Reddish color. Oxidation of blood.

Score: W,S   M,FC   (Hd)   →O—   1.5

COMMENT: There is something rather unsatisfactory about the basic concept of a man with his arms raised for this blot area. The head offers difficulties, and it is necessary to fill in the central white space to provide the body. However, it is a concept frequently enough encountered to suggest that it has a basically accurate match to the blot and should be given a basal rating of 1.5. (Perhaps it is best seen as a conductor of an orchestra with arms raised, black evening suit with white shirt front.) The following credits were added for constructive specifications: 0.5 for the position of the arms; 0.5 for the match of the concept "lungs" to the center red *D* (total now 2.5). The use of color for "lungs" is considered an irrelevant specification since the subject is unable to integrate it well because of the difficulties of position, incompatibility with the concept of X ray, and so on. Credits are subtracted as follows: —0.5 for the "eyes" which are quite out of proportion; —0.5 for the organizational element involved in trying to combine the concept of the human figure and the "lungs." Thus 1.0 is subtracted from 2.5 to give a final form-level rating of 1.5.

Card VIII

PERFORMANCE

I see two animals. Not bears, muskrats. They're not the color of muskrats. They're pink. Makes me think of polar bears. They are slowlike animals anyway.

INQUIRY

S: It is the shape of a muskrat, but polar bears are pink. Just as icebergs are pink. Pink is a frigid color. I think of pink in the Arctic circle.

E: You mean that you think of polar bears as pink?

S: No, they are usually white, but pink is one degree off white.

E: You said they are slowlike.

S: Yes, they are walking, lumbering across the ice.

E: What makes it seem like ice?

S: Ice is a neutral color like this.

Score: D→W   F↔C, FM, C'F   A   P→O   1.0

COMMENT: The basal level is 1.0 for popular animals in motion. Additional credits are given as follows: 0.5 for organization, although this is sufficiently weak that there might be a case for omitting it. No additional credit can be given for precise specifications regarding the movement, for that is included in the popular form level. No credit is given for particular kinds of animal named, for this is not justified in terms of elaborating on the shape. The use of color is so forced and confused that it must be counted as a weakening specification, thus reducing the form level again to 1.0 (Not all forced use of color detracts in the way illustrated here, but at best it is an irrelevant specification.)

For further examples of subtracting credits, refer to pages 216–218 and 223–225.

References

1. Klopfer, B., and Kelley, D. M. *The Rorschach Technique*. Yonkers: World Book Company; 1942.

2. Rapaport, D.; Gill, M.; and Schafer, R. *Diagnostic Psychological Testing*. Chicago: Year Book Publishers; 1945.

CHAPTER 9

Scoring: Tabulation and Use of the Individual Record Blank

The *Individual Record Blank** is a standard and highly convenient form to use when tabulating the information obtained from administering the Rorschach test and preparing the material for quantitative interpretation. The blank consists of six pages, each of which will be discussed below with necessary instructions for filling in the form. (See also pages 638–641.)

Page 1

This page provides self-explanatory blanks for identifying information and for the summary of the appraisal of the personality of the subject.

Page 2: Scoring List

The scoring list enables the examiner to present the scoring symbols in a compact picture, which can easily be scanned. The 10 columns of the scoring list should be filled in as follows:

Column 1: Indicate the number of the card with a Roman numeral, and the number of each of the responses in Arabic numerals. Since no column has been provided for form-level rating, use the extreme left of Column 1. Separate the responses for each card

---

* By Klopfer and Davidson, published by World Book Company.

from those of the next by a horizontal line drawn across all 10 columns.

Column 2:   Record the reaction time at the top of the area used for each card. Beneath it put the position marks opposite the numbers indicating the responses. The position marks are not filled in for every response; one is given for the first response and thereafter for change of position.

Column 3:   Main location score, not more than one per response.

Column 4:   Additional location scores, both the *W* for whole tendencies, additional *S,* and so on, and the locations for additional responses given in the inquiry, rejected responses, and the like.

Column 5:   Main determinant score, only one for each main location score.

Column 6:   Additional determinants, separated by commas if there are several; also determinant scores for additional location scores.

Column 7:   Main content score, one per response.

Column 8:   Additional content scores, including content scores for additional location scores.

Column 9:   Main popular or original scores; many responses will be neither *P* nor *O.*

Column 10:   Tendencies to *P* or *O; P* or *O* scores for additional locations.

Notes

1.   "Tendencies" are indicated with an arrow pointing from the main to the additional column; occasionally the reverse may be indicated when the development of the concept moves from what is scored in the additional column to what is scored in the main column.

2.   Responses that are linked together may be so indicated by bracketing the main scores to the right of the main column. This applies chiefly to location scores, but occasionally also there may be an additional determinant applicable to several main responses and growing out of the organization of them into a loose whole. Similarly, a tendency to an original may be brack-

eted to show that it is the organization that gives the original flavor.

3. Total time should be recorded after the last response of Card X.

4. In the case of minus form-level rating, it is customary to record it not only in the extreme left-hand column with other form-level ratings but also to qualify the determinant with a minus sign (for example, F—, M—, Fc—, CF—).

Page 3:   Tabulation Sheet

This sheet is provided to assist in accurate computation of the quantitative relationships presented on page 4. It is not necessary to use it for brief, simple records, but it is a valuable aid in dealing with long and complicated records. Distinguish the entries in the additional columns from those in the main columns either by circling them, or by using a different colored pencil. The only problem is to distinguish between $F+$, F, and F— in the tabulation. For this purpose $F+$ refers to all form-level ratings of 1.0 or better, and F to ratings of 0.0 and 0.5.

Page 4:   Summary of Quantitative Relationships

The "Psychogram"

Space is provided at the top for a graph showing the distribution of the determinants. Draw a bar graph with unbroken lines for the main scores and dotted lines for the additional scores. If the bar is too high for any one column, indicate it as broken. Units of 1 are usually applicable, but for a long record units of 2 may be necessary. Indicate the units used to the extreme left.

Note the frequencies also, placing the frequency of the main scores at the bottom of the column, and the frequencies of the additional scores at the top preceded by a plus sign.

In the color columns indicate the symbols of the sub-categories preceded by the number of responses so classified—for example, C_{sym}, $F{\leftrightarrow}C$, C/F. Always note the number of minus form-level ratings, if any, in each column. In the M column a note may be made of the content of the responses—such as (H), (Hd), Hd, (A). The average form-level rating for each determinant should also be noted above or below each column.

Various Quantitative Relationships

Total Responses, or R	Fill in the number of main responses given.
Total Time, or T	Expressed in minutes and seconds; the total time for the performance proper.
Average Time per Response, or T/R	Obtained by dividing T by the total number of main responses; expressed in seconds.
Average Reaction Time for Achromatic Cards	Expressed in seconds; rejections are not counted in the calculation.
Average Reaction Time for Chromatic Cards	As above.
F%	Derived by totalling the main F responses, dividing by R, and multiplying by 100.
$\dfrac{FK + F + Fc}{R}$%	Self-explanatory; main responses only are to be used.
A%	Derived by totalling the A and Ad content scores, dividing by R and multiplying by 100.
Number of P	Indicate by stating the number of main populars followed by the number of additionals.
Number of O	Indicate by stating the number of main originals followed by the number of additionals. Indicate the number of $O-$ in each.
(H + A) : (Hd + Ad)	Expressed as a ratio, without reducing the ratio from the totals on each side.
Sum C	Use main responses only. This value gives a weight of 1 to CF, $\frac{1}{2}$ to FC, and $1\frac{1}{2}$ to C.
M : Sum C	Total of main M responses on one side, and the *Sum C* calculated as above on the other. Do not reduce the ratio.
(FM + m) : (Fc + c + C′)	Main responses only; total each side and do not reduce the ratio.
VIII + IX + X%	The number of main responses for the last three cards, divided by R, multiplied by 100. Make a note if the percentage of responses to Card X exceeds 20.

W : M	The number of *W* responses in ratio to the number of *M*'s; use main responses only; do not reduce the ratio.
Succession	Note on the scale the number of systematic successions, placing the notation in accordance with the classification as rigid, orderly, etc. (See pages 314–315 for discussion of succession.)

Estimate of Intellectual Level

1. Check the estimated level of capacity and efficiency.
2. Note the number and average form level of *W*.
3. Note the number and average form level of *M*.
4. Note average unweighted and weighted form level. (See below.)
5. Note number of main and additional *O*'s and any *O*—.
6. Note number of content classifications used outside of *H, Hd, A* and *Ad,* and percentage of responses falling outside these classifications.
7. Note succession.

Manner of Approach

1. Note the percentage of main *W, D, d,* and *Dd* and *S*. Above the blanks left for these percentages, note also the number of responses for each location category and the average form level for that type of location. Above *Dd* and *S* note also the number of main and additional responses for each type of location classified here.
2. In the table below check the level at which each location percentage occurs.

Supplement to Page 4

Form-Level Tabulations

Since the *Individual Record Blank* provides no space for form-level tabulations, it is necessary to supplement the blank with the necessary tabulations and computations to arrive at the figures to be filled in on page 4.

1. The average unweighted form level is obtained by summing

the form-level ratings and dividing by *R*. Only main responses enter into the calculation.

2. The average weighted form-level rating is obtained by multiplying the rating for each 2.5 rating or over by 2, adding the total ratings for the responses under 2.5, and dividing by *R*.
3. Note average (unweighted) form level for chromatic cards and that for achromatic cards.
4. Note differences in form level for heavily shaded cards vs. lightly shaded cards.
5. Find average form level for each determinant category.
6. Find average form level for each location category.

Supplementary Quantitative Relationships

The relationships appearing on page 4 of the *Individual Record Blank* are those traditional in the Rorschach technique. There are, however, certain other relationships which have come to have important interpretative hypotheses attached to them. It is useful to note these in some form supplementary to page 4.

The traditional proportions and percentages listed in the *Record Blank* have been limited to main scores in order to preserve the possibility of comparison of the findings with those of other workers not using additional scores. Such a consideration is not necessary for the newly established proportions which did not exist in the literature before the publication of this system of interpretation.* As a further means of refinement, in all these new proportions, the general principle has been adopted of including all additional scores, giving them a weighting of one-half.

M : FM	Total of main plus additional scores for each, counting each additional as $\frac{1}{2}$. Do not reduce ratio.
M : FM + m	As above.
$\frac{FK + Fc}{F}$	Use both main and additional scores, counting additionals as $\frac{1}{2}$. Leave in the form of a fraction. One-quarter and three-quarters are the critical scores.

* The chief previous publication of this system of interpretation was *The Rorschach Technique* by Klopfer and Kelley.

Achromatic : Chromatic	The Achromatic side of the ratio is found by totalling all the *Fc*, *cF*, *c*, *C'*, *C'F* and *FC'* scores counting additionals as one-half. The Chromatic side of the ratio is found by totalling all the *FC*, *CF* and *C* scores, counting additionals as one-half. This is not the same as Sum *C*.
Differentiated: Undifferentiated Shading	Total all the differentiated shading responses including *FK*, *Fc* and *Fk*, including additionals counted as ½. Compare this with all the undifferentiated shading responses, i.e. *K*, *KF*, *k*, *kF*, *c* and *cF*, counting additionals as ½.
FC : CF + C	Use both main and additional scores, counting additionals as ½, and giving equal weight to *FC*, *CF* and *C*.

Page 5:   Location Chart

See pages 9–10 of this book for instructions for using the location chart. This page is to be filled out during the inquiry.

Page 6:   List of Scoring Symbols

This list is provided for convenient reference.

Pages 2, 3, 4, and 5 of the *Record Blank,* with spaces filled in, are reproduced in connection with the case study given in Chapter 18. See pages 638–641.

Part Two

Interpretation

CHAPTER 10

Quantitative Analysis

Rorschach interpretation is carried out in two major steps, quantitative analysis and sequence analysis, followed by a final step of integrating the findings from these two separate steps in the interpretative process. This present chapter is concerned with quantitative analysis and presents the interpretative hypotheses attached to each of the scoring categories and to the quantitative relationships between them.

The second step in the interpretative process—sequence analysis—depends upon the assumption that the Rorschach performance is an actual sample of the way the individual reacts to his world. The sequence, content, and quality of the responses, and all aspects of the behavior in the test situation, are considered significantly indicative of his reactions to everyday situations. Each response is examined in chronological sequence, both in relationship to the blot material and to the interpretative hypotheses attached to the scoring of the response in question. This is considered an essential step in interpretation, even for the beginner. However, it cannot be treated in any detail until after the interpretative hypotheses of the scoring categories themselves have been dealt with. The process of sequence analysis will be described in Chapter 11. Although, in practice, analysis of content is undertaken simultaneously with sequence analysis, it will be discussed separately in Chapter 13.

The final step in the interpretative process is to bring together those hypotheses that seem applicable to the individual on the grounds of the quantitative analysis of his record with those that have emerged through the sequence and content analysis, retaining those that are confirmed by both analyses and those that are compatible with the total picture, while discarding or modifying others as seems advisable in the light of the integrated picture of the personality that has been built up. Four aspects of this holistic level of interpretation deserve special mention: namely, evaluation of intellectual level, control, creative potential, and the introversive-extratensive relationship. Chapter 12 will be devoted to these evaluations.

This present chapter covers the interpretation of the quantitative summary found on page 4 of the *Individual Record Blank*, together with form-level ratings and certain supplementary proportions for which there is no provision on the *Record Blank* in its present form. (A list of the supplementary proportions is on pages 245–246.) To each of the scoring categories and to many of the quantitative relationships certain interpretative hypotheses are attached, some of which were suggested by Rorschach himself and some of which have emerged through the cumulative experience of later clinicians.

This chapter concerns itself only with the presentation of these interpretative hypotheses and their use in formulating a dynamic picture of the personality functioning of the individual concerned. Questions of the validity of the hypotheses cannot be considered here. The fact that these basic elements of interpretation are termed "hypotheses" is intended to imply that no claim is made for complete or final validity. The Rorschach technique has proved sufficiently useful in clinical work that the clinical examiner seems justified in using this body of interpretative hypotheses pending the conclusion of the extensive investigations that will be necessary to evaluate their relative validity. All of these hypotheses are subject to constant check in clinical use. Experienced psychologists have undoubtedly found some to be more valid than others, though their clinical findings in this respect are rarely reported in the literature. All these hypotheses should be subject to careful scientific investigation, despite the formidable difficulties in validation research with this complex technique (which are discussed in Chapter 14). In this chapter hypotheses that have proved useful in clinical work are presented—with a reminder that their validity has not been firmly established.

In considering the quantitative findings, it is highly important to consider the interrelationships between the various scoring classifications; it is not possible to make a sound interpretation of any point in isolation. Although it is necessary to have hypotheses for each separate scoring category, percentage, and ratio, it is essential that a choice be made between alternative hypotheses and that hypotheses be discarded or modified in the light of the integrated picture that emerges when all the quantitative relationships are viewed in context. This has proved to be one of the chief stumbling-blocks in validation research. Each hypothesis must be investigated; and yet if it is investigated in isolation, the findings are not definitive for the hypotheses as they are actually employed in clinical work. In this chapter the interpretative significance of each scoring category will first be considered separately before proceeding to the important interrelationships between factors. However, since an integrated, holistic view of interpretation is of utmost importance, every effort will be made to cross-reference the various aspects of the findings to assist the examiner to avoid a piecemeal approach.

The interpretation of the quantitative findings will yield a selection of interpretative hypotheses that seem best to fit the particular findings in the individual case. These, by themselves, are of limited value, providing a skeleton or framework only—the "flesh" to be filled in from other sources. Moreover, certain questions are frequently left open since they cannot be decided within the evidence of the quantitative relationships themselves. Two types of check are necessary: (1) the further process of sequence analysis, and (2) as sound an understanding of personality dynamics as is possible in our present state of psychological knowledge. The integration of the findings into some sort of meaningful dynamic picture depends very largely upon the examiner's basic understanding of human personality. Finally, to fill in the "flesh" of the personality in a meaningful way it is highly desirable to consider the Rorschach findings in the context of findings from other psychological tests and case history information. The blind interpretation of the Rorschach protocol without reference to other information may be spectacularly successful when carried out by the highly skilled clinician, but with the less skilled examiner it is likely to be off the mark or at least less useful than it otherwise might be.

Interpretation of the Psychogram

The psychogram shows graphically the frequency of main and additional scores for each of the determinants. The primary basis for interpreting the psychogram consists of the interpretative hypotheses attached to each of the categories of determinants. Overriding this in importance, however, is the body of secondary hypotheses attached to the various interrelationships between the determinant scores, which is summarized in certain of the proportions on page 4 of the *Individual Record Blank,* including the supplementary proportions.

It is logical to deal with each determinant separately in order to present the basic hypotheses before considering the hypotheses attached to the proportions. However, in the interests of perspective, it seems desirable first to refer to the most obvious feature of the psychogram: namely, whether the responses bulk most largely in one area or tend to be distributed over the three main areas of the graph.

If the responses tend to bulk in the left half of the psychogram it indicates that the perception of the subject has been influenced largely by "inner determinants"—movement and use of shading to give vista or depth. These responses have in common the fact that the subject has enriched his perception of the blot with his own imaginal processes, attributing to it something that is not there. Whereas the blots are static and two-dimensional he makes them more lifelike by projecting a kinesthetic element into them or attributing vista or depth to them. The perceiver restructures external reality through his own contribution. The hypothesis is that such a person tends to a relatively great degree of restructuring his world when he perceives it, drawing heavily upon his needs and experience, indeed upon his whole structure of understanding, in doing so. The implication is that he reworks external reality before reacting to it, whether this reworking approaches an enriched understanding of the relationships implicit in reality, at one extreme, or a gross distortion of the facts, at the other extreme.

If the responses tend to bulk in the right half of the psychogram, it means that the perception of the subject has been influenced largely by "outer determinants"—that is, color and the surface use of shading. He is responding freely to all those aspects of external reality that happen to be implicit in the blot material. He is using the "given" as the chief basis of his perception. The hypothesis is that such a person is reactive, tending to respond to external reality as it impinges upon him, with a relative lack of restructuring it in the light of his own needs and experience. Although all perception is the resultant of the properties and organization of the stimulus in interaction with the inner structure of the person, the perceptions that fill up the right half of the psychogram might be said to be relatively stimulus-determined; those that fill the left half are relatively perceiver-determined. The terms *extratensive* and *introversive* are traditionally used in Rorschach work to describe these two major modes of perception; these will be discussed more fully in a later section (see pages 370–375).

If the responses pile up in the center of the psychogram (in the *F* column) this implies that the blots are seen in outline only, and that the perceiver fails both to restructure the material by giving it more lifelike qualities and to utilize to the full the obvious nuances of color and shading that are presented in the stimulus material. This is a limited kind of perception. The hypothesis is that such a person characteristically has a limited view of his world, for any one of a variety of reasons to be discussed later.

A glance at the psychogram will thus give a preliminary notion of the balance between these three modes of perception—whether all three are used in good balance, or whether one or two areas are predominant at the expense of the rest. To fill in the picture it is necessary to consider the determinants and their interrelationships in much greater detail. In the first part of this chapter the interpretative hypotheses that form the basic elements of interpretation will be presented and some reference will be made to interrelationships, although the interpretative hypotheses attached to the ratios, proportions, and percentages will be summarized in the second part of the chapter.

Interpretation of M

In beginning with a consideration of *M* responses, we begin with perhaps the most significant and yet, interpretatively, the most elusive single determinant. Numerous hypotheses are attached to *M* responses, all of which are interlocking, all of which are qualified by other considerations, and which together seem to constitute such an elaborate superstructure of hypotheses that one may feel dismay that they rest on a single process—the perception of human movement in figures seen in the Rorschach ink blots. For a full appreciation of the context in which these interpretative hypotheses should be viewed the reader is referred to Chapter 16, "Rorschach Hypotheses and Ego Psychology."

As a start in understanding the complex body of interpretative hypotheses that has been built up around the *M* response, it should be pointed out that the *M* concept implies three main features: (1) a kinesthetic projection—an enlivening of the blot material by reading into it movement that is not there in fact—which implies an imaginal process; (2) a human concept (or at least one involving human attributes), which implies an ability to see one's world as peopled and consequently to feel empathy with others; and (3) perception at a highly differentiated and usually well-integrated level. All of the interpretative hypotheses stem from one or other of these three features of *M*-perception.

The common condition for all of these features of the typical *M* response is a relatively high level of ego functioning. The imaginal aspect of *M*-production shown in enlivening the blot with movement suggests a relatively free access to fantasy activities, which, within the context of a good tie to reality, indicates a high level of "emotional integration," in which the ego is tolerant of "archaic" or primitive impulses and can freely draw upon these as a source of creative energies.* The empathetic aspect of *M*-production implies a capacity for good object relations, which is both a condition and a result of a high level of emotional integration. Finally, the good tie with external reality, reflected in the high level of differentiation, integration, and accuracy of perception shown in the typical *M* response, in itself suggests a well-developed ego function.

The *M* response thus touches upon all of the most important aspects of the well-functioning personality, bridging the gap between inner resources of drive and fantasy and the outward orientation of reality testing and object relations. Viewed as such, the multiplicity of interpretative hypotheses attached to *M* responses becomes less surprising. Yet the fact that the *M* response taps so many aspects of ego function accounts for the many difficulties found when attempting to apply these interpretative hypotheses to the individual case.

Although it is perhaps most usual for all aspects of ego function to be geared to much the same level, one aspect may be emphasized at the expense of others and this must be taken into account when interpreting the individual record. This can only be done if the *M* responses are viewed in the light of other features of the quantitative findings and are examined in terms of incidence, quality, content, and readiness in the sequence analysis.

M's that are scored as additional rather than main determinants indicate potential resources of imaginative and empathetic capacity upon which the individual is hesitant to draw, usually because of inhibitions resulting from internal conflicts. The implications are that with resolution of the conflicts or relief from strain the personality could better utilize these resources. If few or no *M*'s are given, even as additionals, *M*-capacity may nevertheless be shown through testing of the limits, the readiness of the *M*'s to appear being considered an indication of the degree of availability of the unused resources.

It is suggested that the well-adjusted adult should have three or

---

* For fuller discussion of the concept of "emotional integration" see Chapter 16. For an explanation of the term "archaic," see the Appendix.

more *M*'s, even though he be extratensive, and the adult of superior intellectual capacity or the average introversive adult should have at least five.

Although it is impossible to interpret *M*'s without reference to other determinants, especially *FM*'s and *m*'s, and without consideration of the content, form level and readiness of the concepts involved, the following interpretative hypotheses may be presented as generally attached to the *M* determinant.

Intelligence

HYPOTHESIS: The appearance of *M*'s of good form level is a counterindication of a low intellectual level of capacity, while good quality *M*'s in high number are signs of high intellectual capacity. The implication is that the production of *M* responses is possible only with an individual capable of a fairly high level of differentiation and integration in his perceptual and cognitive functions. (This hypothesis would not apply if the *M*-production were limited to the popular figures in Card III, unelaborated.)

Inability to see *M*'s may be due either to a natural or acquired lack of intellectual differentiation. Therefore, *M* responses are rarely given by young children, feeble-minded subjects, or deteriorated organics. On the other hand, subjects with a high level of intellectual capacity may fail to see *M*'s, the hypothesis being that emotional factors may interfere with the empathy with other people and the utilization of imaginal resources necessary to see live human figures in the blot material.

Imagination

HYPOTHESIS: To the extent to which *M*'s appear in the psychogram, the individual is free to use his imaginal processes to enrich his perception of the world.

Although the basis of this hypothesis is clear, in that the subject is in fact exercising his imagination when he reads movement into a static ink blot, the precise implications of the hypothesis are much more difficult. These difficulties revolve chiefly about the hypotheses of *fantasy* and *creativity,* which reflect the common-sense distinction between imaginative processes as a substitute for dealing with reality and those that are directed towards a reworking of reality towards some creative or constructive end. *M* responses seem to be related to both uses of imaginal processes, and yet the terms fantasy and creativity can be used in certain senses that are not related to *M*'s. The difficulty seems to be that both are blanket terms that have been used to cover a variety of processes, only some of which are related to the production of *M* responses.

The term *fantasy* has been applied to two chief phenomena—"unconscious fantasies," and fantasying as a conscious activity. The psychoanalytic usage of the term usually refers to the "unconscious fantasy"—that is, to inner factors that determine the perceptual response of the individual to a situation. These inner factors are closely related to archaic drives activated by a linkage between some feature of the given perceptual situation and the drive in question, this linkage having been established very early in the subject's life experience and being inaccessible for conscious scrutiny in the ordinary course of affairs. They are thought of as distorting elements in perception, in that the older child or adult is perceiving a situation in terms appropriate to some phase of his early experience that has passed and is no longer strictly applicable. Serious distortion in terms of unconscious fantasy is believed to be reflected by minus form level in conjunction with any determinant and is not specifically linked to *M*-production. The implication is that the perceptual and response tendencies established in infancy and very early childhood have been integrated neither with the more mature aspects of the personality structure nor with external reality, and hence serve to distort perception. Responses with minus form level are, therefore, sometimes described as fantasy-dominated responses, to distinguish them from responses that make an adequate acknowledgment of external reality as represented by the blot structure.

It is believed that *M* responses reflect a more conscious process. Where the *M* responses occur in a record characterized by an inadequate attempt to integrate inner values, impulses, and experiences with the demands and structure of external reality, it is believed that they indicate fantasy activity in the conscious sense—that is, imaginal processes that substitute for dealing with the reality situation. The hypothesis is that wish-fulfilling or escapist fantasy activity is shown by M responses that have a childlike flavor involving A, (A) or (H). The M's of young children are very likely to be of this sort. Indeed, it is often difficult with young children to decide whether to score M or FM for responses attributing to animals action or emotion that, although human-like, is not critically specified as such. The child so automatically attributes human-like feelings to animals that he scarcely could be said to have concepts of animal-like movement as distinct from human-like movement. Adults are more likely to make this distinction, specifying the figures as Walt Disney animals, Alice in Wonderland creatures, or legendary or fairy-tale figures, either spontaneously or in response to inquiry. Where the M responses are predominantly of this type, it is believed that the individual uses his imagination to escape a reality situation by imagining it entirely otherwise rather than by integrating imagination with reality to change the situation in any constructive way.

Finally, while considering the fantasy aspects of M responses, it may be noted that these may have a minus form-level rating, although this is rare. The hypothesis here is that imaginal processes serve to distort reality to such an extent that the ties with reality are seriously loosened. The suggestion is that unconscious determinants of perception are represented in conscious fantasy activity in a manner but thinly disguised; thus in a sense they are accepted by and at least partially integrated with the conscious self or ego but are not integrated with external reality.

Like fantasy, the term *creativity* has been used to cover a variety of processes, of which some seem to be linked to the M response while others are not. It is perhaps because of the failure to specify the particular type of creativity involved that the M-creativity hypothesis has been challenged by research findings. Of these, perhaps the most telling has been the study by Anne Roe [11] which demonstrated that a group of successful painters was not characterized by high M production. There were wide individual differences in the group, some of them having rich production of M's, some producing few or none, with others intermediate between these extremes. It is interesting to observe that all those with rich production of M's were noted for the marked originality of their work. Nevertheless, the studies of Roe and others make it impossible to predict inability to produce works of art from a paucity of M responses. Moreover, it is a commonplace finding that some individuals produce many good M's in response to the Rorschach without showing talent for any kind of artistic achievement.

Many clinicians have attempted to reconcile the difficulty by translating the hypothesis to one of a "creative personality," with implications of a high level of personality integration rather than one of creative output. Schachtel represents this viewpoint when he suggests that "the M responses do not indicate capacity for creative production, but represent a factor in the capacity for creative experience" [12, page 93]. Burchard, in an excellent critical review of the concept of creativity, criticizes this alternative definition, saying: "If we do not know what creative ability is and have no measure for it, the argument that a person may *be* creative but produce nothing of a creative nature has to me rather a metaphysical ring" [5, page 413].

Despite Burchard's well-taken point, the present authors incline towards defining creativity in terms of personality processes rather than output. It would be desirable if an alternative term could be found, but other terms seem to have similar ambiguities. Thus, for example, "constructive" smacks of practical or mechanical ingenuity and "productive" is unfortunately linked to quantity. Creativity, as used in this volume, implies a capacity to integrate archaic impulses or drives within the organization of self and conscious values, and to integrate inner experience with external reality and its demands. This is discussed at greater length in Chapter 12, with reference to "creative potential," and in terms of general rationale in Chapter 16. A brief consideration of the rationale is, however, necessary here in conjunction with the presentation of interpretative hypotheses.

The hypothesis is that M responses of good quality, numbering at least five, involving the perception of real human figures, and in optimal relationship to FM responses, indicate creative potential in that they reflect the ability of the individual to integrate his impulse life with his conscious value system to an extent that the energies stemming from these primitive impulses are available to him, at least to enrich his imaginal processes.

It could scarcely be expected that these energies would be expressed in creative output if the individual did not also have the ability to integrate his inner experience with external reality in terms of mastery—both through the development of appropriate skills or techniques and through an ability to communicate his experience by sharing a common core of reality perception with others. Hence creative output could not be predicted from M responses alone. The creativity indicated by M is a condition for creative output—a necessary but not sufficient condition. Further research is necessary before explicit hypotheses can be advanced except in a very tentative way. However, it seems likely that when good M-production is combined with the ability to produce integrated W responses and good originals in high number—and perhaps especially where there is also an orientation towards the emotional environment expressed by production of FC and CF responses—creative output could be predicted, although this should not necessarily be specified as output in the field of the arts.

It now remains to discuss the "false positives" and "false negatives." By "false positives" reference is made to individuals who produce good M's but are so locked up in themselves that there is nothing resembling creative output. A good example is given by Vorhaus [13] in terms of one of the Rorschach configurations found with children with reading disabilities. This configuration was characterized by good M-production, an optimum $W:M$ ratio, and underproduction of $FM, FC,$ and CF. She suggests:

> These various absences argue that the creative potential (M) is shut off from the outside world. It appears to be merely a private source of richness, neither shared with others nor displayed to them. In this setting, then, M seems to signify the "value system" of the individual, which he must protect from outside intrusion. The suggestion is that the withdrawal of affect that has taken place is a response to a sense of the environment as threatening this value system. [13, page 12]

The "false negatives" refer to individuals, including some in Roe's group of painters, who have output that is recognized as creative in the sense of success in the estimation of others, but who nevertheless fail to produce any adequate number of good M's in their Rorschach responses. The explanation here might be in terms of integration with the outside world being well-developed both in terms of interest and mastery, while the output stems more from intellectual efforts than from deep inner experience. A strong drive for achievement may well meet with success and yet be a compensation for frustration of important basic drives, which are not given much direct or indirect expression in the output itself. This is in contrast to the creative output that itself results from and is an expression of all the energies of the individual, including those from the most primitive layers of the personality. In order to test such an hypothesis it would be necessary to set up external criteria observable somehow in the nature of the output itself. In the extreme cases this should not be difficult. It is quite evident that some output is flavored more by skillful technique, intellectual control, representation of reality, and persistent effort than by any rich imaginative, emotional, and original outpouring. At the other extreme, there are those creative persons who are undoubtedly original, but whose inner primitive energies threaten constantly to get out of control and to overwhelm the personality to the point that it loses touch with reality. The difficulty would be to identify from the output the ideal creative personality, which combines both free access to creative energies and an optimum amount of control.

It is very tentatively suggested that the "false negative" with respect to creative output would be reflected in a Rorschach protocol with great emphasis on W-production, with integrated W's of good form level, and yet an underproduction of M responses. Whether such individuals would direct their output into the arts or into some other field could of course not be predicted.

A word should be added in explanation of the emphasis in the hypothesis relating to creativity, that in order to indicate easily accessible creative potential the M responses should involve the perception of real human figures. It is believed that the intellectual reservations and self-criticism indicated by a stress on *Hd*, *(H)*, and *(Hd)* interfere with the accessibility of creative potential for actual creative output.

It is impossible here to consider all the possible contexts in which *M* responses might appear that would modify the hypothesis of creative potential. Many of them will be self-evident when an attempt is made to bring together the interpretative hypotheses from all aspects of the Rorschach performance of an individual in describing and appraising his personality.

Inner Stability

HYPOTHESIS: The imaginal processes represented by *M* serve as an aid to adjustment by giving stability, in that they represent inner resources upon which the person can fall back in periods of stress, making possible a retreat within himself and hence avoidance of uncontrolled impulsiveness.

All *M*'s of good form level are believed to have this implication, although minus form level itself indicates a breakdown of the control function, an inability to integrate inner experience with reality. Resources implying creativity would obviously contribute to good adjustment to a greater extent than conscious fantasy activity, yet even fantasy can provide a contribution to stability. The readiness of *M*'s to appear, whether the determinant is main or additional, the quality and the content, all contribute to a description of the way in which the inner resources are utilized to give stability in adjustment. Control in terms of available inner resources, or *inner control,* is said to be present if more than five *M*'s are present in an introversive record or more than three in an extratensive record, provided that the form level is good.

A System of Values

HYPOTHESIS: *M* responses indicate an inner system of conscious values of one kind or other, in terms of which the person tends to control his behavior, to guide his satisfactions, and to postpone his gratifications.

In this sense *M*'s in reasonable quantity and of good form quality indicate a long-range orientation, with goals in terms of which the individual can deny immediate satisfactions without feeling too much frustration. The implication is again that a system of conscious values serving such a function is a product of well-developed imaginal activity. How well this value system operates is not shown by the number of M's alone; it is necessary to examine the relationship with other determinants, the quality of the M, its content, readiness, and so on. What the value system is cannot usually be determined from the Rorschach protocol. Clues may sometimes be found through sequence analysis, but usually additional data from other sources are required. It is nevertheless important to ascertain the basis upon which the value system of the individual rests, for this may be crucial in interpreting other aspects of the Rorschach record. For example, sometimes the value system of the individual seems to be built around a drive for achievement, in which case a $W : M$ ratio of 1:1 could not be taken to mean low aspiration level. Sometimes the value system stresses interpersonal or social values. In such cases, emphasis on M with low response to color could not be interpreted as a withdrawal from relationships with other people, although it would imply a lack of emotional dependence on others.

Self-Acceptance

HYPOTHESIS: When M's appear in optimal relationship with FM's and both M and FM are well represented, and where the type of critical tendency implied in (H) and Hd is absent, the individual has achieved an integration between his long-range value system and his impulse life so that both can exist concurrently without undue feelings of guilt or frustration. This implies self-acceptance.

This definition of self-acceptance subsumes much that has been described above: the self-accepting individual is at home with himself, having his creative resources readily available, lacking in any marked inner conflict, and capable of deferring gratifications without feeling frustration—such deferment being in terms of long-range goals and values.

In other terms, M responses may be said to imply a tolerance by the ego for archaic impulses; and optimum balance between M and

FM would indicate how well the ego can not only tolerate but also assimilate these impulses.

Empathy

HYPOTHESIS:　The capacity for seeing human figures in the Rorschach blot materials is related to the capacity for good empathetic relationships with other human beings.

There is considerable empirical evidence that subjects who have had unsatisfactory relationships with both parents tend to be unable to produce *M* responses. Subjects who have had poor relationships with the mother tend to see no adult female figures in the cards, although they may see male figures, or young female figures. Similarly those who have had unsatisfactory relationships with the father tend to lack adult male figures in the Rorschach protocol. Subjects who lack closeness to other people may turn the usual human figures into animals and give *M* responses with (*A*) content. Content with *Hd,* (*H*) or (*Hd*) indicates hostile and critical tendencies, which are believed to obstruct free-flowing empathy and to indicate self-preoccupations that interfere with warm interpersonal relationships.

The Self-Concept

HYPOTHESIS:　Since the quality of the empathy an individual directs towards his social environment tends to reflect his picture of himself, a clue to the self-picture may be found in the quality and content of the *M*.

This hypothesis is more applicable to sequence and content analysis than to the quantitative analysis itself. Note should be made of whether the human figures are seen in vigorous action or in passive posture, and if in action whether this implies hostile and aggressive tendencies or constructive, coöperative relationships. *M* responses with minus form-level rating are considered a sign of defective ego-organization, since here the imaginal responses are directed against reality testing.

Interpretation of FM

Like *M* responses, *FM* responses represent an enlivening of the blot material by the projection of inner resources. *FM* responses differ from *M* responses in two chief respects: (1) they require less intellectual differentiation, and thus may be seen by subjects at all levels of intellectual capacity, provided they are capable of responding to the Rorschach material at all; (2) perception of animal figures does not imply the empathy suggested by the perception of human figures.

HYPOTHESIS: *FM* responses indicate an awareness of impulses to immediate gratification, which, in contrast with the conscious goals represented by the *M* responses, tend to be impulses regarding which the person often lacks insight, understanding, and acceptance. These impulses stem from the most primitive or archaic layers of the personality, either having an instinctual basis or having been acquired very early in the life of the individual—in his pre-verbal years—or both. As such they present a problem of integration to fit them in with the more mature aspects of the personality—the conscious value system and the picture of the self. Therefore, the relationship of *M* to *FM* is highly important for interpretation.

To specify the particular flavor of the impulses represented by *FM* for any one subject is often difficult. Sometimes they have a manifestly hostile and aggressive content; sometimes they are overtly helpless, succorant, and presumably indicate dependency needs. Very frequently it is impossible to specify any particular type of impulse as being characteristic of the subject and presenting a control problem to him. Content analysis of the record as a whole, not merely of the *FM* responses, is often of assistance in rounding out the picture; but as far as the quantitative analysis is concerned, the content of the *FM* is ignored, and the "impulses to immediate gratification" are unspecified.

In general, the hypothesis is that when *FM* are present in any considerable number, impulses to immediate gratification come fairly readily to awareness. This does not mean that they are necessarily accepted by the self, but merely that there is awareness. When a number of the *FM* responses are scored as additionals, either because they did not arise readily or because the movement tended to be considerably restricted, the interpretation is that the individual tends to suppress his more primitive impulses, making a conscious attempt to keep them from awareness. When the subject fails to produce any *FM,* even in connection with the popular animal figures on Card VIII, his readiness to accept *FM* should be explored in the testing of the limits period.

The presence of *FM* in large numbers does not necessarily mean that the individual in fact indulges his impulses to immediate gratification, but rather that he *feels* such impulses whether or not he expresses them in action. A clue to the behavioral expression of these impulses may be found in the *FC : CF* balance. Where *CF* is absent the hypothesis is that the person does not act out the impulses implied in a high *FM* column in the psychogram. Since to feel an impulse without expressing it implies frustration, a high *FM* in the absence of *CF,* and without the optimal relationship to *M* which indicates self-acceptance, indeed seems to indicate frustration. This state of affairs is sufficiently common that some psychologists interpret a high *FM* as a sign of frustration.*

For a more detailed consideration of the interpretation of *FM,* see the discussion of the *M : FM* ratio on pages 288–291.

Interpretation of m

Like *M* and *FM* responses, the *m* response involves projection of movement into the blot material, but here there is a feeling of inanimate or abstract forces rather than the attribution of movement to human or animal figures. The blot is not populated with living figures; it is permeated by the forces of nature or forces of an abstract, spiritual, or mysterious kind.

HYPOTHESIS: The presence of *m*'s in numbers over one or two is a reflection of awareness of forces outside the control of the subject, which threaten the integrity of his personality organization.

These uncontrolled forces frequently come from within the person himself in the form of impulses threatening his value system or

---

* For example, Buhler, C., Buhler, K., and Lefever, D. W. [4] present the hypothesis that *FM* responses represent unsatisfied instinctual needs.

self-picture. In this sense, *m* is said to indicate tension and conflict —conflict between the impulse life and the long-range goals of the individual, and tension due to the effort to inhibit impulse. Thus in many cases *m* seems to indicate a repressive need. On the other hand, *m* may reflect a feeling of helplessness in the face of threatening environmental forces outside his control. In either case *m* is considered to show awareness of a "warning signal"—a warning of forces that threaten the ego-structure either by inundation or by breaking up the integration that is present.

Only when there is a fairly large number of *m* responses present is the awareness of hostile forces considered an indication of serious difficulty in adjustment. The presence of one or two *m*'s is considered a favorable sign for the occupational adjustment, suggesting an attempt to subordinate the impulse life either to long-term goals, to the reality situation, or both. Well-adjusted people tend to produce few *m* responses, presumably having integrated their impulse life with their self-picture and value system and having come to terms with outside threats. However, the absence of *m* in subjects with manifest conflicts is considered a danger sign. Since *m* is believed to indicate awareness of threats or conflicts, the absence of *m* may indicate cessation of struggle towards integration. The presence of *m* in persons with conflicts may indicate unhappy tension, but at least the implication is that the personality is striving to maintain its organization in the face of difficulty.

The relationship of *m* to *M* and *FM* is important for interpretation (see page 291).

Interpretation of K and KF

The rationale of the use of shading is based on the general hypothesis that the way in which the person handles the shading aspects of the blot material is related to the way in which he handles his primary security need and derived needs for affection and belongingness.

When he gives a *K* or *KF* response the person uses shading to give a diffuse, unstructured, but three-dimensional effect to the blot material.

HYPOTHESIS: *K* and *KF* indicate anxiety of a diffuse and free floating nature, reflecting a frustration of affectional satisfactions.

On the one hand, the absence of any specific source of fear or dissatisfaction causes the resultant upset state to be diffuse and unfocussed—that is, free floating. On the other hand, the individual is aware of anxiety and hence has either not yet erected defenses against this anxiety, or the defenses he has built up are an ineffective protection. It is believed that as the person succeeds in defending himself against anxiety feelings, *K* responses tend to disappear. Symptomatic anxiety tends to manifest itself in other ways, especially in the dynamics of handling the chromatic aspects of the blot material.

Since some frustration of affectional need is practically universal and all persons have more or less anxiety from this source, the mere presence of *K* does not indicate anything out of the ordinary. It is only interpreted as a significant amount of anxiety if there are more than three *K* responses or if, generally, the undifferentiated shading responses exceed the differentiated responses (page 291).

Interpretation of FK

When he gives an *FK* response the person is using shading to give the blot material a structured, three-dimensional effect. He sees the material as having depth and perspective with some objects closer to him and others farther away.

HYPOTHESIS: *FK* indicates an attempt by the person to handle his affectional anxiety by introspective efforts, by an attempt to objectify his problem by gaining perspective on it, by putting it at some distance from himself so he can view it more dispassionately.

This is considered a stabilizing influence in that it enables the person to tolerate his own anxiety. *FK* in reasonable numbers are, therefore, signs related to good adjustment, although the balance of *FK* to *F* and *Fc* is to be considered especially (see pages 291–292). Over-production of *FK* indicates a considerable load of affectional anxiety and seems to be characteristic of unhappy worriers.

Although *FK* represents an introspective effort, it is not necessarily a sign of insight. Insight is more likely to be suggested by an optimum relationship of *M* to *FM* and by the quality of self-acceptance implied in good *M* concepts. The absence of *FK* implies neither a lack of insight nor absence of introspection; in the absence of *K* or *k* responses it probably indicates a lack of awareness of affectional anxiety, either because such anxiety is in fact minimal or because the individual has built up mechanisms to defend himself from awareness of anxiety.

Interpretation of k, kF, and Fk

The perceptual activity of the person in giving a *k* response is somewhat similar to that of an *FK* response. He attempts to use the shading to put three dimensions into the material, but this effort falls short of success in that the three dimensions are merely suggested in a two-dimensional plane. The X ray and the topographical map remain flat, although there is an intellectual suggestion of three dimensions. The subject gets away from the formless diffusion of the *K* response without achieving the structured three-dimensional effect of the *FK* response.

HYPOTHESIS: *k* indicates affectional anxiety behind a good front of outward control and is found with subjects who cover up their anxiety with an intellectual cloak.

Fk often appears associated with "phony insight" shown by individuals who are trying unsuccessfully to handle their anxiety by intellectual means, but who have not the kind of emotional insight that enables them to deal effectively with their problems. Such a person can explain exactly what is wrong with him or attempt such an explanation in intellectual terms and yet be unable to help himself through this intellectual appreciation of the problem. *Fk* has also been found with extremely busy people of the executive type; the implication is that compulsive work may constitute a defense to prevent an awareness of affectional anxiety from breaking through.

Interpretation of F

Responses are scored *F* when the subject has utilized only the shape of the blot material in forming his concept, neither availing himself of the chromatic or shading elements presented to him nor enlivening the material by projecting movement into it as a function of his own imaginal processes.

HYPOTHESIS: *F* represents a limited or impoverished type of perception, stripped both of the emotional and affectional nuances implied by the color and shading elements and of the imaginal enrichment which the individual himself might have contributed.

This hypothesis is subject to extension and modification in the light of the place of *F* responses in the bulk of the total psychogram. If *F* responses occur in reasonable numbers with ready use of shading, color, and movement in other responses, the *F* responses themselves do not indicate a generally limited or impoverished view of the world; they indicate that the person is on occasion capable of handling situations in an impersonal and matter-of-fact way, stripped of personal implications. When *F* responses predominate at the expense of color and surface shading responses, but movement (and perhaps three-dimensional shading) responses appear freely, the limitation or restriction seems to apply to a relative insensitivity to the emotional impact of the outer world, while the person remains aware of his inner values, needs, and impulses. If *F* responses predominate at the expense of movement responses, but color (and perhaps surface shading) responses appear freely, there is restriction or impoverishment in the sense of lack of awareness of inner impulses, while the person remains emotionally reactive to the impact of environmental influences. It is only when both "inner" and "outer" determinants are sacrificed to *F* responses that an interpretation of generalized *constriction* is applicable.

Further than this it is impossible to go without considering the relationship of *F* to the other scoring classifications, particularly *M*, *FC*, *Fc*, and *FK*, and form-level rating, and the percentage of *F* responses in the total record.

Interpretation of c

As with the other shading responses, the interpretation of *c* responses relates to the handling of affectional need and to the basic expectation of affection to be received from the outside world. The presence or absence of texture responses and the degree of differentiation involved (*c* vs. *cF* vs. *Fc*) is believed to relate to the degree of awareness and differentiation of the person's needs for affection and dependency. Crude *c* responses are those in which the person seems overwhelmed by the tactual implications of the shading, responding to the shading cards in a mechanical way with undifferentiated texture responses, usually with a concept implying softness and furriness.

HYPOTHESIS: *c* indicates an infantile, undifferentiated, crude need for affection of an essentially physical contact variety.

Crude *c* responses are not found within the "normal range." They are usually found only with patients having serious organic brain damage. The *c* response implies not only an insatiable affectional need, but also a personality so undifferentiated as to be unable to find satisfaction in any interpersonal relationships save those involving the most infantile sort of creature-contact.

Interpretation of cF

Like *c* responses, *cF* responses emphasize the tactual implications of the shading without differentiation either in terms of the shading itself or through using the shading in a context of definite form. They may appear in a record otherwise notable for its immaturity of outlook and control; they occasionally appear in a record that otherwise is highly differentiated and well-controlled.

HYPOTHESIS: *cF* responses represent a relatively crude continuation of an early need for closeness, a need to be held and fondled and a longing for an infantile sort of dependence on others.

This condition may have arisen because there was a serious frustration of affectional need in early childhood, the need having remained an open problem because it has never been satisfied adequately. However, the absence of *cF* does not indicate absence of serious frustration, for some subjects known to have suffered marked deprivation in early mother-child relationships may give no *c, cF,* or *Fc* responses at all. This may mean either that the affectional need has withered away through deprivation and that there is a seriously impaired capacity for affectional relationships, or that deprivation has caused such anxiety that the person must protect himself from recognizing his need for affectional security through a denial mechanism or repression. Sequence analysis and testing of the limits are necessary to throw light on the dynamics underlying absence of texture responses (see pages 346–347).

The presence of *cF* does not necessarily imply an overt manifestation of a childlike seeking for contact; it may merely mean the presence of a craving, an awareness of need. The likelihood of overt expression of this need may be assessed in the light of evidence of controlling factors. Reluctance to accept the contact need is likely when it emerges only in additional scores; control may be shown by subordinating the texture response to some other determinant, or making it part of a well-structured whole. Even where main *cF* responses are scored, control may still be implied by the whole balance of the psychogram and the maintenance of good form level throughout the record. In assessing the capacity of the individual for mature affectional relationships the balance of *cF* to *Fc* is important.

The term "sensuousness" has often been used in connection with *cF*. It has not been introduced into the primary statement of the hypothesis since it tends to mask the essential affectional and dependency implications of *cF*. However, an infantile craving for contact may express itself through sexual relationships.

The content of *cF* should also be taken into account in interpretation. Soft, furry concepts seem to imply greater expectancy of satisfaction than cold, hard, or dysphoric concepts like "snow," "ice," "a piece of rotting wood," "a piece of soggy bread."

Interpretation of Fc

Fc responses, like *cF* responses, reflect an interest in the tactual, textural qualities of the blot material, but an ability to use these aspects in a differentiated way, either in terms of fine differentiations in the perception of the shading or by integrating the texture with definite form. Following the general hypothesis that the use of texture is an expression of awareness of affectional need, the *Fc* response suggests that the infantile craving for contact has been differentiated and refined into a more controlled manifestation.

HYPOTHESIS: *Fc* responses indicate an awareness of and acceptance of affectional needs experienced in terms of desire for approval, belongingness, and response from others, retaining a passive recipient flavor but refined beyond a craving for actual physical contact. It is believed that this is a development essential for the establishment of deep and meaningful object relations and that it occurs only where the basic security needs have been reasonably well satisfied.

The precise interpretation of *Fc* in the individual psychogram depends both upon the qualitative flavor of the texture response itself and upon the relationship of *Fc* to the rest of the psychogram, particularly to *F*. In general, an optimal number of *Fc* in relationship to the rest of the psychogram indicates acceptance of the need for affectional security in terms of awareness of a definite need to relate oneself to other people, to feel part of a group and to belong to it with a sense of acceptance and approval. Immediate gratification is not the goal as it might be with mere sensuousness of the *cF* variety; sensitivity to approval appears instead. The sensitivity reflected by *Fc* betrays its recipient origins in that it is sensitivity to others because of need to receive affection from others. This may mean either sensitivity in the sense of easily hurt feelings, or awareness of any cloud in the emotional atmosphere; or it may imply a tactful awareness of the needs and feelings of other people. The better the control system reflected by the rest of the psychogram, the more likely it is that *Fc* is associated with a tactful sensitivity.

An overdeveloped *Fc* column in the psychogram is believed to indicate that affectional need plays a disproportionate role in adjustment, suggesting either an overdependence on the affection of others or a need for response from too many other people, or both.

The hypothesis is that lack of *Fc* does not imply lack of affectional need but rather lack of acceptance or awareness of it. It is believed that the conditions under which human beings are reared make inevitable the development of a need for affection and security derived from the support of others, whether this need is felt or not. Therefore, the apparent absence of such a need may be interpreted as denial, reluctance to accept it, or as **inability** to feel such a need at all. Just which interpretation is applicable can only be ascertained by sequence analysis and testing of the limits (see pages 344–348).

Both *Fc* and *M* may have implications that the person is capable of empathy in his relationships with other people. However, the empathy indicated by good *M*'s and that shown by good *Fc*'s can be differentiated in terms of the relative presence or absence of recipient flavor. An individual with a well-developed *M* column and little *Fc* in his psychogram may be one with sufficient imaginal capacity and self-acceptance to be able to put himself in the other person's place and see the world through his eyes and yet be little motivated by the need for belongingness and approval, either because his affectional needs have been well satisfied or because of some denial. The empathy indicated by *Fc* retains a recipient flavor.

Different *Fc* concepts are interpreted somewhat differently. Differentiated responses that emphasize soft furriness seem close to *cF* and suggest a contact need, well under control, with some intellectual understanding. Concepts of hard surfaces have a flavor of somewhat more deprivation than those of soft surfaces, but the differentiation in *Fc* implies awareness, intellectual understanding, and control. The more removed the *Fc* concept from concrete and gross textural or contact qualities, the more implication there is of an intellectualization of affectional need—for example, with concepts of differentiated patterns, modelling, carving, and transparency.

An *Fc* score derived from the use of shading as a photographic representation of bright colors involves less acceptance of the need for affection than do concepts closer to touch qualities. In such a case the hypothesis of "abortive sublimation" applies; here the affectional need is likely to be translated into an illusory positive motivation, while the real motive is repressed or projected onto other people. Thus a person may believe he is strongly motivated to sacrifice himself to the service of other people, whereas in fact he demands an affectional response from them. Such a person does not recognize the essentially recipient basis of his own desire to help others; indeed, his helpfulness tends to be limited by his own demands for satisfaction.

Fc— responses indicate a serious distortion of perception caused by a strong affectional need which is badly integrated within the total personality.

Interpretation of C′, C′F, and FC′

The hypotheses attached to *C′* responses are less adequately developed than for any other determinant category. Generally, the use of shading as achromatic color is to be interpreted as a toned-down response to color.

If *C′* responses appear in records that are full of color responses to chromatic areas, this seems to be a simple extension of receptivity to color, implying a rich and variegated reaction to all kinds of stimuli presented in the blot material. Such responsiveness seems characteristic of the artistically impressionable person. However, where *C′* occurs with meager use of chromatic color, it seems to indicate a responsiveness to stimuli from the outer world which can only be expressed in a toned-down, hesitant way. The implication is that responsiveness to outside stimulation has been interfered with by some kind of traumatic experience, resulting in withdrawal. This is known as the "burnt child" reaction. This interpretation is only applicable if the total achromatic responses, including texture responses, outnumber the total chromatic responses two to one (see pages 292–293) .

It has sometimes been suggested that *C′* responses indicate feelings of depression; this may be so when color responses tend to be absent and the content or verbalization of the *C′* responses has a dysphoric flavor. However, this interpretation does not hold when the *C′* responses have a euphoric flavor, which is usually the case in a record where color is used with fair readiness.

General Comments on the Interpretation of Color Responses

Our whole familiarity with pictures, drawings, and diagrams tends to give a set towards distinguishing figures and objects in terms of shape and outline. The appearance of color in the second blot and its reappearance in four subsequent blots presents a problem to the subject. The color is not immediately easy to integrate with form, as is the case with colored photographs and most paintings. The subject's attention is not drawn to color by the examiner; the task does not specifically include dealing with it; he is left free to use it or not as he chooses.

To integrate the color within the framework of the task presents a challenge to many subjects; this is shown by their varying modes of response. Some are drawn to it but are quite unable to "interpret" it and fall back on color naming or description. Others bemoan the fact that they cannot work it in. Others put forth considerable effort to achieve an integration. Still others seem carried away by the color and give concepts determined by color rather than by shape. Some avoid the challenge by avoiding the colored areas as much as they can. A few do not seem challenged. Some take the problem in their stride and skillfully and effortlessly combine color and form. Others completely ignore color and go ahead as though the blots were all achromatic.

Because of this great variation in responses to the chromatic elements in the Rorschach materials, the general hypothesis has been formed that the way in which the subject handles color gives an indication of his mode of reacting to an emotional challenge from his environment which taxes his skill in integrating an outside influence with his activity-in-progress. In one wording or another this is one of the most basic hypotheses of the Rorschach technique. Furthermore, it is generally taken that the chief kinds of emotional challenge met by an individual will be in interpersonal relationships; therefore, the responses to color are to be interpreted to show how the person reacts to the emotional impact of relationships with other people.

Throughout the history of the Rorschach technique considerable attention has been given to the disturbance caused to some subjects by the chromatic elements, this disturbance frequently being called "color shock." Recent studies [1, 2, 8, 9, 10] which set out to test the validity of the concept of "color shock" have demonstrated that (except for the absence of color-determined responses themselves) the responses of a group of subjects to a totally achromatic series of blots are not significantly different from their responses to the usual Rorschach series with five chromatic blots. These studies may well cast some doubt upon the "signs" of color shock used in a statistically diagnostic way. They also, on first consideration, seem to deal a death-blow to the basic hypothesis that color represents an emotional challenge to the subject and to all the secondary hypotheses dealing with the significance of color-determined responses.

Clinicians experienced with the Rorschach tend to brush aside the findings of these studies, since their clinical experiences have convinced them of the general usefulness of the hypotheses attached to the color responses. Moreover, at least one of these hypotheses has been supported by experimental validation [3, 14]: namely, that pertaining to the $FC : (CF+C)$ ratio.

This impasse is perhaps best met by an acknowledgment that the basic color hypothesis need not attach any mystical significance to color as such. Color may be viewed as a striking element presented in the materials, which presents a challenge to the subject in integrating it with form—an interpretation based on form being the implicit understanding of the task. In the absence of color, and indeed simultaneously with the colored elements when they are present, there are other aspects of the blot material that present a similar challenge. One of these is shading (which seems less striking than color to most subjects, although even more striking to others) and another is the extent to which the formal structural qualities of the blot themselves provide a challenge to the differentiating and integrating abilities of the subject. It is not safe to assume that it is color that necessarily causes all disturbances that occur on the chromatic cards. The disturbing feature may be shading, or the formal features of the blot, or indeed it may be some disturbing concept suggested by the particular blot. It is one of the tasks of sequence analysis to investigate causes of disturbance through a study of the whole record in sequence and its relationship to the blot material.

It seems to have been a mechanical use of the "signs" of color shock that has been challenged by the studies of achromatic series. The secondary hypotheses attached to the color-determined responses were specifically excluded from consideration in these studies. The basic color hypothesis stated as above does not seem to be affected by the findings.

To expand the basic hypothesis: the ways in which color is handled in responding to the blots are believed to cast light upon the overt emotional reactions of the subject to the impact of his social environment. In responding to both color and shading the subject is not only interested in the formal outline of the blot reality but also in how that reality is filled in. He responds emotionally to his perceived world. He is in interaction with his surroundings rather than isolated or insulated from them. But, whereas the shading responses are believed to be related to the organization of the affectional need within the personality on the basis of a rationale relating tactual interest to affectional need, the color responses are believed to indicate how the person actually meets an emotional challenge in a behavioral sense.

An examination of the way in which the subject responds to color is traditionally one of the most important features of Rorschach interpretation. Not only are the color responses themselves of interest, but also the particular areas responded to, the sequence of responses, the areas not responded to with color responses and the particular methods of avoiding use of color. These features of interpretation are an important part of sequence analysis and will not be discussed here. The following discussion is limited to the implications of each of the various scoring categories insofar as they can be considered in isolation.

Interpretation of FC

In producing an *FC* response the subject accepts the challenge of integrating the color into a concept of definite form. It is of interest to ascertain how successful this integration is and with what effort it is achieved. The various *FC* scorings reflect these points, and have separate interpretative hypotheses attached to them.

Natural FC Combinations

The *FC* response represents a successful integration of color within a context of definite form, the form level being at least 1.0

and the integration being a "natural" one implying a relative effort-lessness.

HYPOTHESIS: *FC* responses indicate a ready control over emotional impact without loss of responsiveness. This controlled responsiveness implies that the person can respond with both feeling and action appropriate to the emotional demands of the situation.

The appearance of *FC* responses in any considerable number suggests that the person is able to make a pleasant, gracious, and charming response to social situations and to get along smoothly with other people. There is an implication of dependence on other people when *FC* responses are emphasized. It must be important to maintain good relationships with other people for the subject to place so much stress on meeting emotional demands in a graceful manner.

When *FC* responses are the only color responses and are given only as additional responses in the inquiry, somewhat less responsiveness to emotional impact is suggested—the implication being that under the first impact the person tends to withdraw and it is only when he feels more at ease in the situation that his controlled responsiveness begins to emerge. When *FC*'s are scored as additionals to another main determinant, it would seem that the person is capable of controlled responsiveness but is less dependent upon other people than the person who emphasizes *FC* as a main determinant. When *FC* responses are absent there should be an exploration of *FC* capacity in the testing of the limits period; it is of interest to note how readily they can be produced or accepted, and whether natural *FC*'s are given or whether there are tendencies to forced or arbitrary combinations.

The relationship of *FC* to *CF* is an important indicator of control, in this case control over overt expression of emotionality. Preponderance of *CF* over *FC* indicates that emotional reactions tend to be expressed in an uncontrolled fashion. Preponderance of *FC* over *CF* indicates control; this may indeed indicate over-control where *CF* responses are absent or nearly so. Nevertheless, *FC* has been found to be one of the most dependable signs of good adjustment. (For further discussion see pages 296–297.)

Forced FC Combinations, or F↔C

Forced *FC* responses are successful to a degree; they achieve a satisfactory form level, but they do not represent a completely successful integration of color and form since the criterion of a natural combination is not met. The subject seems so struck by the color that he cannot ignore it, even when the form and color do not fit together in any natural way (as, for example, with the "pink animals" on Card VIII). He feels he must resort to some kind of explanation, sometimes ingenious, sometimes labored, to reconcile the incongruity.

HYPOTHESIS: Forced *FC* combinations reflect an effortful emotional responsiveness, in contrast to the smooth responsiveness indicated by the natural *FC* combination. The effort involved implies a certain tension in social relationships, and the unnaturalness of the combination suggests a relative lack of success in maintaining smooth relationships and acquiring easy social techniques.

The responsiveness to emotional impact is emphasized by the very fact that the subject feels it so necessary to work the color into his concept and insists on doing so even though it is difficult. Such a person feels he must involve himself emotionally; he also feels it important to maintain his equilibrium and control. He does not withdraw from interaction with people just because it is difficult to cope with the emotional situations that arise. His very efforts to meet these demands indicate that he is not overwhelmingly preoccupied with his own ego prestige.

Arbitrary FC Combinations, or F/C

In producing *F/C* responses the subject goes through the motions of using color; he forms a concept using color, but one in which the particular color presented in the blot material has no essential relatedness to the concept.

HYPOTHESIS: *F/C* combinations indicate that the subject responds to emotional impact in a superficial, behavioral way that bears no essential relatedness to his own feelings. He responds in terms of what he feels is demanded by the situation, without a true integration of his own response with the reality demands.

This pattern may be found with the person with conventional good manners who lacks the real emotional "feel" of the social situation. In some instances this seems to be a neurotic evasion of the emotional implications of social relationships. *F/C* minus responses sometimes occur with psychotics who think they are behaving normally. If only one *F/C* response is given, and that to Card VIII, the above hypotheses do not necessarily apply, since Card VIII seems especially to facilitate such a response.

FC minus Responses

In the *FC minus* response the subject attempts to integrate color with definite form. He succeeds in integrating the color with an appropriate concept, but his concept does not match the form of the blot.

HYPOTHESIS: An *FC—* response indicates a breakdown in emotional control. It reflects an unsuccessful effort to control emotionality, but an effort nevertheless.

This is not uncommon with children and is of no serious significance. With adults considerable disturbance is indicated, although this may still occur within the normal range of difficulties.

Interpretation of CF

In producing a *CF* response the subject does not attempt to integrate color with definite form. The color is the most striking aspect of the blot area concerned; he lets color determine his response, quite losing sight of his usual objective of identifying objects of definite form, if indeed he had felt this to be a goal.

HYPOTHESIS: *CF* combinations represent an uncontrolled reactivity to environmental impact.

The particular significance of the loss of control varies according to the particular type of color-form combinations produced and to the relationships of *CF* responses to the rest of the psychogram, particularly *C* and *FC*.

Natural CF Combinations

In producing a natural *CF* response the subject is influenced primarily by color rather than by form; if it were not for the color the concept would probably not have been given. It is the color that makes the top detail in Card II look like blood, or the bottom pink detail in Card VIII look like strawberry ice cream. It is as effortless a yielding to the chromatic impact of the blot material as the natural *FC* response is an effortless integration of the chromatic element within a context of definite form. Yet the subject is not totally swept away by the color; an appropriate integration with the form of the blot is not lost, for an indefinite concept is attached to a blot area of sufficiently indefinite shape to be a reasonable match.

HYPOTHESIS: The natural *CF* combination indicates a somewhat uncontrolled but appropriate and genuine emotional response to the reality demands of the social situation.

The natural *CF* combination thus has both positive and negative implications: positively, it may be viewed as indicating spontaneity, while negatively it may be taken as an indication of inadequate control of emotional responsiveness. Again on the positive side, to the extent that *CF* responses appear the individual is capable of acting out his emotional reactions without too tight a control. Yet it is obvious that a certain degree of control is desirable, and *CF* responses may indicate too loose a rein on emotional reactivity. Whether emphasis is to be given to the positive or negative implications of *CF* is to be judged from the rest of the record and particularly from the *FC*: (*CF* + *C*) balance (see page 296) . If *CF* responses occur in the context of the controlled responsiveness indicated by a preponderance of *FC*, the implication is that the person, though usually controlled, is capable of deep and genuine emotional response appropriate in intensity to the strength of the impact. Even though *CF* may outnumber *FC*, there may still be an adequate basis of control elsewhere in the record—that is, through *M, FK,* and *Fc.* In this case *CF* responses would indicate a healthy spontaneity within a context of good control. If *CF* responses occur in a psychogram without signs of adequate control, the implication is that there is an impulsive, uncontrolled acting out of emotional reactions. This is to be expected with young children; with adults it is a sign of emotional immaturity. If *CF* are outnumbered by *FC* the child is believed to be overtrained.

Loss of emotional control does not necessarily imply uncontrolled aggression. The content of both the *CF* responses and the *M* and *FM* responses must be taken into account. Uncontrolled expression of aggression might be expected where the content of the protocol is frequently aggressive and *CF* predominates on the color side. On the other hand, aggressive *CF* responses (explosions, fire, blood, and the like) are very frequently given in the context of a larger whole response, indicating a strong reaction with some control and implying an active mode of adjustment, probably with submerged aggression rather than uncontrolled expression thereof. Passive *CF* responses (flowers, ice cream, and so on), especially in a protocol that lacks other aggressive content, cannot be interpreted as uncontrolled expression of aggression. On the contrary, a preponderance of such *CF* responses seems to indicate a passively reactive personality that tends to be "pushed around" by the conflicting emotional demands of social situations.

If only additional *CF* appear in the psychogram, responsiveness is indicated which the person is hesitant to express outwardly. Absence of *CF* (with simultaneous absence of *C* responses and at least a popular form-level rating) implies lack of emotional interaction with the environment, either because of overly tight control or because of lack of responsiveness. The way color is handled in the testing-the-limits period may cast further light upon the readiness of the person to respond to emotional impact and upon reasons for hesitation in emotional expression.

Forced CF Combinations, or C↔F

Like the *F↔C* response, the *C↔F* response is effortful; but whereas with the *F↔C* response the subject finds it difficult to achieve a natural, smooth integration of color with definite form, in the *C↔F* response the subject finds it difficult to yield to color and give a spontaneous color-determined response. He labors his reactivity to the chromatic impact of the blot material.

HYPOTHESIS: Forced *CF* responses, like $F \leftrightarrow C$ responses, are a sign of an effortful or forced emotional responsiveness. The difference is in the amount of control involved, the $C \leftrightarrow F$ response implying even less success than the $F \leftrightarrow C$ response in maintaining smooth social relationships. The individual feels he must involve himself emotionally, although he is unable to do so while still retaining control.

Arbitrary CF Combinations, or C/F

In producing *C/F* combinations, as with *F/C* combinations, the subject seems to be going through the motions of using color without any essential relatedness between the concept and the particular color presented in the blot material.

HYPOTHESIS: Like *F/C* combinations, *C/F* responses indicate that the subject responds to emotional impact in a superficial, behavioral way that bears no essential relatedness to his own feelings. The difference is in the amount of control involved. Whereas the *F/C* response suggests a superficial, social-veneer type of control, the *C/F* response implies superficiality without successful control. The person seems to need to do something about the emotional demands of social situations but is incapable of a genuine emotional response related to the reality demands of these situations, perhaps because he is too wrapped up in his own problems.

CF Minus Responses

In the *CF minus* response the subject is so struck by the color of the blot that he gives an indefinite color-determined response that is quite inappropriate to the definite shape of the blot area. The color is used appropriately, but there is no effort to reconcile the concept with the form of the blot.

HYPOTHESIS: Like *FC—* responses, *CF—* responses indicate a breakdown of control. They differ in that the latter carry no implication of effort to control. Breakdown of both control and effort is implied and the individual is carried away by emotional excitability to an extent that is irrationally impulsive.

Interpretation of C Responses

As with *CF* responses, in producing *C* responses the subject lets color determine his response. But whereas the *CF* response is at least appropriate in form to the indefinite areas of the blot material, the *C* response is completely color-determined and form considerations go altogether by the boards. Each *C* scoring category represents a different way of handling the color. It is extremely important that the scoring differentiate accurately between the various subdivisions, for they carry with them interpretative hypotheses that differ markedly one from the other.

Pure C, or Crude C

Crude *C* is scored only for a mechanically repeated use of color without any implication of form.

HYPOTHESIS: Crude *C* responses are indicators of a pathological 36 lack of emotional control, emotionality of an explosive, hair-trigger variety. Except in the case of very young children, it is rarely found except with deteriorated organics and hence is considered a pathognomic clue.

Color Naming, or Cₙ

A score of color naming requires generally that naming the colors constitutes the only response to the particular blot in question. The subject acknowledges the color, but he does not integrate it either with form or with meaning. In fact he does nothing with the colors but identify them. This may be a proud accomplishment for the pre-school child but is scarcely an adequate response for an adult.

HYPOTHESIS: The person who names colors is overwhelmed by 37 emotional impact and incapable of handling his reaction with integrated control; nevertheless, he strives to control the situation without coming into real contact with it.

This represents a "magic" way of dealing with an emotional situation, which is essentially ineffectual. The outside world is threatening, the person is powerless to manipulate it, he is compelled to respond emotionally to it; he tries to resolve the intolerable situation by a superficial mode of handling it which gives him the illusion of having dealt with the situation. It is not an uncommon response with young children. However, with adults, C_n tends to be pathological, occurring in feeble-minded or psychotic patients, although it sometimes occurs with disturbed individuals who are not so classifiable. The precise interpretation is supported by examination of the sequence of responses, with particular emphasis on recoverability—that is, following the color naming response with a concept with adequate form level.

Color Description, or C_{des}

Although at first glance color description may seem very similar to color naming, it is a higher-level response. The similarity lies in the fact that the subject does not *do* anything with the color; he does not integrate it either with the form of the blot or into a meaningful concept. The difference lies in the fact that the subject almost invariably shows himself capable of handling the blot material in some other way. This may be all he is capable of doing with color, but it does not mean his perception of the structural qualities of the blot is disrupted. He acknowledges color; he usually cannot integrate it with his concepts, but he produces other concepts. Moreover, his very description seems to be a way of dealing with the color in an intellectual way; he shows that he appreciates it, but holds it off at arm's length.

HYPOTHESIS: Color description responses indicate that the subject is so strongly moved by emotional impact that control is difficult but that he is successful in outward control of emotionality. He is able to control his overt expression, perhaps even to the point of seeming inhibited and reserved. Underneath the controlled exterior, however, there is deep emotionality. The C_{des} person controls by not showing how he feels; in contrast the highly constricted person (with high $F\%$) controls by not feeling.

Color Symbolism, or C_{sym}

In producing a C_{sym} response the subject gives the color meaning, finding an appropriate concept, but fails to integrate color with the form of the blot. In selecting a formless symbolic concept he evades the task of matching his concept to the form of the blot area. At the same time he has the satisfaction of having achieved an intellectual type of performance. A similar intellectualization seems to be involved with FC_{sym} and CF_{sym} responses, although here there is also some regard for the form of the blot (especially in the case of FC_{sym} where there is integration of color with definite form as well as the attachment of symbolic meaning) .

HYPOTHESIS: Like C_{des} responses, C_{sym} responses indicate that the subject is so strongly moved by emotional impact that control is difficult but that he is successful in outward control. There is more intellectual and theoretical flavor to the control effort with C_{sym} than with C_{des}. Similar hypotheses attach to CF_{sym} and FC_{sym}, although FC_{sym} particularly seems to imply a somewhat smoother control— probably because the underlying reactivity is not so strong. The content of symbolic responses is of particular interest for interpretation in the course of sequence analysis, together with the way the symbolic concept is woven into any larger conceptual framework; particular attention is paid to any bizarre flavor it may have.

Interpretation of the Quantitative Proportions

Up to this point the motivational and emotional aspects of personality have been considered only with reference to the determinants considered separately, with relatively little attention to interrelations between the personality characteristics to which they point. The description of the personality as an organized and functioning whole can only be worked out after sequence analysis; nevertheless, an examination of the various quantitative proportions may give some leads to understanding how the motivational and emotional aspects of personality are organized. The structural considerations provided by the quantitative data may form the framework for the qualitative interpretation of the sequence analysis. The content aspect of the sequence analysis particularly is likely to lead to a distorted picture if not firmly anchored in the quantitative findings. Responses with a disturbed and anxious flavor may be taken as indices of less serious disturbance in a subject with a basically well-balanced personality organization than when in a context of a personality with tenuous control. Similarly, innocuous sounding responses may emerge as ominous if it is found that when classified into scoring categories they portray a basically unsound structure. This section presents the basic interpretative hypotheses attached to the various quantitative proportions set forth on page 4 of the *Individual Record Blank* and certain supplementary proportions related to personality organization.

Proportions Relating to Inner Resources and Impulse Life

None of the following ratios may be interpreted unless there are at least three *M* responses.

Ratio of M : FM

1. FM>2M

HYPOTHESIS: Where there are more than twice as many *FM* as *M* responses the individual is ruled by immediate needs for gratification rather than by long-range goals.

This is the expected picture with children, who tend to act on impulse without inhibition and who have little capacity for postponement. An immature behavioral impulsivity cannot be inferred, however, unless *CF* also exceeds *FC,* implying that the individual tends to act out his impulses without socialized restraint. In such a case one might say that the "pleasure principle" prevails in action. Where there are twice as many *FM* as *M,* but there is no color emphasis, and especially if there is not *CF* dominance, it cannot be said that the person tends to act impulsively. There is preoccupation with egocentric needs but these are not overtly manifested in impulsive behavior. The possibility of the formation of psychosomatic or neurotic symptoms suggests itself, but this cannot be confirmed nor can the type of symptom formation be ascertained from the quantitative analysis. The sequence and content analysis may give some clues to these problems, but in many instances other sources of information are necessary to round out the picture.

2. M>FM

HYPOTHESIS: Where *M* exceeds *FM* the impulse life is subordi- 41
nated to the value system of the individual.

Provided that this tendency is not exaggerated a healthy state is
indicated. Thus in cases where *FM* is not less than one-half of *M*
there seems to be an optimum relationship between acknowledgment
of impulse life and integration with the value system. In other words,
the ego is able to tolerate archaic impulses without being overwhelmed by them. Such an individual is expected to possess self-
acceptance and the capacity to defer gratification without undue
frustration, conflict, or inhibition. However, when *FM* is less than
half of *M*, and particularly where *FM* responses tend to disappear
altogether, the hypothesis is that the impulse life is suppressed in the
interests of the conscious values rather than integrated with it. There 42
are implications of tension and inner conflict, excessive control, and
lack of spontaneity. This is particularly serious if *FM* seems to be
replaced by *m*.

3.   M=FM

HYPOTHESIS: Where *M* is approximately equal to *FM* and both 43
are reasonably well-represented, the impulse life is not in conflict
with the value system; the impulse life has neither interfered with
the development of the value system, nor vice versa.

This may indicate mature spontaneity in an individual who has
a well-developed value system which gives him control, but who
within the framework of this control has an easy acceptance of his
own impulses, an easy, happy self-picture. Such an adult could lapse
into childish pranks without damage to his dignity. This could only
be the case where there is freedom to act out the impulses, indicated by a reasonable representation of *CF*. Where *FM* is equal to
M but there is no color, vivacious spontaneity is counter-indicated
and there is the implication of a locked-up concentration on self-
comfort, the value system serving the impulse life. This implies self-
absorption without healthy integration and may also suggest psychosomatic symptom formation.

4. FM between 1M and 2M

Although this is not a balance that is favorable for adjustment, it is so frequently found within the normal range that it cannot have the same implications of infantilism as does a ratio of *FM>2M*. No particular hypothesis attaches to this range of the *M : FM* ratio. One guide to interpretation is whether the numbers of *FM* approach equality with *M* or with *2M*. However, since many mature people have more *FM* than *M*, much depends on the total balance of the psychogram, and upon the quality and content of both *M* and *FM*, in arriving at an interpretation.

5. M and FM Both Few

HYPOTHESES: Where both *M* and *FM* are very few, there is neither simple acknowledgment of impulse nor is imaginal ability available either in the sense of long-range foresight or escapist fantasy. There are two hypotheses to account for this state of affairs. In records where there is mediocre or poor form level the hypothesis of ego weakness is applicable. The fact that impulses are not acknowledged does not suggest that they are not acted out, but rather that the ego has developed so little that the person may act irresponsibly without ego participation. This extreme ego weakness may be found in very young children, psychopaths, or psychotics. However, where the form level is good, the hypothesis of "neurotic constriction" is more likely to apply (see pages 294–295). Here the archaic impulses, reflected directly in *FM* and indirectly through the imaginal processes implied in the *M* response, represent such a threat to the ego that they are not acknowledged. The hypothesis is that repressive processes are involved when both *M* and *FM* are very few, rather than the conscious suppression typical of the record where there are few *FM* responses but a reasonable number of *M*'s.

Ratio of M : (FM+m)

Since *m* refers to the tension and conflict experienced by the individual in attempting to maintain the integrity of the ego integration against disintegrating forces from within or outside the personality, the number of *m* qualifies the interpretation of the *M* : *FM* ratio.

HYPOTHESIS: *FM* plus *m* should not be more than 1½ *M;* a *47* greater number of *FM+m* indicates that the tensions are too strong to permit the person to utilize his inner resources for the constructive solution of his everyday problems of living. When *M* is approximately equal to *FM+m* or a little greater and there are not more than one or two *m,* the implication is that the impulse life is subordinate to and fairly well integrated with the value system and that the individual is able to utilize his inner resources to give himself stability and control.

Proportions Relating to the Organization of Affectional Need

Ratio of Differentiated to Undifferentiated Shading Responses

HYPOTHESIS: Where the undifferentiated shading responses (*K,* *48* *KF, k, kF, c,* and *cF*) outnumber the differentiated shading responses (*Fc* and *FK*), this indicates that the affectional need is so poorly integrated within the personality organization that it constitutes a seriously disrupting influence and a sign of very serious maladjustment.

Ratio of F : (FK+Fc)

Since *Fc* are more numerous than *FK* in the great majority of records, the hypotheses attached to this ratio tend to be a function of the *Fc* component. Where *Fc* outnumber *FK* it seems fairly satisfactory to treat them together. However, where *FK* outnumber *Fc* the hypotheses should be modified in the direction of emphasizing the control of affectional anxiety rather than stressing the awareness and acceptance of affectional need.

1.   (FK+Fc) >¾F

HYPOTHESIS: Where *FK+Fc* exceed three-quarters *F* the need *47* for affection has developed to such an extent that it threatens to swamp the rest of the personality. The suggestion is that early rejection experiences have so inflated the need for being a recipient of affection that a search for response from others plays an undue part in influencing behavior.

2. FK$+$Fc$=\frac{1}{4}$ to $\frac{3}{4}$ F

HYPOTHESIS: Where differentiated shading responses are given in the moderate quantity indicated by the above ratio, the need for affection has developed sufficiently well and is integrated well enough with the rest of the personality organization that it has a sensitive control function, assisting the individual in his interaction with other people without implying a vulnerable overdependency on response from others.

3. (FK$+$Fc)$<\frac{1}{4}$F

HYPOTHESIS: Where the differentiated shading responses are less than one-quarter of the *F* responses there tends to be denial, repression, or underdevelopment of the need for affection. This is believed to stem from rejection experiences serious enough to warp personality development. If the rest of the psychogram is well-balanced and there is good maintenance of form level throughout, it may be that the lack of awareness and acceptance of affectional need has led to lack of personal involvement in interpersonal relationships without threatening the whole stability of personality organization. To the extent that there is insensitivity to shading, or where *Fc—* responses are given and particularly where the rest of the psychogram is unbalanced, the hypothesis is that there is a basic defect in personality organization and the lack of emotional depth is so great as to constitute a major handicap in general adjustment. An examination of shading dynamics through the sequence analysis is essential for an adequate interpretation of the absence or relative absence of differentiated shading responses. (See pages 344–348.)

Ratio of Achromatic to Chromatic Responses

This ratio refers to $(Fc+c+C') : (FC+CF+C)$

1. Achromatic$=$Twice Chromatic

HYPOTHESIS: Where the achromatic responses outnumber the chromatic responses by two to one, the person's responsiveness to outside stimulation has been interfered with by some kind of traumatic experience and withdrawal has resulted. This is the "burnt child" hypothesis. The implication is that need for an affectional response from others is so great that the person is inhibited and toned-down in his overt reactions to others for fear of being hurt or repulsed. There is a resulting overcautiousness in emotional contacts.

2.   Achromatic$=\frac{1}{2}$ Chromatic

HYPOTHESIS: When the shading responses are outnumbered two to one by the color responses, the affectional need does not unduly influence the natural responsiveness to emotional situations and the ability to interact with the social environment. This has an optimal implication when differentiated shading responses are given in moderate quantity and without signs of disturbance and where undifferentiated shading responses are lacking.

3.   Achromatic$<\frac{1}{2}$ Chromatic

HYPOTHESIS: Where the chromatic responses exceed the achromatic responses by two to one or more, the individual tends to act out his emotions. The explanation seems to lie in the fact that he feels relatively little need for approval and affection, and is not held back by related anxieties which might serve as a "brake" for his strongly developed reactivity to emotional stimulation from the environment.

This hypothesis applies particularly to cases where there is also a preponderance of $(CF+C)$ over FC, but should be modified in cases where there is a preponderance of FC over $(CF+C)$. This latter constellation has been noticed to occur with children who are well behaved in the presence of adults but little hellions when adults are absent. It is possible that in adults this constellation may point to an acting-out in conversion symptoms.

Proportions Relating to Constrictive Control

F%, or Percentage of Form Responses

1.   F%=20% to 50%

HYPOTHESIS: Where *F* appears in moderate quantity, the individual's ability to view his world in an impersonal matter-of-fact way serves as an aid to controlled adjustment. He is able to be impersonal on many occasions but has not stripped himself of his responsiveness to his own needs and/or his reactivity to strong emotional impact from outside. The control implications of good form-level rating are pertinent here, for the above hypothesis is inapplicable if there is inadequate integration of perception with reality.

2.   F%>80%

HYPOTHESIS: An overemphasis on form responses to this extent is pathological. Usually it carries the implication that the individual is not sufficiently differentiated in his intellectual function, or is generally so poorly integrated in personality organization, that he is unable to respond to anything but the bare outlines of reality structure, being inchoate in the recognition of his own needs and imperceptive of the nuances of his emotional surroundings.

This is the hypothesis of "natural constriction," or "natural limitations." It would apply particularly if the form-level rating of the *F* responses is at a vague or inaccurate level. This degree of incapability of differentiation might be expected with low mental age, as in very young children or feeble-minded subjects, with severe damage to intellectual function as with organics, or with severe defect in personality organization as with seriously psychopathic personalities.

However, if form level is high the hypothesis of "neurotic constriction" (outlined in the next section) is more likely to be applicable.*

---

* For a fuller discussion of the term "constriction" see pages 364–365. "Constriction" should be viewed as a transitive rather than an intransitive term. One must not lose sight of the processes that are "constricted."

3.   F%=50% to 80%

HYPOTHESIS: Where the emphasis on $F\%$ is less extreme the per- *57* son is likely to suffer from a "neurotic constriction," particularly if the form-level rating is on a high level. Indeed, form-level rating is a crucial consideration, for some subjects with $F\%$ over 80 may be considered neurotically constricted while some with $F\%$ less than 80 may be considered "naturally" constricted on the grounds of form level. The hypothesis of neurotic constriction is that although the person is intellectually capable of a more richly differentiated response to his world, he is inhibited in such response, having repressed his tendencies to acknowledge and respond to his own inner needs and act according to his own emotional reactions. His adjustment rests on stripping the personal and individual components from experience.

Whether this is a relatively stable or unstable adjustment rests upon the amount of anxiety that breaks through, threatening to undermine his defenses. If associated with organized whole responses, neurotic constriction may reflect inhibition through compulsive emphasis on organization and achievement. If associated with emphasis on d and dd, it may indicate a compulsive meticulousness and correctness.

4.   F%<20%

HYPOTHESIS: Where F is underemphasized the person places lit- *58* tle emphasis on maintaining an impersonal, matter-of-fact relationship with his world. If plenty of other control factors are represented, this may indicate a many-faceted personality, creative, spontaneous, sensitive, and well-related to others. If other control factors are poorly represented, a low $F\%$ would indicate inadequate emphasis upon conforming to the demands of reality, a too-highly personalized reaction. In any event the $F\%$ should be at least 10, for even the many-faceted person functions more effectively if some aspects of life are handled in an impersonal way. The implications of inadequate control of a low $F\%$ are confirmed if there are breaks in reality appreciation as indicated by responses with minus form level.

Total of F Plus Differentiated Shading Responses: $(FK+F+Fc)\%$

HYPOTHESIS: This is another indication of degree of constriction. Where the total of *F* and differentiated shading responses exceeds 75 per cent the hypothesis of neurotic constriction is applicable. However, where $F\%$ is near 50 and there is a moderate number of *FK* and *Fc* responses so that the total percentage does not exceed 75, the hypothesis is that the insulated rigidity of constriction is modified and somewhat softened. Through introspective tendencies and/or sensitivity the person with "modified constriction" is able to live effectively in a social milieu without bothering others with his rigidities. However, he will be restrained in his dealings with others, and will find it difficult to make close and warm affectional contacts.

Proportions Relating to Emotional Reactivity to the Environment

Ratio of FC: $(CF+C)$

1. FC>(CF+C)

HYPOTHESIS: This is a sign of control over impulsive expression of emotionality. When *FC* exceeds $CF+C$, but the latter are still represented by at least a few responses, the person is ordinarily capable of a controlled responsiveness to his social environment, responding appropriately with both feeling and action; moreover, he is capable of a deep and genuine response under strong emotional impact. He is not overcontrolled. However, if $CF+C$ is absent or nearly so the hypothesis is that there is excessive control and that the socialized responses tend to be superficial, the person either being unable or unwilling to allow himself a strong emotional reaction even when the situation demands a deep emotional response. The quality of the various types of color responses in terms of forced, arbitrary, or symbolic sub-classifications, and also the form-level ratings, should be used for modification of these hypotheses.

2. FC<(CF+C)

HYPOTHESIS: Where $CF+C$ exceed FC there is weak control over emotionality and the person tends to act out his reactions in overt behavioral expression. This hypothesis is modified by considerations of the sub-classes of color scoring represented.

Sum C

HYPOTHESIS: Sum C is proportional to the degree of overt reactivity to emotional stimuli, whether such reactivity be controlled or otherwise. If Sum C is less than three there seems too little responsiveness to influences from the environment. Otherwise Sum C is rarely considered except in relationship to M and to $F\%$.

Percentage of Responses to Cards VIII, IX, and X

HYPOTHESIS: Whereas Sum C is said to indicate overt reactivity, the percentage of responses to the last three cards, which are entirely chromatic, indicates general responsiveness to emotional stimuli from the environment whether this is expressed in overt reactivity or not.

Statistical expectations* would suggest 30 per cent as the average responsiveness, with neither inhibition by nor stimulation by color. However, since Card X lends itself to more responses by virtue of its facilitation of D responses, 40 per cent is recognized as the upper limit of ordinary responsiveness. Thus, if more than 40 per cent of the responses are given to the last three cards (provided that not more than 20 per cent are given to Card X alone) the hypothesis is that the productiveness of the individual is stimulated by environmental impact, whether he gives overt expression to his emotional reaction or not. If fewer than 30 per cent of the total responses are given to the last three cards, the hypothesis is that the individual is either inhibited in his productiveness under conditions of strong environmental impact or basically lacking in responsiveness to such impact.

---

* Statistical expectations on the assumption that each of the ten cards is equally productive.

*Reaction Time to Chromatic Cards Compared with that
to Achromatic Cards*

HYPOTHESIS: If the average reaction time for chromatic cards exceeds that for achromatic cards by more than 10 seconds this indicates that the individual is disturbed by emotional impact from the environment. On the other hand, a similar excess in reaction time for achromatic cards over chromatic is believed to indicate disturbance by the shading elements and, hence, disturbance when environmental stimuli touch on the area of affectional need.

This hypothesis must be applied very cautiously. It may be that the average reaction time to chromatic (or achromatic) cards has been unduly influenced by a very long reaction time to a particular card, due to a disturbance aroused by some association or feature other than color (or shading) . Card II is classed as chromatic, but the heavy shading may be a disturbing feature for some subjects. The shapes in Card IX are sometimes found to be difficult quite aside from any color considerations. Cards III and X present a problem for the person who feels compelled towards organized whole responses and is uninterested in color concepts (even though he may not be disturbed by color) . Moreover, since both shading and color disturbance may be present in the same individual, an absence of differential cannot be interpreted as an indication of lack of disturbance. In fact, an examination of reaction times card by card during the sequence analysis gives a better picture than can be obtained from the average reaction times.

Proportions Relating to Intellectual Manner of Approach

The interpretative hypotheses connected with the percentages of the various locations are related to the intellectual manner of approach—or *Erfassungstyp,* to use the term originally applied by Rorschach. The structure of the ink blots themselves leads to the expectation that the following percentages of locations will be used:

W%	20%—30%
D%	45%—55%
d%	5%—15%
(Dd and S) %	0%—10%

Normative statistical findings [6, 7] tend to support this expectation. If the individual uses locations within the normal or average range of expectation the hypothesis is that he has a balanced intellectual approach—although this hypothesis may be discarded if there are other findings that make it inapplicable, such as the occurrence of minus form-level rating. Departures from statistical expectations are to be interpreted in the light of other hypotheses relating not only to the extent of underemphasis or overemphasis of the location in question, but also to the other location percentages and to the form-level rating characteristic of the various locations.

Interpretation of $W\%$

A score of W may be achieved in two chief ways. The whole may be achieved by integrating parts that have been differentiated out of the blot—that is, the parts are seen as separate but related. On the other hand, the whole may be seen as global and relatively undifferentiated. Since the form-level rating was designed to show the degrees of differentiation of perception, the organized, integrated wholes may be distinguished from the global wholes on the basis of form-level rating. This distinction is essential for interpretation.

1. $W\%$ over 30%, Form Level High

HYPOTHESIS: An emphasis on W's of good quality is a sign of organizational interest and ability. The person possessing such ability is interested in and capable of viewing the relatively separate facets of his experience as an interrelated whole. This is not found except with persons of superior intellectual ability who have been able to mobilize their capacities to serve their interest in seeing relationships between the various aspects of their experience and making sense of their world. The same abstract, theoretical interest is often indicated by additional W's linking D responses together, even when the $W\%$ is within the average range. However, here there is less implication that a highly integrated view of the world has been achieved.

2.   W% over 30% with Mediocre Form Level but Organizational Effort

HYPOTHESIS: If there is an effort at organization of the differentiated parts of the ink blots which does not serve to raise form perception beyond a mediocre level, there is a reaching beyond the limits of ability to make sense of experience and to seek for relationships. There seems to be a compulsive need to do the big thing in an intellectual sense, to superimpose generalizations on the facts whether they fit well or not. There seems to be an overriding intellectual ambition without the ability to back it up. This may be because the person lacks the necessary intellectual capacity to perceive at an integrated level, or because there are emotional interferences with his ability to sense the essential interrelationships which do exist between the various facts of his experience. This need for intellectual achievement may be viewed as a defense mechanism of a compensatory sort.

3.   W% over 30%, Vague or Indefinite Form Perception

HYPOTHESIS: A stress on vague or indefinite W's indicates little effort to organize experience. This seems to relate not so much to a drive for organization as to a lack of differentiation in perceptual experience, an inability to go beyond a rather global perception of the situation. This finding is common not only with those of mediocre or inferior intellectual capacity, but also with those whose maladjustment has interfered with the constructive use of their intellectual capacities.

4.   W% less than 20%

HYPOTHESIS: An underemphasis on wholes indicates a low degree of interest in seeking relationships between the separate facts of experience and achieving an organized view of the world. However, the particular extensions of this hypothesis will depend upon the balance found with the other locations and upon the form level of the responses. Testing the limits for W-capacity may throw interesting light upon the reasons for the subject's underproduction of W responses.

Types of W Response

The hypotheses presented above are attached to whole responses in general, without consideration of the particular types of whole response involved. Where most of the whole responses are scored *W* these hypotheses apply without modification; where a fair proportion of the *W* responses are scored *W* or *DW* the hypotheses should be modified to take account of the particular processes involved in these responses.

1. W responses.

In producing a *W* score the subject uses most or nearly all of the blot, but cuts off or omits certain portions to suit the needs of his concept.

HYPOTHESIS: A *W* response indicates an interest in organizing experience tempered with an intellectual criticalness prompting the subject to omit from a generalization those aspects of experience that do not fit.

As stated above, this seems a desirable characteristic, and indeed it is if not carried to extremes. However, an overemphasis on *W* would indicate an overcritical and perfectionistic approach which tends to inhibit the processes of generalization and integration.

2. DW Responses

In producing a *DW* response the individual applies to the whole blot a concept derived from one detail, even though the blot as a whole gives no adequate basis for the concept; indeed, the concept is a bad match for the blot as a whole. The subject gives no indication that the discrepancy troubles him.

HYPOTHESIS: *DW* responses indicate a weakness in the link with reality; the subject does not display enough intellectual criticism to prevent him from jumping to erroneous conclusions on the basis of inadequate evidence. *DW* responses are overgeneralizations.

With children this tendency to jump to an erroneous overgeneralization on the basis of one single, striking element of experience is to be expected as a normal phase of development. When this type of response occurs with adults it indicates a serious weakness in reality testing. It occurs with schizophrenics, and very occasionally with non-psychotic subjects, but is always a "bad sign."

3. Tendencies to W

Since the tendency to a *W* always yields an additional *W* score, it is not reflected in the *W*%. However, it must be distinguished interpretatively from the additional *W* score obtained through organization. It is scored when the subject generalizes from one clearly seen detail to the whole blot, but vaguely enough so that he does not achieve an inaccurate fit with the whole blot.

HYPOTHESIS: A tendency to *W* indicates a tendency to overgeneralization, which does not involve the same weakness in reality testing as the similar tendency shown by a *DW*. It shows an interest in integrating experience, without enough intellectual differentiation and criticism to achieve a good integration.

Most adults who overgeneralize produce *D→W* responses rather than *DW* responses, and thereby show a better capacity for reality testing than the young child or the schizophrenic. *D→W* responses are more likely on Card VIII than elsewhere; if the only response of this kind is on Card VIII (for example, animals climbing over something) it is too common to be interpretatively significant.

W:M Ratio

This ratio is believed to give an indication of the extent to which the individual is able to mobilize his creative or productive energies to back up his intellectual interests and ambitions. The ratio itself, together with the quality of the *W*'s and *M*'s involved, throws light on the level of aspiration and related aspects of the personality. It is discussed here because of its obvious relationship with the interpretation of the presence or absence of stress on *W*.

1.   W:M in the Proportion 2:1

HYPOTHESIS: This ratio indicates an organizational interest with enough creative potential to back it up to make it a real drive to intellectual achievement, not a hollow one. The level of aspiration is high, but not reaching too far beyond the productive resources of the individual. The 2:1 ratio is considered optimum, but only where there are at least three *M* responses and six *W* responses.

There are many instances in which this hypothesis seems inapplicable in the light of other hypotheses derived from the Rorschach or in terms of other facts known about the personality in question. Sometimes the hypothesis may be extended to cover these exceptions. For example, an optimum *W:M* ratio is occasionally found with bright non-achievers although the typical non-achiever is more likely to have an excess of *M*. One of the configurations found by Vorhaus [13] in children and adolescents with reading disability was characterized by an optimum *W:M* ratio, which she interprets in this context as a successful "drive for non-achievement." Here it is not a question of lack of capacity to achieve, but of the goal the subject has set himself. In such cases the goal seems to be one of nonconformity; hence non-achievement in conventional terms is a purpose in which the person is succeeding admirably. Although such an extension of the hypothesis can be made in some cases, the many exceptions to the hypothesis that a 2:1 ratio shows optimum level of aspiration make it necessary to use great caution in applying this hypothesis.

2. W>2M

HYPOTHESIS: When *W* is greater than twice *M* the level of aspiration is too high.

One seems on safer ground to interpret an overstress on *W* in comparison to *M* as indicating an overly high level of aspiration, with ambition outstripping the creative resources of the personality. If the ratio approaches 3:1 or higher it must be considered a negative sign. Sometimes it appears that this is indeed due to an overriding ambition, although in many other instances it appears that it is not that the aspiration is so high but that the productive resources of the personality are unduly low. Form-level considerations are important. If the form level is high and there is normal *M* production with overstress on *W*, it seems a case of a superior person with a very strong drive for accomplishment, with perhaps much accomplished, but at the expense of other important satisfactions. If the form level is high but there is underproduction of *M,* the implication is that the aspiration level is too high because the person cannot throw enough of his own creative energies behind his efforts to give solid achievement. If the form level is low, usually also with underproduction of *M,* the hypothesis is more that there is general interference with the use of intellectual capacity (or low capacity itself) so that efforts to gain an integrated view of the world will be ineffective and there will be disappointment in the gap between aspiration and the ability to achieve.

3. $W < 2M$

HYPOTHESIS: When W is less than $2M$, and particularly if the ratio swings to 1:2 in the other direction, the individual has creative potential for which he has not found an adequate outlet or focus.

Here an examination of the qualitative flavor of the M's is important. If the M's have a fantasy flavor—that is, (A) and certain kinds of (H)—it may be that the person is emphasizing escapist fantasy as a substitute for achievement. However, the escapist interpretation of this balance must not be overgeneralized; for $W < 2M$ is frequently found with highly intelligent persons, especially with intelligent and well-educated women, who have excellent W ability but a great production of M which tends to swamp the W. Perhaps the circumstances of the life of the individual do not permit opportunities for achievement fully in line with his capacity. On the other hand, he may feel that to achieve up to the limits of his very high capacity would be at the expense of too many other values in living; hence he lowers his aspiration level below his capacity.

Interpretation of D%

D scores are obtained by breaking the blot up into its most obvious sub-divisions, parts that are easily seen separately from the rest because of the Gestalt qualities of the blot itself. It is as though the subject were aware of the tendency of the blot to subdivide itself and did not resist it by an attempt to pull the parts together.

1. D%>55%, Form Level Good

HYPOTHESIS: When there is stress on the production of *D*'s of
good form level, there is interest and ability to differentiate perceptually, with relatively little interest in integration and organization. This is interpreted as a practical, everyday, common-sense application of intelligence, an interest in the presented, obvious facts,
without much drive to seek relationships between these presented
facts of experience. For a superior person such an approach may
indicate insecurity, a fear of losing his bearings if he does not stick
close to the obvious facts.

2. D%>55%, Form Level Mediocre

HYPOTHESIS: When there is stress on *D*'s of mediocre or poor
form level, it suggests that the person sticks to the practical, everyday, common-sense view of things because he is not capable of a more
integrated view.

3. D%<45%

The interpretation of an understress on *D* depends upon the
form level of the *D*'s and other locations. If the form level is generally low, it may be that the individual is unable to differentiate
between the obvious facts presented by the world around him, either
because he has defective intellectual capacity or because of great emotional disturbance. One would expect to find such an underemphasis
on *D* associated with an overstress on vague, relatively undifferentiated wholes. If, on the other hand, the form level is quite good and
still there is neglect of the *D* locations, the implication is that the
person is capable of differentiation, but lacks recognition of everyday problems and facts. The hypothesis would be extended differently according to whether there was associated with the low *D*% an
overemphasis on *W*, or *d*, or *Dd* and *S*. Schizophrenics characteristically underemphasize *D*, although they may overemphasize either
W or *Dd* and *S*, or both.

Testing the limits for *D* may clarify the reasons why the subject
seems unable to differentiate. For some subjects the whole Gestalt of
the blot seems to have a cohesiveness that makes it difficult to break

it into parts; these subjects would be likely to see, for example, a "cat's face" on Card I and would be unable to see details without covering part of the blot with the hand. Here there seems no question of undifferentiated perception, but rather an inability to see the "trees" for the "woods." With other subjects it may emerge that details can be seen, but the urge to use the whole blot is so great that tendencies to wholes and organized wholes appear even in the testing the limits period; an unusually strong need to organize experience seems responsible for the lack of D. Some subjects betray the concept-dominated nature of their perception in the testing the limits period; the shape of the blot so strongly suggests some dominant fantasy that they are quite unable to utilize the material for any other response. This is most likely to be the case if the response is an original or has minus form elements. On the other hand, if the subject can quite readily accept details when the limits are tested, the neglect of the practical, everyday, common-sense view of things does not seem deep or serious.

Interpretation of d%

A d score is obtained by selecting for the response a small blot area, which is so well-defined that it is statistically usual for it to be selected as a separate part.

1.   d% > 15%

HYPOTHESIS: An overemphasis on d represents not only a differentiated interest in factual things, but also insecurity against which the individual defends himself by clinging to limited areas of certainty for fear of losing his bearings if he departs from them. An emphasis on d often is associated with a pedantic emphasis on accuracy, correctness, and exactness, but sometimes simply reflects a need for certainty, a clinging to the minutiae of life without any pedantic flavor.

2.   d% < 5%

HYPOTHESIS: An underemphasis on d indicates a low level of interest in the minutiae of experience. Lack of d is not particularly significant, for it is a common approach; indeed, the average production of *d* is low—5 to 15 per cent.

Interpretation of (*Dd* and *S*) %

If the percentage of responses using unusual details or space is 10 per cent or less this is not significant, since it is the usual or average finding. To the extent that the (*Dd* and *S*) % exceeds 10 it is important to analyze the type of unusual details and the whole balance of locations used before arriving at an hypothesis.

HYPOTHESES: In general, if the unusual locations are evenly distributed and the overemphasis does not badly upset the whole balance of locations, the hypothesis is that the individual has rich responsiveness to his environment in a perceptual sense, or that he has a flair for the unusual. If *Dd* and *S* are increased at the expense of *W* the interpretation is similar to that of an overstress on *d*—that is, that the individual is too hesitant in drawing general conclusions from fine and detailed observations, that he defends himself against insecurity by clinging to limited areas of certainty. If *Dd* and *S* are increased at the expense of *D* but *W* remains normal, it may indicate an overintellectual approach with too little concern with the obvious, practical facts of experience. If both *W* and *D* drop this seems to indicate a loosening of the ties with reality. Within this general framework of interpretation the following interpretative hypotheses are presented for each of the types of location represented in the (*Dd* and *S*) %.

1.   Emphasis on dd

A *dd* location is characteristically one that is clearly defined in structure, hence clearly demarcated from the surrounding blot material. It is small, sometimes tiny, and probably because of this is not usually selected despite its clear-cut structural qualities.

HYPOTHESIS: An emphasis on *dd* represents obsessional, meticulous, or pedantic trends. The hypothesis is similar to that attached to an overstress on *d:* namely, that this approach is a defense against insecurity through a quest for certainty and a clinging to limited areas for fear of losing one's grip and being carried away into confusion.

2.   Emphasis on de

A *de* location is the edge only of a blot area; if more than the edge is used a *de* cannot be scored.

HYPOTHESIS: A stress on *de* indicates a fear to go into anything too deeply, a fear of becoming involved if one does, and a tendency to skirt the fringe of a situation without coming to grips with it.

This may be found in anxiety states with introversive people. Even though *de*'s are not scored, this type of adjustment sometimes is to be detected through sequence analysis, when one finds that the subject simply skirts the edges of the blot, dealing with the peripheral parts but never plunging into the central portions.

3.   Emphasis on di

A *di* is carved out by the subject from the shaded mass of the blot. Sometimes this seems entirely arbitrary and without justification in terms of the structure of the blot; sometimes there is an adequate basis in terms of fine differentiations in the shading, although these are not usually noticed by the average person.

HYPOTHESIS: If there is little objective basis for the concept in the differentiations in the shading in the blot material, and hence a minus form-level rating, the *di* response is a pathological one, perhaps most characteristic of a schizoid personality fighting against disintegration. If, however, the *di* response is well-seen and hence has superior form-level rating, the hypothesis is that there is anxious preoccupation with matters of interpersonal sensitivity; such a response is most often found with intelligent, artistic subjects who like the shading aspects of the blot material.

4.   Emphasis on dr

The *dr* location is one that is not determined by the Gestalt qualities of the blot. In this respect it is like the *di* and *de*, although without their qualities of insideness and outsideness. The subject chops off an area or combines areas to suit the needs of his concept. The interpretation varies according to the extent to which the subject seems habitually to impose his concept on the blot material, as contrasted with the subject who otherwise demonstrates that he is capable of a flexible variation of response to suit the varying structure of the blot material.

HYPOTHESES: If the emphasis on *dr* is found in a fairly well-balanced series of location percentages, the individual is capable of a highly differentiated responsiveness in a perceptual sense and, hence, has a quick and flexible perceptual approach. If at the same time there is underemphasis on *D* and *W* the hypothesis is that the high degree of differentiation is employed to give a certain arbitrary flavor to perception (seeing things in an unusual or "different" way) which is not conducive to easy communication with other people. A piling up of *dr* responses tends to be characteristic of the records of the compulsive and rigid perfectionist, usually with an excess of *dd* responses also. This pattern seems to stem both from an over-criticalness with respect to form qualities and a need for quantity production that soon exhausts the more obvious subdivisions of the blot, which meet his rigid form requirements.

5. Emphasis on S

The interpretation of *S* depends on how daringly the white space is used. A daring use of white space would consist of a real reversal of figure and ground, a resisting of the usual card pull towards making the blot the figure and the white space the ground. A cautious use of white space is where the subject seems to feel that the gaps should be filled in, or where the spaces are used to represent something that otherwise would be missing in the concept (for example, the eyes of an animal). Intermediate between these is the use of the larger white spaces as part of another concept (windows, lakes, and the like).

HYPOTHESIS: *S* responses are related to an oppositional tendency in the intellectual sphere, the strength of the tendency being related to the daringness in the use of white space. *S* implies an intellectual kind of opposition, a putting of the self across; it is the competitive or self-assertive aspect of intellectuality.

To develop this hypothesis more specifically requires consideration of the total record. The self-assertiveness implied in S may be considered constructive if other locations are used freely, if there is flexible succession, and if the emphasis on S is not exaggerated. However, where there is exaggerated emphasis on S, particularly in main locations that reflect a daring use of S, the hypothesis is that the subject's emphasis on doing things differently and asserting himself competitively or stubbornly occurs at too high a cost to his own balanced perception of reality. Nevertheless, the ability to use white space is considered one indication of ego-strength, the implication being that the personality has resources to resist inundation by environmental forces or motivational confusion.

The general introversive-extratensive balance of the psychogram is also considered. Where there is an introversive balance, the hypothesis is that the intellectual opposition is turned against the self, that the person is competitive in expecting too much of himself and consequently feels inadequate and self-critical. In a context of dysphoric content and lack of control this self-opposition may have a self-destructive flavor. The implication of conscious recognition of inadequacy feelings is reinforced if S responses occur in conjunction with FK. These inadequacy feelings are to be distinguished from the vague, diffuse kind of inadequacy which is more likely to be represented by K or k responses than by S.

Where the record is generally extratensive, the hypothesis is that emphasis on S indicates an oppositional tendency directed towards the environment in an intellectually negativistic way such as argumentativeness, in contrast to purely emotional aggression which is more likely to be represented by a predominance of FM over M and CF over FC. Where the record is neither strongly introversive or extratensive the hypothesis is that an emphasis on S indicates ambivalence and doubt.

In sequence analysis particular attention is given to the unusual treatment of white space. Content symbolism here is generally interpreted in terms of something growing out of oppositionalism.

Other Proportions Relating to Intellectual Aspects

R, or Number of Responses

HYPOTHESES: A small number of responses indicates unproductivity, except where these few responses are good, well-organized wholes. On the other hand, a very large number of responses may indicate not so much a rich productivity as a compulsive need for completion or quantity. Much depends on the ease with which the responses are given and the general balance of the location percentages. A moderately large number of responses is probably optimum. If given easily and enthusiastically they indicate a person perceptually responsive and receptive to the world about him. The average number of responses falls within a range of 20 to 45.

Average Response Time

HYPOTHESES: If the average response time is over one minute this is an indication of slow mental processes, unless the longer time is spent in much elaboration or description of the response. Slow intellectual processes may be due to capacity below average or may be a sign of general depression. An average response time of less than 30 seconds is quick and hurried. Especially if the record is lacking in elaboration or description of the responses, and if the responses themselves are mediocre and obvious, it would seem that for some reason the subject is not really coöperating in the task set for him.

Proportion of $(H+A):(Hd+Ad)$

HYPOTHESIS: If the detail responses are more than half as frequent as $H+A$ it indicates an overcritical attitude. This search for accuracy may well be associated with anxiety, perhaps with obsessive-compulsive characteristics. This tendency to be exacting, critical, or meticulous may be an outlet for hostility. If the detail responses are half as frequent as the $H+A$ or less frequent still this is the usual state of affairs and not to be interpreted except as an absence of a highly over-critical attitude.

P, or Number of Populars

The average number of populars is five, in an average record of 20 to 45 responses [6, 7].

1. Average Number of Popular Responses

HYPOTHESIS: The person who gives the average number of popular responses tends to see the world as others see it, without an undue emphasis upon the conventional view. Such a person has adequate ties to reality, unless this is counter-indicated by some other criterion such as minus form level.

2. Few Popular Responses

HYPOTHESIS: The fewer the popular responses the less able the person is to see the world in the same terms as other people do. This indicates a weakness of the tie with reality and would be confirmed by an unbalanced use of locations, especially a low $D\%$, and by poor form level. It is considered particularly serious if the subject is unable to accept popular concepts even in the testing of the limits period.

The undesirable implications of few P's are modified by an average or higher than average $D\%$ with its implications of ability to meet practical problems in a common-sense way. Additional populars show resources for taking the conventional view which are not usually fully utilized by the subject. Similar resources are indicated by a ready acceptance of popular responses in the testing of the limits period; sometimes the subject is quite capable of seeing populars but did not spontaneously produce them because they did not meet his high standards of form level or because he was striving for originality. These tendencies may be handicaps in adjustment, but do not indicate the same loosening of ties with reality as a more complete inability to see popular concepts.

3. Many Popular Responses

HYPOTHESIS: If eight or more popular responses are given there seems an unusually strong emphasis on seeing the world in the obvious, agreed-upon way. In a person of superior capacity this would imply an overemphasis upon conventionality, perhaps through training or because of fear of error.

O, or Number of Original Responses

The hypotheses attached to this figure vary in accordance with the quality of the original responses, whether they reflect keenly perceived responses with good form level or whether they have a bizarre or inaccurate flavor indicated by an $O-$ score. The superior person tends to have twice as many O's as P's and twice as many additional O's as main O's. If the original responses are fewer than this, he may not be making full enough use of his capacity, especially if there is much scatter in form-level rating. Sometimes one finds an individual with a carefully high form level but lacking any significant number of good O's; the implication is that such an individual is pushing his capacity to the limit, being probably less intelligent than his general level of achievement would indicate. Artistic people may have as many as 25 per cent or more O's. However, if the $O\%$ approaches 50 the implication is that the person is too erratic, unless there are lots of populars and an average range $D\%$. If there are plenty of additional O's and few main O's, the hypothesis is that the individual is not daring enough in using his ability to find a fresh approach to things.

$O-$ responses and the bizarre specifications that give an additional $O-$ score are not so much signs of intelligence as of disturbance. However, in the sequence analysis careful attention must be given to recoverability before an assessment of the seriousness of the disturbance can be made. Moreover, one must distinguish between the $O-$ concept that is far-fetched or queer, showing disregard for what is possible in reality, but matches the blot material, and the $O-$ response that not only violates common sense but also misuses the blot material. The latter type of $O-$ shows a more serious weakening of ties with reality.

A%, or Percentage of Animal Responses

Animal forms are easy to see in the ink blots; therefore, it is quite usual to find a fair number of responses with animal content. The optimum number is considered to be from 20 to 35 per cent. It is an empirical finding that a percentage of animal responses of over 50 tends to be associated either with low intellectual capacity or disturbed adjustment. The hypothesis is that this high an A% indicates a stereotyped view of the world—that is, too narrow a range of interests. This hypothesis may be extended to overemphasis on other content categories—for example, anatomy.

Succession

Succession refers to the order in which location categories are used. The most usual succession is to see first the blot as a whole, then to break it up into one or two large usual details, then perhaps to give a small usual detail or a rare detail or a space response. This succession of W–D–d–Dd (or S) is termed a systematic succession. Some cautious people are equally systematic in reverse order, starting with a small detail with precise form, coming to a larger usual area, and finally achieving a whole response. The succession of Dd (or S)–d–D–W is also designated as systematic. Not all four types of location need be used, but if they are used they must be in either the order W–D–d–Dd (or S) or the exact reverse order. If the card is turned, only the locations used before turning are considered for scoring succession. An unsystematic succession is any violation of the systematic sequence. In some cards succession cannot be termed either systematic or unsystematic—for example, on Card X where several D responses are given and no other locations used, or on a card where only one W response is given and no detail responses at all. The number of systematic successions is counted, then the number of unsystematic successions. If any cards have no succession they are counted either as systematic or unsystematic, whichever classification is the more frequent.

1. RIGID SUCCESSION is indicated by ten systematic successions with no unsystematic cards whatsoever. The hypothesis is that an approach this rigid tends to detract from high intellectual efficiency.

2.   ORDERLY SUCCESSION is indicated by seven to nine systematic successions, the rest being unsystematic. This is considered optimum for intellectual efficiency, implying some systematic approach to situations, but with flexibility.

3.   LOOSE SUCCESSION is indicated if three to six of the successions are systematic, the rest unsystematic. The hypothesis is that this indicates some weakening of control either because of intellectual limitions or by reason of emotional or pathological conditions. However, loose succession is sometimes found with buoyant and intelligent individuals without any particular emotional disturbance.

4.   CONFUSED SUCCESSION is indicated if fewer than three cards have systematic succession. The hypothesis is that this is a sign of an erratic or confused individual.

References

1. Allen, R. M. "The Influence of Color in the Rorschach Test on Reaction Time in a Normal Population," *J. Projective Techniques,* 1951, 15, 481–485.

2. Allen, R. M.; Manne, S. M.; and Stiff, M. "The Role of Color in Rorschach's Test: A Preliminary Normative Report on a College Student Population." *J. Projective Techniques,* 1951, 15, 235–242.

3. Baker, L. M., and Harris, J. S. "The Validation of Rorschach Test Results against Laboratory Behavior," *J. Clin. Psychol.,* 1949, 5, 161–164.

4. Buhler, C.; Buhler, K.; and Lefever, D. W. "Development of the Basic Rorschach Score with Manual of Directions," *Basic Rorschach Standardization Study,* I, 1948.

5. Burchard, E. M. L. "The Use of Projective Techniques in the Analysis of Creativity," *J. Projective Techniques,* 1952, 16, 412–427.

6. Davidson, H. H., and Klopfer, B. "Rorschach Statistics: Part I. Mentally Retarded, Normal and Superior Adults," *Rorschach Res. Exch.,* 1937–8, 2, 164–169.

7. Davidson, H. H., and Klopfer, B. "Rorschach Statistics: Part II. Normal Children," *Rorschach Res. Exch.,* 1938, 3, 37–43.

8. Dubrovner, R. J.; Von Lackum, W. J.; and Jost, H. "A Study of the Effect of Color on Productivity and Reaction Time in the Rorschach Test," *J. Clin. Psychol.,* 1950, 64, 331–336.

9. Lazarus, R. S. "The Influence of Color on the Protocol of the Rorschach Test," *J. Abn. & Soc. Psychol.,* 1949, 44, 506–516.

10. Meyer, B. T. "An Investigation of Color Shock in the Rorschach Test," *J. Clin. Psychol.*, 1951, 7, 367–370.

11. Roe, Anne. "Painting and Personality," *Rorschach Res. Exch.*, 1946, 10, 86–100.

12. Schachtel, E. G. "Projection and its Relation to Character Attitudes and Creativity in the Kinaesthetic Response," *Psychiatry*, 1950, 13, 69–100.

13. Vorhaus, Pauline G. "Rorschach Configurations Associated with Reading Disability," *J. Projective Techniques*, 1952, 16, 2–19.

14. Williams, M. "An Experimental Study of Intellectual Control under Stress and Associated Rorschach Factors," *J. Consulting Psychol.*, 1947, 11, 21–29.

CHAPTER 11

Sequence Analysis

Sequence analysis consists of a card-by-card, response-by-response analysis, in which each response is translated into concepts derived from the basic interpretative hypotheses and considered in relationship to the other responses in sequence, similarly translated, taking into account also the content, test behavior and language and what kinds of response the blot material facilitates. The response is always considered in context, both in the context of the stimulus properties of the blot material and in that provided by the dynamic flow of the record, in which the artificial division of the record into response units disappears and the performance is viewed entirely as process.

Sequence analysis is more easily demonstrated than explained. It requires a phenomenological approach, in which the examiner attempts to feel himself into the subject's world and to view it as he views it, sensing the affect and dynamics of the performance from within. Therefore, the techniques of sequence analysis are extremely flexible; the individual record gives the lead and there is no standardized approach. There is no new list of interpretative hypotheses to be attached to specific features of the record seen through sequence analysis; the examiner adapts and modifies the basic interpretative hypotheses as the dynamic unity of the performance seems to demand.

The fact that each record is viewed as a unique phenomenon requiring a flexible approach has at least two unfortunate consequences, one relating to training and the other to validation. First, since sequence analysis is communicated more by example than as a standardized technique, many instructors hesitate to introduce it to beginners as an essential part of the Rorschach technique. Too often it remains an esoteric art private to experts, leaving for the beginner a mechanical application of interpretative hypotheses with no possibility of using the qualitative and dynamic aspects of the performance as a basis for assembling the hypotheses so that they dovetail into a meaningful picture of a functioning personality. Under such circumstances the description of the personality tends to be cast in the form of a wooden, technical report, full of "ritual terms," which contributes relatively little to an understanding of the individual. Sequence analysis is an essential part of the Rorschach technique, as essential as the interpretative hypotheses themselves.

Secondly, the highly individualized and flexible interpretative approach of sequence analysis presents a formidable problem in validation research. It is necessary to validate the basic interpretative hypotheses, and yet to take them one at a time out of the context of the individual record fails to test out the hypotheses as they are used in practice. Any precise validation of the interpretative hypotheses must somehow take into account the high degree of interdependence of the hypotheses as contributing to the final interpretation. Although a formidable problem, this cannot be taken as an argument against either the value of sequence analysis or the desirability and possibility of careful validation research. This problem will be discussed more fully in a later chapter.

The processes of sequence analysis can best be understood by working through the carefully documented analyses presented in the case material included in Chapter 18 of this volume, and in Volume II. In the present chapter, all that can be done is to set forth some of the considerations that enter into sequence analysis, even though the application of these considerations varies from case to case.

The following twelve points may serve as an aid in sequence analysis:

1. Knowledge of what the blot material on the various cards itself facilitates, in terms of locations, determinants, content, and popular responses.
2. Examination of the use of locations, in terms of succession, organization, and relationship to the blot material.
3. Note of the number of responses made to each card.
4. Examination of the use of determinants, in terms of succession, relationship to the blot material, locations, and content.
5. Examination of form-level rating as it varies from card to card, from response to response, and as it seems to be related to location, determinant, and content.
6. Note of the comments made by the subject during the performance or inquiry, or later during the testing the limits period or after the test is over.
7. Note of the test behavior as it seems related to the blot material or the particular responses.
8. Examination of reaction time and response time as they vary from card to card and response to response, with relationship to the blot material, and the location, determinants, and content of the response.
9. Examination of the color dynamics of the performance, considering not only the color responses themselves but all aspects of response to the chromatic elements of the blot material.
10. Examination of the shading dynamics of the performance, considering not only the shading responses themselves but all aspects of the responses as they vary as the shading varies.
11. A comparion of that which is produced in the performance proper with the material that does not emerge until the inquiry or testing of the limits.
12. Consideration of the relationship between the subject and the examiner and how it may have influenced the performance.

Interpretation of the content of the responses, with relationship to all aspects of the performance detailed above, constitutes such an important aspect of the sequence analysis that it is given a separate chapter. (See Chapter 13.)

1. What the Cards Facilitate

In this section the formal aspects of the blot material will be emphasized (that is, locations and determinants) leaving a detailed consideration of the content facilitated by the cards to Chapter 13.

Card I

W Responses

The popular *W* is the expected response—that is, a winged creature—using the blot as a relatively simple outline. If neither this nor a more organized *W* is given, this point is noteworthy, especially if the subject can give whole responses on other cards. Failure to give the *W* may be due to the impact of the unfamiliar situation, to the heavy shading or the relatively unstructured nature of the blot, to the content the card facilitates, or to habitual modes of perception of the individual himself. Later aspects of the performance may aid a choice between these alternative explanations.

D Responses

Whether or not the popular *W* is given, it is expected that the subject will use the center *D* and/or the side *D*'s, either alone or combining them into an organized *W* or *W*. It is noteworthy if the subject confines himself to *d, Dd* or *S* locations.

M Responses

For subjects who see human figures with any facility, this card should evoke *M* responses, either in the center *D* or in the side *D*'s separately or together. Failure to give *M* responses may be due to any of the considerations outlined in the discussion of *W* responses; or the failure may relate more particularly to difficulty in accepting female figures, since *M*'s here are usually given in the context of a female figure.

Card II

Color Responses

This is the first card in which color is introduced; bright red is presented in such a structure that it is fairly easy to integrate it into a *W* or *W* response. Indeed, it is difficult for the subject to isolate the color from the rest of the blot if he does not wish to use it, particularly in the case of the bottom *D*. Hence, Card II is more likely to produce color disturbance than Card III, where the colored areas are relatively easy to avoid. All the points of importance in the examination of color dynamics are relevant here. How does the subject react to the introduction of color? Can he use it, and if so how? If he cannot use the color, can he use the colored areas? Can he integrate the colored areas into a *W*? Is the form level maintained? And so on.

W Responses

For subjects with some organizational interest and ability this card facilitates an organized *W*, either using the popular animals or human figures in interaction. The card also facilitates a less organized, more global *W*. It is noteworthy if the subject who can give organized *W*'s to other cards gives a global *W* here; also, if the subject who ordinarily gives global *W*'s fails to do so here. Failure is likely to be due to the difficulties presented by the color, but for some subjects the heavy shading of the gray area seems to be the disturbing factor.

FM Responses

Since the popular response to this card is an "animal" response, this card facilitates *FM* responses, being one of the most usual locations for *FM*.

M Responses

Although not to the same extent as Card III, this card facilitates the perception of human figures in movement as a response to the whole of the card. It is noteworthy if subjects who are able to see human figures elsewhere fail to use this location; color disturbance may be the explanation. The sex, clothing, action, and other characteristics of the figures are interesting features for content analysis.

d Responses

The center *d* is one of the most usual small details. For some subjects it seems to have a special phallic significance. It is also a frequent location for an *FK* response—for example, a castle with a path leading to it.

Card III

W Responses

The structure of the card so facilitates the separate use of the entire black-gray area that absence of this location is noteworthy.

M Responses

Human figures in action are more easily seen on this card than on any other. If human figures are seen, the inquiry should always explore their sex and clothing and the meaning of all specific areas within the concept. The sexual characteristics of these figures are of particular interest. To some the figures are clearly women because of their breasts; to others the figures are undoubtedly men because of a phallic protuberance; still others have clear preferences based on clothing. Some subjects seem to betray doubt about sexual identification, being unable to decide whether the figures are men or women. Difficulty in differentiating the role of the sexes is indicated by seeing a man on one side and a woman on the other. The type of action attributed to the figures is also of importance, and whether it is in harmony with the sex attributed to the figures. It is of interest whether the figures are (*H*) or (*A*), indicating certain limitations to empathetic interpersonal relationships. Absence of *M* here is always noteworthy. Inability to see human figures even on this card in the testing the limits phase indicates a serious impairment of capacity to identify with other people. Failure to see human figures in action on this card, on the part of subjects who demonstrate *M*-capacity elsewhere, would indicate some especially disturbing feature specific to this card; the most usual sources of disturbance seem to be color and the sexual implications of the figures.

Color Responses

The center red detail facilitates an *FC* response, usually involving the popular concept of a red bow or red butterfly. However, the structure of the blot makes it easy to separate the colored areas from the rest of the blot and thus to ignore color if the subject is inclined to do so. It is to be noted whether the subject handles color in the same way as he did with Card II.

Card IV

W Responses

This card facilitates a *W* response, often a highly differentiated response involving a human or animal figure such as a giant, monster, or gorilla.

D Responses

The side *D*'s are frequently used, especially as "boots." It is noteworthy if this area is not used, especially if the usual *W* is not given either.

Shading Responses

This card presents a marked shading impact, next in importance to that of Card VI. The way in which the subject reacts to the shading is noteworthy. Disturbance of the usual approach established in the previous three cards may be attributable to the influence of shading.

Card V

W Responses

This card greatly facilitates a *W* response, especially the popular "bat" or "butterfly." Failure to give this response is noteworthy since it is so unusual, particularly if it is not accepted even in the testing the limits period.

FM Responses

If the subject tends to see *FM* at all, it is to be expected here, in connection with the popular winged creature or even in the absence of the popular.

M Responses

Human figures are often seen on this card by subjects with *M*-capacity; however, absence of *M* is not significant unless the subject has already demonstrated his ability in this direction.

Recovery

This is a sufficiently easy card that subjects who have been disturbed on earlier cards may be expected to make a recovery here. It is noteworthy if this is not the case or if disturbance appears here for the first time. If there is disturbance here one possible explanation is that the heavy black surface color upsets the subject who is intolerant of dysphoric or depressive reactions.

Card VI

Shading Responses

If the subject responds to shading at all it is likely to be on this card; failure to do so is noteworthy. The mode of handling the shading should be compared with that for Card IV. Although *Fc* or *cF* responses are the most usual ways of using the shading, *FK* is a fairly common response.

Sex Responses

Although reference to content has been avoided in this section, since this topic is discussed more fully in Chapter 13, it should be noted here that the majority of adults seem to interpret the upper *D* of Card VI as a phallic symbol even though overt mention of this content may be suppressed. Therefore, disturbance to this card may reflect sex disturbance rather than the more usual shading disturbance; or disturbance may seem to stem from both elements simultaneously.

Card VII

M Responses

Perhaps next to Card III this card gives most facilitation to *M* responses, particularly responses involving an adult female figure. If the subject has demonstrated *M*-ability on other cards, failure to give an *M* here, even failure to see the figure as adult and female, may give a clue to disturbed mother-child relationships, especially if the response to the card otherwise shows disturbance.

W Responses

Whether vague and indefinite or well-perceived, this card tends to facilitate a *W* response.

K Responses

A diffusion response to the shading elements of this card is facilitated to such an extent that a *K* response here is of no significance if it is the sole *K* given in the entire performance.

Use of the Bottom Center Area

The use of the bottom center area is of interest. For many subjects the *d* area seems to have vaginal significance. The light gray *dd* immediately below may be used alone or in conjunction with the *d* area for a "little house," with implications of needs for security and dependence. This is a common enough response with children, but when given by adults it seems to point to an unusual longing for a childlike state of security. Both of these common responses should be kept in mind when attempting to assess the significance of the content of a response given to this general area. This is one of the more common areas for an *FK* response.

Card VIII

FM Responses

To see animal figures in the side pink *D*'s and to attribute movement to them is so frequent that absence of this response is noteworthy.

Color Dynamics

This is the first all-colored card; hence it is of interest to see how the subject handles the chromatic element, since he can scarcely avoid use of the colored areas without rejecting the card. Does it seem to confuse his perception to such an extent that he does not see the popular "animals"? Is he so anxious to avoid colored areas that he retreats into the white space or into the more neutral gray or light blue areas? Is color so important to him that he tries to combine it with the "animal" concept, resulting in an $F \leftrightarrow C$? Does he respond to the pastel colors of this card with a passive CF? Or he may use F/C or C/F; this is common enough that it should not be emphasized in interpretation unless repeated elsewhere.

Card IX

Rejection

Although rejection is not sufficiently common to be an expected response, it is more common here than with any other card. Card IX seems to be a difficult one in several ways. It seems to require more than average intellectual capacity to achieve a well-perceived concept here; hence this card may be disturbing to the subject who is intolerant of vague form, yet who lacks the ability to achieve a highly differentiated perception without more assistance from the structure of the stimulus material. It is difficult to achieve a W unless color is used; thus the card may be difficult for a subject with a W drive and mild color disturbance. Shading elements are also prominent. The particular reason for the rejection (or disturbance) in a given case may often be deduced from the way in which the other cards are handled, or explained in testing of the limits.

Color Dynamics

Although entirely colored, this card does not seem particularly to facilitate color responses; if the subject is not confused by the considerations discussed above, he can avoid the use of color quite nicely if he is so inclined. For those who are affected by the color of Card IX, the affect tends to be extreme, either euphoric or dysphoric. Thus some subjects find this a pleasant card and give cheerful color responses, suggesting that they find the emotional impact of their social environment a pleasantly stimulating or exciting influence; other subjects find the color very disagreeable and give responses reflecting this reaction, implying that they find emotional impact disturbing and unpleasant.

Card X

D Responses

The blot areas are so separated on this card that *D* responses tend to be given here if nowhere else. Indeed, a *W* response is noteworthy, indicating either an unusual organizational need or a very undifferentiated type of perception, perhaps due to being carried away by the color.

FC Responses

FC responses are more usual on this card than elsewhere; the "green caterpillar" is the only popular *FC* in the series.

Popular Responses

Failure to give popular responses should always be noted and should be explored in testing the limits in all cases where there are few populars in the record as a whole, and in all instances in which the performance seems disturbed. This card particularly facilitates popular responses; at least two of the three populars are to be expected and should be enquired for in testing the limits if they do not appear.

2. Use of Locations

In sequence analysis a convenient point of departure is an examination of the first location given to each card. Is it the location to be expected because the blot material facilitates it? If not, is this because the habitual manner of approach of the subject departs from the usual obvious use of locations? For example, the subject may cautiously proceed from smaller to larger areas, and repeat this performance on card after card. Or the subject may so fragment his perception as to be incapable of seeing W's, which are the most usual first response to most cards. On the other hand, the approach to the card in question may represent a real divergence from the pattern established with other cards.

If the use of locations departs from expectation, hypotheses are formulated to account for the divergence. Although there may be alternative hypotheses for any one card, the cumulative evidence usually favors one alternative to the exclusion of the others. These hypotheses are usually formulated in terms of what the cards facilitate, drawing upon the basic interpretative hypotheses to explain the significance of the "pull" or impact of each card.

Thus if the subject gives isolated details on the heavily shaded cards although capable of giving W or W responses elsewhere, the hypothesis would be that this use of locations reflects shading disturbance, which would be interpreted to mean that a situation with deep affectional implications tends to disturb his ability to achieve an integrated view of the situation, perhaps further implying that fragmentation is used as a defense mechanism against affectional anxiety.

Following similar logic it would be noteworthy if the subject who could use the expected locations in the achromatic cards tended to approach the colored cards differently. The particular mode of handling color would be interpreted in terms of response to the impact of emotional stimulation of the environment, particularly the social environment. Thus if the divergence from the expected locations comes about apparently because of an avoidance of the colored areas, the hypothesis would be that the subject tends to retreat from emotional involvements. If, on the other hand, the divergence comes about through preoccupation with the colored areas (for example going immediately to the red details on Cards II and III instead of using the usual W or W locations, and perhaps giving several concepts to one location) this would suggest an hypothesis that the subject is unusually responsive to the emotional impact of his social environment.

Color and shading are by no means the only features to which may be attributed an unusual use of locations. Thus a cautious or disturbed succession may be given to Card I because it is the first card and represents the challenge of a new and therefore disturbing situation. Sometimes it seems that changes in approach may be explained in terms of the impact of the human concepts facilitated by certain cards. Thus, for example, an inability to use a *W* location in Card IV—although *W*'s can be given elsewhere, including the other heavily shaded cards—may be interpreted as disturbance caused by conscious or unconscious reluctance to identify with or even to perceive an aggressive, masculine figure such as the usual "giant," "monster," or "gorilla." In other instances the sexual implications of the cards seem to be responsible for variations in the use of locations. Thus sexual disturbance may be shown by a flight away from the usual phallic area on Card VI, with disturbed content or form level; or sexual preoccupation might be indicated by a multiplicity of concepts given for this area even though none were overtly sexual. It is impossible to list all the possible interpretative hypotheses that may be formulated from an examination of the use of locations; these few examples should suffice to show how they are derived from the basic interpretative hypotheses, with some enrichment from theories of personality and object relations.

Quite aside from the first response and the succession of responses and their relationship to what the card facilitates, the process of perception and concept formation manifest in the use of locations is of intrinsic interest. For example, is the integrated perception exemplified in the organized *W* arrived at by an immediate perception of implicit relationships? (This quick perception would be shown by a short reaction time.) Or is integrated perception a more laborious process of synthesizing a whole from the component details? (This is suggested by a long reaction time, after which the subject gives his organized whole.) Does the subject impulsively plunge in and construct the whole as he goes along, or does he keep silence until he can produce a finished response that satisfies him? Does the subject give due weight to the implicit logic of the concept itself in achieving his organized whole? Or is his need for organization achieved only by virtue of extraneous links such as symbolism, far-fetched connections, or mere juxtaposition? Such considerations are of great importance in modifying the interpretative hypotheses attached to $W\%$ and the $W : M$ ratio.

Similarly, the process of differentiated perception may be observed directly through the Rorschach performance. Are the differentiations immediate and obvious, even though they may be obscured in the scoring because of incorporation into a whole? Are they seen only where differentiated perception is easy—that is, where D's are facilitated by the structure of the blot? Or does the subject have great difficulty in breaking up his experience into manageable chunks, perhaps being able to see D's only when the rest of the blot material is covered up? Does the subject show a flexible and rich responsiveness by giving unusual details as joyous afterthoughts, after having used the more obvious areas? Or does he habitually see his world in an unusual way and from an unexpected point of view, as shown by his giving Dd first and in obvious preference to W's and D's? Or does he give the impression of a compulsive striving after more responses and more exotic ones, giving Dd effortfully after having exhausted the possibilities of the more usual locations?

Finally, the total coverage of the blot material is of interest in sequence analysis. Does the subject seem to have a compulsive need for completion, laying down a card only when he has managed to give some sort of response for each part of the blot, even though it be difficult, perhaps with verbalization of the need and the difficulty? Does the subject seem preoccupied with certain blot areas, using them again and again for different responses? If so, the content, together with the kind of content facilitated by that area, may suggest an interpretative hypothesis. Is there some apparent reason for the repeated use of a whole, or other location? Some subjects may give two or more concepts for a whole blot in an effort to improve the quality of the concept or its match to the blot material. Others seem to be striving to give a personally more acceptable response —for example, implying a rejection of aggression by following a response with aggressive content with one that is "nice." Sometimes, on the other hand, a second response represents a breakthrough of disturbance that was controlled in the first response. Another consideration is the degree of objective reality assigned by the subject to his concepts. Some subjects seem to feel that a given blot area can "be" only one thing and that an obvious thing; such subjects are incapable of alternative concepts and resistant to testing the limits. This type of performance suggests the hypothesis of a rigidity in viewing the world, developed through a need for certainty in a flight from freedom. Other subjects reflect flexibility in their free use of alternative concepts; still others display a chronic indecisiveness and ambivalence in their difficulty in choosing between alternatives or resolving incompatibilities.

3. Number of Responses

Closely related to the use of the locations is the number of responses given to each card. Are these evenly distributed, or do some cards seem to provide marked stimulation or inhibition? These variations are interpreted in a similar manner to the use of locations. For example, a marked decrease in response to the chromatic cards may be interpreted as an indication of inhibition of productivity in the face of an external emotional challenge. Or, a subject who gives only one response to Card X, a W—although he normally gives more than one W to a card—may be betraying his need for organizational achievement and showing the difficulty of organizing the relatively isolated parts of this particular card.

4. Use of Determinants

A dynamic analysis of the use of determinants in relationship to the blot material, form level, and content is one of the most important aspects of sequence analysis, and one that enriches considerably the interpretation suggested by the psychogram and related quantitative proportions.

The sequence in which the determinants are used is perhaps of first importance. Generally, the first response to the card would seem to reflect that aspect of the personality organization most readily mobilized in response to whatever challenge the card may be said to represent. If the first response to the cards tends to be an *F* response, this suggests an inhibited control of the first reaction to a situation. On the other hand, if *F* responses tend to follow after responses involving "uncontrolled determinants" such as *CF* or *cF* it suggests that the subject attempts to recover from loss of control by repressive mechanisms; the success of such an effort is reflected by form-level rating. Similarly, the readiness of mobilization of the inner resources represented by *M* responses is suggested by the facility with which *M* responses are given—for example, as the first response to all the cards that facilitate an *M* response, or only as a third, fourth, or fifth response to a card. The ease or difficulty with which the subject acknowledges his impulse life is believed to be shown by the readiness with which *FM* responses are given. Are they given quickly wherever the blots facilitate *FM* responses? Or do these responses seem inhibited, given as later responses, or reluctantly conceded in the inquiry, or with passive or restrained movement?

The change in sequence from one card to another is interpreted in the light of the particular impact believed to be presented by the card in question. Does the subject respond to the shading implications of Cards IV and VI, departing from his usual sequence to give shading responses as the most ready reactions? Or does he proceed as usual, unaffected by the change in the shading impact? Or does he depart from his previous sequence, and still not give shading responses? (This would be shown, for example, by replacing *M*'s and *FM*'s by *F* responses on these cards.) If shading responses appear, in what sequence do they appear? Are they differentiated or undifferentiated? Are they "controlled" by organization into a larger response with other determinants? Does the eruption of a given determinant seem to cause disruption in subsequent responses? Similar considerations are examined wherever there is any marked change in sequence of determinants, interpreted differently according to whatever the disturbing impact seems to be for this card for this subject.

The relationship of the determinants to each other deserves consideration, not only in terms of sequence, but also as they are combined into one response. For example, if *m* responses occur particularly in combination with *CF* responses, or perhaps following *CF* responses, the hypothesis would be that the effort of controlling overt response produces tension which is consciously appreciated by the subject. If on the other hand *m* responses occur chiefly with *K*, *cF*, or *FK*, the hypothesis would be that the conflict and tension are related to affectional need.

Note should be taken of instances where determinants are given in unexpected places yet absent in areas where they are to be expected in terms of what the blot material facilitates. Some subjects give *Fc* responses only to colored areas, failing to produce them where most expected (to Cards IV, VI, VII, and possibly II). This would suggest affectional disturbance of such a degree that the need for affection cannot be acknowledged where the impact is great, as in primary familial relationships, although it can be experienced in relationship to the social environment generally. Even more striking are instances where color responses are given only to achromatic cards, representing a pure projection of something that is not there (and is not scored).

Much can be deduced about the subject's defense mechanisms from a sequence analysis of determinants in connection with location and form level. Are his defenses rigid and brittle? This may be shown by resisting the use of a determinant until it finally breaks through with signs of objective or subjective disturbance. Shifting, flexible lines of defense would be shown by a variety of fairly good responses to the card, with the ability to absorb the disturbance within the context of a well-perceived and well-controlled response.

The determinants should be considered with reference to content, either as implied in the concept itself or as overtly expressed. The interpretative hypotheses attached to *M* responses are selected or modified not only with reference to the content scores of *H*, *(H)*, *Hd*, *(Hd)*, and *(A)* but also in terms of the qualities attributed to the human figures in describing their appearance, action, motivation, feelings, and the like. The hypotheses attached to *CF* responses are much modified in terms of whether the content is active and aggressive, as with concepts of "blood," "fire," "explosions," or whether it is passive, as with concepts like "flowers," "pastel colors." Content analysis is discussed more fully in Chapter 13.

The relationship of the affective implications of the content and that of the language is of interest. Some subjects readily admit that certain concepts are distasteful. Others use quite impersonal language to describe concepts with implicitly disagreeable content, and admit affective implications only when the limits are tested. Still others seem to have developed a defense against the disagreeable, treating dysphoric or threatening content lightly, thus referring to a "perfectly beautiful octopus" or an "amusing mask designed to frighten people," and so on. The relationship of both implicit and overt affective tone to the determinants is itself of interest. If *FM* responses always involve disagreeable concepts or negatively toned language, or both, the hypothesis would be that the subject is aware of his impulse life but finds it distasteful and probably threatening. Similarly, if the *M* responses tend to refer to disagreeable or ridiculous people the hypothesis that *M* indicates empathy would have to be modified. The subject's attitude to his own affectional needs would differ according to whether he describes the shading elements as "lovely" or as "suffocating" or in some other negative terms.

5. Form-Level Rating

The variations in form level throughout the record are of great interpretative significance. The subject who can maintain a superior form level throughout (except perhaps for a few *CF* responses) and yet can give a well-balanced variety of determinants would seem to have a fine control of intellectual function and good but flexible ties to reality. If there are breaks in form level it is important to note where they occur, how bad they are, and how well and how quickly good form level is regained. Thus the subject would be believed to become intellectually disorganized in emotion-producing situations if the first impact of color in Card II reduces the form level to 0.0, or even 0.5 or 1.0. This would seem merely to be an initial disturbance if the subject recovers his intellectual grip on things and gives better form level on subsequent responses to the card. On the other hand, the disturbance would be considered more serious if it does not disappear until the colored elements themselves disappear on Card IV. Disruption of ties with reality are indicated by breaks in form level running into the minus range. Light may be thrown upon the degree of insight into the disturbance by the degree of subjective discomfort accompanying the drops in form level. Does the subject show obvious dislike of the responses with low form level, or is he content or even pleased with his production? If he is pleased with minus responses, does this seem to be delight in a playful disregard of the reality limits (which is possible in a permissive situation) or does it seem to reflect the domination of unconscious elements breaking through to distort the perception of reality? Content analysis of the minus responses may give significant clues about the dynamics of the disturbance.

Despite the importance of the obvious breaks in form level, sometimes subtle impairment of efficiency is only to be detected by comparing the average form level from card to card, from location to location, or from determinant to determinant. The fact that situations with affectional impact tend to lower intellectual efficiency may thus be indicated by lowered averages on the heavily shaded cards, or by lower averages for *Fc* and *FK* responses than for *M, FM, F,* and *FC.*

6. Comments

Some subjects give valuable information in their comments and inquiries, both in the course of the test and in post-test conversation. The following are a few of the types of comment that are of interpretative assistance: expressions of inadequacy, dissatisfaction, or perplexity; comments indicating which cards or concepts are liked or disliked; requests for reassurance or direction; expressions of inability to handle the situation as desired; statements indicating drive or intent to make wholes, use color, and the like; linkages of

concepts with personal experience; side remarks indicating associative links of which the subject may or may not be aware, and
so on.

7. Test Behavior

In any individually administered test the general behavior of the
subject in the test situation is grist for the interpretative mill. Aside
from the familiar features of degree of coöperation, ease or nervous-
ness, enjoyment or anxiety or resentment, and so on, there are certain specific features worthy of note. Does the subject turn the cards?
If he does not, this may indicate a certain rigidity of approach. If
he turns them round and round with little productiveness this may
indicate uncertainty or doubt. If the turning results in responses,
with long pauses in between, this may indicate an effort to squeeze
the last possible concept out of the material, a quantity drive. Sometimes the subject proceeds in an orderly fashion giving responses to
the card first in an upright position, then with it turned sideways,
and then upside-down. Although this would indicate an orderly exploration of the possibilities of the situation, it would suggest less
flexibility than if the cards were turned in a way that seems dictated
more by the material itself than by a predetermined approach. Occasionally the subject turns the card almost immediately; the interpretation of this phenomenon would be entirely dependent upon
the structure of the card and the concept subsequently given. For
example, if Card VIII is immediately turned sideways and the popular *FM* given, this may indicate a respect for logic, in that it makes
it possible to see the popular animal "walking" or "with its head
down looking into water," rather than "standing on its hind legs,"
or "climbing over something." On the other hand, the immediate
turning of Card VI may be dictated by an effort to avoid the phallic
implications of the top *D*.

"Edging the cards" is sometimes to be noted—that is, looking
across the surface of the card rather than holding it at right-angles

to the line of vision. The exact significance of this behavior is not known, but it seems to occur chiefly with highly neurotic or psychotic persons. Touching the cards or stroking the surface may highlight the subject's interest in texture, implying contact need. Finally, note should be taken of the context in which the subject laughs, sighs, or moves restlessly.

8. Reaction Time and Response Time

A slow reaction time to a specific card may often be interpreted as a sign of disturbance caused by whatever particular impact the card is believed to present. Sometimes the reaction time is prolonged because the subject does not state aloud his first concept or concepts; sometimes the perceptual process itself is disturbed. A permissive inquiry or testing the limits may clarify which kind of disturbance is involved and perhaps coax out the suppressed content. Slow reaction time may be due to the fact that the subject takes time to organize or perfect his concept before describing it; this may be detected both from the quality of the response when it comes, and by the fact that the reaction time tends to be slow on the difficult cards but fast on Card V or possibly Card III.

It unduly complicates administration to record the time for each separate response, but note should be taken of any long pauses. If the subject has long pauses between responses throughout the record this may indicate either sluggish or highly effortful production, depending on the quality of the responses themselves. It is the occasional long pause that gives a clue to specific disturbance; the source of the disturbance may be ascertained from studying the location, determinant, and content and its relationship to the blot material.

9. Color Dynamics

The hypothesis relating to color dynamics is that the bright color of Cards II and III and the all-over color of Cards VIII, IX, and X represent the emotional impact of the environment, and that the way in which the subject handles these cards indicates the way he himself adjusts to emotional impact. This hypothesis stems from Rorschach himself; although it is in this sense well established in the Rorschach technique it has been one of the most highly disputed aspects of the technique in statistical validation research. The dispute seems to revolve about the concept of "color shock," which has been held to be a sign of disturbance, particularly neurotic disturbance. Only too often this concept has been handled in a mechanical way by counting up the various "signs of color shock" without due regard to the individualized way in which color is handled in the record. This has happened both in the diagnostic use of the Rorschach and in statistical validation studies. Because "color shock" has been mishandled in this way the term will be avoided here, and attention will be directed to an examination of the handling of color through an analysis of the sequence of responses.

Three considerations are of interest for sequence analysis. First, it is of interest how the person uses color as a determinant, if indeed he does so. Second, if he tends not to use color as a determinant it is important to distinguish between the following dynamic patterns of response, which will be defined below: color choosiness, color shyness, color denial, color avoidance, and disregard for color with objective disturbance. Third, attention should be paid to signs of disturbance occurring on color cards or when color locations are used, distinguishing between subjective and objective manifestations of disturbance. These three sets of considerations are not mutually exclusive. Thus a subject might give a few color-determined responses, with tendencies to avoid using color as a determinant throughout most of the record, with some indications of disturbance on the color cards. However, for the purposes of discussion the three items will be considered separately.

The Use of Color as a Determinant

Least attention will be given here to the use of color as a determinant. The interpretative hypotheses used are derived from those attached to the various color determinant scores, modified in consideration of the location used, the relationship to content, to other determinants, to form level, and to remarks or elaborations indicating pleasure or discomfort—indeed, to all the signs of color disturbance which will be considered below—and, finally, with regard to the occurrence of color-determined responses in the whole sequence of responses.

The most constructive use of color is shown by using all shades of color as presented in the cards without hesitation or disturbance, with some controlling element (which indicates an appropriate and easy meeting of emotional situations), maintaining control yet not retreating from emotional challenge. This would be shown by the ready production of *FC* with a few *CF* responses. A consideration of the natural, forced, arbitrary, or symbolic flavor of the color responses given, together with the readiness with which they are given and the degree of control maintained, will serve to indicate the closeness with which the individual approximates the ideal described above.

Special mention should be made here of responses that make use of color for the concept where the blot material does not suggest it, either as photographically represented color (*Fc*) or as a pure projection. Where the shading is used to represent color photographically, and where *Fc* can be scored, the hypothesis is one of "abortive sublimation" as outlined on page 274. Where the color is projected on an achromatic area without justification in terms of the shading, or where it is projected on a blot area of an entirely different color (there being no question of color blindness), the fantasy-dominated quality of the response suggests a serious loosening of the ties with reality and an inappropriate manifestation of affect.

Tendencies Not To Use Color as a Determinant

If color is used little or not at all in determining the responses given to color cards, it is of importance to distinguish between the following patterns:

a. Color *choosiness,* shown by a tendency to use only the milder colors and to retreat from the colored areas in Cards II and III. The hypothesis is that this indicates some disturbance in the face of emotional challenge, with a certain reluctance to become involved emotionally.

b. Color *shyness,* shown by general reluctance to use colors, even leaving out color elements in concepts. If this occurs without objective disturbance in responses using colored locations, the hypothesis is that it indicates a lack of emotional dependence on others but no disruption in the face of emotional challenge.

c. Color *denial,* shown by concepts suggesting the use of color but with marked avoidance in the inquiry of admitting that the color elements had anything to do with the response. Thus, for example, the subject may see animals fighting on Card II but deny the use of the red areas as blood; or he may give the response "Hair ribbon" to the center red detail on Card III but insist that it was just the shape that determined the response. If there is denial, it is of interest to see whether it is maintained consistently throughout, or applies to the strong colors on Cards II and III with some use of milder colors on the last three cards, or is combined with strong color responses such as blood, fire, and explosions. The hypothesis is that color denial is a sign of ego strength, in that the emotional impact is resisted; however, the degree of objective disturbance and the presence or absence of breakthrough of uncontrolled color responses will modify this hypothesis.

d. Color *avoidance,* shown by failure to use the color locations. It is of interest to note whether this is carried consistently throughout with a tendency to use only the white space or grayish areas in the last three cards, or is shown only on Cards II and III, with submissive acceptance on Cards VIII, IX, and X in terms of color responses such as color designs, flowers, patterns, pastel shades. The hypothesis is that color avoidance suggests a desire to retreat from situations involving emotional challenge. If this is combined with submissive acceptance of color on Cards VIII, IX, and X it would indicate that there are emotional situations with which the individual cannot cope, but that his tendency to avoid such situations enables him to maintain a certain amount of control.

e. *Disregard* for color with objective disturbance, with use of colored areas, but with the concepts not implying the use of color. This implies less control than color avoidance, in that the individual cannot control even through retreat. It is difficult to say whether or not this type of response implies more maladjustment than that in which objective disturbance occurs with the use of color determinants. Both are disturbed types of performance; but disregard for color implies a lack of awareness of the emotional situation that is touching off the difficulties, whereas the use of color as a determinant, although with disturbance, at least implies a conscious awareness of and responsiveness to emotional impact.

Color Disturbance

Color disturbance may be either subjective or objective, or both. Certain features of the response to color cards clearly point to one type of disturbance or the other; other features are ambiguous and might be caused by either objective or subjective disturbance. Since the interpretative hypotheses attached to objective disturbance are quite different from those attached to subjective disturbance, and since both kinds of disturbance are lumped together in most lists of "signs of color shock," it is little to be wondered at that statistical research has shown the "signs" to be of doubtful validity.

Indications of Subjective Disturbance

Subjective disturbance is betrayed by the remarks and explanations of the subject referring to the color or by the way in which the concepts given to color areas are described. The subject finds the color unpleasant or distressing and either says so in indirect remarks or shows his discomfort in the unpleasant connotations of the concept the colored area suggests to him. The hypothesis is that this indicates a conscious appreciation of disturbance in situations with emotional impact. When it occurs without objective disturbance the implication is that the subject is able to maintain his intellectual efficiency in dealing with emotional situations despite his feeling of discomfort. The absence of subjective disturbance may indicate absence of discomfort in emotional situations because of competence in dealing with them; this would be expected of the well-adjusted person who would show his competence by absence of objective disturbance.

Indications of Objective Disturbance

The following indications of objective disturbance are all reflected in formal scoring: lowering of form level on colored cards or for colored areas, changes in the succession of locations on colored cards, changes in the use of determinants on colored cards or for colored areas, and failure to see populars on colored cards. It should be understood that all of these indications show changes in the direction of lowered efficiency of function when faced with the colored cards. Changes in the opposite direction are worthy of note and are interpreted as increase of effectiveness of function under the stimulation of emotional impact from without.

Of the indications listed above, the most significant is a drop in form level. Changes in succession of particular interest here are those that indicate a regression from integrated to fragmented perception, or from differentiated to undifferentiated perception, or those that show a breakdown from a systematic or orderly approach to a confused or chaotic one. Interesting changes of determinants would reflect either a constrictive process with F responses replacing the movement or shading responses that had previously been freely given, or a weakening of control; in the latter case a drop in form level would also occur.

The hypothesis is that objective disturbance indicates a lowering of efficiency in emotional situations, the seriousness of the change being indicated by the extent of the formal disturbance. Breaks into minus form level indicate the most severe disruption of efficiency. When objective disturbance is combined with subjective disturbance the implication is that the person maintains conscious appreciation of his difficulties, and usually shows some attempt to handle emotional challenge, be it only through retreating. Where it occurs with no sign of subjective discomfort—particularly when minus-form-level responses are the criterion of disturbance—this indicates a disintegration of efficiency under emotional impact, with no insight into the difficulty, and hence serious weakening of ties with reality.

Indications of Either Subjective or Objective Disturbance

There are several indications of disturbance that might indicate either subjective or objective disturbance, or both. Careful testing of the limits is usually necessary to determine which is the case.

Increase of reaction time to the chromatic cards or long pauses between responses may indicate either type of disturbance. If the delay is due to the deliberate suppression of an unpleasant concept which the subject does not wish to mention to the examiner, and a search for a more acceptable concept to substitute for it, the disturbance is clearly conscious—that is, subjective. If, on the other hand, the delay is due to a true disruption of perception in which there is a blocking or inhibition, the disturbance is best characterized as objective.

Rejection of one or more color cards or a marked decrease of responses to color cards may reflect similar alternatives. If the rejection is to avoid mentioning a distasteful concept such as a sexual concept with blood on Card II, the disturbance is subjective. Similarly, a decrease in responses to a given card may indicate a similar suppressive process. If the rejection or decrease in responses is due to a genuine inhibition or blocking of perception, the disturbance is objective. In the latter case the depth of blocking should be tested by ascertaining the ability of the subject to accept concepts suggested to him in testing the limits.

Content of the response may also indicate either type of disturbance. Unpleasant or dysphoric responses may be given in several ways. If they are obviously productive of discomfort in the subject they indicate subjective disturbance, even though this may not be clear until the testing-the-limits period. Some subjects attempt to disguise their discomfort by presenting their concept in light or sophisticated terms, with control maintained as shown by maintenance of good form level. This must be distinguished from "cold-blooded use of hot color concepts," in which case there is a poor form level with disagreeable or uncontrolled content (such as unpleasant anatomical concepts, explosions, disintegrations) with no sign of subjective disturbance. This indicates a serious shallowness of affective reactions.

Although it is outside the scope of this present chapter to deal with the diagnostic significance of the various patterns to be detected in the sequence analysis, certain diagnostic features of color disturbance should be mentioned as having obvious relevance to the above discussion. Absence of both objective and subjective disturbance is characteristic of the well-integrated personality standing in a good relationship with its environment. Slight subjective disturbance without objective disturbance is common within the normal range. Marked subjective disturbance is characteristic of neurotic adjustment; increasing accompanying objective disturbance is found with the more serious neurotic conditions. As subjective disturbance decreases with continuing objective disturbance the range of psychotic disorders is approached. The chief diagnostic category that may cause difficulty is that of psychopathic personality where both objective and subjective disturbance may be lacking and a pseudo-normal record be given; in this case some estimate of the depth or shallowness of affect and the capacity for object relations is an essential supplement.

10. Shading Dynamics

The general hypothesis underlying an analysis of the shading dynamics is that the way in which the subject handles the shading elements of the blot material throws light upon the way he handles his own affectional needs. The entire series of ten cards is considered, not just those cards that are entirely achromatic. On Cards II and III there are large achromatic areas; on Card II, particularly, the shading is heavy. Moreover, in the colored areas in these cards and in the all-colored cards there are differentiations in shading. Any heavily shaded area in any one of the ten cards is of interest as representing an affectional impact to the subject, one that may arouse his basic security needs. His response to the area in question may show either how these needs are experienced or how his defenses are mobilized to deal with such impact.

First, it is of interest whether the subject uses shading as a determinant and, if so, how he does it. Secondly, if he tends not to use shading as a determinant it is important to ascertain whether this is a matter of denial, evasion, or insensitivity. Finally, as in the case of color dynamics, attention is turned to the degree of disturbance aroused by the shading and whether this is expressive merely of subjectively experienced discomfort or whether it is manifested through the lowering of efficiency of function—that is, through objective disturbance.

The Use of Shading as a Determinant

If shading is used as a determinant it is of interest how it is combined with form (that is, differentiated and undifferentiated use of shading) and whether the shading suggests texture, vista, diffusion, or a three-dimensional concept reduced to a two-dimensional plane. The interpretative hypotheses attached to the shading determinants apply throughout the sequence analysis and are modified in consideration of the relation of the shading response to location, other determinants, content, form level, remarks, readiness, and the like.

The locations used for shading responses are of especial interest. Does the subject use only the areas most frequently responded to—that is, the heavily shaded areas of Cards VI and IV? Or does he respond freely to the shading on other areas as well? Or does he fail to use shading in the usual heavily shaded areas but produce shading responses in lightly shaded or colored areas—for example, "clouds" for the pink *D*'s on Card IX or "furry animals" on Card VIII? In general, it may be useful to equate the most heavily shaded areas to the most highly loaded affectional impact of primary object relations, while the lightly shaded areas, particularly those that are colored as well, represent the more attenuated affectional impact of less emotionally loaded social relationships. This hypothesis must, however, be used with caution, for considerations other than the heaviness of the shading itself seem to play a part. Thus Card VII, whether because of the vaginal formation at the bottom of the card or because of the forms suggesting female figures, seems frequently to present strong impact, although the shading is relatively light.

Tendencies Not To Use Shading as a Determinant

If shading is used as a determinant very rarely or not at all, it is of importance to distinguish between the following patterns:

a. Shading *denial,* shown by the production of at least two responses to heavily shaded areas, these responses suggesting the use of shading but with marked avoidance in the inquiry of admitting that the shading elements had anything to do with the response. This denial may be carried into the testing-the-limits period with strong resistance to accepting shading as a determinant. Thus, for example, the subject may give animal skin responses to Cards IV and VI but state that this response was determined by the shape only, with outright rejection of the idea that the shading might have made it seem "furry." Sometimes, in their manner of denial of their use of shading subjects may betray their sensitivity to shading—for example, by pointing out that there is too much contrast between light and dark for it to seem like fur. Shading denial is considered the most ego-defensive response to shading, indicating a conscious conflict about acceptance of affectional need. As with color denial, it is considered a sign of ego strength.

b. Shading *evasion,* shown by one of the following ways of handling shading: (1) Using the shading stimuli on the heavily shaded cards but not in the most usual and most conspicuously shaded areas; for example, calling the bottom center of Card IV an "animal skin" instead of the rest of the card, or giving a shading-determined response to the top center D in Card VI rather than to the large lower area. (2) Giving a usual response to the shaded areas, such as an "animal skin" or "fur-bearing animal," and justifying the response in the inquiry by pointing to the ragged or fuzzy edge rather than emphasizing the texture of the blot. (3) Using the common shading areas but with vague shading responses of a content suggesting an attempt to avoid direct contact sensations; for example, in Card IV, "about the only thing I could see would be maybe something under water." During testing the limits, the subject who evades shading will show little or no resistance in accepting the usual justification of shading responses. The hypothesis is that shading evasion indicates reluctance to accept one's need for affection, with the emphasis on repressive mechanisms rather than conscious denial. This is believed to stem from early experiences of rejection or deprivation and to result in difficulties in forming satisfactory object relations, although not to the extent of the severe impairment shown by shading insensitivity.

c. Shading *insensitivity,* shown by no reference to shading in either the performance proper or in the inquiry, with minimal use of the concepts that subjects usually connect with the shading stimuli (clouds, animal skins, and the like). Even the insensitive subject may respond "animal skin" to Card VI, however, because of the shape of the blot. In testing the limits he either may not understand the most explicit explanation of the possible use of shading stimuli or may show very little interest in it, without any marked resistance to the idea. In any case, he will not be able to apply the principle of shading differences to another card because he is not sensitive to such differences. Shading insensitivity is the most seriously disturbed pattern of response to shading. The hypothesis is that it indicates such an early and severe deprivation experience that the need for stable dependent and affectional relationships either has never been properly mobilized or developed, or it has been severely repressed; in either case the capacity for any deep or meaningful object relations has been very seriously impaired.

Shading Disturbance

It is perhaps more difficult to attribute disturbance on any given card to the shading elements than it was even in the case of color disturbance. In certain instances it is quite clear, however. For example, remarks showing discomfort about the shading are obvious signs of subjective disturbance. Concepts clearly suggesting the use of shading (whether this is accepted or denied) which are described in unpleasant terms may be considered evidence of subjective disturbance—that is, disturbance indicating conscious uneasiness in the area of affectional need. At the other extreme, *Fc* minus responses are clear indications of objective disturbance attributable to shading. Other signs of objective disturbance are (1) changes in the direction of less efficient function with respect to form level, succession of locations, or use of determinants, and (2) failure to see populars, not only on Cards VI and IV but also on Cards I and V and perhaps on Card II. As with color disturbance, there are other indications that may reflect either objective or subjective disturbance, or both: namely, long reaction time to achromatic cards and especially in the case of the most heavily shaded cards (VI and IV); long pauses between responses, particularly when the subject is trying to use heavily shaded areas; marked reduction of responses to the heavily shaded cards; and rejection of one or more of the achromatic cards. Finally, the content of the response itself may indicate shading disturbance, although it is not always clear whether this is objective or subjective. Indeed, it is often difficult to ascertain whether the disturbances described above are in fact directly attributable to the shading elements, although this hypothesis should always be entertained and examined in the light of other evidence both within the Rorschach performance and from other sources.

Subjective shading disturbance seems to indicate frustration of affectional needs that is well-appreciated by the subject. A more severe disturbance with objective signs of loss of efficiency of function seems to indicate a more deep-seated deprivation or rejection, with more ingrained maladjustment as a result. As indicated earlier, the most serious deprivation experiences are reflected in shading insensitivity, where there is no subjective disturbance apparent and where whatever objective signs of inefficient function there may be are not directly attributable to the presence of shading—for indeed, the subject does not seem to be affected by the shading elements at all.

11. Performance Proper vs. Inquiry vs. Testing the Limits

Going on now to the next item, comparison of the performance proper with the inquiry and the testing of limits, the general hypothesis is that the performance proper indicates the resources readily available to the subject in a relatively unstructured situation where specific demands, direction, and support are lacking. The additional material that emerges in the inquiry is interpreted in the light of what is available after he becomes more settled in the situation, the interaction with the examiner perhaps playing a facilitating or inhibiting role. Sometimes the subject becomes freer in the inquiry, either better able to draw on constructive resources or able to drop his defenses and let go his control. Sometimes he is threatened even by a non-directive inquiry and tends to become defensive or to retract. In any event, the comparisons between the two sections of the protocol are of interpretative significance.

Whereas the analogy period is designed to help the examiner with scoring, the testing-the-limits period is intended to highlight interpretation, giving the examiner opportunity to observe the response of the subject when he is progressively pushed in directions he did not take in the earlier part of the test. The general hypothesis is that testing the limits will tap the aspects of the adjustment not readily available to the subject, giving an opportunity to estimate the extent of potential. Since the testing of the limits is tailor-made to suit the particular protocol, it is extremely difficult to list specific hypotheses. In practice, the examiner will find that these specific hypotheses emerge quite readily from the basic interpretative hypotheses.

12. The Relationship between Subject and Examiner

Although the establishment of rapport is taken for granted as an important aspect of administration of any individual test, it is too infrequently realized that the relationship between the subject and the examiner has also an interpretative significance. Any holistic interpretative procedure should take account of the subject-examiner relationship as just as much part of the total context as the stimulus material itself. However, the influence of this aspect of the test situation has been inadequately explored; it is not known in detail just what influence on the test performance is provided by the personality of the examiner, the expectations of the subject regarding the test, the previous acquaintanceship with the examiner, and the role of the examiner in the total life situation.

Nevertheless, account should be taken of the possible influence the examiner may have had upon the performance, having regard for the dynamics of the particular subject involved. Such obvious considerations may apply as, for example, that an adult male subject may be inhibited in expressing overt sexual content to a young female examiner, and hence should not necessarily be considered more inhibited than another subject who has established a man-to-man relationship with a male examiner. Less obvious are the considerations relating to the underlying object relations of the subject and the way in which the personality or role of the examiner, real or fantasied, may influence his performance. An examiner with an authoritarian manner, testing under authoritarian conditions, may well have an inhibiting effect on many subjects, tending to produce a more constricted picture of personality than would be the case with an examiner who can in fact establish the highly permissive relationship intended in the Rorschach technique. On the other hand, a highly permissive examiner may be cast into an authoritarian role by the subject, and the same type of result obtained. Moreover, different subjects might well be expected to respond differentially to the same authoritarian examiner, some becoming inhibited, some challenged to higher intellectual production, others perhaps striking out aggressively through both the formal and content aspects of the protocol.

It would be a useful exercise for Rorschach examiners to compare notes regarding the particular bias or flavor that seems to emerge from the records of the general run of subjects they examine, especially when these subjects are drawn from the same population and the records are checked for uniform application of scoring principles. It is probably only through some such exercise, or research similar to that of Lord [1], that the examiner may learn to know the constant factor his personality introduces into the testing situation so that he may take it into account in his interpretations. Indeed, such an exercise would be pertinent in all individual testing; there is no reason to believe that tests of cognitive function are free from influence by subject-examiner relationship.

References

1. Lord, Edith. "Experimentally Induced Variations in Rorschach Performance," *Psychological Monographs,* 1950, No. 316, Vol. 64, #10.

CHAPTER 12

Evaluation of Intellectual Level, Control, Creative Potential, and the Introversive-Extratensive Relationship

It is a customary part of Rorschach analysis to estimate the levels of intellectual capacity and efficiency of the subject. This is not considered a substitute for a test of general intelligence—although for some purposes such an estimate might be all that is required, thus making an intelligence test unnecessary. That the estimate of intellectual capacity is frequently in close agreement with the findings of other psychometric methods provides evidence for the validity of the hypotheses upon which the estimate is based. There are, of course, discrepancies in the findings, but these cannot be taken as a general indication of unreliability of either test or the invalidity of either method. On the contrary, the differences between the kind of situation presented by the usual intelligence test and that presented by the Rorschach or other projective technique lead to the hypothesis that the IQ reflects the performance of the subject in a structured situation whereas the intellectual estimate from the projective technique indicates his performance in an unstructured situation. The intelligence test is described as "structured" because a clear task is presented to the subject, a task that he is urged to perform as well or as quickly as he can and a task having obvious linkages with similar demands in academic or occupational situations. The projective technique is said to provide a relatively "unstructured" situation in that the test situation is highly permissive, the subject being reassured that he can do what he pleases with the material and that there are no right and wrong answers. It is only to be expected that some subjects will blossom out in a permissive situation although they may be anxious, inhibited, or overly matter of fact in the more structured intelligence test. Other subjects tend to flounder in a situation where the limits are vague and there is no certainty regarding what is really expected of them; such subjects would feel on familiar ground in the more structured situation and respond with more confidence and effectiveness.

The intellectual estimate derived from the Rorschach performance is primarily based upon the intellectual level of the perceptual process as it may be deduced from the concepts given. This level depends relatively little upon knowledge assimilated in the life experience. It is assumed that vague, global perception reflects a relatively low level of capacity, and that the more refined and differentiated the perception the higher the level of intelligence. The level of integrated and organized perception is considered the highest level of all. Since these features are rated as form level, this step in scoring is the most important basis of the intellectual estimate.

Despite the fact that the IQ was intended to be a measure of intellectual capacity, it is generally acknowledged by psychologists that capacity can only be measured as it reflects itself through ability—through what the individual has learned to do. The IQ may thus be considered a measure of general ability, indicating the general extent to which the individual has realized his potential. Although an analysis of sub-test scatter may provide an indication of discrepancy between ability and capacity, this is of controversial significance, mixed up as it is with diagnostic considerations. When the IQ is used as a basis of prediction of academic or occupational success, it is what the person can readily mobilize that is of importance, and the distinction between ability and capacity does not matter particularly. However, in the clinical situation it is often of great importance to distinguish between actual and potential limits of function; it is for this type of problem that the Rorschach estimate is of particular value.

The hypothesis is that the limit of capacity is at least as high as that indicated by the best response given in the test, although it may indeed be higher. On the other hand, the general level of the responses throughout the record indicates the level at which the intellectual resources are usually available—the habitual level of efficiency with which the person operates. The "worst" responses in the record are believed to indicate the extent and frequency with which the person loses his intellectual grip on reality and becomes incompetent in integrating his perception with the reality situation. As a supplement to the estimate of intellectual efficiency a description is given of the particular strengths and weaknesses manifested in the intellectual function of the individual.

Hypotheses Relating to Intellectual Estimate

The following aspects of Rorschach performance are considered when estimating intellectual capacity and efficiency:

1. Form-level rating.
2. Quantity and quality of M responses.
3. Quantity and quality of W responses.
4. Quantity and quality of O responses.
5. Variety of content.
6. Succession.

1. Form-Level Rating

Form-level rating is the most important basis of the intellectual estimate. The hypothesis is that the form level varies directly with intellectual level, and that the highest form level obtained gives an indication of the level of capacity or potentiality, whereas the average form level indicates the general level of efficiency of intellectual function—that is, the extent to which potential is realized. An examination of the changes in form level through sequence analysis is believed to provide clues to the type and source of disturbance of intellectual function.

Tentatively, it is suggested that even one response of:

Form level 4.0 indicates very superior capacity,
Form level 3.0 indicates superior capacity,
Form level 2.0 indicates average to slightly above average capacity.

One difficulty with this set of hypotheses is that occasionally one or two responses indicating superior capacity may be given by subjects diagnosed as mentally defective. Before concluding that this is obvious evidence of invalidity of the hyopthesis that form level reflects capacity, it would seem wise to consider the growing weight of evidence that the IQ is far from being a constant figure presumably set by the genetic limitations on intellectual growth. Clinical evidence suggests that mental deficiency resulting from organic damage or disease leaves a jagged profile of abilities and defects, even though the general level of ability may average out as very low. Even more important, there is a gradual accumulation of clinical evidence that early deprivation or serious emotional disturbances may prevent the individual from manifesting more than a fraction of his capacity either in general intelligence tests or in his general adjustment to life. It is a common clinical finding that therapy often results in an increase in IQ, particularly with children. From this kind of evidence it seems reasonable to form the hypothesis that with some individuals there is a great discrepancy between the limits set by capacity and the level at which the individual habitually functions. The hypothesis is that even one response of 2.5 form level counterindicates a diagnosis of simple feeble-mindedness. If other indications point to a very low level of intellectual efficiency, the examiner would seem faced either with an individual with very uneven capacities resulting from organic disease or damage, or one who has been prevented from realizing his intellectual potential through severe emotional disturbance. Although a social diagnosis of "feeblemindedness" may be justified in terms of the individual's incapacity to maintain himself in society, the differential diagnosis is of importance in detecting individuals who may be able to respond to therapy or special training.

The second chief difficulty with the hypotheses relating to the estimate of intellectual capacity comes from within the Rorschach performance itself. To a certain extent the spontaneous elaboration of responses reflects personality trends as well as capacity. Some subjects give careful elaboration of their concepts, attaining a high form level in an effortful fashion; others lightly mention well-seen concepts, bothering little to justify the match of concept to blot material, perhaps because it seems self-evident that the match is good. High form level effortfully obtained would indicate both superior capacity and a straining to keep intellectual performance close to the limits of capacity. If an estimate of capacity is to be obtained for the casual subject, however, he must be encouraged by non-directive inquiry to elaborate his responses beyond what may be necessary for scoring locations and determinants. However, mere elaboration does not necessarily raise the form level. Some records that appear at first glance to be "very intelligent" are found to be full of highly personalized and over-ideational elaborations; these are counted as irrelevant specifications since they have nothing to do with the keenness of perception which is the basis of form-level rating and the estimate of intellectual capacity.

In records where there is not a great variation in the form level from one response to another, the average form level is considered an indication of intellectual efficiency. An average weighted form level from 1.0 to 1.4 represents the average level of function, indicating a moderately differentiated perception of the Rorschach material. Below this average there would be an inferior level of mental efficiency with a large proportion of the responses undifferentiated, vague, and global. An average weighted form level of 1.5 to 1.9 indicates a fair proportion of well differentiated responses and, hence, an above-average level of function. Very superior intellectual efficiency is indicated by an average form level above 2.0; achieving this level requires a large proportion of responses that are very well differentiated, or well organized, or both.

If there is great scatter in the form level it is more difficult to estimate a general level of intellectual efficiency characteristic of the individual. Here it seems more meaningful to describe the processes that make for inefficient function and their apparent causes. This description may be derived from sequence analysis in which form level is considered with reference both to the blot material and to all other aspects of the response.

Minus form level deserves particular mention. Accurate perception results from an integration of the structural characteristics of the stimulus material and the meaning attached to it by the person in the light of his present needs and past experience. The hypothesis is that minus form level is due to an exaggeration of the personal contribution to perception at the expense of adequate acknowledgment of the structure of "reality" as represented by the blot material. Thus minus responses may be described as concept-dominated or fantasy-dominated. They represent a distortion of reality in terms of the concept the subject imposes upon the material. Interpretatively, therefore, they represent something more than mere low level of intellectual function; a loosening of the ties to reality is always involved. This does not imply that the appearance of minus responses is an invariable indication of psychotic function, even though it is characteristic of psychotic records. Much depends upon the other aspects of the record, with recoverability an important consideration. The content of the minus response may provide an important clue to the cause of the distortion of perception, indicating the kind of fantasy, need, or concept that engrosses the subject to the extent that he misinterprets his world in terms of it.

Descriptive tendencies represent an opposite emphasis in that the structure of the blot material is given undue weight and the subject fails to integrate it with his own apperceptive background. These may be described as blot-dominated responses. They seem to represent a safe line when there is difficulty in integrating stimulus and meaning. The hypothesis is that this is a mechanism by means of which the subject protects himself against breaks with reality; sensing the danger of being guided by his own interpretation, he clings to reality, even though his failure to achieve meaningful perception means that he cannot make an adequate adjustment to the reality to which he clings. It is not surprising to find descriptive tendencies alternating with minus responses in the same records.

2.   Quantity and Quality of M Responses

The more *M* responses, the farther they go beyond the obvious, and the richer the variations from the usual responses, the more brilliant the intellectual function. Subjects of barely average intelligence rarely give *M* responses except to Card III. The imaginative and empathetic function shown by *M* responses is apparently characteristic of superior capacity. However, lack of *M* responses cannot be interpreted as an indication of low intellectual capacity where other indications point to the contrary; indeed this is a common sign of emotional disturbance among superior adults. In such a case lack of *M*'s would indicate intellectual efficiency below the level of capacity, the particular flavor of the inefficiency being an inhibition of imaginal function and an inability to achieve empathetic identification. This adjustment may permit efficient function in non-creative academic pursuits or in practical achievement, but it suggests inefficient function in the emotional and social aspects of adjustment and a blockage in creativity.

The quality of *M* responses is important in interpretations; minus form level tends to indicate a serious lack of control over the imaginal function—a lack that, in itself, represents a serious break in intellectual efficiency.

3.   Quantity and Quality of Whole Responses

A high level of intellectual function is indicated by a fair number of *W* responses of good quality. This implies form level high enough to indicate good differentiation and organization of perception, with stress upon the recognition of relationships inherent between the differentiated parts of the material perceived. The reverse implication is given by a large number of global or undifferentiated whole responses, which indicates either a low level of intellectual capacity or considerable emotional interference with efficiency of function. The absence of any significant number of *W*'s would not in itself be grounds for estimating capacity at a low level;

this may be found with an over-cautious, over-meticulous approach associated with high form level. In such instances the lack of *W*'s would point to a weakness in function in organized perception, in seeing relationships, and a general difficulty in mobilizing resources towards an integrated achievement.

4. Quantity and Quality of Original Responses

Characteristic of free use of resources and a high level of intellectual efficiency is a large number of original responses, main and additional, which have good form level and lack both strain and bizarre elements. Where the capacity is estimated to be high on other grounds and there is much scatter in form level and fewer originals than should be given by a subject of high capacity, the implication is that intellectual efficiency is considerably lowered, and that there are resources that the individual cannot mobilize in ordinary functions. On the other hand, if there is a paucity of originals and a carefully high form level throughout, the implication is of efficiency of function pushed close to the limits of capacity; such an individual is probably less intelligent than his general level of achievement would suggest. Paucity of main *O*'s with plenty of additionals would indicate that the individual is too cautious and modest in exploiting his capacities for full efficiency of intellectual function. Bizarre originals and minus responses indicate severe disturbance of intellectual function and loss of efficiency, but not necessarily a low level of capacity.

5. Variety of Content

Subjects of defective or mediocre intelligence characteristically give a large proportion of animal responses, since animal forms are very easy to see in the blot material. However, a high *A%* is not necessarily an indication of low capacity; it indicates a limitation of efficiency of function through a narrowness in the range of interests or lack of flexibility in interpretation, or both. It is considered optimum if the *A%* falls between 20 and 35, with at least 25 per cent of the content being outside the categories *H*, *Hd*, *A*, and *Ad* and spread over at least three other content categories. Such a spread indicates a flexibility of approach and a range of interpretative background that contributes to the efficiency of intellectual function.

6. Succession

An orderly succession is considered a contribution to the efficiency of intellectual function in that it shows enough system in approaching new situations so that past experience can be mobilized to assist, yet enough flexibility to modify the approach as the differences in the situation may demand. A rigid succession is considered a limitation in efficiency since it implies that the same approach is carried over from one situation to another without due regard for modifications demanded by new aspects. On the other hand, a loose succession, and especially a confused succession, often indicates a weakening of intellectual control—a haphazard approach dictated by this or that feature of the situation, without sufficient continuity to ensure a sustained effort towards a successful conclusion.

Finally, in describing the efficiency of function the skillful examiner will draw broadly upon the whole picture of the personality, utilizing all aspects of analysis to give a rounded account of the strengths and weaknesses of function as they may serve to modify intellectual efficiency.

The Evaluation of Control

The concept of control is an important one in Rorschach interpretation, being a criterion of the effectiveness of general adjustment to life situations. It is the "negative" aspect of good adjustment. The hypothesis is that the individual must have sufficient control over both his impulses and their overt expression to be able to avoid the dangers presented by the reality situation and to find successful ways of satisfying his needs. Although control is thus a necessary condition of good adjustment it does not guarantee satisfaction; indeed, the overcontrolled person may be too inhibited to satisfy his basic needs or to realize his creative potential.

It is of interest to estimate not only the degree of control of which the subject is capable but also the particular bases upon which his control rests. Three modes of control are distinguished: (1) outer control, (2) inner control, and (3) constricted or repressive control. Running through the consideration of these various modes of control is the indication of the extent to which the individual can effectively keep his grip on reality, represented by form level. Nearly all the features that contribute to the evaluation of control have already been dealt with in earlier sections. This section, therefore, will provide a summary of earlier hypotheses that contribute to the evaluation of control.

1. Outer Control

Outer control refers to the control of overt behavior or expression. It is close to "self-control" as popularly defined, for the implication is that the individual feels impulses and tendencies to react which he refrains from expressing overtly. There are various modes of outer control. Some individuals control their outward behavior by virtue of having learned socially acceptable ways of feeling and expressing their feelings so that control is an effortless matter; others can remain outwardly calm only by bottling up their emotions and failing to give them expression; still others maintain outward control by insulating themselves from emotional impact by withdrawal or repression.

There are three modes of outer control:

a. Socialized Control

(1) $FC>(CF+C)$ is a sign of controlled responsiveness, a socialized control of emotional expression indicating a tendency to feel and act appropriately to the social demands of the situation, while still being responsive and emotionally involved. If CF is absent or nearly absent the implication is that there is socially skilled expression, but a minimum of real emotional involvement. (See pages 296–297.)

(2) $F \leftrightarrow C$ indicates an effort to respond emotionally while still maintaining control, the effort involved implying a certain tension in social relationships and the forced nature of the color com-

bination suggesting some difficulty in maintaining a smooth and easy social technique. (See page 280.)

(3) F/C is a sign of a superficial and ungenuine socialized control; the person responds in terms of what he feels the situation demands, without relation to his own feelings. (See page 281.)

b.   "Bottling-up" the Emotions

(1) C_{sym} and C_{des} both indicate that the individual is strongly moved to emotional reaction but manages to keep the response bottled-up without overt expression. Such individuals may appear quite calm, even inhibited on the surface. (See pages 286–287.)

(2)   Where CF is subordinated to an elaborate whole response or a vista response it appears that the individual feels strong emotional response, but through a larger view of the situation or introspective effort manages to refrain from overt expression, even though the emotional response bubbles close to the surface.

c.   Control through Withdrawal or Insulation

(1)   Achromatic>Chromatic. Where the achromatic responses outnumber the chromatic responses, this indicates that the individual is maintaining control of outward expression of emotion by virtue of detaching himself from emotional impact by withdrawal from genuine emotional involvement. Such persons would have difficulty in expressing their emotional and affectional impulses even when they really wished to do so. Where the achromatic responses outnumber the chromatic responses by two to one the "burnt child" hypothesis applies. (See pages 292–293.)

(2) $M>2$ Sum C and $F\%>50$. Where these proportions are found the hypothesis is that control is achieved by both withdrawal and repression with too little affective energy remaining in emotional contact with the social environment.

There are four signs of inadequate outer control:

a. $(CF+C)>FC$ is considered a sign that there is inadequate control of emotional expression, implying that impulses tend to be acted out directly in a behavioral sense without adequate control in terms of social demands. (See pages 296–297.)

b.   Achromatic$<\frac{1}{2}$ Chromatic. Where the chromatic responses exceed the achromatic responses by 2:1 or more, there is a tendency to act out the emotions. (See page 293.)

c.   Minus form level in color responses indicates inadequate control of emotional expression, with impulses acted out without adequate control in terms of reality perception.

d.   Sum $C>2M$ and $F\%<30\%$. With this set of proportions the hypothesis is that outer control is tenuous, and there must be a very good balance within the color responses themselves to guarantee adequate outer control, especially where there are fewer than four M responses.

2.   Inner Control

The implications of inner control are that the person has enough inner resources to enable him to meet emotional impact by delaying action long enough to gain control over outward expression of behavior. The chief sign of inner control is M. For inner control at least three M responses are required for the average person, and at least five M for the introversive person. The content of the M responses gives information about the way in which a person uses his inner resources as a mode of control, whether in terms of a long-range value system, through empathetic understanding of others, through intellectual criticism or escapist fantasy. (See pages 254–264.) Similarly the evaluation of the relationship between M and FM or $FM+m$ gives an indication of the balance between ego values and impulse life. (See pages 288–291.) However, even when the M responses are not in optimum relationship to FM and m, or where the content gives a flavor of escapist fantasy or an intellectually overcritical approach, the minimum number of M responses of good form level is considered an indication of inner resources sufficient to give a control function. Minus responses indicate a weakness of control of imaginal processes and their integration with reality, and hence invalidate any interpretation of M responses as having a control function.

3. Constrictive or Repressive Control

The hypothesis is that the individual utilizing constrictive or repressive control manages to control outward expression by virtue of controlling the very feelings, emotions, and impulses that prompt to uncontrolled behavior. Viewed in this way, "constriction" is a transitive rather than an intransitive term. Thus the individual personality may be said to constrict, limit, or repress certain responses, although it would blur the picture to say that the personality is "constricted." This is one consideration that made it desirable to distinguish between "natural constriction" in which the personality is in fact limited by influences of endowment or development or both, and "neurotic constriction" in which the person actively (although not necessarily consciously) limits his response.

In general, there are three major types of process that the person may "constrict." He may suppress or repress his impulse life, thus constricting his imaginal processes (which derive from impulse); this would be indicated by an increase of F responses at the expense of movement responses. He may constrict his awareness and acceptance of affectional need, indicated by an increase of F responses at the expense of shading responses. Or he may constrict his outward reactivity to emotional impact, shown by a dearth of color responses. However, it is only when he tends to constrict or inhibit all three types of process that the F responses dominate the record to an extent that he may be said to rely chiefly upon constriction as a mode of control. When constrictive control predominates, not only the outward expression is inhibited but also the inner response.

However, it is considered that some capacity to strip a situation of personal implications is an aid to adjustment, enabling effective impersonal action in routine situations. Therefore an $F\%$ between 20 and 50 is considered optimum, provided that the form responses are of good quality; the hypothesis of constriction does not apply within these limits.

Two signs of constrictive or repressive control may be noted:

a.   An overemphasis on constrictive control is indicated by an $F\%$ in excess of 50, provided the responses are of good form level.

The hypothesis is that control is achieved at the expense of desirable responsiveness, flexibility and imaginativeness, even though efficient intellectual function is indicated by good form level. This is considered a brittle adjustment, since it is presumed that needs and emotional reactions will continue to exert an influence even though they are not permitted a conscious role in reality perception. Since optimum adjustment can only be achieved by a genuine integration of needs with reality demands, it represents a distortion to interpret the reality situation without reference to needs, just as there is distortion if the needs unduly affect reality perception. (See also pages 294–295.)

b. A modified constrictive control is indicated when $F\%$ is close to 50, when $FK+Fc$ is between $1/4$ and $3/4$ of F, and when $(FK+F+Fc)\%$ does not exceed 75. The hypothesis is that introspective tendencies and affectional sensitivity are sufficiently developed that constriction is softened and the adjustment less brittle. However, this adjustment would seem to be at the expense of close affectional relationships, emotional involvements and the adequate utilization of creative potential. The "negative" or control aspects of adjustment are emphasized at the expense of the "positive," creative, and constructive aspects. (See also pages 292 and 296.)

There are three signs of inadequate control:

a. When $F\%>50$ with vague or indefinite form level the control is inadequate. This may be because the individual is relatively undifferentiated in his intellectual function or badly integrated in personality organization or in a severe anxiety state. Occasionally this feature is found with the cautious, evasive neurotic, whose very evasiveness may be said to constitute a mode of control. For this reason this hypothesis must be used with caution, and in the context of other findings.

b. Minus form level responses generally indicate a weakening of ties to reality and hence inadequate control.

c. When $F\%<20$ the hypothesis is that there is too little emphasis on an impersonal, matter-of-fact relationship with the world for sufficient control to be maintained, unless plenty of other control factors are represented, such as *M, FK, Fc* and *FC* responses with good form level. (See page 295.)

The Evaluation of Creative Potentials

Perhaps because the Rorschach technique has been used so frequently with an emphasis upon psychiatric diagnosis, and hence upon the symptoms or defects in personality function, interpretative stress is all too frequently placed upon the negative aspects of personality—upon liabilities, maladjustments, or illnesses. Since the Rorschach technique gives a view of the person-as-a-whole in action, it is simply a matter of the kind of spectacles worn by the observer if the strengths and potentialities are not seen just as clearly as the weaknesses and defects.

Attention has already been drawn to two sources of strength, in the sections on the estimate of intellectual capacity and efficiency and on the evaluation of control. However, these two aspects may be considered background factors, the intellectual functions being a tool, and control a necessary condition of good adjustment; they do not cover the positive aspects of mental health.

In the Rorschach technique these positive aspects have been described as "creativity." The implications of creativity for actual creative output have been discussed in Chapter 10 in conjunction with the interpretative hypotheses attached to *M* responses. The very features of personality organization that offer a good prognosis for creative output are the hallmarks of the well-integrated personality capable of meaningful interaction with its environment. The creative person is an emotionally mature person who feels at home in the world and with himself. He can maintain himself in society and make to it a constructive contribution which is at the same time deeply satisfying to him. He can live on a coöperative, mutually contributing basis with other people, and he finds satisfactions for his various needs and realizations of his aspirations within this framework. There are two chief aspects to "creativity" thus defined—those referring to the realization of inner creative resources and those referring to object relations. These correspond to the two aspects Erich Fromm [1] attributes to a "productive orientation"—productive work and productive love.

Since a fully developed creativity or productive orientation represents an ideal to be realized, evaluation concerns itself with questions of more or less closely approximating the ideal rather than with presence or absence of creativity. Hence the evaluation of creativity covers not only an examination of the record for signs of creativity already developed, but also for signs of potential which may be further developed, although perhaps only under very favorable circumstances. One aspect of assessing potential is to consider material elicited in the inquiry or in testing the limits as indicating potential resources not as fully available to the personality as that which emerges from the performance proper. Other indications of creative potential will be considered under the two chief headings that follow.

1. Imaginal Resources

The constructive use of the imaginal resources can ideally result in the development of the following:

a. A flexible and constructive use of the imagination to manipulate the possibilities of the reality situation and thus to solve problems and arrive at fuller satisfaction of needs.

b. A long-range orientation given by a system of values in terms of which the person not only can control his behavior and postpone his gratifications but also guide his satisfactions.

c. An integration of impulsive urges with the long-range value system so that both can exist concurrently without undue feelings of guilt or frustration.

d. The liberation of intellectual potential towards a creative achievement that serves those values attached to self-realization as well as satisfying the more basic needs.

Evaluation of Creative Potential in Imaginal Resources

(1)   *M* Responses

HYPOTHESIS: *M* responses of good quality, involving the perception of real human figures, and in optimal relationship to *FM* responses, indicate a constructive use of the imaginal resources to achieve a creative adjustment as defined by the points listed above. Even though the *M* responses are reluctantly conceded, or involve intellectual reservations shown by the use of *Hd* or *(H)*, or have a fantasy flavor shown in *(A)*, or are not in optimal relationship to *FM*, they may nevertheless be considered potential sources of creativity—resources which, though not immediately available to the personality, are not so deeply buried or undeveloped as to be inaccessible. The better the quality, the readier the response, the better the relationships with *FM*, and the more spontaneous the activity expressed in the *M* responses, the more nearly the ideal of creativity has been realized.

(2)   *m* Responses

HYPOTHESIS: Since the full development of creative resources is frequently hampered by conflict within the personality, the appearance of *m* responses is an indirect indication that inner resources exist which might be released for more creative use if the conflict could be relieved. Moreover, *m* may be considered a source of strength since it indicates that the individual has not abandoned himself to dissociation and disintegration and is still striving towards an integration of impulse life with his ego values, however rudimentary the latter may be.

(3)   *FM* Responses

HYPOTHESIS: Since *FM* responses may be considered a potential source of *M* responses and all that is implied in *M*-capacity, they are a source of creative potential—although it may be that the individual will not realize this potential without optimum circumstances, perhaps including considerable assistance. The hypothesis is based on the assumption that *M* responses reflect a tolerance of the ego for the primitive impulses that are the basic source of the creative energies. A first step towards ego-tolerance of impulses is awareness of the impulses themselves—an awareness implied in the *FM* response. Hence the hypothesis is that the person with *FM* in his psychogram has greater creative potential than the person who lacks even this degree of integration of ego and impulse life.

2. Object Relations

Since it is impossible for any person to grow to maturity without being dependent on other people, or to maintain himself as a mature adult without coöperative relationships with other people, it is inconceivable that any definition of the creative personality could omit reference to object relations. Indeed, the conditions of human development are such that a need to achieve a close and harmonious relationship with at least one other person is built deeply into the motivational system; moreover, the conditions under which the human being must live, even the mature adult, are such that the establishment of coöperative relationships is a necessary condition for the accomplishment of other goals and the satisfaction of other needs. A "creative" relationship would be defined as one to which the person contributes and from which he derives a sense of belongingness; It is thus a mutually contributing relationship.

Evaluation of Creative Potential in Object Relations

(1) *M* Responses

HYPOTHESIS: The capacity for seeing real human figures in action is related to the ability to use the imaginal resources in an empathetic way, so that the person is able to imagine how another person is feeling, what his needs may be and how he views the world. A capacity for empathy is postulated as a necessary condition for an ideally coöperative and contributing relationship. Although the perception of human figures that are limited in life, wholeness, reality, or acceptance indicates that the use of the imagination falls short of empathy, nevertheless *M* responses of all kinds indicate potential empathy.

(2) *Fc* Responses

HYPOTHESIS: Even though the sensitivity shown by *Fc* responses falls short of the empathetic identification implied in the full-bodied *M* response, it still shows an ability to accept recipient affectional needs, which is a first step towards the formation of mature object relations. Hence the appearance of *Fc,* even in numbers that indicate an overdeveloped need for affection, suggests an orientation towards forming object relations.

(3) *FC* Responses

HYPOTHESIS: Since *FC* responses indicate a socialized responsiveness towards the emotional impact of the social environment, they suggest an interest in relationships with other people, as well as social skills which help in forming and maintaining good relations. Following the same trend of argument, color responsiveness in general may be considered creative potential, although the less fully developed it is and the less socialized the mode of perception, the less the potential has been realized.

The Introversive-Extratensive Relationship

Identification of the "experience type" or "Erlebnistyp" is a traditional aspect of Rorschach analysis, having been given much emphasis by Rorschach himself. This involves classifying individuals as more or less introvert, extravert, or ambivert. Much misunderstanding has attached to this classification; for the definitions of the terms differ very considerably from the popular psychological usage, which refers to traits such as those measured by the Bernreuter Personality Inventory. Popularly speaking, the introvert is withdrawn, shy, socially inept, and apt to overindulge in fantasy to the extent of being schizoid or at least neurotic, whereas the extravert is the stereotype of the well-adjusted American, socially skilled, participant, dominant, and confident. These definitions bear so little relationship to the Rorschach meaning of introversion-extraversion that they are best forgotten. Indeed, it is usual to use the terms introversive (rather than introverted) and extratensive (rather than extraverted) to make it clear that it is the Rorschach definition that is implied.

According to Rorschach usage, the markedly introversive person is one who has a well-developed imaginal function, either in terms of fantasy, long-range goals, or acknowledged impulses, while his responsiveness to and involvement with the outer world are reduced. To translate the Jungian concept of a libido turned inward, it might be said that the major portion of motivational energy tends to be discharged within the personality itself. He reacts more through cerebral or autonomic processes and less through striped muscles than the extratensive person. More important, he tends to restructure the world in terms of his own values and needs. He reads much of his own interpretation into reality. At worst this leads to distortion of reality; at best it is invaluable in enabling him to deal with reality more effectively, since he is not bound by the immediate structure of the reality situation but is free to imagine it as different and to shape a course designed to make it so. The well-adjusted introvert is not withdrawn or retiring; he is self-sufficient. While capable of good object relations, he is not overly dependent on other people because he has well-developed inner resources. He may get along very well with people and enjoy social contacts.

The markedly extratensive person, on the other hand, is one who is highly responsive to his environment, either in terms of overt emotional expression or affectional warmth of feeling, or a mere passive submission to forces coming upon him from without. The passively extratensive person accepts the reality situation as he finds it, whether he perceives it clearly or not. He tends to restructure it little in terms of his own needs. He is easily stimulated; he is reactive rather than striving. The well-adjusted extratensive person is not passively reactive. He is creative in his relationship to objects and people external to him and strives towards goals that he has staked out in the external world, while the goals of the introversive person have a more personal, developmental significance.

Generally speaking, the Rorschach concept does not imply that introversion is less well adjusted than extraversion. Indeed the opposite implication is suggested by the fact that imaginal function is considered such an important aspect of creativity, and inner resources are believed to be a very helpful basis of control. Important as interpersonal relationships are, it would seem that the healthy self-acceptance and empathy, which only well-developed imaginal function can give, are essential for creative object relations. However, the estimate of adjustment must be considered quite independent of the introversive-extratensive balance; neither the extravert, the introvert, nor the ambivert has a corner on good (or bad) adjustment.

The Rorschach concept of introversion-extratension does not imply an "either-or" notion, in the sense of a fixed amount of libidinal energy so that the more that is attached to inner objects the less is available for outer attachments. On the contrary, personalities are viewed as differing in the amount of energy that is free for canalization either towards inner objects or values or towards outer objects, or both. A highly developed inner value system does not prohibit rich and varied object relations. If one were to sketch an ideal personality, one would probably postulate a balance between introversion and extratension, with a well-developed imaginal function and value system, rich emotional responsiveness, and an adequate integration with reality. However, a mere balance between introversive and extratensive tendencies is not necessarily well-adjusted, for this balance may be found with constricted or pathological tendencies, characterized by impoverished inner resources and faulty emotional responsiveness.

Proportions Relating to Introversive-Extratensive Balance

1. M : Sum C

HYPOTHESIS: When *M* responses outweigh the Sum *C* by 2 : 1 there is an introversive balance; whereas when Sum *C* outweighs *M* by 2 : 1 there is an extratensive balance. Something approaching a 1 : 1 ratio is perhaps most common.

Extreme introversion may be due to a retreat from emotional complications, although there seem to be some cases where there is no suggestion of traumatic experiences that could have led to retreat. There seem to be two chief periods of life when the balance tends to swing in an introversive direction, provided that there is a superior level of intellectual function: (a) in adolescence; and (b) from the age of about 30 to 35 when there seems to be a consolidation period for the revaluation of inner resources. This secondary phase of introversion serves to prevent panic reactions in middle age.

Extreme extratension is believed usually to reflect an attempt to solve problems by a flight into reality. The inner impulse life constitutes such a threat that the person defends himself by gearing himself entirely to reality demands.

2. $(FM+m) : (Fc+c+C')$

HYPOTHESIS: $FM+m$ responses indicate introversive tendencies not fully accepted by or available to the subject at the time, and hence represent a potentiality. The rationale is that all movement responses relate to imaginal function, and that since M genetically develops from FM, these responses may be considered an M-potential. Similarly, the hypothesis is that the achromatic responses indicate extratensive tendencies not fully accepted by or available to the subject at the time, and hence represent a potentiality for greater emotional reactivity. The rationale here is that achromatic responses are toned-down emotional responses and indicate an orientation towards the social environment in terms of feeling if not overt response. If the feeling is present, potentially there is response.

If this ratio is in the same direction as M : Sum C it confirms and strengthens the impression given by the latter. If it is at variance with M : Sum C there are several hypotheses from which to choose. It might be that the subject is in a state of transition from introversion to extratension, and the second ratio indicates the direction in which the change is progressing. An equally reasonable supposition might be that the ratio indicates the direction in which the person is retreating. Or it might indicate a persistent secondary orientation which the person has been unable to realize, but which remains as a source of conflict. In any event a discrepancy in the direction of the ratios reflects a conflict in tendencies within the personality, although the specific significance of this may remain obscure.

3.   Percentage of Responses to Cards VIII, IX, and X

HYPOTHESIS: The percentage of responses to the last three cards which are entirely chromatic indicates general responsiveness to emotional stimuli from the environment. Some subjects tend to "dry up" when presented with the color cards, others respond with the same productiveness as they did to the other cards, while still others seem stimulated even though they may not use the color in their responses. (See page 297.)

If less than 30 per cent of the responses are given to the last three cards the hypothesis is that the individual is withdrawn from reactivity to emotional impact from the environment, either because he is confused or threatened and withdraws as a defense, or because he has a long-standing mode of adjustment involving little emotional involvement. If more than 40 per cent of the responses are given to the last three cards the hypothesis is that there is actual or potential responsiveness to the emotional implications of the environment. If there is potential responsiveness only, as indicated by little use of color, the hypothesis is that there is a conflict between natural responsiveness and conscious attitudes, a repression of emotional responsiveness.

If the percentage of reponses to the last three cards goes in the same direction as the other signs of introversion-extratension it would seem that the indicated direction of balance is of such long standing that it might be termed "natural."

In conclusion, it must be said that the concept of experience balance is one of the most difficult to fit meaningfully into a picture of the functioning personality, perhaps because the theoretical basis from which it is derived is little understood by most examiners. Moreover, it seems to be equally difficult to validate, even in terms of clinical validation, again probably because the judgment of introversion-extratension is strange to most clinicians and thus the clinical criterion is obscure. Certainly validation in terms of personality inventories of popular psychological concepts would be quite irrelevant. Examiners who find it to be a step in interpretation that adds little or nothing to their understanding of the function of the individual personality are well-advised to omit it, since the processes involved are quite well covered by a careful analysis of the psychogram and the application of interpretative hypotheses attached to the various determinants and their proportions.

References

1. Fromm, Erich, *Man for Himself.* New York: Rinehart & Co., Inc.; 1947.

CHAPTER 13

Interpretative Hypotheses Derived from the Analysis of Content

General Principles

The essential process of interpretation of any clinical appraisal instrument consists of the constant formulation of hypotheses or guesses. As the evidence for a given hypothesis increases, more confidence is placed in it. As evidence appears to the contrary, the hypothesis may be eliminated from consideration. This process goes on throughout the entire analysis of structure and content of the Rorschach as well as during the interpretation of other clinical tests and case history materials. Taking this into consideration, we need not fear the tenuousness of any given hypothesis derived in any one stage of assessment of the materials.

The kinds of hypotheses to be presented in this chapter are based on the whole backlog of dynamic personality theory as well as the clinical experiences of many people with whom the present writer has been associated. They are presented not as facts, but as working hypotheses, hunches, or guesses which become available for experimental investigation with their appearance in print. Contributions to this area have been made by Due and Wright [2], Goldfarb [3], and Hertzman and Pearce [4]. The work on "content analysis" by Lindner [6] is less suitable for individual personality study.

In assessing the personality of any given individual, we may test the worth of any given interpretation by checking the internal consistency of the various hypotheses derived both from the analysis of content in the Rorschach and the analysis of structure as outlined in the preceding chapters. Many of the kinds of variables involved in this analysis appear in the interpretation of such other clinical tests as the Thematic Apperception Test, sentence completion tests, and various expressive tests (such as the Draw-A-Person Test). In addition to this, we have case history materials available for comparative purposes, although it should be pointed out repeatedly that many of these hypotheses, derived from projective techniques, are not capable of being verified or discredited by knowledge of overt behavior.

A problem that continually arises in the analysis of content is, of course, the knotty one of level of awareness. If, for example, much aggressive activity is seen in the test protocol, what does this mean? Is the person acting out this aggression? Is he inhibiting it, repressing it, sublimating it, having a reaction formation against it? No easy answer has been found to this problem. However, there are at least two methods by which we can come closer to a solution. The first consists of a comparison of projections with conscious attitudes, such as may be obtained from answers to a sentence completion test or a case history interview. This permits us to compare attitudes and feelings of a conscious nature with those that may or may not be close to awareness. It has been pointed out by many clinicians that it is merely interesting for a Rorschach and case history to agree, but highly important when they do not. The implication is that where the Rorschach is able to tap levels of the personality not revealed in the ordinary interview situation, it is making a real contribution to personality assessment.

Another possible approach to gauging the level of awareness of feelings, needs, and attitudes revealed in the Rorschach technique is the one suggested by Tomkins [8] in regard to the Thematic Apperception Test. The concept he introduces is that of "distanciation." He points out that the identification is conscious to the extent that the person identified with in the TAT is of the same age, sex, color, era, and so on, as the subject telling the stories. He hypothesizes that any way of making the hero more distant from oneself by having a different sex, a discrepant age, another time in history, is a way of pushing the fantasy away from conscious awareness. This concept has already been transferred to the Rorschach test by Due and Wright [2], and will be discussed in more detail below.

The last general point that should be raised here is the importance of sequence in analyzing content. The term "sequence analysis" has generally referred to a study of the sequence not in terms of content alone, but also in terms of structure—that is, we are interested in the sequence of form levels, location categories and determinants (as described in Chapter 11). However, one of the most important uses of sequence analysis may well be an attempt to understand the symbolic or projective meaning of the actual responses as they follow each other both within and between cards. A skilled interpreter is often able to judge a great deal about the individual subject by this method. The exact application of sequence analysis will be taken up later in this chapter.

Human Figures

Probably the most fruitful sources of hypotheses in the content area are human figures perceived in the Rorschach test. This has been pointed out in other sections of this book and in the paper by Hertzman and Pearce [4], and the need for carefully inquiring about all details of such responses has been emphasized. The more that is known about the perception of such responses, the richer a source of information they will be.

One problem that must be considered from the outset is that of gauging the difference between attitudes expressed towards other people and those expressed towards the self. Basically, of course, there is no difference. The etiology of both kinds of attitudes lies in the early experiences of the individual in interaction with his environment. Attitudes towards others may often be the result of projected feelings of one's own, whereas attitudes towards the self may be essentially the reflections of the perceived feelings of others. However, it may be helpful for practical purposes to propose a way of making a distinction. We might say that a generally introversive type of individual, as gauged from the record as a whole, would be more apt to be concerned with himself, whereas an individual who generally is more reactive to those around him would be apt to express attitudes about them. This would provide a rough yardstick for interpreting the material surrounding the perception of human figures in the test in this regard. Where such responses are completely missing, the absence of empathy might be suspected. ("Empathy" refers to the ability of an individual to accept or identify with others.) At the same time, complete failure to perceive human figures would imply a lack of conscious control over one's own feelings and impulses.

Often, subjects tend to be preoccupied with certain parts of the body as opposed to others. Many subjects, for example, will stick to the perception of heads or faces, ignoring the greater part of the body. The hypothesis that might be brought forward here is that such individuals tend to preoccupy themselves with the external or persona qualities of human beings, tending to more or less ignore the more physical or biological aspects. This type of perception is often found in the records of people using the mechanisms of intellectualization or compulsion. The opposite interpretation might be made of an individual whose tendency was to conspicuously omit the head area. Such people might have difficulty in the intellectual aspects of interpersonal relationships and prefer to relate to others on a more primitive or biological level.

A tendency to perceive various minor parts of the body discretely may again be indicative of a compulsive attention to detail accompanying an inability to deal effectively with other people. This is especially true of those discrete parts that are directly or indirectly sexual in significance. Seeing many genitalia in the Rorschach is characteristic of an individual whose aim it is to prove to the examiner and the world in general that he is sufficiently mature to be interested in such things. This attempt is usually designed to cloak a preoccupation with pregenital sexuality and a complete inability to effectively carry out either heterosexual or homosexual relationships. The perception of various pregenital areas may be directly related to an individual's inability to progress beyond their level. References to ani and buttocks, as well as peering eyes, are frequently found in the records of paranoid individuals, whereas breasts occur in the records of those frustrated in regard to receiving affection from a mother or similar important person. Seeing discrete parts of human figures may also occur as an "oligophrenic" response (where the majority of subjects see a whole figure) accompanying feeble-mindedness or a definite looseness of the intellectual ties to reality.

One of the common problems in our culture is the problem of the sexual role. Margaret Mead [7] has amply demonstrated in a recent book that the concepts of masculine and feminine roles in our culture are by no means as clear-cut and definite as they might have been at one time. Consequently, the sexual role has become a problem area for nearly every individual. Some subjects avoid this problem by referring to their human figures as "persons," indicating their unwillingness to face the problem of identification. Whenever a particular sex is specified, it is always interesting to note the reasons given for the perceived figure being that sex. Sometimes they may be quite incongruous. For example, the figures in Card III may be men because they have a bulging vest or are wearing high-heeled shoes. This kind of identification of the men leads us to think that men, in the frame of reference of this subject, have rather feminine characteristics. A better reason for their being men might be that they are formed as such, are garbed in masculine clothing, or are engaging in a masculine type of activity. Occasionally, subjects may be quite overtly confused and point out that the figures have both male and female attributes, or they may solve the dilemma by making one of the identical figures a man and the other a woman. A more subtle way of gauging difficulties in the identification of sex is in terms of the kind of activity projected into the perceived figures. Carrying baskets, for example, may be considered a feminine type of activity, whereas bowing to one another with top hats is more characteristic of men. Where a woman is perceived clearly and unambiguously, but the activity in which she is engaged is a masculine one, it may lead us to suspect some confusion on the subject's part. These difficulties, as indicated on the Rorschach, may lead us to formulate certain hypotheses concerning the etiology or history of the subject's present attitudes. For example, a home in which the mother plays a dominant role and the father is weak or otherwise irresponsible often produces such confusion. The loss or separation of the parents at an early age may also be a causal factor. In older subjects, it may be well to scrutinize the choice of marriage partner in order to see whether the subject has unwittingly attempted to re-establish the psychological situation of his early days in his own home.

The kinds of activities engaged in by the perceived human figures are also capable of other kinds of interpretation. When much aggression is taking place (as with people fighting or attacking one another) it may be indicative of the presence within the subject, at some level, of severe feelings of hostility against the world. Aggression can in turn be divided into physical aggression, oral or verbal aggression, and aggression present only by very indirect inference. It must be reiterated at this point that no movement responses can be interpreted as being necessarily analogous to observable behavior. The blots, although objectively possessing color and shading, are stationary; therefore, any movement projected into them is an expression of the person's inner life and not a reaction to the actual world. This inner life may or may not reflect itself in behavior.

Further material may be inferred from a study of the affect expressed during the perception of or inquiry about human figures or parts thereof. The Rorschach consists of inkblots and not of pictures of people; therefore, when ugly or beautiful, menacing or seductive people are perceived, it is strictly a projection of the subject's own feelings about human beings. In clinical practice, the most useful way to approach the interpretation of such phenomena is to compare the Rorschach performance with as many known factors as are available about the important individuals in the subject's life. Blind interpretation of Rorschach content is not encouraged except for research or demonstration purposes, since the Rorschach material becomes much more meaningful in the light of other information.

The concept of distanciation discussed above is very relevant to the interpretation of human figures. The two most common distanciation methods are making the human figures animal-like and making them mythical. These are both ways in which the individual can project the actions and affects of human beings into figures not really accepted as such, thereby making them more distant from awareness. By attributing animal-like characteristics to humans the individual identifies less closely with them. By making them mythical the individual is attributing human traits to unreal or imaginary human figures, thereby again removing the situation from his own particular frame of reference so that it will be less close to home. An extreme example of distanciation is the perception of the figures in Card III as "the shadows of the silhouettes of two ghosts of puppets."

Animal Figures

People tend to identify less readily with animals than with human figures. Although the kinds of affects or attitudes expressed in regard to animals may represent the fantasy life of the individual, these fantasies are apt to be less close to awareness and therefore less readily available as a means of adjusting to the environment. In terms of a continuum of distanciation, animals would represent even more distance than mythological or unreal human figures.

In terms of this kind of reasoning, the interpretation of perceived animals on the Rorschach has usually been in terms of inner drives or affects that are currently unrelated to adjustive or creative capacities and therefore present in almost all subjects. Animals are perceived in the records of subjects of all ages and of both normal and abnormal subjects. They may represent potential adjustive techniques, but are not now available for this purpose. The use of animal per cent *(A%)* on the *Individual Record Blank* refers to one use of animal content in interpretation—namely, to indicate a certain paucity of interests or stereotypy in thought content. However, it should be clearly kept in mind that stereotypy in thinking can be indicated equally clearly by a high percentage of any other content category. Even in the case of animal per cent, its significance may be attenuated by interesting or unusual ways of perceiving animal figures—for example, ascribing human-like activities and attributes to them.

The meaning of perceiving various different kinds of animals is rather a speculative matter but has been studied to some extent by

Goldfarb [3]. Certain kinds of animals, such as tigers, lions, panthers, are usually thought of as rather fierce and wild. In describing them, a subject may be referring to certain rather bold and aggressive tendencies in himself which he is attempting to handle in some way. It will then be interesting to note whether the kind of activity in which these animals are engaged is commensurate with the fierce characteristics usually attributed to them. Other kinds of animals, such as foxes and rodents, are usually associated with a more subtle kind of aggression, characterized by cunning, and may be interpreted accordingly. Some animals are characteristically thought of as being passive, such as cows and sheep. Many other such stereotypes exist. However, making the assumption that the individual subject is attributing such characteristics to the animal he is perceiving is a hazardous procedure. It is always best to try to discover in each case what the subject has in mind in regard to any given kind of animal. If this has not become clear as a result of the inquiry, it may well be worth while to pursue the point by requesting animal associations during the testing-the-limits procedure. With further experimental work in this area, it may become possible for us to rely more routinely on stereotypes such as the ones described above.

From the kind of animal and the kind of activity perceived, it may thus be possible for us to formulate certain hypotheses concerning the strength and consistency of certain basic instinctual drives. The assumption made here—which is indeed a central one in Rorschach theory—is that everyone has certain personality needs, such as aggression and passivity. The question is not whether or not these needs are present, but the particular role they play in the particular individual being described. Only thus will we be able to describe the individuality of a subject and avoid having our interpretations emerge as meaningless verbal stereotypes.

Anatomical Concepts

Content of an anatomical sort is very frequently encountered. Depending on the way it is described and the context and sequence in which it occurs, it may have a variety of meanings. A number of kinds of pathology are accompanied by a concern about the human body

—for example, conversion hysteria, hypochondriasis, or actual somatic illness. Also, anatomical concepts described in great detail and with the use of long words may serve as an attempt to deal with feelings about oneself so as to impress others with technical knowledge. Often, anatomical concepts occur in association with colored areas, especially in Cards VIII, IX, and X. In this context, they may be interpreted as a direct reaction to what seems to the subject to be an emotionally loaded situation. They may, for example, occur in the form of F/C or C/F responses, indicating a certain stereotyped way of dealing with emotions as well as the use to which one's body is being put in this regard. On the other hand, the content of anatomy may remain and the color may be disregarded. In this case, somatic preoccupations have actually replaced affect, as is commonly the case in conversion hysteria. The extent to which rational control has been maintained under such circumstances can be gauged by the definiteness, indefiniteness, or bizarre nature of the form accuracy of the responses.

A particular kind of anatomical response is the X-ray response, often associated with the use of Fk or FK. In this case, we may be dealing with an attempt on the part of the perceiver to probe more deeply into his body, or the psyche which it may symbolize, so as to discover more about himself. Thus the anatomical response would represent an introspective tendency. Seeing anatomy in the form of skeletons or skulls may represent certain masochistic or depressive tendencies on the part of the individual.

It should be kept in mind that there are many cases in which an individual really has good reason to be preoccupied with his body and its functions, so that the presence of anatomical responses alone cannot be considered a pathological indicator or even very much of an expression of individuality. It is only by considering the kind and quality of anatomical perception in addition to the use of determinants in connection with it that we are able to find the interpretation of such responses diagnostically helpful.

Sexual Symbolism

Sexual symbolism can be approached in two main ways. The first is in terms of responses that may be symbolic of sex, and the second is the interpretation of responses in areas usually associated with sex. Both of these are hazardous procedures and should be employed with caution.

"Sex," as used in the Rorschach, has the broad meaning employed by Freud but misinterpreted by many of his followers. The term refers to the ways the individual has of dealing with himself and others in terms of his basic biological tendencies. It is important to keep in mind that we have done little to aid in the understanding of a case by boiling other contents down to sexual meanings. This procedure will take on significance only if the sexual concepts serve as springboards for further predictions and generalizations. Sexuality, however, may be a specific problem in many cases in our particular culture, because our culture has produced this effect by inhibitions and restrictions unacceptable to the individual personality. The difficulty of describing the normal sexual role for a person in our culture has already been mentioned.

Certain responses are quite obviously of a symbolic nature and therefore readily recognized as such. Examples of these are snakes, totem poles, and the like. Other responses appear to have an obvious symbolic significance to a given interpreter in a given situation. Responses with personal symbolic meaning are often unusual in terms of area, content, or form level. In the opinion of the present writer, individual interpreters should feel free to make guesses about such symbolic meaning any time they wish—providing these hunches are not included in a formal report of the findings unless the evidence along these lines accumulates throughout the perusal of the Rorschach and other materials to the extent that inclusion seems justified.

The second approach is to study responses given to areas usually associated with sex. Some of the more common of these areas are the following: center *d* and bottom *D* on Card II; extension on lower "leg" area and swelling on "chest" areas of the usual figures on Card III; top *d*, side *d*, and bottom *D* on Card IV; top *D*, center area and bottom opening on Card VI, and the center *d* on Card VII. Whether paying attention to these areas will be useful in the interpretation of a given response depends entirely on the subject's way of dealing with them. The subject may, for example, conspicuously avoid, or give a number of responses to, these areas, indicating that they have a special importance to him. The particular reactions he has to these areas may, in any given case, be clearly symbolic of sexuality. Or there may not be enough evidence for us to make any use of this approach to interpretation in any individual case.

A good example of the use of the "area" approach and its possible utility is given by the responses of three subjects who served as demonstration cases. The interpretative meaning will be obvious, if these are considered as perceptions of a phallic symbol. The interpretation of the top *D* on Card VI was, by each subject, as follows:

1. "A beautiful, ornately carved bedpost—a gorgeous object, but completely useless." (Male, age 17)
2. "A beautiful, shiny streamlined train with big shiny headlights. It's coming right at me." (Female, age 19)
3. "Oscar, the Academy Award winner." (Male, age 38)

There are cases in which the various extensions on the cards are dealt with in a conspicuous manner either by making much use of them or leaving them out whenever possible. This, of course, has meaning in terms of an intellectual approach on the part of the individual, which is critical and relies on compartmentalization as a way of coping with anxiety. Whether this is also indicative of feelings of inferiority or of a preoccupation with phallic sexuality would have to be determined on the basis of the specific content in which such reactions are embedded. The meaning of actual sexual responses has been discussed above. Whether the presence of many sexual responses is associated with any kind of actual activity of either a genital or pregenital sort can be determined best by studying such responses in relation to the color dynamics and form level of the record as a whole, since these aspects of Rorschach performance are most directly analogous to behavior. The writer's view is that the presence of a great many genital responses most usually serves as a cloak for pregenital preoccupations which the individual is attempting to screen. He wishes to appear more mature both to himself and to others. An overt preoccupation with pregenital responses, on the other hand, is more frequent in the case of serious disintegrative disorders than in other kinds of records.

Evasive Responses

Certain kinds of responses seem to be quite affectively neutral to most subjects. A common example of this kind of response is the geographical or map response. When a subject says that a given area looks like a map, a rock formation, clouds, or the like, he is close to letting us know that it really does not look like anything in particular. If we can consider such responses as near rejections, they become very useful in analysis of sequence. We may go on to assume that something in the card disturbed the individual to the extent that blocking was produced. This may be either a preceding response in the same card, one in the preceding card, or something about the stimulus value of the cards *per se*. This latter point will be discussed in detail later in this chapter.

Miscellaneous Categories

The categories of responses discussed above are those most frequently discussed in the literature. There are numerous other kinds of percepts possible on the Rorschach. It may be useful to indicate some of the hypotheses associated with them, although these hypotheses are of a very tenuous nature.

1. *Buildings* may be considered representative of the human body or its achievements. Someone who perceives beautiful, stately buildings may think of himself quite differently than someone who is prone to see rotten, crumbling shacks. This is the same principle, essentially, as that involved in the use of Buck's H.T.P. technique.

2. *Nature responses* sometimes seem to reveal attitudes on the part of the subject about certain elemental forces in himself. This is especially true when an individual perceives such phenomena as explosions and volcanic eruptions. Such responses, usually associated with *m,* are indicative of a feeling of helplessness and lack of voluntary control in dealing with powerful instinctual urges.

3. *Masks* may be rather concretely interpreted as indicative of the human persona. The feeling of the individual subject about this peripheral aspect of personality may be gauged by the methods he uses in handling such concepts during the test. An overemphasis on such responses may indicate an overemphasis on persona values.

4. *Emblems* may express the submission of the subject's own needs to authority and may serve the purpose of emasculating animal and human figures by making them part of an emblem or coat of arms. When thus perceived, the necessity of projecting movement into them is no longer present. Thus, the expression of inner drives can be avoided.

5. *Man-made objects* are useful primarily for discovering the subject's immediate preoccupations. These may have special meanings when compared with material available from other sources.

6. *Clothing,* especially when seen as separate and apart from human figures, may be indicative of a concern with peripheral or surface aspects of other people or relationships with them. The specific area of interest again can be gauged from the kind of clothing.

7. Responses like *fire* and *blood,* usually associated with a rather labile use of color, are indicative of uncontrolled affective reactions. The specific meaning of such reactions can best be judged by regarding them in the context of their particular sequence.

Content Frequently Occurring in the Ten Cards

In this section, an attempt will be made to discuss the kinds of hypotheses that may be derived from some of the content that has been found to occur most frequently in the ten cards. The list here is not intended to be exhaustive or even representative except in terms of the present writer's own experience. It is the hope in presenting this material that from the examples cited here and the general discussion already given in this chapter, the reader will be able to form certain general principles in interpretation which he can apply to the analysis of any kind of content.

Card I

Card I has the special stimulus property of being the first aspect of a new and relatively unstructured situation. The content and structure of the first response may therefore reveal the subject's initial reaction to such a situation.

The most typical kind of content in this card is the popular concept of a winged creature. If this concept is perceived, it would seem to indicate an ability on the part of the perceiving subject to think along the line that most people do in a similar situation. Certain details about the perception that can be brought out during the inquiry may be used to form additional hypotheses. The making of irrelevant changes (changes that do not add to the form level) may be characteristic of an intellectual pseudo-critical attitude or a feeling of insecurity about reality.

White space may be used as a part of the popular concept or by itself, and the degree to which the individual is able to reverse the figure and ground has the usual meaning about the strength of and control over oppositional tendencies towards himself or others.

Among the other frequent ways of interpreting the blot as a whole is a response of a face, such as a cat or a jack-o-lantern. The affect connected with this response may lead the observer to feel that the subject is frightened of the world. Anatomical interpretations of the total blot may also be made and are characteristic of people concerned about their body and/or its potency. The amount of intellectual control in the face of such concern may be gauged from the specificity of the descriptive statements and the accuracy of form.

The large side *D*'s of this blot may be interpreted as profiles, whole human figures, or animals. If profiles are seen here and elsewhere, the individual may tend to be overcritical and to emphasize the intellectual aspects of interpersonal relationships. Seeing whole figures, most usually called witches, may have a specific meaning, depending on the way the figure is described and the affect expressed towards it. Seeing witches, for example, may lead the observer to hypothecate a feeling of threat from older, rather unpleasant women. In the case of animals, we would be interested in the kind of animal and its activity as well as the details of perception. The subject's method of dealing with the various extensions, for example, may be related to his ability or inability to accept and make use of his instinctual drives.

The central area of the blot is commonly interpreted as some sort of human or human-like figure. It is most commonly considered a female figure and may be seen as either dressed or undressed. If the figure is seen as dressed, the concept of a transparency may be involved. If transparent clothes are mentioned, it may lead us to suppose that the individual is preoccupied with the idea of seeing through the outer aspects or persona of people. Seeing this figure from the rear, calling it a hooded figure, monk, nun, or the like, may be considered ways of avoiding the specification of sexual characteristics, since the differences between men and women are less pronounced under these circumstances. Describing the figure as being pulled about or otherwise engaging in action over which it has no apparent voluntary control may lead us to think of schizoid or obsessive tendencies within the perceiving subject. All of these hypotheses may turn out to be quite erroneous as the evidence accumulates, or they may be borne out. However, much may be gained by adding this kind of interpretative hypothesis to the kind derived from the analysis of structure.

Other details frequently used in the card include the upper inner *d*'s interpreted as hands. This may be related to a feeling of helplessness or a need to cling if the elaborations lead to this kind of feeling. On the other hand, they may be described as being aggressive or threatening. Storm clouds seen within the blot may reveal a feeling of pessimism or fear. Tiny usual and unusual areas around the periphery may be interpreted as faces of various kinds, the attendant hypotheses being as described above.

Card II

Card II is unique in introducing for the first time affective loading in the form of color as part of the stimulus. The criteria for gauging emotional disturbance have been described in Chapter 11. They include long reaction time, evasion of colored areas, or disturbance in content. Here we are concerned with the latter. Psychotic individuals will tend to demonstrate objective color disturbance by loss of their intellectual contact with reality, manifested by pronounced drops in the form level. Adequate responses in the first card will be replaced by bizarre and idiosyncratic responses in this one. The particular content of these peculiar responses may reflect the focus that these individuals' difficulties are taking—as, for example, anatomical or sexual concepts. People with less disintegrative kinds of emotional disturbances do not show such drastic changes but may substitute responses in which the affective components play the major role for those dominated by essentially controlled or form factors. Among the uncontrolled or irrational ways of reacting to color, we may distinguish passive responses, such as plants or flowers, from more explosive or aggressive responses, such as fire and blood. These may occur in the records of both normal and abnormal subjects. However, the passive responses are more characteristic of anxiety states, the latter of conditions in which acting out of symptom formation is a prominent feature.

The popular response to this card is that of the two animals, one on either side. Here, again, we are interested in the type of action and interaction as well as the specifications involved. When a subject is sufficiently aware of the nuances of the stimulus card to see these animals with a textured skin, we may infer a greater amount of sensitivity than where such elaborations are attached to areas more commonly associated with texture. Another common response using the total blot is that of two human or human-like figures, often called clowns. The use of the latter concept provides an opportunity for the controlled use of color (FC), although this is not a necessary part of the concept. The way sex is specified, the type of action injected into the picture, the type of clothing, and so on, will all provide rich clues and should be inquired for diligently. The specific idea of clowns, if repeated, may be associated with an attempt to regard others or oneself as foolish or ineffectual. Seeing the heads or the bodies alone may give us ideas concerning the relative importance of intellective and non-intellective aspects of human functioning to the perceiving subject.

The center d and the bottom D are often associated with sexual material. Even responses not of a sexual sort may be considered as symbols, provided the evidence is sufficiently clear and borne out in other cases (that is, giving many responses to the center *d* may be indicative of the great attraction that phallic sexuality has for this individual in spite of an inability to deal consciously with such material). Using the center *S* for a sexual concept is rather more unusual and may be a sign of disturbance.

Card III

Card III is the second one in the sequence of colored cards. An ability to deal more adequately with this card may reflect an ability on the part of the individual to adapt gradually to an emotional situation. Recoverability may be demonstrated by an increasing accuracy of the responses, the use of color for more constructive purposes, and the disappearance of disturbance in the content. If an individual shows more disturbances of this sort on Card III than on Card II, it may be due to the special stimulus properties of this card, such as the popular human figures in it.

These popular human figures, the only ones in the whole series of cards, make this card particularly valuable for the analysis of content. Inquiry concerning them should always reveal their sex and clothing and the meaning of all the specific areas within the concept. Being unable to perceive human figures in this area altogether is so unusual as to lead to a hypothesis that the perceiving subject is unable to accept or identify with others. Intermediate between a rejection and whole-hearted acceptance of this concept are the various kinds of distanciation responses, such as seeing the figures as dressed-up animals, shadows, or comic strip characters. Various difficulties in the identification and acceptance of a sexual role may be indicated by such details as not specifying the sex of the figures, referring to the two symmetrical figures as being of different sexes, or attributing both male and female characteristics to the same figure. The action of the individuals is also of importance. It may be masculine or feminine, either being appropriate to or conflicting with the stated sex of the figures. On the other hand, it may be involuntary, due to some centrifugal or other forces, leading the observer to hypothesize feelings of inner tensions or the presence of obsessions over which the subject has no control.

The center red *D* provides one of the two popular *FC* combinations in the series of cards. The subject's ability to form adequate social relationships may be gauged in part from his handling of this detail. Interpreting this particular area by giving an anatomical or vague form response may be considered somewhat more unusual and more disquieting than in the case of other colored areas.

The upper red *D*'s are often called animals, which may lead to varying hypotheses depending on the kind of action projected and the method employed by the subject in dealing with the long extensions involved. The lower center *D* may be organized as part of the human figures, or it may become two Negro heads when the card is rotated. Seeing people of another race may be considered another attempt at distanciation. The way such people are described may reveal important attitudes about minority groups which, in turn, may reflect feelings of insecurity or potency on the part of the subject.

Card IV

Card IV has sometimes been referred to as the "father card." It does possess many characteristics associated with the concept of father, and many times important attitudes along these lines may be gauged. However, there are many cases in which the formulation of hypotheses in this area would be extremely difficult on the basis of the kind of content utilized. In the opinion of the present writer it is unnecessary and unfruitful to stretch empirical reasoning to the point where every reaction to Card IV is interpreted as a reaction to father or authority. The card possesses other important stimulus characteristics, including the first introduction of pronounced shading and several areas frequently associated with sex.

The kinds of interpretations of the blot most directly relevant to hypotheses about authority relationships are the perception of the whole blot as a giant man, ape, or monster, or the interpretation of the side *D*'s as boots. A preoccupation with parental relationships should not blind us to the evaluations of such responses in terms of the role of masculine aggression in the person himself.

Guesses about the role of sexuality in an individual may be made on the basis of his handling of the lower center D (often interpreted as a tree stump or head of an animal) or the side d (called snakes, dancing ladies, wilted lettuce, and so on) or the top d (called a plant or face of some sort). A phenomenon sometimes observed is seeing a symbol of one sex in an area usually associated with the other— that is, a phallus may be seen in the top d of this card. Where shading and sexuality occur together, sexuality may be considered by that subject as a reciprocal and coöperative act. This is an example of the way in which the analysis of content and structure may work together in the formulation of a hypothesis.

This card contains no popular concepts; however, the concepts most frequently seen are an animal skin for the W, or the above-mentioned boots. Extreme blocking or total rejection of the card may be due to disturbance by any one of the elements mentioned above. The specific aspect or aspects disturbing an individual subject can be determined only by further probing his reactions to the card during the testing-the-limits procedure.

Card V

Card V is unique in having an extremely common concept associated with it. This, of course, is the winged creature usually called a bat or a butterfly. As noted in Chapter 11, this response is so frequent that an inability to see it, even during the testing-the-limits procedure, is considered most peculiar. The hypothesis in this case would be that the individual's ties to reality are rather weak. The various extensions on the card may be used as part of this concept, or they may be pointedly removed. The interpretation here would be the usual one mentioned above. Expressions of affect in regard to this response may also be useful; that is, the animal may be seen as hovering or otherwise in a threatening position, which may be how the subject views the world. Endowing a neutral object with affect, such as seeing a brightly colored butterfly here, is a rather concrete example of the mechanisms of projection at work. Projection without conscious control, as illustrated here, is characteristic of serious pathology.

A complete inability to see concepts on this card is rather unusual. A unique property of the card, which may result in its rejection, is its intensive and massed black color. The black may produce a phenomenon that has been called "grey-black shock" by Beck [1]. This implies, in part, an inability on the part of the individual to deal with the more somber aspects of his environment—an intolerance for feelings of depression.

The central area in this card may be interpreted as a human or animal figure or figures, whereas the side outline areas may be interpreted either as profiles or whole human figures. Here, as elsewhere, sexual identification, clothing, and affect expressed towards the figures are important and will all lead to the strengthening of previous hypotheses or the formulation of new ones. Sometimes a figure in the center is seen as hiding behind or cloaked by some material in front. This might be related to fear of the environment or one's role in it. The side *d*'s, often interpreted as crocodile heads, provide an opportunity for the expression of aggression, especially of an oral sort.

Card VI

Card VI is particularly characterized by the frequency with which sexual associations are made to it, either in direct or symbolic form. The top *D* is frequently called a penis or else an object having rather evident phallic significance (see above, page 386). An ability to utilize this area by giving a response to it or including it with the rest may be thought of as being indicative of the acceptance of masculine sexuality on the part of the perceiving subject. The subject's specific attitudes about phallic sexuality may be further demonstrated in his elaborations of the concept. The center line in the lower part of the blot may be thought of as an area symbolizing feminine or vaginal sexuality. Frequently, the affect displayed towards and the elaborations concerning this area may be interpreted accordingly. Two contrasting perceptions might be: "A beautiful, fruitful valley surrounded by rolling hills," and "An animal split open with an axe." Usually, only the smaller opening at the bottom of the card is interpreted directly as a vagina. Extending this concept to the large center area may be suggestive of an emphasis on the grosser aspects of sexuality.

Particular disturbance in reaction to this card is frequently due to its sexual implications. However, it may also be related to a difficulty in dealing with the shading nuances with which the card is plentifully supplied. The popular concept here is that of the animal skin, and some initial clue as to the importance of sexuality in the subject's reaction to the card may be gotten from his ability or inability to include all portions of the card in the popular response. Whether a reaction to shading is absent or not being expressed can be ascertained, of course, during the testing of the limits procedure.

The small detail in the center of the card, often called a nest and eggs, might lead to the hypothesis that the individual feels unable to cope with the adult world and is preoccupied with reproduction or infantile objects. The D's on either side, interpreted as a king's head, may be related to attitudes towards authority and a high level of aspiration. Here again, the perception of color in the upper D, when seen as a butterfly, is a rather unusual kind of projection and should be scrutinized carefully.

Card VII

Card VII has also been given a specific label by some. It has been called the "mother card." The reasoning in regard to this point is similar to that described in regard to Card IV. Many aspects of the card are often associated with femininity, but such interpretation should always be made in context and not automatically.

The upper third of the card, with or without the middle third, is often interpreted as two figures, most often referred to as women. If the individual sees children or animals rather than women, this may also be important. A general tendency to see only infantile or animal objects, especially when a positive affect is associated with them, may be indicative of an immature level of social development. Such a person can express affect only towards lesser or toy-like objects, but cannot tackle adult heterosexual relationships with any expectancy of success. Another common way of seeing female figures is by turning the card and viewing it as a whole, which often makes it possible to see the figures as headless, if the perceiver is so inclined. This, as in other cases, would lead the observer to assume that the emotional aspects of relationships surmounted the intellectual in importance in the perceiving subject.

Responses given to the center *d* often seem to have rather evident meaning if this area is considered as symbolizing vaginal sexuality. For example, the area may be interpreted as an open or shut zipper, gate, tiny human figure, or the like. Formulating hypotheses about a person's basic sexual attitudes on the basis of this kind of evidence is justified only when other sources of information are available for comparative purposes. The interpretation of the light gray area just below the *d* as a "little house" deserves special mention, as it often is associated with a desire to seek the comfort and security of an earlier stage.

The total blot is very commonly interpreted as clouds. Although responses of this sort are frequently thought of as being associated with feelings of unsureness, vagueness, or anxiety, we would be less inclined to formulate such a hypothesis on this card. This is because the giving of common responses, as such, provides less opportunity for making interpretations about the individuality of the perceiver. However, any unusual methods of handling such concepts is of importance.

Card VIII

Card VIII is a totally chromatic card which follows a series of black and white cards. Any marked changes in content here might be interpreted as being due to this change in affective tone. Possible ways of reacting to the color here are various. An individual may use the color to distinguish areas from one another, indicating a highly stereotyped way of dealing with affective stimuli. Such responses are usually anatomical or geographical in content. Anatomical reactions, when given to this card and not to any of the previous ones, are especially significant, as they indicate the subject's return to somatic preoccupations under conditions of emotional stress. Passive ways of giving in to the color may include the perception of flowers or plants, whereas a constructive way of using the affective properties of the blot is illustrated by the response "tropical butter-fly" to the bottom *D* area. Attempts to make use of the color in regard to the popular concept of animals in the side *D*'s result in forced or arbitrary affective reactions more often than not.

These animals are another response sufficiently frequent to warrant the kind of hypothesis suggested for the bat in Card V if they are *not* perceived. A critical attitude towards this particular response, such as stating that it is only very roughly like an animal, would be particularly unusual and probably characteristic of very critical people. The degree of aggressiveness of the action imputed to the animals is important insofar as it departs from the ordinary description of them and thereby becomes an expression of individuality. A way of robbing the animals of their vitality, for example, is to make them part of an emblem.

Another common response to this card is to perceive part of a tree in the upper *D,* which provides an opportunity for using color constructively. Although some observers have hypothecated a difference in the interpretative significance of reactions to the so-called cool colors (green and blue) as opposed to the warm colors (red, pink, yellow), no experimental evidence is available for such a conjecture. The center area in this card is very frequently interpreted as an anatomical concept. Such an interpretation would, therefore, be considered of lesser significance than if given elsewhere.

Card IX

The giving of no responses to this card is a frequent occurrence in emotionally disturbed individuals. This may be due to the complex color and shading properties of the blot as well as to the scarcity of usual concepts. When responses are given to this card, however, they are, in many cases, highly unusual and extremely worthwhile from an interpretative point of view. Since this section claims to deal only with usual or ordinary kinds of content, illustrations of this point will have to occur in other sections of the book. Some fairly common responses are the following: Witches or clowns in the upper orange area, perhaps related to an interpretation of other people or oneself as threatening, foolish, or otherwise unwholesome and unacceptable. Some sort of human head in the bottom pink area of the card; this is usually called a man's head, but may be called an infant's or embryo's head when the individual is inclined to emphasize infantile love objects in his own thinking. The green area is sometimes interpreted as a face and occasionally arouses such affect as to result in its being termed stupid, vapid, or otherwise inferior.

Although explosions, when perceived in the Rorschach, are usually indicators of uncontrolled affect on the part of the perceiving subject, this is not so true when the reaction is to this card. This statement, again, is based on the empirical observation that such an interpretation of Card IX upside down is a frequent one, especially since the public has seen pictures of atomic bomb explosions.

Card X

Card X provides an unusual opportunity for those subjects who are hindered from making good perceptions only by their difficulty in organizing complex blot materials. Here they are faced with a number of discrete situations, each of which can be interpreted by itself. Consequently, many individuals are able to reveal much more flexibility, initiative, and spontaneity in their reactions to this card than previously. Of course, it may have the opposite effect on other subjects. The opportunity for integrating affective and rational reactions is provided by such common responses as the green caterpillars in the bottom *D*, blue birds in the center *D*, brown deer in the side brown *D*, yellow dogs in the center yellow *D*. Opportunities for projecting movement occur in connection with the responses mentioned above plus such other responses as jumping sheep in the top green *D*, fighting insects in the top *D*, crawling spiders in the side blue *D*. Human beings may be seen in the pink *D* area. Especially common is the perception of them as sucking at something, which, when taken together with other evidence, may be related to an emphasis on oral or dependent kinds of methods of dealing with the world.

Thus, Card X by itself may be thought of in terms of a preliminary testing-of-the-limits kind of procedure. Subjects previously lim-

ited in the full utilization of their resources by the complexity or
novelty of the materials may blossom out here. Blocking on this
card in the case of individuals with potentially at least average intelligence is indicative of severe impairment due to emotional factors.

Testing the Limits

Hypotheses concerning content made during an interpretation of
the responses to the ten cards may be considerably amplified and
added to during the testing-the-limits procedure. Some of the points
that can be covered are:

1.   If an individual has been unable to spontaneously perceive
very frequent responses during the test proper, it is very important
to find out whether he will be able to accept such responses with
some encouragement. His ability to do this may answer the question
of whether he is merely being intellectually critical or whether his
thinking is of a disintegrative sort.

2.   Specific kinds of content may be tested for. If an individual
has been unable to see human beings or animals during the examination proper, he would be encouraged to do so in this part of
the test. The extent to which pressure will have to be brought to
bear, or support given, before he can accept some of the more ordinary human concepts will provide a clue to the strength of his
inhibitory withdrawal or rejection mechanisms. Once a given concept has been added by the subject to his own frame of reference,
further clues may be gotten by continuing the usual type of inquiry.

3.   Any responses that seem to have a specific symbolic meaning
to the subject, especially if they occur frequently, can be further
clarified by requesting free associations to them. This is not suggested as a routine procedure, but as one that can be of considerable
help in sharpening up certain hypotheses in specific cases.

4.   By asking the subject to place the cards in piles, it is often
possible to discover the particular aspect of the blot that is most
important to the individual. That subject most concerned with the
objective aspects of outer reality is apt to divide the cards on the
basis of the principles of color. A more introspectively oriented in-

dividual is apt to use content as a dividing principle. Irregularities in the process of concept formation may reveal further interpretative clues.

5. Asking the subject to give affective ratings of the cards—for example, asking him to select the most and least liked—will often give more detailed information about certain crucial responses given in the previous examination.

Conclusions

The aim of this chapter has been to formulate certain principles that may be used in setting up interpretative hypotheses on the basis of an analysis of the content of Rorschach responses. The application of these principles to some of the more common concepts perceived in the ten cards has been intended as a purely illustrative demonstration. It is hoped that the process of hypothesis formulation here described will enable the reader to make some constructive use of the content of any response he gets on the Rorschach test. The more unusual these responses are, the more they deviate from the stereotypes described here, the more important an expression of individuality they will be.

The point of view expressed here is that an attempt to deal with the content of Rorschach responses as symbolic is justified under certain special circumstances. These conditions require that the individual constantly check himself by comparing the hypotheses formed on this basis with one another, with hypotheses derived from an analysis of structure, and with hypotheses formed on the basis of other tests and case history materials. The result will be a series of formulations which will permit a rather thorough assessment of the personality and will be of considerable aid in clinical diagnosis. This approach contrasts with the empirical nosological method described by Lindner [6]. This latter method, though possibly useful in distinguishing diagnostic groups from one another, is of very little use in the assessment of individual personality characteristics. In fact, its concrete application in the individual case could be quite dangerous and misleading. There is no substitute in Rorschach interpretation for the careful and thorough evaluation of every response, both in terms of its own structure and content and as part of a larger configuration.

References

1. Beck, S. J. *Rorschach's Test*. New York: Grune & Stratton, Inc.; 1944.

2. Due, F. O., and Wright, M. E. "The Use of Content Analysis in Rorschach Interpretations," *Rorschach Res. Exch.*, 1945, 9, 169–177.

3. Goldfarb, W. "The Animal Symbol in the Rorschach Test and an Animal Association Test," *Rorschach Res. Exch.*, 1946, 10, 121–129.

4. Hertzman, M., and Pearce, J. "The Personal Meaning of the Human Figure in the Rorschach." *Psychiatry*, 1947, 10, 413–422.

5. Klopfer, W. G. *Suggestions for the Systematic Analysis of Rorschach Records*. University of California at Los Angeles: The Student Store (mimeographed) .

6. Lindner, R. M. "The Content Analysis of the Rorschach Protocol," in Abt, L. E. and Bellak, L. *Projective Psychology*. New York: Alfred A. Knopf, Inc.; 1950.

7. Mead, M. *Male and Female*. New York: William Morrow & Company; 1949.

8. Tomkins, S. *The Thematic Apperception Test*. New York: Grune & Stratton, Inc.; 1947.

Part Three

Theory

CHAPTER **14**

Problems of Validation *

The basic thesis of this chapter is that it is more productive to view the Rorschach technique as a method of observation and appraisal than to class it as a "test" of personality. It is legitimate to ask the question "Is it valid?" regarding a test that purports to measure some aspect of personality. However, regarding a method of observation the appropriate questions are: "Is it useful? Is it productive?" After a sample of the functioning of an individual has been obtained by means of the method, and a complex description and appraisal has been produced as a conclusion, two further questions may be asked: either "Is this a valid account of the functioning of this person?" or, "Are the assumptions and hypotheses upon which the conclusions are based valid ones?"

It is assumed that the problem of validation of the Rorschach technique transcends that of ascertaining the truth and accuracy of the individual personality description; the basic question concerns the validity of the interpretative hypotheses upon which the appraisal of personality function is based. Therefore, it is proposed

---

* This chapter has grown out of a paper read at a meeting of the General Section of the British Psychological Society in February, 1951 [2].

Note: Since it is not proposed in this chapter to attempt a comprehensive review of the voluminous literature on Rorschach research, the reader is referred to reviews by Bell [11], Hertz [62, 63], Piotrowski [112], and Rickers-Ovsiankina [118], also to the bibliographies included in the books by Rorschach [123], Beck [9], Frank [45], and Klopfer and Kelley [80], as well as to the bibliography appended to Volume II of this present work.

405

that the validation of the Rorschach technique should follow the familiar scientific process of the validation of hypotheses rather than the pattern of test validation. Viewed in this way, it becomes an obvious expectation that through validation research hypotheses will become modified, extended, refined, and corrected—not merely accepted as valid or rejected as invalid.

From this point of view there is no sharp dividing line between validation research and the clinical use of the Rorschach technique; the process of development and modification of hypotheses through everyday clinical use, which has been going on since the Rorschach technique was originated, is in validation research greatly extended and supplemented by the use of systematic scientific controls and techniques. Nor is there any sharp dichotomy between validating Rorschach hypotheses about personality function and validating any other such hypotheses. Validation research cannot be separated entirely from more basic research into personality function and development. Improvements in methods of observation facilitate advances in the understanding of the functions observed; advances in the scientific understanding of the function facilitate refinements in the method of observing it and the interpretation of the significance of what is observed. In this context, validation of the Rorschach technique is a continuing process; indeed, the technique itself is continually changing through the validation process.

Within this frame of reference it is proposed to discuss certain methodological problems involved in the validation of the Rorschach technique. These problems have been increasingly recognized in the course of the past few years; there have already been a number of careful discussions of validation in the literature, including those by Benton [14], Cronbach [28, 29], Ferguson [38], Hertz [60], Korner [82], MacFarlane [90], Rosenzweig [125, 126], Rotter [132], Sarason [138], Schafer [145], Schneider [146], and Vernon [159], which have already played a part in focussing validation research on a more productive level. However, before discussing methodological problems, it seems desirable to consider a few of the differences in viewpoint which have added to the methodological difficulties, and which have helped to make the question of the validation of the Rorschach technique a controversial one.

Differing Viewpoints towards Validation

There are many who work with the Rorschach technique who feel little or no urgency about the validation of the technique. Working under the practical pressures of rendering a service, they have welcomed the Rorschach technique as a helpful instrument of personality appraisal and have come to feel a certain inner conviction that it is valid, with perhaps a few reservations about details. For the service job it is necessary to accept both theoretical formulations and technical devices as working hypotheses and tools, going ahead as though they were valid. It is difficult at the same time to maintain a sound scientific skepticism about the validity of these hypotheses and tools, testing out their validity whilst working with them and welcoming systematic research in other quarters. The clinical psychologist may insist that the very fact that the Rorschach technique "works" (that it is helpful) is a testimonial of validity. On the contrary, the fact that the method has seemed helpful enough to gain such widespread use should point to the value of extensive validation research to ascertain how it "works" as well as it does, what its errors and limitations are, and generally to refine and improve it as a tool. The inner conviction of validity that comes to the worker as he uses the technique may be personally reassuring, but it must be held as scientifically suspect. This danger has often been pointed out—that the descriptions of personality emerging from techniques such as the Rorschach may be cast in such vague and general terms that they have too broad an applicability; moreover, the fact that they are found to "fit" the individual patient either by the examiner or by the patient himself may lead to an erroneous impression of validity. Forer [41] has recently demonstrated the "fallacy of personal validation" by presenting to students a "personality description" made up of statements culled from newsstand publications but purporting to be the "results" of a test previously administered to the class; the students accepted a very high proportion of the component statements as applicable to themselves, despite the fact that the "descriptions" issued to all students were the same.

The Rorschach examiner has good grounds for replying that it is incorrect to class the Rorschach technique with fortune-telling devices simply because both are subject to the fallacy of "personal validation." The Rorschach technique rests on a phenomenological rationale. The appraisal of personality or the prediction of future behavior do not rest on the basis of lines on the palm or the fall of the cards—which have no demonstrated connection with the personality or behavior of the subject—but upon a sample of his actual behavior, following the rationale common to all psychological tests that a generalization may be made from behavior in the test situation to behavior outside the test situation. Thus, if the subject displays great ability in organizing his perception of the Rorschach blots it seems reasonable to predict that he will generally display ability in organizing his perception of the world. Similarly, if he approaches the Rorschach material piecemeal, selecting isolated, small, clear-cut details as the basis of his concepts, it is reasonable to suppose that he will show the same characteristics in his perception of his life situation.

Reasonable although this approach may be, it begs the question of validation. It could not be assumed that ability to solve arithmetical problems had any general predictive value regarding academic success or general problem-solving ability unless this value was demonstrated; indeed, it is well known that simple mechanical arithmetical computations do not have this broader predictive value. Thus, it is necessary to ascertain the limits within which the generalization from a sample of behavior does in fact hold. Does a subject's "organizing ability" as sampled by his Rorschach performance extend to organizing the use of his time, organizing group activity, and organizing his thinking? Or does it merely refer to his ability to see relationships between various aspects of his perceived world? Or does it perhaps have no generalized significance beyond perception of the Rorschach material itself? These are questions to be answered through validation research. The phenomenological rationale of the Rorschach technique should be viewed as a promising basis for the formulation of interpretative hypotheses, but the rationale does not make it possible to dispense with research to ascertain the limits of the generalization.

Some critics scorn the phenomenological basis of the interpretative hypotheses as "reasoning from analogy"; apparently they assume that all analogy is false. The possibility must be held open that some phenomena *seem* like others because they *are* in fact like them, involving the same processes and arising from the same antecedents. Perception of such similarities may prove to be the starting-point for an advance in scientific understanding. Analogy can be misleading where it is inapplicable, and helpful where it is applicable. The applicability of the analogy must be tested, however. Empirical test through practical use may lend some support, but is no final substitute for a more systematic scientific testing.

Validation of Tests vs. Validation of Hypotheses

It has been held by some that the projective techniques should not be used until their validity has been demonstrated according to the criteria employed with other psychological tests. This position is a natural one if the projective techniques are viewed as essentially similar to other psychological tests. It is traditional in the field of psychological testing that validation should proceed hand in hand with test construction, and that some more or less adequate degree of reliability and validity must be demonstrated before the test is offered for general use. The test is viewed as a finished whole, for which some estimate of validity may be obtained within a limited period of time. It may be judged valid enough to be used, or too invalid to be helpful, or reasonably valid for some purposes but not for others. The test is not viewed as a changing and developing instrument of appraisal; indeed to change the test would spoil its standardization. Changes can only be accomplished by "revision"; the revised version is in fact a new test.

Projective techniques are used as "tests" of personality and manifest a number of similarities to other psychological tests, but the differences are crucial enough to recommend that projective techniques be considered another genus among the family of appraisal methods. The chief similarities are that all individuals are observed in a controlled and standardized situation in which the structural characteristics of the individual are to be considered the independent variable and the resultant performance the dependent variable, and that generalizations are made from the sample of behavior taken in the test situation to the function of the person in his everyday life. Here the resemblance ends.

The typical psychological test deals with one variable or function, and attempts to provide a means of placing all tested individuals on a continuum with respect to that function. The fact that a few tests deal with several variables and several continua at once does not change the essential basis of the approach. Projective techniques such as the Rorschach deal with n functions or variables and attempt to describe the individual in terms of a dynamic pattern of interrelated functions or variables. This multiplicity of interrelated and interdependent variables constitutes the most important difference between projective techniques and other types of psychological tests and presents one of the greatest problems of validation.

Attached to each variable is at least one interpretative hypothesis. Different sets of interpretative hypotheses have been presented by different workers with the same type of projective material. With the Rorschach ink blot material there have been developed a number of sets of interpretative hypotheses, not only those presented by Rorschach himself, [123] but those of Beck [9] and Rapaport [117] as well as those presented in this present book and its antecedent [80], to mention only those most commonly used in the English-speaking world at the present time.

That there should be differences between the hypotheses of various clinicians inevitably follows from the fact that these hypotheses in the first instance grew up empirically from clinical observations and experience. That there should be a large common core follows partly as a suggestion of the validity of the hypotheses as formulated separately by different individuals, and partly because there is a rapidly accumulating literature, of both clinical impressions and controlled scientific observations, which has been influential in casting certain of the hypotheses into a common mold. The fact remains that the task of validation pertains to the various sets of interpretative hypotheses rather than to any prototype interpretation originally attached to the test material itself.

Evidence of the invalidity of any one hypothesis or set of hypotheses cannot be generalized to the test material as the basis of a method of investigating personality, nor to the other interpretative hypotheses advanced by the same or other individuals. Critics of the Rorschach technique seem sometimes to feel that to prove the invalidity of one hypothesis somehow disposes of the entire technique as invalid. To them the Rorschach technique must seem to have a certain Hydra-headed resilience. To lop off one hypothesis has no effect on the vigor of the others; indeed, in the place of the hypothesis disposed of, others are developed which are free from the defects of the original one. There is nothing irregular about this phenomenon; scientific understanding characteristically advances through the testing out, discarding, modification, and refinement of hypotheses.

With the foregoing as introduction, let us now consider the major problems of validation of the Rorschach technique, problems shared by projective techniques generally. These problems may be classified under five main headings:

1. Problems pertaining to the interrelatedness of the interpretative hypotheses.
2. Problems related to the nature of Rorschach concepts and their communicability.
3. Problems stemming from the time-consuming nature of the Rorschach technique, and the short-cut methods often used to overcome this drawback.
4. Problems related to reliability.
5. Problems related to the outside criteria against which hypotheses are to be checked.

1. Problems Pertaining to the Interrelatedness of Interpretative Hypotheses

The personality appraisal that is the end result of the analysis of the performance of an individual in response to the Rorschach materials represents the integration of a large number of different interpretative hypotheses, each one of which may influence the applicability of the others. The Rorschach technique is holistic rather than atomistic. This is not to imply that the interpretation is based on a total, unanalyzed impression growing out of clinical experience. On the contrary, a great deal of highly differentiated perception on the examiner's part has gone into the analysis. The final interpretation, however, is in the form of a dynamic sketch of the way in which the personality functions; the interpretation forms a highly integrated and articulated whole. This fact introduces a very serious difficulty when it comes to validation, for in the tried-and-true method of scientific investigation one variable at a time is explored through a range of variation. The beginner, learning the Rorschach technique, is first presented with a series of discrete hypotheses attached to the various scoring classifications. At first glance these present themselves as hopeful starting points for validation research. However, the beginner soon learns that each separate hypothesis is applicable only within a certain range of configurations and is modified by the particular configuration in which it appears.

To exemplify this problem in perhaps its simplest context, let us consider the question of assessing intelligence from the Rorschach performance.* Rorschach [123, page 56] originally suggested certain features as indicators of a high level of intelligence, including a large percentage of clearly visualized forms $(F+\%)$,† many kinesthetic responses (M), many whole responses (W), and a small percentage of animal responses $(A\%)$. Altus and Thompson [6] investigated this set of hypotheses, correlating each "sign" separately with scores on a group intelligence test. Coefficients of .35 and .45 respectively were found for M and W, while neither the $F+\%$ nor the $A\%$ seemed significantly related to the criterion. These results seem likely to be minimal in view of the fact that a group administration of the Rorschach and a group intelligence test were used, while a very narrow range of ability was represented by the population of college students. Most important, however, is the fact that in practice these "signs" of intelligence are never considered singly. The estimate of intelligence is made from the various factors con-

---

* See pages 352 ff. of this volume.

† In this book the practice of finding $F+\%$ has been discarded in favor of the average unweighted and weighted form-level rating. $F+\%$ would refer to the percentage of responses receiving a form-level rating of 1.0 or higher.

sidered in combination and within the context of the rest of the personality. It is well known that neurotic but highly intelligent persons may give few *M* responses, and that many subjects of mediocre or low intellectual level may have a high proportion of *W* responses. Moreover, the hypotheses have been refined since Rorschach's original formulation; the intellectual estimate is based not merely on the number but also on the form level of the *M* and *W* responses. In other words, Altus and Thompson were not testing the hypotheses connected with the intellectual estimate as they are actually used, and the integrative nature of the process of estimation was left out of consideration entirely. Vernon [159], on the other hand, found a correlation of .78 between the Binet test and an estimate of intellectual level based on a combination of features, although he confirmed that the separate components correlated poorly.

A study by Holtzman [68] is pertinent here. Taking the ratios *CF* : *FC* and (*CF*+*cF*+*2C*) : (*FC*+*Fc*) as indicators of impulsiveness or lack of control in social situations, he correlated these ratios with pooled ratings of impulsiveness made by residence-mates of the subjects. Taken separately, both of these "indicators" showed negligible correlations with the criterion. However, when a score was assigned on the basis of a number of different aspects of the protocol given weightings on an empirical basis, a correlation of .49 was obtained, which was significant at a 2 per cent level of confidence. Holtzman concludes that impulsiveness may be revealed in a number of different ways, depending upon the individual personality structure, but that behavioral impulsiveness may, nevertheless, be predicted if a number of different variables are considered in interrelationship.

The fact that interpretative hypotheses are modified by the context of the configuration in which they appear presents a difficult dilemma in planning validation research. On the one hand it may be argued that if the discrete hypotheses cannot be shown to have some valid basis, a judgment based on the integration of these hypotheses can scarcely be valid. On the other hand, it seems equally justifiable to insist that validation research is irrelevant unless it tests out the hypotheses as they are actually used in practice. There is probably no simple or single solution to this problem.

"Matching" Studies vs. Validation of Discrete Hypotheses

There have been various attempts to test the validity of the Rorschach technique by holistic methods, chief of which involves "matching." The essentials of the "matching" method are that a number of judges are required to match personality sketches drawn from an analysis of the Rorschach performance with personality sketches written on the basis of some other type of experience with the subjects involved, such as that of a teacher or therapist. Vernon [159] obtained a contingency coefficient of .833 ± .0315 using a matching method, which indicates a high degree of similarity between the personality pictures involved. However, he points out in another paper [160] that the coefficient of contingency is affected by several conditions: namely, the training of the judges and hence their reliability, the heterogeneity of the sample, and the number of elements to be matched. These considerations probably explain the varying degrees of validity shown by different "matching" studies. Thus Krugman [83] reports an average contingency coefficient of .830 between Rorschach appraisals of problem children and sketches based on case reports, while Hunter [70] reports that only 5 out of 50 Rorschach reports on private school children were matched correctly by all judges with personality descriptions written by teachers. However, Krugman did not control the heterogeneity of her matching groups, while in Hunter's study the sample was a highly selected one and a number of her personality sketches were said to be closely similar.

Palmer [106] emphasizes the importance of validating the interpretation rather than establishing the relationship of discrete scores with some outside criterion. He designed a study permitting a comparison between the results of a holistic matching approach with the results of one in which discrete interpretative statements were matched. In the matching procedure the therapist who had been treating a patient was asked to select the patient's Rorschach report from among five other reports carefully selected as neither very similar nor very different. In 11 of 28 cases the selection was made correctly, which yields a contingency coefficient of .434, significant at the 3 per cent level. In the item-analysis procedure he devised

34 multiple-choice items designed to cover the chief areas of personality function dealt with by Rorschach hypotheses. The multiple-choice items were checked independently by four experienced Rorschach examiners on the basis of the Rorschach performance and by the therapist on the basis of his acquaintance with the patient. No significant degree of agreement was found between the two sets of item checks, although the Rorschach judges were in fairly reliable agreement among themselves. Agreement was not superior in the case of the 11 patients who had been correctly "matched" to agreement in the case of the others. Palmer suggested, however, that there were two chief problems to be overcome before this method could be tested out adequately. He felt his particular check list was inadequate and could be much improved, while other indications pointed to the fact that the different conceptual frameworks within which the Rorschach examiners and the therapists operated had prevented them from checking the items on a comparable basis.

Cronbach [28] criticizes matching techniques because they cannot indicate the degree of rightness and wrongness of each prediction, and because either matching or mismatching may be based on small coincidences. He acknowledges the importance of the configuration of scoring features, and indeed of the qualitative features of the Rorschach protocol, in arriving at the appraisal of the personality but recommends breaking the description down into its component statements and testing these against an outside criterion. In the study quoted by Cronbach, the Rorschach examiner made various predictions about the problem-solving approach of Ph.D. candidates in psychology, which later were to be checked against the report of the Ph.D. adviser as the criterion. This suggested approach overcomes the difficulties of the check-list, which is too rigid an instrument to represent the nuances of the interpretative statements with any accuracy. However, it would not necessarily overcome any problems inherent in congruency of concepts and fluency of communication between the Rorschach examiner and the outside judges.

Despite the holistic nature of the Rorschach appraisal there seems little alternative to a careful testing of the interpretative hypotheses one by one, not merely to establish the degree of validity of the present hypotheses but also to correct, refine, and extend the hypotheses themselves, thus shaping a more valid basis of interpretation. There is no simple answer to the problem posed by the interrelated and interdependent nature of these hypotheses, nor is there any one solution that would be equally applicable to all hypotheses. Some are more easily isolated for independent research than others. With some hypotheses it should be possible to validate the "estimate" or the interpretation, even though it seems unsatisfactory to test the component parts. With other hypotheses it should be quite possible to test the component parts, provided that due caution is observed in formulating the subhypotheses. Thus, to return to the problem explored by Altus and Thompson [6], the "estimate" of level of intellectual capacity can be checked against the outside criterion of a good individual intelligence test; a correlation coefficient falling short of a one-to-one relationship would be satisfactory evidence of validity, since this estimate purports to indicate an optimum level of function rather than the average effective level of function. It would be interesting to make separate estimates of capacity and efficiency and check both against the outside measure. A careful exploration of this sort would not only serve as validation research for the Rorschach technique but also should throw new light upon the whole problem of what an intelligence test measures. At the same time, there is no reason why the separate bases of the intellectual estimate should not be checked against the outside criterion, with two major cautions: (1) the sub-hypotheses should be those actually used in the technique (for example, the relationship of the IQ to the number of W responses *of good quality* should be checked, not merely the number of W responses as such) and (2) the range of population used should be appropriate to the hypothesis (for example, in testing the relationship of the $A\%$ to the outside criterion the population should have a wide spread, since the original hypothesis was derived from the observation that the $A\%$ tended to be high with feeble-minded subjects; in this connection one would scarcely expect the $A\%$ to differentiate between various levels of above-average capacity).

Both validation research and normative research in the Rorschach technique have been handicapped by a fallacious notion of objectivity in research. On this account both types of research have usually dealt with the raw quantitative findings pertaining to scoring categories. Correlates have been found for $W\%$, for $F\%$, for M responses, and so on, despite the fact that *there are no unqualified interpretative hypotheses attached to these values as such.* It would be as easy, for example, to explore the correlates of the various kinds of whole constructions, taking form-level rating into account, as it would be to study $W\%$ as an over-all classification. $F\%$ could be explored, taking into account form-level rating, the various levels of the percentage purported to be critical, and even the various contexts in which $F\%$ occurs—that is, with and without differentiated shading responses, with and without other signs of control, and the like. When studying M responses, it would be quite possible to distinguish between M and M—, and between M responses associated with H, (H), (A), Hd, and (Hd) content. These various refinements and differentiations are just as "objective" as the W, F, and M classifications themselves. The reason why such differentiations are not usually made in normative and validation research is difficult to ascertain. One possible explanation may be that many studies try to cover everything even though crudely, rather than attempting to sort out thoroughly the hypotheses involved in any one area.

Statistical Difficulties

A major reason for emphasizing the feasibility of testing the interpretative hypotheses separately, with due caution in formulating the hypotheses to be tested, is the fact that current statistical methods do not lend themselves readily to the handling of patterns of interrelated variables. As Cronbach [29] says:

> A major gap between psychometric and clinical methodology at the present time is the insistence of the clinician that the full meaning of results on many tests can be understood only through study of interrelated patterns of scores. The conventional statistical methodology is unable to cope with patterns in a way approximating clinical pattern interpretation. The result is that research on many clinical problems and tests is incomplete or unsatisfactory. [29, page 149]

However, it is probably unduly pessimistic to assume that statistical methods cannot be adapted to meet the problem. Cronbach proceeds to offer a method of pattern analysis which can cope with two-score or three-score patterns—a method that offers some assistance in Rorschach validation research, although it by no means solves the whole problem.

Ferguson [38] believes that the difficulties of interrelated variables could be overcome by working with the interpretation rather than with "scores," treating the Rorschach examination and the Rorschach examiner as an inseparable combination and using configurational analysis, drawing upon statistical techniques already in existence. He suggests that the solution lies in multiple regression techniques, with adaptations for curvilinearity where necessary. To treat the test-examiner combination as one does not provide an insurmountable handicap in satisfactory research, for the reliability of the test-examiner instrument itself could be tested.

Other suggestions about the adaptation of statistical techniques to meet the problems of the Rorschach technique and other multivariable tests have been made by Eichler [36], Mensh [95], Rabin [113], Zubin [167], and by Cronbach in two further articles [30, 32]. The problem does not seem an insoluble one, although the solution is made more difficult by the fact that clinicians, on the whole, have a very rudimentary knowledge of statistics while psychological statisticians usually have an inadequate knowledge of the nuances of Rorschach interpretative hypotheses. A teamwork approach seems indicated to overcome these difficulties.

Validation of Hypotheses Related to Sequence and Content Analysis

There seems no reason why the testing of interpretative hypotheses should be limited to those that are attached to the separate scoring categories and quantitative proportions. Validation research has tended to ignore the hypotheses used in sequence analysis and content analysis. Neither of these two analyses should involve judgments too intuitive or mystic to be testable. A few studies have ventured into these areas—unfortunately only a few. McLeod [92] tested the hypothesis that the perception of the Rorschach blots becomes both more highly differentiated and a better match to the blots with increasing chronological and mental age, using matched groups of four-, five-, and six-year-olds. He distinguished fifteen different types of responses* which varied in degree of differentiation and match to the blot, including, among others, arbitrary responses, perseverative responses of various kinds, confabulatory responses, inaccurate outline responses, crude determinant responses, populars, and superior form-level responses. He found significant differences between the three age levels in the direction indicated by the hypothesis.

Elizur [37] devised a simple method for scoring the content of the Rorschach protocol for anxiety and hostility and found these scores to agree reasonably well with outside criteria derived from questionnaires, self-ratings, and interviews. Although his intention was to develop a score for these two aspects as an adjunct to the standard Rorschach technique, his study at the same time serves to test hypotheses commonly employed in content interpretation.

Pascal, Ruesch, Devine, and Suttell [107] asked 237 subjects to point out parts of the blots that could be male or female sexual organs, in a special "testing of the limits" procedure. Their findings provide a check for the areas hypothesized to have sexual significance in sequence and content analysis, whilst a study of the relationship of the responses given in the protocols to the content of the sex responses given in the special phase of limits testing provides a check on hypotheses relating to sexual symbolism.

Meer and Singer [94] in a suggestive although not crucial study asked 50 subjects in a special "testing of the limits" phase to select a card that could represent a "father card" and one to represent a "mother card." The subjects were asked for reasons for their selections and then were requested to rank the cards on the basis of likes and dislikes. It was found that Card IV, and to a lesser extent Card II, were selected as "father cards," while Cards VII and X were selected as "mother cards" significantly often. The authors point out that this finding does not answer the question whether the responses to these cards may be taken as expressing attitudes towards the

---

* See Klopfer and Kelley, *The Rorschach Technique*, pages 88–91.

parents in question, even for the subjects for whom these cards have an acknowledged significance.

Conclusion

In conclusion, it is suggested that the problems pertaining to the interrelatedness of interpretative hypotheses have been exaggerated beyond their real magnitude (which in itself is formidable enough) by superficial or overambitious attempts to explore a great many hypotheses in one and the same study, working with unqualified single scores rather than with refined interpretative hypotheses, and confining interest to "quantitative" scoring categories, to the neglect of modifications of interpretation stemming from sequence and content analysis. It would seem better to explore the ramifications of one hypothesis or one set of closely related (or contrasting) hypotheses at a time, in studies particularly designed to highlight the function under consideration. Attention should be given to exploration of the various suggestions that have been made for adapting statistical techniques to meet the needs of handling interrelated variables and to the development of new statistical avenues of approach. However, even with single-variable statistical techniques much can be done, provided that the work is based on refined interpretative hypotheses, on judgments or estimates made by the examiner, or even upon combination "scores" rather than on the simple, isolated scores that have formed the basis of so much rather sterile and controversial "validation research" up to the present time.

2. Problems Relating to Concepts and Their Communicability

Another problem, which is probably even more fundamental than that presented by the interrelatedness of the variables, is that of communication of the concepts basic to the interpretative hypotheses. MacFarlane [90] cautions that a *sine qua non* of validation research is an explicit statement of the concepts so that they can be subjected to a validation test. Her view stresses the point that the Rorschach concepts postulating inner processes underlying the overtly observable responses to the blot-material are scientific constructs, serving as tools; they should not be reified, by attributing to them a reality beyond the processes from which they are inferred. Rorschach examiners have found it difficult to state their underlying concepts explicitly, in terms intelligible to others. Perhaps no other single feature of the Rorschach technique has caused more misunderstanding, indeed exasperation; this is clearly illustrated in a diatribe by Thurstone [157] in which he points out that Rorschach workers are isolated because of their concepts and jargon. He urges the translation of these concepts into "currently known concepts" where this is possible.

A further difficulty is that even where the Rorschach concepts seem to be identical or closely related to concepts in everyday use or current psychological theory, the similarity may be only superficial; this is the case even with clinical and psychoanalytic concepts, which may seem very closely allied to those that are basic to many of the interpretative hypotheses in the Rorschach technique. The problem of "translation" of concepts is essentially the same one that faces the Rorschach examiner in trying to communicate his clinical findings to those who are not familiar with the Rorschach technique. He may learn to phrase his findings in language that is meaningful to the clinicians with whom he works, and they in turn may gain a fuller understanding of Rorschach concepts. However, a smooth and congenial working arrangement, and the clarification of communication that is brought about by focussing on the particularities of the individual case, may often cloak the fact that the Rorschach examiner and his colleagues are using a common language to talk about processes that are overlapping but far from identical. This basic gap in understanding may occasion no more than an incidental feeling of frustration in a smooth-running clinical situation; validation research serves to throw it into relief.

Basic Concepts and Research Planning

The most serious difficulty occurs when the psychologist planning the research has a faulty understanding of the Rorschach hypotheses. A considerable degree of expertness, based on special training and experience, is necessary before the research worker can assimilate the communicable basis of interpretation embodied in the Rorschach technique and thus test out the interpretative hypotheses in the form in which they are cast for use in clinical practice. Every attempt has been made in this present book to state the interpretative hypotheses as explicitly as possible so that they are in fully communicable form; yet it is anticipated that they will prove to be imperfectly stated for full communication to those who are not intimately acquainted with the way subjects perform in perceiving the Rorschach materials. To one steeped in Rorschach technique many concepts have an automatic operational definition. Thus, to refer back to previously cited examples, "an organized approach" is immediately reminiscent of the way in which a subject goes about integrating the separate parts of the blot to form a single complex concept, and "preoccupation with details" may immediately summon up the picture of a subject who focusses on small, clear, confined areas of the blot, being unable to "see the woods for the trees." The very translation of these operational definitions into language that is meaningful *in the same terms* to the non-expert is itself to be hoped for as a by-product of validation research.

The degree of expertness with the Rorschach technique that is necessary for planning research to test out the interpretative hypotheses in any crucial or even relevant way is unfortunately not common among those who have a good working knowledge of experimental and statistical techniques. This is a handicap to validation research which is certainly no less serious than the fact that those who are expert in the Rorschach technique tend to be weak in statistics and experimental design. Not only do statistical experts such as Cronbach [30] shudder at the inadequate statistical techniques that are characteristic of Rorschach research (and indeed were more characteristic before Cronbach published his helpful criticism), but Rorschach experts are equally dismayed by the large number of investigations that seem quite lacking in pertinence to the interpretative hypotheses they purport to test because the hypothesis has been imperfectly understood by the investigator.

At the risk of unfairness in singling out any particular example of this very common fault, one might point to an investigation by Holtzman [67] which tested certain Rorschach hypotheses against pooled ratings of shyness and gregariousness. Four hypotheses relating to introversive-extratensive balance were tested on the assumption that extratension would express itself behaviorally in gregariousness. Since there seems nothing implicit in the concept of experience-balance that justifies this interpretation, the fact that his findings were essentially negative seems quite irrelevant to these hypotheses. Further, he derived an hypothesis that shyness would be related to the ratio of achromatic to chromatic responses— $(Fc+c+C')$: $(FC+CF+C)$ * —from the following statement: ". . . the point of real 'contact shyness' or overcautiousness in emotional contacts is reached if the total number of achromatic responses is at least twice the total number of bright color responses" [80, page 230]. It must be confessed that this statement, taken out of context, seems to justify Holtzman in his formulation of the hypothesis; however, the hypothesis was not intended to deal with the behavioral expression of shyness, but rather with the internal reluctance of the subject to become emotionally involved on a dependency or interdependency basis with other people. Holtzman concludes from his study that the "results strongly indicate the need for considerable caution in evaluating shyness or gregariousness by the Rorschach test." The conclusion is unexceptionable; the implication that basic Rorschach hypotheses were tested by the study is, however, quite erroneous.

Basic Concepts and Evaluation of Research Findings

Even when the research is not steered in an unproductive direction by a misunderstanding of the interpretative hypotheses it is designed to test, the discussion of the results often gives the clinician the impression that straw men are set up merely to be knocked

---

* See pages 292–293 and 362 for the interpretative hypotheses attached to $(FC+c+C')$: $(FC+CF+C)$.

down. The research author states an oversimplified or incomplete interpretative hypothesis, tests it out, finds it oversimplified or incomplete, and proceeds to restate it in much the same terms as had been used all along in clinical work. Thus the research, instead of indicating the invalidity of the hypotheses in question, in fact is a testimonial to their validity.

In their discussion of the results of an extensive investigation comparing a number of different clinical groupings including "normals," Buhler, Buhler, and Lefever [20] seem particularly prone to stating their conclusions in this misleading way. For example, they test the hypothesis that the size of $F\%$ is an indication of the strength of super-ego function.* If this hypothesis is true, it is argued, clinical groups believed to be characterized by strong super-ego development, such as obsessive-compulsives and hysterics, ought to show high $F\%$, and those such as psychopaths who have inadequate super-ego function should show low $F\%$. Although obsessive-compulsives as a group did indeed support this version of the $F\%$ hypothesis, hysterics were found to have low $F\%$ and, perhaps more serious, psychopaths were found to have high $F\%$. On the face of it, this seems to imply that the interpretative hypothesis attached to $F\%$ was invalid. The authors go on to discuss the importance of taking form level into account, and finish by reformulating the hypothesis, relating $F\%$ to the awareness and assimilation of reality. It is not clear where Buhler, Buhler, and Lefever found their original hypothesis, for they state merely that "some authors have considered that the Ego and Super-ego trends are represented by the Rorschach signs M and $F\%$." It is manifestly untrue that any such hypotheses were used widely by experienced clinical psychologists without consideration of the form level of the responses, and without a realization that high $F\%$ was common not only with psychopaths but also with young children, organics, and other subjects with inadequate control over impulse, and that low $F\%$ was frequently found with hysterics. Moreover, the reformulation of the hypothesis is highly reminiscent of Rorschach's original formulation [123, page 23]. There is no question that Buhler, Buhler, and Lefever have rendered useful service

---

* See pages 294–295 and 364–366 for the interpretative hypotheses proposed for $F\%$.

in checking interpretative hypotheses by the method of group comparisons in a more comprehensive and systematic way than was done in antecedent studies; their findings provide confirmative evidence for a large number of interpretative hypotheses and diagnostic suggestions. However, most of the hypotheses "exploded" by the study were either serious oversimplifications, or hypotheses misrepresented by having been taken out of the context of their various limitations and qualifications.

Basic Concepts and Outside Criteria

Quite aside from difficulties that the misunderstanding of Rorschach concepts may occasion in the planning of validation research and the discussion of the findings thereof, problems arise whenever the outside criterion involves an appraisal of the characteristic in question on other-than-Rorschach grounds. Thus, Holtzman, in the study quoted above, would have found it extremely difficult to explain clearly to students living in residence the exact basis upon which they should rate each other for introversion, extratension, and "contact shyness" in order to make their ratings pertinent to the Rorschach hypotheses. The difficulty is reported in a non-hypothetical case by Palmer [106] to whose study reference was made earlier. He discovered that although Rorschach examiners had a fair degree of reliability among themselves in filling out a check-list of interpretations on the basis of individual Rorschach protocols, and therapists had a similar degree of reliability in filling out the check-list on the basis of a case report, the Rorschach examiners and the therapists showed negligible agreement.

> Each set of judges used their particular clues and concepts consistently and reliably when considering their respective data. The two sets of judges did not agree significantly on the concepts which were not central to their separate considerations, especially when these concepts were isolated from the context of the whole structural pattern—as was required on the check list. [106, pages 22–23]

It must be remembered that this result was obtained despite the fact that a significant degree of agreement had been found between Rorschach examiners and therapists by the matching technique.

Of interest in this connection is a study by Grayson and Tolman [52] on the semantic difficulties in communication between clinical psychologists and psychiatrists. They investigated this problem by asking psychologists and psychiatrists to define words in common use in pychological reports, such as "abstract," "aggressive," "bizarre," "compulsive," "control." They conclude:

> The range of individual differences is great for both groups, though greater for psychiatrists than psychologists. . . . In spite of a fairly high modal value in both groups for most of the words, only rarely do as many as 75% of the responses fall into a single category. Thus, although a central core of meaning tends to prevail, wide variations occur. . . . The most striking finding of the study is the looseness and ambiguity of the definitions of many of these terms. . . . The semantic confusion is a product of the vagueness of our present grasp of deep psychological meanings, a vagueness shared alike by psychiatrists, psychologists and authoritative sources. . . . The lack of precision seems to stem from theoretical confusion in the face of the complexity and logical inconsistency of psychological phenomena. Verbal discrepancies can only be reconciled by a deeper understanding of these underlying phenomena which will require many years of careful, penetrating and analytical psychological experience. [52, pages 228–229]

It does not seem too much to hope that validation research on the Rorschach technique could make a contribution of some magnitude to obtaining this "deeper understanding of underlying phenomena" at the same time that it serves to refine and make more explicit the various interpretative hypotheses.

In the meantime, a helpful line of approach would seem to lie in cross-comparisons with other projective techniques, an approach suggested by Thurstone [157]. Common perceptual determinants would seem to influence the subject's handling of different projective materials, and yet manifest themselves in different ways because of the differences in the materials. Such cross-comparisons have to date been limited almost entirely to case studies. For example, Ainsworth and Boston [3] quote comparative Rorschach and Children's Apperception Test protocols of a child whose relationships with his mother are known to have been deeply disturbed by prolonged separation in early childhood. To cite one example of the cross-comparisons that emerge from this study, an underlying process of "constriction" is inferred from a high percentage of *F* responses with poor form level on the Rorschach and from CAT stories that are essentially enumerative-descriptive, with interpretation occurring only with prodding and then reflecting a seriously limited ability to attribute to the characters needs or feelings on the basis of which action is determined. An hypothesis that these two types of performance are functionally linked should be checked by systematic comparisons with an adequate sample. The expected linkage would not so much "validate" the interpretative hypotheses in question as make more explicit in operational terms what is implied by the concept of "constriction." (A second hypothesis would, of course, be required to deal with the "constriction" to be inferred from a high percentage of *F* responses with high form level, which would be expected to be linked with TAT stories dealing either with conformity or punishment themes. For a discussion of these two kinds of constriction, see pages 294–296, 364–365.)

Conclusion

In summary, the problems relating to concepts and their communicability make it necessary to caution that validation research should be planned and the results discussed by those who have more than a superficial understanding of the basic concepts involved in Rorschach interpretative hypotheses, and that great care should be taken, in selecting an outside criterion against which to test an hypothesis, to be sure that one is chosen and formulated so as to provide a relevant basis for the test. It is expected that concepts will become clarified and more easily communicable through examination of the "correlates" brought to light through validation research; in the meantime, there is a strong case for comparative studies with other techniques designed to make more explicit their common underlying concepts.

3. Problems Relating to Short-Cut Methods

The Rorschach technique is designed for individual administration. Although large-scale adaptations of the Rorschach technique have been devised, the interpretative hypotheses that form the backbone of the technique have been formulated on the basis of the materials as perceived by subjects in the context of an individual test-situation. The application of these interpretative hypotheses to derive a description and appraisal of the individual subject involves an intensive and very time-consuming investigation. Odom [104] reports that the time required to carry through an average test, including administration and all steps of analysis and reporting, is a little less than four hours (sometimes less than two hours or more than eight hours may be required, depending upon the complexity of the response pattern of the individual). Although, presumably, beginners may take longer than this, he quotes experts as considering this a conservative estimate even when applied to themselves. With this time-involvement for a single subject it is easy to understand why so many investigations have been based on a number of subjects falling somewhat short of the ideal for proper sampling and statistical measures of significance.

Some research workers attempt to overcome the limitations imposed by the time-consuming nature of individual administration by using group methods of administration and abbreviated, hence necessarily mechanical, methods of analysis and interpretation. The most frequently used group methods are the Group Rorschach Test and the Multiple-Choice Rorschach Test developed by Harrower and Steiner [56]. The most popular short-cut method of analysis is the inspection technique developed by Munroe [101], which may be used either with individual or group administration [102]. Harrower and Munroe both contribute discussions of their techniques to the book on projective techniques edited by Abt and Bellak [1]. These shortcut methods offer promise of usefulness as screening devices in situations where it would be impractical to use individual methods of administration and interpretation. However, the interpretative hypotheses formulated on the basis of individual administration cannot be assumed to be applicable automatically to group methods. These seem best treated as separate techniques to be validated more or less independently of the parent technique. This is recognized by Singer [148] who entitles his monograph "The Validity of a Multiple-Choice Projective Test in Psychopathological Screening," although in fact it uses the Rorschach ink blots in a group method presented as an alternative to the Harrower Multiple-Choice Rorschach.

Group methods rely for interpretation upon statistically established differentiations between groups, such as those reported by Ross [127, 128, 131]. A multiple-choice screening test based on the Rorschach material is essentially a psychometric test in that it requires standardization based on item validation using criterion groups; the only legitimate use of Rorschach hypotheses is to guide in the original choice of items. Other group methods are less obviously new tests. Nevertheless, it seems dangerous for three reasons to draw freely upon the usual interpretative hypotheses to interpret the results. First, it is not self-evident that the group test situation offers the same background for the perception of the blots and reporting thereon as that offered by the individual method. Secondly, a short-cut method of administration has given quite a different basis for scoring the protocol than that provided by the individually administered inquiry. Finally, and insofar as short-cut methods of analysis are also used, it can be misleading to base the appraisal entirely upon the interpretative hypotheses attached to the various quantitative frequencies, percentages, and proportions without modification in the light of sequence and content analysis. Moreover, as pointed out earlier, there are no interpretative hypotheses attached to the various scoring classifications *as such*.

Although it may well be that short-cut methods of administration and analysis are well-justified for practical screening purposes where it is out of the question to employ full clinical-type procedures, it is confusing when they are used in normative or validation research into the Rorschach technique. It is usually forgotten that the norms or the evidence of validity or invalidity found are applicable to the short-cut method rather than to the Rorschach technique as such, even though the author may have been careful to point this out.

Short-Cut Methods in Research into "Color Shock"

In no area of crucial validation research has the confusion occasioned by short-cut methods been better exemplified than in researches designed to ascertain the role of color.* Lazarus [85] investigated the phenomenon of "color shock" in a well-designed test-retest experiment in which subjects were asked to respond both to the standard series of cards and to a special achromatic series. Group administration was used and quantitative findings quoted for each scoring category and for each "sign" of color shock. He found few differences between the two series. The $F\%$ was higher with the achromatic series and there were fewer total responses for the color series, although the differences were significant only for the achromatic cards. He selected the 30 per cent of the group manifesting the greatest number of "signs" of color shock and dealt with them separately. Again there were more responses and higher $F\%$ with the achromatic series; he found also that there was a significant increase in P with the achromatic series, but only for those blots that are also achromatic in the standard series. He found a poorer form level on the chromatic blots, due largely to responses making direct use of color—that is, $FC-$ and $CF-$. He concludes that color does not significantly affect either the scoring categories or the chief indices of "color shock." He suggests that the effects attributed to color shock are partly a result of difficulty of integration of form and color (the only function of color in the test) and partly due to the fact that the blots differ in "difficulty." Sappenfield and Buker [137] in a similar study found that the distributions of percentages of responses to the all-colored cards (VIII, IX, and X) did not differ significantly from the distributions obtained from these cards in an achromatic series.

The immediate response of many clinical psychologists to these two

---

* For a discussion of the interpretative hypotheses attached to the use of color, see pages 275–287.

studies was critical both because group methods had been used and because the samples were confined to normal subjects who would not be expected to manifest color disturbance to the same extent as a more maladjusted sample. However, these results were confirmed by other studies using individual administration. Allen, Manne, and Stiff [5] in a study with 25 normal students investigated 13 signs of color shock but found no major differences between a standard and an achromatic series. Nor did they find signs of color shock to be at all common in their sample. Allen [4] investigated reaction time as an isolated sign with the same population and found no significant differences attributable to color. Meyer [97] reported that there were no differences between two groups of 71 and 78 normal subjects, one of which was given the standard series and the other an achromatic series, but found that 83 per cent of his population showed "neurotic color shock" according to the usual "signs." Dubrovner, Von Lackum, and Jost [33] found no differences in productivity or reaction time between the standard and achromatic series given to 30 nurses. Perlman [109] found no differences with respect to the (VIII, IX, X) %, but suggested that the D characteristics of these cards may still make the interpretation hold that this percentage is related to responsiveness to the environment. Buker and Williams [21] in a study with 21 schizophrenics found that reaction time was the only significant difference between the chromatic and achromatic series, decreasing with the latter. Rabin and Sanderson [115] compared the effect of the standard order of presentation of the cards with that of a reverse order. They found that the standard order produced richer records characterized by more accurate responses. However, they found that some cards were consistently more difficult, as indicated by long reaction time, while others consistently produced a greater number of responses regardless of the order of presentation. These difficult cards—rather than the unexpected impact of color—seemed to account for sudden increases in reaction time or lowering of productivity.

Some of these authors suggested that these findings invalidated the whole concept of "color shock," while others discussed various possibilities which might account for the fact that color indices are found to be clinically useful although color does not seem to be the operative factor. This series of studies left the impression with many who were unfamiliar with the Rorschach technique (and perhaps with some Rorschach examiners as well) that the Rorschach color hypotheses had been proven invalid in these seemingly definitive studies.

A helpful by-product of these studies was the important emphasis on the fact that the various cards in the standard series differ in "difficulty," a fact that should be taken into account in sequence analysis. This emphasis culminated in the normative study reported by Sanderson [135] who established reaction time norms for each of the ten cards and suggested that disturbance should not be inferred on the basis of reaction time unless the reaction time of an individual falls outside the range of $\pm 2\sigma$ for that card.

There is still the important objection that the findings of these studies had little bearing upon interpretations based on an examination of color dynamics in a careful sequence analysis. Whether group or individual administrations were employed in these studies, all used short-cut methods of analysis limited to separate scoring categories or indices. They are pertinent, therefore, to the validity of hypotheses relating to short-cut methods of administration and/or analysis; they are only indirectly relevant to the validity of the hypotheses used in a careful clinical-type analysis. A further disadvantage of the short-cut methods used in these studies is that they provide little basis for refining the hypotheses relating to "color shock" or the effect of color generally, though some suggestions are offered as possibilities. Although validation evidence is valuable as such, it is less valuable than evidence pointing out in what ways the hypothesis in question is valid or invalid. There have been several further studies designed in such a way that this kind of question can be answered better. Three of them used short-cut methods, but the methods were specially designed for the exploration of the color area rather than being adopted merely as time-savers or to facilitate the use of statistics.

Siipola [147] used cut-outs of twenty areas of Rorschach blots presented both in their original chromatic form and in achromatic reproductions. Her analysis covered chiefly reaction-time, responses to the question "How did you like this blot?", and the content of the responses given. She concluded that the effect of color seems to depend upon whether the color of the blot is appropriate or inappropriate for the concept suggested by the shape of the blot. When the color was appropriate to the usual concept (s) suggested by the blot, it seemed to have a mildly reinforcing effect in that it made common concepts more common in the chromatic than in the achromatic versions. In about 20 per cent of the responses, however, the colored blots seemed to have a disruptive influence, with symptoms suggestive of conceptual conflict and behavioral disorganization. These seemed to occur when the color was inappropriate for the concept (s) suggested by the shape of the blot. In all but two of the blots she found the presence of color to increase reaction time. Finally, she found that color tended to increase the affect, sometimes in a positive and sometimes in a negative direction, and that the achromatic reproductions tended to be more neutral and less affect-laden.

Wallen [162] deals with Rorschach's original hypothesis that color shock is "associative stupor" resulting from the impact of color. He abandoned the standard procedure, administering the Rorschach cards individually with the simple question: "Do you like this card?" He experimented with various groups using reversed vs. standard order, upright vs. inverted presentation, and an achromatic series compared with the standard series. With normal (stable) subjects he found that inverting the cards had no appreciable effect, that subjects tended to like the cards towards the end of the series rather than those at the beginning both in the standard and reversed order of presentation, and that Cards VIII, IX, and X were more frequently liked in their colored version and Cards II and III were more frequently liked when achromatic, despite the fact that there were no differences in percentages of cards liked between the achromatic and chromatic series.

He tested out the effects of the chromatic vs. achromatic series with two groups of unstable subjects. He found that the unstable subjects liked the chromatic cards less frequently than did the normal subjects, especially in the case of Cards II and IX. In the achromatic series it was Cards VI and IV among the achromatic cards and Cards III, IX, and X of the normally chromatic cards that were less popular than with normals. It would appear that there are several factors possibly involved in the differences in "likes" between the stable and unstable groups: (1) the color, especially in Card II, (2) the shading in Cards VI and IV, and (3) the contour and organization in Cards III, X, and especially IX.

The effect of color in determining the dislikes was tested out with another group of unstable subjects by giving pairs of achromatic and chromatic plates and inquiring whether there was a preference, This group showed a relative dislike for the colored versions of II, III, and IX, especially II and IX, while there was no difference with respect to VIII and X. The reason most frequently given for disliking the colored cards was that the red looked like "blood." Wallen concludes that color may produce unpleasant affect, through associations, which tends to break through controlling mechanisms in the case of unstable subjects. He suggests further that it is not color as such that tends to produce this unpleasant affect, but color in the special shapes in which it is presented in the blots; this would also be the case with shading or gray color. Finally, there seems to be a special role played by the shape and organization of the blot, Card V being preferred because it is more easily seen as something and Card IX being disliked frequently because it is difficult.

Rockwell, Welch, Kubis, and Fisichelli [120] pointed out that the various definitions of color shock in the literature differed greatly in their implications. They contrasted particularly the definition given by Beck [9], who describes color shock as a startle response, and that originally given by Rorschach [123]. Rorschach describes it as emotional and associative stupor occurring on the all-colored plates, particularly Card VIII, shown by a long pause without associations, and considers it a pathognomonic sign of psychoneurosis indicating a neurotic suppression of affect. In order to settle between these definitions Rockwell et al. measured the changes in palmar skin resistance of subjects responding to the Rorschach cards. They reasoned that if color shock was essentially "startle" it would manifest itself by a marked change of galvanic resistance within the first five seconds of presentation of a color card, this change presumably being greatest in the case of Card VIII. But if color shock was "emotional and associative stupor" (they reasoned) it should be analogous to neurophysiological shock and should manifest itself by inhibition of the action of the sympathetic nervous system, which would be reflected by a small change of galvanic skin resistance on the color cards, particularly on Card VIII.

Three groups of 10 subjects each were used, the first consisting of students who were free from color shock in terms of Rorschach's criteria, the second consisting of students who manifested marked color shock, and the third group being composed of psychoneurotic patients all of whom manifested color shock. The cards were presented individually, projected on a screen. Each card was shown for 90 seconds only, so that there would be a comparable time period within which to measure the changes in palmar skin resistance from one card to the next. A standard inquiry followed the performance proper, during which galvanometric measurements were discontinued. The "startle" hypothesis was ruled out because no group showed a sudden, marked lowering of skin resistance, analogous to a startle response, for any card. The findings supported Rorschach's definition of color shock as emotional and associative stupor, in that there were smaller deflections indicating lowered skin resistance on Card VIII than for any other card for the group of students who showed color shock. The non-color-shock group showed galvanic changes, for both Cards VIII and IX, which were about the mean for all cards. In terms of inhibition of associations, the hypothesis was also supported by the fact that the non-color-shock group gave more verbal responses than either of the other two groups, especially to the color cards. The non-color-shock group showed less change in palmar skin resistance for all cards except Card VIII than did the color-shock group of students, although not as little as the psychoneurotics, who also gave the fewest verbal responses. The authors interpret these findings to suggest that the psychoneurotic patients manifest a "holding back," a generalized inhibition of emotional responsiveness in the test, due to a more complete mobilization of defense mechanisms than either of the other two groups. The color-shock group of students they consider potentially psychoneurotic, with greater emotional instability and no sweeping inhibitory defenses. It is this group that showed a marked inhibition of automatic responsiveness to Card VIII and hence color shock, whilst the color-shock reaction of the psychoneurotic patients tended to be masked by their generalized inhibition.

With the above findings as a background, Rockwell, Welch, Kubis, and Fisichelli [121] proceeded to examine the effect on both verbal responses and galvanic skin responses of retesting with an achromatic series of slides. In this study two student groups were used, one manifesting color shock according to Rorschach's criteria and one free from color shock. Both groups increased their verbal responses in the retest with the achromatic series; when color was absent the two groups could not be differentiated in terms of their verbal responses, whereas previously the non-color-shock group had given more verbal responses, especially to the color cards, than had the color-shock group. In the retest the non-color-shock group showed a greater increase in verbal responses to the cards that are normally achromatic, a finding confirmed by Lazarus [85]. These authors interpreted this finding as a demonstration that the change from the familiar color to the unfamiliar achromatic card was itself inhibiting, an explanation that does not seem adequate since Lazarus got similar results when he controlled the order of presentation by giving the achromatic series first with half of his subjects. The non-color-shock group showed higher autonomic responsiveness on the retest than to the standard colored series, whilst the color-shock group whose autonomic responsiveness had already been high with the colored series did not increase further. The authors conclude that the non-color-shock group had a general inhibition of responsiveness as a defense mechanism on the first test (although to a lesser extent than the psychoneurotic group), which lessened on retesting, and that the color-shock group differed in that they could not mobilize their defenses so well.

A final study may be quoted as having a bearing on the color-shock controversy, although it is not especially pertinent to the question of short-cut methods. Sarason and Potter [139] compared the reactions to color in the Rorschach with performance on the Kohs Block Designs, which, of course, involve color. The subjects were 31 problem children, divided into three groups. Group A had a mental age equivalent, on the Kohs test, 18 months or so above their mental age as measured by the Stanford-Binet test. Group C were 18 months or more lower in mental age on the Kohs test than on the Binet. Group B included the remainder, whose Kohs performances were within 18 months plus or minus of their Binet mental ages. That the differences between A and C were not due to a depressed Binet mental age for Group A is suggested by the fact that Group A were found to be more intelligent than Group C.

Group A was found to give few color responses on the Rorschach, and only one minus response to the color cards as well as one minus response to the shading cards. The form level was remarkably stable with both color and shading cards. The lack of color disturbance on the Rorschach was manifested also in the Kohs test by the fact that 5 of the 7 subjects passed at least the 17th design. Group C was found to give more color responses of all kinds than either of the other two groups, and was the only group to give C_n, C_{des}, or FC— responses. Queer combinatory wholes occurred with 6 subjects (as compared with one subject of Group A) and these were confined to the color cards. Moreover, 13 of the 14 subjects had lower form level for the color cards than for the shading cards. This group's performance on the Kohs test was very poor, 9 of the 14 subjects being unable to get beyond the 3rd design. Group B was similar to Group A in that few color responses were given and few queer combinatory wholes. However, 5 of the group of 10 gave minus responses to color cards while 5 gave minus responses to shading cards, with similar division with respect to general drops of form level on color vs. shading cards. Sarason and Potter conclude that emotional reactions interfering with intellectual functioning are associated with color in both the Rorschach and Kohs Block Designs, although it is not clear whether this is a direct effect of color or whether it is due to difficulty in obtaining a visual grasp of figure-ground relationships when color is introduced.

The studies by Siipola, Wallen, Sarason and Potter, and Rockwell et al. yield evidence that color has a differential effect upon the perceptual processes of different groups of subjects, interfering with the efficiency of perception of some and having no disturbing effect on others. These results seem to be contradicted by the studies using "short-cut" methods—those by Lazarus, Meyer, Buker and Williams, Allen, Manne and Stiff, and others, who contrast the scores and indices obtained with a standard series of blots with those obtained from an achromatic series. There seem to be a number of factors contributing to the apparent contradictions between the two sets of studies.

1. It would seem that different hypotheses about color shock or color disturbance have different implications, as shown by Rockwell et al. It may well be that there are different kinds of "color disturbance" of which Rorschach's classical "color shock" is one. Allen et al., Meyer, and Buker and Williams did not set out to test any particular formulation of the "color shock" hypothesis or to focus upon any particular kind of color disturbance; on the contrary they culled from the literature all sorts of different criteria and tested them out either separately (when in actual practice the whole configuration of the record would have been considered) or lumped them together as Meyer did without regard for the fact that they may have tended to cancel each other out. This may in part explain why Allen et al. find little evidence of "color shock" with normal subjects while Meyer found it to occur with 83 per cent of his normal population.

2. The "short-cut" method studies were not well-designed to throw light upon those very "signs" that emerged as most significant in the studies that focussed on processes, such as affect, content, reaction time, and form level. In fact, reaction time was found by Buker and Williams to be longer with the chromatic than with the achromatic series, while the group method of presentation used by Lazarus made it impossible for him to measure reaction time.

3. The "short-cut" studies did not examine the very group of subjects who are hypothesized to be most prone to color shock, namely neurotics, but focussed rather upon "normals." Buker and

Williams swung over to schizophrenics. On the other hand, Rockwell et al., Wallen, and indirectly Sarason and Potter, make it clear that some classes of subjects are very differently affected by color than others, with "unstable normals" or neurotic subjects responding differently from stable normals. Only one of the "short-cut" studies even made a distinction between color-shock and non-color-shock groups in their relative performances with the achromatic and standard series; Lazarus did, in fact, find a significant difference in that the color-shock group dropped in form level on the color cards in the standard series, whereas the non-color-shock group did not.

4. From the "short-cut" studies the major conclusion emerges that cards differ in the degree of perceptual difficulty and that this is responsible for the "shock" that has been attributed to color. However, these studies were in no way designed to highlight color disturbance and to distinguish it from disturbance due to other factors such as shading, associations, or difficulty. To discover that other factors contribute to disturbance should not invalidate the hypothesis that color may be a disturbing factor. It seems highly likely that the various sources of disturbance tended to cancel each other out in the "short-cut" studies, with "card difficulty" emerging as the most important common factor—at least with the normal populations on which most of these studies were based. This difficulty would also occur if "signs" of color shock were used on a mechanical basis for diagnosis or for statistical differentiations between groups. It seems certain that there are different sources of disturbance (color, shading, "associations," perceptual difficulty, and the like) which may manifest themselves in similar ways (by increased reaction time, decrease in number of responses, drops in form level, and so on). It also seems highly probable that any one source of disturbance (such as color) may manifest itself in different ways on different cards with different subjects. In the clinical use of the Rorschach technique it would therefore seem highly important to make a careful examination of the sequence and content of the responses as well as the scoring categories and test behavior in order to ascertain what kinds of influences seem to disturb the particular subject

in question and how the disturbance is expressed, defended against, and recovered from. In validation research it seems very unproductive to test "signs" or hypotheses through studies that cannot sort out the variables concerned, that cannot elucidate the processes involved, and that provide no basis for refining hypotheses or substituting new hypotheses for those that seem invalid.

With respect to "color shock" the following findings seem quite clear, especially through the studies that threw light upon the processes involved in perceiving colored blots. Color does not disturb the perception of all subjects. It seems more likely to disturb the perception of "unstable normals" and psychoneurotics than that of either "stable normals" or psychotics. Some "normal" subjects seem to have their perception facilitated by color where form and color are easily integrated (Siipola) . One way in which color can disturb perceptual efficiency is by making it difficult to perceive clear forms when color is present (Sarason and Potter) , or by making it difficult to integrate the concept suggested by the color of the blot with that suggested by the shape (Siipola) . It also seems clear that the presence of color may lengthen reaction time (Siipola, Buker, and Williams) . It seems likely that subjects who are disturbed by color will give fewer responses than those who are not, although a general inhibition factor may enter in to obscure differentiations (Rockwell et al.) . Siipola provides some evidence that the colored blots are more affect-laden than their achromatic versions, but Wallen's findings make it clear that other factors (on Cards IV and VI) may produce strong negative affect as well. One of the ways in which color may be disturbing emotionally is through the concepts it suggests (Siipola, Wallen) . Finally, there is evidence to support the hypothesis that color suddenly appearing after a number of achromatic cards may, with some subjects, lead to inhibition of autonomic responsiveness (Rockwell et al.) . All of these findings, together with the heavy weight of impression from the clinical use of the Rorschach technique, lead to an acceptance of the position that color *can* make a difference in perception, despite the studies of standard vs. achromatic series of blots, which seem to demonstrate that it does not do so, but which do not provide an opportunity to examine the perceptual processes involved. What is not yet clear is whether all the above indications of disturbance and the various processes associated with color disturbance occur at one and the same time, or whether there are different kinds of color disturbance, perhaps one being Rorschach's classic "color shock," perhaps another being the arousal of unpleasant associations, perhaps another being disturbance in the perception of clear form. The hypothesis has been presented (pages 341–344) that there are at least two classes of color disturbance that may occur together but often occur separately: namely, *subjective* disturbance characterized by unpleasant affect and manifested by exclamations, behavior or content reflecting unpleasantness; and *objective* disturbance, which may or may not be associated with unpleasant affect and which is manifested chiefly by disturbances in form level. It is certain that further light on the question is more likely to be thrown by studies that highlight the perceptual processes of the individual than by studies that deal mechanically with scoring categories and indices.

Conclusion

In conclusion, it is suggested that a differentiation be made between short-cut methods, which obscure the processes involved, and other departures from standard clinical procedure which highlight these processes for the purposes of intensive exploration. Only the former seem unsuitable for validation research, except insofar as they are used to test out the validity of group techniques and quantitative "signs" that have been proposed as differentiating between groups.

4. Problems Relating to Reliability

In the context of psychometric tests it is commonly stated that although a test may be reliable without being valid, it cannot be valid without being reliable. It would seem, therefore, that an evaluation of the evidence of the reliability of the Rorschach technique should have preceded any discussion of the problems of validation. In fact, attempts to assess the reliability of the Rorschach technique have themselves brought to light many problems, some of which are shared by psychometric tests but which are highlighted when viewed with reference to projective techniques.

Methods of Testing Reliability

Early studies of the reliability of the Rorschach technique attempted to use all three of the classic tests of reliability: split-half method, alternative forms, and test-retest. Because of the small number of "items" represented by the ten blots and because of the fact that the standard series of blots was originally selected because the blots differed markedly in "stimulus quality," it would seem reasonable to reject the split-half method as unsuitable. The mere fact that an odd versus even splitting of items would leave one half with two chromatic blots and the other with three would seem to rule out the possibility of using this method. Nevertheless, it has been tried, with varying results.

Vernon [158] reported a correlation of .91 for the number of responses for the two halves, but found that other scoring categories and relationships fell short of reliability. He suggested, and Cronbach [30] later agreed, that the number of responses in the record should be controlled when testing for reliability since variations in this number tended to distort the results; reliability was higher, he reported, for records containing more than 30 responses. Hertz [58] found an average coefficient for all scoring categories of .829 using the split-half method, and concluded that the various scoring categories and relationships were reliable on the whole—enough so to make the Rorschach test a reliable instrument.

Thornton and Guilford [156] investigated the reliability of "Erlebnistypus" scores by the split-half method. The Rorschach was administered to two groups of students under different conditions. With one group the instructions were given printed on a card with no discussion and no subsequent inquiry. For this group the reliability coefficients were high, that for M being .919 and that for sum C being .938. The second group was given fuller instructions by word of mouth and were permitted to ask questions; an inquiry was included; time limits were imposed in the performance proper.

Under these conditions the reliability coefficients were unsatisfactory, being .768 for M and .655 for Sum C. Unfortunately, the design of the experiment did not permit of judgment regarding which difference in conditions seemed responsible for the different reliabilities. However, for the total group it was found that the ratio M : Sum C would place the subject in the same "Erlebnistypus" group (that is, coartative, ambiequal, dilated, extratensive or introversive) in 55 per cent of the cases—a per cent that seemed well above chance expectations.

The trend of opinion is currently away from the split-half method, with Hertz herself saying: "Because of the global nature of the test, it is not possible to split it and work with isolated variables." [63, page 316]

A proposed alternative form of the Rorschach materials was devised by Behn [10] with a manual prepared by Zulliger [168]; Harrower and Steiner [57] have proposed a second. Swift [152], working with pre-school children, retested with the Behn series after an interval of seven days. She found high reliability coefficients for most of the scoring categories and quantitative relationships, although a few were quite low: namely, $W\%$, (VIII, IX, X) %, and especially FC. The marked difference in these features led her to caution against using the Behn series as an entirely satisfactory alternative form. Eichler [35] also found the reliability coefficients for retest with the Behn series to compare favorably with those obtained for retest with the standard series, but further analysis showed that the Behn series facilitates the production of more FM responses and has a slight tendency to produce more shading responses and animal responses and fewer F, M, and H responses. Buckle and Holt [19] came to much the same conclusion. They found a high similarity of pattern between Rorschach and Behn scores as established by analysis of variance and chi squares, but when the ten pairs of blots were compared large specific differences were found.

Again thinking along traditional lines, it was long considered that retesting was not a satisfactory method of testing for reliability because of a possible memory factor. There have been at least two ingenious attempts to rule out this factor. Kelley, Margulies, and

Barrera [74] used 12 electric convulsive therapy cases who had complete amnesia for a testing immediately prior to shock yet were free from confusion resulting from shock when tested two hours later. The psychogram seemed unchanged and the diagnostic impression the same. The only shifts of more than one response were found in the following: *R, D, F%,* (VIII, IX, X) % and *P.* The authors caution that these factors seem less stable than others, hence small shifts should not be interpreted as significant. Griffith [53] found four patients with Korsakoff's syndrome who seemed to have complete lack of recall for testing within 24 hours. The test-retest protocols were found to be very similar, the reaction times relatively the same, and original, autistic content stable.

That responses are remembered from previous testing was demonstrated by Swift [152], who found that an average of 47 per cent of the responses were remembered by pre-school children after 30 days. An even higher percentage could be expected to be recalled by adult subjects. Her reliability coefficients ranged from .15 for (VIII, IX, X) % to .83 for *A%,* whereas the range for a retest after only 14 days was from .52 for (VIII, IX, X) % to .74 for *W%.* When corrected for attenuation the range of coefficients was raised, ranging from .59 to .83. However, the fact that Eichler [35] found the retest coefficients with the Behn series to be as high as when the retest involved the standard series suggests that the memory factor does not increase reliability and hence does not lead to a spurious reliability. Eichler's test-retest coefficients for the standard series range from .45 for *A%* to .82 for *W* and *M.*

The criterion of split-halves has been preferred in the case of psychometric tests because it assumes neither a stable function nor identical testing conditions. If alternative forms are administered at the same session the same conditions would be met. The retest criterion is complicated by possible differences in testing conditions. An experimenter employing this criterion can only avoid assuming a stable function by using a very brief interval between tests, which, of course, would emphasize the memory factor. The fact that, despite the memory factor, the reliability coefficients of the various scoring categories are not ideally high—some, indeed, being very low—makes it desirable to look behind the coefficients themselves to find out what factors are responsible for changes from test to re-test. This involves abandoning the traditional methods of investigating reliability, and putting the Rorschach technique to a more crucial test than that involved with split-half methods or alternative forms.

Are the Traditional Criteria of Reliability Sufficient?

Instead of arranging the reliability test in such a way as to minimize any instability of the functions reflected, it seems of crucial importance to test the limits of stability of whatever functions are being examined by the Rorschach technique. Instead of trying to arrange identical testing conditions, or assuming them, is it not more important to examine the stability of the results obtained under varying conditions? Instead of testing reliability under conditions that must inevitably mask the influence of a variety of factors in shaping the test performance, would it not be more helpful to try to separate out the various influences so that a better understanding is obtained of just what functions *are* reflected in the Rorschach protocol? Instead of trying to prove the Rorschach a reliable technique, is it not more significant to find out to what extent and under what conditions the Rorschach technique yields unreliable results? Discovering these facts would provide a basis for obtaining more reliable and valid individual appraisals when using the technique. With this point of view, further attempts to explore the reliability of the Rorschach technique should not be viewed as expedients used because the traditional criteria are difficult to apply, but as improvements upon the traditional criteria in that they represent more searching tests of reliability than have traditionally been employed with psychometric techniques. Indeed, if applied to these also, such tests might lead to more reliable and valid use of the techniques in question.

As a perceptual technique for exploring personality function, the Rorschach method, through the utilization of ambiguous or unstructured materials, draws attention to the perceiver's own contribution to perception. Since standardized materials are used, dif-

ferences between individuals in modes of perception may not be attributed to the "stimulus" differences inherent in the materials
being perceived. However, it does not seem permissible automatically to attribute all differences in perception to a "personal constant" which the perceiver brings to all perceptual situations. It may
be that the situation within which the perception takes place contributes to differences in perception; notable points here would be
the influence of the interpersonal relationship between examiner
and subject, or failure to structure a permissive situation. Moreover,
it cannot be conceived that the whole of the perceiver's contribution
is a constant, uninfluenced by other perceiver factors such as set,
needs of the moment, emotional state, and so on. Indeed, it is possible that the assumption of an important "personal constant" basic
to projective techniques is faulty, and that the functions reflected
in the test performance are essentially unstable ones—in which case,
of course, the test performance would lack predictive validity.

Does the Rorschach Performance Reflect a Stable Function?

It has often been suggested that the Rorschach technique taps the
"basic personality structure." Since this structure is assumed to be
a highly stable function, this view implies that stable results should
be obtained through retesting. There seem to be two problems here:
whether personality structure (or whatever it is that the Rorschach
taps) is indeed an unchanging function, and whether the technique
taps this function alone and is uninfluenced by any other factors,
either dyamic factors pertinent to an understanding of the personality or factors accidental to the particular test situation.

The whole predictive value of any test or technique rests upon
the relative stability of the function measured or assessed. Yet it
would not square with the main line of psychological theory to
postulate a complete stability of personality or its influence upon
perception. On the other hand, it is not congruent with either
clinical experience, or learning theory, or personality theory to deny
the existence of some relatively stable organization which gives a
thread of continuity to experience and behavior. Developmental
changes would be expected, and changes resulting from major life

influences. Shifts and changes of emphasis could be expected even within the framework of a relatively stable organization. Moreover, it could not be expected that the whole of the relatively stable core of organization would reveal itself at any one time or under any one set of circumstances. Validly to reflect a relatively stable core of organization, the Rorschach technique should reveal developmental changes and changes attributable to major environmental changes, particularly when there is reason to believe that these changes have resulted in an inner reorganization. The Rorschach results would be suspect either if they were identical (or highly similar) when major changes intervene between test and retest, or if no continuity were found between test and retest.

Perhaps because of the influence of traditional conceptions of reliability, there have been few retest studies of children during a period of rapid development. It was reported above that Swift [152] retested pre-school children after varying time-intervals. With a 14-day interval she found coefficients (corrected for attenuation) ranging from .59 to .83. However, with a 10-month interval the coefficients were lower, ranging from .18 to .53. Swift turns attention to factors that seem to work against reliability: namely, small R's, low frequency of responses in many scoring categories, and variability in interest and attention span in the retest situation. It is proposed that her results could be interpreted as evidence in the direction of validity in that there were significant continuities over a 10-month interval during a period presumed to be one of rapid development; this seems a more significant finding than the moderate reliability coefficients found with a short interval.

Indirect evidence of developmental changes is provided by the various normative studies* which compare the performances of different age-groups, even though the same children have not been followed through longitudinally. However, the only long-term, large-scale retesting program reported to date is the University of Cali-

---

* Among the normative studies of children may be listed those by Carlson [22], Ford [40], Hertz [59], Kay and Vorhaus [73], Kerr [76], Klopfer and Margulies [81], Meyer and Thompson [98], Paulsen [108], Rabin and Beck [114], Ranzoni, Grant, and Ives [116], Sunne [150], Swift [153], Thetford, Molish, and Beck [154], and Vorhaus [161].

fornia Institute of Child Welfare "Guidance Study." McFate and Orr [91] report on trends with increasing age for 194 subjects who were tested four times between their 11th and 18th birthdays. These trends include an increase in unusual details, popular responses, human movement responses, and total number of responses, with a decrease in *FM* and *cF* responses—all of which are compatible with the interpretative hypotheses attached to these scoring categories. The two chief expectations that were not fulfilled, at least with this age range, were an increase in *FC* responses with a decrease in *CF,* and a decrease in *A%.* Future papers are promised on the changes shown by individual children, relating the Rorschach performances to life-history material.

Crucial evidence on the stability of the functions reflected by the Rorschach could be derived from test-retest studies paralleling life history, both within the developmental period and in adulthood. So far the only studies of this sort are those examining the changes in Rorschach performance that parallel psychiatric treatment. However, a major difficulty with these studies has been a lack of adequate criteria for judging the changes attributable to treatment independently of Rorschach changes. Indeed, many of the studies have used the Rorschach as a tool for exploring the effect of treatment, rather than using treatment changes as an outside criterion against which Rorschach changed may be checked; some studies aim chiefly at the establishment of Rorschach "signs" for predicting a favorable response to treatment.

Brosin and Fromm [17] report a general impression of stability of manner of approach and experience-balance over a lapse of time and through therapy. Rioch [119] reported on the "before and after" protocols of 36 patients undergoing psychoanalytically oriented intensive psychotherapy. She states that there are changes in content and feeling tone that are quite meaningful in the light of changes reported by the therapist, but difficult to formulate in general terms and therefore open to the danger of distortion by prejudice. However, certain general trends can be formulated. In the case of the out-patients the therapist and Rorschach examiner were in complete agreement with respect to the incidence of improvement.

These patients showed a marked shift in the $FC : (CF+C)$ balance towards FC, an average increase in $F\%$ from 56 to 63, a decrease in $W\%$, and an increase in populars. In the case of the hospitalized patients there was agreement in 10 of the 22 cases regarding the extent and direction of the changes during therapy; in the other cases the therapist thought there was improvement on the basis of a "social recovery" while the Rorschach examiner could detect no improvement in the perceptual distortions in the protocol. However, in 5 of the cases where it was agreed that improvement had occurred, there was an increase in CF with a decrease in $F\%$. These changes seemed to indicate an increased emotional accessibility, even though it was troublesome and ill-adapted to the environment. Despite these trends and other individual changes, Rioch reports that tests and retests were, on the whole, more alike than different.

Harris and Christiansen [55] compared pre-therapy Rorschach performances with ratings from therapists regarding responsiveness to treatment of 53 patients who were given brief psychotherapy because of delayed recovery from disease, operation, or the like. No statistically significant differences were found between those rated "good," "indifferent," or "poor" in terms of response to therapy. Here the intent was to establish predictive criteria rather than to examine changes attributable to treatment; no post-treatment Rorschach examination was given.

Piotrowski [110] reports that schizophrenics who improve through insulin treatment show improvement in Rorschach performance characterized by increased speed and ease of interpretation, better verbal form and logical content of responses, better distinction between relevant and irrelevant, increased number and quality of movement responses, more FC responses, better-seen percepts reflected in an increased $F+\%$ and better organization. An examination of the pre-treatment Rorschach records indicated that the patients who subsequently recovered were very inefficient before treatment, with poor concentration, very uneven performance with good percepts but extensive and uncontrolled associations, and some responsiveness to color although of an uncontrolled variety. The pre-treatment records of the patients who did not improve through treatment were characterized by an earnest attempt to do well, by an even performance level with poor percepts but controlled elaboration, and by a lack of color interference. On the basis of these findings he set up "signs" on the basis of which the response to therapy might be predicted. He reported [111] that 88 per cent of 60 cases were predicted correctly, with clinical estimates as the criterion of improvement through treatment.

Graham [51] reports the following tendencies in retests after hypoglycemia therapy: increased R, a slight tendency for $F+\%$ to more nearly approximate the optimum, increased number of patients who give at least some kinesthetic responses, fewer CF and C responses, fewer coarctated records and a trend towards less heavily extratensive records, and fewer shading responses. She did not find that more patients gave FC responses after treatment, but that those who did produce FC responses produced more after treatment. The results of treatment were rated by the physician. The number of subjects were too small to make statistically reliable comparisons of the pretreatment Rorschachs of those who responded well to treatment with those of patients who responded poorly. However, the chief distinguishing mark of those who responded well to treatment seemed to be more frequent shading responses, despite the fact that treatment tended to reduce the incidence of shading responses.

Kisker [78] reports that insulin shock or metrazol convulsive therapy resulted in a smaller number of minus form level responses, improved succession, and a decrease in D and $Dr\%$. However, he reports that even with recovered patients there remain certain elements of psychotic patterns in the Rorschach performance, which makes one question whether shock therapy has brought about any deep restructuralization of the personality pattern. Halpern [54] compared a group of schizophrenics who did not respond favorably to insulin therapy with a group who responded with satisfactory adjustment maintained for at least a year after treatment. The pretreatment Rorschachs differed in that the improved group had more responses, a higher Sum C, more c, C', and K, more movement responses, and more human concepts. Both groups responded to treatment with some changes, the unimproved group with more CF and

C responses and a less complete lack of *M* responses, while the improved group showed an increase of *FC* responses. Both groups retained a "schizophrenic" flavor to their records, however.

Ross and Block [130] review the use of projective techniques in the evaluation of neurosurgical treatment. They conclude:

> It seems unfortunate that so many of the studies so far reported have fallen short in some important respect from the most carefully controlled and yet qualitatively discriminating use which could be made of the Rorschach technique. Those who have reported qualitative impressions have failed to establish significant changes in comparison with controls. The statistical studies, on the other hand, have been somewhat mechanically applied without due consideration of constellations in the Rorschach performance which might be correlated with particular operative results. It is rare to find the combination of a regard for statistical criteria with a penetrating understanding of the dynamic patterns displayed in Rorschach records and a sensitivity to the modifications which would be expected if the operation should bring about a change in personality integration. [130, page 402]

In general, these studies seem to show certain changes concomitant with response to treatment within the context of some continuing stability of pattern. If the Rorschach reflects "basic personality structure," treatment does not appear to effect a complete reorganization of personality structure. In any event there appears to be continuity from test to retest even with considerable change in surface adjustment, with some modification of pattern to parallel the externally observable changes. A major handicap in this field is, however, a lack of precise formulations of the personality changes that have, in fact, been effected by treatment; so there is no truly satisfactory criterion against which to check the interpretative hypotheses connected with Rorschach changes. It can only be urged that further attention be given to test-retest studies of the same individuals over a period during which specific changes could be expected to have taken place in personality function. Only through such testing out of the Rorschach technique can information be obtained relevant to the degree of stability of the functions studied, an essential requirement before the "reliability" of the technique can be appraised thoroughly.

"Testing the Limits" of Reliability

A number of productive studies have been directed towards an examination of the influence of factors other than stable personality factors upon the Rorschach performance. The most frequent pattern of these studies has been to retest under conditions so designed that they will facilitate a major change in performance if the individual's perception of the ink blots and his verbal report thereon are in fact influenced by unstable factors attributable either to ongoing processes in the organism or the test situation, or both. Such studies seem best designed to show within what limits the Rorschach technique is reliable rather than to arrive at some absolute judgment of reliability.

(1)   *Extreme Unpredictability of Performance*

Since schizophrenic patients are notoriously unpredictable in daily-life performance, Holzberg and Wexler [66] thought that a test-retest study with schizophrenic patients would provide a crucial test for the Rorschach technique, and that high reliability coefficients could only be obtained if the Rorschach gets at some underlying stable organization. With 20 schizophrenic patients reliability coefficients were found to be significant at the 5 per cent level for most of the scoring categories, low coefficients seeming to be a function of infrequency of responses in the scoring categories in question. There were no significant differences between the means of test and retest findings, except in the case of the reaction time to chromatic cards. This last finding suggests that the inhibiting effect of color becomes lessened on retest. There were some qualitative differences between the test and retest protocols for individual patients, but these were not great enough to make it difficult to identify the individual. Matching was significant at better than the 1 per cent level.

(2)   *The Influence of "Set"*

Despite the fact that high reliability coefficients have been obtained for various kinds of personality tests based upon statements an individual makes about himself, it has long been recognized that these tests are particularly vulnerable to the deliberate intention of the subject to present himself in a favorable or unfavorable light. Fosberg set out to test the assumption that the Rorschach technique was not subject to this source of unreliability. The pattern of his study [42, 43] was to present the Rorschach cards four times to the same subjects: first, under standard conditions; second, asking the subject to attempt to make the best possible impression; third, asking him to attempt to make the worst possible impression; and, finally, under standard conditions again. Unfortunately, the statistical techniques used by Fosberg in these studies were unsound (as Cronbach [30] points out) ; hence his conclusion, that the Rorschach technique is resistant to "faking," is open to question. He reports further [44] that an inquiry from each subject into how he had tried to "fake" his results confirmed the impression that there is no sound *a priori* basis whereby the subject could deliberately shape his responses in such a way as to affect materially the quantitative findings. Most frequently the subjects tried to do so by altering the number of responses, being erudite, or giving only the obvious responses, and including or omitting sexual references.

Carp and Shavzin [23] set out to verify Fosberg's findings, giving the test twice to 20 subjects, once asking them to make a good impression and once asking them to make a bad impression. The experimenters did not undertake to test whether the subjects succeeded in altering their records in the desired direction, but only in the extent of changes between the two testings. They found that there were differences, but these were so diverse in direction that they tended to balance out; only Beck's Z score yielded a difference significant at the 5 per cent level. They found correlations ranging from .16 to .97. The content categories seemed most subject to manipulation; low correlations were also found for *W, M, CF,* and *Sum C.* Chi square techniques were used to compare each subject with himself. Of 20 subjects only three managed to alter their patterns to an extent significant at the 5 per cent level; two made alterations to an extent approaching significance—the 10 per cent level. They conclude that some subjects are successful in altering their Rorschach performance to a significant extent. It would seem necessary to undertake further exploration into this problem, with emphasis upon the effect the experimentally altered "set" might have upon the examiner's interpretation of the performance and not merely upon the quantitative findings, and upon what kinds of subjects are successful in altering their performances, and in what direction.

Another extension of the problem of reliability is the question of the vulnerability of the Rorschach technique to special "tips" regarding how to alter the Rorschach performance so as to make a good or bad impression. This has been the emphasis of Hutt [71] and his associates in the exploration of the effect of varied experimental sets on Rorschach test performance. Hutt, Gibby, Milton, and Pottharst [72] report the findings of a study in which four equivalent groups of subjects were retested under different conditions. A control group was retested under standard conditions. It was required of the subject in each of the three experimental groups on the occasion of the second test to tell everything he saw and, in addition: (a) to pay particular attention to the segmented areas of the blots, (b) to find as many human movement responses as he could, and (c) to give only good form, but to combine form and color in giving responses and to give as many human movement responses as possible; each condition applied to one of the experimental groups. The third condition was designed to produce a conflicting state of "set." With the control group the reliability coefficients were highly variable for the different scores, the lowest coefficients being —.13 for $F+\%$ and .08 for FC, and the highest being .81 for $F+$ (in absolute not percentage terms). Oddly enough, the reliability coefficients found with the experimental groups were higher than those for the control group. The general pattern of changes from test to retest suggested that anxiety, constriction, and withdrawal tendencies decreased; the authors caution that this change would have to be taken into account before attributing test-retest improvement to the effect of any intervening therapy. The subjects who had been asked to give emphasis to detail responses were successful in increasing $D+Dd$ by 18 per cent at the expense of a decreased W of 50 per cent, both changes being statistically significant. The subjects who had been asked to emphasize M responses produced 100 per cent more M's on the retest, these being of good quality, neither cheap nor hazy. There was also an alteration in $M : Sum\ C$ and a decrease of W and $A\%$. Gibby [47] reports in more detail on the findings of this study, with particular emphasis on the intellectual variables. With conflictful instructions (emphasis on good form, FC, and M simultaneously) there was a decrease in W and R, but no change in D or Dd. (The findings with respect to FC, M, and other non-intellectual variables have not yet been published.)

Gibby [47] explored further into the kind of individuals who were able to effect the greatest changes in their performance under specific instructions. Those subjects in the control group who changed the most with respect to D and Dd on retest were found in their original Rorschachs to have higher W and M and lower $D+Dd$. They seemed to be relatively "mature" and "rich" personalities, neither rigid nor constricted. On this basis Gibby devised a "stability score" by means of which he was able successfully to predict those individuals in the experimental groups who would be able to effect most change under experimentally altered instructions, except that his predictions did not hold with the group given conflictful instructions. Hutt, Gibby, Milton, and Pottharst [72] conclude that with normal subjects there is vulnerability to experimentally induced sets; hence the simple, unrefined psychogram should be interpreted with caution. They acknowledge that less capacity to shift might be found with pathological subjects, a suggestion quite in line with the clinical impression that the more maladjusted the subject the less possible it is to induce him to change his mode of perception in the testing of the limits period.

Coffin [25] produced evidence in the same direction as the Hutt studies. He gave a group of students deliberate misinformation regarding the Rorschach "signs" pointing to occupational success. Individual Rorschach tests showed a significant tendency for the subjects to respond in the suggested direction.

Luchins [89] retested a group of 103 subjects with "negative clinical findings" giving particular emphasis to the testing of the limits period. He summarized the subject's comments pertinent to rea-

sons for not having been able to give, in the earlier phases of the
test, responses that they were later able to give in the limits period.
Such reasons were: distinterested attitude, fear of test or tester, misunderstanding of instructions, an unsuccessful attempt to see the
responses in question, effects of past experience, or a literal-minded
interpretation of instructions. He emphasizes the importance of investigation during the limits period of why the subject did not give
certain types of responses during the test proper.

Schachtel [142] points out that despite an attempt to structure the
test situation to be wholly permissive, each subject will define it in
terms of his own needs, wishes, and fears. He suggests that there are
two ways of dealing with this fact. One way is the traditional one of
trying to increase the reliability of the test by attempting to reduce
the influences that may provoke subjective definitions of the test
situation, and (since this factor cannot altogether be excluded) trying to evaluate its influence so that its effect on test behavior may
be discounted. The other way is to exploit the fact that the subject's set influences his Rorschach performance, by using this set
as a valuable source of insight into his personality structure and
attitudes. The implication is that the definition the subject gives a
permissive situation is itself an important "constant" in his approach
to undefined situations. Some subjects characteristically define such
situations in authoritarian terms, some are characteristically competitive, others are chronically resistant. These various definitions
have effects upon performance, specifically upon number of responses, reaction time, sequence, form level, use of locations, content, and test behavior; and indirectly they influence the use of
determinants. However, these effects can be distinguished and interpreted. For example, short records are given both by some competitive subjects and by resistant, evasive subjects. The short records
of the competitive subject would be characterized by an attempt
to make his record well-organized, with clear form perception, a
"masterpiece," while that of the resistant subject would be per-
functory or listless. Similarly, a long record may be given either by
one who is coöperative and cheerful, enjoying the test, and oriented
towards the test materials rather than towards himself and the im-

pression he is making, or by one who has defined the test situation in authoritarian terms as a pressure situation, interpreting the requirement in quantitative terms. However, these two kinds of approach may be easily distinguished in terms of other aspects of the test record and test behavior.

The various studies on experimentally induced sets seem to show that the Rorschach technique is not wholly resistant to deliberate efforts on the part of the subject to change his pattern of response, especially where specific instructions are given regarding how he can change it, and particularly in the case of normal, flexible subjects. It would seem that this is not a serious limitation to reliability, for these experimental conditions are extreme ones, which push reliability to the limits. However, this does not minimize the importance of "set" and "definition." It is important to recognize that the subject will define the test situation for himself and that this definition will have an effect on his performance. As Schachtel points out, there are clues to the subject's definition within his test performance, which provide important interpretative material. However, to exploit sources of "unreliability" in this way requires very careful analysis of the performance, with due emphasis upon qualitative nuances and upon the interrelationships between various aspects of the performance. A wooden kind of interpretation based upon quantitative findings separately considered leaves the subject's set merely a source of unreliability rather than a source of valuable information. The studies on experimentally induced sets should be taken as serious indicators of the importance of including a testing-the-limits period, not only with rigid, maladjusted subjects but also with the well-adjusted, flexible subject with whom the limits phase of testing is often neglected. Not only would the limits period qualify generalizations to be made from quantitative analysis when it is found that shifts can easily be made, but also the degree of capacity to shift would itself seem to be a significant finding. Although it is entirely likely that subjective definitions of the test situation cannot be ruled out, it seems important, nevertheless, to emphasize pre-test structuring of a permissive situation so that the subjective definition the subject does in fact give the situation may be viewed against a background of having made every attempt to present him with a permissive situation.

(3) Influence of the Test Situation

Studies where experimental changes have been made in the test situation confirm the importance of the test situation as a part-determiner of the Rorschach performance, making it impossible to claim that the Rorschach taps basic functions of the personality without being influenced by here-and-now conditions and processes. (Any such claim would seem untenable, in any event, on purely theoretical grounds.) Kimble [77] administered the Rorschach to 14 subjects individually, first under standard conditions and then in a social situation with other people present. Composite records derived from each of the two situations were compared. She found that the social situation produced more W responses, fewer S responses, and—most significant—a shift of the experience balance in an extratensive direction due to an increase in $Sum\ C$, significant at the 2 per cent level. This, she concluded, confirmed Rorschach's hypothesis that the experience balance can be affected by the subject being "in a good humor," and in any event made it impossible to think of the personality apart from the environment. This finding does not throw doubt upon the reliability of the Rorschach technique (since it is not standard practice for other people to be present) so much as it tends to confirm the hypothesis that color responses are related to social responsiveness. Moreover, it emphasizes the importance of exploring the test situation as an interpersonal situation; for if the performance can be affected by the introduction of other people it would seem impossible to insist that the social situation inherent in the examiner-subject relationship can be ignored.

Lord [88] carried through a well-designed study using 36 college students in which each subject was tested under three conditions: (1) a standard test situation, (2) a situation in which preliminary tests of other kinds were administered under conditions designed to make the subject feel rejected and a failure, and (3) one in which preliminary tests were administered under conditions designed to make him feel accepted and successful. Each administration was undertaken by a different examiner, all three examiners being female. The study was designed to evaluate the relative effects of retesting as such, of experimental alteration of the emotional atmosphere of the test situation, and of the personality of the examiner.

The retesting factor was found to be least important. The changes from test to retest were decreased response time, decrease in W responses, and increase in "refined control," which could be interpreted as resulting from decreased anxiety and increased mastery over a challenging or threatening situation. There was an increase of M responses in the second test, but a decrease in the third test, which the author attributes to the effect of boredom attending the third testing. The effect of the rejecting, disapproving test atmosphere was to increase $A\%$, decrease P's, decrease M's, decrease (VIII, IX, X) %, and to increase FK and S responses. In general, the performance could be described as less imaginative, less responsive, more stereotyped, and characterized by more self-questioning and more resistance against feelings of inadequacy. The effect of the warm, accepting, permissive test atmosphere was to increase $R, M, P,$ and again FK responses, but to decrease $A\%$. In general, the records were "richer," showing fuller use of all aspects of the blot material.

However, the effect of the artificially altered test atmosphere was much less than the effect of the three examiners themselves. One examiner had the effect of decreasing $R, FC, CF, Fc,$ and C' and of increasing $W\%$. $F\%$ was also higher and C responses were more numerous. This examiner seemed to produce a threatening, frustrating situation. This finding was somewhat confirmed by an outside description of her as the coldest, most inflexible, most "masculine" of the three. The second examiner had the effect of reducing $F\%$, $(FK+F+Fc)\%$, and $W\%$, of facilitating C responses, and increasing $K, FK, M, FM, Fc, C', H, Hd,$ and Ad and the use of all blot areas except W. This pattern seemed to imply an intellectual challenge, with attendant anxiety, but with easy rapport and less need to control. This examiner was described as flexible and feminine, "bubbling" and sympathetic. The third examiner produced effects on the Rorschach scores intermediate between the other two, although with least *FK*, *M*, and *FM* and the highest *Sum C* and $(FK+F+Fc)\%$. She thus apparently did not stimulate intellectual activity, nor provoke undue anxiety, although she seemed to evoke well-controlled emotionality. She was the youngest of the three, and described as the most feminine, softest, and most nearly an ideal, protecting mother-figure.

Lord's findings are confirmed by Baughman [8] who examined 633 records obtained by 15 examiners (unfortunately the reliability of scoring was not checked or controlled). Baughman found that some examiners contributed much more heavily to the variance than others, who seemed in effect interchangeable. In 12 of 22 scoring categories there were differences significant at the .001 level. Among the most stable categories were *W*, *A%*, *P*, *CF*, *C*, *M*, and *m*, with detail responses and *FM* and *FC* apparently most influenced by the examiners (or their scoring).

These studies tend to lend credence to the criticism that has often been put forward by therapists: namely, that the Rorschach technique neglects the influence of the subject-examiner relationship as a determiner of the Rorschach performance, in effect ignoring the transference aspect of the test situation. However, the fact that it has been demonstrated that different examiners have differential effects does not mean necessarily that the subject-examiner relationship is neglected, nor is it inherent in the Rorschach technique to ignore the influence of this relationship. Nor does the fact of examiner-influence mean that the Rorschach technique is more vulnerable to this influence than other tests or methods. These studies do point up the practical importance for the examiner of arriving at a sound estimate of the way his personality has affected the performance of the individual subject, and emphasize the scientific desirability of further investigations that undertake a thorough personality appraisal of various examiners to ascertain both their constant effects on groups of subjects and their differential effects on subjects of varying personalities.

Conclusion

In summary, the studies of reliability and of the effects of retesting under varying conditions would seem to indicate that the various functions tapped by the Rorschach technique have a fair degree of stability (although some seem more stable than others), but that the perception and verbal performance of the subject on the test may be influenced by factors extraneous to these relatively stable functions. In view of the fact that it would seem untenable to hold that perception in any test situation could be exclusively a product of the interaction of the constant test material and the "personal constant" of the subject's personality without any influence from background factors in the total test situation or from ongoing processes in the individual, it does not seem that these studies point so much to the absolute unreliability of the method as to certain limitations of reliability, which in turn suggest ways in which the method may be *used* to produce more reliable and valid interpretations.

5. Problems Relating to Criteria

The problems discussed so far might be described as background problems in validation research. We turn now to the most basic problem—that of the criteria against which the interpretative hypotheses are to be checked. This is perhaps the most formidable problem of all; were criteria available for assessing personality characteristics, these criteria themselves being of irreproachable validity, there would be little problem of validation. Despite the fact that such criteria are non-existent, and that to find even moderately satisfactory criteria involves considerable caution and ingenuity, there has been a large amount of research which may be said to throw some light on the validity of the Rorschach technique. This research may be classified into the following groups: (1) diagnostic studies, (2) group comparisons, (3) factorial studies, (4) "single variable" studies, (5) studies involving experimentally induced states, (6) clinical studies, and (7) prediction studies.

(1) Diagnostic Studies

Diagnostic studies relevant to validation are of two main kinds: those that check the accuracy of a diagnosis based upon "blind analysis" of the protocol, and those that test the validity of "diagnostic signs" proposed as a basis for differentiating between diagnostic groups.

An example of the "blind diagnosis" type of study is that by Benjamin and Ebaugh [13]. This involved diagnoses made on the basis of the Rorschach protocol, sometimes without even a glimpse of the patient himself, and always without access to any other information. The criterion of validity was the diagnosis arrived at by the psychiatric conference on the basis of the usual clinical procedures. In 39 out of 46 cases the Rorschach diagnoses were in complete agreement with the final diagnoses; in the remaining 7 there was no serious discrepancy. This represents a higher degree of agreement than one would expect usually to result from different psychiatrists arriving independently at a diagnosis, unless they had agreed in advance upon the diagnostic classifications to be used and the criteria thereof. It would indicate that Benjamin and Ebaugh, working within the framework of diagnostic categories used in their particular setting, and backed by extensive diagnostic experience, were able to arrive at a diagnosis, on the basis of the sample of performance elicited by the Rorschach ink blots, that was nearly always in agreement with a diagnosis based on the more usual samples of performance elicited in the psychiatric interview.

The qualifications implied in the above statement indicate the limitations of the diagnostic study in providing a criterion of validity. Diagnostic classification is a difficult criterion, since the bases of classification differ considerably from one psychiatric setting to another. As Ross [129] points out, diagnostic labels imply sharp lines of distinction between disorders, where in fact one classification shades into another with much overlapping. Moreover, psychiatric diagnostic classification is based on empirical and symptomatic considerations which bear only indirect relationship to personality structure. Schafer [144, 145] implies that psychiatric diagnosis from the Rorschach or other psychodiagnostic tests and techniques is not a direct judgment, but rather involves an intermediate step. An appraisal is first made of the modes of functioning of the personality on the basis of the test protocol; then, working from a knowledge of what processes of thinking and acting are characteristic of various diagnostic groupings, a diagnosis is made.

A variation of the "blind diagnosis" approach, which avoids the difficulties attendant upon diagnostic classification, is illustrated by Hertz and Rubenstein [64] who report a high degree of agreement between the "blind" interpretations offered by Hertz, Klopfer, and Beck with respect to a single Rorschach protocol. However, this study does not so much pertain to the validation of interpretative hypotheses as to the reliability of interpretations offered by proponents of different systems of scoring and interpretation.

Another variation is illustrated by the Case of Gregor [12] prepared for a symposium on projective techniques. Gregor was tested by a large number of different tests and techniques. His various test protocols were interpreted "blind" by clinicians expert in each of the various techniques. The symposium gave the impression of a remarkable degree of congruency among the various interpretations and with the case history and diagnostic findings, although an item by item comparison was not carried through, and the case history material was unfortunately meager.

However, all these "blind" interpretations and diagnoses seem to be more of a *tour de force* to impress the skeptic than to represent a serious attempt to test out the basic hypotheses upon which both interpretation and diagnosis are based.

There is a very large group of studies, much too numerous to mention here, dealing with the establishment of and testing out of diagnostic "signs" which will differentiate on a significant statistical basis between different diagnostic groups. A classified bibliography of such studies has been drawn up by Bell [11, pages 138–146]. Only one will be quoted as an example, namely, that by Miale and Harrower-Erickson [99] in which nine signs are proposed as characteristic of neurotic records and distinguishing them to some extent from those of normal subjects. These signs have been tested out in many subsequent studies which showed both that they were valid in distinguishing groups of neurotics from groups of normals, and that their usefulness is much limited by the fact that similar signs are manifested by patients with organic brain disease, schizophrenia, psychosomatic disorders of various kinds, and indeed by some normal subjects. They are characteristic of the neurotic group but not exclusive to it.

Even where statistically significant differences between groups can be established, these differences are of relatively little use in individual diagnosis, at least when used in a mechanical rather than in a clinical way. Generally, those signs that seem exclusive to the given diagnostic group are so rare even with that group that many cases would be missed in diagnosis; or they are shown by enough patients in other diagnostic groups for errors of commission rather than omission to be made. Thus, "contamination" of responses has held up as a fairly dependable sign of schizophrenic process in thinking, but it is by no means always found in the protocols of obvious schizophrenics. On the other hand, nearly all schizophrenics give responses with minus form level; but minus responses are given also by organics, other psychotics, neurotics, and occasionally by normal subjects.

In general, diagnostic studies involving both systematic and unsystematic clinical observations have proved very useful as a source of interpretative hypotheses, but involve difficulties as sources of stable and valid outside criteria in validation research. It is not to be wondered that this is so, for there are many individual differences, and important ones, between patients included in the same diagnostic classification; and there is much fluidity of boundaries between diagnostic groups. It is perhaps indirect evidence of the validity of the Rorschach technique that it fails to establish clear-cut differentiation between diagnostic groupings while yet showing some undeniable relationship to them.

The importance of diagnostic "signs" should not be belittled. They may be useful as screening devices and as such their validity should be checked. Even though it appears that their validity is limited as a basis for individual diagnosis when used in an automatic or mechanical way and without due consideration for the general configuration of the record, they nevertheless are very help-ful to the Rorschach examiner in building up a basis of diagnostic judgment. Moreover, the Rorschach differences between diagnostic groupings may throw light upon the nature of the disease processes as they influence perception. However, the chief point to be made here is that to establish the validity of diagnostic "signs" would still not establish the validity of the basic interpretative hypotheses of the Rorschach technique; the validity of "signs" is a separate valida-tion problem.

(2) Group Comparisons

Studies of the characteristics of the Rorschach performance of groups are extremely common in Rorschach research, either involv-ing the comparison of two or more groups, or the description of a single group but implying a comparison with normative data or with the hypothetical normal record. Usually such group compari-sons limit themselves to statistical treatment of the various scoring categories and quantitative proportions and omit consideration of qualitative differences. These studies overlap with diagnostic studies, for many of the groups studied are diagnostic groupings, either of psychiatric or psychosomatic disorders. Other studies, however, com-pare various age groups, delinquent vs. non-delinquent groups, oc-cupational groups, and so forth.

These group comparisons are rarely, if ever, designed primarily as validation studies. Some are exploratory studies intended to ascer-tain whether the Rorschach protocols of individual members of a group do indeed yield a common denominator which could be said to be characteristic of the group. Some assume the validity of Ror-schach hypotheses, using the Rorschach technique as a method for describing the personality characteristics of the group. Some are intended to provide normative data. Others are designed as a basis for setting up or testing diagnostic "signs" or predictive indices.

Group comparisons have been invaluable as a source of interpre-tative hypotheses, perhaps particularly those involving various diag-nostic groups. Indirectly, they also provide an opportunity for the evaluation of the validity of certain interpretative hypotheses, even though they may not have been designed specifically to test these hypotheses. Because of this lack of intention in the design of the study, it is rare that a group comparison is sufficiently crucial to lend strong positive support to the claim for validity of any given hypothesis, but rather support is to be found in the general congruency of the Rorschach findings with "common-sense" or theoretical understanding of the differential characteristics of groups. Thus, the changes in frequency of Rorschach scores with different age groups lends this kind of generalized support to claims for validity. For example, the control indices $FC : (CF+C)$ and $M : FM$ might be expected to change with age in the direction of greater control. The fact that CF and FM responses are found to predominate over FC and M responses with younger in contrast to older groups does not provide explicit validatory evidence for the interpretative hypotheses attached to these determinants. However, had the younger groups been found to have a preponderance of FC and M scores this would have provided crucial evidence of the invalidity of the control hypotheses. Thus, group comparisons are a means of detecting grossly invalid hypotheses, and sometimes provide a basis for the delimitation of the generality of interpretative hypotheses. This point may be illustrated by citing a few examples.

Reference has already been made (in Chapter 10) to the contribution made by Roe [122] in her study of artists in delimiting the hypothesis that M responses are related to "creativity." Her findings that M responses were, if anything, less frequent with a group of high-ranking artists than would normally be expected, and that there were few "creative personalities" in the group as defined in terms of the whole Rorschach performance, made it necessary to specify that the Rorschach concept of "creativity" referred to personality rather than to output in the sense of artistic production.

Another example is provided by the comparison of delinquent and non-delinquent groups undertaken by Schachtel [143]. He found that a group of delinquents gave significantly fewer S responses than a matched group of non-delinquents, thus invalidating any extension of Rorschach's hypothesis that S responses indicate an oppositional tendency to imply opposition in the sense of the anti-social tendencies characteristic of delinquency, an extension that has sometimes been made.

More frequently, the group comparison can provide neither a crucial negative nor a crucial positive test of validity, but rather an indication of more or less congruency of Rorschach findings with differences otherwise known to exist between groups. A notable example is the study by Goldfarb [48] who assessed the effects of early institutional care on personality development by comparing adolescents who had spent the first three years of their lives in an institution with subsequent foster-care and a matched group of adolescents who had been cared for by foster-mothers from early infancy. On the basis of a large number of indicators, including intelligence tests, concept formation tests, a social maturity scale, speech ratings, ratings based on test behavior, ratings of behavior in a frustration situation, and caseworkers' evaluations, the two groups were found to be significantly different. The institution children were found to be inferior in every respect, with particular emphasis upon defective capacity for abstract function and a great impoverishment of capacity for the formation and maintenance of normal affectional relationships. Their behavior was characterized by an aggressive, distractible, uncontrolled pattern. Their mental performance tended to be aimless, unreflective, situationally determined, and generally at an unproductive, undifferentiated level.

With such marked differences in terms of all other criteria— differences reflecting basic differences in personality organization— it would be a serious indication of invalidity of Rorschach hypotheses if equally marked differences were not apparent in Rorschach performance. However, the Rorschach findings are generally congruent with the findings of tests and ratings. The institution group show significantly more crude color responses, confabulatory responses, poor originals, fewer M responses, and poorer form level than the group raised in foster homes [49]. Their records are uneven, with the occasional gleam of unfulfilled possibility in single responses, with a consistent extreme attitude of passivity and conspicuous absence of tension [50]. In comparison with schizophrenic children, to whom they are very similar in Rorschach performance, the institution group show both fewer popular and fewer original responses, fewer perseverative responses, fewer total responses, and less variability in form level. Goldfarb suggests that these differences result from the profound anxiety of the schizophrenic child in comparison with the extreme passivity of the institution child [49].

Levi [86] compared the Rorschach patterns of physically handicapped patients who responded poorly to rehabilitation treatment with those who responded well. He found that those who gave 60 per cent or more anatomical responses had great difficulty in rehabilitation, and interpreted this heavy weight on *At* as an indication of narcissistic withdrawal. Notable among those who responded well were those who showed either normal Rorschach patterns or patterns interpreted as indicative of great neurotic guilt, characterized by a very high $F+\%$ and a large number of aggressive animal responses. Here the Rorschach findings are generally congruent with expectations stemming from theory, but there is no crucial evidence of the validity of the interpretative hypotheses.

Morris [100] compared the pre-treatment Rorschachs of patients who improved under metrazol therapy with those who did not, the judgment of improvement being based on criteria such as parole, discharge, or better hospital adjustment. As a result of the comparison he set up prognostic "signs" which, he predicted, would raise the rate of improvement from 44 per cent to 78 percent if patients were selected for treatment in accordance with the "signs." The "signs" were based on the findings that the unimproved group gave in their pre-treatment test more anatomy responses, more poor originals, fewer total responses, fewer *D, S,* and *FC* responses, and had a lower $F+\%$ than the improved group. For crucial evidence of the validity of the interpretative hypotheses associated with the "signs" there should be some indication of how it is that the personality characteristics indicated militate against successful response to metrazol therapy.

Klebanoff [79] compared the Rorschach findings of a group of 60 soldiers suffering from operational fatigue with normative findings. He found them characterized by low R, frequent rejections, shading emphasis, high $F\%$, high $A\%$, poor form level, low responsiveness to color, and a total absence of M responses in 72 per cent of the records, with only 5 per cent of the records showing more than one M response. These findings add up to a picture of constriction of reactivity and generalized rigidity as a fundamental reaction to anxiety, a picture of withdrawal with integrity of the ego. These findings, he implies, are congruent with expectations.

McReynolds [93] selected 50 Rorschach concepts that are generally accepted by Rorschach examiners to be clearly positive or negative signs of good adjustment. These concepts were proposed to 214 subjects individually tested, some of whom were "normal" and some of whom were clearly "abnormal." He found that the normal group "saw" a significantly higher proportion of the concepts believed characteristic of good adjustment, while the abnormal group "saw" a significantly higher proportion of those believed characteristic of maladjustment.

These few examples of group comparisons serve to illustrate the point that this method tends to throw only indirect light upon the validity of interpretative hypotheses. It is necessary to know in advance the crucial psychological distinctions between groups before group differences may be used as crucial criteria against which interpretative hypotheses may be tested, although occasionally, as illustrated by the studies by Roe and Schachtel, the obvious group characteristics may provide such crucial distinctions—in these examples, creative output and delinquency, as objectively demonstrated. On the whole, the Rorschach technique has been used to increase an understanding of the crucial psychological distinctions between groups, rather than being validated against crucial distinctions already known.

(3) Factorial Studies

Factor analysis seems better suited to exploratory studies than to the validation of interpretative hypotheses, although it has been proposed by Wittenborn as a method of testing the validity of basic assumptions.

Wittenborn [164] argues that the factorial composition of the Rorschach scoring categories should reflect the basic scoring distinctions if these are valid ones (although why this should be so is not clear). Thus, he argues, the major factors to emerge from an analysis should be a color factor, a movement factor, a vista factor, and a texture factor, as well as a general productivity factor, if basic Rorschach assumptions are valid ones. His analysis based on the individual records of 92 undergraduates shows factors cutting across the basic scoring distinctions between determinants. He concludes that Rorschach distinctions between M and color scores (CF and C) are justified since Factor III, which has high loadings for CF and C as well as W, K, and FK (and which seems to refer to lack of perceptual control), is distinct from Factors I and IV, both of which have high M loadings. However, he does not believe it justified to think of FC, CF, and C as similar in implications (presumably as indicating emotional responsiveness) since FC is more closely associated with M and possibly other control factors in Factor I (which has high loadings for O, FC, Fc, C', M, and m) than with the other color determinants which bulk large in Factor III. He also finds a general productivity factor in Factor IV, with high loadings for Dd, D, d, S, M, FM, F, Fc, and R. He offers no particular explanation of Factor II, which has high loadings for K, c, C, P, and O.

To check that these findings were not merely a product of the fact that the subjects were college students, the study was repeated for 160 clinic and hospital patients [165]. This study supported the previous findings, in Wittenborn's opinion. Factor B reflects lack of perceptual control, with heavy positive weights for CF, W, c, C, K, and C'. Factors C and D seem to represent features combined in the productivity factor in the student population. Factor C has high positive weights for R, Dd, d, D, and F particularly, and seems to be due to the presence in the sample of highly constricted patients, while Factor D has heavy weights for FM, M, D, R, FC, C', and FK, which Wittenborn identifies with movement responses. He goes on to make the suggestion that the behavioral implications of the FC response have been mistakenly interpreted by Rorschach workers. Factor A was unanticipated by the student data, comprising chiefly original and space responses, which Wittenborn takes to be characteristic of seriously disturbed individuals. He concludes that the usual scoring and interpretative distinctions between the vista, texture, and color determinants are not supported, that a more basic distinction is on the grounds of perceptual control, that only the movement responses cluster together to form a separate factor, and that the fact that this cluster includes *FC* responses suggests that a considerable revision is required of the hypotheses attached to *FC* and color generally.

It would seem that the major positive finding of this study is a confirmation of the importance attached in the Rorschach technique to a distinction between responses where the determinant is controlled by form considerations and responses where the form considerations are less important than the determinant. It is unfortunate, therefore, that form-level ratings were not also included in the analysis. However, it does not seem self-evident that a factor analysis should indeed yield factors based on the main classes of determinants; hence Wittenborn's conclusion that his study invalidates the "usual scoring and interpretative distinctions" between the vista, texture, and color determinants does not seem justified. Indeed, the basic rationale which views these all as "outer" determinants would lead one to expect a certain clustering together. The "social adjustment" implications of *M, FC,* and *Fc* would seem to make the linkage found between them in the student population a reasonable one and not to imply a need for a major revision of hypotheses. Wittenborn's interpretation of Factor A (based chiefly on original and space responses) as being a factor relating closely to mental illness does not seem justified, particularly since no distinctions were made with respect to form level. In short, Wittenborn's study illustrates vividly the weakness of factor analysis in validation research: namely, the difficulty of obtaining agreement regarding the interpretation of the factors derived.

Hsü [69] undertook a factor analysis of content scores and language used in the Rorschach responses of 76 children, and derived six factors exclusive of residuals. He avoids difficulty in interpreting by giving a highly descriptive account of the factors, as follows: I, facility in the use of words and verbal associations about human figures; II, nouns, non-human context, and an apparent relationship with lower intelligence; III, faces, especially human faces; IV, facility with verbs and adjectives; V, "bat" responses; and VI, human responses.

Sandler and Ackner [136] carried out a factor analysis of content categories, using 50 psychiatric patients. Four factors were derived and then correlated with ratings of symptomatology and previous personality of the patients and with a few case history items. Factor I was a productivity factor. Factor II had at the positive pole internal anatomical responses and at the negative pole external objects such as architecture, emblem, apparel, and ornament. Factor III was also bi-polar, with animated percepts, especially faces, at the positive pole and inanimate percepts at the negative pole. Factor IV was difficult to interpret, but seems to imply defensive percepts at the positive pole and well-defined human parts at the other. The comparisons with psychiatric ratings were too detailed to be reported here; only one example will be given. Factor I was positively correlated with a secure, productive previous personality, with present symptomatology of disjointed speech, incoherence, flight of ideas, and the like. It was negatively correlated with a dependent, evasive, tense previous personality characterized by giving up easily, and with present symptoms including anorexia, negativism, hysterical attitude, an anxious, depressive picture. On the whole the psychiatric ratings seemed significantly associated with the Rorschach factors

It seems fairly clear that the chief function of factor analysis in Rorschach research at the present time is as a source of interpretative hypotheses rather than as a validating device, despite Wittenborn's conclusion that his study invalidates certain of the basic interpretative hypotheses. Hsü's analysis does not seem particularly helpful since the factors were not linked up with other criteria and their significance is not self-evident. On the other hand, the factors derived by Sandler and Ackner are more meaningful for having been correlated with psychiatric symptoms, and seem promising as a basis for new interpretative hypotheses attached to the content of responses. It is to be hoped that a similar study will be undertaken with normal subjects.

A basic difficulty in factorial studies of Rorschach variables is that of interpreting the factors derived. This difficulty is overcome in well-designed factorial studies of testing matrices by inserting into the test battery tests in fair number for each of the factors that are hypothesized in advance. These hypotheses are then validated by seeing whether the expected factors do in fact emerge, and are revised if the findings reflect other than the expected clusterings. Rorschach factorial analysis does not permit of advance planning so that all hypothesized factors are adequately represented. On the other hand certain factors seem to be "put in" by virtue of the selection of the population to be tested, the influence of which tends to be known imperfectly in advance. Thus, Wittenborn's patient population yielded a factor with heavy loadings for original and space responses. Wittenborn believes this to reflect the abnormality of the population. An alternative explanation might be that this factor reflects the presence in the population of some patients with considerable ego strength, which is manifested by perceiving things "differently." There is no basis in the data for deciding whether either of these interpretations is correct, although the correlation of factors with outside criteria might well help to throw light on interpretation, as shown in the study by Sandler and Ackner.

(4) "Single Variable" Studies

This group of research projects are classed as "single variable" studies because they characteristically select one interpretative hypothesis at a time and check its relationship with some relevant outside criterion.

There have been relatively few studies where the outside criterion was a psychological test, for the obvious reason that the interpretative hypotheses relate to functions for which tests have not been developed. One exception is, of course, the intellectual estimate (and the scores upon which it is based) which can be checked against an intelligence test. The findings of Vernon [158] and Altus and Thompson [6] have already been discussed on pages 412–414.

Other studies comparing Rorschach findings with test scores have sought to find "test correlates" rather than arranging a crucial test of any specific interpretative hypothesis. Thompson [155] studied the relationships between Rorschach movement responses and the items of the Minnesota Multiphasic Personality Inventory; the two main "correlates" that emerged were between M responses in small details and items indicative of a lonely, withdrawn maladjustment, and between FM responses in excess of three and items indicating irresponsible, aggressive, distractible trends. Clark [24] focussed on color responses as they related to the scores on the MMPI scales; he concluded that CF responses were delated to impulsiveness and lack of social consciousness, while $Sum\ C$ was related to hypomanic trends and overconfidence. Fonda [39] correlated S responses with the Guilford-Martin Personnel Inventory and the Guilford-Martin factors GAMIN, finding as the only significant correlation a coefficient of .809 with "?" responses on the Inventory. He interprets this finding with reference to the concept of "response set" advanced by Cronbach [27, 31], concluding that both S responses and a response set to choose the "?" answer may be interpreted as a critical kind of intellectual opposition.

These three studies would indicate that the "test correlates" of Rorschach scoring categories may provide indirect evidence of the validity of the interpretative hypotheses attached to them through a reasonable sort of "congruity of findings." However, before "test correlates" can provide crucial evidence of the validity of Rorschach hypotheses the validity of the interpretation of the test finding itself should have been first well-established. Even then there would be the question of appropriateness of the test as a criterion of the validity of the Rorschach hypothesis with which it is compared. For example, Thornton and Guilford [156] find that the "Erlebnistypus" scores on the Rorschach are not significantly correlated with any of the scores of the Nebraska Inventory, which includes the factors of "social introversion," "thinking introversion," emotionality, masculinity, and arrhythmia. For this to be evidence of invalidity of the Rorschach "introversion-extratension" hypotheses, it would first have to be established that *if* these hypotheses are valid, the related "scores" *must* correlate with the various factors of introversion and emotionality measured by the Nebraska Inventory. Otherwise, the easy reply is that the two sets of scores may simply refer to different kinds of responses.

In the absence of pertinent tests, some investigators have relied upon rating scales as the criterion against which Rorschach hypotheses can be checked. Reference has already been made to the studies by Holtzman [67, 68] which used pooled ratings by residence-mates of the subjects and that by Elizur [37] which employed self-ratings as well as questionnaires and interviews. A few further examples will be noted below.

Gardner [46] investigated hypotheses referring to impulsivity, checking various Rorschach factors against ratings by acquaintances and ratings based on the subjects' responses to the Rosenzweig Picture-Frustration Test. He found the following correlations to be statistically significant:

Acquaintanceship ratings	$(C + CF): FC$	$\rho = .879$
	$(CF + C): R$	$\rho = .865$
	$(FC + CF): R$	$\rho = .788$
	Sum M: Sum C	$\rho = .788$
	$P: R$	$\rho = .680$
Ratings based on Picture-Frustration Test	$(CF + C): FC$	$\rho = .815$
	$(CF + C): R$	$\rho = .680$
	$P: R$	$\rho = .855$

It may be noted that these ratings were made by psychologically trained raters, which may explain the significant positive relationships with Rorschach indications of impulsivity in comparison with the negligible relationships found by Holtzman [68] who used pooled ratings by residence-mates who were without psychological training.

Benton [14] quotes an unpublished thesis by Fitzgerald, who checked the hypothesis that $FC > CF$ indicates socialization of the expression of emotional reactions, using as the outside criterion a pooled rating of social adaptability. A rank-difference coefficient of 0.5 was found, indicating a moderate but significant relationship.

An exploratory study was undertaken by Rust [134] on correlates of the movement response, using the Levy movement cards, a special series of ink blots which specially facilitate M responses. M as an indicator of intelligence was checked against various levels of MA, CA, and IQ with children from 7½ to 16 years of age, but no significant differences were found. M as an indicator of "creativity" was checked against ratings of children by their art supervisors; a small but significant negative relationship was found, confirming the conclusions drawn by Roe [122] from her study of artists that M responses are not predictive signs of creative output. M as a sign of adjustment was confirmed by finding it to be significantly less frequent with schizophrenics and neurotics than with normals. Studies of patients with frontal lobe ablation showed, as the only significant finding, an increase in M following the removal of Brodman's Area 9.

Reference should be made also to studies testing the generality of the preference for color or form, which is reflected by the Rorschach ratio $FC : (CF+C)$; see pages 296–297. Oeser [105] presented his subjects first with a colored geometrical figure (a red triangle, for example). He then made a tachistoscopic presentation of eight colored geometrical figures arranged in a circle, having at one pole a figure matching the original one in color but not in form (a red circle), and at the other pole a figure matching the original in form but not in color (a blue triangle). The subjects were asked to select the figure that matched the original figure. He found that some subjects showed a consistent preference for the figure matching the original one in color, and that on the Rorschach they gave many color responses, particularly CF and C responses. Other subjects would consistently select the figure matching the original one in form; on the Rorschach these subjects gave either no color responses or only FC responses. Ruesch and Fensinger [133] found that subjects with many color responses on the Rorschach chose a variety of colors in drawings and spread these colors liberally over the surface of the paper, whereas subjects with few or no color responses on the Rorschach tended to make drawings using only one color and to use the color to mark the outline rather than to fill in the surface. An earlier study indirectly related to the $FC : (CF+C)$ is that by Brian and Goodenough [16] who showed that there are important age-differences in whether color or form are the preferred bases of matching geometrical figures. With children two years of age or younger matching is done largely on a basis of perseveration; but where there are consistent non-perseverative trends the matching is chiefly on the basis of form rather than color. Perseveration rapidly disappears and color becomes the preferred basis of matching with pre-school children, reaching a peak at four and a half. Then gradually form becomes predominant, until adulthood when 90 per cent of the subjects match on the basis of form rather than color. These findings seem closely in line with age-trends for color versus form preference, although it seems likely that the special group of adults used in this study showed a larger proportion of form-dominance than would be found with the general population.

Some of the most ingenious validation studies used experimental stress as the criterion of validity. Baker and Harris [7] set out to test the hypotheses that the $FC : CF$ ratio and $F+\%$ are indices of control. Working on the assumption that weak control would tend to give way under strain and result in less coördinated behavior, they produced stress by laboratory methods and measured loss of control in terms of loss of coördination in speech as indicated by word intelligibility and intensity variations. A correlation coefficient of .45 was found for $FC : CF$ and one of .41 for $F+\%$, although the small number of subjects precluded statistical significance.

Williams [163], using 25 subjects, investigated the predictive value of $F+\%$ and form-color integration as indices of control, the outside criterion being maintenance of intellectual efficiency (measured by the digit symbol test) in an experimentally induced stress situation. $F+\%$ was found to be correlated to the extent of .61 with the criterion, although the $F+\%$ to the colored plates alone was found to have a higher correlation, .72. The relationship of an index of form-color integration with the criterion was found to be .35, which falls slightly below the level of statistical significance with this number of subjects. However, the multiple r based on $F+\%$ and the form-color index was .82, which shows the latter index to be far from negligible.

Smith and George [149], using the Multiple-Choice Group Rorschach Test tested the hypotheses that $M : FM$ and $F\%$ are indices of control, using as a criterion the decrement of efficiency in performance on a digit symbol and information test when the tests were repeated after severe criticism of the previous performance. The correlation of $M : FM$ with the criterion was positive but not statistically significant. A significant non-linear relationship was found between $F\%$ and the criterion. Between 30 and 50 the $F\%$ shows a positive relationship with control, but with $F\%$ over 50 the control breaks down. There is also a suggestion of a break at 30%, indicating that subjects with a low $F\%$ may have good control. (Smith and George attribute this to control factors indicated in the $M, FK, Fc,$ and FC responses of a rich record, a reasonable conclusion for normal subjects of superior intelligence.) These relationships they take as clear confirmation of the Klopfer hypotheses relating to $F\%$ as an indication of control.

Brower [18] used experimental criteria, but since the significance of the criteria themselves is obscure, the study must be considered exploratory rather than a crucial test of interpretative hypotheses. Using 36 students he measured diastolic blood pressure, pulse pressure, and pulse rate before and after an experimental situation involving mirror drawing using direct vision, then mirror vision, then blindfolded. The pre-experimental diastolic blood pressure was found negatively related to FC; the post-experimental diastolic blood pressure was found negatively related to (VII, IX, X) %; the post-experimental pulse pressure was found positively related to F and (VIII, IX, X) %, while the pre-experimental pulse rate was found positively related to F. His descriptive conclusions are that higher constrictiveness and repressiveness are related to higher pulse rate prior to the experiment and to higher pulse pressure after the experiment; lower level adjustment to reality (FC) is related to higher residual blood pressure prior to the experiment; the higher the extraversial reserve—that is, (VIII, IX, X) %—the higher the post-experimental pulse pressure and the lower the diastolic blood pressure.

It has often been assumed that it is impossible to test the validity of one hypothesis at a time, because the Rorschach hypotheses are interrelated and the judgment involved in the application of each hypothesis derives from an examination of various interrelated aspects of the subject's performance. The "single variable" studies to date have been successful enough to contradict this assumption and to demonstrate that it is feasible to test one hypothesis at a time. The interrelatedness of *hypotheses* does not present the same kind of limitation that is presented by the fact that any one hypothesis is likely to involve a number of "scores." If the examiner's estimates or the interrelated scores themselves are checked against an outside criterion the difficulty may be overcome. This leaves as the major difficulty that of a suitable outside criterion. The experimental stress criteria have yielded the most clear-cut results to date, probably because the behavioral implications of the Rorschach hypotheses have been clear in the case of hypotheses related to "control." Ratings, particularly those by trained examiners, have seemed possible criteria for the testing of hypotheses with a behavioral reference, although negative results cannot be taken as crucial evidence of invalidity because of the limited reliability and validity of the ratings themselves. For the most part, the "single variable" studies have been limited to those hypotheses that are most obviously easy to check against an outside criterion. There remain many hypotheses and sub-hypotheses that will require either an extension of the hypothesis to predict the way in which the "inner dynamics" will be expressed in behavior, or the devising of a special test or situation as criterion—or both.

(5) Studies Involving Experimentally Induced States

A further type of validation study is that in which the state of the subject is experimentally modified at the time that he is examined by the Rorschach technique to see whether the artificially induced state is reflected in a changed Rorschach performance. Pre-experimental performance or a matched control group is used as a basis for comparison.

Eichler [34] sought to ascertain whether Rorschach performance under conditions of experimental stress would be reflected by an increase in the various indices of anxiety that have been proposed by various workers. He matched groups on the basis of the Behn-

Rorschach, and gave the control group the standard series of plates under standard conditions. The subjects in the experimental group were first given subtraction problems with intermittent electric shocks and then were given the Rorschach under the threat of further and stronger electric shock, although no shock was in fact given. Using the Hertz scoring categories [61] he found that some of the alleged indices of anxiety differentiated significantly between the stress group and the control group. Shading weight increased, W responses decreased, the total number of responses decreased, and oligophrenic details increased. Constriction as indicated by $F\%$ decreased, concomitant with the increase in shading responses. Certain other indices moved in the expected direction although the differences were not statistically significant: populars and color weight decreased and the number of rejections increased. He found the following indices to be non-differentiating: Dr, M, A, Ad, Hd, Anatomy, and shading shock. He concluded that experimentally induced anxiety offered evidence of the validity of certain indices of anxiety, but that it could not provide crucial evidence of the invalidity of the other indices which proved to be non-differentiating. It may be that these other indices reflect another kind of anxiety, or result from anxiety prolonged over a period much longer than that aroused in the experimental stress situation.

Hypnosis provides another method for artificially altering the state of the subject while undergoing the Rorschach examination, although hypnotic studies are open to the question of whether the hynotically induced state is comparable enough to the "genuine" state to provide validation evidence. Lane [84] checked the hypothesis that M responses are related to creativity by building up through repeated hypnotic suggestions the capacity of a subject to relive the "creative and introversive" role on command, this increase in creativity being a goal much desired by the subject as a result of treatment. When it had been established that the subject could assume this role under hypnosis, she was given the Rorschach first under standard conditions, then under hypnosis with the "creative and introversive" suggestion, and finally under hypnosis without suggestion. Under the influence of this general suggestion in the second testing (with no suggestions specific to perception of the Rorschach material) not only was there a marked increase of M responses, and hence a shift of the experience balance in an introversive direction, but also a marked increase in number of responses, original responses, a better reality sense, fewer W responses, fewer populars, and a lower $F\%$. All of these changes are compatible with the hypotheses relating to a creative and productive personality.

Sarbin [140], also using one subject, administered the Rorschach under the following four conditions: first under hypnosis with the suggestion to the subject that she was Madame Curie, then under hypnosis suggesting that she was Mae West, then under hypnosis without suggestion, and finally under standard conditions. When under the "Madame Curie" suggestion 21 of the 40 responses were "scientific" in content; in the "Mae West" state the subject gave 22 of 33 responses involving "costume"; in the hypnotic state without suggestion 15 of the 35 responses were associated with France, which was interpreted in the light of the subject's ambition to be an interpreter in the diplomatic service. In the normal state not one response was associated with any of these types of content. Sarbin concludes that an "Aufgabe" was set up in the hypnotic states, even in the situation where one had not been suggested deliberately. In these "Aufgabe" states the ratio between W and D was shifted towards W, and Z scores increased in comparison with the normal waking state. $A\%$ ranged from 12 to 20 in the hypnotic states, whereas it was 54 in the normal waking state. Five populars were given in the normal waking state, but few when the subject was under hypnotism. Otherwise the records were similar. It might be argued that the subject would have no way of feeling herself into the personalities of Madame Curie and Mae West except on a superficial level, which is reflected in the content changes; the "personality structure" reflected by the psychogram was unchanged.

A more pertinent study is that by Levine, Grassi, and Gerson [87] who administered the Rorschach to one subject nine times, first under standard conditions, then under hypnosis seven times with a variety of moods suggested to the subject, and finally under hypnosis suggesting a "normal" serene and composed mood. The first and last records were almost identical, which the authors take as evidence that the hypnotic state itself does not change the record. Under the influence of the hypnotically induced mood-changes, however, there were a number of shifts, all of which seemed in line with expectations from diagnostic group comparisons. For example, when a depressed mood was suggested there was a marked decrease of movement and color responses and a greatly increased $F\%$. When a depressed but conflictful mood was suggested there were similar changes but with an increase of m responses. Hypochondriacal fears resulted in decreased M and FM, increased m, no FC, 6 CF and 10 anatomy responses. Intense apprehension resulted in greatly increased Dr responses, decreased M, and increased shading responses, with some color responses still present. Gay, high spirits resulted in a more mediocre record than that obtained under normal conditions, with increased W, decreased d, FM greater than M, $F\%$ decreased from 44 to 17, and one C response. The authors conclude that although there is a stable core running throughout all records, the Rorschach performance is sensitive to changing conditions, attitudes, and emotional states. Although only one subject was studied in this thorough way, the results point up the importance of taking into consideration in the interpretation of the record the emotional state of the subject at the time of testing, and not attributing to "basic personality structure" features of performance that may be due to temporary emotional states.

Counts and Mensh [26] attempted to induce conflict and hostility towards one of the Rorschach examiners by means of post-hypnotic suggestion in a study using five subjects. The performance on the Rorschach under conditions of artificially induced hostility toward the examiner was compared with a previous test under standard conditions and with two subsequent tests after the suggestion had been removed. There were some changes from the initial to the second examination, especially an increase in S responses. But this and the other changes tended to persist in subsequent tests and, therefore, may have been due to simple retesting. The authors conclude that the personality structure remained stable despite hypnosis and despite the fact that psychiatric interviews indicated that the post-hypnotic suggestion had been effective in changing a "surface" hostility level. A possible explanation of the differences between this study and the others quoted above was the difference between post-hypnotic suggestion and suggestion operative during the hypnotic state itself, perhaps particularly because the subjects reported by Lane, by Sarbin, and by Levine, Grassi, and Gerson were completely amnesic for the Rorschach examinations given under hypnosis.

Finally, attention may be drawn to two studies in which hypnosis was used to induce age regressions. The first study, by Bergmann, Graham, and Leavitt [15], pointed to Rorschach changes concomitant with age regression but did not utilize any other criteria to indicate that age regression had in fact been obtained. Mercer and Gibson [96], however, used the Stanford-Binet vocabulary test and drawings rated on the Goodenough scale to establish that the intellectual level of performance in each testing was compatible with the age to which the subject had been suggested to regress. The Rorschach was administered four times, three times with age regression, to 6, 10, and 14 years respectively (these years being suggested in terms of key events in the subject's life) and a fourth time under standard conditions. In each case the Rorschach production seemed consistent with the age level in question. Of major interest was the way in which certain of the original and disturbed responses in each testing were found to be strikingly related to disturbing events of the life experience of the subject at that age—events that had been discussed in the course of therapeutic interviews.

In general, the studies on the effect of artificially induced states on the Rorschach performance tend to support interpretative hypotheses. However, they point to the sensitivity of the test to "set" and temporary emotional states, thus emphasizing the need for caution in interpreting the performance, the need for taking into account the subject's state at the time, and the need for care in establishing rapport and structuring the situation so as to establish the desired set and to put the subject at his ease.

(6) Clinical Studies

In the introductory paragraphs to this chapter it was stated that there is no sharp dividing line between validation research and the clinical use of the Rorschach technique. However, the chief emphasis of the discussion of validation has been, up to this point, upon non-clinical methods and criteria. This should not be taken to imply that the clinical field is barren of aid to scientific validation research. Indeed, in the present state of our knowledge there are some hypotheses that probably can be checked only against clinical criteria. It is true that these criteria tend to be less reliable and explicit than would be ideally desirable and that they involve many problems of communication. It is also probably true that a mere checking back and forth between Rorschach data and clinical material can provide no definitive evidence of the validity of interpretative hypotheses. Nevertheless, just such a checking back and forth seems at the present time to be the most promising method for refining certain of the Rorschach hypotheses towards reformulation in more precise and behavioral terms so that they can then be checked with all the proper scientific safeguards.

Young and Higginbotham [166] undertook to check a variety of interpretative indices, using as their outside criterion the behavior of 21 boys at a psychiatric summer camp as evaluated by trained clinical workers. They found that simple quantitative enumeration of single determinants did not match up with the behavioral judgments on the whole, although there was congruency of the findings when Rorschach judgments were based on the total configuration of the record. The best single determinant in predicting behavior was found to be FC, which related to socialized control as hypothesized. The ratio $(FM+m) : (Fc+c+C')$ and (VII, IX, X)% were found to be more closely related to introversive and extratensive tendencies than the $M : Sum\ C$ ratio. (This seems a reasonable finding in a group of children who are disturbed and with whom M responses would probably be few in most instances.) The intellectual estimates not only checked closely with IQ in 16 of 19 cases, but also where the estimate deviated from the IQ it was found to agree qualitatively with the picture of functioning at the camp better than did the IQ. The authors imply that the chief value of their study was to emphasize the superiority of judgments based on the configuration of the whole record to inferences drawn from the various scores and proportions separately. The study would have been very much more valuable had they been able to suggest a behavioral extension of the interpretative hypotheses in the light of the excellent opportunity provided by the setting for comparing hypothesized inner dynamics with overt behavior.

When the Rorschach technique is used in a clinical setting there is no guarantee that Rorschach hypotheses will be checked against clinical material in any crucial way, even to the extent undertaken by Young and Higginbotham. In many clinical settings the Rorschach is used only in the diagnostic procedure with no systematic attempt to check Rorschach findings against subsequent findings about the patient as a result of treatment. The only material available at the purely diagnostic level tends to be lacking in detail and incomplete to the extent that there is no critical basis for checking on agreements or discrepancies between test findings and history and interview material. The pressure of work tends to eliminate the possibility of a follow-up check even where highly detailed records of material emerging in subsequent treatment sessions are accessible to the psychologist. Yet the observations of the patient during treatment—whether this be in terms of general behavior, or further history elicited in interview, or responses to the therapist or the therapeutic group—provide a rich source of accurate knowledge about the patient, information that is extremely difficult to obtain by direct observation of the individual in ordinary life activities. This material has been neglected, at least as material for systematic studies.

A study by Hertzman and Pearce [65] illustrates both the advantages and drawbacks of clinical validation studies. These authors undertook an investigation of the significance of the way in which human figures are identified and described in the Rorschach protocol. Protocols were obtained from twelve subjects prior to the beginning of intensive psychotherapy. After a median lapse of ten months each human-figure response was checked with the therapist to ascertain what meaning it could have had for the subject in the light of the attitudes expressed, in the course of therapeutic interviews, towards himself and the key figures in his life. Hertzman and Pearce state that the responses likely to have personal meaning were easily picked out from the protocols. However, even with the assistance of the therapist it was not always possible to interpret what the meaning could be, although this was more easily done in the case of subjects giving a relatively large number of human responses than for subjects who gave few; 85 per cent were identified in the former group and only 54 per cent in the latter. The investigators suggest that subjects giving few human responses need to avoid self-awareness and need not to know their deeper attitudes towards others. By far the greatest number of human responses, in cases where the meaning could be identified, seemed to reflect attitudes towards the self; some seemed to reflect attitudes towards the parents; while a few seemed to reflect a general attitude towards the world.

It is easy to criticize this study on a number of counts, chiefly the subjectivity of the judgment of the therapist of the subject's attitudes and the subjective distortion that might be a factor in a judgment of the congruency of the therapist's and psychologist's opinion. Moreover, it is not known to what extent attitudes towards self and others are merely two sides of one medal. Nevertheless, it would seem that a check against material collected by the therapist might be a better criterion for the subject's attitudes towards himself and others than any other available criterion, certainly better than isolated interviews or questionnaires or self-ratings.

Earlier in this chapter it was suggested that Rorschach studies of patients undergoing treatment would provide criteria for examining changes in Rorschach performance in comparison with changes known to have been effected through treatment. It was pointed out that a major disadvantage at present is that the criteria of changes due to treatment are themselves ill-defined. It was further seen that Rorschach studies of patients undergoing treatment seemed to reflect an indecision between using response to treatment as a criterion against which Rorschach changes could be checked, or using Rorschach changes as a criterion for the effect of treatment. Moreover, there seemed to be a tendency to shape the study towards setting forth Rorschach "signs" on the basis of which response to treatment could be predicted, without any apparent attempt to elucidate how it is that certain "signs" seem related to successful or unsuccessful response to treatment. A more useful approach to treatment as a criterion would seem to be to trace relationships between performance in the Rorschach and performance during treatment, not merely the ultimate "effect" of treatment.

Sutherland [151] suggests that the patient's response to the transference situation in both individual and group therapy is a valuable criterion against which the performance in a projective test situation should be checked. Such a check, he suggests, would be helpful in building up a basis for assessing the importance of the transference situation in testing itself. It might be added that a check between the Rorschach worker and therapist should yield as a by-product an improvement in communication of Rorschach findings in terms intelligible to and useful to the therapist. Most important, the detailed account of the patient's behavior and verbalization under treatment should provide an invaluable basis for ascertaining some of the behavioral and attitudinal correlates of the Rorschach performance. After such correlates have been established on some systematic basis, the performance in the therapeutic situation could provide an outside criterion for prediction studies. It is premature, however, to suggest prediction of behavior under therapy as a major method for validating the Rorschach technique at the present time. The behavioral correlates of Rorschach performance first must be worked out on some basis more communicable than that which rests upon the clinical experience of the individual worker.

(7) Prediction Studies

The most crucial and demanding criterion of validity is the prediction of the behavior of the individual case. This criterion has been used little in test validation, except perhaps in a private and clinical way without systematic coverage of a number of subjects. Psychometric test validation has remained largely on a basis of statistical prediction of a large group of cases—with little or no attention paid to the few exceptions—if the general trend points to the validity of the test. It is not statistical prediction that is under discussion at this point, but rather the precise prediction of the behavior of the individual case under specified conditions. Since it has been proposed that the approach to the validation of the Rorschach technique should not be as a whole, indeed not as a "test," but rather should proceed by testing the component interpretative hypotheses, and since the clinical use of the Rorschach is geared towards the understanding of the individual rather than as a statistical screening device, it is entirely appropriate to view the prediction of the individual case as a criterion of validity—indeed, the ultimate criterion.

Approach through prediction promises certain important advantages. Subjects can be tested individually and interpretation carried out using the full resources of the technique, since the numbers of subjects could be kept small where exactness of prediction rather than statistical tendencies are involved. The prediction could be made on the basis of integration of a number of interpretative hypotheses, although the precise basis of the prediction would have to be stated. The design of the experiment could exploit the sensitivity of the instrument to change by predicting changed behavior under changed life conditions, or by experimentally varying test conditions and predicting the result.

Although some writers who have considered the problem of Rorschach validation consider that any attempt to depart from the holistic basis of interpretation is improper, others such as MacFarlane [90] and Sargent [141] propose prediction as the best and perhaps the only satisfactory method of validation of techniques such as the Rorschach. Myers [103] extends this point of view to cover all clinical hypotheses. Yet there are formidable difficulties to be encountered with this approach, perhaps greater than with any other approach to validation.

One major difficulty is in ascertaining the exact conditions towards which the prediction is made, and in knowing in advance the precise demands these conditions would make on individuals of varying personalities. The failure to have made this extension of understanding would seem to have been a prominent factor in the failure of a recent large-scale attempt reported by Kelley and Fiske [75] to predict the success in training in clinical psychology of a number of post-graduate students from a large variety of bases, including the Rorschach technique. Sarason [138] points out that another drawback in this prediction study was that the subjects came to the selection situation with varying sets and involvements. He cautions that prediction from a test to another situation must take into account not only the test results but also all the various determinants in the test situation and the extent to which they entered in to determine the test results. Such factors include instructions, purpose of testing, time and place of testing, the examiner, and attitudinal factors related to previous learning. Thus, it is necessary to have precise knowledge both of the situation one is predicting from and that to which the prediction is made. It is entirely likely that present knowledge of the effect of set, personality of the examiner, and other "test determinants"—inadequate though it may be—is more precise and reliable than present knowledge of the psychological demands and conditions of situations towards which predictions might be made, especially knowledge of the ways in which those conditions and demands might be expected to affect personalities of various kinds.

A further source of difficulty that has been touched on previously is that the Rorschach hypotheses themselves are rarely formulated in such a way that the behavioral implication is clear-cut. To test the validity of the present hypotheses against a prediction criterion would involve the extension of the hypothesis; to demonstrate the invalidity of the extension would not necessarily demonstrate that the underlying hypothesis itself was invalid. New extensions would have to be made and tested out. If one of these extensions were found to be a satisfactory basis of prediction, it would be the extended hypothesis that is found to be valid rather than the underlying one. This is not to imply that a method of validation by successive clinical predictions, such as that suggested by Rosenzweig [125], would not be possible or valuable. It must be recognized, however, that validation research of this kind would be basic personality research, involving the formulation, extension, and modification of hypotheses, not merely the validation of ready-made hypotheses. In investigating how certain modes of responding to test material are related to behavior of individual subjects in specified situations one is faced with a special case of the basic problem of psychological science. When validation research is formulated in this way, it is manifestly impossible to insist that the "test" should be "validated" before it is used.

As Rosenzweig [124] suggests, a first step in the approach to prediction from psychodiagnostic techniques would be inquiry into the various levels of behavior represented by the test responses so that a distinction between them may be established. According to Rosenzweig, Level I is that of self-critical or censored responses from which one may predict towards other situations in which the subject is self-consciously critical. Level II is that of overt behavior; if the subject manifests in the test situation a certain type of overt behavior, one may predict that he will behave similarly in similar externally defined situations. Level III is that of implicit behavior, which requires interpretation from the manifest content of the response to underlying factors. Although projective techniques are geared primarily to Level III, the responses in the projective test situation may be in part at either of the other two levels. From which level is prediction to be made? Does manifest aggressive content in the test performance mean that the subject will act aggressively, even when self-critical, and hence is self-accepting in this respect? Or does it mean that he will behave aggressively without accepting his aggression, perhaps not even recognizing it? Or does it mean that he feels hostile, but does not express it in behavior? Or does it mean that there is unconscious hostility that finds indirect outlets of expression?

Korner [82] holds that projective techniques not only explore perceptual processes but also explore needs and fantasies. She suggests that it is a frequent clinical error to predict too literally from fantasy to reality behavior. She queries whether it is the purpose of projective techniques to predict reality behavior and suggests that the contribution which they "make in the area of diagnosis and fantasy exploration is sufficiently valuable in and of itself to justify their use." She concludes:

> Instead of deploring the fact that fantasy and reality behavior do not necessarily correspond, as we currently seem to be doing, we can use projective techniques as a short-cut to a person's fantasy and ideational life, which then can be compared and examined in the light of his present and past actual behavior patterns. After all, is it not in the adaptations, the compromises and the balances achieved between needs or fantasies and the demands of reality, that we find the key to personality at work? [82, page 627]

Korner is concerned chiefly in her paper with the use of projective techniques. She says, regarding prediction:

> For prediction, ego psychology has to solve two important problems, problems which are so complex that perhaps they never will be solved. The first one is the detection of all the innumerable variables which are at work in the process of an individual's reality adaptation to a need. It is probably not only the existence of these variables but also their interaction which determines what form his adaptation will take. The other problem is to find the secret of ego synthesis which probably consists of an organismic process involving more than the sum of the variables at work, and which possibly is at the root of all the clinical discrepancies. . . . [82, page 625]

There would seem to be a point of resolution of the impasse between those who insist that precise prediction of individual behavior is the only satisfactory criterion of the validity of the Rorschach interpretative hypotheses and those who, like Korner, imply that the predictive criterion is an impossible one in our present state of knowledge about personality function. To achieve this resolution requires the recognition that the validation of the hypotheses about personality functioning derived from the Rorschach test performance is inextricably linked with basic research into the functioning of the individual personality. There is at present no adequate basis for the selection of truly crucial outside criteria for the validity of Rorschach hypotheses. Such criteria can only gradually be developed as knowledge of personality increases. It is proposed that the Rorschach technique is a tool useful in basic personality research, although obviously not the only tool. It would seem presumptuous for either the Rorschach enthusiast or the Rorschach critic to insist that the validation of this tool should take precedence over basic personality research. The lack of established validity as a tool of personality research is by no means limited to the Rorschach technique; the same difficulty of "the outside criterion" applies to all. It therefore seems reasonable to take the viewpoint that validation of the tools should proceed with and through the basic research in which they are used. The tools are important, but to place whole emphasis on perfecting the tools distracts attention from the basic task for which they are designed. Prediction cannot be denied as the ultimate criterion of validity of the technique, but it should be remembered that through prediction one is testing an hypothesis about the functioning of an individual personality. Validation of the hypothesis serves two purposes: validation of one component of the technique, and extension of knowledge about personality.

As may be seen, prediction is not the only approach to the validation of the interpretative hypotheses that make up the Rorschach technique. Although the other approaches have limitations and defects, they may be used as a basis for the refinement of hypotheses, for elimination of the more obvious over-generalizations, and specification of the more obvious conditions within which the hypothesis holds. Although precise prediction is perhaps only an ideal towards which psychological science aspires, it is not fitting to reject it as an impossible goal. As our knowledge of personality functioning becomes more precise, this knowledge will be reworked into the tools for investigating personality, making them more precise. In the meantime, the Rorschach technique must be considered a partly finished and continuously developing method, available for investigations into the development and function of the individual personality, and to be brought to a more finished state through use in such investigations.

References

1. Abt, L. E., and Bellak, L. *Projective Psychology*. New York: Alfred A. Knopf, Inc.; 1950.

2. Ainsworth, Mary D. "Some Problems of Validation of Projective Techniques," *Brit. J. Med. Psychol.*, 1951, 24, 151–161.

3. ——, and Boston, M. "Psychodiagnostic Assessments of a Child after Prolonged Separation in Early Childhood," *Brit. J. Med. Psychol.*, 1952, 25, 169–201.

4. Allen, R. M. "The Influence of Color in the Rorschach Test on Reaction Time in a Normal Population," *J. Proj. Tech.*, 1951, 15, 481–485.

5. ——; Manne, S. H.; and Stiff, M. "The Role of Color in Rorschach's Test: a Preliminary Normative Report on a College Student Population," *J. Proj. Tech.*, 1951, 15, 235–242.

6. Altus, W. D., and Thompson, G. M. "The Rorschach as a Measure of Intelligence," *J. Consult. Psychol.*, 1949, 13, 341–347.

7. Baker, L. M. and Harris, J. S. "The Validation of Rorschach Test Results against Laboratory Behavior," *J. Clin. Psychol.*, 1949, 5, 161–164.

8. Baughman, E. "Rorschach Scores as a Function of Examiner Difference," *J. Proj. Tech.*, 1951, 15, 243–249.

9. Beck, S. J. *Rorschach's Test* (2 vols.). New York: Grune & Stratton, Inc.; 1944.

10. Behn-Rorschach Tafeln. Bern: Hans Huber.

11. Bell, J. E. *Projective Techniques.* New York: Longmans, Green & Company; 1948.

12. ——. "The Case of Gregor: Interpretation of Test Data," *Rorschach Res. Exch. & J. Proj. Tech.*, 1949, 13, 433–468.

13. Benjamin, J. D., and Ebaugh, F. G. "The Diagnostic Validity of the Rorschach Test," *Amer. J. Psychiat.*, 1938, 94, 1163–1178.

14. Benton, A. L. "The Experimental Validation of the Rorschach Test," *Brit. J. Med. Psychol.*, 1950, 23, 45–58.

15. Bergmann, M. S.; Graham, H.; and Leavitt, H. C. "Rorschach Exploration of Consecutive Hypnotic Age Level Regressions," *Psychosom. Med.*, 1947, 9, 20–28.

16. Brian, C., and Goodenough, F. "The Relative Potency of Color and Form Perceptions at Various Ages," *J. Exp. Psychol.*, 1929, 12, 197–213.

17. Brosin, H. W., and Fromm, E. O. "Some Principles of Gestalt Psychology in the Rorschach Experiment," *Ror. Res. Exch.*, 1942, 6, 1–15.

18. Brower, D. "The Relation between Certain Rorschach Factors and Cardiovascular Activity before and after Visual-motor Conflict," *J. Gen. Psychol.*, 1947, 37, 93–95.

19. Buckle, M. B., and Holt, N. F. "Comparison of Rorschach and Behn Ink-blots," *J. Proj. Tech.*, 1951, 15, 486–493.

20. Buhler, C.; Buhler, K.; and Lefever, D. W. "Development of the Basic Rorschach Score with Manual of Directions," Basic Rorschach Standardization Study I, 1948.

21. Buker, S. L., and Williams, M. "Color as a Determinant of Responsiveness to Rorschach Cards in Schizophrenia," *J. Consult. Psychol.*, 1951, 7, 196–202.

22. Carlson, Rae, "A Normative Study of Rorschach Responses of Eight-year-old Children," *J. Proj. Tech.*, 1952, 16, 56–65.

23. Carp, A. L., and Shavzin, A. R. "The Susceptibility to Falsification of the Rorschach Psychodiagnostic Technique," *J. Consult. Psychol.*, 1950, 14, 230–233.

24. Clark, J. H. "Some MMPI Correlates of Color Responses in the Group Rorschach," *J. Consult. Psychol.*, 1948, 12, 384–386.

25. Coffin, T. E. "Some Conditions of Suggestion and Suggestibility," *Psychol. Monogr.*, 1941, 53, #41.

26. Counts, R. M., and Mensh, I. N. "Personality Characteristics in Hypnotically Induced Hostility," *J. Clin. Psychol.*, 1950, 6, 325–330.

27. Cronbach, L. J. "Response Sets and Test Validity," *Educ. Psychol. Measmt.*, 1946, 6, 475–494.

28. ——. "A Validation Design for Qualitative Studies of Personality," *J. Consult. Psychol.*, 1948, 12, 365–374.

29. ——. "Pattern Tabulation: a Statistical Method for Analysis of Limited Patterns of Scoring with Particular Reference to the Rorschach Test," *Educ. Psychol. Measmt.*, 1949, 9, 149–171.

30. ——. "Statistical Methods Applied to Rorschach Scores: a Review," *Psychol. Bull.*, 1949, 46, 393–429.

31. ——. "Further Evidence on Response Sets and Test Design," *Educ. Psychol. Measmt.*, 1950, 10, 3–21.

32. ——. "Statistical Methods for Multiscore Tests," *J. Clin. Psychol.*, 1950, 6, 21–26.

33. Dubrovner, R. J.; Von Lackum, W. J.; and Jost, H. "A Study of the Effect of Color on Productivity and Reaction Time in the Rorschach Test," *J. Clin. Psychol.*, 1950, 6, 331–336.

34. Eichler, R. M. "Experimental Stress and Alleged Rorschach Indices of Anxiety," *J. Abnorm. Soc. Psychol.*, 1951, 46, 344–355.

35. ——. "A Comparison of the Rorschach and Behn Ink-blot Tests," *J. Consult. Psychol.*, 1951, 15, 185–189.

36. ——. "Some Comments on the Controlling of Differences in Responses on the Rorschach Test," *Psychol. Bull.*, 1951, 48, 257–259.

37. Elizur, A. "Content Analysis of the Rorschach with Regard to Anxiety and Hostility," *Rorschach Res. Exch. & J. Proj. Tech.*, 1949, 13, 247–284.

38. Ferguson, G. A. "Approaches to the Experimental Study of the Rorschach Test," *Canad. J. Psychol.*, 1951, 5, 157–166.

39. Fonda, C. P. "The Nature and Meaning of the Rorschach White Space Responses," *J. Abnorm. Soc. Psychol.*, 1951, 46, 367–377.

40. Ford, Mary. *The Application of the Rorschach Test to Young Children.* Minneapolis: University of Minnesota Press; 1946.

41. Forer, B. R. "The Fallacy of Personal Validation," *J. Abnorm. Soc. Psychol.*, 1949, 44, 118–123.

42. Fosberg, I. A. "Rorschach Reactions under Varied Instructions," *Rorschach Res. Exch.*, 1938, 3, 12–31.

43. ——. "An Experimental Study of Rorschach Reactions under Varied Conditions," *Rorschach Res. Exch.*, 1941, 5, 72–84.

44. ——. "How Do Subjects Attempt to Fake Results on the Rorschach Test?" *Rorschach Res. Exch.*, 1943, 7, 119–121.

45. Frank, L. K. *Projective Methods.* Springfield, Illinois: Charles C. Thomas; 1948.

46. Gardner, R. W. "Impulsivity as Indicated by Rorschach Test Factors," *J. Consult. Psychol.*, 1951, 15, 464–468.

47. Gibby, R. G. "The Stability of Certain Rorschach Variables under Conditions of Experimentally Induced Sets: I. The Intellectual Variables," *J. Proj. Tech.*, 1951, 15, 3–26.

48. Goldfarb, W. "The Effects of Early Institutional Care on Adolescent Personality," *J. Exp. Educ.*, 1943, 12, 106–129.

49. ——. " Rorschach Test Differences between Family Reared. Institution Reared, and Schizophrenic Children," *Amer. J. Orthopsychiat.*, 1949, 19, 624–633.

50. ——, and Klopfer, B. "Rorschach Characteristics of 'Institution Children,'" *Rorschach Res. Exch.*, 1944, 8, 92–100.

51. Graham, Virginia T. "Psychological Studies of Hypoglycemia Therapy," *J. Psychol.*, 1940, 10, 327–358.

52. Grayson, H. M., and Tolman, Ruth S. "A Semantic Study of Concepts of Clinical Psychologists and Psychiatrists," *J. Abnorm. Soc. Psychol.*, 1950, 45, 216–231.

53. Griffith, R. M. "Test-retest Similarities of the Rorschachs of Patients without Retention, Korsakoff," *J. Proj. Tech.*, 1951, 15, 516–525.

54. Halpern, Florence. "Rorschach Interpretation of the Personality Structure of Schizophrenics Who Benefit from Insulin Therapy," *Psychiat. Quart.*, 1940, 14, 826–833.

55. Harris, R. E., and Christiansen, C. "Prediction of Response to Brief Psychotherapy," *J. Psychol.*, 1946, 21, 269–284.

56. Harrower, M. R., and Steiner, M. E. *Large-scale Rorschach Techniques.* Springfield, Illinois: Charles C. Thomas; 1945.

57. ——, and Steiner, M. E. *A Manual for Psychodiagnostic Ink Blots.* Springfield, Illinois: Charles C. Thomas; 1949.

58. Hertz, Marguerite R. "Reliability of the Rorschach Ink-blot Test," *J. Appl. Psychol.*, 1934, 18, 461–477.

59. ——. "Rorschach Norms for an Adolescent Age Group," *Child Develpm.*, 1935, 6, 69–76.

60. ——. "The Validity of the Rorschach Method," *Amer. J. Orthopsychiat.*, 1941, 11, 512–520.

61. ——. "The Scoring of the Rorschach Ink-blot Method as Developed by the Brush Foundation," *Rorschach Res. Exch.*, 1942, 6, 16–27.

62. ——. "Rorschach: Twenty Years After," *Psychol. Bull.*, 1942, 39, 529–572.

63. ———. "Current Problems in Rorschach Theory and Technique," *J. Proj. Tech.*, 1951, 15, 307–338.

64. ———, and Rubenstein, B. "A Comparison of Three 'Blind' Rorschach Analyses," *Amer. J. Orthopsychiat.*, 1939, 9, 295–315.

65. Hertzman, M., and Pearce, J. "The Personal Meaning of the Human Figure in the Rorschach," *Psychiatry,* 1947, 10, 413–422.

66. Holzberg, J. D., and Wexler, M. "The Predictability of Schizophrenic Performance on the Rorschach Test," *J. Consult. Psychol.*, 1950, 14, 395–399.

67. Holtzman, W. H. "Validation Studies of the Rorschach Test: Shyness and Gregariousness in the Normal Superior Adult," *J. Clin. Psychol.*, 1950, 6, 343–347.

68. ———. "Validation Studies of the Rorschach Test: Impulsiveness in the Normal Superior Adult," *J. Clin. Psychol.*, 1950, 6, 348–351.

69. Hsü, E. H. "The Rorschach Responses and Factor Analysis," *J. Gen. Psychol.*, 1947, 37, 129–138.

70. Hunter, M. E. "The Practical Value of the Rorschach Test in a Psychological Clinic," *Amer. J. Orthopsychiat.*, 1939, 9, 278–294.

71. Hutt, M. L. "Assessment of Individual Personality by Projective Techniques," *J. Proj. Tech.*, 1951, 15, 388–393.

72. ———; Gibby, R.; Milton, E.; and Pottharst, K. "The Effect of Varied Experimental Sets on Rorschach Test Performance," *J. Proj. Tech.*, 1950, 14, 181–186.

73. Kay, L. W., and Vorhaus, P. G. "Rorschach Reactions in Early Childhood: Part II. Intellectual Aspects of Personality Development," *Rorschach Res. Exch.*, 1943, 7, 71–77.

74. Kelley, D. M.; Margulies, H.; and Barrera, S. E. "The Stability of the Rorschach Method as Demonstrated in Electric Convulsive Therapy Cases." *Rorschach Res. Exch.*, 1941, 5, 35–43.

75. Kelley, E. L., and Fiske, D. W. "The Prediction of Success in the VA Training Program in Clinical Psychology," *Amer. Psychologist,* 1950, 5, 395–406.

76. Kerr, M. "The Rorschach Test Applied to Children," *Brit. J. Psychol.*, 1934, 25, 170–185.

77. Kimble, G. A. "Social Influence on Rorschach Records," *J. Abnorm. Soc. Psychol.*, 1945, 40, 89–93.

78. Kisker, G. W. "A Projective Approach to Personality Patterns during Insulin Shock and Metrazol Convulsive Therapy," *J. Abnorm. Soc. Psychol.*, 1942, 37, 120–124.

79. Klebanoff, S. G. "A Rorschach Study of Operational Fatigue in Army Air Forces Personnel," *Rorschach Res. Exch.*, 1946, 10, 115–120.

80. Klopfer, B., and Kelley, D. M. *The Rorschach Technique.* Yonkers, New York: World Book Company; 1942.

81. ———, and Margulies, H. "Rorschach Reactions in Early Childhood," *Rorschach Res. Exch.*, 1941, 5, 1–23.

82. Korner, Anneliese F. "Theoretical Considerations Concerning the Scope and Limitations of Projective Techniques," *J. Abnorm. Soc. Psychol.*, 1950, 45, 619–627.

83. Krugman, Judith I. "A Clinical Validation of the Rorschach with Problem Children," *Rorschach Res. Exch.*, 1942, 5, 61–70.

84. Lane, Barbara. "A Validation Test of the Rorschach Movement Interpretation," *Amer. J. Orthopsychiat.*, 1948, 18, 292–296.

85. Lazarus, R. S. "An Experimental Analysis of the Influence of Color on the Protocol of the Rorschach Test," *J. Abnorm. Soc. Psychol.*, 1949, 44, 506–516.

86. Levi, J. "Rorschach Patterns Predicting Success or Failure in the Rehabilitation of the Physically Handicapped," *J. Abnorm. Soc. Psychol.*, 1951, 46, 240–244.

87. Levine, K. M.; Grassi, J. R.; and Gerson, M. J. "Hypnotically Induced Mood Changes in the Verbal and Graphic Rorschach, a Case Study," *Rorschach Res. Exch.*, 1943, 7, 130–144.

88. Lord, Edith. Experimentally induced variations in Rorschach performance. *Psychol. Monogr.*, 1950, 64, #316.

89. Luchins, A. A. Situational and attitudinal influences on Rorschach responses. *Amer. J. Psychiat.*, 1947, 103, 780–784.

90. MacFarlane, Jean W. Problems of validation inherent in projective methods. *Amer. J. Orthopsychiat.*, 1942, 12, 405–410.

91. McFate, M. Q., and Orr, F. G. Through adolescence with the Rorschach. *Rorschach Res. Exch. & J. Proj. Tech.*, 1949, 13, 302–319.

92. McLeod, H. A Rorschach study with pre-school children. *J. Proj. Tech.*, 1950, 14, 453–463.

93. McReynolds, P. "Perception of Rorschach Concepts as Related to Personality Deviations," *J. Abnorm. Soc. Psychol.*, 1951, 46, 131–141.

94. Meer, B., and Singer, J. L. "A Note on the 'Father' and 'Mother' Cards in the Rorschach Ink-blots," *J. Consult. Psychol.*, 1950, 14, 482–484.

95. Mensh, I. N. "Statistical Techniques in Present-day Psychodiagnostics," *Psychol. Bull.*, 1950, 47, 475–492.

96. Mercer, Margaret, and Gibson, R. W. "Rorschach Content Analysis in Hypnosis: Chronological Age Regression," *J. Clin. Psychol.*, 1950, 6, 352–358.

97. Meyer, B. T. "An Investigation of Color Shock in the Rorschach Test," *J. Clin. Psychol.*, 1951, 7, 367–370.

98. Meyer, G., and Thompson, J. "The Performance of Kindergarten Children on the Rorschach Test: a Normative Study," *J. Proj. Tech.*, 1952, 16, 86–111.

99. Miale, F. R., and Harrower-Erickson, M. R. "Personality Structure in the Psychoneuroses," *Rorschach Res. Exch.*, 1940, 4, 71–74.

100. Morris, W. W. "Prognostic Possibilities of the Rorschach Method in Metrazol Therapy," *Amer. J. Psychiat.*, 1943, 100, 222–230.

101. Munroe, Ruth L. "Prediction of the Adjustment and Academic Performance of College Students by a Modification of the Rorschach Method," *Appl. Psychol. Monogr.* 1945, #7.

102. ———. "Projective Methods in Group Testing," *J. Consult. Psychol.*, 1948, 12, 8–15.

103. Myers, C. R. "Prediction in Clinical Psychology," *Canad. J. Psychol.*, 1950, 4, 97–108.

104. Odom, C. L. "A Study of the Time Required To Do a Rorschach Examination," *J. Proj. Tech.*, 1950, 14, 464–468.

105. Oeser, O. "Some Experiments on the Abstraction of Forms and Color," *Brit. J. Psychol.*, 1932, 22, 287–323.

106. Palmer, J. O. "A Dual Approach to Rorschach Validation: A Methodological Study," *Psychol. Monogr.*, 1951, 65, #325.

107. Pascal, G. R.; Ruesch, H. A.; Devine, C. A.; and Suttell, P. J. "A Study of Genital Symbols on the Rorschach Test," *J. Abnorm. Soc. Psychol.*, 1950, 45, 286–295.

108. Paulsen, A. "Rorschachs of School Beginners," *Rorschach Res. Exch.*, 1941, 5, 24–29.

109. Perlman, Janet A. "Color and the Validity of the Rorschach 8–9–10%," *J. Consult. Psychol.*, 1951, 15, 122–126.

110. Piotrowski, Z. A. "Rorschach Manifestations of Improvement in Insulin Treated Schizophrenics," *Psychosom. Med.*, 1939, 1, 508–526.

111. ——. "The Rorschach Method as a Prognostic Aid in the Insulin Shock Treatment of Schizophrenics," *Psychiat. Quart.*, 1941, 15, 807–822.

112. ——. "A Rorschach Compendium," *Psychiat. Quart.*, 1947, 21, 79–101.

113. Rabin, A. I. "Statistical Problems Involved in Rorschach Patterning," *J. Clin. Psychol.*, 1950, 6, 19–21.

114. ——, and Beck, S. J. "Genetic Aspects of Some Rorschach Factors," *Amer. J. Orthopsychiat.*, 1950, 20, 595–599.

115. ——, and Sanderson, M. H. "An Experimental Inquiry into Some Rorschach Procedures," *J. Clin. Psychol.*, 1947, 3, 216–225.

116. Ranzoni, J. H.; Grant, M. Q.; and Ives, V. "Rorschach 'Card Pull' in a Normal Adolescent Group," *J. Proj. Tech.*, 1950, 14, 107–133.

117. Rapaport, D. *Diagnostic Psychological Testing.* Chicago: Year Book Publishers; 1944 (Vol. I), 1946 (Vol. II).

118. Rickers-Ovsiankina, Maria. "Some Theoretical Considerations Regarding the Rorschach Method," *Rorschach Res. Exch.*, 1943, 7, 41–53.

119. Rioch, Margaret J. "The Use of the Rorschach Test in the Assessment of Change in Patients under Psychotherapy," *Psychiatry*, 1949, 12, 427–434.

120. Rockwell, F. V.; Welch, L.; Kubis, J.; and Fisichelli, V. "Changes in Palmar Skin Resistance during the Rorschach Test: I. Color Shock and Psychoneurotic Reactions," *Mschr. Psychiat. Neurol.*, 1947, 113, 129–152.

121. ——; Welch, L.; Kubis, J.; and Fisichelli, V. "Changes in Palmar Skin Resistance during the Rorschach Test: II. The Effect of Repetition with Color Removed," *Mschr. Psychiat. Neurol.*, 1948, 116, 321–345.

122. Roe, Anne. "Painting and Personality," *Rorschach Res. Exch.*, 1946, 10, 86–100.

123. Rorschach, H. *Psychodiagnostics* (Transl. by P. Lemkau and B. Kronenberg). New York: Grune & Stratton, Inc.; 1942.

124. Rosenzweig, S. "Levels of Behavior in Psychodiagnosis with Special Reference to the Picture-Frustration Study," *Amer. J. Orthopsychiat.*, 1950, 20, 63–72.

125. ——. "A Method of Validation by Successive Clinical Predictions," *J. Abnorm. Soc. Psychol.;* 1950, 45, 507–509.

126. ——. "Idiodynamics in Personality Theory with Special Reference to Projective Methods," *Psychol. Rev.,* 1951, 58, 213–223.

127. Ross, W. D. "A Contribution to the Objectification of Group Rorschach Scoring," *Rorschach Res. Exch.,* 1943, 7, 70–71.

128. ——. "A Quantitative Use of the Rorschach Method," *Amer. J. Psychiat.,* 1944, 101, 100–104.

129. ——. "The Relation between Rorschach Interpretation and Clinical Diagnosis," *J. Proj. Tech.,* 1950, 14, 5–14.

130. ——, and Block, S. L. "The Use of Projective Techniques in the Evaluation of Neurosurgical Approaches to Psychiatric Treatment," *J. Proj. Tech.,* 1950, 14, 399–404.

131. ——, and Ross, S. "Some Rorschach Ratings of Clinical Value," *Rorschach Res. Exch.,* 1944, 8, 1–9.

132. Rotter, J. B. "The Present Status of the Rorschach in Clinical and Experimental Procedures," *J. Personality,* 1948, 16, 304–311.

133. Ruesch, J., and Fensinger, J. "The Relation of the Rorschach Color Response to the Use of Color in Drawings," *Psychosom. Med.,* 1941, 3, 370–388.

134. Rust, R. M. "Some Correlates of the Movement Response," *J. Personality,* 1948, 16, 369–401.

135. Sanderson, H. "Norms for 'Shock' in the Rorschach," *J. Consult. Psychol.,* 1951, 15, 127–129.

136. Sandler, J., and Ackner, B. "Rorschach Content Analysis: An Experimental Investigation," *Brit. J. Med. Psychol.,* 1951, 24, 180–201.

137. Sappenfield, B. R., and Buker, S. D. "Validity of the Rorschach 8–9–10%," *J. Consult. Psychol.,* 1949, 13, 268–271.

138. Sarason, S. B. "The Test Situation and the Problem of Prediction," *J. Clin. Psychol.,* 1950, 6, 387–392.

139. ——, and Potter, E. H. "Color in the Rorschach and Kohs Block Designs," *J. Consult. Psychol.,* 1947, 11, 202–206.

140. Sarbin, T. S. "Rorschach Patterns under Hypnosis," *Amer. J. Orthopsychiat.,* 1939, 9, 315–318.

141. Sargent, Helen D. "Projective Methods: Their Origins, Theory and Applications in Personality Research," *Psychol. Bull.,* 1945, 42, 257–293.

142. Schachtel, E. G. "Subjective Definitions of the Rorschach Test Situation and Their Effect on Test Performance. Contributions to an Understanding of Rorschach's Test. III," *Psychiatry,* 1945, 8, 417–448.

143. ——. "Notes on Rorschach Tests of 500 Juvenile Delinquents and a Control Group of 500 Non-delinquents," *J. Proj. Tech.,* 1951, 15, 144–172.

144. Schafer, R. *The Clinical Application of Psychological Tests.* New York. International Universities Press, Inc.; 1948.

145. ——. "Psychological Tests in Clinical Research," *J. Consult. Psychol.,* 1949, 13, 328–334.

146. Schneider, L. I. "Rorschach Validation: Some Methodological Aspects," *Psychol. Bull.,* 1950, 47, 493–508.

147. Siipola, Elsa M. "The Influence of Color on Reactions to Ink Blots," *J. Personality*, 1950, 18, 358–382.

148. Singer, M. "The Validity of a Multiple-Choice Projective Test in Psychopathological Screening," *Psychol. Monogr.*, 1950, 64, #314.

149. Smith, S., and George, C. E. "Rorschach Factors Related to Experimental Stress," *J. Consult. Psychol.*, 1951, 15, 190–195.

150. Sunne, D. "Rorschach Test Norms of Young Children," *Child Develpm.*, 1936, 7, 304–313.

151. Sutherland, J. D. "Some Notes on the Use of Projection Tests." A paper read at a meeting of the Royal Medical Psychological Association, Nov. 7, 1952 (not yet published).

152. Swift, Joan W. "Reliability of Rorschach Scoring Categories with Preschool Children," *Child Develpm.*, 1944, 15, 207–216.

153. ——. "Rorschach Responses of Eighty-two Preschool Children," *Rorschach Res. Exch.*, 1945, 9, 74–84.

154. Thetford, W. N.; Molish, H. B.; and Beck, S. J. "Developmental Aspects of Personality Structure in Normal Children," *J. Proj. Tech.*, 1951, 15, 58–78.

155. Thompson, Grace M. "MMPI Correlates of Certain Movement Responses in the Group Rorschachs of Two College Samples," *J. Consult. Psychol.*, 1948, 12, 379–383.

156. Thornton, G. R., and Guilford, J. P. "The Reliability and Meaning of Erlebnistypus Scores in the Rorschach Test," *J. Abnorm. Soc. Psychol.*, 1936, 31, 324–330.

157. Thurstone, L. L. "The Rorschach in Psychological Science," *J. Abnorm. Soc. Psychol.*, 1948, 43, 471–475.

158. Vernon, P. E. "The Rorschach Inkblot Test, II." *Brit. J. Med. Psychol.*, 1933, 13, 179–205.

159. ——. "The Significance of the Rorschach Test," *Brit. J. Med. Psychol.*, 1935, 15, 199–217.

160. ——. "Matching Methods as Applied to the Investigation of the Personality," *Psychol. Bull.*, 1936, 33, 149–177.

161. Vorhaus, Pauline G. "Rorschach Reactions in Early Childhood, III. Content and Details of Preschool Records," *Rorschach Res. Exch.*, 1944, 8, 71–91.

162. Wallen, R. "The Nature of Color Shock," *J. Abnorm. Soc. Psychol.*, 1948, 43, 346–356.

163. Williams, M. "An Experimental Study of Intellectual Control under Stress and Associated Rorschach Factors," *J. Consult. Psychol.*, 1947, 11, 21–29.

164. Wittenborn, J. R. "A Factor Analysis of Rorschach Scoring Categories," *J. Consult. Psychol.*, 1950, 14, 261–267.

165. ——. "Level of Mental Health as a Factor in the Implications of Rorschach Scores," *J. Consult. Psychol.*, 1950, 14, 469–472.

166. Young, R. A., and Higginbotham, S. A. "Behavior Checks on the Rorschach Method," *Amer. J. Orthopsychiat.*, 1942, 12, 87–94.

167. Zubin, J. "Introduction: Symposium on Statistics for the Clinician," *J. Clin. Psychol.*, 1950, 6, 1–6.

168. Zulliger, H. *Einführung in den Behn Rorschach Test.* Bern: Hans Huber, 1941.

CHAPTER **15**

Implications of Some
Contemporary Personality Theories
for Rorschach Rationale

In the introduction to the monograph in which he presented his "experiment," Rorschach wrote in his characteristically direct and unpretentious way:

> At the outset it must be pointed out that all of the results are pre-dominantly empirical. The questions which gave rise to the original experiments of this sort (1911) were of a different type from those which slowly developed as the work progressed. The conclusions drawn, therefore, are to be regarded more as observations than as theoretical deductions. The theoretical foundation for the experiment is, for the most part, still quite incomplete. [64, page 13]

When one considers the fact that these words were written more than 30 years ago, and that some thousands of persons have worked with Rorschach's test since then, producing a bibliography that now runs to over twelve hundred items, it is sobering to note how well the last sentence quoted could describe the situation today. There have been some stirrings during the past ten years, however, starting with Rickers-Ovsiankina's important presidential address [61]. Dissatisfaction with our lack of theoretical underpinnings for the Rorschach method has grown, and there have been calls for increased attention to theory from persons both within clinical psychology and outside it [for example, 12, 56, 60, 72, 75; see also 19, 49, 67].

The Importance of Theory

Perhaps it would be worth-while to ask some naïve questions:
Why do Rorschach workers need to bother about theory? Hasn't
there been enough empirical clinical research with the test to show
that most of the clinical tradition of its interpretation is valid? Isn't
the traditional way of looking at it good enough? There are four
main points to be made in answer to these questions:

1.   First, just from the practical viewpoint, a theoretical understanding of the psychological processes that are involved in the Rorschach performance can give much greater *flexibility* to our efforts
to analyze and diagnose personalities, at the same time *checking wild
speculation*. If we restrict ourselves to looking for and interpreting
patterns the significance of which has been demonstrated in empirical research and in our clinical experience, we will be helpless when
faced with a new problem or an atypical case—as most of them seem
to be! If instead we fall back on hunch and our "clinical intuition,"
we are flying blind with instruments whose accuracy is completely
unknown; without theory, flexibility becomes fluidity. Actually,
every time we rely on clinical feel in a novel situation we apply
some theory or other, but an implicit and perhaps unconscious one.
On the other hand, the more that we can construct a theoretical
rationale for a test in terms of the psychological processes involved,
the more freedom and scope we have in considering the unique
pattern of each case—the ways in which the discerned elements interact to produce this particular set of test results. For theory enables us to *deduce* and *predict* about new situations, and to modify
and improve our principles through testing such deductive predictions.

2.   It follows directly that theory can have a great value in *teaching* the use of the Rorschach. A skilled and intuitive clinician will
have great difficulty in communicating to his students anything of his
interpretative ability unless he is able to reflect on his experience
and draw from it general principles—which is exactly one stage in
the process of theory-formation. In teaching, if we do not emphasize

the memorization of arbitrary-seeming equivalences (to caricature: color = affect, shading = anxiety) but rather give the student an understanding of what is going on in the patient as he responds to the blots, through emphasis on systematic rationale, we can get away from the all-too-prevalent "cook-book method" of Rorschach interpretation. No amount of preaching that the test is a Gestalt and that no factor can be interpreted without considering its context can be effective in counteracting this rigid, mechanical attempt to categorize patients, unless the student learns how he can use psychological tests as a way of studying on-going processes in persons who are variously structured. Our ability to achieve this result will depend very largely on the extent to which we have a theoretical understanding of the Rorschach.

3. A third practical value of a systematic theoretical understanding of our tests (for these remarks apply to all psychological testing, not just to the Rorschach) is in *facilitating communication* between colleagues. The logical positivists have taught us what a large part of theoretical science consists of putting ideas into systematically clear language. As Rapaport says, without a theoretical rationale "the tests and test results must remain meaningless to the psychiatrists" [59, page 5]. The development of systematic theory means refining and sharpening the concepts we use to describe personality and giving them clear operational significance. Nothing could do more for the acceptance of clinical testers by their colleagues in other disciplines, and also in academic psychology, than tightening up our concepts in this way and relating them to other aspects of psychology. And it must be admitted that even old friends and colleagues in clinical testing have difficulty sharing their insights about the Rorschach in the present relatively atheoretical babel of jargons.

4. Finally (and in the end, most importantly), theory enables our science of human behavior to grow in an orderly and efficient manner. It provides a structure within which individual contributions fit together and produce a comprehensible and intelligible totality instead of a disjointed heap. It guides research by pointing out areas of little knowledge, where work is necessary for further

progress. Only with the aid of the logical order given by theory is it possible to *prove* or *disprove* empirical propositions. All of this means that the Rorschach method can become a part of the great body of scientific advance only when research with it is planned and executed with the aid of clearly formulated theory. With adequate theoretical linkages, the Rorschach can contribute to our understanding of many aspects of personality—particularly perception, association, thinking, and their pathology.

Theorizing is a very necessary activity, then; but it also has its dangers when it is not followed up by systematic (preferably experimental) checking. Theory is such a scientifically respectable enterprise (and a difficult enough one, too) that when a person has labored through a translation of factual observations, hunches, and speculations into the systematic terms of a formal system, he often heaves a very human sigh of relief and sits back with the feeling of a job well done. "Now I *understand* what is going on," he thinks, "because it is elegantly stated here in an orderly and abstract vocabulary."

Danger is hidden in just this feeling of closure. The job is only *begun* at the stage when the theory is written out. If a theory does not lead more or less directly to systematic and controlled observations of a new kind, it is a static structure of quite limited value. A superstructure of theoretical rationale (or rationalization) may be built on quite erroneous observations and may perpetuate entirely mistaken hunches, unless it is tried in the fire of experiment.

This criticism may be levelled against even such otherwise admirable "Contributions to an Understanding of Rorschach's Test" as Schachtel's [66, 68, 69, 70], which are required reading for anyone seriously interested in the test. Though they lack systematic rigor, these articles are the fruit of a sustained and very sensitive attempt to set down some hypotheses about the psychological processes that bring about many aspects of the Rorschach performance. In the very artistic form of these utterances lies their weakness; they give the reader a feeling of completeness and self-sufficiency, rather than impressing him with the hypothetical nature of what is proposed and the need for someone to verify or refute it.

Perhaps it is unfair to Schachtel to single him out in this way. The fact is that no one who has written on the rationale of the Rorschach test has oriented his hypotheses toward empirical testing—with the possible exception of Rorschach himself. He tried always to understand what was going on in the mind of the patient to produce the test result, and he carried out a number of little experiments and proposed others to test some of his hypotheses. [See, for example, 64, pages 53–54.] His remark that "such problems need much further study" has unfortunately been disregarded,* even though the quality of validation research has been improving in recent years, with the development of research designs more nearly adequate to clinical realities.

Let us take it as granted that theoretical foundations for the Rorschach technique are necessary, and that they must be tested as they are built, by means of prediction and controlled observation. More attention to such problems will, incidentally, be very likely to improve the practical clinical work of Rorschachers who grapple with them.

But it may be asked whether those who clamor for more attention to theory are not expecting too much, considering the state of affairs in personology and psychology generally today. There is no one theoretical position that is universally accepted; there are, instead, many competing schools and systems. Some command respect because of their rigor, some because of their vigor; and at times it seems that formal elegance varies inversely with explanatory and predictive power. It is probably safe to say that the dominant theoretical position in clinical psychology is more or less psychoanalytic; but psychoanalysis as a theory is a sprawling, undisciplined, and mostly unsystematized mixture of brilliant insight, dogma, wild speculation, shrewd system-building and indispensable single concepts. Its enormous literature has only rarely been surveyed and pulled together in any usable form. Is it surprising, then, that Rapaport's monograph [60] represents the only major effort to apply psychoanalytic concepts in working out a rationale for the Rorschach?

Quite a number of theoretically-minded psychologists have un-

---

* Except in the researches of Zubin and his associates [see 75].

dertaken to bring conceptual order into the wilderness that is the problem of personality. They are too numerous for all of them to be given the hearing they deserve. For the purposes of this chapter the field has been narrowed by considering only those who have explicitly dealt with personality,* and further by choosing only those whose ideas seem most important.

Some Definitions

It may well be that the modest-sounding request that a rationale for the Rorschach be provided is going to turn out to be a demand for a better theory of the total personality than any we have today —one that is broad enough to take into account the kinds of behavior inferred from the test, and finely enough differentiated to explain specific perceptual-associative acts. It would seem that a personology should have this much scope to deserve the name. The study of personality has been considered by many people to be a subdivision of the broader science of psychology, corresponding perhaps to perception or to learning in its claims to be a legitimate special field of investigation (and thus deserving of a separate chap-

---

* By this criterion we shall have to omit both the contemporary heirs of behaviorism, who have little to offer to our quest, and men like Heinz Werner [74], who have a great deal. Many of Werner's ideas have been incorporated into Murphy's theory, and will find their way into our discussion at that point. As for behaviorism, the problems we are trying to solve are the very kind that are most vexing to stimulus-response psychology. Pattern perception, similarity and generalization, for example, are hard enough for the post-behaviorists to handle in simple laboratory situations with rats; but when it is a question of how elements of experience and behavior that have only a meaningful congruity may be related, often without there being any apparent possibility for directly learned connections—then it is really hard lines for this widely prevalent school of American psychology. The habit approach, with the assumption of broad identities of elements, could possibly explain why a person who generally perceives things as a whole (having been rewarded for doing so) would give W responses to a Rorschach card. But why would the "habit" of perceiving things as a whole be related to ability at abstraction, or to paranoid grandiosity? It is this kind of metaphorical transfer that old-fashioned CR and S–R theorists fought most vehemently. The fact is, also, that they have implicitly recognized the limitations of their theoretical tools and have stuck to the areas where they can operate well: rote learning, rat motivation, and other relatively simple problems. With a few exceptions, they recognize that their theories have a long way to go before they can even approach complex problems of personology.

ter—usually the last one!—in the introductory text). This tradition is passing. As more people have become seriously interested in personology, its boundaries have been pushed out to take in more and more of the older "special fields" in psychology. At the same time, the dividing lines between such areas as motivation and perception, which seemed so patent and fixed while we were still suffering from the residual effects of faculty psychology, have begun to waver and melt. The attacks of doughty universalists like Krech [38] have put on the defensive anyone who would still want to maintain them as separate branches of psychology. It is still possible in a science to single out by abstraction a particular aspect of a unified organism, and to study it; but one has to recognize that this is only a *conceptual* separation, and that in the real world any one aspect of organismic functioning, such as perception, is no more independent from the total than is another, such as anabolism.

Many lines of evidence—from psychosomatic medicine, from experimental psychology, from psychopathology—point to a complex, interpenetrating though incomplete unity of the human organism. But there is specificity, too. Self-contradiction and inconsistency are at least as characteristic of human beings as their opposites. If this is the kind of phenomena with which we are dealing, it seems more and more inevitable as the evidence piles up that a new science of personality will become necessary to provide a conceptual frame broad enough to encompass the facts. As Angyal has convincingly argued [3] this new science must provide concepts suitable for describing and working with the behavior of the organism as a whole in its inextricable relationships with its social, cultural, and physical environment (the "biosphere"). The most important part of that environment is the other people with whom the organism interacts, so those sciences that deal with patterns of human relationships (social psychology, sociology, and social anthropology) must be drawn into the orbit of personology. Furthermore, the new science of personality must embrace and interrelate much of medicine and its basic sciences, physiology and anatomy, and all of psychology (including psychoanalysis and psychopathology). The day is gone forever when the study of personality could be considered to be the attempt to speculate about and to measure a few of the emergent general trends of behavior (traits).

So far this broad new personology exists mainly as a program. Must progress in Rorschach theory wait on the completion of the grand structure? The answer would seem to be "No." We can learn from existing personologies, even if they are incomplete approximations to the ideal set up here. Further, any well-defined problem may be directly attacked, both empirically and theoretically, if we use concepts that are not only suitable to the immediate data but also may readily be fitted into a broader framework. Scientific progress does not have to wait for complete integrated systems of ideas; in fact, the useful ones usually come late in the game.

This is what "personology" will mean, then: a complete science of the behavior and inner functioning of individual human beings in a social context.*

What about a second term, that which is to be related to personology—"the Rorschach"? It may seem at first thought that everyone who reads this book will understand what *that* means. Still, it may be useful to make explicit the way that the present writer understands the word. It is going to be necessary to limit the scope of this discussion and it must be made clear that the emphasis on perception here is *not* due to a concept of the Rorschach as a purely perceptual test. The Rorschach is, of course, not a test at all in the old sense, any more than any of the other so-called projective techniques. It is a partially controlled method of observing human beings in a specific situation, in order to learn as much as possible about their personalities. Accordingly, the complete Rorschach record will contain far more than the responses. First, it will record *all* of the subject's *verbalizations* (and as much as possible of the examiner's). Then it will include the *nature of the situation*—both objectively and as subjectively defined by the examinee—including the purpose for which the test was given; what kind of *interpersonal relationship* came about between the two persons; *observations* of

---

* "Inner functioning" is added to make it clear that "pre-behavioral" events in the organism—thoughts, impulses, affects, dreams, fantasies, unconscious mental operations—are just as much the subject matter of personology as overt observable action.

the subject's mood, his gestures, facial expressions, his behavior both in handling the cards and otherwise; and any *special attendant circumstances* that may have affected the performance (such as interruptions, unusual conditions of lighting, non-standard physical surroundings). We cannot have just a theory of Rorschach responses, though they will play a major role; we must be able to understand all that can readily be observed and recorded of the interpersonal interaction and the subject's reaction to the situation. Sooner or later, in attempting to trace the determinants of any abstracted portion of a person's behavior when taking the test, we should come to a point where no further progress could be made without considering more of the totality that was violated by our original, somewhat arbitrary, decision to attend to just one part of it—for example, only what the subject says.

Implications of Current Personality Theories for an Understanding of the Rorschach Technique

Any attempt to come to grips with the problem of developing Rorschach theory might start from either of two beginning-points. One could go carefully through what has been written about the test and its applications, and through the "oral tradition" of Rorschach interpretation, extracting all theoretical statements, and looking constantly for implicit theorizing and for the implications that certain empirical findings and ways of thinking about the Rorschach have for personality theory. Or one could begin with personality theories as they exist today, and examine the contributions that they have made or seem suited to make to an understanding of the Rorschach.

The former, the more inductive approach, might in the long run be the more creative one. Although bringing out into the open many of the implicit assumptions that are used by Rorschach workers today might make a number of them fall of their own weight, many other interesting propositions about personality would emerge. These might conceivably be integrated into something that could provide a useful "small-package" theory, if not a complete person-ology. But the task would be too great for a single chapter. It is in the deductive direction that this chapter will head, seeing how much progress toward a rationale for any of the many aspects of the Ror-schach can be made starting from each of a number of current, widely known personologies.

In considering each theory, it will be good to ask certain general questions, besides looking into its more specific contributions. To begin with, a rather dogmatic position will be taken—that a theory must be *organismic* if it is to offer more than a partial treatment of Rorschach problems. A purely psychological theory could not ex-plain the effects of brain injury on Rorschach performances, for example. This does not mean that a personology *has* to have an explicit theoretical model of the brain's functioning, but such a model is an additional property much to be desired. In his discus-sion of the papers at a 1949 symposium on "interrelationships be-tween perception and personality," Tolman devoted himself en-tirely to a call for brain models. "The important point, as I see it," he said at that time, "is that a model (whether almost good physiol-ogy or almost wholly 'pseudo') has certain specific intrinsic proper-ties attributed to it by its authors. And it is by following out the consequences of these attributed properties that one is led to wider predictions than those already found empirical relations with which we start" [73, page 48].

We shall expect further that the most helpful theories will be those that contribute to our understanding of *psychopathology,* or at least are able to assimilate and conceptualize findings from this field. If a personology is tailored only to the contours of the "normal" per-son, we should not be surprised to find embarrassing conceptual gaps when we try to fit it to the diagnostic problems in which the Ror-schach finds its greatest day-to-day usefulness. An adequate struc-tural-functional theory, on the other hand, will contain in itself implications for various kinds of personality organizations, normal and abnormal.

Then we shall want to know two principal points about the theory's concepts. First, are they *operationally enough defined* (or definable) to make feasible their experimental use and the verification of the theory's propositions? And, second, do they provide us with a useful *vocabulary* for describing individual personalities? For one of the great defects in current Rorschach interpretation is the vague, elusive, and non-specific kinds of concepts used. Too often, reports contain a mishmash of assorted terms from several theories, with a generous sprinkling of words and phrases more or less unique to Rorschachers—like "unconscious living," "promptings from within," "coarcted," "extratensive" (which, as noted in Chapter 12, is *not* the same as extraverted, but which lacks—as all these expressions do—any clear and unambiguous referent in clinical observation).* Ideally, a theory would provide a set of systematically interrelated terms which could be used to pin down any significant aspect of observable behavior, thought, or affect.

Finally, it will at times be necessary to make other brief evaluations of methodological points. One vexing question, which keeps bobbing up in the consideration of one theory after another, is: *What is theory and what isn't?* It is not always easy to tell. If someone writes, in a book supposedly on the theory of personality, that people see what they want to see, is this then a theoretical formulation, or is it merely an empirical generalization? Does such a statement take on any more of the character of theory if the phenomenon described is given a name? Or must there be further hypotheses about the process that is involved, or systematic linkage to a consistent set of concepts? The present writer is inclined to want to go as far as these last questions imply, but then it is hard to know what constitutes "systematic linkage," and so forth, short of a tightly-knit hypothetico-deductive system like Hull's. Repression, for example, is a good deal more than a name for the phenomenon that Nietzsche had described as memory's yielding to pride; it is a complex hypothetical process involving an elaborate set of assumptions about psychic structure and function. By contrast, consider the effect of motivation on perception. As will be shown, almost every theorist whose work is examined here has noted somewhere or other the obvious fact that visual perception is affected at times by wishes,

---

* The use of technical terms in reports is discussed in Chapter 17.

fears, interests. But very few, if any, have gone much farther than to name this process and demonstrate it experimentally.

Turning to more specific questions, we shall ask what each theory has to say about perception. Despite the point, made in the preceding section, that there is much more to the Rorschach performance than a set of visual percepts, it seems desirable to rein ourselves in this much lest we follow the example of Stephen Leacock's hero, who mounted his horse and galloped off in all directions. Furthermore, the perceptual side of it contains most of what is specific and unique about the Rorschach among our clinical tools. We shall be particularly concerned to find out whether or not each theory concerns itself with *individual differences* in modes of perceiving, what it suggests as the determinants of such differences, and what it says about ways in which the influences of such determinants are mediated. How far have the currently prevalent theories of personality gone in exploring or postulating relationships of this kind? The whole "New Look" movement in perceptual experimentation, as Krech has conveniently christened it [38], involves the idea of tracking down determinants of the variation in standard perceptual phenomena—variation that was regarded in the older experiments as simply "experimental error." It seems reasonable to hope, therefore, that some of the more recent developments in personality theory will have relevance to this quest. Finally, we shall consider briefly what each author has had to say directly about the Rorschach test.

G. W. Allport

Allport's definition of personality includes the statement that it is a "psychophysically neutral" structure,* and in other definitions too he maintains this nominally organismic standpoint. In practice, however, the theory is almost exclusively concerned with the psychological dimension of the human organism. Psychosomatic problems are simply beyond the scope of Allport's undertaking. He makes almost no reference to the level of neurological processes.

---

* This phrase was taken from William Stern, to whose personalistic psychology Allport acknowledges indebtedness for many aspects of his own personology.

Add to this the fact that Allport's theory is explicitly one for the normal personality only, and it is plain from the start that its value for our purpose must be quite limited. Indeed, not only has he made no contribution to our understanding of psychopathology, but he considers that psychopathology can give us little or no help in dealing with problems of the healthy personality.

Although Allport's first experimental work was in the field of perception (eidetic imagery), and though many of his students have done important work in "New Look" perceptual studies [for example, 14, 55], he has never said much about the perceiving aspect of the person. There are only three references to perception in the index to *Personality, a Psychological Interpretation,* none of which is concerned with individual differences. Nor has his interest shifted much towards perceptual problems in more recent publications.

Nevertheless, two basic propositions in Allport's theory are relevant to the Rorschach. First, Allport has been one of the earliest and staunchest advocates of the view that individual behavior is *consistent, unified,* and *generalized;* he has been one of the stoutest foes of behavioristic atomism. Personalities are to varying degrees unitary, he says, but behavior must be understood in terms of consistent dispositions called *traits,* not specific habits. Traits, in turn, are of two types: motivational or driving, and expressive—transmitting the style of a personality. Second, traits are conceived of as *organizing, selective* forces. They "select the stimuli to which they respond, even though *some* stimulus is required for their arousal" [1, page 206]. Though Allport does not seem to have made any specific statement that traits may cause distortion as well as selection in perception, this is clearly his belief. He quotes from Theophrastus (ca. 300 B.C.) a character sketch of "The Coward," in which a perceptual distortion due to a characteristic motive was observed: "At sea, he thinks cliffs are pirates . . ." [2, page 201].

The first of these conceptions (the consistency of behavior) underlies our practice in a good deal of Rorschach interpretation. When we conclude that a person who uses many rare details in the test is finicky, quibbling, over-concerned with fine points, we are proceeding on the assumption that his behavior is consistent, that it is determined by such highly general dispositions that if a person is concerned with the minute here, he must be the same in all other departments of his life. Likewise, conclusions based on succession, productivity (R), originality of responses, verbalization, and to some extent content, are of a similar sort: if the subject, compared to others, is orderly, brimming with ideas, banal in his associations, if he elaborates his percepts tediously, or if he talks about a limited range of topics, we assume that he acts similarly when faced with most other situations, no matter how different they may be. In fact, a fair amount of what is found in reports based on the Rorschach consists of such descriptions of *expressive traits.**

Allport has been less interested in and impressed by the achievements of Rorschach testing than most of the other authors we shall consider; the test is mentioned only three times in his basic book and then in a brief and somewhat disparaging way. Curiously enough, his main objection (expressed in lecture courses) was that the test constituted too slight a sample of behavior from which to make such far-reaching generalizations. Not *that* much consistency could be assumed, he thought; behavior is determined more situationally, and also by momentary dispositions such as the task-attitude the subject happens to take. If he were to hear his own trait theory quoted to justify certain aspects of Rorschach interpretation, he would very likely consider it an inappropriate exaggeration.

The second principle—that traits guide perception selectively—might be invoked to explain the particular content that a person finds in the blots. Interests, values, and attitudes are among the moving forces that cause an artistic person to see the center space in Card II as a ballerina, while an ardent fisherman sees it as a ray, and so on. On a less obvious level content may be determined by the general value orientations that Allport, following Spranger, has done so much to bring into psychologists' ken: the religious, theoretical, esthetic, economic, political, and social. Thus, an intense social value might be expected to cause selective perception of human

---

* Bellak [9, 10] was perhaps first to note the relevance of this concept. Rorschach behavior includes, according to him, adaptive, expressive, and apperceptive (projective) elements, not just the last.

figures, perhaps engaged in helping activities. Since Allport and Vernon have provided us with a test, the Study of Values, this formulation characteristically has at least the value of being easily testable. Allport has encouraged his students to do a good deal of experimental work within the general bounds of his system.

There is little else that Allport's theory can contribute to help our understanding of the Rorschach. The experiments just referred to do little more than demonstrate in ingenious ways how perception *can* be influenced by personal values, attitudes, and the like. His system does not provide us with a set of useful analytic categories for describing behavior, for Allport is opposed to the search for general variables of personality that may be used to characterize all comers. We violate the uniqueness of personality when we try to ask of everyone to what extent he has, for example, feelings of inferiority, Allport says, overlooking the fact that the logical consequence of this position is a neologism for each "individual trait" that is discovered in a subject.

Further, since his theory is not concerned with the detailed study of perceptual or associative processes, it fails to provide us with concepts that might be useful in such studies, and is not even congenial to developments of this kind. Closely examined, those of his concepts and explanations that have been used here have little theoretical content. They are mainly restatements of what has been the common knowledge of intelligent men since at least Theophrastus' day. The concept of trait is basic to Allport's system, yet it is open to serious methodological objections. It merely names the fact that a certain degree of consistency in behavior is empirically found by postulating a special inner disposition. To be sure, dispositions in the personality *do* modify perception, but *how?* Without some answer to that question, trait theories such as Allport's can give us no real help in extending our understanding of the Rorschach.

Kurt Lewin

Topological and vector psychology has some promising features as a theory for our purposes, even though Lewin does not seem to have written anything about the Rorschach test. To begin with, his basic formula, $B = f\ (P,\ E)$, is a constant reminder to us that behavior must be explained always in terms of forces deriving from the environment (E) as well as from within the person (P). In field theory, E is not the objective physical environment; it is the subject's "private world," his own world as he sees it and as it has effects on him. Since L. K. Frank [20] has told us that the Rorschach and other projective techniques are *par excellence* ways of getting at the subject's private world, this might appear to be a happy beginning.

Unfortunately, however, Lewin does not provide more than occasional hints to guide us in constructing the life space out of what he called "the hull of physical facts" [45]. It is not that he failed to recognize this as a problem; he was simply more interested in problems of action than those of perception, and wanted to explain overt behavior in terms of an already created personal world. Consequently, we find at the outset that the very problems that are central for Rorschach theory are passed over in Lewin's field theory.

From inspection of a typical topological representation of the person, showing differentiated inner-personal regions corresponding to such functional unities as needs, and outer regions of the person which are denoted *perceptual-motoric*, one might think at first that the solution lay in studying the effects of inner-personal regions on this perceptual periphery. Thus, one might think that an aroused need, such as hostility, could influence perception in the following wise: a need is conceptualized as an inner-personal region in a state of tension; in the topological-vector model, tension tends to spread from one region to others with which it is connected (adjacent), being restrained by the degree to which boundaries between regions are rigid.

So far, so good. But we cannot conceptualize seeing the small upper central detail in Card II as a bullet in terms of a spread of tension from an inner-personal region to the adjacent motoric-perceptual region. Lewin is quite explicit about this. *"Instead of linking the need directly to the motoric* [-perceptual regions], *the need is linked with certain properties of the environment. The environment then determines the motoric"* [46, page 108; italics in the original]. Lewin goes on to admit that "it is somewhat difficult to understand how a force acting on a person in a certain direction can produce a change in the structure of the environment" [46, page 109]. This question was never satisfactorily answered in topological psychology. Lewin simply goes on: "If one links force with need and sees the primary effect of a need in the change of [the] psychological environment (valence), it is understandable that a need may result in a structural change of the environment as naturally as it may result in locomotion" [46, page 109].

Even if we were content just to accept this last statement, the system has no way of distinguishing one need from another. Because of Lewin's strong ahistorical emphasis, he constructed a system that was limited to momentary dynamic constellations. As such it was excellent for representing the kind of interpersonal situation created in Rorschach testing, and for clarifying the complex nature of this apparently simple relationship for Rorschach examiners. But it had no place for the representation of enduring features of personality, no vocabulary for discussing the personality trends that we usually diagnose from the Rorschach.

There are a few exceptions. The concepts of differentiation and rigidity may characterize the personality, and are readily coördinated to features of the topological representations. Kounin [37] has, for example, derived a number of predictions about behavior from the theory of rigidity and has verified them. With some difficulty, his formulations might be extended to predict rigid succession in the Rorschach; but it seems impossible to relate rigidity as he and Lewin saw it to other "indications" of rigidity, such as the production of many rare detail responses (assuming for the moment that this is a valid relationship). On the other hand, Lewin's concept of fluidity (having conceptual properties just the opposite of rigidity) is a useful one in thinking about certain kinds of pathological responses. If we assume that one of the effects of schizophrenia is to reduce the rigidity of boundaries between cognitive regions corresponding to a person's conceptual organization of his memories, it is possible to predict some of the kinds of looseness in association that this fluidity brings about. Thus, contamination responses and certain kinds of peculiarities of verbalization can be understood as being the result of such fluidity that what should be kept separate cannot be, and the patient confounds and confabulates from an inability to maintain adequately firm boundaries between conceptual regions.*

As Murray and Angyal have taught us, personality is not just a cross-section of a person in the specious present. It is a Gestalt extended in time, and "a satisfactory analysis of personality requires a biographical tracing through of the main branches of personality organization." This is a good rule for us to remember when, in our enthusiasm for the richness of the cross-sectional picture that the Rorschach allows us to paint, we start claiming that it is a test of the *total personality*.

It may seem paradoxical that so firmly ahistorical a thinker as Lewin should have made basic contributions to genetic psychology, but it is a fact. He was among the first to apply the concepts of differentiation and integration of biologists like Coghill to an understanding of human development. Topology was an excellent means through which to represent the three principal developmental stages as Lewin described them from his direct observations of young children, and by which to derive certain properties of these stages. (1) Much of the neonate's behavior could be understood by thinking of him as a very simple total structure, reacting in diffuse and massive ways because of the *lack* of appreciable differentiation. This primordial unstructured unity was followed by (2) the differentiation of the person into relatively independent action systems (regions). And finally (3) unity could be attained again through intercommunication and connectedness of the differentiated regions, forming a hierarchical or other type of integration.

This brief summary of some of Lewin's teachings about personality development is presented here to give credit where credit is due, even though he did not apply them to perception in a way that would be helpful to us. Later on, we shall see how Murphy has taken this basic three-stage developmental conception and has extended it

---

* It is quite possible that a good many other equally applicable ideas may be found in Lewin's earlier work—particularly the series in *Psychologische Forschung*, which is published in German.

and combined it in ways that are helpful to our present purposes with similar ideas that Heinz Werner had been independently developing.

A few final evaluative remarks: The rigor and hypothetico-deductive structure of Lewin's system, always closely geared in with experimentation, might urge us to try to develop new aspects of it to encompass those of our problems that it neglected, for in many ways it is a model of methodological excellence. But by its very nature it resists the attempt, say, to graft on to it concepts about the enduring personality; their absence is no oversight. Even its formal elegance loses luster when we notice that most of the theory's explanations have to be *post hoc,* since the knowledge that would be necessary to predict in its terms is rarely obtainable ahead of time. Further, it is a purely psychological theory with no way of linking up psychological to neurophysiological phenomena and brain mechanisms. Some of Lewin's students have made fruitful use of the system in studies of psychopathology, but always as a kind of special tool for handling limited problems. It is not suited to the basic spadework of explaining abnormal behavior comprehensively.

As a sort of concluding footnote on Lewin, it might be noted that one reason for his neglect of perception may well have been the fact that his colleagues Köhler, Koffka, and Wertheimer had concentrated so much of their effort within this very field. By the same token, they tended to leave problems dealing with the total person up to him; the concluding section on personality in Koffka's monumental *Principles* [36] is brief—barely three pages—and disappointing. There are many features of Gestalt psychology that look hopeful for Rorschach rationale (for example: emphasis on organization, the supersummativeness that is invoked in pattern-analysis, careful analysis of perceptual phenomena in terms of a definite brain model, the theory of traces), but its formulations are consistently aimed at the general case. Thus, the subtle and complex propositions of Koffka and Köhler about the process of recognition are not directly helpful because they never suggest how individual variations might come about or what might determine them. Koffka says nothing, for example, about ways in which motivation may affect perception. As

Bruner puts it, "Gestalt theory has means of handling variables like set, motive, value and past experience [in their influence on perception] . . . But it has not exploited these means" [13, page 306]. It is probably not accidental that quite a few leading Rorschach workers have their main allegiance in academic psychology to the Gestalt school, but so far none of them has been able to add much to our understanding of the test through attempts to apply Gestalt principles to it.

Andras Angyal

At first glance, Angyal's "science of personality" [3] seems to be a good potential source of theoretical underpinnings for the Rorschach. Here is an uncompromisingly holistic theory, one that does not merely pay lip-service to the concept of "the organism as a whole" but makes a serious attempt to approach each of the problems that is taken up from a genuinely organismic standpoint, not just a psychological one. The science of personality, Angyal tells us, cannot deal with mental phenomena only, or even with a combination of subjective data and social behavior. It must look for truly organismic, psychophysically neutral data of its own, as well as find ways to integrate the segmental data of the partial sciences of psychology, physiology, sociology, and the like.

In accordance with this outlook, Angyal proposes to deal with psychosomatic problems according to the following formula: not "physiological disturbances produce psychic disturbances," nor vice versa, but rather "physiological disturbances produce organismic changes, one manifestation of which is psychic disturbance." For example, in the studies of schizophrenia that were carried out under his direction at Worcester State Hospital [5], withdrawal in schizophrenia was conceived of as an organismic process, which could be —and was—studied in its sociological, psychological, and physiological aspects. Angyal does not, however, provide us with a brain model.

To an even greater degree than many other theories, Angyal's has the disadvantage of dealing very largely with general propositions and broad trends of personality organization. The book *Foundations for a Science of Personality* is modestly and appropriately titled; it is a programmatic statement of foundations, and does not contain a great deal of specific elaboration. As far as it goes, it is nearly impeccable methodologically.

In his discussion of perception, Angyal says: "Perceptions are not passive reflections; the organism elaborates them actively according to certain biological needs. Perceptions, and mental phenomena in general, are not mere labels but inherent parts of the organismic total process" [3, page 67]. This is fine, as is his advice that psychology should "relate the conscious phenomena to non-symbolic personality processes." Angyal is pointing in the direction in which we wish to travel, but he has hardly more than set his feet upon the path. Again, he discusses briefly the fact that past experience can play a large part in determining present perception, but does not go any further into the mechanism of this effect than to remark, "There is an astonishingly small amount of reality in our perception of each new situation and an astonishingly large amount of fantasy created through an organization of past experiences" [4, page 181].

His discussion of perception is exclusively in terms of the general case; nowhere does he point out the ways in which individual differences may come about in such aspects of the process as the way in which the organism elaborates and constructs a percept, or what specifically might determine such differences. For example, in discussing intersensory effects, he notes that a number of aspects of visual perception are based partly on kinesthesis; but he gives no hint that there may be individual differences in the extent to which kinesthetic and visual elements blend in a percept—and of course, therefore, he says nothing about what such individual differences might signify.

In his "law of continuity of system action," Angyal formulates clearly a common fallacy in personology, the one that is involved when we try to understand the Rorschach by means of correlations such as those that one investigator found between vista responses and somatotype: "If one neglects the intermediary steps one may bring into relationship members [of the system, personality] so distant that the connection between them remains entirely incomprehensible. Their only value is that of a statistical correlation the basis of which requires further investigation" [4, page 182]. Such, of course, is the situation with respect to most of our clinical knowledge about the Rorschach. It is regrettable that Angyal has not gone further in providing the "intermediary steps" for which we are looking.

One of the most original contributions Angyal has made, possibly one of highest importance, is his theory of the *integration of wholes*. He demonstrates the proposition that a Gestalt cannot be derived from *relationships* between parts, but only from a *system principle*, which organizes them. This conclusion leads to a sophisticated argument about the substitution of system action for causality (in the sense of specific cause-effect relationships) —one that is difficult to condense here. The reader is referred to the original discussion [3, pages 243–302]. The aspect of this theoretical development that is relevant for our purposes is its opening up a new logical aid to our understanding of the way that diverse aspects of the organism's functioning may be interdependent.

An example from the Rorschach may make this possibility clearer. Suppose that it has been well established that sensitivity in interpersonal relationships is highly correlated with the occurrence of certain kinds of shading responses. In ordinary causal thinking, this is very difficult to comprehend. Surely we cannot argue that either phenomenon directly causes the other. They seem to be effects of a common cause. But where are we to look for such a causal agent, which can produce sensitivity to nuances in such very different aspects of living?

One type of solution looks toward the brain model as the ultimate explanatory tool. Krech, a principal advocate of this position [38, 39, 40] argues that a unitary neurophysiological process (a "Dynamic System") in the brain corresponds to any organismic event, which has perceptual, emotional, conative, and other aspects, all shaped by this common cause. Hebb [26] has raised some rather formidable arguments against this position, and recent developments in neurology [for example, 54] tend to support him, though as an answer to the present problem his own alternative brain model seems to be fraught with just as many difficulties.

The other kind of solution, the one Angyal proposes, boldly by-passes the specific neural events involved and deals directly with the behavior of the whole organism. According to this view, the organism is itself a *unitas multiplex,* a system of systems. The parts that may be involved in any of its constituent systems may hail from any department of the organism's total business. They are organized by occupying positions in the system, not by specific causal relationships. By means of the formula

*part*₁ affects *system* leads to change in *part*₂

it is possible to get around the knotty logical problem of relating events that are conceptualized in different universes of discourse.

To return to our example, it seems faithful to the spirit of Angyal's discussion to hypothesize a system principle that we might call *sensitivity to nuance.* Empirically we could trace the boundaries of the system by investigating the consistency of various types of behavior (including, if desired, individual differences in sensitivity of physiological response) as well as the Rorschach responses and the interpersonal skills, in a group of persons in whom the correlation seemed to hold true. Thus, we could at the same time advance our understanding of personality and of this specific kind of Rorschach response. The motto might be, "understanding through finding the *position* of a kind of Rorschach behavior in a *personality system,*" rather than "understanding through finding *causes* of a kind of Rorschach behavior." This approach seems to deserve most careful trial.

In fact, the program of experimentation in perception being carried on by Klein and his associates [30, 31, 33], which will be described below, is using essentially this approach in a very fruitful way. Instead of the term *system principle,* Klein prefers to speak of *Anschauung* or *perceptual attitude,* but he acknowledges the essential identity of his conception and Angyal's [29, page 333].

Henry A. Murray

The creator of the TAT—the Rorschach's nearest rival among the projective techniques—might very well be expected to produce a theory of personality that would shed a good deal of light on the obscure theoretical problems we are considering. Curiously enough, this is not the case. Although Murray's is one of the richest and most detailed of personologies, brimming to excess with novel concepts and borrowings from other theories, its focus is on different problems.

In many respects, Murray's personology is a variant of psychoanalysis, and it shares with Jungian and with early Freudian psychology a preoccupation with dynamics at the expense of structure. The concept that is most closely associated with Murray's name is *need*. A very large share of Murray's theoretical thinking and of his practical experimental work has been focussed on this concept. Early in *Explorations in Personality* we are told that " a need or an emotion may determine the direction of attention and markedly influence the perception and apperception (interpretation) of external occurrences. To influence sensory and cognitive processes a need must be some force in the brain region" [53, page 66]. There is indeed a fair amount of emphasis, in Murray's theoretical writing, on the brain; in his more recent formulations, the brain as the principal organ of personality receives even more emphasis [35]. Yet a study of Murray's work leads one to the conclusion that this emphasis on the brain is more a matter of general conviction than it is something that he has had to develop in order to explain any experimental findings, or to make any predictions.

It is as if, in sketching out his theory, Murray had built himself a magnificent palace containing all kinds of rooms, courts, foyers, and halls, and then had decided to live and work primarily in the basement, with the boilers and dynamos. He has provided us with an organismic theory, which potentially can bring together data from all the sciences of man, and has filled with elaborate conceptual furniture only a few sections of it, primarily those dealing with needs and sentiments. But his personology is outstanding for the job he has done in providing a relatively consistent and operationally defined vocabulary of concepts for the systematic description of personality in its many dimensions.

In connection with the brief paragraph (quoted above) on the effect of needs on perception, Murray cited Sanford's work on the influence of hunger and an experiment of his own in which he demonstrated that children perceived a set of photographed faces as markedly more malicious after a frightening experience than before it. In the theoretical section of the paper reporting the latter experiment, Murray has some interesting remarks to make about perception, particularly the perception of faces. He argues that when one looks at the face of another, "there must be some retinal stimulation which is not translated into conscious perception, but which, nevertheless—through some other effects—determines apperception" [52, page 546]. About the nature of these other effects he says: "physical changes are activated in the body of the subject which are the sort that may be cognized as feelings, emotions, and kinesthetic sensations" [52, page 546]. These unattended-to activations, Murray argues from observations of young children, seem to appear ontogenetically before clear visual perceptions. Murray continues: "the point is that certain physical features of the object which the subject does not consciously perceive are nevertheless physically affecting his body, and though he may be unable to report upon these internal happenings, they are nevertheless affecting his conscious appraisal of the object." He suggests that unconscious imitation may be involved, as well as learning, and leaves open the possibility of an unlearned physiognomic responsiveness.

The aspect of this theorizing that needs to be emphasized here is the fact that Murray points out that people *differ* in the extent to which "these intermediary physical processes" are involved in their perceptions of others, and proposes that this may be a source of differences in people's abilities to judge character.

In discussing the results of his experiment, Murray hypothesized that "the bodily processes operative in the subjective experience known as fear were aroused . . . these in turn mobilized the integrated images and categories (the more general imaginal meanings). Then, when the test was presented to the children, the photographs which fulfilled the requirements of sufficient similitude functioned as foci for the projection of these images and categories" through the mediation of two processes: preferential perception and perceptive projection. "By *preferential perception* we refer to the unconscious (unintentional) process by which attention is directed to objects in the environment similar to the traces (or images) integrated with the aroused emotion" [52, page 557]. Perceptive projection is a process in which the influence of the aroused images is so strong as to result in distortion or illusions.

"These phenomena can be best explained," Murray goes on, "by the hypothesis of activated traces or unconscious images. The traces which are integrated with the bodily processes which make up the emotional state are there, as it were, below consciousness—ready to appear as conscious imagery or to modify events which are conscious, namely, perception and apperception" [52, pages 557–558]. Later on, Murray returned to this trace theorizing, spelling out the assumed process in a little more detail. ". . . Traces (images) of cathected objects in familiar settings become integrated in the mind with the needs and emotions which they customarily excite, as well as with images of preferred modes." An aroused need tends to make the organism "seek or avoid, as the case may be, the external objects that resemble the images with which it is integrated. Failing in this, it projects the images into the most accessible objects. . . . The thing 'out there' looks like or is interpreted to be the cathected image of the need integrate" [53, page 110]. Therefore, "the press of projected imagery may be used as an index* of imaginal or inhibited need tension" [53, page 260].

For all of its sketchiness, this is about as well developed a theory of the processes underlying the appearance of certain kinds of content in the Rorschach as exists. Murray's experiment shows very nicely how a persisting emotional state can dynamize perception, and also how the nature and extent of this effect depend upon the particular personality involved. His purpose, however, seems to have been simply to demonstrate the kind of effect that he knew to exist, not to study it more intensively nor to try to follow up the indications of structural differences in the subjects that led them to respond differently. This comment is not meant to imply that he should have pursued this tack instead of exploiting the basic phenomenon as

---

* Elizur has done exactly that in developing measures of anxiety and hostility in Rorschach content [17].

he did in a series of ingenious researches into the motivations of normal subjects, but rather to point out that the particular direction of his interest prevented his theory from developing in the ways that would interest us in the present context. Nevertheless, Murray should be credited with having not simply concerned himself with a theory of the general phenomenon of projection; in addition to this, he has pointed out aspects of the process that may give rise to individual differences, and he has been interested in the extent to which different persons do actually make use of the process.

Gardner Murphy

In Murphy, we have a personologist who has a great respect for the Rorschach, a familiarity with the kind of work that is done with it, and a conviction that it has important lessons to teach us about personality. It is possible that all of this is in some way a background for his pioneering in the "New Look" movement in perception. Back in the early 1940's, when perception was for most clinical psychologists still just a battleground where Gestalt experimentalists locked horns with conditioners, Murphy was teaching the influence of idiosyncratic drive-makeup on "the personal outlook," and was (with his students) carrying out experiments to investigate this interrelationship.

It is not surprising, then, to find in his book, *Personality* [50], a good deal more about both the Rorschach and perception generally than in any of the other theories being considered here. But it is a pleasant surprise to find him also constantly pointing out *ways* in which individual differences in perceiving may arise. For its pertinence, therefore, Murphy's theory deserves a particularly careful hearing.

To begin with, Murphy resembles Allport more than he does Lewin or Angyal as a theorist. He is as eclectic, as willing to listen to anyone and to try to incorporate the best he has to offer, as could be desired. His aim is at inclusiveness rather than rigor, at building a framework (however loose) within which all relevant empirical data may be arranged rather than at providing a tight logical structure from which hypotheses may be deduced. Certain main dimensions or formative principles may be discerned in this framework, however. Important among them are an emphasis on the *learned* nature of mature behavior, and on the role of the *drive: "the ultimate elements in personality structure are the needs or tensions"* [50, page 641; italics in the original]. It is an organismic theory, and one that lays great stress on development. A final merit: it is congenial to, and frequently calls for, formulations of theoretical problems in experimental terms for verification or disconfirmation.

Murphy's whole discussion of "the perceiver" is pervaded with constant attention to the origins of individual differences. He discusses many determinants of such differences: for example, variations in the receptors, in the cyto-architecture of the brain, in learning, in link-ups with idiosyncratic motor patterns; but his main points may be organized under two headings—the effects of drives and drive-structure, and perceptual aspects of the three basic developmental levels (see the above discussion of Lewin).

According to Murphy, drives or motives may affect perception in two principal ways. First, individual differences in strivings are chiefly important in determining the kinds of unique learning experiences a person will have, his predilections for certain kinds of experience, and his selective focus on those aspects of the world that have special relevance to his developing conative pattern. Positing a general human need for anchorage, for perceptual stabilization, Murphy describes how it interacts with a particular pattern of an individual's strivings to produce selective awareness.

While a person's motivational structure undoubtedly does channel and organize his experience in such ways, Murphy overstates the case. His calling it a "fact that the structure of motive patterns tends to become the structure of cognitive patterns; the perceived world pattern mirrors to a considerable extent the organized need pattern within" [50, page 351] is a more unqualified and sweeping statement than the present stage of perceptual research warrants.

Similarly, there is too direct a jump to the desired conclusion in his statement about the Rorschach that "in general, the details perceived as figure against the background of the rest of the ink-blot pattern (and the card as a whole) are directly suggestive of the individual's drive structure" [50, page 346]. Would that Rorschach interpretation *were* that simple! Such an hypothesis has never been proved, and clinical experience suggests that it is quite unlikely.

The second kind of influence of needs on perception delineated by Murphy he calls *autism*. This is a name for the tendency of motives to cause cognitive processes to move in the direction of need satisfaction, noticeable particularly when the stimulus structure is weak. (This is a restatement of what we have found in most theories—some version of the notion that we see what we want or fear to see, which may be used to explain individual differences in a few kinds of Rorschach content.) It operates in a number of ways: direct facilitation (lowering thresholds), raising thresholds, selective attention, and also by guiding associative and mnemonic processes. Further, there may be individual differences in *general* susceptibility to autism. Such differences would undoubtedly be related to aspects of personality structure, though Murphy does not go this far in speculation. It is possible that the degree of a person's general predisposition to autistic perception could be gauged from his Rorschach responses, perhaps yielding an index to structural as well as contentual aspects of personality. All of this is as yet, of course, no more than a speculative glance in a direction where research is urgently needed.

Murphy speaks welcome words of caution against assuming too much autistic determination of perception. Not every percept is a window into the unconscious—or even the conscious—drive-organization. For perception is a *bipolar process,* "which is organized in terms of saliences both of the world without and the world within" [50, page 353]. By varying experimentally the dominance of exteroceptive components (those representing the "real situation") over interoceptive and proprioceptive ones, Murphy and Hochberg [51] hypothesize, we can bring about perceptual behavior that ranges all the way from complete autism to complete realism. Thus they seem to follow the Gestalt assumption that pure exteroceptive perception is organized by the figural properties of the field, and conceive of personal organizing influences only in terms of afferent impulses from within the body. The work of Klein and Holzman [see particularly 30] casts much doubt on this formulation, with its neglect of possible central organizing factors that are more akin to sets than they are to sensations. Actually, in chapters five and six of *Personality* [50], Murphy has made as strong a case as anyone for the conception of motives as states involving almost all the tissues of the body, with major biochemical aspects directly affecting the central nervous system, not just states in which interoceptors and proprioceptors are stimulated.

Murphy mentions a second check against autistic effects, besides the structuring pull of outer reality. Even when outer forces are relatively weak, perception is still not entirely the pawn of momentary states of desire or deprivation. The need for secure anchorage in perceptual stability is still operating to maintain a constant environment. The general effects of the need-structure, spoken of above, tend to continue. Finally, the highest developmental level, that of integration (to be discussed below) "tends to achieve homeostasis or stability and offers maximal resistance to change" [51, page 341].

Thus, the theory of autism raises the same warning signals that have been hoisted by other theories about the effects of motivation on perception: one should be careful in Rorschach interpretation to look out for the fact that a temporary and uncharacteristic state of strong need, fatigue, joyful anticipation, or the like, may have some effect on the responses, particularly their content, which the unwary psychologist might interpret as an enduring characteristic of the person. Recent experiments of Hutt and his collaborators [28] show a variety of ways in which these temporary states can affect Rorschach protocols; studies such as that of Brozek et al. [11] and of McClelland and Atkinson [7, 47] indicate that the effects of aroused needs on perception are not at all simple or easy to predict. Nevertheless, Murphy's stress on the stability-giving effects of enduring needs helps provide a theoretical basis for the assumption that a single Rorschach protocol may be a legitimate basis on which to make statements about general personality trends.

On the question of "micro-process"—just *how* the need does influence perception, or how perceptual stability is attained—we get some help, but not a great deal. Murphy repeats Murray's important point that need precedes perception, and determines *where* we shall look and to what we shall attend. Then, "needs determine how the incoming energies are to be put into structured form. Perception, then, is not something that is first registered objectively, then 'distorted' " [50, page 377]. But in spite of his general friendliness to attempts at neurological explanation, and his way of systematically implicating all levels of the organism, Murphy goes no further than other theorists considered here in offering specific hypotheses about ways in which these interactions take place in the brain.

Let us turn now to the second general basis on which Murphy's contributions to perceptual theory are organized: the three levels of development. As described by Werner and Lewin, they were an initial undifferentiated phase of global unity, a stage of unorganized differentiation, and a final state of integrated organization of the sub-parts. Murphy develops a great deal of his argument in terms of these three developmental levels, marshalling a host of data from all the regions in which personality has been explored, consistent with this unifying model.

It is important to note that Murphy does not use these concepts only when taking up child development. "The fact seems to be that the adult mind is functioning all the time at all three levels, but that each individual has his own proportion, his own balance of the three" [50, page 344]. Murphy does not go very far in telling us what in turn determines how much a person uses each of the levels, but it is not difficult to use this conception, to build on it, in conjunction with Rorschach findings.

First, to restate these levels in perceptual terms: "At the first stage of perception . . . drive satisfaction or drive frustration yields affects that are fused or blurred with cognitive dispositions in the physiognomic process, the whole being a global reaction. . . . At the second stage, the cognitive structure begins to move into the foreground, and objects are recognized but are *acceptable* or *unacceptable*. . . . At the third stage, affective elements are wrought into the total picture in which cognitive integration has been or is being achieved" [50, pages 365–366]. Murphy and Hochberg add the assumptions that "exteroceptive, interoceptive, and proprioceptive components enter fully and on an equal footing, but not always with equal weight, into the dynamics of perception" [51, page 335], and "that in the most primitive forms of perception all three sources of sensory information are present in an undifferentiated or partly differentiated state and that subsequent differentiation gradually achieves more and more separation of these factors . . . in primitive stages, perception of environmental objects would prove inextricably fused with the motion, position, and feeling state of the observer" [51, page 336].

What are the implications of these formulations for the Rorschach? First of all, it is easy to assign different types of responses and reactions to the test to the three levels. Clearly belonging to the lowest order of undifferentiated perceptual-affective-impulsive functioning are the most diffuse types of reactions to the blots: emotional exclamations not followed by definite percepts, and vague descriptive comments ("a smudge"; "take it away—an awful mess"; "it just gives me a feeling of doom"). Since Murphy posits a relative unity of the person, in which perceptual development is of a piece with total organismic development, we have a basis for understanding such responses as indicating regressive or primitive functioning of the personality. This is in good agreement with clinical experience.

Even when responses are formed, we know that many patients give us vague global W's in which there is no differentiation or integration of parts (Rapaport's W_v). Often (as in responses like "dirt," "snow," "cloth," "flowers," "paint") determinants like texture, color, and shading seem to play a large role in these fuzzy, formless percepts—determinants which suggest the fused operation of various sense modalities and qualities. Following Werner [74], we should expect to find that the people who to the largest extent perceive this way are young children, regressed psychotics, or other patients who have been forced to retreat from a differentiated and integrated stage of development. The fact is that such responses are indeed characteristic of certain severe organic cases, of chronic schizo-phrenics, and of young children.*

Corresponding to Murphy's second stage, that of differentiation, would be most responses to details and many ordinary, "instanta-neous" whole responses with definite content but without any par-ticular inner articulation (Rapaport's W_o). Finally, the perceptual equivalent of the highest, the integrated developmental stage would be responses in which differentiated sub-parts are combined and organized into large unities (Beck's Z, [8], Rapaport's $W+$). This gives us a rationale for understanding the empirically found rela-tion between the amount of Z, or the number of well-organized W, and level of intelligence and personality integration. Murphy even suggests specifically that the "over-all organizing capacity" that is necessary to achieve the highest level of development "cannot at present be measured, except in the crude ways provided by the com-parison of whole responses and details in the Rorschach technique" [49, page 360 f.]. But this is going too far and too fast on the basis of theoretically assumed relationships. Not only would we need a more sophisticated approach to organizing activity than something like a W/D ratio, but we lack the factual basis in validation research for calling any Rorschach measure one of general "integrating *power.*"

The three main ways in which form and other determinants are combined (for example, C, CF, FC) also parallel the basic three stages of development. Consider, for instance, three responses to the lower detail in Card VIII. A typical pure C response ("blood") is undifferentiated, an immediate global associative response to an apparently diffuse sensory impression. A CF response like "masses of flowers," contains a minimum of differentiation, which we recog-nize in scoring subordinate aspects of form, but the general petal-

---

* Mention should be made here of an unpublished paper presented at the Chicago convention of the American Psychological Association, September 1951, by Howard Friedman (23), in which a number of hypotheses very similar to these were derived from Werner's developmental theory and verified with groups of young children, re-gressed schizophrenics, and normal controls. Significant differences in the predicted directions were also found for organized, good-form responses.

like forms that are implied and may be described by the subject are not organized in any way, as may be seen from the fact that a definitive form is not used. Finally, if the same area is seen as "two-toned sweet peas, orange and pink," there is not only definite differentiation, but also the color is integrated in the percept appropriately with a definitive shape. We should expect to find good FC responses correlated with intelligence, too, therefore; and again the prediction from the theory is borne out. Murphy recognizes, incidentally, that all three levels of functioning may usefully operate in a mature person, and he certainly does not imply that a well integrated adult should have nothing but highly integrated percepts.

Notice that nothing has been said specifically about *affective* adaptation. Murphy offers us no theoretical basis on which to predict a relation between color and affect.* Yet mature, integrated behavior would be predicted from the presence of not only $FC+$ but good FC', Fc, FY [see 8], FCh [see 60], $F(C)$ [see 64], and similar combinations of accurately perceived form with various types of sensory impression. In fact, it is a logical implication of this theory that in carrying the C–CF–FC sequence systematically throughout the scoring of determinants the criteria for classifying should be the degree of presence or absence of differentiation and integration.

In conclusion, it is only fair to mention again the fact that the concepts of differentiation and integration were not invented by Murphy nor first applied by him to personology; his debts to Lewin and to Werner are particularly heavy here. He uses those concepts, however, in a way that gives them a central importance in his discussion of perception and personality, so that it is easiest to see their relevance to Rorschach theory in his formulation.

Psychoanalysis

For the most part, Rorschach workers have relied chiefly on psychoanalytic concepts and hypotheses in their daily clinical work. Psychoanalysis furnishes much of the vocabulary (unfortunately not a very operational vocabulary) in which reports are written. Without

---

* Nor does any other theory considered here. The main contributions to this particular problem are summarized by Rickers-Ovsiankina [61] and Schachtel [68].

its principles of psychodynamics there would be no mortar with which to hold together the (sometimes too lofty) edifices of inference that we erect to reach diagnostic and prognostic conclusions about patients. But does this close relationship mean that psychoanalytic theory can provide a sufficient basis for an understanding of the Rorschach?

When we say "psychoanalysis," even in the narrower sense of a theory of personality, we still refer to an enormous literature as compared to the few volumes that have been written on any other personology. Freud's writings alone cannot be mastered in less than years of study, and they are only the core of an output that has poorly defined limits and many contributors. It must be admitted by anyone who has an acquaintance both with this literature and with methodological principles that much of its theorizing is loose, poorly integrated, and of questionable scientific merit. A final difficulty in the way of anyone who wishes to find out "what psychoanalysis says" about any particular topic is that Freud frequently changed his ideas, discarding formulations that seemed unsatisfactory and producing new ones without taking the trouble always to point out what was superseded. Nor have change and progress in psychoanalytic thinking stopped with his death.

As a result, contradictions and confusions are not hard to find within the bounds of what is generally called psychoanalysis, even leaving aside contributions of the movements that have branched off from the Freudian mainstream. Attempts to apply and develop the theory through systematic experimentation have had the greatest difficulty in finding operational definitions that capture the essence of the concepts' meanings in the context of the theory and at the same time lead to propositions that are verifiable under controlled conditions of observation. When all this is said and done, however, the present writer must frankly admit what would show between the lines anyway, that psychoanalysis remains for him the most nearly adequate and most indispensable body of personological theory that we have.

Here are some of the merits that urge this conclusion. First, Freud's thinking never neglected the brain and the physiological facets of the organism. When he laid down the main outlines of his theory too little was known to allow him to construct a valid brain model; nevertheless, the attempt that he made in the seventh chapter of *The Interpretation of Dreams* [21] had some insights in it that are just now being confirmed by direct experiment on the brain. (See Penfield's demonstration [54] that memory and conscious perception have different locations in the brain—a proposition logically derived by Freud.)

Freud wanted not only to help patients; perhaps most of all he wanted to construct a theory that would explain human behavior with a thoroughness that had never been attempted before. It is true that he was so fascinated by his tremendous discoveries in the realm of unconscious psychic determinants of behavior and thought, particularly in their pathological forms, that he wrote at times as if the psychological level of analysis alone was sufficient; but he referred at many times to the hope of developing a set of neurological concepts that would be adequate to carry the load of psychological distinctions and connections that he had made. Today, as a result, some analysts are working with the vanguard of researchers in neurophysiology and brain anatomy, trying to integrate the researchers' new findings with those of psychoanalysis [for example, 42]. And a psychoanalyst, Erikson, has written a book that contains perhaps the most thoroughgoing and viable organismic synthesis of somatic, psychological, and social determinants of human functioning yet to appear [18].

It is hardly necessary to mention the overwhelming indebtedness of modern psychosomatic medicine and psychopathology generally to psychoanalysis. Its psychodynamic formulations, as mentioned above, are indispensable to anyone who wants to understand anything more than the outer surface of personality. Finally, recent developments in ego psychology [25, 41, 57] offer the hope that some of the traditional problems of academic psychology, such as perception, will now be drawn more actively into the orbit of psychoanalytic thinking and research.

David Rapaport's Contribution

When we come to the question of applying psychoanalytic theory to the perceptual problems that the Rorschach poses for us, it is obvious that this is a task of quite a different magnitude than similar exercises with the other personologies that have been considered here. Under the circumstances, it is fortunate that a few years ago a thorough scholar of psychoanalysis set himself the task of writing a rationale for the Rorschach test in almost all of its details. Any reader with a serious interest in the topic of this chapter can hardly do better than to read the sections on rationale in Rapaport's monograph [60, pages 6–12, 89–94, 101–114, 120–122, 125–126, 128–129, 131–135, 138–142, 153–156, 159, 166–169, 176–177, 182–184, 188–193, 211–215, 233–244, 265–267, 282–289, 294–305, 315, 319–320, 323–326, 329–331; see also 338–366]. It is the most comprehensive, sustained, and serious attempt yet made to provide an understanding of what Rorschach responses are all about in terms of an integrated theoretical standpoint. One does not have to agree with Rapaport's methods of administration nor share his preferences in scoring to profit from these discussions.

It is obvious that Rapaport's well over 100 pages of discussion cannot be adequately summarized here. Not all of it draws directly on psychoanalytic theory, however, and furthermore much of it consists of the detailed application of a relatively few general principles. It will be worth our while, therefore, to survey briefly the aspects of psychoanalysis that Rapaport calls on, and to see how he uses them.

There are two main concepts that Rapaport uses in setting up hypotheses about the ways in which various aspects of the Rorschach performance come about: *associative processes* and *perceptual-organizing processes*. Only the former is to any great extent derived from psychoanalysis; most of Rapaport's ideas about perceptual organization have their roots in Gestalt psychology, since Freud wrote very little about the process of perception. These two are abstracted aspects of a unitary process, in which an intimate interaction is assumed to take place between the perceptual and the associative aspect.

Percepts derive their meaning from the associative processes in which they become embedded . . . percepts and images are clues or points of orientation for the thought processes; they indicate necessary changes of direction and points of termination, they bind the association processes to the necessities of reality, they prevent them from running wild and being directed only by subjective wishes. Thus percepts and associations in the smoothly functioning organism are mutually dependent upon each other, mutually stimulate, guide, and limit each other.*

In approaching the task, Rapaport turns to the processes that take place in the subject when he looks at an ink blot. His ideas about these processes in turn come from a theory of thinking that is predominantly (though not entirely) psychoanalytic.† The processes take place in a complex apparatus that is structured and directed by basic needs and interests, modified by old experiences and "set" by recent ones. The first vague perceptual impressions from the blots set off associative processes. "These processes, like all thought processes, can be approached from the point of view of concept formation, of memory, and of the triad of attention, concentration, and anticipation" [60, page 92]—all being aspects of thinking pointed out by Freud. Memory and conceptual thinking come into play as the associative process seeks a realm of content within which the vague impression can be located, resulting in the arousal of some kind of memory image. In the properly functioning person, this is checked back against the perceptual impression, helping to organize it further. "The perceptual potentialities and limitations of the inkblot act as a regulating reality for the association process" [60, page 93 f.].

From the nature of the responses, we can determine how flexibly and adequately, or how impulsively and unrealistically, the perceptual and the associative processes interact. Rapaport's rationale for the location of responses, the form level, and to a large extent for M, is worked out primarily in terms of these two basic concepts. One of the weakest parts of his discussion introduces hypotheses about "perceptual imbalance" to help account for M, but this has

---

* David Rapaport, Merton M. Gill, and Roy Schafer, *Diagnostic Psychological Testing,* Vol. II (The Year Book Publishers, Inc., 1946), page 92. Used by permission.
† Since he wrote this discussion of the Rorschach test, he has worked out this theory in considerably more detail and published it in the final chapter of his recent book [57].

nothing to do with psychoanalysis. In the case of form level, he calls on a more convincing conception of a "critical controlling function" involving judgment and reality testing. He introduces the idea of "preparatory phases" of a response, which helps us understand certain responses (for example: fragmentary, *Do* * percepts) as due to the stopping of the process in a preparatory phase, when the organism is unable to carry out the total task due to limitations of organizing capacity by anxiety, obsessive defenses, or native endowment.

Thus, Rapaport's method is to consider how processes of these kinds must be involved in bringing about any specific kind of response, and then to examine how these processes in turn are affected by various kinds of personality characteristics and psychopathology. The analytic concepts serve as intervening variables to make intelligible the empirically-discovered relations between Rorschach behavior and more general characteristics of the person. This, as the present writer sees it, *is* the function of rationale.

Central to Rapaport's presentation of the psychoanalytic theory of thinking is the concept of *delay*. Only when our ancestors found it possible (or necessary) to hold back the immediate gratification of impulse did thought itself, as trial action, become possible, according to Freud's hypothesis. As applied to modern adult man, the concept of delay does not just mean a lapse of time between impulse and action, but a "long-circuiting" of impulse so that it is brought into harmony with realistic considerations. "In quick and alert subjects the amount of temporal delay may be almost negligible; nevertheless, a complete and responsible psychological process has occurred . . ." in which " 'formal characteristics' of reality can be regarded and unconscious impulses constrained from discharge to allow 'testing of reality' " [60, footnotes on pages 190, 189]. It is the linking of delay to regard for formal characteristics that enables Rapaport to use this concept in developing a rationale for form and color responses.

_____

* "Oligophrenic (oligophrenic = feeble-minded) small detail responses (*Do*) are those interpretations in which only a part of the body is seen by a subject, though others see the whole body clearly in the same part of the figure in question." [64, page 40. See also 34, page 329, footnote.]

Following Werner [74], Rapaport says:

> The primitive and the child tend to apperceive objects of their environment in terms of physiognomic characteristics, affective characteristics, and usefulness; but our culture apparently has forced adults to apperceive objects of the environment in terms of their formal characteristics. That is to say, formal characteristics and their relationships become our guide in life, and not our affective reactions to the things about us: we are trained from childhood on to be "objective."
>
> From the Ego-psychological point of view, the form responses refer to processes of formal reasoning which should pursue their course without anxiety and affects intruding into and disrupting them. Form responses apparently represent . . . the conflict-free sphere of the Ego. Therefore, they stand for the autonomy of the perceptual and thought processes . . . from encroachments by unconscious factors. Finally, . . . the coming-about of form responses represents a capacity for delay of discharge of impulses. . . .*

Accepting the empirical fact that color seems to have the same kind of impact on the psychic apparatus that affective impulses do, Rapaport uses the above rationale to work out an explanation, in terms of the psychoanalytic theory of drives and affects, of the varieties of color responses, and the meaning of different kinds and amounts of form responses. Some of the interrelationships of form and shading in responses are treated in the same way, after a connection between anxiety and the chiaroscuro aspects of the cards has been made: partly through a presumed symbolism, partly through the assumption that the heavily-shaded cards are more disturbing because actually harder to articulate perceptually.

The rationale of content is worked out primarily in terms of the associative processes, their wealth or stereotypy, their vagueness or specificity. About the specific correlation of animal responses with weak, banal associations, Rapaport remarks: "the symmetry of the ink-blots is one of the crucial factors. . . . We experience the greatest variety of non-geometrical forms, which nevertheless have some symmetry, in the world of animal life" [60, page 295]. Being easiest to conceive, such responses indicate the least originality and activity of the associative processes. Similarly, he explains popular and

---

* *Op. cit.*, pages 188–189. Used by permission.

original responses in pretty much the usual way, without much reference to analytic concepts.

Rapaport's main innovations in Rorschach scoring have to do with the way the patient *verbalizes* his responses. Primarily, these scores refer to typical ways in which schizophrenic thought disorders manifest themselves in the test. The basic concept that is introduced to help us understand these bizarre types of verbalization is pathological increase or loss of distance from the card, which again is not derived in any direct way from psychoanalytic theory, and cannot be more than mentioned here.

Such a brief summary can hardly do more than indicate with a few schematic strokes the kinds of considerations on which Rapaport draws in working out detailed hypotheses about the meanings of most aspects of the test performance, and hypothetical intervening variables that establish meaningful links to parts of personality structure and pathology.

The Problem of Projection

What about the psychoanalytic concept of projection? It has not been referred to in any of the above discussion, for Rapaport does not actually use it in any of his detailed rationale for specific aspects of the Rorschach. He does use the concept in a very broad sense, however, in what he calls "the projective hypothesis" underlying all projective techniques. His position here is similar to that of many other authors, who use projection in the general sense of processes that create a private world.*

There are already a great many discussions of projection in relation to projective techniques [for example, 9, 10, 44, 60, 70]. There is not much that is new to add to them. Bellak [10, page 10] has pointed out the fact that Freud used projection not only in the familiar sense, as a defense mechanism characteristic of paranoia, but also in a very generalized way, comparable to the usage it suffers in contemporary clinical psychology. Freud wrote:

---

* Though in a recent paper (presented at the 1952 convention of the American Psychoanalytic Association in Atlantic City), "Projective Techniques and the Psychoanalytic Theory of Thinking," he expressed views that are somewhat closer to the position taken here.

But projection is not specially created for the purpose of defence, it also comes into being where there are no conflicts. The projection of inner perceptions to the outside is a primitive mechanism which, for instance, also influences our sense-perceptions, so that it normally has the greatest share, in shaping our outer world. Under conditions that have not yet been sufficiently determined even inner perceptions of ideational and emotional processes are projected outwardly, like sense perceptions, and are used to shape the outer world, whereas they ought to remain in the inner world. [22, page 857]

In spite of this *ipse dixit,* the writer is inclined to agree with van Lennep [43] that "psychology has no need of a mixture of categories; the need is for sharper differentiation." Particularly is this true when extension results in a loss of clarity. In its narrower Freudian usage, projection is an intelligible process, the dynamics of which have been described in detail. Extended to the point where it merely points to the fact that a person puts his individual mark on almost everything he does, projection is forced to abandon the job it can do well and take on something that is already better handled by other, broader conceptions (for example, see the basic Lewinian formula, quoted above).

The fact is that a person's unique qualities manifest themselves in his Rorschach responses in a variety of ways, apparently using many different processes and mechanisms. One of these processes seems to be at work when a person who has powerful ego-alien homosexual impulses sees the two figures on Card III as two men grabbing at each other's erect penises, and then angrily accuses the examiner of trying to upset him by showing him such disgusting pictures. This kind of thing is not too rarely encountered in testing paranoid schizophrenic patients. Clearly, the mechanism involved is projection. To understand the ways in which other aspects of this man's "private world" may be discerned from his Rorschach performance (for example, when he also gives a number of sharply seen space responses), we would have to call on entirely different kinds of mechanisms.

Psychoanalytic Theory and the Interpretation of Content

Probably the main purpose for which Rorschach interpreters try to get help from psychoanalytic theory is in understanding the significance of content. Rapaport's position on this issue is a rather extreme one: "The psychologist who expects to find in it [that is, Rorschach content] direct manifestations . . . of the content of the patient's problems will be sorely disappointed. Only in very sick patients, or in cases with acute isolated problems, does the content become directly revealing; but then it reveals nothing of which the patient is not conscious or could not tell us in a few moments without the test" [60, page 102]. There are bases in psychoanalytic theory as well as experience for concluding that content is more revealing than this statement claims.*

To go into this matter of content, we must first review quickly a few psychoanalytic concepts. The primitive non-logical form of thinking found most unmistakably in dreams and in schizophrenic language is called *primary process,* in contrast to the *secondary process*—rational, logical thinking. As the name implies, the primary process is the kind of thinking characteristic of young children. With the slow development of reality testing and other ego functions, a person becomes able to think in terms of the secondary process to a progressively greater extent.

One important characteristic of the primary process is that it takes place mainly in terms of *isolated visual images* [57, page 390, footnote 95]. Words are also involved at times, but just as the essential features of dreams are mainly the visual presentations, so it is with the primary process generally. The *symbols* that seem to form an archaic language of the unconscious all consist of pictures: isolated, concrete representations—for the relationships between them cannot be visualized. It seems that such visual images play a crucial part in unconscious psychic life.

This fact could readily lead us to the conclusion that a task which requires the subject to visualize occupies a peculiarly strategic posi-

---

* For an even more detailed psychoanalytic rationale of content interpretation, parallel to this discussion but arrived at independently, see the forthcoming book on the interpretation of the Rorschach by Roy Schafer.

tion. Add the fact that the ink blots offer complex stimulus configurations that are literally non-representative, yet are richly enough varied and differentiated to offer objective support for almost any kind of seen experience. Add further the encouragement of the instructions to see anything, it doesn't matter what, and to produce unrelated images (instead of connected narrative, as in the TAT), and we have a situation that is about as conducive to primary process visual thinking as anything could be—granted the state of full waking consciousness, which in healthy persons tends strongly to maximize the secondary process components of thought.

An essential point about symbols is that the dreamer or the testee only rarely sees through them to the latent content. Therefore, they offer a prime opportunity for psychic formations that would be consciously unacceptable if undisguised to slip into awareness, always urged on by the instinctual drives. When the task is to say what a blot looks like, rather than simply to gaze into space and think of something, or to say whatever comes into one's mind without some external focus on which to concentrate, the self-awareness of the subject is diminished and he is tacitly offered a projective excuse for his thoughts: "It's not I who have such thoughts; you can see what I'm talking about right there in your ink blot." Thus it is *theoretically* possible for the subject's deepest conflicts to find at least indirect and symbolic expression in his responses.

In actuality, of course, people differ tremendously in the kinds of defenses they rely on, and accordingly in the degree of directness with which they can express instinctual or conflictual ideas and still keep them ego-alien. Defensive armoring is so rigid and extensive in some persons that hardly anything of direct or indirect symbolic significance can get through. At the other extreme are patients who are nearly defenseless, and who pour out a torrent of more or less symbolic expressions of their motivational life in primary process terms.

The facts that the blots do have some structure and that certain configurations (the popular responses) are widely recognized by the people of any one culture, help to prevent the Rorschach cards from becoming veritable dream-screens, and allow defensive people something obvious and safe to which to cling. In any response, then, there is almost always some influence of the physical possibilities of the blots, but also (at least theoretically) some expression of unconscious material.

From the above reasoning, we can conclude at once that a study of Rorschach content, the extent to which conflictual material is directly expressed in it, symbolized, or not even adumbrated, can give us useful information about the subject's defenses: how rigid and impermeable they are, how adequately they keep out of consciousness and interpersonal communication violent archaic fantasies that would better remain unconscious, how naïve or intellectually sophisticated the subject is, and so on.

We can conclude also, that Rorschach records will differ greatly in the extent to which we can profitably approach them from the standpoint of content analysis. This seems to be true, in spite of some Rorschachers' contention—supposedly derived from the universality of meaning claimed for certain symbols in psychoanalysis—that reactions to certain cards or certain areas have a fixed and universal significance. The school of content interpretation that proceeds from the assumption that reactions to a specific card can be taken to give the pattern of the subject's relations to his mother or father is in fact without adequate justification in psychoanalysis, though it is often presented as if it were based on psychoanalytic theory [48].

It is not always clear in Freud's writings that he conceived that there might be a continuum of intermediate stages between the ideal types of the primary and secondary process, but Hartmann [25] has made this conception quite explicit. Similar to it is another continuum in modern ego psychology, from the most primitive instinctual impulses through various of their derivatives to "ego-interests" that may operate largely in the conflict-free sphere of the ego, and with "secondary autonomy" of their drive origins [24, 58; see Allport's concept of functional autonomy, 1]. Further, it has been recognized [25, 41] that motives at almost any level in this hierarchy can operate preconsciously in a primary-process kind of way [see Rapaport's discussion, 57, page 405]. Hence, it follows that the processes described above by means of which repressed instinctual impulses might find their way into consciousness via Rorschach responses, apply also to motives on almost all hierarchical levels. (Of course, there is no need for completely ego-syntonic values and attitudes, such as an interest in art, to take indirect routes when there are no barriers on the main highway.)

Digressing for a moment, we might harken back to the fact that all theories we have considered have in one way or another recognized the influence of motives on perception. Is it not surprising, then, that it is so difficult to assess a subject's main conflicts, his strongest needs, his interests and values, from a Rorschach protocol? For the fact is that many a record—particularly the brief, unoriginal, stereotyped ones—contains an assortment of rather standard goods, being much like the protocol of another subject, while the two people themselves may not be nearly so similar to one another. At this point, we have to remember again what was said about defenses and the reality principle. It is perfectly possible for a person—even a coöperative one— to stick to what the blots actually resemble most closely and reveal little about himself other than that he has a certain kind of defensive structure, one that prevents his unique motivational pattern from expressing itself in this particular performance. We should never forget that in a standard 10-card Rorschach we are taking a tiny sample of behavior, even though it may be a very strategically located kind of behavior. Within the microcosm of this test an amazing amount may find expression, *if* the subject is productive (for he himself determines to no mean extent how large a sample it will be) ; but even in 100 responses a man with a thousand interests cannot express them all. There are more ways of getting around defenses than one, however—which is a major reason for using not just one test, and not just projective tests, but a well-rounded battery.

Returning to the interpretation of content, another analytic concept may help us find the kind of responses that are most freighted with personal significance—identification. Identification is not just an introjective process by which a child incorporates images of relationships with his parents [18, page 54], nor just a mechanism of defense. It is also an active process that is very frequently involved in smoothly-functioning, empathic relationships with other people.

For empathy may be defined psychoanalytically as a process of relatively brief identification whereby, in conscious or unconscious fantasy, one merges himself with another to understand and share the other's feelings and attitudes. When a human figure is seen in the blot, then, and is endowed with attributes of life—movement, desires, thoughts, feelings—it seems fairly safe to assume that some process of empathic* identification is involved. These, of course, are the M responses, about which Rorschach wrote that "they must stand in the closest relation to what is generally spoken of as the unconscious" [64, page 208]. The present writer does not share Schachtel's conviction that kinesthetic sensations of how the other person must *feel* have been demonstrated to be an essential part of such a response, but this is a matter about which it is futile to argue and for which an empirical test would be hard to devise.

Nevertheless, Schachtel has described, far better than can be done here, how important basic attitudes and strivings may be diagnosed from movement responses, following psychoanalytic principles [70]. In an earlier article, he does a similarly laudable job in describing the interpretation of form-determined responses [66]. The distinction between dynamic and detached form perception that Schachtel describes may well be coördinated to primary and secondary process, though he does not use these Freudian concepts. According to Kris, the degree to which thought is organized according to the primary versus the secondary process is a function of the extent to which the cathectic energy being used by the organism in thinking has been *neutralized* or bound [41; see also 25].

Now if we could get an adequate operational definition of neutralization (desexualization, deaggressivization), we might have a concept that could be quite useful in relation to the Rorschach. Hartmann suggests that it not only means "different modes or con-

---

* Not just theoretical considerations but also factual findings urge the use of this term. The writer has criterion ratings of the empathy shown by a group of 46 psychiatric residents in their handling of patients. Pooling the ratings of their supervisors, he selected the top eight and bottom eight men from this group, and found them to be significantly different in their production of M responses on the Rorschach test that had been given them when they applied for residencies. The most empathic group averaged a little over 5.6 M, the least empathic a little more than 3.4; t for this difference is 2.18, significant at about the .02 level (one-tailed test).

ditions of energy" (a notion that is difficult to make meaningful)
but also "the degree to which certain other characteristics of the
drives (such as their direction, their aims) are still demonstrable"
[25, page 87]. As a tentative first approximation, therefore, it might
seem reasonable to suppose that a thought product is the result of
neutralized cathectic energy to the extent that evidences of any kind
of libidinal or aggressive aims are lacking in it.

Reasoning in this way, the writer set up a rough scoring scheme
and tried it out on a number of Rorschach protocols. In effect, each
response was rated on the extent to which the content itself or anything about its verbal elaboration involved oral, narcissistic, anal,
voyeuristic, exhibitionistic, urethral, phallic, homosexual, or other
libidinal aims, *or* any manifestation of aggression, personal or impersonal, and including deteriorative, destructive contents. From these
scores, it was possible to derive a total "neutralization" index, dividing by R. (This index would probably correlate rather highly with
a ratio of "detached" to "dynamic" forms, as defined by Schachtel.)
After this scoring had been applied "blind" to a number of Rorschachs,* the extensive data that were available on the personalities
and work performances of these men were examined. It had been
predicted that the subjects whose responses were most pervaded with
more or less explicit libidinal and aggressive overtones would have
the greatest difficulty in working with the emotional problems of
patients.

The prediction was fairly well borne out. The least-neutralizing
subject was one who had done poorly and had had to seek psychotherapeutic help to continue his residency, while some of the others
who had lowest neutralization scores had left the residency program
or even the field of psychiatry. Naturally, there were many reversals;
success in psychiatric work is dependent on a large number of factors, some quite independent of anything this procedure might
have been measuring.

---

* Of the same subjects in a Research Project on the Selection of Medical Men for Psychiatric Training, on which the author has been working in collaboration with Dr. Les-
ter Luborsky in the Research Department of The Menninger Foundation. The project
is at present supported by a grant from the New York Foundation.

One surprising reversal caused a useful revision. One of the best residents in the group had one of the poorest neutralization scores. But he was a sensitive, rather creative fellow, composed and quite well-adjusted; he gave no outward signs of being driven or threatened by instinctual impulses. Then an important statement by Kris came to mind: "During many types of productive processes . . . the ego may use the primary process and not only be overwhelmed by it" [41, pages 488–489]. Studies of humor, of art, and other creative activities led him to this idea of "regression in the service of the ego." Thus, regression from secondary to primary process thinking may occur as a sign of pathology; or, conversely, it may indicate ego strength! For it is a sign of health and flexibility to be able to relax one's controls, playfully or productively to let thought wander freely without feeling threatened by the danger of being overwhelmed by unconscious fantasies and wishes if one lets go for a minute.

Going back to this particular Rorschach protocol, it differed from others with similar neutralization scores in giving evidence that the subject felt free, not driven or threatened; he was quite sensitive to physiognomic and movement impressions yet maintained an excellent level of form accuracy. Some of his responses with aggressive content are given with humor and a rather artistic touch; he enjoyed taking the test. Thus it was possible to understand the apparent inconsistency in terms of Kris's concept of regression in the service of the ego.

This brief and inadequate account of preliminary steps in an attempt to derive a neutralization index is presented principally to show how rather abstract theoretical considerations may usefully increase our understanding of our day-to-day clinical results.* This particular line of approach may in the long run not turn out to add anything, but it serves as an example of one way in which person-

---

* A fuller report of this work will be published later. The matter cannot be dropped here, however, until the obvious fact is mentioned that the index as described above neglects the crucial problem of *defenses*. It seems certain that the degree of positive results reported here was possible only because small samples of subjects were used who had been selected from the larger group on the basis of relatively homogeneous kinds of defenses, as indicated by formal aspects of the psychogram. It would be extremely difficult to make any sense out of such a content-based index in terms of neutralization if one compared Rorschachs from persons with quite different defensive structures.

ality theory can have direct applications to Rorschach work. And it illustrates one way of working with theoretical conceptions—seeking operations by which they can be measured, predictions made and tested—a procedure that has been too little followed in psychoanalytic personology.

Suggested Directions for Rorschach Research

The study just described illustrates one type of research that might well be carried out more extensively with the Rorschach—a type that may contribute both to personality theory and to our use of the test. In the remaining pages, a few other lines of research will be suggested.

First, however (since W should precede D), a few generalizations. Looking back over the various trails we have traversed, we can see that a great deal, perhaps most, of what is distinctive about the Rorschach has so far escaped the conceptual nets woven by contemporary personologists. We can do something with location, content, verbalization, even succession. But when it comes to determinants, the aspect of scoring where Rorschach's genius showed itself most brilliantly, our theories can give us little help. Most of our hypotheses about their significance in terms of emotional responsiveness, ideational activity, introspectiveness, tact, and what not, remain essentially as empirical generalizations without theoretical linkages or support. They continue to constitute a challenge to personology— a challenge that is, however, muffled and not yet inescapable, because the facts have not all been well established. There surely can be little quarrel about the intimate tie-ups between experiences of color and of affect, but validational studies on the other determinants have for the most part either yielded negative results (as in the sad story of M and creativity; see 62, 63, 65) * or they have simply not yet been done with adequate methods. Theory cannot make much progress unless it has some definite facts to work with. Vague hunches, statements of a general relationship that leave unclear what the form

* See the discussion of creativity in other chapters of this volume—pages 256–262, 366–370, 568, 576–578.

and limits of the tie-up may be—these do not ordinarily provide solid enough bricks for theory-building.

Validational studies of the kinds recommended by Hertz [27] are needed, then, though they will not in themselves appreciably advance our *theoretical* understanding, however useful and necessary they may be for our practice. Preferably they should be done by investigators who have read and thoroughly digested Cronbach's important articles on method [15, 16]. But beyond these conventional horizons, we should encourage work that has not taken a pledge of allegiance to the Rorschach, research that will follow its own natural course wherever that may lead. The research worker who is guided by his curiosity about the trends that develop in his data, often in surprising ways, will accomplish more eventually than the one who is guided by a directive, for example, to provide a rationale for the *M* response.

The main technical problem that the ingenuity of future researchers will have to cope with is how to get at the intervening variables, the mediating processes, between general life-trends and specific perceptual-associative reactions. It is recommended that they be thought of as "organizers," or "system principles," but quite different conceptions may prove more satisfactory. It may still be too soon for this kind of concept to be teased out of a brain model, but it is to be hoped that someone will try. And whatever kind of theory investigators may favor, let them try to be explicit about it and try to derive predictions from the theory as stringently as possible beforehand. The most desirable state of affairs is a constant growth of theory and experiment, each suggesting new developments in the other and forcing changes.

Now for the specific suggestions. First, let us review the research ideas that have grown directly out of our discussions of the half dozen personologies that have been reviewed here. *Allport's* theory suggests a study of the content of responses offered by people who differ in their value orientations, as measured by the Allport-Vernon *Study of Values*. The hypothesis to be tested would be that people who are otherwise generally similar but who differ in the values that they espouse will tend to see in the neutral blots things, persons, and activities that are relevant to their strongest values. About the only other kind of research that Allport's approach would lead us to would be case studies in which congruence between characteristics of a subject's Rorschach performance and of his other behavior would be sought. The disadvantages of this kind of research, however, are that it is impossible to *prove* anything this way, and that the relationships are essentially *post hoc.*

It seems worth while to investigate *Lewin's* concept of rigidity with the methods worked out by Kounin, and relate it to supposed Rorschach signs. As a matter of fact, this is a concept that is found in almost all of the theories, usually with slightly different meanings. Different operations might be derived from the various theories and all applied to the same subjects; then we might get some idea of the theoretical framework in which the rigidity that shows up in the Rorschach best fits.

A study (of sensitivity to nuances) based on *Angyal's* approach has already been outlined in the discussion of his theory, above.

On the whole, *Murray* seems to have most to offer by way of method. His technique of clinical research, in which a team of many investigators study a relatively small group of subjects, pooling their data and the contributions of their different backgrounds and training, is ideal for validational research, if the results of the Rorschach are kept separate from the team's assessment of the subject's personalities. Murray's bold plan [see 53] of using the composite portrait of each subject, not just to correlate rated variables to Rorschach scores, but as a basis of individualized *predictions* of how each subject will react in a given situation, might well be applied to the Rorschach.

The kind of study suggested by *Murphy's* theory as well as Murray's is to arouse some need experimentally and see what it does to readministered Rorschachs, in the manner of McClelland and Atkinson [47]. Such studies of autism would have greater value if some systematic account were taken of differences in personality structure. Thus, hunger might have quite different effects on perception in people who accept and others who repress and deny their orality.

The *psychoanalytic* concept of neutralization, and the scoring scheme briefly described above for gauging it, might be further explored along the following lines: First, the method might be modified to take account of context, particularly with emphasis on the degree of the subject's enjoyment of the testing experience, and the kinds and degree of defensiveness shown. Then, it might be applied to Rorschachs given to persons of the same general defensive types, but in different states of consciousness, such as extreme fatigue (to test Silberer's hypothesis [71] that such states in themselves are conducive to an increase in primary process thinking), those induced by various drugs and by hypnosis. Again, it might be used in experiments with groups of subjects chosen by an independent criterion of ego strength, who would be tested with the Rorschach once in the usual way, and then with instructions to "let yourself go, get as wild and woolly as you can," to test Kris's hypothesis about the ability of a strong ego to "regress" creatively.

Finally, there is a group of miscellaneous experimental ideas without any pure theoretical parentage but with some reasonable hope of offspring. One easily recognizable ancestor that they have in common is the conviction that issues concerning the Rorschach test can often be more easily and relevantly studied in the experimental laboratory, outside of the usual test situation.

It might be helpful to start with certain classical perceptual phenomena and study individual differences in groups having different kinds of known pathology, as specific as possible (that is, not "neurotics" versus "schizophrenics"). For example, Rorschach studies of depressives suggest that they perceive color less vividly than people who are not depressed. A direct attack on this problem might be made with one of the following kinds of design. One might test the differential thresholds of neurotically depressed patients for the perception of small amounts of color added in a gray color wheel, preferably having each patient serve as his own control after improvement, or using patients with clinically differentiated degrees of depression. Another approach might be to prepare a number of figure-ground drawings with contours given by differences in saturation or color contrast with other stimulus attributes held constant; the score would be how high in a graded series you would have to go before the patient recognized the figure. Still another, an indirect way of getting at the impressiveness of color to people suffering various kinds of affective disorders, would use the kind of design worked out by Restorff to study trace aggregation [36, pages 482 ff.]. Series of paired associates are given to a subject to learn—for example, homogeneous nonsense syllables—except that one pair is printed in color. Ordinarily, the color produces a high degree of salience and thus of improved retention. The hypothesis would be that, if the colored pairs give a subject a slighter advantage than normally occurs, he must have a less vivid color experience.

Then, there might be value in a series of studies in which subjects were tested not only with the Rorschach but in situations of the kind that the Rorschach is supposed to represent. For example: seeing if subjects who give many vista responses and those who give none differ in judgments of depth or distance in stereoscopic perception of three-dimensional space; or studying via one-way mirror the reactions of persons who give many *Fc*, and persons who give none, when left alone in a room containing a number of objects with a variety of textures (alabaster figures, gnarled wood burls, fur rugs, and the like). Qualitative observations, plus subsequent requests for introspective reports, of extreme subjects in such situations might tell us at least whether or not these kinds of Rorschach responses have anything to do with the kinds of experiences from which they take their names. Independent studies of the same subjects' dependent needs and how they handled them could test the hypothesis about the significance of *Fc* presented in an earlier publication [34]. In this same category might fall attempts to measure muscle potentials of subjects who give many *M* responses versus those who give none, when observing the cards—to see if there is any possibility of measuring directly the disputed kinesthesias.

Another kind of research on the movement response would attempt to follow up the leads given by Arnheim in a recent article [6]. He links the *M* experience up with an esthetic experience of "visual dynamics"; from the examples given, it should not be hard to devise tests of sensitivity to good and bad composition, varying sys-

tematically the kinds of factors that he mentions, relating them to
M-productivity.

Somewhat similar is the type of research that is being carried on
by Klein, Gardner, Holzman, and Schlesinger in the Research Department of The Menninger Foundation [29–33]. Working within
a general psychoanalytic framework of assumptions, they are seeking to find organizing principles of cognition, which they propose
are ego-controls. The procedure might best be described by reference
to a series of experiments that led to the isolation of such a principle,
or *Anschauung,* which Klein calls "tolerance (vs. intolerance) for
perceptual instability." These experiments [32, 33], incidentally, are
excellent examples of a fresh approach to using the Rorschach in
research, throwing light on both the test and on the perceptual phenomena under study.

On the basis of preliminary exploratory work with the phenomenon of apparent movement (or *phi*), Klein and his co-workers
formed the hypothesis that individual differences in ease of getting
the movement experience were related to a general tolerance for instability and change in the stimulus field. Extending this conception
to the Rorschach, they hypothesized that a person who easily tolerated
instability would have an attitude of "form-lability," feeling free to
see what occurred to him and to elaborate his percepts. The opposite
pole, form-boundedness, was spelled out in Rorschach terms as a
lean, constricted, carefully accurate record, in which the subject
stuck to what was safe and sure. Groups of subjects were selected by
going through a large number of Rorschach protocols and picking
the extremes on this dimension. The subjects were then tested for
the *range* of time intervals between successive presentations under
which they could see apparent movement, using a number of different stimulus pairs. Extremely significant differences in the predicted direction were obtained. Incidentally, it is interesting that a
re-examination of the Rorschach data from the subjects who had the
highest and lowest scores on the range of apparent movement shows
that they are not well distinguished in terms of the *M* response. There
is no difference in $M\%$, and in both groups there are persons with

no *M* and with five or more, though the total frequency is higher in the subjects who easily got the apparent movement experience.

A characteristic feature of this kind of experimentation is that the authors did not let the matter rest with the original hypothesis verified. Instead, they went on to *explore* the limits of the hypothesized Anschauung of tolerance for instability *within* the perceptual area. In a second experiment, they used the apparent movement experience to separate extreme groups, and tested them with a number of other perceptual experiments: autokinesis, the distortion of the visual field by wearing aniseikonic lenses, fluctuating reversible-perspective figures, a binocular rivalry situation, and flicker fusion. Not all of these phenomena turned out to be highly interrelated, but a consistent core of perceptual effects continued to be correlated with each other and with the Rorschach "form-boundedness," though not with any one of the standard scoring categories.

By continuing to work with an expanding circle of experimentally defined phenomena, it is possible to implicate an increasingly wider range of behaviors that are unified by a single organizational principle, and to sharpen and focalize the nature of this principle. Viewed in the context of related perceptual phenomena, aspects of the Rorschach can be better understood in perceptual terms. Then, following Angyal's formula, inferences about organismic system principles can be drawn, from which in turn it will be possible to predict kinds of congruent behavior in quite different regions of the personality.

For these reasons, the kind of research that Klein and his group have been doing may prove extremely valuable to the Rorschach worker as well as the personality theorist. This will be true *even if* it means drawing new dimensions from the test; perhaps *especially because* would be more apt. The Rorschach is so rich and complex a slice of behavior that further progress in its use may well involve the isolation of new types of scores, the possibility of which is only half-glimpsed at present, as well as further understanding of the old, familiar, but still challenging ones.

References

1. Allport, Gordon W. *Personality, a Psychological Interpretation.* New York: Henry Holt & Company, Inc.; 1937.

2. ———. *The Nature of Personality, Selected Papers.* Cambridge, Mass.: Addison Wesley; 1950.

3. Angyal, Andras. *Foundations for a Science of Personality.* New York: Commonwealth Fund; 1941.

4. ———. "The Holistic Approach in Psychiatry," *Amer. J. Psychiat.,* 1948, 105, 178–182.

5. ———; Freeman, H.; and Hoskins, R. G. "Physiologic Aspects of Schizophrenic Withdrawal," pp. 254–258 in Tomkins, Silvan S. (ed.) *Contemporary Psychopathology.* Cambridge: Harvard University Press; 1943. (Reprinted from *Arch. Neurol. Psychiat.,* 1940, 44, 621–626.)

6. Arnheim, Rudolf. "Perceptual and Aesthetic Aspects of the Movement Response," *J. Personality,* 1951, 19, 265–281.

7. Atkinson, John W., and McClelland, David C. "The Projective Expression of Needs. II. The Effect of Different Intensities of the Hunger Drive on Thematic Apperception," *J. Exp. Psychol.,* 1948, 38, 643–658.

8. Beck, Samuel J. *Rorschach's Test. Vol. I. Basic Processes.* New York: Grune & Stratton, Inc.; 1944.

9. Bellak, Leopold. "The Concept of Projection," *Psychiatry,* 1944, 7, 353–370.

10. ———. "On the Problems of the Concept of Projection," pp. 7–32 in Abt, L. E., and Bellak, Leopold (eds.) *Projective Psychology: Clinical Approaches to the Total Personality.* New York: Alfred A. Knopf, Inc.; 1950.

11. Brozek, Josef; Guetzkow, Harold; and Baldwin, Marcella V. "A Quantitative Study of Perception and Association in Experimental Semi-starvation," *J. Personality,* 1951, 19, 245–264.

12. Bruner, Jerome S. "Perceptual Theory and the Rorschach Test," *J. Personality,* 1948, 17, 157–168.

13. ———. "One Kind of Perception: A Reply to Professor Luchins," *Psychol. Rev.,* 1951, 58, 306–312.

14. ———, and Goodman, C. C. "Value and Need as Organizing Factors in Perception," *J. Abnorm. Soc. Psychol.,* 1947, 42, 33–44.

15. Cronbach, Lee J. " 'Pattern Tabulation': A Statistical Method for Analysis of Limited Patterns of Scores, with Particular Reference to the Rorschach Test," *Educ. Psychol. Measmt.,* 1949, 9, 149–171.

16. ———. "Statistical Methods Applied to Rorschach Scores, a Review," *Psychol. Bull.,* 1949, 46, 393–429.

17. Elizur, Abraham. "Content Analysis of the Rorschach with Regard to Anxiety and Hostility," *J. Proj. Tech.,* 1949, 13, 247–284.

18. Erikson, Erik H. *Childhood and Society.* New York: W. W. Norton & Company, Inc.; 1951.

19. Faterson, Hanna F., and Klopfer, Bruno. "A Survey of Psychologists' Opinions Concerning the Rorschach Method," *Rorschach Res. Exch.*, 1945, 9, 23–29.

20. Frank, Lawrence K. *Projective Methods*. Springfield, Ill.: Charles C. Thomas; 1948.

21. Freud, Sigmund. *The Interpretation of Dreams*, pp. 179–548 in *The Basic Writings of Sigmund Freud*. New York: Modern Library, Inc.; 1938.

22. ———. *Totem and Taboo*, pp. 807–883 in *The Basic Writings of Sigmund Freud* (A. A. Brill, ed.). New York: Modern Library, Inc.; 1938.

23. Friedman, Howard. "Perceptual Regression in Schizophrenia, an Hypothesis Suggested by the Use of the Rorschach Test." Paper presented at the convention of the American Psychological Association, Chicago, 1951.

24. Hartmann, Heinz. "Ego Psychology and the Problem of Adaptation," pp. 362–396 in Rapaport, David, *Organization and Pathology of Thought*. New York: Columbia University Press; 1951.

25. ———. "Comments on the Psychoanalytic Theory of the Ego," *Psychoanalytic Study of the Child*, 1950, 5, 74–96.

26. Hebb, Donald O. *The Organization of Behavior*. New York: John Wiley & Sons, Inc.; 1949.

27. Hertz, Marguerite R. "Rorschach Twenty Years After," *Psychol. Bull.*, 1942, 39, 529–572.

28. Hutt, Max L.; Gibby, Robert; Milton, E. O.; and Pottharst, K. "The Effect of Varied Experimental 'Sets' upon Rorschach Test Performance," *J. Proj. Tech.*, 1950, 14, 181–187.

29. Klein, George S. "The Personal World through Perception," pp. 328–355 in Blake, Robert R., and Ramsey, Glenn V. (eds.) *Perception: An Approach to Personality*. New York: The Ronald Press, Inc.; 1951.

30. ———, and Holzman, Philip S. "Perceptual Attitudes of Leveling and Sharpening: Relation to Individual Differences in Time Error," *Amer. Psychologist*, 1951, 6, 257. (Abstract.)

31. ———, and Schlesinger, Herbert J "Where is the Perceiver in Perceptual Theory?" *J. Personality*, 1949, 18, 32–47.

32. ———, and Schlesinger, Herbert J. "Perceptual Attitudes toward Instability: I. Prediction of Apparent Movement Experiences from Rorschach Responses," *J. Personality*, 1951, 19, 289–302.

33. ———; Schlesinger, Herbert J.; and Gardner, Riley. "Perceptual Attitudes toward Instability: Prediction from Apparent Movement Responses to Other Tasks Involving Resolution of Unstable Fields," *Amer. Psychologist*, 1951, 6, 332. (Abstract.)

34. Klopfer, Bruno, and Kelley, Douglas M. *The Rorschach Technique*. Yonkers, N. Y.: World Book Company; 1942.

35. Kluckhohn, Clyde, and Murray, Henry A. (eds.) *Personality in Nature, Society, and Culture*. New York: Alfred A. Knopf, Inc.; 1948.

36. Koffka, Kurt. *Principles of Gestalt Psychology*. New York: Harcourt, Brace, & Company, Inc.; 1935.

37. Kounin, Jacob. "Experimental Studies of Rigidity. I and II." *Character and Pers.*, 1941, 9, 251–282.

38. Krech, David. "Notes toward a Psychological Theory," *J. Personality*, 1949, 18, 66–87.

39. ———. "Dynamic Systems, Psychological Fields and Hypothetical Constructs," *Psychol. Rev.*, 1950, 57, 283–290.

40. ———. "Dynamic Systems as Open Neurological Systems," *Psychol. Rev.*, 1950, 57, 345–361.

41. Kris, Ernst. "On Preconscious Mental Processes," pp. 474–493 in Rapaport, David, *Organization and Pathology of Thought*. New York: Columbia University Press; 1951.

42. Kubie, Lawrence S. "Some Implications for Psychoanalysis of Modern Concepts of the Organization of the Brain," *Psychoanal. Quart.*, 1953, 22, 21–68.

43. Lennep, D. J. van. "The Four-Picture Test," pp. 149–180 in Anderson, Harold H., and Anderson, Gladys L. (eds.) *An Introduction to Projective Techniques*. New York: Prentice-Hall, Inc.; 1951.

44. ———. *Psychology of Projective Phenomena*. New York: Grune & Stratton, Inc.; in preparation.

45. Lewin, Kurt. *A Dynamic Theory of Personality*. New York: McGraw-Hill Book Company, Inc.; 1935.

46. ———. *The Conceptual Representation and the Measurement of Psychological Forces*. Durham, N. C.: Duke University Press; 1938.

47. McClelland, David C., and Atkinson, John W. "The Projective Expression of Needs: I. The Effect of Different Intensities of the Hunger Drive on Perception," *J. Psychol.*, 1948, 25, 205–222.

48. Meer, Bernard, and Singer, Jerome L. "A Note on the 'Father' and 'Mother' Cards in the Rorschach Inkblots," *J. Consult. Psychol.*, 1950, 14, 482–484.

49. Munroe, Ruth L. "Considerations on the Place of the Rorschach in the Field of General Psychology," *Rorschach Res. Exch.* 1945, 9, 30–40.

50. Murphy, Gardner. *Personality: a Biosocial Approach to Origins and Structure*. New York: Harper & Brothers; 1947.

51. ———, and Hochberg, Julian. "Perceptual Development: Some Tentative Hypotheses," *Psychol. Rev.*, 1951, 58, 332–349.

52. Murray, Henry A. "The Effect of Fear upon Estimates of the Maliciousness of Other Personalities," pp. 545–560 in Tomkins, Silvan S. (ed.) *Contemporary Psychopathology*. Cambridge: Harvard University Press; 1943. (Reprinted from *J. Soc. Psychol.*, 1933, 4, 310–329.)

53. ———, et al. *Explorations in Personality*. New York: Oxford University Press; 1938.

54. Penfield, Wilder. "Memory Mechanisms," *AMA Arch. Neurol. Psychiat.*, 1952, 67, 178–191.

55. Postman, Leo; Bruner, Jerome S.; and McGinnies, Elliott. "Personal Values as Selective Factors in Perception," *J. Abnorm. Soc. Psychol.*, 1948, 43, 148–153.

56. Rabin, Albert I. "Validating and Experimental Studies with the Rorschach Method," pp. 123–146 in Anderson, Harold H., and Anderson, Gladys L. (eds.) *An Introduction to Projective Techniques*. New York: Prentice-Hall, Inc.; 1951.

57. Rapaport, David. *Organization and Pathology of Thought*. New York: Columbia University Press; 1951.

58. ——. "The Autonomy of the Ego," *Bull. Menninger Clin.*, 1951, 15, 113–123.

59. ——; Gill, Merton M.; and Schafer, Roy. *Diagnostic Psychological Testing.* Vol. I. Chicago: Yearbook Publishers; 1946.

60. ——; Gill, Merton M.; and Schafer, Roy. *Diagnostic Psychological Testing.* Vol. II. Chicago: Year Book Publishers; 1946.

61. Rickers-Ovsiankina, Maria. "Some Theoretical Considerations Regarding the Rorschach Method," *Rorschach Res. Exch.* 1943, 7, 41–53.

62. Roe, Anne. "Painting and Personality," *Rorschach Res. Exch.*, 1946, 10, 86–100.

63. ——. "A Psychological Study of Physical Scientists," *Genet. Psychol. Monogr.*, 1951, 43, 121–239.

64. Rorschach, Hermann. *Psychodiagnostics.* Berne, Switzerland: Hans Huber; 1942.

65. Rust, Ralph M. "Some Correlates of the Movement Response," *J. Personality*, 1948, 16, 369–401.

66. Schachtel, Ernest G. "The Dynamic Perception and the Symbolism of Form," *Psychiatry*, 1941, 4, 79–96.

67. ——. Review of *The Rorschach Technique*, by Klopfer, B., and Kelley, D. M., *Psychiatry*, 1942, 5, 604–606.

68. ——. "On Color and Affect. Contributions to an Understanding of Rorschach's Test. II," *Psychiatry*, 1943, 6, 393–409.

69. ——. "Subjective Definitions of the Rorschach Test Situation and Their Effect on Test Performance. Contributions to an Understanding of Rorschach's Test. III," *Psychiatry*, 1945, 8, 419–448.

70. ——. "Projection and Its Relation to Character Attitudes and Creativity in the Kinesthetic Responses. Contributions to an Understanding of Rorschach's Test. IV," *Psychiatry*, 1950, 13, 69–100.

71. Silberer, Herbert. "On Symbol-Formation," pp. 208–233 in Rapaport, David, *Organization and Pathology of Thought.* New York: Columbia University Press; 1951.

72. Thurstone, L. L. "The Rorschach in Psychological Science," *J. Abnorm. Soc. Psychol.*, 1948, 43, 471–475.

73. Tolman, Edward C. "Discussion," *J. Personality*, 1949, 18, 48–50.

74. Werner, Heinz. *Comparative Psychology of Mental Development.* Revised edition. Chicago: Follett Publishing Company; 1948.

75. Zubin, Joseph. "Personality Research and Psychopathology as Related to Clinical Practice," *J. Abnorm. Soc. Psychol.*, 1949, 44, 14–21.

CHAPTER **16**

Rorschach Hypotheses
and Ego Psychology

The function of the concluding chapter in this part on theory is twofold: (1) to attempt to develop a common frame of reference for the many interpretative hypotheses set forth in Part Two ("Interpretation") and (2) to consider how the development of a Rorschach rationale and the construction of a personality theory can stimulate each other.*

Basic Observations and Assumptions

The statement on personality theory made in *The Rorschach Technique* † indicated that the Rorschach is a useful instrument, regardless of what theory of personality the clinician espouses. Looking back over the interval that has elapsed since then, the statement sounds more naïve than modest.

---

* The literature references in this chapter were contributed by Jack Fox, Los Angeles, California.

† "It is unnecessary for our purposes here to become entangled in the warring camps fighting for their particular theories of personality structure. The general psychological assumptions made in Rorschach interpretation are so few and simple that nobody will have any compunction about accepting them." [28, page 221]

The following statement from the *1946 Supplement* [28] shows increasing sophistication.

> The application of the Rorschach method from Rorschach's first publication up to the present time has not been predicated upon any particular theory of personality. Nevertheless, a number of the newer publications indicate that the use of the method is having a stimulating effect on the development of such a theory. [28, page 434]

Ego psychology has become the common meeting ground in the recent development of the various dynamic personality theories. At the same time, it has become more and more apparent that the concepts of ego psychology are relevant to the special contribution the Rorschach technique can make to the understanding of personality.

A number of personal experiences during the last ten years have strengthened the tendency of this author to focus on ego psychology in connection with his efforts to develop a Rorschach rationale. The most painful but—fortunately—very rare experiences involved a few cases which manifested dramatic behavior, such as homicide. Such behavior, obviously, is important for the understanding of the individual personality, yet the Rorschach records of the individuals concerned did not reflect it at all. Closest scrutiny of the records and the circumstances surrounding the commission of these acts seemed to reveal that they were committed in such states as epileptic furor, toxic conditions, or extreme panic. Thus, it appeared that these acts were neither ego-syntonic nor ego-alien, but rather the products of a temporary yet complete dissociation of the ego structure. The acts were thus completely disconnected from the ego of the individual.

Other cases, more helpful to the clinician—and, fortunately, much more frequent than the above—are those showing an extreme discrepancy between the general nosological picture they present overtly and symptomatically and the ego structure, as revealed in the Rorschach records. Such a discrepancy between two sets of observations usually indicates that neither observation reflects the total reality. Prognostically this may have either positive or negative implications.

A discrepancy with negative prognostic implications is exemplified by patients with predominantly hysterical symptoms. Their Rorschach records may indicate the absence of the ego capacities usually associated with predominantly phallic psychosexual development, which supposedly underlies such symptoms. The final clinical judgment may lead to a diagnosis of "schizoid personality, covered up by a thin hysterical overlay." This is also the case where pseudo-adjustment covers up the lack of real ego strength. For instance, some subjects whose social and economic achievements surpass the average, produce Rorschach records that indicate emotionally impoverished, almost emaciated personalities. Such "pseudo-normal" personalities are so brittle that they break easily under unexpected strain.

Positive prognostic implications are provided by the Rorschach records of overtly psychotic individuals, which show a relatively well-integrated ego picture without the usual indications of schizophrenic disintegration such as erratic variations in form level, grotesque use of color without subjective discomfort, or bizarre originals. Such an "unpsychotic" Rorschach record is sometimes so astonishingly at variance with the overt symptomatology that hardly anybody making a "blind interpretation" of the record would diagnose the symptoms correctly. Closer examination of the case history usually shows that an extraordinary strain in the life situation caused a psychotic break. Such temporary psychotic breaks sometimes accompany extreme battle fatigue. It should be noted, however, that such breaks usually manifest themselves in the form of hysterical dissociations rather than in schizophrenic disintegration.

The psychological implications of these observations are threefold: (1) The Rorschach record usually seems to reflect the ego organization, as it is shaped by the level of maturation, the character formation, and the symptomatic ego defenses of the individual. (2) The ego organization may not always be easily recognizable in overtly observable behavior. (3) The breakthrough of "archaic" or "pre-phallic" forces into behavior is visible in Rorschach reactions only to the extent to which such breakthrough is mirrored in the existing ego organization.

Observations of cases that illustrate point (2) led to the development of the Rorschach Prognostic Rating Scale (RPRS). This scale will be discussed in detail in Chapter 19.

The only substantial statement with regard to the relationship of Rorschach hypotheses and ego psychology in the literature is one by David Rapaport:

> The psychology of thought processes is a part of Ego psychology. If a breakthrough of *unconscious* modes of thinking occurs, it should prompt the projective tester to draw on psychoanalytic theory concerning such a breakthrough and the nature of unconscious processes. But the patterns characteristic of conscious thought processes are unexplored by psychoanalysis, and the next-of-kind to them are defense mechanisms—the subject matter of psychoanalytic Ego-psychology. To draw on the theory of the latter with utmost caution, and to attempt to mold a theory of observed thought-patterns so that they and the known patterns of defense mechanisms will elucidate each other and be welded into one common theoretical framework, is the great unsolved task of projective testing.*

The present writer would like to amplify and modify this statement in the following directions: Rapaport has amply demonstrated the justification of his contentions by showing the theoretical and practical value of studying in great detail the nuances of the thought processes revealed in Rorschach reactions, especially with regard to their ego-defensive meaning. He has given insufficient attention, however, to the non-intellectual, constructive ego functions, the "reasonable ego" of Otto Fenichel [8] and others or the "critical ego" of Milton Wexler [49].

There is one further modification. The writer is inclined to follow the idea of C. G. Jung [26] when he considers the "Self" a part of the personality organization, separate from the ego, yet in interaction with it.

* David Rapaport, Merton M. Gill, and Roy Schafer, *Diagnostic Psychological Testing,* Vol. II (The Year Book Publishers, Inc., 1946), page 11. Used by permission.

Jungian Modifications of Freudian Ego Psychology *

Jung's concept of the Self visualizes a second center of personality which, in most adults, is less conscious and less differentiated than the ego.

While the ego is the mediator between outer reality and the forces of the unconscious, the Self has a mediating position between the ego and the "archaic forces" of the unconscious (see Appendix). The ego is trying to defend the conscious life of the personality against any threats from these forces, or to neutralize such threats. The Self, on the other hand, tries to make contact with these same forces and to amalgamate and absorb as much of their creative power as the conscious personality can afford.

The ego, in its major functions, is outside the sphere of the unconscious forces and in opposition to them (opposition, here, does not necessarily imply negative contradiction but may involve a constructive relationship). The Self is within the realm of the unconscious, and a part of it. The Self can become conscious only in symbolic form, and usually only in rare moments.†

---

* The ideas expressed in the second and third sections of this chapter present no particular claim for originality by the author; nevertheless, they may appear rather new to many readers, maybe even startling to some. One of the major reasons for this unintentional effect is the fact that the conceptual context from which these ideas stem is not easily accessible.

Summaries of the Freudian and Jungian approaches to the development of Ego and Self in available textbooks and introductory publications are by necessity too oversimplified to offer an adequate basis for a critical evaluation of these ideas. More explicit formulations of their conceptual context are spread through a voluminous literature, made uninviting to the uninitiated reader by semantic and terminological barriers.

Any attempt to present the conceptual context for these ideas within the framework of this chapter would have obviously overstrained this framework. Literature references seem an inadequate device for the reasons just mentioned. As an obvious compromise solution, the Appendix to Volume I offers a summary of the Freudian and Jungian approaches, drawing on the writings of Fenichel and others [8, 12, 34].

† When these moments become too frequent, a fate like that which befell Van Gogh may overcome its unfortunate victim. The genius Goethe, who had an extreme degree of Self contact as seen symbolically in "Faust," did not have his ego swallowed by the Self because in his case the Self contact was counter-balanced by equally well-developed skills in the mastery of reality situations. Goethe was, therefore, able to reach a high degree of self-realization.

The Self has its own symbolic representation in dreams, myths, and artistic expressions. These symbols of the Self, as Jung has pointed out repeatedly, are closely related to religious symbols.

The difference between the Freudian and the Jungian theoretical approaches seems less marked than one might think at first glance. The solution of certain theoretical, psychoanalytical antinomies is bringing the two views closer together.

One of Jung's most disputed notions about the Self is his idea that the Self is an inherited archetype. When we consider what psychoanalysts have brought to light about ego structure and development in the last few years, Jung's position appears much less controversial. Rapaport, for instance, has the following to say about the genetic development of the ego:

> Note the circularity: The ego is both born out of the conflict, and party to the conflict. How can we explain this seeming contradiction? The answer can be seen in the study of infants in the individual differences between infants which are present from the very beginning of development, suggesting inborn personality determinants *in nuce*. It may be seen on one of Freud's last papers, "Psychoanalysis, Terminable and Interminable," in which he directly postulates inborn, inherited ego factors. It can be seen also when we consider that after all psychology has found some general laws of perception, memory, and learning which show some inter-individual consistency. . . . Memory, perception, and motility have already been existing and functioning before conflict ever occurred. Here then we see apparatuses which antedate conflict, and may become the core of ego development. Indeed we know that these appartuses may remain, in many cases, outside of conflict later on also. . . .
>
> Indeed, rereading material like that summarized by Heinz Werner in his *Developmental Psychology*, clearly suggests an initial, undifferentiated phase in which percepts are physiognomic, concepts are syncretic, and experience is diffuse.
>
> The inborn ego apparatuses, and their integration in the ego, which, just like the id, develop from an originally undifferentiated matrix by differentiation, provide a way out of the paradox described above. [36, pages 117–118]

Rapaport's formulation is quite similar to the conceptualization of ego development by the English Jungian, Michael Fordham [9, 10].

Fordham postulates the existence of a developing, undifferentiated infantile Self. This infantile Self serves as the matrix from which the ego "buds" during the pre-school years. The infantile Self is an archetype and is unconscious—as is, apparently, the "originally un-differentiated matrix." In the process of maturation, the "de-inte-gration" of the infantile Self apparently parallels the process of differentiation. Later, after their integration, one of the main functions of these ego nuclei is to stimulate the re-integration of the Self through the process of self-realization. The emphasis on self-acceptance in dynamic and non-directive psychotherapy aims specifi-cally at the facilitation of this process.

A difference remains, however, in that the Freudian approach in-cludes the Self in the ego, while the Jungian approach prefers to include the ego in the Self.

In either case, it seems that during the later stages of its develop-ment, the Self can be quite easily distinguished from the ego phe-nomenologically. Take, for instance, the intriguing case described by Robert Holt (in Chapter 15) of the psychiatric resident with the "regression in the service of the ego." In a personal communication, Holt further elucidates this process in the following manner:

> As I understand it, using one's unconscious energies in creative self-expression is sublimating these energies; but sublimation is only an-other term equivalent to neutralization. I think in the Freudian scheme, we always think of "the archaic forces of the unconscious" as at least a potential threat, against which we must defend ourselves. But defense is not the same thing as neutralization, though some forms of defense involve greater or less degree of neutralization. I would sum it up by saying that when we find thinking that shows evidences of operating with freely mobile (not bound) energy, in which the influence of per-ceptibly libidinous or aggressive aims is apparent, we must speak of this as regression, since it is thinking that partakes more of the nature of the primary process than does most waking, everyday thought. Such thinking and such regression may or may not be healthy; if it is under-taken freely and without subjective feelings of threat or anxiety, then it is a creative use of unconscious forces and is regression in the service of the ego. When it is a forced manifestation, arousing anxiety and/or defenses, then it represents some degree of break-through of the uncon-scious forces and is to be looked on as pathological. [24]

Phenomenologically, it is more appropriate to describe the situation as follows: The individual has reached the stage of self-realization where the archaic forces of the unconscious are no longer a threat that has to be neutralized; they have become, instead, a source of creative self-expression. The drive impulses reflecting archaic forces are not only accepted here but are recognized as an essential part of the Self; namely, as that part of the Self which is the essential source of productivity even though, and because, it is outside the realm of conscious ego control. The ego can only control the channels of expression through which the drive impulses can become productive, not the productive energy itself. In addition to the usual channels of productivity, such as art or science, one of the most important channels of expression is self-realization. This self-realization may express itself in "Leistung" (productive achievement) or mature love, and it may also express itself in a comfortable relationship to one's Self, which makes the individual a "Rock of Gibraltar" in his social setting (see also the discussion on the evaluation of creative potentials in Chapter 12).

To sum up: Instead of speaking of a regression in the service of the ego, we could speak of the ego functioning in the service of self-realization. In line with the limitation of this chapter to ego psychology, we will not pursue the phenomenology of the Self any further in this context, but now limit our attention to the relationship of the ego and the Self, which contributes the process of self-realization to the constructive ego functions (the "Auseinandersetzung" between ego and Self which is also the goal of therapy).

The Constructive Ego Functions

The constructive ego functions may be described in the symbolic figure shown on page 569.

The importance of basic security for the further development of the personality has been strikingly demonstrated by William Goldfarb [13–21], John Bowlby [5, 6], and René Spitz [41, 45], and has been given much emphasis in the writings of Margaret Ribble [38] and Lauretta Bender [2, 3, 4]. The sum and substance of all their

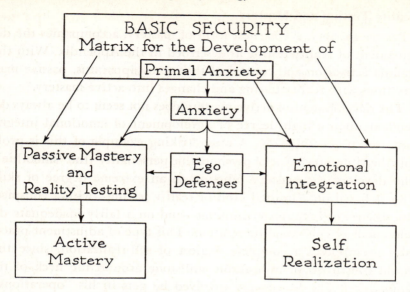

researches seem to indicate that the "oceanic feeling" (see Appendix) of the newborn infant cannot simply be abandoned to the onslaught of primary anxiety without irreparable damage to the soma and psyche of the infant. The protective care of an adult envelops the infant and his emerging ego through the demonstration of affection and creates thus the indispensable "basic security" which replaces the oceanic feeling.

It seems that the gratification of the infant's security needs is a prerequisite for the development of constructive ego function. On the other hand, the more these basic needs are frustrated, the more these ego functions tend to become crippled. Unfortunately, it appears that this kind of damage to the developing basic ego functions is almost irreversible.

The unavoidable primary anxiety that even the best-cared-for child suffers in our culture is the prime mover for the development of reality testing and emotional integration out of basic security. As long as this anxiety remains within tolerable and absorbable limits, it serves the useful purpose of promoting constructive ego functions. If it exceeds these limits, it may either destroy or cripple the whole ego structure, or promote the cancerous growth of ego-defenses.

Reality Testing and Mastery

Passive mastery, the earliest form of mastery, accompanies the development of reality testing as described in the Appendix. With the gradual activation and control of the motor apparatus, passive mastery fuses with reality testing and changes into active mastery.

The development of active mastery does not seem to be always dependent upon a high degree of development of emotional integration (see pages 571–573). A most striking example of this is probably the "imposter" type of psychopathic personality (the "smoothie") who develops the mastery function to an extreme degree of skill. This is based on a limited kind of reality testing—with a conspicuous absence of long-range thinking—and on a fairly inadequate development of emotional integration. This type of adjustment practically presupposes a complete neglect of self-realization, since this would constitute an unbearable millstone around the neck of the "smoothie." The less deeply involved he gets in his "operations," the more smoothly can he operate. From an objective point of view, this kind of adjustment can also be called "defensive," in the sense that offense is the best defense. However, such "defense" completely lacks the emotional characteristics of the conscious strain that accompanies the consumption of life energies in ego-defensiveness.

The most important role that reality testing plays in the development of constructive ego functions is in its contribution to the differentiation of the other functions. Not only does mastery need fusion with reality testing to transform itself from the passive to the active phase, but in addition the development of emotional integration and self-realization is inconceivable without the contribution of reality testing (this will be described later).

Another less generally accepted aspect of reality testing should be added. We usually conceive reality testing as an intellectual process. However, we are able to test the reality of an emotional situation without the benefit of intellectual processes. Observations made on very young children who respond to the less obvious emotions of adults lend support to such an assumption of emotional reality testing. Jung includes this assumption in his thinking when he describes feeling along with thinking as a "rational function," meaning by this that they are two different forms of reality testing.

The primary role of reality testing is to establish a safe balance between the individual's internal need structure (drive impulses) and the external stimulus conditions, within the process of perception. In order that the individual may survive, it is imperative that the projective element (the influence of the internal need structure) in perception be limited to a safe level, thus permitting the development of long-range reactions and secondary thought processes.

Emotional Integration

Emotional integration represents the necessary counterbalance for the process of differentiation of an originally undifferentiated primitive organization through endless steps of "de-integration" [9, 10] and re-integration to the complicated structure of the personality organization of the adult human being in our culture. At any one of these steps, the current state of integration, of wholeness, has to be modified to make room for new development. It seems understandable that a considerable amount of basic security is necessary to facilitate the canalization of the available life energies into this repetitive process of overcoming a temporary state of "de-integration" and to re-establish the wholeness of the personality organization on a new level.

Thus, provided there is an adequate amount of basic security, the available life energy can flow into the construction of a strongly unified, highly differentiated, and hierarchically ordered system of personality organization. An individual who is organized in this manner is able to gratify his needs appropriately, to relate all spheres of living to one another in a meaningful manner, and to profit maximally from his experiences because he is able to establish connections between them (intercommunication between regions, Lewin [30]). Our concept of emotional integration is thus organismic. Appropriateness of feeling in the fullest sense of the word is probably the most outstanding behavioral representation of emotional integration, while compartmentalization or division of feelings is the most conspicuous expression of its impairment, even within the limits of normal adjustment.

If there is not a sufficient amount of basic security then part of the available life energy is used in defensive maneuvers to protect the developing organism from being inundated by anxiety. As a consequence thereof, there is less life energy available for the construction of a unified personality organization. Depending on the degree of early deprivation, the personality organization remains more or less "de-integrated," fragmented, compartmentalized, loose-jointed, or dissociated. In such cases, we speak of an impairment of emotional integration.

This state of affairs was recognized over sixty years ago by Pierre Janet in his description of the hysterical personality.

> This limitation of the field of consciousness is but a manifestation of the general cerebral exhaustion which has often been admitted. This exhaustion, we think, is described with more precision when we say: *It is a special moral weakness, consisting in the lack of power on the part of the feeble subject to gather, to condense, his psychological phenomena, and assimilate them to his personality.* [25, page 502. Italics in original.]

While Janet considers the hysteric as being dissociated in part, he considers the demented to be almost wholly dissociated. Mayo, describing Janet's ideas on this subject, puts it as follows:

> He admits at once that a dissociation of functions might be claimed equally as a character of dementia; but in dementia one finds a mere "dust heap" of ideas, habits, instincts replacing the systematic constructions of the normal. The dissociation of hysteria, he says, is distinguished from mental deterioration of a dementia type by the fact that "in spite of the dissociation the function itself remains almost undamaged." [31, page 46]

Emotional Integration and Ego Defenses

We see now that, within limits, there is a reciprocal relationship between emotional integration and ego defensiveness. If we think in terms of a relatively limited amount of available life energy, then it can be used up either for constructive purposes or it has to be invested in defense mechanisms (the emotional problem of butter or guns). The more available life energy is consumed in ego defensiveness, the more one or several of the constructive ego functions will suffer in their effectiveness. This relationship, however, holds true only within a medium range of "ego strength." Where the development has been severely crippled from the start, as in highly schizoid personalities, or has been later destroyed by traumatic ego dissociation, the capacity for emotional integration and the development of ego defenses are both simultaneously crippled or destroyed. When the capacity for emotional integration is impaired to such an extent, it is still possible for the remaining life energy to be used in a limited kind of reality testing, as observed in schizoid and psychopathic personalities. The maximal development of the constructive ego functions, in turn, limits the need for the use of ego defenses.

Within the medium ranges of "ego strength," where the capacity for emotional integration is not too severely impaired, it seems that any strain in personality development and functioning must first exhaust the life energy available for emotional integration (by its absorption in defenses) before such strain can impair the capacity for reality testing.

Self-Realization

The concept of self-realization, as used here, stands semantically about midway between the colloquial concept of self-realization, which is almost identical with mere self-acceptance, and the rather exalted concept of self-realization as the ultimate phase of the individuation process, as C. G. Jung describes it [26]. Sometimes the term "self-actualization" is used in the sense in which self-realization is used here.

Self-realization is based on a fairly high degree of development of the capacity for emotional integration. As long as emotional responses serve merely the purpose of getting along with others, "keeping out of trouble," they involve very little of the Self of the individual. In fact, the more the individual approaches the ideal of a "Babbitt," the more easily will he be able to get along superficially. On the other hand, the more the individual permits his capacity for

emotional integration to involve himself in his work and in interpersonal relations and to commit deeper and deeper layers of his
emotional being, the more he will be able to realize himself in, and
through, these relationships.

Early manifestations of self-realization are well-known to the
educator. They are the periodically heightened attempts at self-assertion, the developmental phases of negativism and stubbornness,
which make their appearance at the end of the first year of life, and
during the third, seventh, and fourteenth years. These early forms
of self-assertion reflect a strange role of "will power" (the subjective
aspects of self-assertion) in the development of ego functions. The
will power of an individual from its earliest appearance in passive
mastery comes time and again into opposition with the existing mode
of living, forces its de-integration, and then through re-integration,
commences a new phase of ego development. The passive mastery
destroys the undifferentiated Gestalt of the "oceanic feeling" and thus
provokes further development of reality testing. The stubbornness
and negativism of the various later phases destroy the kind of dependency relations that exists in each of these phases and thus indirectly contribute, step by step, to the process of differentiation
and interaction of the ego and the Self. Finally, the will power of the
strongly developed, well-integrated ego is faced with the archaic
forces of the unconscious, which form the indispensable raw material of the Self, and reaches its most important "Auseinandersetzung"
with these forces. In this see-sawing battle between the ego and these
elusive but powerful forces the process of self-realization takes place.
In its early development, the ego had to gain and maintain its integrity in dealing with the outside reality. Now, this integrity has to
be gained and maintained in dealing with the forces of the inner
world. A weak ego remains permanently a mere mouthpiece of these
forces. The strong ego is not simply "identified" with these forces;
it recognizes their power, but does not permit them to swallow it.

At the adult level, self-realization expresses itself in the ability
to form and sustain personalized, differentiated, and reciprocal emotional ties, the ability to put oneself into one's work (Freud's "Leistung"), and finally in the ability to utilize the archaic forces of the
unconscious for creative purposes. In these ways, self-realization leads

to a further deepening and broadening of the function of emotional integration.

In order to be oneself, one's personality organization has to be pretty well "in one piece." Only a person with an optimal degree of interaction between all spheres of living, and intercommunication between all parts of the personality organization, can develop the seed-crystals for the formation of a structural and functional intimacy of the ego and the Self. In this way, self-realization takes over the function of an internal reality testing, stripping the Self concept more and more of its defensive and distorting aspect until one comes closer and closer to the difficult moment when one really faces one's Whole Self. Few people in our culture come even close to this goal without the help of intensive psychotherapy.

An additional prerequisite is that the ego defenses should not absorb too much of the available life energy. This, in turn, presupposes that the archaic forces of the unconscious are not experienced as too threatening.* In terms of observable behavior, the most reliable indicator that an individual has reached an advanced stage of self-realization is the presence of humility. The humility of a person who is really at home with himself simultaneously conveys the relative absence of ego-defensiveness, the directness of one who is not afraid to commit himself, and an awareness of all the overwhelming forces without and within, which drive home the smallness of the individual and his relative insignificance. This concept of humility does not contain any suggestion of moral guilt.

Rorschach Indicators of Ego Functioning

The Rorschach Prognostic Rating Scale (RPRS, see Chapter 19), mentioned earlier, represents an attempt to focus on the most important clues in Rorschach reactions for the evaluation of ego strength. The practical purpose that led to its development plays only a minor part in our present considerations. Its didactic and research functions are stressed here.

---

* An interesting explication of this point of view is contained in a recently published lecture by Abenheimer [1].

Obviously, the majority of the interpretative hypotheses made explicit in the chapters on interpretation are in many ways connected with the evaluation of ego functioning. However, for a long time most of the experienced clinicians who use the Rorschach for diagnostic and prognostic purposes have been using other clues in addition to those formalized there. Probably, the vast majority of such other clues are individual in character, understandable only in the context of the specific record and through intensive case study, and defy any attempt to be described in categorical terms. The RPRS represents an attempt to salvage as much as possible from these methodological frustrations by describing those clues that might be applicable in many cases. One of the outstanding characteristics of such clues is the fact that they represent a point of confluence of formal and content aspects of Rorschach data. Among others, Holt discovered in his Rorschach research project on neutralization (reported in Chapter 15) that he had to combine the content-symbolic indications of libidinous and aggressive drives with the form-level characteristics of these same responses in order to get an adequate picture of the ego strength of his outstanding subject. The same is true throughout Rorschach interpretations. Only this combination enables us to distinguish between the breakthrough of unconscious forces and their creative use. The breakthrough interferes with reality testing, while the creative use reflects a fusion of reality testing and self-realization.

This first attempt to relate Rorschach clues to ego psychology may do well to follow the rating categories of the RPRS, because this might facilitate the design of experimental and clinical projects aimed at the validation of the relation between Rorschach clues and the various aspects of ego functions.

Hypotheses Used in the RPRS

1. The Human Movement Responses

The selection of M as one of the six components of the RPRS is, first of all, based on the hypothesis that M is an indicator of inner stability. This hypothesis relates M to the ego function of emotional **integration.**

Secondly, upon the basis of the hypotheses about self-acceptance and empathy, M is also related to the capacity for self-realization. In this connection, the readiness to use M is probably a more specific indicator of self-realization than the quantity and quality of M. This readiness is expressed in a number of ways: (1) in the sequence in which the responses are given—that is, whether M responses are at or near the beginning of a series of responses to a given card, or near the end of such a series; (2) in the free use of M opportunities. Sometimes subjects give a few M responses to blot areas in which such responses are rather unusual, while they overlook the more obvious areas; (3) most M are given in the performance proper and not in the inquiry; (4) human action is not qualified by attributing it predominantly to figures with animal or mixed human-and-animal characteristics; (5) the subject does not feel the need to qualify his M responses by emphasizing the medium of representation ("sculpture of," "drawing of," and so on).

The rationale underlying these hypotheses about M can be summarized in the following way: (1) The ability to see human beings or any kind of creatures in human-like action presupposes a tendency to identify with human beings. (2) The enlivening of a response, which is involved in seeing M, presupposes a relatively free access to the energies stemming from archaic forces, using these as creative inner resources to enrich the intellectual life of the subject. (3) The gratification resulting from such use of inner resources has a beneficial effect on the frustration tolerance of the subject, irrespective of whether he has the ability to use his fantasy activity for actual creative productions or is merely able to work through in fantasy his emotional needs and tensions, gaining daydream satisfactions. The underlying assumption for all these hypotheses about M can best be described as "ego tolerance for archaic forces." (See also Chapter 10, pages 254–255.)

There is an optimal area for the function of M as an indicator of "inner stability." Even when reality testing is unimpaired (no $M-$) an excess tendency to daydream limits the total adjustment capacity of the individual. Such a tendency may be found in persons who have over-invested in their drive for self-realization, while they neglect the development of skills devoted to the mastery of reality situations.

One of the most frequent imbalances in the Rorschach records of such people is marked excess of *M* over *W* responses. This constellation is rather frequently found among students of psychology at the beginning of their careers. There is a marked preoccupation with inner experiences in such individuals, which leads to a temporary neglect of the development of ways and means to utilize these experiences in the organization of factual material for the purpose of dealing skillfully with reality situations. In fact, sensing any pressure towards investing life energy in such reality functions is often resented; consequently the establishment of smooth social relationships suffers.

2. Animal Movement Responses

The hypothesis that *FM* indicates impulses for immediate need gratification makes it clear that *FM* is closely associated with the handling of "stress tolerance." The unfolding of emotional integration is dependent upon the development of stress tolerance because only in the extent to which immediate need gratification can be postponed are opportunities provided for the facilitation of this process. Both over-defensiveness towards and too easy acceptance of one's drive impulses interfere with the building up of stress tolerance since both attitudes reflect the existence of mechanisms that reduce tension before such tension has had an opportunity to come fully to awareness and to be accepted. Thus, if drive impulses are handled too much like a "hot potato," or if the subject is carried away by his drive impulses without any real effort to handle them, no flexible stress tolerance can develop. In this way, the quantity and quality of *FM* reflect an important aspect of emotional integration. How freely animals are permitted to come to life, how vivacious their actions are, and the extent to which the seeing of animals is balanced by other movement, color, and shading determinants, particularly in the same responses—all these are major clues which reveal to us the ways and means by which an individual deals with his drive impulses and the extent to which he has been able to integrate them into his ego organization.

The role of *FM* as an indicator of ego strength is also related to the comfort, or lack of comfort, the subject feels with regard to his drive impulses. The empirical assumption that serves as a basis for this idea may be formulated in the following way: (1) Drive impulses find their natural, symbolic representation in myths, dreams, and idiomatic expressions involving animal behavior. (2) An attitude of conscious rejection of drive impulses leads to an avoidance of conceptualizing animals in action, which is an unfavorable factor in terms of adjustment capacity. (3) An over-acceptance of drive impulses (excess of *FM* over *M*) without the modifying tendency to "humanize" them, gives the total personality picture a flavor of "infantilism." Such excess is, therefore, moderately unfavorable in terms of total ego strength.

These considerations lead to the assumption that an optimal range for the production of *FM* exists. The weighted score is constructed accordingly. Less weight is given to the top score than in the case of *M*, since the total positive contribution of this area to ego strength seems to be of less importance than that of *M*.

3. The Inanimate Movement Responses

The assumption underlying the interpretation of *m* can be summarized as follows: The tendency to conceptualize inanimate movement in Rorschach responses expresses an awareness of conflict which might exist either between different impulses within the personality, or between the impulses of the individual and some frustrating forces in his environment. This awareness serves as a "warning system" against seeking immediate gratification for such impulses. A prerequisite for the functioning of this warning system is the capacity to anticipate internal or external conflicts. Where such anticipation is lacking, as in personalities "who don't learn from experience," no such conflict awareness exists and little or no *m* is produced. Therefore, only individuals with fairly well developed emotional integration seem to be able to give *m* responses.

As support for this assumption, the following research observations may be mentioned: more *m* was found in the records of subjects successful in flight training [32] and mechanical shop work [35]. Success was achieved by some individuals in the first study

who otherwise would have been expected to have considerable difficulty in adjustment due to overimpulsiveness $[(CF+C) >FC]$ but
were able, with the help of their conflict-awareness (m), to time
and channelize their impulses in accordance with the demands of
their tasks.

Two types of m responses make the largest contribution to ego
strength: (1) The description of natural or mechanical forces which
overcome the force of gravity; and (2) affective expressions projected symbolically onto inanimate objects.

Gravity responses, and responses describing the operation of abstract forces without the quality of expression, indicate less ego
strength than the responses discussed above, but still show that there
is enough libidinal investment to keep the warning system intact.

4. The Shading Reactions

Shading responses can best be described as showing how the individual organizes his need for affection. The whole range of attitudes to one's need for affection, from insensitivity, evasion, and
denial to full acceptance, finds expression in the large variety of
ways of responding to the shading effects in the stimulus material.

The underlying rationale can be formulated in the following
steps: (1) The shading effects create in most subjects some kind
of "contact sensation." (2) This "contact sensation" evokes in the
subject his need for basic emotional security (to be held, to belong).
(3) This need, in turn, evokes the prevailing emotional response to
this need in the life of the individual (anxiety, acceptance, denial,
and so on). (4) Conversely, this prevailing emotional response influences the conceptual use of the shading stimuli.

In this way, the shading dynamics allow us to infer the status of
the affectional matrix from which all the constructive ego functions
spring forth. Vorhaus states:

> The shading responses are divided into the usual headings: the dif-
> ferentiated (Fc and FK) and the undifferentiated (K, k, c). Several
> sub-divisions occur, the greatest number being in the Fc area. Only
> when Fc is used to indicate something warm, soft, or transparent does

the score reach 1. *Fc,* when used for something cold or hard, is ½. The most favorable condition for emotional integration (one of the four components listed in the definition of ego strength) seems fulfilled in relation to the first mentioned *Fc.* The individual who, in early childhood, has experienced life in its soft, warm aspects had, even in that early time, laid the foundations for ego development. [47]

Within the positive *Fc* responses, we can further distinguish whether the *Fc* score is based (1) on the internal organization of the shading with an indefinite outline, or (2) on the definiteness of the outline, filled in by undifferentiated shading, or (3) on a combination of definite outline and internal organization. Obviously, the last represents the highest level of integration of the need for affection, which leads to the ability to enter into differentiated emotional relationships. This is the case also with internal organization of shading within an indefinite outline, but the lack of form implies some difficulty in finding the appropriate partner in reality. The lack of internal organization in the shading response of the second type reflects the kind of emotional relationships prevailing in our culture, where the emotional contacts seem superficially well-established but lack depth and internal differentiation. This is progressively more true and more pervasive when responses have to be scored *cF* and *c.*

A number of shading reactions permit us to gain insight into ego-defensive formations.

> *Fc* denial also scores ½; I think also because the very need to deny suggests a "whistling in the dark" maneuver, by an individual who, in fact, *has* developed *Fc,* but because he has been traumatized, dares not use it. From the point of view of ego strength, the potential is there. In therapy, he may learn that the outside world does not always threaten. [47]

Fc responses in which shading is used as a representation of bright color represents a milder form of what is called, in another publication [27, page 46], "abortive sublimation." As such, it is not only an expression of energy-consuming ego defenses, but one of those insidious devices of resistance which make the actualization of unused ego strength particularly difficult.

The individual pictures himself as a loving and giving person who has been stopped from expression by the harshness of a rejecting world. Resistance to therapy is indicated here. Why should one change an adaptation in which one is so absolved from blame? [47]

Other shading reactions reflect the lack of well-articulated ego defenses. To quote Vorhaus [47] again:

In considering the fact that K receives a zero rating on this scale, it is interesting to contrast it with m (where the weighted score goes as high as 2). Whereas m suggests the kind of inner uncomfortableness which many therapists consider to be the motivating factor in successful therapy, the diffused heavy nature of the anxiety indicated by K has an unproductive quality settling on one in an enveloping manner (as distinct from spurring one on to attempts to find peace and mental ease).

5. Color Reactions

While the shading stimuli seem to reflect the way in which an individual handles his "emotional expectations," color responses seem rather to reflect the subject's way of handling "emotional actualities"; or, in other words, color reflects his way of responding to the emotional impact of an actual life situation. Experimental psychology has yet to unravel the many threads of connection between color and emotionality, although a host of studies on color shock have turned up some interesting data (see Chapter 14). The rationale underlying the relationship of color and emotional responsiveness can be formulated in the following manner: (1) The readiness to react to this aspect of the stimulus material expresses the ability to respond to an emotional challenge from the environment. (This seems to be true also for the various degrees of emotional responsiveness.) (2) The attention given to the color stimuli seems to make the stimulus material appear more like a "real" object, or a representative piece of outer reality rather than just a symbolic piece of paper. (The tendency to be interested in the color appears to be correlated with the tendency to "recognize" rather than "interpret" the blot material.) (3) The individual's prevailing method of dealing with emotional challenges from without (whether withdrawal, shyness, reticence, impulsiveness, explosiveness, aggression, or submission) and the depth or intensity of his emotional response (whether bland, forced, over-easy, heated, cold-blooded, earthy, or passionate) are both revealed in the nuances of the color responses.

If these assumptions are valid, their contribution to the total ego picture can be described as follows:

Color reactions are related to emotional integration. While shading reactions reflect more clearly the basic development of this capacity (its matrix), the color reactions indicate what the individual is actually doing with his integrative capacity in various life situations. For this reason, deficiencies in shading reactions have more serious implications for prognosis and adjustment than deficiencies in color reactions; the former seems to reflect serious disturbances in the *capacity* for warm interpersonal relations, while the latter appears to point toward disturbances in the *mechanics* of interpersonal relations. Thus, while shading reactions have more of a basic importance in the evaluation of ego strength, the color reactions broaden the picture considerably by showing how the capacity for emotional integration is deployed in interpersonal relations, revealing their depth and intensity.

Depths

The Rorschach clues that reveal depth of feeling, as distinguished from intensity of feeling, can be described as follows:

NATURAL COLOR. The color concepts are characterized by the use of natural color, as contrasted with a bland or forced use of color. The subject who easily finds natural objects that carry the color of the blot material suffers least from the effects of intellectualization and therefore is able to enjoy the full benefit of his capacity for feeling, while such mechanisms interfere with the free emotional exchange between a person and his environment and with the development of deep emotional object relations.

The *forced* use of color, as in the use of the pink color in Card VIII for "bears walking in the sunset," expresses both the effort of the subject to respond to the color and, even more, his feeling of being under an obligation to respond to the color; this does not counterindicate depth of feeling but interferes with its full expression.

The *bland* use of color shows no such effort. On the contrary, the subject has the tendency to see any number of colored areas as colored butterflies without any sense of discrimination for specific color values, just because the blot areas have the approximate form and are colored. This is an attitude of paying easy lip-service to emotional responsiveness. It is an off-hand and uninvolved responsiveness which reflects a basic incapacity for real involvement. These bland Rorschach responses must be distinguished from the responses of anxiously submissive or sentimental people who may also cling for a while to the idea of colored butterflies; but generally they also produce a few submissive *CF* responses in the same record, while the bland subjects feel perfectly satisfied that they have done their part by giving a few colored butterflies.

The natural use of color must be distinguished from a merely conventional use of color, or form-color combinations, such as seeing the red butterflies on Cards II and III. It should extend beyond the use of just one response like the popular green worms on Card X or the red hair-ribbon on Card III.

SPONTANEITY. Spontaneity in the use of color prevails over reluctance. While the natural use of color emphasizes the free flow of emotional exchange between the individual and his environment and implies the relative absence of obstacles, spontaneity in the use of color places the emphasis upon the immediacy of the emotional exchange. This spontaneity must be carefully distinguished from an impulsive use of color. This can be done with the help of the form level characteristics of the responses: Impulsiveness in the use of color is more likely to be associated with superficiality and is commonly found in intense or heated color reactions given with little consideration for form specifications. Spontaneity is expressed in Rorschach responses primarily by the ease with which the color is combined with the formal properties of the blot area and by the absence of any form of delay for such color responses. (For the ways in which delay manifests itself see the discussion of *M* in this chapter.)

Since, not infrequently, subjects capable of deep emotional reactions suffer from some degree of "affect shyness" and are, consequently, incapable of communicating their deep emotions easily, thus using color quite sparingly in the Rorschach record, the absence of spontaneity in the use of color seems to be a less detrimental indication of lack of depth of emotionality than the absence of a natural use of color and the absence of permeability of other determinants by color.

PERMEABILITY. Hermann Rorschach was the first to point out that what he called "oscillation" between the use of movement and color was a sign of the achievement of the highest level of emotional maturity [39]. Such a permeability of color with movement and/or shading in one concept points toward the connectedness of the emotional responsiveness of the individual with his basic need for security and his self-realization.

Intensity

Intensity of emotions is an expression of the intensity of drive impulses. The conceptual model for emotional intensity is the concept of "pressure" in hydrodynamics. In colloquial terminology, the term "strength of emotion" is unfortunately used to describe both the intensity or pressure with which an individual experiences emotion and its impact upon other people. This impact, however, depends a great deal more upon the depth of feeling and the degree of total involvement of the carrier of emotion than upon the mere intensity of emotion. Intensity of emotion is subjectively felt primarily as "heat" of feeling, whether it be love or hate, and does not necessarily have a strong impact upon the object of the emotion, except in extreme states.

Naturally, depth of feeling does not exclude intensity; but intensity does not necessarily include depth. Usually, such intense emotions are not appropriate to the situation and the relationships of the people involved. Depth of feeling, however, is always in contact with the objective reality of the emotional situation because it includes some emotional reality testing of which the subject is not necessarily intellectually aware.

The capacity for intense emotions depends largely upon individual differences in temperament; but any strong frustration or crucial emotional decision can raise the intensity of feeling to a high pitch, regardless of temperamental dispositions.

In contrast to emotional depth, emotional intensity is apt to be inimical to integration. Where intensity of emotion is not balanced by depth of feeling, it rests upon a lack of self-realization and a weakness of integration. The abandon of an immature adolescent, for example—or, still more, that of an aggressive psychopath—turns the ego into the mouthpiece of archaic forces and away from its potential role as a servant of a well-crystallized Self. In extreme cases, this type of intense emotional reaction becomes highly ego-alien and may develop into a real threat of ego-dissociation. The terrific fear of their own intense emotional impulses that many incipient schizophrenics experience, bears witness to this; so do the panic reactions that develop out of many anxiety states, and sometimes lead to hysterical dissociation or amnesia.

The most important Rorschach clue for such intense emotional reactions is the "hotness" of color concepts, most often expressed in concepts such as "blood" and/or "fire." As long as ego organization is still fairly well intact, such "hot" color responses are regularly accompanied by strong indications of intensely-felt subjective discomfort.

The indications of subjectively-felt discomfort disappear with a corresponding decline in the ability for emotional integration. They are replaced by a detached use of hot color concepts. While the destructive effect of the intensity of the emotion on both emotional integration and reality testing is visible in serious breaks in the form level of the responses, the subject seems to be perfectly comfortable with it. The following response to Card II will illustrate such a situation: "This is an animal which has been run over by a car. You can distinctly see in which direction the car traveled, because the lower center red portion was the point of first impact, while the upper red marks represent the tire marks the car left behind when it went on." The color stimulus induces the subject to use color freely without any compunction or sign of subjectively-felt discomfort as expressed in the detached, legalistic way the accident is described; free use of color expresses impulsive intensity, but the detached formulation reveals lack of depth and personal commitment.

The emotional reactions of children present a special problem with respect to their depth and intensity. The child's emotions are deep in one sense in that he is wholly involved; but since the extent of differentiation and integration of his personality development is limited, the emotions are not deep in another sense. He seems to react wholly, but he has not the resources to tolerate long-lasting involvement. With too much distress, a "catastrophic reaction" takes place; consequently the defense against distress is impoverishment of personality.

6. Form Level

Form-level variations in the Rorschach responses seem to be our main clues for the reality testing aspect of ego strength. Form-level considerations were permitted to influence the total prognostic rating in two ways: (1) Minus scores reduce the weighted scores of the five other components of the rating scale. (2) The total form level adds a separate sub-score heavily weighted by the occurrence of the actual minus scores. At the same time, the absence of any indication of deficiency in reality testing produces a positive contribution to the final prognostic rating.

The rationale underlying these assumptions is simply that the various degrees and types of disturbance in thinking due to deficiencies in reality testing will be expressed in the way in which the form characteristics of the stimulus material are utilized by the subject.

The outstanding clue for the "firmness" of reality testing is the evenness of the form level, regardless of whether the subject's intellectual endowment is low, mediocre, or superior. Naturally, to some extent the propensities of the ten cards to influence the form-level characteristics must, however, be taken into account. Thus Card III may produce a higher form level than Card V, regardless of any emotional implications of either card.

The contribution of the form-level clues to the total ego picture is probably more significant on the minus side than on the plus side. This is so because positive form-level ratings are so highly influenced by intellectual capacity, which—clinically speaking—has only a very slight and indirect relationship to ego strength. For instance, the difference between an average form level of 1.5 and 2.5 may reflect merely a difference in intellectual capacity and none in ego strength, provided that both records show the same degree of evenness of form level and an absence of minus ratings.

The Systematic Meaning of Rorschach Hypotheses for Ego Organization

Using our diagram of the constructive ego functions (page 569) as a point of departure, we can schematically relate the main areas of Rorschach hypotheses to specific areas of the diagram.

The developmental sequence of form-level characteristics—magic perseveration, confabulation, confabulatory combination, minimal (popular) level of specification for basal form level—reflects the ontogenetic development of reality testing and mastery from their emergence from the common matrix to their establishment as relatively independent functions.

The varieties of shading responses—from the completely undifferentiated enjoyment of contact sensations to the highly differentiated, subtle use of shading, via the circuitous routes of diffuse shading—reflect the efforts of the growing individual to differentiate his original longing for basic security and to channel his energies into a highly intricate system of emotional responsivity.

The entire range of color reactions—from the naïve, uncritical color confabulations, to impulsive and controlled, aggressive and submissive, hot and cold, deep and intense color reactions—reflects the constant efforts of the individual to integrate and deal effectively with the drive impulses from within and the emotional challenges from without, as well as his efforts to fuse emotional integration with reality testing.

The area of movement responses picks up in the schema with considerable overlap where the color dynamics leave off. These responses reflect the development of the "inner life" of the subject from his early attitudes to his drive impulses to the flowering of self-realization.

1.   Reality Testing and Mastery

For the obvious reason of difficulty in communication, the earliest phases of normal ego development that can be caught in Rorschach reactions lie in the period of transition from the primary to the secondary process. The magic perseveration represents the earliest form of Rorschach reactions and is obtained from children between two and four years of chronological age (the minimum mental age for these reactions is probably three years). The child picks up some clue from the presentation of the first card or from the total test situation and utilizes it as a picture-word concept, such as airplane, doggy, mountain, or "daddy" (in the latter case possibly for no better reason than that the toy seems to belong to daddy). As soon as the child receives some sort of approval for this sort of "achievement," he uses this first word like a magic wand to give the same meaning to the remaining nine cards. He may look carefully at the card, but make no use of the differences in the stimulus material. This kind of Rorschach response mirrors the emergence of a primitive form of mastery over a puzzling reality situation.

Subsequent chronological steps in Rorschach reactions are the interspersing of some other responses in a chain of perseverations, the rejection of most of the cards with a somewhat appropriate response to a few cards, the combination of two or three different chains of magic perseveration—all reflecting an increasing degree of reality testing, which modifies the primitive passive mastery function. This modification takes the following path: the predominantly passive mastery of the magic perseveration, which contains only one active step of picking up the clue, transforms itself step by step into a more active form of mastery, until as we see the final stage of this process in the Rorschach records of gifted adults, the organization and specifications show the smoothest coöperation of reality testing and active mastery, enriched by a fusion with emotional integration and self-realization. This was described earlier as permeability.

2.   Emotional Integration

The earliest Rorschach phases of the emergence of the function of emotional integration out of the need for basic security can be reconstructed theoretically only from the records of extremely regressed, pathological cases. The normal child is unable to communicate his responses to the Rorschach cards or even to focus his attention on this kind of stimulus material during the early period of his development in which his longing for basic security is expressed in total dependence upon an all-enveloping, warm and loving mother figure.

The most impressive pathological case in the experience of this writer was the famous subject in Dr. R. Brickner's study [7], who several years earlier had lost both his frontal lobes through severe tumors necessitating a bilateral lobectomy. It was surprising how much of the intellectual functioning was still left under these conditions. However, emotionally he was reduced to the status of a good-natured, dependent, but mischievous two-year-old child who loved to wallow in undifferentiated sensuous gratifications. He saw completely undifferentiated animal skins in five of the Rorschach cards. At the same time, he saw in Card III the usual two men who told the butterfly between them to go and get them a glass of beer (one of his symptoms was "Witzelsucht").

The earliest communicated response to shading shows a mixture of cF and Fc. This represents a considerably differentiated need for affection and belongingness.

Again, as in the development of the mastery function, the gradual fusion of reality testing with the need for affection constitutes the major development of emotional integration. One phase of this development—and, as pointed out previously, the prevailing one in our culture—is reflected by giving more consideration to the outline of a shaded area. This modification still lacks the depth of feeling that would be expressed in a more differentiated concern for the internal structure of the shaded area (a form of emotional reality testing), but at least it expresses some consideration of whether the external circumstances permit the expression of the relatively undifferentiated need for affection.

Similarly, the development of emotional integration is represented in the change from K to k response. The free-floating anxiety, expressed in undifferentiated diffuse shading responses like fog or smoke, is one of the most important forces that promote the growth of emotional integration. In most human beings this state of free-floating anxiety is purely transitional and is quickly resolved through the development of ego defenses or through progressive integration. The intellectualization of free-floating anxiety, prevailingly expressed by seeing X-ray pictures or topographical maps, represents an only mildly effective compromise between the development of more substantial ego defenses and further integration.

A more effective way of utilizing free-floating anxiety for the promotion of further integration is the use of introspection as an emotional balance wheel. This attitude is expressed in the Rorschach by marked interest in shading stimuli, using them in the elaboration of vista responses. This was first recognized in the records of a group of physicians who went through the first few months of their personal training analysis; their anxious preoccupation with their "inner landscape" expressed itself this way.

An adequate organization of the basic need for affection is the prerequisite for the establishment of effective intercommunication between the various areas of emotional experience. If the need for affection is poorly organized, a constant inner pressure is created which lowers frustration tolerance, develops defensive "ego involvements," so that there is a constant confusion in emotional relations with other persons, and which weakens reality testing by giving undue weight, in perception, to the basic need component. This results in a compartmentalization or division of feeling which becomes, in the majority of individuals in our culture, a painful obstacle to further emotional integration. These are the processes that express themselves in the shading responses.

The most common expressions of such difficulties are the various forms taken by the inability to use the shading stimuli as a determinant.* The relatively most favorable of these non-scorable reactions is shading denial, expressing an inability of the subject to accept his own dependency needs even in the symbolic form of shading stimuli. Such an attitude certainly slows down emotional integration; but there seems to be at least enough strength to put up a

---

* See "Delineation," Part Four, page 696.

struggle, promising a fair chance for overcoming the obstacle with some help.

A less favorable picture is indicated by an evasive use of shading. Subjects who show this reaction still feel their dependent needs, but so little expectation of satisfaction that they try to circumvent the whole issue. Symptomatically, a frequent form of such circumvention is an addiction to alcohol or drugs. Emotional re-integration in such cases, even with the help of psychotherapy, proves much more difficult than where shading is denied. In the earlier development of these individuals, emotional integration has never advanced sufficiently to establish a requisite depth of feeling, even for therapeutic transference situations.

The least capacity for emotional integration, indicated by a more or less total insensitivity to shading, is found in subjects whose longing for basic security has been traumatized so early and so extensively that the whole capacity to feel a need for affection has become crippled.

An important step in the further development of emotional integration is the fulfillment of the task of dealing with our drive impulses appropriately and of permitting them to find expression by the establishment of rich emotional relations with our fellow human beings. This aspect of emotional integration is reflected in color reactions.

When impulses appear uncontrollable or the specific goals of gratification are too unacceptable, the expression of drive impulses is blocked and further integration is checked. This is the case to an even greater extent where a weak ego organization has given up any further attempt to fight the impulses and has chosen dissociation as the only way out, or has retreated into a de-personalized, conventional sham existence.

In the case of blocking, the excessive consumption of available life energy in a complicated system of neurotic defenses deprives the individual of the necessary energy for further integration. This is expressed in Rorschach reactions by extreme discomfort with color and shading stimuli, which interferes with the appropriate productive use of these stimuli.

In the case of dissociation or retreat, disturbances evoked by emotional stimulation are no longer felt subjectively but express themselves objectively in the undesirable weakening of reality testing. Mostly we find this in psychotics. In other cases it leads to the conventional or bland use of color, expressing an excessive investment in what Jung calls "Persona"—meaning the tendency to live a conventional role according to what one thinks other people expect one to do, without a feeling for personal values or commitments.

3. Self-Realization

With the immediately preceding statements, we have already touched the transition from emotional integration to self-realization. The personality organization just described exemplifies the fact that a mediocre or limited emotional integration practically precludes the emergence of self-realization. On the other hand, an adequate emotional integration—with sufficient depth of feeling, adequate handling of one's need for affection, and an appropriate fusion with reality testing—is the fertile ground from which self-realization can emerge.

Its main expression in Rorschach reactions is a favorable balance between the various types of movement responses. As described previously, m is mainly useful as an expression of conflict awareness, a control mechanism balancing the threat of drive impulses. *FM* simply expresses the general attitude of the subject to his drive impulses. An accepting attitude toward this aspect of our inner life is necessary for the emergence of self-realization. If we are unable to accept such an important part of ourselves, we are unable to establish adequate contact with our inner resources. The M responses simultaneously represent self-acceptance and a capacity to commit ourselves in relationship to others. Consequently, M responses must balance the other types of movement responses in order to express a favorable condition for self-realization. Such a balance is indicated, in the records of those adults who have above average intelligence, by the presence of at least five M and by a proportion in which the sum of *FM* and m is not greater than twice the M score and not less than the sum of M.

It is more difficult to find clues for the degree of self-realization in the records of less intelligent subjects. In such cases, we have to rely more on the spontaneity of whatever M is produced, and on the indications for depth of feeling.

Considering that self-realization is genetically the latest of the constructive ego functions, it becomes understandable that the production of M, its main representative, does not usually occur in children below the age of eight, and does not reach its climax until late adolescence (see the chapter on children's records in Volume II).

For further Rorschach clues for self-realization, see Chapter 12, pages 366–370, the section headed, "The Evaluation of Creative Potentials."

4. Ego-Defensiveness

In the clinical chapters of Volume II the ego defenses specific for the various nosological categories, if any, and the way in which they are represented in the Rorschach, will be discussed under the heading "Differential Diagnosis." For the time being, it seems more important to present a fairly comprehensive picture of the Rorschach clues for ego-defensiveness in general, regardless of the specific ego defense mechanisms employed by any given subject.

Let us return to our basic assumptions about ego psychology and recall that we have to conceive the constructive and the defensive ego as competitive polarities which vie with each other for the available life energy. The state of competition when ego defenses make more and more inroads into the life energies available for the constructive ego is demonstrated in the Rorschach by a mounting expression of subjectively-felt discomfort in the subject's dealing with color and shading stimuli. Ranked in terms of increasing ego-defensiveness, it appears that this discomfort expresses itself, at first, more easily in color reaction, and then equally in color and shading reactions. Finally, one finds instances where the subject appears to be more uncomfortable in his dealings with shading stimuli than with color stimuli. The ego organization of such subjects shows, characteristically, fairly deep erosions in the constructive ego functions; these are covered up by superficial adaptations, as, for example, in some cases of hypochondriasis and in severe obsessive-compulsive character neuroses. The degree of recoverability from color and shading disturbances in Rorschach reactions is a valuable indicator of the limits of ego-defensive erosion. Where the subject can make a constructive use of color and shading after disturbance in the performance proper, possibly even in the same card, the erosion is very mild. If the recovery occurs only in the inquiry, emotional integration faces more difficulties. Finally, if recovery is only possible under the conditions of testing the limits, the interference with the integrative process is most marked.

These statements about the significance of recoverability are also applicable to the process of self-realization, as expressed in the subject's handling of movement responses, and to some extent even in the use of form elements (recognition of irrational form elements during the inquiry and testing the limits).

The distinction between subjectively-felt discomfort and objectively observable disturbances in color and shading reactions (as, for example, the detached color response mentioned above) become of paramount importance in the evaluation of ego strength for prognostic purposes. The point at which the subjective discomfort begins to vanish and gives way to objective color and shading disturbance seems to represent the exact borderline between neurotic and psychotic adaptation. It is the point where the attack shifts from the exhausted capacity for emotional integration to the function of reality testing, and this finds its expression in the Rorschach in breaks in the form level.

The strange consequence of these assumptions and observations is the clinical fact that, so long as the subject remains close to the nebulous border area of normal and neurotic adjustment, the existence of subjectively-felt discomfort in dealing with color and shading stimuli, indicating ego-defensive efforts, appears as a negative indicator for the total adjustment of the individual; but it changes into a hopeful sign for recoverability and into an indicator that unused ego strength is still available, the more closely the subject approaches the dangerous borderline between neurotic and psychotic personality organization.

References

1. Abenheimer, K. "Anal Symbolism," *Guild Lecture 72*, The Guild of Pastoral Psychology, London, 1951.

2. Bender, Lauretta. "There is No Substitute for Family Life," *Child Study*, 1946, 23, 74.

3. ———. "Psychopathic Behavior Disorders in Children," in Lindner, R. M., and Seliger, R. V. (eds.) *Handbook of Correctional Psychology*, New York: Philosophical Library, Inc.; 1947.

4. ———, and Yarnell, H. "An Observation Nursery," *Amer. J. Psychiat.*, 1941, 1158–1174.

5. Bowlby, J., *Maternal Care and Mental Health*. Geneva: World Health Organization: Monograph Series, 1951.

6. ———. "Forty-Four Juvenile Thieves, Their Characters and Home Life," *Internat. J. Psychoanalysis*, 1944, 25, 19–53.

7. Brickner, R. M., *The Intellectual Functions of the Frontal Lobes*. New York: The Macmillan Company; 1936.

8. Fenichel, O. *The Psychoanalytic Theory of Neurosis*. New York: W. W. Norton & Company, Inc.; 1945.

9. Fordham, M. Lecture notes from his seminar on *Archetypal Images in Childhood*, held in Los Angeles, Spring 1952.

10. ———. "Integration and Disintegration and Early Ego Development," *The Nerv. Child*, 1947, 6, 266–277.

11. ———. "Analytical Psychology Applied to Children," *The Nerv. Child*, 1946, 5, 134–145.

12. Freud, S. "Analysis Terminable and Interminable," *Internat. J. Psychoanalysis*, 1937, 18.

13. Goldfarb, W. "Rorschach Test Differences Between Family-reared, Institution-reared, and Schizophrenic Children," *Amer. J. Orthopsychiat.* 1949, 19, 624–633.

14. ———. "Variations in Adolescent Adjustment of Institutionally Reared Children," *Amer. J. Orthopsychiat.*, 1947, 17, 449–457.

15. ———. "Effects of Psychological Deprivation in Infancy and Subsequent Adjustment," *Amer. J. Psychiat.*, 1945, 102, 18–33.

16. ———. "Psychological Privation in Infancy and Subsequent Adjustment," *Amer. J. Orthopsychiat.*, 1945, 15, 247–255.

17. ———. "The Effects of Early Institutional Care on Adolescent Personality: Rorschach Data," *Amer. J. Orthopsychiat.*, 1944, 14, 441–447.

18. ———. "Infant Rearing as a Factor in Foster Home Placement," *Amer. J. Orthopsychiat.*, 1943, 13, 162–166.

19. ———."The Effects of Early Institutional Care on Adolescent Personality (Graphic Rorschach Data) ," *Child Development*, 1943, 213–222.

20. ———. "The Effects of Early Institutional Care on Adolescent Personality," *J. Expl. Education*, 1943, 12, 106–29.

21. ———. "Infant Rearing and Problem Behavior," *Amer. J. Orthopsychiat.*, 1943, 13, 249–265.

22. Hartmann, H. "Comments on the Psychoanalytic Theory of the Ego," *Psychoanalytic Study of the Child,* 1950, 5, 74–97.

23. ——. "Psychoanalysis and Developmental Psychology," *Psychoanalytic Study of the Child,* 1950, 5, 7–17.

24. Holt, R. Letter to the author of this chapter.

25. Janet, P. *The Mental State of Hystericals.* New York: G. P. Putnam's Sons; 1901.

26. Jung, C. G. *Psychological Types or the Psychology of Individuation.* New York: Harcourt, Brace & Company, Inc.; 1923.

27. Klopfer, B. "The Rorschach Technique," in *Military Clinical Psychology,* Departments of the Army and the Air Force, 1951 (TM 8–242, AFM 160–45).

28. ——, and Kelley, D. M. *The Rorschach Technique.* Yonkers: World Book Company; 1942, 1946.

29. Kris, E. "Notes on the Development and on Some Current Problems of Psychoanalytic Child Psychology," *Psychoanalytic Study of the Child,* 1950, 5, 24–46.

30. Lewin, K. *Conceptual Representation and the Measurement of Psychological Forces.* Durham: Duke University Press; 1938.

31. Mayo, E. *Some Notes on the Psychology of Pierre Janet.* Cambridge: Harvard University Press; 1948.

32. Molish, R. H. Unpublished study.

33. Neumann, E. *Ursprungsgeschicts Des Bewusstseins.* Zurich: Rascher Verlag; 1949.

34. Nunberg, H. *Practice and Theory of Psychoanalysis.* Nervous and Mental Disease Monographs, New York, 1948.

35. Piotrowski, Z. A., et al. "Rorschach Signs in the Selection of Outstanding Young Male Mechanical Workers," *J. Psychol.,* 1944, 18, 131–150.

36. Rapaport, D. "The Autonomy of the Ego," *Bull. Menninger Clinic,* 1951, 15, 113–123.

37. ——. *Diagnostic Psychological Testing.* Chicago: The Year Book Publishers, Inc.; 1946.

38. Ribble, Margaret. *The Rights of Infants: Early Psychological Needs and Their Satisfaction,* New York: Columbia University Press; 1943.

39. Rorschach, H. *Psychodiagnostics: A Test Based on Perception.* Bern: H. Huber; 1942.

40. Schilder, P. *Mind: Perception and Thought in Their Constructive Aspects.* New York: Columbia University Press; 1942.

41. Spitz, R. A. "Anxiety in Infancy: A Study of Its Manifestation in the First Year of Life," *Internat. J. Psychoanalysis,* 1950, 31, 36–41.

42. ——. "Autoerotism: Some Empirical Findings and Hypotheses on Three of Its Manifestations in the First Year of Life," *Psychoanalytic Study of the Child,* 1949, 3 and 4, 85–120.

43. ——. "Grief, a Peril in Infancy." Film (1947). Available through New York University Film Library.

44. ——. "Anaclitic Depression: An Inquiry into the Genesis of Psychiatric Conditions in Early Childhood," *Psychoanalytic Study of the Child,* 1946, 2, 313–342.

45. ———. "Hospitalism: An Inquiry into the Genesis of Psychiatric Conditions in Early Childhood," *Psychoanalytic Study of the Child,* 1945, 1, 53–74.

46. Sullivan, H. S. "Conceptions of Modern Psychiatry," *Psychiatry,* 1940, 3.

47. Vorhaus, Pauline G. "Rationale for the RPRS." Unpublished paper, read before the convention of the Western Psychological Association, Fresno, California, April 26, 1952.

48. Waelder, R. "The Principle of Multiple Function," *Psychoanalytic Quart.,* 1936, 5, 45–62.

49. Wexler, M. "The Structural Problem in Schizophrenia: The Role of the Internal Object," in Brody, E. B., and Redlich, F. C. (eds.) *Psychotherapy with Schizophrenics.* New York: International Universities Press; 1952.

Part Four

Reporting of Findings

CHAPTER **17**

Principles of Report Writing

The Purpose of a Psychological Report

The purpose of a formal written report is to communicate certain kinds of data to specified individuals or groups. The data are usually derived from behavior in a standardized situation (in this case, the Rorschach technique). The assumption is made that from the individual's behavior in this particular situation it is possible to predict his behavior in situations not directly observed. However, as demonstrated in the preceding sections of this book, some data derived from the Rorschach are not necessarily equivalent to directly observable behavior.

It should be kept in mind that the material obtained from the interpretation of tests or diagnostic techniques may be, at best, offered in the form of guesses or hypotheses. If there is such a thing as a psychological "fact," it certainly cannot be inferred from such a brief observation of the personality. Therefore, the test report, especially when not integrated with case history material, would indeed be presumptuous were it not to specify the tentative nature of the personality analysis made.

The test report has diagnosis as its purpose only in the broadest sense. What we are attempting to assess is the total configuration of the personality—its strengths and weaknesses, assets and liabilities, adaptive and maladaptive techniques. Our emphasis is on whatever

601

dynamic forces are enabling the personality to maintain the degree of homoeostasis manifested in its adjustment to the environment. If the pattern that evolves bears a striking similarity to one of the common nosological syndromes, this similarity can be pointed out. However, nosological identification, as such, is not the purpose of either the test report or the clinical psychologist. Such a decision, if it is of any importance at all, must be made by that individual having the final responsibility for the disposition of the case at hand. If this person happens to be the psychologist, his conclusion should not be based on test data alone.

Reports may be delivered orally or in writing. Oral reports have certain advantages, as noted below.

Oral Reports as a Problem in Communication

Referrals from an Outside Agency

The psychological clinician frequently gets referrals for psychological examinations from agencies and individuals that he is not connected with by virtue of his particular position. The level of sophistication of these referrants will vary greatly. With referrants whose level of sophistication about the Rorschach is fairly low, two main dangers exist: (1) They may be overly skeptical about the test and use the findings in an inappropriate or minimal manner. (2) They may have too much faith in the test and fail to take into account the fact that its predictive powers have not been fully clarified by research.

For these reasons it is preferable in instances of this kind to discuss the results of the examination orally. Even a brief telephone conversation is preferable to a written representation of the findings, since the written report might be ambiguous. It is in the exchange of data between the referring individual and the psychological clinician that the status of the patient can be clarified. The level of personality being tapped by various aspects of the Rorschach can be fitted into the frame of reference of the individual referring the patient, and the psychologist can gain increasing insight into the nature of his instrument by discovering something about the patient's behavior outside of the examining situation. The referrant may subsequently desire a written summary for his own files. A written report might well prove dangerous if made without some knowledge of the whole case history (see the discussion of blind reporting, below). Needless to say, it should be made clear, if necessary, that such written summaries are not for the eyes of the patient but only for the eyes of the referrant.

Self Referrals

Requests for Rorschach or other psychological tests occasionally come from private individuals or the parents of children. If the psychologist has diagnostic responsibilities only, his task is simply to refer these patients to whoever is taking on the consulting or treatment responsibilities. If this job is that of the psychologist alone, he faces the problem of integrating the test findings into his general way of dealing with the problem as presented. In this instance it is probably best to use the test information as a part of a general formulation of the dynamics to be used in advising or treating the patient. If particular concern is expressed by the patient about the test results it is best to give fairly superficial kinds of interpretation, which are apt to be consciously acceptable to the individual and not particularly anxiety-provoking. In these cases it has usually been found that an emphasis on the intellectual aspects of the personality, thought contents, characteristic ways of reacting to stressful situations, and the like, can be discussed most easily. It should be kept in mind that some aspects of the Rorschach are apt to be of an unconscious nature, dealing with repressed material, and should not be brought out except in the context of intensive psychotherapy, and after the establishment of substantial rapport. It need hardly be stated that giving a written report to a patient is an extremely dangerous and harmful thing to do and may cause much grief, both to the patient and to the psychologist.

Referrals by Team Members

Referrals made by the colleagues of a psychological clinician in a team setting present certain special problems. Thorough communication with psychiatrists and other referring agents may be especially important at the beginning of a professional relationship. It is at this time that the psychologist must demonstrate his ability to make an unique contribution to the understanding of any given patient and toward a general comprehension of psychodynamics and psychopathology. This may be accomplished by careful and thorough demonstrations of the psychological tests and the methods of analysis used in conjunction with them. Since it will not always be possible to have such thorough discussions of every case, written reports become an extremely relevant method of communication. The special problems of communicating in written form are discussed in the next section.

Written Reports as a Problem in Communication

Submitting a report to someone else in written form places certain limitations on the free flow of communication with that individual. Questions arising in the mind of the recipient of the report cannot be discussed. It is not possible under these circumstances to exchange ideas that would enhance the understanding, on the part of both the reporter and the recipient of the report, of the case in question. The psychological reporter, without knowing the exact thinking of the individual with whom he is attempting to communicate, will have more difficulty in meeting his needs in the situation.

The Problem of Blind Reporting

Some individuals make it a practice to report psychological data, especially if based on the Rorschach, without any reference to, or indeed any knowledge of, case history material. The present writer considers this a satisfactory method when used for either research or demonstration purposes. If, however, the report is to be used for a serious clinical purpose, which will affect the life of the subject or patient in some important way, this procedure is very hazardous. It might, indeed, be termed unethical. The Rorschach, like any other psychological test, is no crystal ball that analyzes the personality with complete accuracy. Even if it were, the psychologist might find it desirable to emphasize or de-emphasize certain aspects of the interpretation if he knew the case history. It is suggested, therefore, that no written report be submitted without some knowledge of the situation of the patient outside of the examination room.

The Question of Technical Language

If we are to successfully communicate with those to whom our reports are directed, it is obvious that we must employ language comprehensible to them. This requires that any language too technical for their frame of reference must be translated into plainer English. We must remember that many of the terms that we employ with facility, and that seem commonplace to us, are not so to other people. The most extreme kind of technical language, of course, is language related to the test in question (extratensive, high $F\%$, overemphasis on W, and so on). Incredible as it may seem, this sort of jargon is to be found in some test reports. Next come terms technical to the field of psychology or to some particular kind of psychological theory (Oedipal strivings, masculine protest, castration anxiety, and fixation). It seems hardly necessary to point out that for someone not familiar with or sympathetic to the particular theories in question, this kind of terminology would represent an almost insurmountable barrier to understanding. Next in order of technicality are words comprehensible to most physicians but incomprehensible to lay people who might receive test reports (for example: schizophrenia, psychoneurotic, affective).

In certain circumstances the use of all these various kinds of technical language may be excusable. The use of language exclusive to the test should be restricted to reports directed to practicum supervisors who are unable to personally go over the tests with their students. The second kind of language may be used in reports to psychoanalysts or adherents to any other specific school of thought with which the psychologist finds himself allied. The third kind of technical language can generally be used in any medical setting. In situations other than these (as when a report is written to lay individuals not trained in the field of mental hygiene, such as school teachers, case workers, probation officers) the reports must be written in plain, ordinary English. It is the contention of the present writer that all data that can be inferred from the Rorschach test can be reported in this way and that an exercise of this kind is, indeed, most profitable to the psychological report writer. Too often, technical concepts become a substitute for understanding rather than a method of expressing it.

Organization

A common way of organizing a psychological test report is according to sources of information. In such a system, one paragraph may be devoted to interpretation of the Rorschach, another to an interpretation of the Thematic Apperception Test, and so on. In a report based exclusively on one test, such as the Rorschach, there may be an organization based on the various ways of analyzing this test. For example, there may be a paragraph consisting of an interpretation of the psychogram, another based on the sequence analysis, and still another dealing with the question of pathological indicators.

All these ways of organizing a report may, perhaps, have some meaning when submitted to a person supervising the work of a clinical psychology student, but they are completely meaningless to anyone else. An inherent evil in such a report is the repetition of much data and a complete lack of integration of the various hypotheses submitted.

A much better way of organizing a report would be in terms of areas of the personality. In this way, the emphasis would be on the patient rather than the tests. This would make the psychological test report comparable to reports by psychiatrists and other personnel evaluating the case. An example of the kind of organization that might be used is given on pages 608–610.

The Use of Test Data

The role of the psychologist, as here conceived, is that of an individual who has been asked to offer his professional opinion about a given case. There is no reason to assume that his competence is in question or that "evidence" needs to be brought forward to substantiate his claim.

The use of test data as the bulk of the report has little meaning to anyone, including other psychologists. If the individual is able to go no further than to report scores, ratios, presence of diagnostic "signs," and the like, he should not be submitting reports at all.

Another matter is the use of test data for illustrative purposes. If the report is to go to other agencies where it might come to the attention of psychologists, these psychologists might be interested in more specific information than is contained in the formal report. The report writer may wish to give them some idea of the actual flavor or style of the individual's productions by citing examples. However, there is little reason to cite any examples at all when submitting reports to members of other professions. Most of the kinds of examples we could cite might be incomprehensible to them and offer little more than evidence of our own insecurity about our interpretations. Where illustrative material in the tests is utilized, it might better be placed in the form of footnotes, so that an individual could read straight through the personality descriptions and skip the examples, if he so desired.

The Need for Flexibility

Above all other things, the psychological test reporter should remember that stereotypy is very undesirable. Little is revealed about the individuality of a patient if all the cases passing through the hands of a given psychologist are described as having "latent homosexuality," "masturbatory anxiety," "difficulty in interpersonal relationships," "ambivalence about the mother," and so on. It seems desirable to specify in each instance the importance of these various factors, if they exist, and the particularly unique way that the individual has in dealing with them. In any given case, the writer may well wish to focus on a particular problem mentioned by the referring colleague. Reports may be short or long, detailed or sketchy, depending on the particular needs of the situation. To whom the report is to go, how much time the individual has to prepare it, how confident he is of his interpretations, how much attention will be paid to his opinions—these are all important factors to consider.

Suggested Content of a Rorschach Report

Below are some general areas that might be discussed in a Rorschach report. They provide a sample kind of organization. By no means is this the only organization or the one that should be used at all times. However, as can be seen, the focus is on personality areas rather than ways of analyzing the test.

A. Intellectual Factors in Functioning

1. Intellectual potentialities.
2. Intellectual efficiency.
3. Degree and quality of impairment or deterioration, if any.
4. Ways of dealing with practical problems.
5. Ability to conceptualize or engage in abstract kinds of mental activity.
6. Ability to accept conventional lines of thinking.
7. Ability to conceive of original ideas and put them into effect.
8. Range of interest.
9. Intellectual ties to reality.

B. Affective Factors in Functioning

1. Availability of inner resources as a means of adjusting.
2. Strength and quality of inner drives.
3. Amount of conflict between inner drives.
4. Reactions to emotional stimulation from others.
5. Ways of handling affectively toned situations.
6. Ability to maintain control under stress.
7. Kind and degree of anxiety.
8. Prevailing mood and consistency of mood.

C. Roles and Relationships

1. Self-concept, feelings of security and insecurity, satisfaction and dissatisfaction.
2. Aspirations and their relationship to potential achievements.
3. Kind and amount of concern about the self, including criticalness and introspective tendencies.
4. Ways of relating to members of the same sex, including older, younger, and contemporary individuals.
5. Ways of relating to members of the opposite sex, including older, younger, and contemporary individuals.
6. Basic sexual role identification of the individual, consistency of his role-playing.

D. Diagnostic Formulation

By diagnosis is meant an integrated picture of the personality structure as revealed by the Rorschach test. The process of putting the personality into various categories, such as neurotic versus psychotic, introversive versus extraversive, hysteric versus obsessive, is part of an older psychological frame of reference. Even though we may occasionally make such statements, they have relatively little meaning to us. Our present conception of the personality is that of a dynamic interaction of forces which tend to bring about a certain method of adapting to the environment. We would here describe the individual's basic conflictual patterns, the adaptive and maladaptive mechanisms he has employed to cope with them, and the resultant kind of overt personality picture. It is especially important, if possible, to specify the latter; such a picture may serve as the psychiatrically trained physician's only means of comparison between the Rorschach report and his own observations.

E. Prognostic Statement

The prognostic statement is meaningful only in the kind of situation in which the patient or subject might find himself in the future. Prognosis could be discussed in relationship to various kinds of therapy or in terms of the possibility of spontaneous remissions. A prognostic formulation would usually include some over-all estimate of the individual's maturity, mental health, ego strength, or whatever one chooses to call it. The assumption here is that a mentally healthy climate will not encourage the growth and development of functional disorders.

Conclusion

In this chapter, an attempt has been made to discuss certain issues about report writing. The emphasis has been in discovering what the purpose of a report might be and how such a purpose might best be served. The problems in delivering oral or written reports have been conceived of primarily as problems between the reporter and the referrant with whom he is attempting to communicate. Some suggestions have been made as to how such communication might be facilitated, and a schema for organizing the report has been included for illustrative purposes.

CHAPTER ![18]

Illustrative Case Study

This chapter presents a case study intended to illustrate the processes of scoring and interpretation recommended in earlier chapters. The case is presented in the following order. First, the protocol is given, including the inquiry, analogy period and testing of the limits. Next each response is scored, with comments on any points of particular interest or difficulty with respect either to the scoring or the inquiry. Then the interpretation of the quantitative findings is worked through, followed by a detailed account of the processes of sequence and content analysis. The interview material is then considered, succeeded by an integration of the interpretative hypotheses with the interview findings. Finally, there is a summary, which might be used as a case report. The case as a whole is thus intended to illustrate in detail the processes involved in inquiry, scoring, interpreting, and reporting on the record of an individual case.

The case was selected in the light of this purpose. The record covers a fairly broad range of scoring categories. There are some flaws in the inquiry, but by and large it was thorough enough to make the scoring clear-cut—an advantage in an illustrative case. This also seemed a good record to illustrate sequence analysis, both because of the way in which the locations were handled and because a fair amount of original content was included. Another advantage of this case for illustrative purposes is the detailed interview material available, against which the hypotheses formulated throughout the

611

interpretative process could be checked. Finally, it seemed desirable that this record be drawn from the normal range of adjustment, to balance the cases included in Volume II as illustrating various diagnostic classifications.

It should be noted that the Rorschach examination was given after a series of counseling interviews, so that the subject was well known to the examiner at the time of the testing. In a way, this fact is a disadvantage for didactic and illustrative purposes, since the reader might find the analysis of the Rorschach more convincing or impressive if it had been done in a "blind" fashion. On the other hand, the use of the Rorschach technique diagnostically without any other knowledge of the patient is not advocated. The blind analysis of any particular test protocol is a useful teaching device, but it does not correspond to the realities of clinical practice, nor should it be expected to. When the Rorschach is used for diagnosis it should be interpreted in the light of all available information about the subject, including the history material and findings from other tests.

The present study cannot be considered typical of the diagnostic use of the Rorschach because the examiner had an exceptional amount of information about the subject. History material was available in more detail and in better perspective than would be revealed by the one or two interviews possible in most clinical situations. Also, the fullness and clearness of the history leave no room for illustrating the processes the examiner would go through in attempting to integrate the Rorschach interpretation with interview findings in which there was suppression and distortion. Nevertheless, the advantages of the record as an illustrative study outweigh these disadvantages.

In order that this case record may be used as a teaching device—the reader attempting to form hypotheses on the basis of the protocol—the scoring and interpretation will be considered before the history material is presented. At this point it is enough to state that the subject is an unmarried woman, aged 24. She was in her third year of university and living at home with her family at the time of the Rorschach examination.

Rorschach Protocol

The Rorschach protocol follows. Then, on pages 638–641, there are reproduced pages 2, 3, 4, and 5 of the *Individual Record Blank* for this subject.

Card I—23″

PERFORMANCE	INQUIRY
∧ 1. A map of something.	1. *Location:* Upper outer projections plus outside portion of uppermost projections.
Must I use the whole, or can I use bits?	S: It is like Newfoundland.
(E: Either. It's up to you)	E: What about it makes it seem like Newfoundland?
(long pause)	S: It is jutting out.
∨ 2. Part looks like a horse's head, but it has an extra bump on its nose.	2. *Location:* Projection on the left lower side, just inside the small knob-like extension.
	S: This little bit here (pointing to the "bump on the nose") kind of spoils it.
	E: Was it just the shape?
	S: Yes.
(long pause)	E: How much of the horse do you see?
	S: I don't see much of it; just the outline of the head.
⌐ 3. Another part is a dog's head. The mouth of a dog.	3. *Location:* Tiny projection on right lower side, just outside the small knob-like extension.
	S: It is a yapping dog.
∧ 4. Another part is a turtle's head. (long pause)	4. *Location:* Tiny projection on left side often seen as the nose of a man.
	E: Can you describe it?
	S: Just the head. Just the shape.
5. Two white spots in the center look like two figures in a picture that is over at a friend's house. A picture of Old England. Two people.	5. *Location:* Upper pair of white spaces.
	S: Two old monks. They have no shape, just as in the picture. Just the outline.

INQUIRY (*continued*)

Analogy Period:
E: Here in Card II you saw two women talking and here in Card V you saw an old man writing with a quill. How was it with the monks?
S: They remind me of the picture, and I can't remember the picture. They just are.

Card II—21″

PERFORMANCE

∨ 1. It is something like the head of a crab. Something we had in zoology.

(long pause)

∧ 2. Looks like a . . . almost like a picture on Christmas cards of a man done up in a muffler with a fur cap.

(pause)

3. The same part could be two women talking over a fence or something. They have terrific hats or hairdos or something.

(pause)

< 4. The head of a Scottie.

INQUIRY

1. *Location:* Lower red, turned to top of card.
E: What about it made it seem like a crab?
S: The feelers and the color. It is a lobster. It is like a diagram of a lobster.

2. *Location:* Tip of upper red detail.
S: Here just where the dark red shading is.
E: What about it made it seem like a fur cap?
S: The shading, not the color.
E: How do you see the man?
S: It was just the outline.
E: What about it reminded you of a Christmas card?
S: The fur cap. You don't see them around.

3. *Location:* Upper red portions for the women and upper gray center *d* for fence.
S: They are facing each other and their hands are up.

4. *Location:* Bottom outer projection with card turned sideways.
S: I couldn't figure out what was in his mouth.
E: What about it makes it look like a Scottie?

S: It is clear-cut and regular, just like a soap carving.
E: It was just the outline then?
S: Yes.

∧ **5.** The center is like a turtle only the shell is not quite all there. It slopes away too quickly.

5. *Location:* Center white space.
S: The head and tail. The shell should be rounder.
E: How do you see the turtle?
S: It is just there. It should have its feet out too.

Card III—50″

∧ 1. Two people bending over floor or ground or something. They are more like cartoons, for they look more like animals than people actually.

(pause)

2. The center looks like a red bow. Nothing else.

(pause)

3. Two red things on the side could be spirits or demons from a fairy story. They are hanging anyway.

(long pause)

1. *Location:* All black-gray portions.
S: The heads seem more like a bird's head, and the feet seem more like an animal's hoof. They are cartoons because of the way they are standing in the picture.
E: Where is the ground or floor?
S: Here. (Pointed to lower center *D*.)

2. *Location:* Center red detail.
S: It was the shape and the shading. The shading of the lighter part in the center, and a little bit on the edge. But it is red here.

3. *Location:* Outer red details.
E: Are they human-like or animal-like spirits or demons?
S: The head and hands are human-like, but the rest . . . goodness knows.
E: You said they were hanging?
S: Yes, because of this (pointing to the upper projection). Just the fact that that thing is there.
Analogy Period:
E: (After having inquired for *M* in I.5) How was it here?
S: I can imagine more now than I did at the time. I can imagine putting bad ideas into his head, and his tongue is sticking out.

PERFORMANCE (*continued*)

∨ 4. Two people back to back.

4. *Location:* Lower center gray.
S: Two heads, just the heads.
E: Tell me more about them.
S: They are like African natives. The shape and the shading like fuzzy hair.

Card IV—32″

PERFORMANCE

∧ 1. Two dogs lying down. They look like Airedales.

INQUIRY

1. *Location:* Lower side light gray.
S: Here is the head. They are just sitting down.
Analogy Period:
Here on Card VI the shading made it seem like a kitten's paw. Was it the same with these dogs?
S: No, I used the shading just to distinguish them. It was the outline.

2. Part of a flower.

(long pause)

2. *Location:* Uppermost portion.
S: It was the shading. I don't know what flower it is.
E: How was it the shading?
S: It gave depth to the petals.

3. The leaves are coming down the side. Bending over.

3. *Location:* Upper side extensions.
S: It is not the right kind of leaf for that kind of flower.
E: Did you see it as belonging to the flower?
S: No.
E: What about the blot made it seem like leaves?
S: Just the shape.

∧ 4. Some tall person saying something to a child or someone sitting down,
< lower. The tall person is definitely standing up. The chair is behind. (pause)

4. *Location:* Lower side light gray.
S: Head, hands, chair. Here is the smaller person.

∧ 5. Looks like a large pair of boots.

5. *Location:* Lower side light gray, but omitting the upper part of this portion.
S: A boot. Toe and heel. The shape not the shading. The shading breaks into it.

6. Tails to an evening suit. They are awfully long and one would trip on them.

6. *Location:* Entire lower two-thirds of blot.
S: The boots and then the tails would be in here. They are even more like . . . College gowns. This is all they have left.
E: What about it made it seem like tails or gown?
S: Just the shape.
E: Are they on someone?
S: I don't connect a person with them.

Card V—8″

PERFORMANCE

∧ 1. Looks like a rabbit's head.

INQUIRY

1. *Location:* Top portion with extensions.
E: What about the blot made it look like a rabbit's head?
S: The two ears. The shape.

2. Looks like rabbit's feet stretched out at the side too.

(pause)

2. *Location:* Side extension without adjacent thin extension.
E: What about it made it seem like rabbit's feet?
S: The shape, and perhaps the shading a little bit. It helped it stand out. It is rounded.

3. Looks a little bit like a bat, I guess.

(long pause)

3. *Location:* Whole.
E: What about it makes it seem like a bat?
S: The shape.
E: How do you see it?
S: Stretched out. Just the shape.

4. Looks like cliffs down at B——. And then a piece of land, low land, jutting out into the lake.

(long pause)

4. *Location:* Right quarter of side, with light gray extensions.
S: This (pointing to light extension) is lower land than this because of the shading.
E: Where would you be when you see it?
S: You are in it and above it.

PERFORMANCE (*continued*)

5. An old man writing with a quill.

INQUIRY (*continued*)

5. *Location:* Side bump usually seen as nose and moustache of a profile.
S: It is a lovely face with moustache and eyebrows, square face, ear. I used the shading here. His head and no neck. Here is the quill pen.
E: When you said you used the shading, what did you mean?
S: I got the details from the shading. It just served to distinguish it. It could be a photograph too. He is not as alive as the others.

Card VI—20″

PERFORMANCE

∧ 1. Some kind of insect or bug at the top. It's got wings, anyway.

(pause for 30 seconds)

2. Looks like pictures looking down from an aeroplane. A highway or traintracks going through flat ground on each side, and further out from that forests or hilly ground.
(pause for 44 seconds)

3. That head is not right for a turtle. A turtle's head and an insect body.

4. The wings look like part of a leaf. The lower two-thirds of a maple leaf.

5. That side almost looks like our kitten's paw, except for the end there where there is too much.

INQUIRY

1. *Location:* Entire upper portion.
S: Here are the wings.
E: What about the blot made it seem like an insect?
S: Wings, head, feelers. Just the shape.

2. *Location:* Lower portion omitting all projections.
S: That is the shading.

3. *Location:* Uppermost detail, without wings or whiskers.
S: Just the head. The shape.

4. *Location:* Lighter part of upper portion.
S: The shape.

5. *Location:* Lower lateral extension.
S: The shading. There is a burr on the end. It looks furry. Very soft.

Card VII—28"

PERFORMANCE	INQUIRY
∧ 1. Rather like two impish pixies in stories we used to have in Brownies. (long pause)	1. *Location:* Upper two thirds. S: The shape and shading on the face. The head doesn't seem quite right. E: Is the pixie all there? S: It is mainly the heads. It is just there.
2. Like a volcano. It is very small. The other mountains around it aren't very distinct. (pause)	2. *Location:* Tiny uppermost detail of inner portion of bottom D. S: It is a high volcano. The volcano because of the shape, and the shading makes the other mountains distant. E: How did you mean the shading makes the other mountains distant? Is it that they are misty, or that they just look farther away? S: They're not misty. Just farther away.
3. I think it is a paw or a foot held out. It has claws, but not very large claws. (long pause)	3. *Location:* Outermost side projections. S: It might be a rhinoceros' foot. It is partly the shading. It is rounded. E: When you say "held out," did you mean it belongs to an animal? S: Yes, as when you teach a dog to shake hands. E: What did you mean when you said it was partly the shading? S: The shading makes the claws stand out.
4. This is far-fetched but it looks something like Spain or some other country jutting out and surrounded by water.	4. *Location:* Middle third, left, without projection. S: It was the shape. It doesn't include the paw.
5. Looks as though looking through mountains. I don't know what the center part is. Mountains in the distance. A barricade or something between them. It doesn't look right. Lake on the side and barricade reflected in the lake. (pause)	5. *Location:* Dark center bottom detail and light portions above and below it. S: The mountains are distant, the shading. There is a lake here (pointing to lower portion) and a reflection in the lake.

PERFORMANCE (*continued*)	INQUIRY (*continued*)
V 6. A lion's head. (long pause)	6. *Location:* Middle third, right, upside-down. S: He could have a paw. A dancing lion. The shading here. A lovely head. E: How was it the shading? S: The nose looks rounded, the rest doesn't.
< 7. Same one as the lion's head is a camel, the hind part of it. I like the pixies.	7. *Location:* Upper two-thirds, without uppermost projection, card held sideways. S: The head is not right but here is the hump. Just the shape.

Card VIII—80″

PERFORMANCE	INQUIRY
⊲ 1. An angry wildcat. Angry is not quite the word. (long pause)	1. *Location:* Right pink detail. S: This one looked angry. The shading makes the face look angry, and the other one is the raccoon, which is more playful and inquisitive.
∧ 2. Something the same effect as the night we saw the Northern Lights. A curtain effect, hanging in folds.	2. *Location:* Blue middle portion. S: The shading. Hanging in folds. E: Which kind of Northern Lights did you mean? The flickering ones or the ones that are just there, not moving? S: I hadn't thought. It looks as though it could change. E: When you said it was the shading here hanging in folds, how did you mean that? S: It looks like a theatre curtain, but you couldn't go up and touch it. I didn't use the color.
3. Two needles, knitting needles with knitting between.	3. *Location:* Top gray. S: The needles are here (pointing to tiny uppermost projections). Looking more at it . . . the lines aren't right. E: What made it seem like knitting? S: The needles chiefly.

4. A mixture between a lampshade and an umbrella.

4. *Location:* Top gray, middle blue and center line extending downwards.
S: The orange is the handle, yet the orange part has a definite shape. Made it seem like a lamp, and these two little pieces here connected it with an umbrella, the ribs.
E: I'm not sure just how you see it. Did you use this part too (pointing to orange)?
S: No, except for the handle. It is stained or something.

5. Something like shells in the center. Can't make it out quite. Very fine shells.

5. *Location:* Upper center rib-like portion.
S: The white part. The shape and the shading coming in. White shells.

4. If this thing is an umbrella it has a rip down the center. Or a stain or something spilled down there.

6. The bottom is like a snapdragon. Partly because of the color.

6. *Location:* Lower center part of bottom *D*.
S: Here is the part you can snap.

> 7. On this side it looks more like a raccoon. Doesn't look mad. It is looking at something on the ground.

7. *Location:* Left pink *D*, card sideways (See Inquiry for 1.)

V 8. The orange and pink could almost be a two-toned sweet-pea.

8. *Location:* Lower pink and orange.
S: The color.

9. In a way it looks like snow over a bank. Icebergs, but powdery snow, soft on top.

9. *Location:* Lower orange, card upsidedown.
S: The softness of the orange part. Not the color, it would be white. It is hanging down. The shading.

Card IX—40″

PERFORMANCE

∧ 1. Two old people or witches both talking at once. Won't listen or agree with the other person. Both trying to get the last word. (long pause)

2. Looking down on the highway. On both sides there is something all lit up. Could be a stadium. One on each side of the track, when they don't need two.

> 3. Looks like a woman trying to put a great huge screw into a table. The table is very small, smaller than the screw. Almost looks like mother bear in Goldilocks and the Three Bears.

4. Some kind of small dog running for all it is worth.

∨ 5. Fireworks or something going up and coming down in a spray for-
< mation.
∨

INQUIRY

1. *Location:* Orange portion.
S: Hat looks like witches. This one could be an old man with a large, red nose, and hands out to hold attention.

2. *Location:* Center line and the two spaces near it, one on each side of the line.
S: The white part makes them seem lit up. The white looks bright. Intense brightness.
E: You said you were looking down on it?
S: It looks very small, like the movies looking down from a plane.

3. *Location:* Left green detail.
S: Here is the head of the screw, screw, table, big bow at the back and the shape of mother bear.

4. *Location:* Lower white space, left.
S: The white. Ears and tail and everything seems out behind.

5. *Location:* Light streaks in lower pink.
E: What about it made it seem like fireworks?
S: Going up here and coming down here.
E: I wondered if the color had anything to do with it.
S: No. It was the shading. It is these white parts in the shading. It could have been white and black.
E: What about it made it seem like a spray?
S: Something to do with the whiteness. Something intangible.

Card X—65″

PERFORMANCE

∧ 1. Some kind of small dog. I can't figure out what kind.

2. Grasshopper.

(long pause)

3. Some kind of flower. I don't know
∧ . . . iris . . . or what kind it is.
>
∨ (long pause)

∧ 4. Some kind of animal out of a book, goodness knows what. It is discussing something by a tree. It has queer horns.

∨

> 5. Some kind of caterpillar.

(long pause)

INQUIRY

1. *Location:* Inner yellow.
   S: It's cute. Looks happy, prancing. The darker part could almost be his ear.
   E: You had trouble figuring out what kind it is?
   S: I tried to make it into a Peke, and it didn't work. The light color. But perhaps it helped make it a happy dog.

2. *Location:* Outer, upper green.
   S: The green ones. The color and shape.
   Analogy Period:
   E: At the end you said the whole card seemed alive. Could you show me the things that made it seem so.
   S: (pointing to grasshopper) This seems alive.

3. *Location:* Lower green.
   S: It was the shading. They are not all there though. The two last petals. A hollow flower.
   E: How did you mean it was the shading?
   S: In the turning back of the petals.

4. *Location:* Top gray.
   S: Storybook animals, saying things in human words.

5. *Location:* Pink portion.
   S: This part here looks like it because of the shading. It is not distinct. Just there and that's all.
   E: What made it seem like a caterpillar?
   S: The shape and the shading. The head stands out.
   Analogy Period: (see X,2)
   S: This one is alive too.

PERFORMANCE (*continued*)   INQUIRY (*continued*)

6. A wolf's head.

    6. *Location:* Upper, inner part of outer blue.
    S: Nose, ears, eye.
    E: Was it the shape?
    S: Yes and the white for the eye.

∧ 7. Part of the petals of a pansy.

    7. *Location:* Center blue.
    E: What about it made it like a pansy?
    S: The shading. You can almost see a pansy face. Part lighter and part darker. It could be any color.

8. Two faces with definitely turned up noses.
This whole card seems alive.

    8. *Location:* Inner side of pink *D*'s.
    S: Nose, forehead, chin. They're cute.

Total time, 57 minutes.

Testing the Limits

W: E: Can you see anything in the whole card (pointing to Card I)?
     S: Could be witches with wings.
     E: Can you see anything in this whole card (Card II)?
     S: Two people dancing, a square dance. Seeing them at a distance helps.

CF: E: Some people see things that are just color with no particular shape. Can you see anything like that?
     S: Here in this card (Card III) it could be blood. My demons. It might have helped make them demons. . . . I like blue. This could be a spider (Card X), which I can't stand, so I kept looking for something nice in the blue.

Fc: E: Can you see anything that might be animal skins?
     S: (Pointed to VI, IV, and V). The shading here, but I used the shading more to make the various parts . . . to distinguish them.

P: E: (Quite spontaneously) Oh, here is a rabbit's head, I didn't notice before. But I don't know what these could be (pointing to darker green of lower center *D* in Card X).

Discussion of Scoring and Inquiry

Card I

1. *Scoring:*   dr   F   geo   0.5

COMMENT: A *dr* is scored since the area used is more than the upper, outer projection usually scored *d,* yet less than the upper side usually scored *D.* The subject implied nothing beyond shape, and hence *F* is scored, and the inquiry was not pushed further. Despite the fact that the subject mentioned a definite geographical concept, it is assumed that anything "jutting out" would have been compatible; hence the form level is rated 0.5, indicating a semi-definite concept.

2. *Scoring:*   dd   F   Ad   O   1.5

COMMENT: The blot area used is clearly demarcated in terms of its peninsular position and is not a *d,* hence is scored *dd.* The inquiry was pursued to elicit anything beyond "just shape." This was probably undesirable since the subject said nothing implying movement, and the use of such a small area usually precludes any determinant other than *F* unless particularly stated by the subject. A form-level rating of 1.5 is given; a particular species of animal was mentioned and there is a particularly good match with the blot area. Nothing was added for the "bump on the nose," since this is not considered a constructive specification.

3. *Scoring:*   dd   FM   Ad   O   1.5

COMMENT: As with the previous response this is scored *dd.* A main *FM* is scored for animal movement even though only part of the animal is seen. The specification of movement implying an open mouth raised the form level above the popular level to 1.5.

4. *Scoring:*   dd   F   Ad   O   1.5

COMMENT: The form level presents the chief problem here. Although there are no specifications, a rating of 1.5 seemed justified since a specific animal form was mentioned that was an excellent match to the blot area used.

5. *Scoring:* S   F   (H)   →O   1.5

COMMENT: The inquiry was carried into the analogy period to determine whether *M* should be the determinant, since the subject shows *M*-capacity elsewhere and her vague performance left the matter in doubt. However, the response to questioning in the analogy period makes it clear that her concept was too vague to justify scoring *M*. (*H*) is scored since the human figures are seen in a "picture," and thus their reality is qualified. The form level is 1.5, the basal level for human concepts. The concept does not justify a main original, since it is not highly unusual to see human figures in this white space location. However, the concept "monk" had not been encountered before in this examiner's experience; hence a tendency to an original was given.

Card II

1. *Scoring:* D   F→FC   (Ad)   1.0

COMMENT: The chief scoring problem here is whether *FC* should be main or additional. Although "lobster" suggests that the color was used, the change from "crab" to "lobster" did not occur until the inquiry; therefore, an additional *FC* seems the best scoring. Any implication that the content should be scored "food" is denied by making it a diagram, hence an (*Ad*) .

2. *Scoring:* dr   Fc   (Hd)   O   2.5

COMMENT: The use of shading as the main determinant is clearly established in the inquiry. (*Hd*) is scored because it is part of a human in a picture. A basal form-level rating of 1.5 is given for a human concept, with .5 added for each additional specification of cap and muffler.

3. *Scoring:* dr   M   Hd   3.0

COMMENT: A *dr* is scored for the combination of *D*'s and *d*. To the basal rating of 1.5 is added .5 for the organizational relationship implied in the "talking," .5 for the fence, and .5 for the hats or hair-dos. An additional .5 is not added for the "hands are up" because this seems to be the same specification as the "fence" given in the performance proper. The inquiry might have dealt with the question of color for the hats by non-directive questioning, but the fact that both hats or hairdos were suggested seemed to imply that only shape and position were involved.

4. *Scoring:* d   F   Ad   O   1.5

COMMENT: An addition of .5 was made to the popular 1.0 form-level rating for the specification of a particular kind of dog matching the blot area very well indeed. The inquiry was pursued to establish the possibility of shading contributing, but the subject's reply seems to rule this out.

5. *Scoring:* S   F   A   O   2.0

COMMENT: Since a turtle has a very distinctive shape, a basal rating of 1.5 is given, with .5 extra for the "tail." No additional is given for the "head" since this is included in the basic concept; the comments about the shell are considered to be irrelevant specifications.

Card III

1. *Scoring:* W   M   (H)→*A*H   P   1.0

COMMENT: The content is the chief point of interest here with *H* immediately qualified by "like cartoons" to (*H*), and then qualified still more to some mixture of animal and human, scored *A*H. This tendency is indicated by the scoring. The "bird's head" and "hoof" are considered irrelevant specifications for the concept "people"; hence the form-level rating is not raised beyond the basal level of 1.0 for a popular response.

2. *Scoring:* D   FC,Fc   obj   P   1.0

COMMENT: Despite the fact that more attention is given to shading than to color in the inquiry, *FC* is made the main determinant and *Fc* additional, partly because color was mentioned in the performance proper, and partly because color is in any event given precedence should the emphasis be equal. The popular form level of 1.0 is given; the additional comments add to the determinants, but do not refer to any essential aspects of the concept "bow."

3. *Scoring:* D   F   (H)   1.5

COMMENT: It may be noted that the inquiry first attempted to establish the content as (H) or (A). Then it was ascertained that *m* was not implied in the notion of "hanging," since this just accounted for the projection. The analogy period made it clear that movement was not attributed to the figures spontaneously enough to warrant scoring *M,* even as an additional.

4. *Scoring:* D   F,Fc   Hd   2.0

COMMENT: The effectiveness of a highly non-directive question is shown here. The use of shading is recognized by an additional *Fc* since it applies to only part of the concept, the hair.

Card IV

1. *Scoring:* D   FM   A   2.0

COMMENT: Since this subject used *Fc* for similar concepts, and since dogs seen in that area are often seen as furry or hairy, the analogy period was used to ascertain whether shading entered into it. The subject's reply made it clear that the shading simply served to demarcate the blot areas used. A main *FM* was scored because a definite posture was mentioned, even though it is a passive posture. A basal form level of 1.5 was given for mentioning a specific breed of dog which matches the blot well, and .5 was added for the posture.

2. *Scoring:* d   Fc→FK   Pl   1.0

COMMENT: A problem presents itself regarding scoring the determinant here. The shading is clearly used by the subject, and she states: "It gave depth to the petals." However, with a small, compact object like a flower it seems that the rounded effect must be primary, even though there is also a space effect. Therefore, *Fc* with an additional *FK* is scored.

3. *Scoring:* d   F   Pl   O   1.0

COMMENT: Although the subject said "bending over," she said nothing in the inquiry to indicate any feeling of gravity about the concept. Therefore *F* was scored, not *Fm.*

4. *Scoring:* D   M   H   →O   3.0

COMMENT: The inquiry here should have been pursued further. The subject gives enough to establish a main *M* and a high form level, but might have been induced to specify the sex of the figures if she had been asked to describe the figures or tell more about them.

5. *Scoring:* dr   F   obj   1.5

COMMENT: These are not the usual boots which take up the whole lower side gray. They use even less than the lower side light gray, and hence are scored *dr.* An extra .5 is given to the form level rating for specifying the "heel."

6. *Scoring:* W   F   obj   →O   1.5

COMMENT: The concept suggested the possibility of an *M,* but the subject made it clear in the inquiry that a human concept was not involved. Although this examiner has encountered occasional responses describing a man in an evening suit, the original twist of having the evening suit alone seemed to justify a tendency to an original.

Card V

1. *Scoring:* d   F   Ad   1.5

COMMENT: There seems no problem here.

2. *Scoring:* d   Fc   Ad   1.0

COMMENT: A main *Fc* is scored for the use of shading, even though the subject said "perhaps the shading a little bit"; the subsequent comments seem to justify a main score. "Stretched out" might imply an *FM,* but this was not pursued in the inquiry and cannot be scored since it may be merely a positional specification.

3. *Scoring:* W   F   A   P   1.0

COMMENT: The subject did not indicate animal movement despite a fairly directive question. "Stretched out" in this connection is not considered grounds for *m,* especially since she says "just the shape."

4. *Scoring:* dr   FK   N   →O   1.0

COMMENT: Here the shading is used in a landscape concept to give differences in the height of land. This seems to justify an *FK* response, although the concept is a curious mixture of vista and aerial view.

5. *Scoring:* d   M,Fc   Hd→ (Hd)   O   3.5

COMMENT: A score of *M* is definitely indicated here because of the postural implications. Later in the inquiry the subject tends to rob the concept of life and says it could be a photograph. This, however, is indicated in the scoring by showing a tendency towards (*Hd*) rather than qualifying the score of *M*. An additional *Fc* is scored for the use of fine differentiations in the shading to give features. Although the "moustache" and "eyebrows" might conceivably be given merely by the outline, the "ear" must be based on the use of shading.

Card VI

1. *Scoring:* D   F   A   1.5

COMMENT: An extra .5 is given to the form-level rating for the "feelers," the "head" and "wings" being covered in the popular level of 1.0.

2. *Scoring:* dr   FK   N   1.0

COMMENT: Although quite large, the location should be scored *dr* rather than *W,* since the entire lower portion would be scored *D* had this subject used it. The only other possible alternative would be a *di,* but this was discarded since the concept could not be described as "carved out" of the heavy shading area so much as an extension of a *D,* the vertical center portion which is the focus of the concept. The form-level rating is 1.0 for the highway running through country. The extra specifications of "forest" or "hilly ground" establish the determinant rather than adding to the form.

3. *Scoring:* dr   F   Ad   1.0

COMMENT: This is scored *dr,* being less than a *D* and more than a *d.*

4. *Scoring:* D   F   Pl   →O   1.0

COMMENT: Although a "leaf" would be scored 0.5 as a semi-vague outline, a concept as definite as a "maple leaf," which matches the blot area well, warrants 1.0.

5. *Scoring:* d   Fc   Ad   O   2.0

COMMENT: A basal level of 1.0 is given for the "kitten's paw." An additional .5 is given for the furriness as an essential component of the concept, and another .5 for the "burr" as an ingenious way of reconciling the concept with the shape of the blot.

Card VII

1. *Scoring:* D   F→M,Fc   (Hd)   1.5

COMMENT: To score even an additional *M* is open to question. It was done on the basis of expression implied by "impish," with a subject who has shown capacity for seeing *M*. The inquiry should have picked up this point and the question should have been asked: "What about it makes it seem impish?" Again the *Fc* should have been inquired about, although it seems entirely likely that it was used to differentiate the features, perhaps also giving them a rounded effect. Since it applies only to the face—that is, part of the blot area—it must be given an additional rather than a main score.

2. *Scoring:* dr   FK   N   O   1.5

COMMENT: Although this is a very small location, it is *dr* rather than *dd* because it is not clearly demarcated by the "Gestalt qualities of the blot." The clumsy question in the inquiry was designed to ascertain whether *K* entered in as well as *FK,* but the response makes it clear that the shading gave distance without implying diffusion. The "volcano" alone would have been 1.0, but the organizational tendency introduced by "other mountains" adds .5 to the form level.

3. *Scoring:* dd   FM,Fc   Ad   →O   1.5

COMMENT: The inquiry was successful in establishing that animal movement was implied in "held out." An additional *Fc* is scored for the shading used to give a rounded effect.

4. *Scoring:* dr   F   geo   1.0

COMMENT: The *dr* is scored rather than *D* because the projection is cut off to improve the match of concept to blot. The mention of a definite country with a geographical outline similar to the blot area used raises the form level from vague to definite.

5. *Scoring:* d   FK   N   →O   2.0

COMMENT: The *FK* is scored because the distance effect is attributable to shading. A basal rating of 1.0 is given for "mountains," with .5 added for the "barricade" and .5 for the "lake."

6. *Scoring:* D   F→FM,Fc   Ad   →O   2.0

COMMENT: Although only the head was seen in the performance proper, the concept was enlarged to include the front-half of the lion, seen in action. This, in effect, is a new concept emerging in the inquiry; therefore an additional rather than a main *FM* is scored. The inquiry should have been pursued to ascertain whether it was in "human-like" or "trained animal-like" action. Since this was not done, it is assumed that the determinant should be *FM* rather than *M*. The lion's head is not an unusual concept, but the front half of a dancing lion has an original flavor and hence was scored as a tendency towards an original.

7. *Scoring:* D   F   Ad   O   1.5

COMMENT: Here again the subject extends the location in the inquiry, starting with the hind part of a camel and ending with the whole camel.

Card VIII

1. *Scoring:* D   F→FM,Fc   A   →P   1.5

COMMENT: The major problem is whether responses 1 and 7 should be scored as one response or two. Even when differences are seen between the two animals they are usually scored as one response, and always as one if they are seen in relationship. However, the second animal was not mentioned until much later in the performance, with the card held in another position, and the scoring of the determinants differs somewhat. Therefore, they were scored as two responses. The tendency to *FM* is given rather than a main *FM* since the movement is reduced to an expression, and only a tendency to a popular is scored on that account. The additional *Fc* is scored for the implied use of shading for the face of the animal, although the inquiry should have ascertained how the shading was actually used.

2. *Scoring:* D   FK   N   O   1.0

COMMENT: *Fc* is ruled out by placing the concept at a distance. The choice between *K* (for diffuse light) and *FK* (for a structured vista response) was settled in favor of the latter, especially since a 1.0 rather than a 0.5 basal rating is indicated by the good match of the blot to what seems to be seen as a distinctively structured natural phenomenon. It must be admitted, however, that one could make a case for a *KF* score with form level 0.5. The inquiry for movement was somewhat lacking in finesse, so the reply was taken as evidence against *m*—although, had it been given spontaneously in response to a non-directive question, an additional *m* score would have been justified.

3. *Scoring:* dd→D   F   obj   →O   1.5

COMMENT: The focus of the concept is the "needles" in a *dd* area, although there was a tendency to extend the concept to the whole *D*. The extra .5 was given to the form-level rating for organizational activity.

4. *Scoring:* D   F   obj   O   2.0

COMMENT: Here again the problem is to decide whether there should be one or two responses for the "lampshade" and the "umbrella." The inquiry might have been pushed further. However, although the subject implied that she would use the orange part for the lampshade, she replied to a definite inquiry that she used only the gray, blue, and center line *D*'s. It seemed that the "umbrella" was the central concept, particularly since "ribs" and "handle" were specified and the lampshade was mentioned only as a certain dissatisfaction about the form. Hence it was scored as one response, an "umbrella." There is undoubted difficulty about scoring alternative concepts such as this one. It is neither clearly two responses, nor is it clearly one, nor is it a merging of the two such as one finds in a "contamination."

5. *Scoring:*   S,D   FC′, Fc A_{obj} →O   1.0

COMMENT: The rib-like *D* was used as an additional location, and must be scored since *Fc* is involved. It was taken that the shading gave a rounded effect, which should have been confirmed by inquiry; however, this seems typical enough of this subject to justify an additional *Fc* score. *FC′* is taken to be the main determinant for the concept of "shells," especially since they are specified as white shells in the inquiry.

6. *Scoring:*   dr   FC   Pl   →O   1.5

COMMENT: The definite shape of the "snapdragon" as a flower concept, matching the blot so exactly, gives both an FC score and a form-level rating well beyond the vague level of many flower concepts.

7. *Scoring:*   D   FM   A   P   1.0

COMMENT: FM is scored for the posture "looking down," hence a main *P* is given. Although often the mention of a definite animal would raise the form-level rating to 1.5, in this case no reason was given why this looked like a "raccoon" especially, and it was taken that it had been labelled such to distinguish it from the "angry wildcat." That is, it was more determined by the need to find a quiet, small animal in contrast, than by the form of the blot.

8. *Scoring:*   D   FC   Pl   1.5

COMMENT: A good *FC*.

9. *Scoring:*   D   cF   N   O   0.5

COMMENT: Here the difficulty is deciding between a *cF* with a basal rating of 0.5 and an *Fc* with a basal rating of 1.0. This is certainly a borderline concept. The subject meant to imply form in her comments "over a bank," "hanging down." Yet it was felt that a bank of snow (or even an iceberg) could be any shape, and cF would be the better scoring.

Card IX

1. *Scoring:* D M H→(H) 3.5

COMMENT: A basal level of 1.5 was given for a human concept, .5 for "talking at once" and the organization implied, .5 for hat, .5 for nose, and .5 for "hands out to hold attention."

2. *Scoring:* S,D FC′,FK Arch, N O 1.5

COMMENT: The S was made the main location because the "stadium" seems to be figure and the rest ground. The "brightness" must be scored $FC′$ rather than K because it is the whiteness that makes it bright rather than the shading. The FK presents some problem, since it is not clear that the shading was used; however, despite the fact that she explains the aerial view in terms of "it looks very small," this concept is applied to a shaded area and is of a kind that makes it seem very likely that shading contributed, especially since this subject has already shown a tendency to use FK.

3. *Scoring:* D M (A)←H O 3.5

COMMENT: The content is the chief point of interest here. The fact that a human concept was turned into a fairy-tale animal is shown by giving an additional H with an arrow pointing to a main (A).

4. *Scoring:* S FM A O 3.0

COMMENT: A basal level of 1.5 was scored for the specific animal, with .5 added for the "ears," another .5 for the "tail," and .5 for the movement, which is an essential part of the concept.

5. *Scoring:* S,dr mF,C′F fireworks O 0.5

COMMENT: In the inquiry the examiner leaped to the conclusion that the subject intended to use the whole pink bottom D, and hence assumed that color was the determinant. This shows the danger of making such assumptions because other subjects have given similar concepts; for it emerged that this subject used a very rare location —namely, the light streaks in the lower pink, with the surrounding area as background. Although it might be argued that the trace of light color in these streaks would make them a *dd* rather than an *S,* her emphasis that they were white, and the fact that "whiteness" was focal in her concept, seemed to justify a scoring of a main *S* and an additional *C'F*. The additional *dr* was given because the background is part of the concept, "could have been white and black." Inanimate movement is clearly the main determinant. The only remaining question is whether this concept is definite enough in shape to score *Fm, FC'* with a form-level rating of 1.0 or better, or whether it is a vague concept that could be any shape. The latter was preferred on the assumption that all that was required of the shape was curving lines—hence the *mF, C'F,* and 0.5 scoring.

Card X

1. *Scoring:* D   FM   A   2.0

COMMENT: The inquiry indicates that the subject tried to integrate color into the concept but could not reconcile the color with the shape. An additional FC_{sym} is a possibility, but since she spoke of "light color" rather than yellow, it was felt better to omit a color score.

2. *Scoring:* D   FC,FM   A   1.5

COMMENT: A main *FC* score is clearly indicated. An additional *FM* is given for the movement implied in her general remark at the end of the performance proper and specified in the analogy period.

3. *Scoring:* D   Fc→FK   Pl   1.0

COMMENT: *Fc→FK* is scored for the "turning back of the petals," implying a rounded effect with a tendency to depth. A basal form level of 1.0 is given for a definite flower that is a good match for the blot.

4. *Scoring:* D   M   (A)   2.0

COMMENT: The *M* score for a story-book animal was justified by the subject's spontaneous explanation in the inquiry.

5. *Scoring:* D   F,Fc,FM   A   1.0

COMMENT: The main determinant cannot be *Fc* since the shading is used for only part of the "caterpillar," nor can it be *FM* when this determinant was not established until the analogy period. *Fc* and *FM* are therefore scored as additional to a main *F*.

6. *Scoring:* dr,S   F   Ad   2.0

COMMENT: The additional *S* is given for the "eye," but not an *FC'* because it was taken that she meant the "white for the eye" as she stated, rather than the white of the eye.

7. *Scoring:* D   Fc   Pl   →O   1.0

COMMENT: The shading is used to differentiate the distinctive face of a "pansy" and hence is scored *Fc*.

8. *Scoring:* dr   F   Hd   2.0

COMMENT: The basal form-level rating is 1.5 for the concept of "face," plus .5 for "turned-up nose."

Testing the Limits

COMMENT: The subject's difficulty in using wholes and the fact that no *CF* responses emerged made these points obvious ones to test. Although *Fc* did emerge no "animal skins" had been seen, and it was desired to test the subject's tolerance for this concept. She saw enough populars that these were not necessary to test; but it was interesting that none emerged on Card X, although she did see a non-popular "caterpillar" in the pink. Her reason for not seeing the "spiders" emerged in testing for *CF,* and her difficulty with the green area was clarified in her comments about the "rabbit's head."

Pages 2, 3, 4, and 5 of the *Individual Record Blank* for this examination are reproduced on the following pages.

SCORING LIST

Card No. and Number of Response	Time and Position	Location Main	Location Add	Determinant Main	Determinant Add	Content Main	Content Add	P—O Main	P—O Add
I	23"								
0.5 ①	∧	dr		F		qeo			
1.5 ②	∨	dd		F		Ad		O	
1.5 ③	⌐	dd		FM		Ad		O	
1.5 ④		dd		F		Ad		O	
1.5 ⑤		S		F		(H)			→O
II	21"								
1.0 ①	∨	D		F→FC		(Ad)			
2.5 ②	∧	dr		Fc		(Hd)		O	
3.0 ③		dr		M		Hd			
1.5 ④	<	d		F		Ad		O	
2.0 ⑤	∧	S		F		A		O	
S **III**	50"								
1.0 ①	∧	Wx		M		(H)→AH		P	
1.0 ②		D		FC	Fc	obj		P	
1.5 ③		D		F		(H)			
2.0 ④	∨	D		F,	Fc	Hd			
S **IV**	32"								
2.0 ①	∧	D		FM		A			
1.0 ②		d		Fc→FK		Pl			
1.0 ③		d		F		Pl		O	
3.0 ④	⌃̌	D		M		H			→O
1.5 ⑤	∧	dr		F		obj			
1.5 ⑥		Wx		F		obj			→O
U **V**	8"								
1.5 ①	∧	d		F		Ad			
1.0 ②		d		Fc		Ad			
1.0 ③		W		F		A		P	
1.0 ④		dr		FK		N			→O
3.5 ⑤		d		M	Fc	Hd→(Hd)		O	
U **VI**	20"								
1.5 ①	∧	D		F		A			
1.0 ②		dr		FK		N			
1.0 ③		dr		F		Ad			
1.0 ④		D		F		Pl			→O
2.0 ⑤		d		Fc		Ad		O	
U **VII**	26"								
1.5 ①	∧	D		F→M,Fc		(Hd)			
1.5 ②		dr		FK		N		O	
1.5 ③		dd		FM	Fc	Ad			→O
1.0 ④		dr		F		qeo			
2.0 ⑤		d		FK		N			→O
2.0 ⑥	∨	D		F→FM,Fc		Ad			→O
1.5 ⑦	<	D		F		Ad		O	

Card No. and Number of Response	Time and Position	Location Main	Location Add	Determinant Main	Determinant Add	Content Main	Content Add	P—O Main	P—O Add
VIII	80"								
1.5 ①	⌐	D		F	→FM,Fc	A			→P
1.0 ②	∧	D		FK		N		O	
1.5 ③		dd→D		F		obj			→O
2.0 ④		D		F·		obj		O	
1.0 ⑤		S	D	FC'	Fc	Aobj			→O
1.5 ⑥		dr		FC		Pl			→O
1.0 ⑦	>	D		FM		A		P	
1.5 ⑧		D		FC		Pl			
0.5 ⑨	∨	D		cF		N		O	
IX	40"								
3.5 ①	∧	D		M		H→(H)		O	
1.5 ②		S	D	FC'	FK	Arch	N	O	
3.5 ③	>	D		M		(A)←H		O	
3.0 ④		S		FM		A		O	
0.5 ⑤	∨	S	dr	mF	C'F	fireworks		O	
X	65"								
2.0 ①	∧	D		FM		A			
1.5 ②		D		FC	FM	A			
1.0 ③	∨	D		Fc→FK		Pl			
2.0 ④	∧	D		M		(A)			
1.0 ⑤	>	D		F	Fc,FM	A			
2.0 ⑥		dr	S	F		Ad			
1.0 ⑦	∧	D		Fc		Pl			→O
2.0 ⑧		dr		F		Hd			
T=57min									

(right margin flags: U at Card VIII; S at Card IX)

[2]

TABULATION SHEET

Scoring Symbols	I Main	I Add	II Main	II Add	III Main	III Add	IV Main	IV Add	V Main	V Add	VI Main	VI Add	VII Main	VII Add	VIII Main	VIII Add	IX Main	IX Add	X Main	X Add	Total Main	Total Add
LOCATION																						
W { W / W̄ / DW }					1		1		1												3	
D			1		3		2				2		3		6	(2)	2	(1)	6		25	(3)
d			1				2		3		1		1								8	
Dd { dd / de / di / dr } (dd)	3												1		1						5	
Dd { dr }	1		2				1		1		2		2		1			(1)	2		12	(1)
S	1		1												1		3			(1)	6	(1)
Main Total	5	+	5	+	4	+	6	+	5	+	5	+	7	+	9	+	5	+	8		=59	
DETERMINANTS																						
M			1		1		1		1					(1)	2		1				7	(1)
FM	1						1						1	(1)	1	(1)	1		1	(2)	6	(4)
m (m,mF,Fm)															1						1	
k (k,kF,Fk)																						
K (K,KF)																						
FK								(1)	1		1		2		1			(1)		(1)	5	(3)
F { F+ }	3		3		2		3		2		3		4		3							
F { F }	1																		3		27	
F { F- }																						
Fc			1			(2)	1		1	(1)				(3)		(2)			2	(1)	6	(9)
c (cF,c)															1						1	
C (FC',C'F,C')															1		1	(1)			2	(1)
FC { FC / F/C }				(1)	1										2				1		4	(1)
CF { CF / C/F }																						
C { C / Cn / Cdes / Csym }																						
Main Total	5	+	5	+	4	+	6	+	5	+	5	+	7	+	9	+	5	+	8		=59	
CONTENT																						
H	1				2		1										1	(2)			5	(2)
Hd			2		1				1				1						1		6	
A			1				1		1		1				2		2		4		12	
Ad	3		2						2		2		3						1		13	
Aobj													1								1	
At																						
Sex																						
Obj					1		2								2						5	
Pl							2								2		1				5	
N									1		1				2		2		1		7	
Geo	1										2		1					(1)			6	(1)
Art and Des															1		1				2	
Arch																						
Emblem															1						1	
Clouds																						
Blood																						
Fire																						
Mask																						
Abstract																						
~~At~~						(1)																(1)
fireworks																	1				1	(1)
Main Total	5	+	5	+	4	+	6	+	5	+	5	+	7	+	9	+	5	+	8		=59	
POPULARITY-ORIGINALITY																						
P					2				1						1	(1)					4	(1)
O	3	(1)	3				1	(2)	1	(1)	1	(1)	2	(3)	3	(3)	4			(1)	18	(12)

[3]

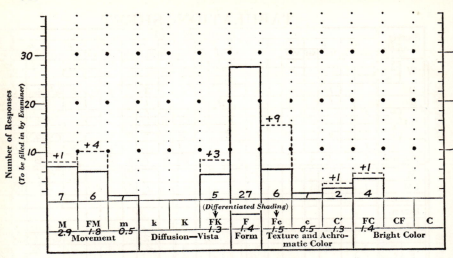

RELATIONSHIPS AMONG FACTORS

Total Responses (R) = *59*

Total Time (T) = *57'*

Average time per response $\left(\dfrac{T}{R}\right)$ = *60"*

Average reaction time for Cards I, IV, V, VI, VII = *20"*

Average reaction time for Cards II, III, VIII, IX, X = *51"*

$\dfrac{\text{Total F}}{R}$ = *46* F%

$\dfrac{FK + F + Fc}{R}$ = *64* %

$\dfrac{A + Ad}{R}$ = *43* A%

Number of P = *4 + 1*

Number of O = *18 + 12*

(H + A) : (Hd + Ad) = *17 : 19*

sum C = $\dfrac{FC + 2\,CF + 3\,C}{2}$ = *2*

M : sum C =   *7 : 2*

(FM + m) : (Fc + c + C') =   *7 : 9*

$\dfrac{\text{No. of responses to Cards VIII, IX, X}}{R}$ = *37* %

W : M =   *3 : 7*

Succession :

    Rigid   Orderly   Loose   Confused

(Place a check mark at the appropriate point on the scale above)

Estimate of Intellectual Level

Intellectual Capacity	Intellectual Efficiency
....Very Superior	....Very Superior
✓..Superior	ʃ..Superior
....High Average	....High Average
....Low Average	....Low Average
....Dull Normal	....Dull Normal
....Feebleminded	....Feebleminded

Note that this estimate is based mainly on the following:
— number and quality of W   *av. unweighted form level* = 1.6
+ number and quality of M   *av. form level (achr.)* = 1.5
+ level of form accuracy   *av. form level (chr.)* = 1.7
+ number and quality of O   *av. weighted form level* = 2.0
— variety of content
— succession

dd = 5
dr = 12 + 1
s = 6 + 1

Manner of Approach

W(*3* /*5* %) D(*25+3*/*42* %) d(*8*/*14* %) Dd and S(*39* %)
f.l. *1.5*   *1.6*   *1.7*   *1.4* or *1.6*

Enter the location percentages in the spaces above. Compare these percentages with the norms shown in the box below, by placing a check mark opposite the appropriate range of percentages.

((W))	(D)	d	Dd and or S
< 10% ((W))	< 30% ((D))		
10–20 (W)	✓30–45 (D)	< 5% (d)	
20–30 W	45–55 D	✓5–15 d	< 10% Dd S
30–45 W	55–65 D	15–25 d	10–15 Dd S
45–60 W	65–80 D	25–35 d	15–20 Dd S
> 60 W	> 80 D	35–45 d	20–25 Dd S
		> 45 d	✓ 25 Dd S

LOCATION CHART

Interpretation of Quantitative Findings

It is proposed to discuss the interpretation of the quantitative findings without reference to the background material; an integration with the interview material will be undertaken later (pages 679–685). The following procedure seems desirable in the process of interpretation: First, formulate hypotheses about the personality of the subject solely upon the basis of the quantitative findings; then check the interpretation, choosing between alternative hypotheses and modifying hypotheses, by a comparison with the findings of sequence and content analysis and finally with the history material, integrating all sources of information so as to arrive at the picture that seems best to fit all the available facts. Since the presentation here is intended to describe the processes through which the examiner goes in working out his interpretation, neither the mode of presentation nor the order in which the various aspects of the Rorschach performance are discussed should be taken as a model for reporting. For the sake of convenience it is proposed to deal with the quantitative findings in roughly the same order in which they are discussed in Chapter 10.

The Psychogram

A first glance at the psychogram (page 640) shows that the responses bulk in the central area and on the left, with the color area on the right-hand side containing few responses. This immediately suggests that this subject is not reacting freely to her environment as it impinges upon her but rather tends both to limit her responsiveness and to restructure her world in terms of her own needs.

Movement responses are seen to be fairly well represented, with $M:FM$ amounting to 7:6, or $7\frac{1}{2}:8$ when additionals are counted in with half-weight. On the face of it, this proportion approximates an optimum balance, implying both a well-developed value system and a ready acknowledgment of impulses towards immediate gratification, with little conflict between them. However, this hypothesis can be accepted only in terms of a potentiality for development under favorable circumstances. The fact that there are 4 additional *FM* responses indicates some reluctance to give ready, free responses of this sort. This is taken to show a tendency to inhibit the acknowledgment and expression of the more primitive and less well-understood impulses. These impulses are not only subordinated to the long-range goals and values of the subject (indicated by a preponderance of main *M*), but there seems to be a tendency to suppress impulses in the interests of maintaining the value system. There seems to be over-inhibition, rather than the self-acceptance that should be implied by an optimum *M:FM* ratio. This interpretation is supported by the fact that the *F%* is as high as 46. The conflict between the value system and impulse life, suggested by a tendency to suppress *FM* responses, is not reflected, however, in over-production of *m*. One *m* response is a "normal" expectation. The implication is that the system of defenses utilized by this subject is fairly effective in protecting her from painful awareness of conflict with respect to her less well-understood impulses. The quantitative findings themselves give no indication of the nature of the impulses prominent in this subject's motivational system; for this the sequence and content of the responses must be considered—and perhaps also the interview material.

Considered in isolation, the fact that $7+1$ *M* responses are produced raises the possibility that the creative potential of this subject. is readily accessible. However, the applicability of this hypothesis seems limited by the fact that the scoring list shows only one unqualified *H*—with the other responses involving *(H)*, *Hd*, *(Hd)*, *AH*, and *(A)*—suggesting that intellectual reservations and self-criticism tend to hamper creativity. Another negative indication is the *W:M* ratio of 3:7, which represents an imbalance between the creative potential shown by the *M* responses and the organizational interest implied by *W*. Something is hampering this subject from finding an outlet for her creative potential. This hypothesis is given special emphasis since the imbalance of the ratio is due rather to an unusually low number of *W* responses than to an unusually rich production of *M* responses. It seems entirely likely that her imaginal function is concerned with fantasy solution to her problems or escape therefrom. If sequence analysis can throw light on the difficulty in seeing relationships, it should help to explain why imaginal capacity is absorbed in unproductive fantasy rather than in constructive ways.

Despite the fact that the context in which the *M* responses appear limits the applicability of the hypotheses of creativity and self-acceptance, this many *M* responses suggest that this subject's imagination is active enough to lend stability to her adjustment, providing inner resources upon which she can fall back in periods of stress. Moreover, this number of *M*'s indicates an inner system of values of some kind or other which serves as a guide to satisfactions and a basis of control in terms of which gratification can be postponed. The quantitative findings alone give no clue as to the nature of these values; possibly the content analysis or the interview material will throw light on this. The effectiveness of the value system as a basis of orientation and deferment seems somewhat limited, however, by the fact that the *M*'s are given somewhat reluctantly, only twice as the first response to a card (see scoring list) and are qualified by *Hd*, *(H)*, and the like, indicating self-criticism.

The same limitations of the *M* responses also suggest a limitation in the ability to feel empathetic identification with others. Whatever the implications of color and shading responses with respect to interpersonal relationships, it would seem that this subject clearly falls short of optimum capacity for mature, contributing, interdependent relationships with others. Clues to the reasons for this limitation, and the ways in which she views other people, may be found in sequence and content analysis. Moreover, content analysis may likewise throw light on the nature of the self-picture. Nevertheless, the number and form level of the *M* responses alone suggest an ego-organization strong enough to rule out the possibility of psychosis or severe neurosis.

Before leaving the left hand side of the psychogram, the diffusion and depth responses must be considered as indications of the extent and mode of handling affectional anxiety. The absence of *k* and *K* responses cannot be interpreted as an absence of anxiety, because of the marked tendency to produce *FK* responses $(5+3)$, which, insofar as they indicate a tendency to handle affectional anxiety by an introspective attempt to understand it, imply the presence of some considerable amount of affectional anxiety to be handled. This number of *FK* is unusually high, suggesting that introspective effort is carried beyond effective bounds. The limitations of self-acceptance shown in the *M:FM* ratio and the lack of organized *W*'s suggest that this introspective effort does not imply any great success in achieving an insightful view of the self. The hypothesis of the "unhappy worrier" seems to fit the *FK* emphasis.

The right side of the psychogram is believed to give indications of the nature of the subject's emotional relationships with her environment, particularly with respect to interpersonal relationships. The marked emphasis on texture responses is the first noteworthy feature, with 6+9 *Fc* and 1 *cF*. This suggests a strong awareness of affectional need, enough beyond the average expectation to indicate an exaggerated need for affectional response from others. Clinical experience would lead to the suggestion that there has been some deprivation of affection in primary familial relationships, probably in mother-child relationships, but that this deprivation was neither early enough nor complete enough to lead to a serious defect in capacity for affectional relationships. The hypothesis is that the resulting exaggeration of affectional need would be expressed in a strong need to feel belongingness and closeness to others, in a need to be approved by others, and in a recipient and dependent orientation. The one *cF* supports the notion of a recipient and dependent orientation, implying some residual infantile need for affectional contact. It might be expected that the *Fc* emphasis would give a basis of sensitivity to other people and consequent tact in interpersonal relationships, especially since it is within the context of good control. However, there is a possibility that this sensitivity may also manifest itself in easily hurt feelings. It is expected that a consideration of shading dynamics and the content of shading responses will throw further light upon the way in which the affectional need of this subject is organized within her personality.

The proportion of undifferentiated to differentiated shading responses is seen to be 17:1, counting additionals as ½. This tends to confirm the previous hypothesis that psychosis or severe neurosis may be ruled out and that this subject is in the normal or mildly neurotic range of adjustment.

There are $2+1$ C' responses. This is not readily interpretable in isolation. However, these do not seem to indicate a rich receptivity to all aspects of environmental stimulation because of the relative paucity of color responses, with a *Sum C* of only 2. On the other hand, there is evidence that the hypothesis of the "burnt child" is applicable, since the ratio of achromatic to chromatic responses $[(Fc+cF+C'):(FC+CF+C)]$ is $14:4\frac{1}{2}$—that is, the achromatic responses outnumber the chromatic responses by more than 2:1. This further confirms the hypothesis that there has been deprivation in affectional relationships resulting in a withdrawn kind of adjustment in which there is considerable responsiveness in the "feeling" sense—responsiveness that can be expressed or acted out only in a very toned-down, hesitant manner. Whereas the emphasis on *Fc* indicates great desire for affectional response from others, the relative lack of color responses suggests that this desire is concomitant with a reluctance to let herself go in establishing emotional ties with other people.

Although the responsiveness to the social environment is reduced in its overt manifestations (as shown both by the achromatic-chromatic balance and the low *Sum C*) there is some responsiveness of a well-controlled sort, shown by $4+1$ *FC* responses and a complete absence of *CF* or *C* responses. Although the subject is unable to "act out" emotional reactions, she would seem to be able to express well-socialized feelings in a pleasant, graceful, and controlled manner. The presence of this number of *FC* responses confirms the hypothesis of a normal range adjustment, slanting the emphasis to normal rather than neurotic. Further light will be thrown on this whole area in the sequence analysis. Color disturbance should be watched for because the reaction time to the color cards is considerably more than that for the achromatic cards, although this fact alone seems too little to support an hypothesis of "neurotic color shock."

Introversive-Extratensive Balance

The three pertinent proportions here are the $M:Sum\ C$ of 7:2, the ratio $(FM+m):(Fc+c+C')$ of 7:9, and the (VIII, IX, X) % of 37. The $M:Sum\ C$ ratio shows an emphasis on the M side of greater than 2:1, indicating a markedly introversive adjustment at the present time. This would imply that the subject is more dependent on her own values, needs, fantasies, and experiences in perceiving her world than she is upon the nature of the actual presented stimulus. She tends to restructure her world in perceiving it, although the fact that this is not carried to the point of loosening of ties to reality is indicated by the good form level throughout the record and the presence of $4+1$ popular responses. The implication of this ratio alone would be that she is not dependent on other people in particular or upon the impact of the environment in general to give direction to her behavior.

However, this hypothesis is somewhat contradicted by the second ratio, which suggests an even balance between introversive and extratensive trends, with a very slight trend in the extratensive direction. Moreover, the whole discussion of the implications of the shading responses builds up a picture of a person highly dependent on affectional response from others, even though hesitant in the expression of her own responsiveness. The resolution of this apparent contradiction is to be found in the "burnt child" hypothesis, suggesting that the trauma of partial deprivation of affection has led her to retreat to an emphasis on her own inner life and away from full emotional participation with the social environment—the retreat nevertheless being characterized by a hesitant reaching out towards a fuller participation. The hypothesis that a more even balance between introversive and extratensive trends is "natural" to this subject (that is, before the "trauma" causing the withdrawal) is confirmed by the fact that the (VIII, IX, X) % is within the average expectancy.

Control

In discussing the implications of the movement, shading, and color proportions the topic of control has already been touched upon. This subject may be said to have "outer control"—control of emotional expression—in that the ratio $FC:(CF+C)$ is $4\frac{1}{2}:0$ and the achromatic-chromatic ratio is $13\frac{1}{2}:4\frac{1}{2}$. Indeed, this degree of outer control was thought to indicate over-control and over-cautiousness in emotional contacts. Further, the fact that M is more than twice *Sum C* and $F\%$ is nearly 50 would indicate that there is too little affective energy tied up in emotional relationships and too much in inhibition and withdrawal. The picture of over-control is found also on the movement side. The subject approximates "inner control" in that $M:(FM+m)$ is $7\frac{1}{2}:9$, but the tendency to suppress FM responses shown by 4 additionals suggests an inhibitory over-control. Finally the $F\%$ of 46 itself approaches the range of "constriction," in this context indicating chiefly a marked limitation of responsiveness to external impact. This subject tries to handle the anxiety aroused by environmental impact (and also by inner impulses) by attempting to strip the world of its implications in terms of needs and emotional relationships and to deal with it in an impersonal, matter-of-fact way. This "constriction" is within the normal range, however, shown both by the fact that it falls short of 50% and by the ratio of $(FK+Fc):F$ and the $(FK+F+F)\%$. $(FK+Fc)$ is approximately half of F (17:28) while F responses plus differentiated shading responses are less than 75% of the total, 64% to be exact. This suggests "modified constriction," which seems to bridge the normal to mildly neurotic range, and which indicates that the subject's introspective tendencies and sensitivity enable her to get on fairly effectively in social relationships, although she limits her responsiveness to an extent that she would find it difficult to establish close, warm, unrestrained affectional contacts.

Intellectual Manner of Approach

The use of locations shows a very marked overstress on Dd and S (39%), with a concomitant underproduction of W (5%) and a very slight underemphasis on D (42%). This imbalance in itself is marked enough to indicate serious disturbance, but such an hypothesis cannot be entertained in the light of the fairly well-balanced psychogram and the good form level. However, the low $W\%$ indicates a marked weakness in this subject's interest and/or ability in seeing the relationships between the various aspects of her experience. The form level is high enough to rule out the possibility that she lacks the intellectual capacity for an integrated view of the world. Of the 3 *W* responses, 2 are cut-off wholes; this, together with the overemphasis on *Dd* and *S* would also suggest that she is intellectually capable of integrated perception, although she fails to use her capacity in this direction.

The significance of the *Dd* and *S* responses is of primary concern in interpreting the understress on *W*. The overstress on *Dd* and *S* cannot be interpreted as inadequate acknowledgment of reality demands because the $D\%$ approximates normal production, and there are a well-maintained form level and a number of popular responses approaching average expectancy. The ties with reality seem quite good. The *Dd* consist of $12+1$ *dr* and 5 *dd*. The possibility that the over-production of *dr* might be a reflection of a quick and flexible perceptual approach seems ruled out, despite the confirmation given by $18+12$ original responses. The average time per response is 60 seconds, this time being used up in long pauses rather than in extensive elaboration of her concepts. Thus there does not seem enough fluency to support the hypothesis of quick, flexible perception; indeed, the performance seems somewhat labored and forced, as though the subject felt compelled to meet some inner standard of quantity of responses and found it difficult to do so. Another possibility is that the *dr* constitute an arbitrary approach, with a striving to be original and impressive. This hypothesis would be supported if the sequence analysis shows that the responses have an arty, intellectual, or clever flavor. In this case, however, the *dr* responses seem to imply much the same thing as a *dd* emphasis, since a glance at the location chart shows that they are chiefly in small areas. This implies a clinging to small areas for fear of losing her bearings. This hypothesis is supported by the fact that there are 5 *dd*, a $d\%$ of 14, and an emphasis on details in the $(H+A):(Hd+Ad)$ ratio of $17:19$. Finally, the $F\%$ of 46 is compatible with the hypothesis that the subject is preoccupied with the minutiae of her perceived world as a defense against anxiety. In this light the understress on *W* could be interpreted as a tendency to fragment her experience in order to avoid seeing relationships, because of a fear of what she would find should she seek to tie the various aspects of her experience together. The sequence analysis should provide an occasion for a test of this hypothesis.

The number of space responses is 6+1, which is quite high and indicates a "daring" use of space with a complete reversal of figure and ground. The hypothesis that this might be a constructive form of self-assertion is counter-indicated by the fact that there are too many S responses and not a free enough use of W and D. Nevertheless, this stress on S would indicate a considerable degree of ego-strength, a resistance against inundation either by environmental impact or inner impulse. Since the S responses occur in an introversive context the hypothesis would be that they indicate self-critical tendencies. This is confirmed by the self-criticism implied in the $(H+A):(Hd+Ad)$ ratio, and by the introspective trend shown by the $5+3$ FK. However, the secondary orientation in a more extratensive direction suggests the possibility that the "oppositional tendency" implied in S may be directed in some measure towards the environment. The lack of CF and C responses rules out the likelihood of any "acting out" of aggression. There is the possibility that both the S responses and the critical tendencies implied in the $(H+A):(Hd+Ad)$ ratio represent some acceptable outlet for aggression. In the sequence analysis particular attention should be paid to the context in which space responses appear, and to their possible symbolic significance, to throw further light on their interpretation.

Intellectual Capacity and Efficiency

The average weighted form level is 2.0, which places the estimate of the intellectual capacity of this subject at the lower limit of "very superior." This is confirmed by the fact that the form-level ratings range as high as 3.5 and that there are 7 responses over 2.0. Other indications of high capacity are the fairly large number of M's of good form level, a large number of originals (18+12) none of which have minus rating, and the fact that there is a fair range of content (39% outside the categories H, Hd, A, and Ad). In a subject with an emphasis on small details and a rather high $F\%$ there is the possibility that the form level may be misleadingly high, due to an overstress on quality, which would be reflected by extensive elaboration of the responses. This point should be checked in sequence analysis.

There are indications that this subject does not operate at a level compatible with an intellectual capacity approaching the very superior level. Her organizational weakness, her tendency to fragment her experience, her over-critical trends, her inhibited adjustment, and her weakness in the constructive or creative use of her imagination have already been mentioned. The loose succession might suggest a loosening of ties to reality; however, it is likely that this is a product of her avoidance of organization because the form level, $D\%$, and production of populars all point towards a reasonably good tie with reality. Control is adequate; indeed there seems to be over-control. Therefore, it may be concluded that her loss of intellectual efficiency falls within a reasonably normal range, although she is hindered in making full use of her high-level capacity.

Creative Potential

This subject might be characterized as an "unhappy normal." There are undoubted difficulties in adjustment, but these should not be overemphasized at the expense of recognition of her considerable "creative potential." She has good imaginal capacity which seems already to be utilized in giving a long-range orientation to her adjustment. What is to be hoped is that she can make still better use of this potential in a more creative use of her imagination, an improvement of her ability to see relationships, and a larger measure of self-acceptance. Despite the qualifications she gives to her M responses she has at least potential empathy. Her Fc responses indicate a strong orientation towards forming relationships with other people, while the FC responses indicate social skills and an interest in maintaining smooth interpersonal relationships. All of these trends suggest at least a potential capacity for warm and mature relationships, despite the fact that she is at present over-dependent in the sense of an exaggerated affectional need and over-cautious in forming emotional ties.

Summary of Hypotheses

1. There is a tendency to subordinate impulses in the interests of long-range goals and values, with over-inhibition of the acknowledgment and expression of impulses.

2. Although there is some awareness of conflict, her defense mechanisms seem to be working effectively to protect her against too painful an awareness of conflict.

3. Her imaginal resources and values are well enough developed to give stability of adjustment.

4. She is too inhibited and self-critical for a ready access to her creative potential. A tendency towards fantasy solutions is suspected.

5. The ego-organization is strong enough to place this subject in the normal or mildly neurotic range of adjustment.

6. There is considerable affectional anxiety, with much emphasis upon introspection as a method for dealing with it. However, it is suggested that her insight is limited, at present, chiefly by her fear of seeing relationships between various aspects of her experience.

7. There is an exaggerated need for affectional response from others, believed to stem from deprivation in affectional relationships, presumably mother-child relationships. This deprivation was neither complete enough nor early enough to produce any serious defect in her capacity for object relations.

8. Her affectional need implies a sensitivity to others, probably both in the sense of a capacity for tact and in terms of a tendency to be hurt easily.

9. Deprivation in affectional relationships (to the degree that she has experienced it) has led her to withdraw from full emotional participation with her environment, to be somewhat too hesitant in forming emotional ties, and to express her feelings in a very toned-down manner, despite a reaching out towards fuller participation.

10. There is adequate control—indeed over-control—which, however, does not reach the point of clear-cut neurotic "constriction."

11. There is a marked weakness in seeing the various aspects of her

experience as related. This tendency to fragment her experience is believed to be a defense against the anxiety that would be aroused by seeing those aspects as related.

12. The ties with reality are good.

13. There is a strong "oppositional tendency" which may be interpreted as an indication of ego strength. It also may indicate both a self-critical tendency and a way of expressing aggression in an acceptable way, since this subject must be inhibited in "acting out" aggression.

14. There is superior intellectual capacity, approaching the very superior level; but the effective level of intellectual function is at present below capacity, although this loss of efficiency seems to be within the normal range.

15. This subject may be characterized as an "unhappy normal" with considerable creative potential both for a more constructive use of her imaginal resources and for more mature, more meaningful, and warmer interpersonal relationships, although her empathetic ability is at present limited by critical trends.

Sequence and Content Analysis

The analysis of the sequence and content of responses may assist in answering the following questions, which were left open in the interpretation of the quantitative findings:

1. What is the nature of the impulses this subject tends to inhibit as incompatible with her value system? That is, what do the *FM* responses represent?

2. What is the nature of her value system? What are the long-range goals in the interests of which she denies herself ready acknowledgment of her impulses?

3. What lies behind her difficulty in seeing the various aspects of her world as interrelated? Why does she tend to fragment her experience, keeping the various aspects of it in separate compartments?

4. What can be inferred about her attitudes towards and her relationships with other people from the human figures she sees in

the blots? What sex are the figures? What age? What characteristics have they?

5. From an examination of the "color dynamics" what further may
be said about her reactions to the emotional impact of her social
environment?

6. From an examination of the "shading dynamics" is it possible to
add to the picture given by the quantitative findings about the
organization of her affectional need?

7. Are there further clues to the nature and direction of the "oppositional tendency" shown by her space responses?

8. Does the way in which she elaborates her responses confirm the
intellectual estimate made from the quantitative findings?

Card I

The first striking feature of the series of responses to Card I is the
sequence of locations. A glance at the location chart shows that this
subject does not come to grips with the main blot area at all, but
rather skirts the edges, picking out an isolated detail here and there,
and finally plunges into the white space. The performance on this
card is a vivid illustration of the reluctance this subject feels about
seeing the various aspects of her experience as related. Her choice
of tiny detail locations so limits the scope of her perception that there
seems to be a distinct aversion towards gaining an integrated view
of her world.

The first important question to be asked is why she fragments
her experience to such an extreme extent. This card facilitates the
perception of large areas—wholes or large usual details. She seems
to get as far away from these usual areas as possible, selecting projections and finally a pair of white spaces for the locations of her responses. It seems desirable to reject any hypothesis that the choice of
projections signifies preoccupation with phallic areas; the content
of her responses suggests a denial of "body" (she sees three heads of
animals) ; moreover the fact that the last response is a space response
suggests that she is avoiding something rather than making a positive
choice in her selection of locations. One explanation would be that
the choice of locations represents a shading avoidance. This would

imply that she is retreating from the impact of affectional relationships when that impact is heavy, as it would be in primary affectional relationships—that is, mother-child relationships.

A second possibility is that she is avoiding the areas in which human figures are usually seen by subjects with M-capacity. When asked in the testing-the-limits period whether she could see anything in the whole card, this subject responded with "witches with wings." On the basis of this response the hypothesis might be formed that this card represents a "bad" mother-figure for this subject. In keeping to the periphery of the card this subject both avoids involvement with the "bad" mother-figure and retreats from the impact of affectional demands in mother-child relationships represented by the heavy shading. This hypothesis can be tested out through an examination of the sequence of responses in other cards, but in the meantime it provides a helpful background against which the content of the responses to Card I may be viewed.

The first response is an evasive, vague geographical response with a 0.5 form level, which she attempts to make more precise by suggesting a specific geographical location (Newfoundland). To have such a vague response follow a fairly long reaction-time would suggest that considerable anxiety has been aroused by this first blot. In part this anxiety may be due to the impact of the new situation represented by the test; but it seems likely that the retreat from the impact of the "bad" mother and acknowledgment of her need for affectional response is also involved, especially since she retreats to the "wings" of the "witches" seen in the testing-the-limits period. It is interesting to note that the choice of geographical content is Newfoundland, a cold, rocky, and forbidding country.

After the first response, the subject requests a further definition of the task presented by the test. This need for guiding rules in a permissive situation is interesting in view of the fact that the subject had previously reported to the examiner for weekly non-directive interviews for well over a year and thus should have felt at home in a permissive situation. The fact that she did not feel at home seems to reflect a very strong need for authority and direction.

After having been assured that she could use either the whole blot or "bits," she proceeded to choose "bits." That this is a preference for tiny, isolated areas rather than a complete inability to see wholes is shown in the testing-the-limits period. Thus the hypothesis advanced when analyzing the quantitative findings should be modified to indicate that she is capable of seeing the various aspects of her world as related, but she prefers not to. Perhaps she first saw the "witches with wings," found them unpleasant, and so retreated to the smaller areas. That she is capable of this kind of reaction is shown by her comment that she saw the blue areas in Card X as "spiders," but since she wanted to find something nice in the blue area she hunted for something else. The implication is that she prefers to close her eyes to painful or unpleasant facts related to her relationship with her mother, and does not want to see the relationships implicit in these facts. The long pauses between responses tend to confirm the hypothesis that she sees more things in the blot area than she mentions in her responses.

The fact that she persists with the task in the face of difficulty until five responses are given makes it seem that she has subjectively defined the test-situation as an authoritarian one in which a certain quantity of responses is expected of her. Indeed, the modal number of responses to all the cards is five.

The second response to Card I indicates a certain intellectual criticalness, in that she points out the extra "bump" on the "horse's nose" as well as limiting herself to *Ad* content. This critical approach seems inhibiting for she can give only an *F* response. However, *FM* emerges in the third response even in a very tiny area with *Ad* content. The "yapping" action suggests oral aggression of a rather toned-down sort. This gives the first clue to the nature of the impulses this subject tends to inhibit—they are aggressive impulses. If we are correct in our interpretation of the quantitative findings as indicating an exaggerated affectional need stemming from a partial deprivation or rejection experience in primary familial relationships, probably in mother-child relationships, clinical experience would lead us also to expect ambivalence in dependency relations. Rejection tends to arouse hostility, which tends to be suppressed or repressed because of the threat it provides to the highly valued dependency relationship. We are inclined to view the oral aggression shown by the "yapping dog" response as related to the hostile component of an ambivalent mother-child relationship. The intellectual criticalness implied in all three *Ad* locations, including the fourth response of a "turtle's head," is probably an acceptable channel through which aggression may be expressed.

For her last response this subject plunges into the white space, avoiding the shading. She sees "monks"—suggesting an idealized, desexualized human figure. The empathy shown by this response is very slight, because no movement is attributed to the figures and they are in a "picture." The fact that this response occurs in a white space links it to an "oppositional tendency." In the context of the mother-significance which Card I seems to have for this subject it is suggested that the identification with an idealized, desexualized figure may represent a protest reaction against her mother.

Finally, it seems possible to confirm that the intellectual estimate has not been set too high because of a "forced" form level of a subject who is striving for high quality. This subject does not elaborate her responses in any compulsive striving to impress the examiner with quality.

Card II

The hypotheses advanced in the analysis of Card I tend to be confirmed by the performance on Card II. Again the subject skirts the edges of the blot, using somewhat larger areas on this card but completely avoiding the heavily shaded main area of the blot, and again plunging into the white space for the fifth response. Like Card I, Card II facilitates *M* responses for subjects with *M*-capacity, and the human figures are often seen as women. This subject turns the card upside down before giving her first response; in so doing she avoids the human figures as well as retreating from the shading to the color area.

Color does not seem to disturb this subject; indeed, her first response not only shows a preference for the colored areas to the shading area but also shows a capacity for socialized control of responsiveness to the emotional impact implied by color. The content of the response, however, suggests a certain uneasy, over-intellectualized flavor ("something we had in zoology"). This avoidance of shading with preference for color suggests that this subject feels more at home with the emotional impact of her social environment than in the more demanding primary relationships, and indeed escapes from one to the other. This preference for colored areas is interesting in view of the psychogram, which shows a low weighting on color responses. The explanation for low color production does not seem to be that she is disturbed by color and avoids colored areas.

In her second response she goes to the other colored area, and to the extreme tip of it. Color is not used, probably because it is incompatible with the *Hd* concept. It is interesting that she can use the shading in this colored area although she has completely avoided shaded areas. The hypothesis would be that she can accept her need for affection when socially stimulated, whereas she finds it difficult to do so within primary familial relationships. Again the human figure is male rather than female and, as with the "monks" on Card I, the details are vague (there is a "muffler" but the face is not described), no movement is attributed to it, and it is made unreal—a picture, a Christmas card. This again shows a limitation of empathy, this time suggesting that it is the intellectual criticalness implied in the *(Hd)* that is responsible; it seems easier to acknowledge a need for warmth and affection in seeing the fur of the "cap."

In the third response, and after a pause, she finally produces an *M* response, "two women talking over a fence." It seems likely that this response was seen before but not mentioned, and that it was from this concept as well as the shading that a retreat was made in the first two responses, first by turning the card and then by using the extreme tip of the area later used for the women's heads. (This is the same mechanism that was overtly described in the testing of the limits with respect to the "spiders" on Card X.) That it is a conscious reluctance to deal with the concept rather than disruption of form perception is seen by the fact that the form level of the response is high, and indeed there is a quite remarkable feat of organization involved in using the top *D*'s and the center *d* while avoiding the main blot area. This confirms the hypothesis of Card I that this subject is capable of seeing relationships but prefers to view the various aspects of her world as isolated, perhaps particularly where relationships with her mother are concerned. As with the previous movement response (the "yapping" dog on Card I) the action is oral. However, the fact that she can attribute movement to adult female figures, even though she is intellectually critical as shown by the *Hd,* implies a certain capacity for empathy with the mother-figure, and therefore confirms the hypothesis that deprivation of affection did not enter in so early and so completely that the capacity for affectional relationships (in this case empathetic relationships) was prevented from developing. Moreover, in the testing-the-limits period she shows a more complete empathetic capacity by seeing an entire human figure in vigorous action—"two people dancing"—although even here she shows some difficulty in identification by not specifying the sex. She comments: "Seeing them at a distance helps." When the cards are seen at a distance the shading is less apparent. It seems that the shading prevents her at first from seeing the women as whole. This fits in with the general hypothesis that the affectional impact of the mother-child relationships is disturbing to her, and may now be seen as interfering with empathy.

Although the subject is unable to see the popular animals in the shaded area, she displaces the response to a small detail area seeing the "head of a Scottie" as her fourth response. Again the mouth is the focus of interest, as it was with the dog in Card I. The sequence of responses here is interesting. From the women's heads (mother-figure) she retreats, avoiding the shading (reluctance to accept affectional need) to an *F, Ad* response (an inhibited, critical response) with an oral emphasis (dependency). Avoidance, withdrawal, criticalness, and inhibition seem to be defenses against affectional anxiety.

A similar defense is shown in the fifth response, the "turtle," which gives a flavor of passive resistance to her withdrawal, a stubborn "staying put" while withdrawing into her shell. The fact that the location is *S* confirms the notion that the "turtle" is a symbol of resistance, a protest reaciton against her mother's influence. The fact that this is the second "turtle" response given suggests that it is an important fantasy symbol for this subject.

With respect to color dynamics there is no apparent subjective disturbance, in that there is no discomfort expressed about the color and no overtly unpleasant flavor to the concepts. Nor does there seem to be "objective disturbance" attributable to color. The reaction time is no longer than it was for Card I; the form level is good, with three responses of 2.0 or higher; the sequence of locations established in Card I is not upset. Therefore, the hypothesis is that this subject is not upset by emotional impact from her social environment except by the affectional impact of mother-child relationships, which relates to shading dynamics rather than to color dynamics.

Card III

The first noteworthy feature is the long reaction time. This does not seem to be due to the problem of integration provided by the broken-up Gestalt of this blot with the separate red details; this subject has not shown enough interest in integrating her perception for this explanation to seem reasonable. Her admission in the testing-the-limits period that the side red details might be "blood" makes it possible that the delay in responding may be due to the influence of the red color and its interference with good form perception; however, if this was the disturbing feature it might have been expected also to influence the reaction time to Card II. The most likely explanation seems to be that she saw the popular human figures first and most vividly, but hesitated to accept them because of the critical reservations which she verbalizes: "They are more like cartoons, for they look more like animals than people actually." She is so preoccupied with the fact that the heads are like "birds' " and the feet like the "hoofs" of animals that she pays little attention to the movement. This would suggest that intellectual criticalness, an acceptable channel for inacceptable hostility, interferes to a considerable extent with her ability to empathize with other people, and also with the constructive use of her undoubted imaginal capacity. It may be noted that she does not specify the sex of the figures; they are merely "people" like the figures she mentions in the testing-the-limits period for Card II. This may indicate reluctance to identify herself with any clear-cut sexual role.

On Card III this subject uses the large areas of the blot much more freely than she did with Cards I and II. Either she can abandon her skirting-of-the-edges approach as she becomes more familiar with the situation, or the lighter shading on Card III and the way in which it is broken up may be responsible for the fact that she can use the shaded areas more freely. The performance on the subsequent heavy shading cards should prove crucial in deciding between these alternative explanations.

The performance on Card III reinforces the previous hypothesis that she is not disturbed by the emotional impact of social relationships, represented in the blots by color. The integration of form and color in the popular "red bow" implies a socialized control of emotional responsiveness. Moreover, she again uses shading in a colored area, while she has not yet been able to use shading in an achromatic area. This reinforces the hypothesis that she can acknowledge her need for affection in her less demanding social relationships, whereas she cannot do so in the more emotionally loaded relationship with her mother.

The third response reinforces the impression that she is willing to use the colored areas. However, the testing-the-limits period implies that she first saw the side red details as "blood," but that she rejected the *CF* response in favor of the "demons." This implies a reluctance to "act out" emotional responses, although the fact that the *CF* came out readily in the limits period shows a potential capacity for "acting out" which modifies the extremely tight picture of emotional control given by the psychogram. That it is hostility that she is reluctant to express is shown by the response to questioning in the analogy period. "I can imagine putting bad ideas into his head, and his tongue is sticking out." The impression is of a helpless, ineffective, childishly oral mode of expressing aggression.

The fourth response is noteworthy as the first use of shading in an achromatic area. The "fuzzy" quality of the textural response implies a not-too-highly intellectualized awareness of affectional need. The tendency to limit empathetic identification through intellectual criticalness is again implied in the fact that she sees just the heads of the African natives, not the whole figure in action.

It may be noted that she does not use white space in Card III as she did in Cards I and II. Perhaps this is because she has been better able to use all the shaded areas; perhaps it is because this card does not have mother-significance for her; perhaps it is merely because there is no area of white space completely surrounded by heavy shading.

Card IV

After a long reaction time the subject returns to her skirting-of-the-edges approach. She goes first to the most lightly shaded area of the blot, then uses two peripheral and projecting areas, returning later to the lightly shaded area. It is only in her last response that she becomes bold enough to use a larger portion of the blot, and even here she fails to use the whole. The fact that the use of locations is a little bolder than it was for Card I suggests that the anxiety aroused by a new situation was a component of the inhibited timidity of her handling of Card I. However, the fact that she skirts the edges of the heavily shaded fourth card after her freer handling of the more lightly shaded third card reinforces the hypothesis that her tendency to fragment her experience and her reluctance to see the relationships between the separate aspects of her experience is due to acute insecurity in her affectional relationships.

Her first response is well-seen, her third "dog." She might have been expected to use shading for the concept of "Airedale dog" since she had done so for the "fuzzy hair" of her Africans in III.4. The fact that she did not do so reinforces the hypothesis that she finds it difficult to acknowledge affectional need in situations having a heavy affectional impact. She uses shading for her second response, a "flower," but receives an $Fc \rightarrow FK$ score, suggesting that anxiety is aroused by heavy affectional impact which she tries to handle by introspection rather than by free acknowledgment of her need for affectional response. Her third response, "leaves," seems a carry-over from the "flower" although her "flower" is so fragmented that the "leaves" are seen in an area too far separated to be integrated with it. Although these two locations are often found to have sexual significance, it seems likely that this subject is attracted to the locations because they take her away from the heavily shaded main blot area rather than because of any preoccupation with sexual symbols.

The fourth response is highly suggestive of a mother-child concept, but the figures are described as a "tall person" and "a child or someone." This would seem to indicate reluctance to identify herself whole-heartedly in the mother-child relationship, and yet there seems to be some capacity for empathetic identification with the mother-figure. As in Card II the action is "talking," suggesting an oral interest and hence a recipient, dependent orientation.

For many subjects this card suggests a strong, aggressive, often threatening, masculine figure, which often seems to represent the father-figure. This subject approaches a perception of a masculine figure, but is unable to use the whole blot and sees only the superficial aspects—the clothing, not the man. In the fifth response she reduces the "boot" that is usually seen in the large side *D*'s to something more like a mere shoe seen in the lightly shaded area; this seems to be due to her avoidance of the heavily shaded areas. Many subjects go from perception of the boots to perception of a whole man, but this subject merely sees more clothing without connecting a person with it. The implication of the content is that the man would be rather a foolish figure, with either long tails to his suit that he might trip over or a college gown so tattered that there is little of it left. The concept suggests that she lacks a relationship with a strong masculine figure and is somewhat critical in her attitude towards males.

A highly important feature of the performance on Card IV is that the form-level rating of her responses holds up at a fairly high level. With the hypothesis of affectional disturbance, a breakdown in form level might have been expected on this card; but she continues to give well-seen responses ranging from popular unelaborated form level to distinctly superior. This suggests successful control, perhaps a little too tight, but not so tight that movement and shading responses are precluded. It would appear that her skirting-of-the-edges approach functions as a successful defense mechanism.

In the testing-the-limits period she spontaneously points out that Cards VI, IV, and V might be "animal skins" because of the shading. This confirms the previous hypothesis that it is possible for her to use the whole card, but that she prefers not to do so. In this case it would seem that she prefers not to acknowledge affectional need as freely as an "animal skin" response would imply.

Card V

Although this card has a strong "pull" towards a W response, this subject continues with the skirting-of-the-edges approach that she has used for every card to date except Card III. That the reaction time is short suggests that she does not even see the W as a "bat" until later.

She first sees a "rabbit's head." Like the other animal forms seen so far (dog, horse, and turtle) this is a non-aggressive creature, perhaps a pet. This seems to fit in with the hypothesis that this subject suppresses hostility. The second response seems to be a carry-over from the first. It is perhaps an illustration of the difficulty she has in integrating her experience that she sees the head and feet of the rabbit in areas that cannot reasonably be brought together for a whole rabbit. Again she can produce Fc in a lightly shaded area, confirming the hypothesis that she can acknowledge her need for affection when the affectional impact of the situation is not too strong.

Her reluctance to see wholes is demonstrated by her third response. Whereas most subjects seem to feel that the whole blot looks very much like a "bat" (or a "butterfly") this subject says it "looks a little bit like a bat, I guess." However, it is a W response, the only W in the protocol that is not cut off.

From it she veers off to the edge of the blot, and gives an FK response, indicating a desire to put her affectional anxiety at a distance and to gain perspective on it. Judging from the vague and nearly unsuccessful nature of the form perception, it would seem that this introspective effort does not meet with much success.

Her fifth response is a well-seen $M,$ the fourth to appear in the protocol, and, like the others, having an original flavor in location and content. Like the others, it appears somewhat late in the response to the card, indicating a certain cramping or inhibition in empathetic identification with others and in the creative use of imaginal processes. Here she gives a masculine figure, but it is an "old man," denied full reality ("it could be a photograph"). Like the "monks" in Card I, this figure seems to lack the full flavor of masculinity, indicating that there is no strong masculine figure with whom she has formed a relationship.

With her predilection for projections it is noteworthy that this subject does not use the lower d area. In view of the fact that young children often see this as a "biting mouth," it is possible that the latent content of this area is too aggressive for her to use, since she does not seem to be able to express oral aggression except in a very toned-down way—"talking," "yapping," or "sticking the tongue out."

Card VI

With her tendency to avoid heavily shaded areas and with her lack of apparent disturbance in using areas that often have sexual significance, it might have been predicted that this subject would use the top D for her first response. She does, in fact, see the top D as an "insect" before making her first real sally into a heavily shaded area, which she does in her second response after a very long pause. Although she readily acknowledges that Card VI might be an "animal skin" in the testing-the-limits period, this relatively bold sally into the shading has an FK rather than an Fc or cF emphasis, with a clinging to the center line. Both of these elements of the response seem to represent ways of coping with the affectional anxiety aroused by the shading. This implies a defense mechanism, which seems to work reasonably well judging from the fact that the form-level rating does not drop below 1.0.

After another long pause she gives her third "turtle" response, which, in view of the previous hypothesis, suggests a passive resistance reaction as a defense against the pressure felt in affectional relationships with her mother. A fourth response, "part of a maple leaf," is given to a lightly shaded part of the top D area, without use of the shading. Only in the fifth response, given to a projection, can she give acknowledgment to her need for affection. It is a "kitten's paw . . . furry, very soft." This escape from heavy shading to a projection, with a response involving a non-aggressive, pet animal, is familiar by now. However, even here her intellectual criticalness is alert, for she feels she must deal with the bump on the end of the projection "where there is too much"; this she handles more successfully than the "bump on the horse's nose" of Card I, making it a "burr" on the "kitten's paw."

Card VII

Since the hypothesis seems well established that the central problem in the adjustment of this young woman is in her relationship with her mother, it is of particular interest to see how she handles Card VII—a card that seems to have "mother-significance" for many subjects. It specifically facilitates perception of female figures for subjects with *M*-capacity. This subject fails to identify the figures as adult; she sees childish "pixies" instead. The emphasis is on the heads, and she fails to use the whole card. Moreover, the empathetic element of the concept is reduced both by making them imaginary figures and by the fact that the movement is inhibited to the extent that it emerges only as an "impish" expression reminiscent of the "demons" on Card III, which had bad thoughts and stuck their tongues out. There is a tendency to use texture in a highly intellectualized way to differentiate facial features.

Her second response is given, after a long pause, to a very unusual location. The content, "volcano," is also unusual on this card. Working on the hypothesis that this card has "mother-significance" for her, the "volcano" may be taken as denoting a potentially explosive component in her relationship with her mother, suggesting a recognition of the danger of eruptions of hostile emotion. The shading is used to give an effect of distance, implying affectional anxiety handled by an attempt at introspection.

After this sally into the lower area she retreats to a projection and sees an animal's paw "held out," with the implication of a pet animal seeking a response from a human. Her intellectual criticalness demands a recognition of the fact that it is a clumsy sort of paw (she attributes it to a "rhinoceros"), but it is clear that the association is with a dog, which seems a favorite animal of hers. Texture (that is, affectional need) can be acknowledged in this context.

The geographical content of the next response may be interpreted as an evasive, defensive response to anxiety. Her intellectual critical-ness makes it necessary for her to cut off part of the blot area used, to refer to the response as "far-fetched," and to make it a specific country, Spain.

The fifth response follows without noticeable pause, suggesting that the concept has been formulated before but not overtly given. The location is the lower center area—a fact that is of particular interest in a subject with manifest affectional disturbance. Young children frequently see this area as a "little house," and adolescents and adults with regressive and dependent yearnings give concepts for this area that seem to be linked with their needs for affectional security. In this light the *FK* response with its implications of distance and affectional anxiety seems quite appropriate for this subject. The concept of a "barricade" suggests that she feels as though there were a barrier between herself and her mother as far as expression of affectional feelings is concerned. Whereas the "volcano" response emphasizes the hostile component, this response brings in the seeking-for-affection component of the ambivalent relationship to her mother.

In most other cards to date she has given five responses, but with Card VII she seems unwilling to end on the "barricade" note. She seems to search for something else (probably something "nice") although the pauses indicate that the search is an effortful one. Both of her next responses reflect an inhibition of impulse, which may be attributable to the anxiety implicit in her relationship to her mother. First she sees a "lion's head"; in the inquiry she expands this into the front part of a lion and attributes movement to it. Then she sees "the hind part of a camel," which in the inquiry is expanded into a whole camel although she is unable to read in movement and is highly critical of the shape. Expressing dissatisfaction with these labored responses, she says "I like the pixies," as though she did not like her other responses.

Finally it may be noted that on this card, which like Card III is lightly shaded and rather broken up, she is able to use the various locations more freely than she has been able to do on the cards with heavy shading.

Card VIII

It is of interest to attempt a prediction of the kind of performance that might be expected from this subject on Card VIII, on the basis of the hypotheses formulated to date. From the hypothesis that her characteristic skirting-of-the-edges approach was due to the need to avoid heavily shaded areas, a much freer use of locations would be expected on Card VIII, the first card without black-gray shading. Judging from her performance on Cards II and III, there should be no difficulty in using colored areas and in producing *FC* responses, although *CF* responses would not be expected. On the hypothesis that she finds hostility and aggression inacceptable, it would be expected that she would not see the popular animals as predatory.

At first glance the expectation that she would not be disturbed by color seems to be contradicted by the reaction time of 80 seconds, the longest reaction time in the protocol. However, this might be explained by the difficulty occasioned by the hostility implicit in the content of the first response, the "angry wildcat." This is the first hint of overt aggression to appear in the protocol. Instead of showing open aggression (fighting) or sublimated aggression (striving), as many subjects do, this subject inhibits aggression by reducing the movement to mere expression and by drawing a sharp distinction between the "angry wildcat" in the pink *D* on the right-hand side and the "raccoon" who is "playful and inquisitive" in the pink *D* on the left-hand side. She even gives further qualification of aggression in her comment that "angry is not quite the word."

A glance at the location chart confirms the prediction that she uses all areas much more freely in this card. This tends to confirm the hypothesis that her earlier skirting-of-the-edges approach was due to shading avoidance. However, although she uses the colored areas freely, she shows initial preference (except for the popular animals in the first response) for the "cooler" colors. She goes first to the blue area, then to the gray, then combines them, and finally uses the center white space before venturing into the orange-pink area at the bottom. She does not use color in her first four responses to Card VIII; in the fifth response she uses achromatic color before giving an *FC* in her sixth response.

The second response, "Northern lights," is an *FK* response, rein-forcing the impression that she is sensitive to shading in colored areas. Indeed, this response implying affectional anxiety may have been a reaction against the suppressed hostility of the "angry wildcat." The third response, "knitting needles," has a *dd* flavor, although she is able to extend her concept to include the whole top gray area. She is criti-cal of the shape, however. In the fourth response she becomes more ambitious, attempting to integrate the top gray, middle blue, and even the orange portions as well, although she seems finally to leave out the lower part except for the center line. She is critical of this attempt to integrate her experience, and even here she has a *dd* em-phasis in her interest in the "stain." The "lampshade-umbrella" con-cept is confused, implying that she is not particularly skillful in sort-ing out her experiences, getting tangled up in inessentials. The "ribs" and the "handle" make it seem an "umbrella," despite the fact that a "lampshade" would have been a better general match for the lower area which she seemed interested in using.

In the fifth response, "white shells," she uses color, although it is *FC'*. In the sixth, and later in the eighth response, she gives good *FC* responses, with a gentle, graceful flavor to them, indicating socialized control of emotional expression. The intervening response, the "play-ful, inquisitive raccoon," successfully eliminates the inacceptable hos-tility of the "angry wildcat."

The last response to Card VIII is of particular interest. Here in the "warm" color, she gives the kind of relatively uncontrolled tex-tural response that she would not acknowledge under the impact of heavy shading. If the hypothesis is correct that this young woman has a highly ambivalent relationship with her mother (which arouses much anxiety and unacceptable hostility) and that she has an exag-gerated need for affection, it is reasonable to suppose that there might also be more than a hint of an infantile sort of craving for contact in affectional relationships. The "animal skins" (which might have been *cF* responses) that she sees in the testing-the-limits period for the heavily shaded Card VI, IV, and V are not seen (or not acknowledged) in the performance proper or the inquiry. Yet here, in the orange area, she gives a *cF* response, which she strives to bring under control by making it seem of definite form: "snow over a bank . . . hanging down." The major emphasis is a *cF*, however, with "powdery snow, soft on top." The coldness implicit in the concept of "snow" would suggest that no gross sensuousness would be manifested, but rather a wistful yearning for affection, perhaps expecting little response.

Card IX

The first response to this card is an *M*, confirming the hypothesis that this subject has all the constructive potential implied in *M*-capacity, but also that there is something wrong with her empathetic identification with both adult female and adult male figures. The concept is that the "witch" (mother-figure) and "old man" (a not particularly strong or masculine father-figure) are arguing. Her critical attitude towards both figures is implied in the description of the action. Moreover, she points out that the "old man" has a "large, red nose," scarcely a desirable feature. Although other subjects may see these figures as fighting or throwing things at each other, these figures are merely arguing, confirming our hypothesis that this subject has a toned-down way of expressing aggression and that she has a predominantly oral-dependent orientation. The fact that a male figure is attributed to one side of a symmetrical blot area and a female figure to the other side confirms the previous suggestion that this subject has no clear-cut sexual role with which she identifies wholeheartedly, and that she is somewhat confused in her perception of sexual roles, attributing masculine and feminine functions to the same figures.

The implication that the first response has something quite personal to communicate about her object-relationships is confirmed by the fact that the second response is an original response, involving white space and an introspective use of shading. Following the hypothesis that the *S* response implies an "oppositional tendency," this second response seems to represent a protest reaction against the human figures about which she has been so critical in the first response.

Her critical attitude and lack of complete empathy with her mother are then confirmed by the third response, in which a woman is seen in a rather ridiculous activity and then is turned into a fairy-tale "mother bear." However, the fact that the subject has high form level for both her first and third responses—and that she can see mother figures at all—suggests that the disturbance is not so profound as to indicate very serious maladjustment.

Assuming that there is now fair evidence that the use of white space by this subject represents a tendency to oppose her mother, with a flavor of protest and passive resistance, it would seem that the highly original, well-seen, "dog" response which follows implies some symbol of resistance to the mother.

The last response to this card is also a highly original *S* response with "fireworks" content and an *m* determinant, indicating that the oppositional response to her mother is a conflictful one full of latent explosiveness. The fact that *CF* is not given here would indicate that she can feel opposition and hostility to her mother but is unable to act it out. She is too dependent on her mother and her mother's approval and affection to express the hostility she feels.

Card X

The growing hypothesis that the "dog" is an important personal symbol in this protocol is confirmed by the fact that it is the first response to Card X; following a long reaction time, it is given to a relatively obscure *D*, used by most subjects only in later responses. Both this dog and the one preceding it on Card IX have a flavor of spontaneity in their action. This may indicate that the impulses she tends to inhibit include child-like, happy, spontaneous ones, as well as hostile and threatening ones.

The second response is a somewhat unusual *FC* response, which, although it confirms the hypothesis that this subject is capable of the socialized and controlled responsiveness implied by *FC*, raises the question of why she does not give further, more usual, *FC* responses to this card. One reason seems to be the predominance of her sensitivity to shading, with its implications of affectional need. This sensitivity is shown in the third response, "some kind of flower . . . turning back of the petals," and in the seventh response, "part of the petals of a pansy." The implication of oral aggression in mother-child relationships is another possible source of inhibition of socialized responsiveness, as suggested by the fourth response, "story-book animals . . . discussing something by a tree." The rejection of hostile expression is shown in the fact that the creatures are "discussing" not even quarrelling. In general, it would seem that this subject is too preoccupied with her own problems to fulfil the turning out towards her social environment of which she seems capable. Her failure to see populars on this card rather emphasizes her preoccupation with inner problems.

In the testing-the-limits period she makes it clear that she was able to see at least two populars, the "spiders" in the outer blue D's and the "rabbit's head." Her rejection of the "spiders" is interesting. "I like blue. This could be a spider, which I can't stand, so I kept looking for something nice in the blue." She uses a small dr with additional S in the blue area for a "wolf's head"; but the small location, and the Ad, preclude the possibility of giving overt expression to the hostile impulse implied in the content. The popular caterpillars do not seem to be perceived because of her difficulty in sorting out her perception; they are too close to the "rabbit's head" and interfere with her perception of it. Yet they seem displaced to the pink area, where they are seen with a shading interest.

Interview Material

As mentioned at the beginning of this chapter, the subject is an unmarried woman of 24. At the time the Rorschach record was obtained she was a third-year university student. She had been known to the examiner for a year before this; having first sought advice about her study methods, she then continued to come regularly for help in working out better relationships with her family, particularly her mother.

She is a petite, attractive girl with a shy but friendly manner. She seems capable of warm relationships with other people, having not only made good contact with the examiner but having at least two very close friends. She had good relationships with her classmates. She enjoyed college life, either as an enthusiastic spectator or in a participant role behind the scenes. When she feels at ease with friends she can chatter away vivaciously. However, on many social occasions she can only smile, being too inhibited to speak. She is an active member of a "high" church, teaching a children's class, belonging to the choir, and helping the "Sister" with various church activities. The parish is in an old part of the city, with a considerable proportion of members in deprived economic circumstances. The subject feels very much identified with the parish and is eager to help with community work.

She intended to take a course in child care after graduation from the university, and has done so. She would like to devote herself to work with underprivileged children in her own parish, if there is a vacancy for her. Her vocational plans absorb her to the extent that she expresses no interest in boys, love, or marriage. However, she enjoys mixed company and has occasional dates, although no boyfriend.

Her intelligence level is superior (IQ 125). Her academic work was satisfactory but not brilliant. She studied hard, achieving satisfactory grades with considerable effort.

At the time that the Rorschach was administered she lived at home with her mother and a sister five years younger. There had been an older sister but she died at the age of two, before the subject was born. Other members of the household were her maternal grandfather and an elderly female cousin. The maternal grandmother had died about 18 months earlier.

The mother runs a shop which sells art supplies, reproductions of paintings, and a few original water colors and oils. The shop was originally established by the maternal grandmother, who ran the business and delegated a subordinate role to the grandfather. The parents are separated, the father living in a boarding house and visiting his family once every week or so. He is employed, but the subject is not sure what he does.

Family Background

The maternal grandfather had been a scholar of some distinction who contributed articles to literary reviews. However, following a nervous breakdown he gave up his former interests. He and his wife moved to their present home, and she set herself up in the shop. Her choice of an art shop grew out of an interest in painting—previously only a hobby. The maternal grandmother is described as an extremely dominating woman, who "ran" her husband, daughter, and two grandchildren and all their activities. The subject says: "My mother was always completely tied to her mother's apron strings, and now she wants to tie me to hers. Sometimes I feel that I will never get away, and then I will be caught for life, just as she was."

Her mother is also described as a very dominating woman, snobbish, nagging, suspicious, and of unpredictable mood. When she is upset about something, the whole household is upset; when she is cheerful everyone relaxes and can scarcely believe it. The subject says: "Living with mother is like living on top of a volcano; it is likely to blow up at any moment." The mother's health is not very good, and the subject feels obliged to help her in the house—though she resents this housework as interfering with her academic work. The mother works hard both in the shop and at home. Her income enables them to live fairly comfortably, but there is not enough money to keep the old house in good repair.

The father is rather a shadowy figure. His wife saves up odd jobs for him to do when he comes to visit, and "bickers" with him. The subject feels that she is like her father, and idealizes him; but she states that when she is alone with him she finds very little to say and really knows very little about him. The paternal grandparents are described in glowing terms, but the subject does not see them often and gives no exact information about them.

Early History

This subject recalls her early childhood as ideally happy. She paints herself as a spontaneous, lively child, who came home from kindergarten bubbling over with songs to sing to a responsive and sympathetic mother. She feels that, at five years of age, her whole life changed when her father lost his job and the family moved to this city, father to live with his parents and the subject and her mother to live with the maternal grandparents. The reason given for the separation was they could not afford their own home while the father was jobless and neither set of grandparents had enough room for the whole family. The fact that the parents have never subsequently lived together suggests that they do not want to do so, although the subject still clings to the economic explanation.

Her early days in her grandparents' home are recalled as extremely unhappy. She missed her father. Shortly after their arrival another child was born, and mother was completely preoccupied with the new baby and her own troubles. The grandfather's nerves were so bad that the five-year-old was constantly being "shushed" and had to tiptoe about and speak in whispers. He could not tolerate her childish songs of which she had been fond; in fact, he would not allow any music in the house. The subject states that the bottom dropped out of her world. Things have never been the same. Her dearest wish is that her parents could be reunited; somehow (she thinks) the happy days of early childhood would thus be automatically reinstated.

Not much was said about her school years. She attended a school in a well-to-do district, and felt inferior because she lived on the wrong side of the tracks. She attended Sunday school and enjoyed this and the children's choir more than anything else. The church and its activities have been her home away from home. Indeed they have been more "homelike" than home itself, for the subject often complains: "If only I could feel 'at home' at home!" Holidays were spent happily out of town, with a variety of relatives and parent-surrogates about whom the subject feels very warmly.

The whole history is dominated by the mother: desire for her approval, fear of her unpredictable changes of mood, despair when she disapproves, resentment at her interference, and bitter jealousy of her sister, who is felt to be the mother's favorite.

Later Events

Some friends of the family became concerned about the way in which the subject was dominated by her mother and urged her to join the air force during the war, so easing the way towards her enlistment that she did enlist and was posted to a distant city. She very much enjoyed her life in the service. She got along well with the other girls and enjoyed their companionship. She became a non-commissioned officer, doing high-grade clerical work with considerable responsibility for accuracy and secrecy. She loved the feeling of emancipation, although at first she felt guilty that she could just leave the barracks without needing to tell anyone where she was going or what she was going to do.

Upon discharge, she decided to take advantage of the provisions for veterans' training and go to a university to prepare herself for work with children. Although the training allowances would have made it possible for her to attend a university away from home, she felt that "there was no excuse" for going to another university and, much as she hated it, returned home. She expected her mother to be very pleased with her decision to seek a university education; but she found to her distress that her mother was quite scathing about her probable inability to get through college, and wanted her to become a stenographer. "The trouble was that mother didn't have the idea herself." The subject has resisted mother's suggestion that she become a stenographer, despite the fact that she enjoys clerical work.

The taste of freedom she had in the service made settling down again at home quite intolerable. She felt that she could hardly wait to get away, but that first it was necessary to get her university degree so that she could then go overseas to take a course in child care. She said: "The ocean would be none too wide between myself and mother."

Attitudes and Problems

The subject pictures her family as constantly bickering. There is overt hostility between the two girls. Although the sister is felt to be the mother's favorite, both come in for much nagging, supervision, and recrimination. The mother, the grandfather, and the cousin seem to be in a perpetual three-cornered quarrel over trifles. The subject feels she can scarcely bear to be in the family circle. If she has no excuse to leave the house, she goes to her room and closes the door. If she is not permitted to withdraw, she at least attempts to withdraw into herself and insulate herself from the rest.

The subject feels that her mother interferes with her life in every respect. She nags her to invite friends home, and then embarrasses her daughter by her behavior and infuriates her by critical remarks after the departure of the company. The mother opens all the subject's mail and inquires into every detail of her social activities. The mother tries to direct all her activities and is so persistent that open rebellion brings no solution. The subject takes a role of passive resistance. "I just dig in my toes and won't budge, although I don't dare say anything."

The only bright spot at home is the subject's little dog, upon whom she lavishes affection and from whom she receives a gratifying response. The mother accuses her of loving the dog more than she loves her mother. This simply makes the subject more demonstrative towards the dog, for she is acutely embarrassed when her mother demands affection. She says that sometimes she feels that she would like to confide in her mother and to feel close to her, but "there is such a barrier between us."

Her attitudes towards her mother are ambivalent to a high degree. She dislikes being with her; indeed, when forced to sit beside her in church or at the movies she feels stifled to the point of actual illness. One of the chief reasons for wanting to sing in the choir at church is that she can thus avoid sitting beside her mother. Yet the subject greatly values her mother's love and approval. "I would do anything to please my mother." The subject herself sums up the situation by saying that all her goals have been set either to please her mother or as a reaction against her mother's domination. She is not sure that even her most treasured ideals and ambitions are not motivated by rebellion. In spite of being a staunch churchgoer, the mother has shown herself quite disapproving of her daughter's interest in church and church activities. For this reason the subject keeps a good deal of it to herself, although she would dearly love to be able to talk to her mother about it.

Needless to say, the subject feels very guilty about her rebellious and hostile feelings, though not too guilty to acknowledge them freely in interview. She feels guilty also about her marked feelings of jealousy and rivalry towards her sister. These emotions, together

with her constant feeling of frustration at her inability to emanci-
pate herself, often lead to periods of depression.

Although in interviews she was quite ready to air feelings that
were painful to her, the subject was not equally free to acknowledge
cause and effect relationships and tended to cherish illogical, fantasy solutions to her problems. For example, she has one fantasy
in which her father comes home to live, and the whole atmosphere
of the household changes: the mother is happy again; since she has
her husband she will no longer want to have her daughter by the
apron strings, and the daughter will be free to move out to the room
vacated by her father, letting her father have her room at home. She
has often felt bursting to tell her mother to ask her father to come
home; but she is afraid that her mother will say that the does not
love him, and this she cannot bear to hear or to believe. She can
acknowledge painful feelings in herself; she finds it extremely difficult to acknowledge painful facts about her parents.

One problem that preoccupied her was that, though she was a
member of the choir and attended regularly, she was unable to
sing. She knew the parts, and could sing them when she was alone
or in full choir, but could not utter a note by herself or when she
had to carry a part alone or with one or two other members. She
attributed this symptom to the fact that she was not allowed to sing
as a child because of her grandfather's nerves, and to the connection with the unhappy change in her life. She measured her progress
in adjustment by the gradual release from this inhibition.

This young woman considers herself fortunate always to have had
some older relative or friend in whom she had confidence. For many
years the chief figure of this sort has been the "Sister" at the church,
who understands her difficulties and gives her sympathy and emotional support even while being able to maintain good relationships
with mother too. "Sister" is the subject's ideal; it is after her that
she wants to model her character and her life pattern. Another
close friend and source of support is her paternal aunt. About a year
after the time of the Rorschach examination the aunt invited the
subject to come to live with her, thus providing the opportunity for
the subject to move away from home. Despite her yearning to get

away from home, it seemed impossible for her to do so until she had a secure home to move into; she could not face going entirely "on her own."

At the time of the Rorschach examination the subject was making progress in the solution of her problems. Shortly afterwards, she graduated from her university course and began training in child care, which she enjoys very much. Now that she has finally taken the first major step towards emancipation by moving away from home, she is much happier and feels that she will eventually be able to get along harmoniously with her mother, at a distance.

Integration of Sequence Analysis with Quantitative Findings and Interview Material

Since the examiner was familiar with the interview material before undertaking an analysis of the Rorschach performance of this subject, it probably has not been possible to avoid being influenced by previous knowledge of the subject, despite an attempt to work out and present the findings independently of the interview material. The choice between alternative interpretative hypotheses has probably been particularly influenced by this previous knowledge. However, whether an interpretation has been undertaken "blindly" or not, as a final step there should be an attempt to integrate the Rorschach interpretation with the other information that is available about the subject, as well as to draw the interpretations from the quantitative findings and the sequence and content analysis together. It is proposed to undertake both of these processes in this section, before finally drawing together the findings into a summarized statement that could serve as a report.

The sequence analysis was pinned to the major hypothesis that this subject's focal problem is a feeling of rejection by her mother with consequent feelings of deprivation of affection. This hypothesis would have been suggested by the *Fc* emphasis in the psychogram, even had nothing been known about the subject apart from her Rorschach performance. Moreover, clinical experience would suggest an exten-

sion of the hypothesis to the assumption that the deprivation in affectional relationships did not occur so early or so completely as to
seriously interfere with her capacity for object-relations. The interview material confirms this hypothesis, in the statement by the subject that her early childhood was very happy and that everything
seemed to change when she was about five years old. The feelings of
rejection are confirmed in her description of her mother's preoccupation with her own problems, with the new baby, and with the attempt to keep the child quiet in order to meet the requirements of
the grandparents.

In the sequence analysis the hypothesis was formulated that the subject feels great hostility towards her mother, which she can acknowledge but cannot express overtly nor accept as a desirable part of her
self-picture. The *FM*'s were thus identified, in part, as hostile impulses. The strength and inhibiting nature of this resentment is confirmed by the interview material in that the subject feels stifled to the
point of illness when sitting beside her mother in church or theater.
The shading avoidance in the heavily shaded cards was interpreted
as an escape from the strong affectional impact of mother-child relationships. The history material makes it clear why that impact is so
disturbing. The combination of resentment with a great dependence
upon her mother's approval, and a deep desire for an affectional response from her mother, produces a highly-charged, ambivalent relationship, which she finds well-nigh intolerable. Her mother demands a show of affection that the subject cannot express, and tries
to dominate every aspect of the subject's life. Her desire to emanci-
pate herself and thus escape the conflictful relationship is interfered
with by her extremely dependent orientation.

The content of various responses seems to reflect various facets of
this ambivalent relationship. The dependent orientation is suggested
by the oral emphasis in many of the human and animal responses.
The "barricade" in Card VII is matched by the subject's statement
that she feels a barrier between herself and her mother, which prevents the close and confiding relationship that is desired. The "volcano" on Card VII is matched by her statement that living with her
mother is like sitting on top of a volcano.

There seems little doubt that the "bad" mother, shown in the Rorschach by the "witches" and other adult female figures, is uppermost in the subject's conscious attitudes. Nevertheless, her deep yearning for a "good" mother is implied in her overwhelming desire to gain her mother's approval and in her search for "good" figures outside her home. Card IX seems to give a picture of home life, with the mother (witch) and the grandfather (old man with the red nose) both talking at once, neither being willing to listen or agree with the other and both trying to get in the last word. Card IV, with the "tall person" talking to the child, also seems to be a picture of mother-child relationships in the light of the history. The grandfather may well be the prototype for the "old man writing with the quill pen," which appears in Card V. The fact that the grandfather, a weak and dominated figure, is the only male figure in the immediate family circle would go far towards explaining the lack of any strong masculine figures in the Rorschach performance. The father is an idealized fantasy figure; the real father is known very slightly. Perhaps this is why in Card IV she sees the clothing but not the man. The shadowy "monk" in Card I may be related to the idealized father-figure, although it may also symbolize the church as a "good" parent-substitute. In either case the fact that it appears in a white space seems to link this symbol with a protest reaction against mother.

For this girl who feels so overwhelmed by the incessant bickering of the household and the continuous critical and dominating talking of her mother, it is not surprising to find "talking," "yapping," "discussion," and "arguing" to be the chief types of action attributed to the human and animal figures in the Rorschach protocol.

The interview material confirms the interpretation that this subject's emphasis upon sexual areas of the blot-material did not imply an overt sexual interest. The suggestion made in the sequence analysis that she has difficulty in identifying herself with a clear-cut sexual role, and tends to portray the female figures as relatively aggressive and the male figures as relatively passive and unreal, is borne out by the interview material. The Rorschach picture is quite compatible with the interview picture of a young woman brought up in a household where the women were the dominant and domineering figures and the men were reduced to unimportance. Her lack of interest in "dating" and her identification with the idealized mother-figure of the "Sister" make it quite convincing that she lacks overt sexual interest.

In the analysis of quantitative findings it was impossible to specify the exact significance of the *FM* responses, which were to some extent inhibited or suppressed. In the sequence analysis it was suggested that these impulses included chiefly aggressively hostile impulses, oral needs, and needs for happy, childish, spontaneous activity. Of these impulses, it would seem that only the hostile impulses are incompatible with a conscious system of values and tend to be suppressed. Nevertheless, the sequence analysis gave the impression that non-hostile oral impulses and spontaneity were inhibited, especially within the context of mother-child relationships. This fits in with the interview evidence of inhibition of oral satisfactions and spontaneity, not only in relationship with her mother but also carrying over into her difficulty in talking freely except to intimate friends and her inhibition in singing.

The Rorschach itself throws little direct light upon the nature of the value system of this subject, except that hostile aggressiveness is inacceptable. By inference, it would seem likely that the value system would be geared to "people" because of the strong *Fc* emphasis. The interview material gives a much clearer notion of her conscious goals and values, in terms of her need to be of service especially to deprived children and her deep desire to work in the community in which she has already sunk her roots. All of these may be viewed as related to her affectional frustrations in her relationship with her mother. Her vocation seems tied to her search for the "good" mother. Her needs for belongingness have been generalized beyond her family into the church and community. Her need to give service seems to stem from her need for an affectional response from others.

The defenses that emerge so clearly in the Rorschach performance have their counterparts in the interview material. She defends herself against the anxiety aroused by the ambivalent nature of her relationship with her mother by preferring to close her eyes to unpleasant facts, and by failing to see obvious relationships between these facts.

The most striking instance is her refusal to accept the fact that her mother and father do not love each other and do not want to live together. She tries to see things that are "nice." Her *dd* and *dr* emphasis was seen in interview in her dwelling with enthusiasm on isolated minor events. Indeed, her chief conversational charm was built up around her ability to notice and describe an interesting "snippet" of an observation or happening. Her life is a series of minor pleasures, anticipated intensely and either enjoyed thoroughly or found to be intensely disappointing.

Fitting in with her desire to see her world as nice is her tendency to find fantasy solutions for her problems. This was deduced from the psychogram because of her undoubted imaginal ability, which seemed to have limitations in terms of creative outlet. The interview material gives vivid confirmation of this hypothesis in her fantasy emancipation through father coming home to live and thus making it possible for her to leave home.

The interview material shows clearly that she searches for substitute sources of security, belongingness, and affection in friendships and identifications outside the home, with emphasis upon substitute mother-figures. This fits in with the tendency to be able to acknowledge *Fc* in colored or lightly shaded areas, while she is not able to do so in the heavily shaded areas. It also fits with the fact that she is able to see adult female figures in the Rorschach blots; the mother-child relationship has not been so disturbed as to prevent the development of empathetic identification, even though it hampers the fullness of such identification through hostile impulses and intellectual criticalness.

The dog as an affectional object and symbol of protest against her mother emerges clearly in the interview material. In retrospect it is interesting to examine the "dog" responses on the Rorschach and the way in which they emerge in tiny projections or in white spaces following either a shading avoidance reaction or the description of a female figure. (Note I.3, II.4, IV.1, IX.4, and less directly VII.3. In X.1, on the other hand, the "dog" seems more a symbol of happy spontaneity.)

The interpretation of the "turtle" symbol in the Rorschach, with

particular emphasis on II.5, as indicative of passive resistance in protest against the affectional impact of mother-child relationships, is supported by the interview material. The subject describes her attempt
to withdraw from the bickering and demandingness of her mother
into her own room or into herself, saying: "I just dig in my toes and
won't budge, although I don't dare say anything."

The intellectual criticalness that is so noticeable in the Rorschach
performance has some counterpart in the interview material. Here it
is chiefly expressed as criticalness of her mother, her grandfather, her
sister, and the cousin—although, at least in interview, it was expressed relatively rarely in connection with other people. Interest-
ingly enough, one of the things about her mother of which she is most
critical is her mother's criticalness.

The introspective effort implied in *FK* seems quite compatible with
the subject's seeking for help through counselling. Indeed, the counselling itself may have resulted in exaggerating her introspective
tendencies.

Both the quantitative findings and the sequence analysis suggest
that the defenses of this subject are working reasonably well. The psychogram shows adequate control, indeed over-control, while the form
level of the responses is high. Despite the fact that her intellectual
efficiency is limited by certain of these defenses—her difficulty in seeing relationships, her avoidance of recognizing painful facts, her criticalness, her inhibited adjustment, and her fantasy solutions—there
seem nevertheless to be a strong ego development and a resistance to
breakdown. The history facts confirming this interpretation are
chiefly her ability to complete her university course and to embark
upon postgraduate work, despite her anxiety and preoccupation with
her own problems.

The intellectual estimate checks fairly well against the IQ of 125,
although a guessed optimum IQ would have been slightly higher. It
may be that her capacity is indeed higher than the IQ, since the measure of intelligence was a group test and she might have done slightly
better in an individual test with good rapport. The effortful per-
sistence and desire to meet the standards, which she read into the
test situation, checks with her approach to academic work.

The handling of color in the Rorschach test fits in with the interview material fairly well, although there are some aspects that are not immediately obvious. The lack of *CF* responses checks with an obvious inability to "act out" her emotional reactions, especially with respect to overt hostility against her mother. She feels angry but does not dare do or say anything. The fair number of *FC* responses checks with the fact that she has a charming, graceful social manner, despite inhibition and shyness. The chief puzzle is that a person so extremely dependent on others should produce so few color responses. The dependent orientation is shown on the Rorschach in terms of oral content and *Fc* emphasis. It would seem that it is the shading emphasis in this case that should be interpreted as extreme dependence upon others, with the emphasis on affectional dependence, while the relative lack of color would be interpreted as a lack of full emotional participation with other people because of intense preoccupation with her own needs and problems. The conflicting trends in the introversive-extratensive ratio seem intelligible in this light. The primary $M : Sum\ C$ ratio reflects the fact that she tends to restructure her world in perceiving it rather than reacting to it as "given." The secondary $(FM+m) : (Fc+c+C')$ ratio shows the strength of her emotional dependence upon an affectional response from others.

The chief gap in the Rorschach protocol is that there are no direct reflections of the intense sibling rivalry revealed in the interview material. However, this might well have been inferred from the rest of the personality picture built up in the Rorschach interpretation.

Summary

This young woman has considerable strength in her personality organization, and much potential for good adjustment. It is necessary to draw particular attention to her resources if she is to be seen in good perspective, for her difficulties are pervasive enough that they could otherwise be overemphasized. Her intellectual capacity borders on the very superior level; and although she does not make full use of this capacity, she still operates on a level of efficiency well above average. She is capable of a long-range orientation and can defer immediate gratification in the interest of her long-range goals and personal values. She is trying to achieve a better adjustment by better understanding of herself. She has capacity for good interpersonal relationships, being sensitive to the needs and feelings of others and capable of some degree of empathetic identification with others. She is a pleasant person, able to manifest grace and charm in her social behavior. She is well controlled and unlikely to break down to any serious extent, even under considerable stress and strain. Her adjustment falls within the normal range, despite the fact that she is sometimes quite unhappy and manifests certain mildly neurotic trends. Her difficulties must be seen against the background of these very considerable resources.

The chief problem of adjustment focusses on relationships with the mother. She has feelings of rejection and deprivation, which suggest that there has been a partial deprivation of affection but neither early enough nor complete enough to interfere with the development of capacity for mature object-relationships. She is dependent upon her mother's approval, longs for a closer and more affectionate relationship, yet feels a barrier hampering affectional interchange. There is considerable hostile aggression felt towards the mother, which is not expressed in overt action. It nevertheless makes the whole mother-child area one that is ambivalent and highly charged. It tends to dominate her whole orientation.

She tries to defend herself against the anxiety stemming from mother-child relationships by holding the various aspects of her experience in separate compartments as though she were afraid of what she would find out if she put two and two together. She seems to be capable of insight into the relationships between the various facts of her experience but to fragment her world by preference. The fragmenting tendency hampers her intellectual effectiveness, since she is unable or unwilling to gain an integrated view of her major life problems; this tendency has carried over to be a characteristic way of handling experience in general. This, together with an intellectual criticalness that seems to stem from her hostility towards her mother, keeps her from mobilizing her quite considerable imaginal ability towards the constructive solution of her problems or towards creative achievement. Rather, her ability is used to spin fantasies which provide escape from or solution of her problems—she imagines how nice everything would be if it turned out the way she would like. It must be emphasized, however, that this fantasy life has not seriously weakened her ties with reality. There is no flavor of psychotic processes.

She is a dependent and recipient person with strong needs for the affection, approval, and emotional support of other people. Her sensitivity and social skill pave the way for some ease in interpersonal relationships, but she is at present too highly recipient and too preoccupied with her own problems to be able to realize fully mature, contributing interaction with others.

Despite her ambivalence towards her mother she is to some extent able to identify herself empathically with adult female-figures. However, she seems to be lacking any relationship with a strong, masculine figure. Perhaps because of this she does not seem to identify herself with any clear-cut sexual role. There is little overt sexual interest or anxiety.

Her control is excessive to the point of over-inhibition. Not only does she suppress hostile impulses and reactions, but she is inhibited in the expression of happy and spontaneous impulses. This would make for a certain shyness and restraint in her behavior.

Her resources of strength and the underlying stability of her personality suggest a good prognosis. The loosening of her over-adjusted control would facilitate the mobilization of her resources. The chief limitations upon her ability to benefit from counselling or therapy are her tendency to fragment her experience and her reluctance to face painful facts and to see relationships between important aspects of her experience.

CHAPTER 19

Rorschach Prognostic Rating Scale *

The Rorschach Prognostic Rating Scale is a preliminary attempt to use the Rorschach to predict a patient's response to psychotherapy. *All* responses and specifications occuring in the performance proper and the inquiry are treated alike. (Thus, both main and additional responses are included in the ratings.)

The rating scale described in the following pages is an attempt to measure the adjustment potential of the individual on the basis of the responses he makes to the Rorschach cards. It is based upon the manner in which the patient uses shading, color, and movement, as well as the accuracy and definiteness with which he sees his concepts. At the end of the scale is an interpretation of the meaning of the scores obtainable, given in terms of groups, from the poorest risk in psychotherapy to the best.

The various sections of the rating scale may make it possible to differentiate the concept of ego-strength in its most important components: reality testing, emotional integration, self-realization, and mastery of reality situations. These components may in turn be related to particular areas of adjustment. No attempt has yet been made to relate the theoretical ego-strength components individually to the separate sections of the rating scale. The experimental use of this prognostic rating scale during the last two years has been merely an at-

* The first portion of this chapter was published as an article in the *Journal of Projective Techniques,* 1951, 15, No. 3. The authors of this article are Bruno Klopfer, Frank J. Kirkner, Wayne Wisham, and Gertrude Baker.

tempt to compare the total prognostic rating of patients with their total responsiveness to psychotherapy.

The weighting assigned to each response was empirically determined on the basis of clinical judgment and has been frequently revised. Research is under way at this time to determine by a multiple-regression technique the more precise weighting that will be required for greater accuracy in predicting a patient's response to psychotherapy.

Ordinarily, when we speak of a patient's "promise" in psychotherapy, we are concerned with the amount of ego-strength, which, though not immediately available to the patient, may become available or mobilized through psychotherapy. In this context "unused ego-strength" simply refers to the developmental or adjustment potential of a person.

At this point we have no means to rate or estimate the unused ego-strength by itself. What we hope to rate by means of the prognostic rating scale is the combined total of (1) the adjustment level or available ego-strength (which usually corresponds closely to the nosological category similar to the basic Rorschach score of the Buhlers', and (2) the unused portion of the developmental and adjustment potential. In utilizing this criterion for the selection of patients for therapy it is also necessary to consider the type of disorder the patient manifests.

Usually, psychotic patients or those with severe character disorders will have the lowest rating; conversely, neurotic patients will be found in the upper ratings. Generally, then, the treatment potential does not differ greatly from the clinical picture. However, an important point is that there is a minority of patients who do have more unused ego-strength than their nosological category would in itself suggest. We have all encountered patients who show a favorable discrepancy between the diagnostic "label" attached to them and their ability to profit by psychotherapy. These are the patients who will show the greatest relative improvement in therapy. The difficulty, of course, has been in identifying such patients.

With those patients who show a gratifying recovery in psychotherapy, a repeat Rorschach may yield a total rating higher than the original one. This is because the actual ego-strength has been augmented. But the original discrepancy between the clinical picture and ego-strength will have diminished. The inference made here is that un-used ego-strength is not a fixed quantity, but that successful psychotherapy adds to the adjustment potential.

This rating scale is offered to our professional colleagues for experimental use, with the hope that it will prove useful in stimulating further research on the problem of selection of therapy patients.

A. Human Movement Responses

Each *M* response is rated according to the three criteria below; then the *average* of these three ratings is assigned to that response.

CRITERIA   RATING

1. Amount of movement in space, described or implied
   a. Increasing living space 1
      (dancing, running, talking together, pointing)
   b. Decreasing living space .... ½
      (bowing, kneeling, crying, crouching, and all Hd responses)
   c. Merely alive (sleeping, lying down, sitting, balancing) ... 0
2. Freedom in seeing movement
   a. Spontaneously sees action 1
   b. Uses intermediary means of representing movement ..... ½
      (picture of someone walking)
   c. Reluctantly given in inquiry or follows only from the logic
      of the situation 0
3. Cultural distance
   a. Real people of immediate cultural milieu 1
   b. Culturally distant real people; culturally popular fantasy
      figures; and figures whose clothing or equipment practi-
      cally conceals their human form .... ½
      (Ubangis, Mickey Mouse, Superman, diver in diving suit)
   c. Unusual fantasy figures or culturally and/or historically ex-
      tremely distant 0
      (Neanderthal men)

The average ratings of all the *M* responses are added algebraically, counting each *M—* response as —1. The resulting raw score is converted into a weighted score by this table:

M RAW SCORE	WEIGHTED SCORE
5 to 10.9	3
3 to 4.9 or 11 to 15.9	2
1 to 2.9 or 16 to 20.0	1
Less than 1 or more than 20.0 . . . .`.	0
Less than 0 (any minus score) . . . .—1	

B. Animal Movement Responses

Each *FM* response is rated according to the three criteria below and then the *average* of these three ratings is assigned to that response.

CRITERIA	RATING
1. Amount of movement in space	
a. Increasing living space	1
(running, jumping, growling at each other)	
b. Decreasing living space	½
(crouching, stooping, bending over)	
c. Merely alive	0
(sleeping, lying down, sitting, standing)	
2. Freedom in seeing movement	
a. Spontaneously sees action	1
b. Uses intermediary means of representing movement	½
(picture of an animal flying or climbing, totem animal)	
c. Reluctantly given in inquiry or follows only from the logic	
of the situation	0
3. Cultural distance	
a. Existing animals common to the culture	1
(dog, bear, cat, crab, elephant, lion, spider, cat, monkey)	

b. Existing rare animals, common extinct animals, or culturally popular fantasy animals .... ½
   (octopus, dinosaur, Mickey Mouse)
c. Unusual fantasy or culturally extremely distant animals .. 0
   (Pegasus, Push-me-pull-me, Cerberus, amoeba)

The average ratings of all the *FM* responses are added algebraically,
counting each *FM*— response as —1. The resulting score is converted
into a weighted score by this table:

	WEIGHTED
FM RAW SCORE	SCORE
2 or more	1
1 to 1.9; or if raw score FM is twice raw score M or more ...	0
0 to 0.9	—1
Less than 0 (any minus score)	—2

C. Inanimate Movement Responses

Each *m* response is rated according to one of the criteria below.

CRITERIA	RATING
1. Natural and mechanical forces	
a. Counter-gravity	1
(explosion, rocket, mechanical motion, geyser, volcano)	
b. Due to gravity	½
(falling, rock poised precariously)	
2. Abstract forces	
a. Expressions projected onto inanimate objects	1
(pumpkin with devilish expression)	
b. Repulsion or attraction	½
(This keeps two people apart or brings them together; this	
is the center from which all power emanates)	
c. Dissipation	0
(Card VIII, lower *D*, melting ice cream; Card IX, deterio-	
rating mess)	

The ratings of all the *m* responses are added algebraically, counting each *Fm—* as —1. The *m* raw score is then converted into a weighted score by this table:

m RAW SCORE	WEIGHTED SCORE
3 to 5.9	2
1 to 2.9 or 6 to 10.0	1
0 to 0.9 or more than 10.0	0
Less than 0 (any minus score)	—1

D. Shading Responses

Each shading item is rated according to the weightings below. The individual ratings are added algebraically. The total thus obtained is multiplied by 3 and divided by the total number of shading entries. This is done regardless of whether these entries are ratings for single responses or for characteristics of the total record. This figure is then used as the total weighted score for shading responses.

RESPONSES	RATING
Fc (warm, soft, or transparent)	1
FK	1
Fc denial	½
Fc (cold or hard)	½
K, KF	0
Fc (shading used as color)	—½
Fk, kF, k	—½
cF	—½
Fc—	— 1
FK—	— 1
Fc (diseased organ)	— 1
c	— 1
Characteristics of total record:	
Shading evasion	—½
Shading insensitivity	— 1

E. Color Responses

Each color item is rated according to the weightings below. The individual ratings are added algebraically. The total thus obtained is multiplied by 3 and divided by the total number of color ratings. This figure is then used as the total weighted score for color responses.

RESPONSES	RATING
FC (color is important, essential and meaningful part of the concept)	1
CF (explosive or passive)	½
C_{des}	½
Color denial	½
C_{sym} (euphoric)	½
Unscorable color remarks expressing discomfort	½
(Card II: that red doesn't mean anything)	
F↔C (forced, overeasy bland)	0
F/C, C/F	0
C_{sym} (dysphoric)	—½
Color in diseased organ	—½
CF (explosive but given without any sign of affect)	—½
FC—	— 1
CF—	— 1
C, C_n	— 1
Color contamination	— 1

F. Form Level

Each response is rated for form level in the usual manner. Then the *average* form-level rating is used as a weighted score except for the following modifications:

1. The occurrence of any "weakening" specifications anywhere in the record (specifications where 0.5 is subtracted from the form-level

rating of any response) reduces the weighted form-level rating for the entire record by 0.5.

2. The existence of discrepancies between the lowest form-level rating for any response in a record, provided it is a minus score, and the highest form-level rating for any response in the same record of at least 3.0, reduces the weighted form-level rating for the same record by 1.0.

3. These two may be cumulative in the same record. That is, where both occur in a record, 1.5 is subtracted from the average form-level rating.

G. Final Prognostic Score

The final prognostic score is the sum of the six separate weighted scores described above. Tentatively, the following meanings have been assigned to different ranges of prognostic score:

RANGE	GROUP	MEANING
17 to 13	I	The person is almost able to help himself. A very promising case that just needs a little help.
12 to 7	II	Not quite so capable as the above case to work out his problems himself but with some help is likely to do pretty well.
6 to 2	III	Better than 50-50 chance; any treatment will be of some help.
1 to — 2	IV	50-50 chance.
—3 to — 6	V	A difficult case that may be helped somewhat but is generally a poor treatment prospect.
—7 to —12	VI	A hopeless case.

Delineation of Some Concepts Used in the Rorschach Prognostic Rating Scale

Increasing and Decreasing Living Space

These terms are a modification of Rorschach's flexor and extensor movements. It seems preferable to use the physical relationship between the individual and his environment as a point of departure, rather than the activity of specific muscles, especially since both types of muscles are involved in any movement. Any activity that increases the living space by means of an outgoing movement (such as running) or through outgoing communication (talking together) therefore belongs to the first category. Any movement that decreases the amount of space used by the body (for example, kneeling) or has a withdrawing tendency in regard to communication (crying) belongs to the second category.

Shading Denial, Shading Evasion, Shading Insensitivity

These three forms of *not* using the shading stimuli constructively can be differentiated in the following way.

In the case of *shading insensitivity* no reference to shading occurs either in the performance proper or in the inquiry. None of the concepts are used that subjects usually connect with the shading stimuli. In testing the limits the insensitive subject may either not understand the most explicit explanation of the possible use of shading stimuli, or show very little interest in it. However, there is usually no marked conscious resistance to the idea.

Shading evasion is expressed in various forms:

1. The shading stimuli may be used in the strongly shaded cards but not in their most usual and most conspicuously shaded areas. (For example, the bottom center of Card IV may be called an "animal skin" instead of the rest of the card; or the top center D in Card VI may be used instead of the large lower area.)
2. The shaded areas are used in a more usual manner; but as an answer to the question "What made you think of an animal skin?"

the subject will point in the inquiry to the ragged or fuzzy edge rather than emphasize the texture of the blot.

3. The common shading areas are used, but the quality of the shading responses is vague and indicates in content symbolism an attempt to avoid direct contact sensations. (Example, in Card IV: "About the only thing I could see would be maybe something under water.")

4. In testing the limits the shading evader will show little or no resistance in accepting the usual justification of shading responses.

Shading denial presupposes the production of at least two of the usual shading responses in the usual areas during the performance proper. In the inquiry the subject will go to any length to avoid mentioning the usual shading stimuli. In testing the limits he might even refuse to accept as possible or logical the usual justification for shading responses.

Rationale Implications

Shading denial obviously represents the most ego-defensive response to shading, indicating a conscious conflict about the subject's need for affection. Shading evasion shows some reluctance to accept one's need for affection. Shading insensitivity is the most detrimental form of unresponsiveness to shading.

Shading Used as Color

The use of shading as a symbolic representation of bright colors, or as a photographic achromatic reproduction of these colors, represents one of the instances of "abortive sublimation" (see page 581). The bright colors have to be mentioned spontaneously and specifically by the subjects in order to justify the negative rating. A simple description of the surface characteristics as a "beautiful patterning" does not suffice.

Color Denial

The prerequisites for establishing this category are: (1) A response is given to one of the colored areas (like "hair ribbon" to center red in Card III) in which the majority of subjects would spontaneously mention the color as one of the determinants. (2) There is an outright denial by the subject during the analogy period of the inquiry that color could have been used as a determinant for the response.

Rationale Implications

This attitude shows more ego-defensiveness than does an over-easy use of color. It therefore carries a more positive rating as compared with the latter.

Color Contamination

Most of the truly contaminatory responses (like Rorschach's "grass-bear" in Card IX) contain color as one of the contaminated elements. All the prerequisites for a true contamination must be fulfilled, namely: (1) The two contaminated determinants must be located in the same blot area. (2) The contaminated concept must be not only unrealistic, but also actually meaningless or silly. (3) The subject should not display any feeling of humor or lack of seriousness in regard to the concept.

"Weakening" Specification

The "weakening" specification can be inaccurate in one of two ways: it either attaches to the concept a characteristic that does not exist in reality for the sole purpose of making use of a stimulus detail located in this area (as by adding a second tail to an animal), or it utilizes, for elaborating a specific part of a concept, an area that cannot be used for this purpose without qualifying references (for example, calling the top center d of Card I the "face" of the "bat" without being able to explain in the inquiry the split between the two round bumps). In either case such an inaccurate specification should not destroy the form level of the rest of the response.

Use of the Rating Scale

During the two years since the RPRS was first published, the suggestion that the scale be used experimentally has been widely accepted—judging from informal communications. The gist of these communications can be described as encouraging for the clinical use of the scale and stimulating for further clinical research with it. Systematic reports of these experiences are just beginning to appear in print. Eight references are listed below [1–8].

References

1. Johnson, E. Z. "Klopfer's Prognostic Scale Used with Raven's Progressive Matrices in Play Therapy Prognosis," *J. Proj. Tech.*, 1953, 17, 320–326.

2. Kirkner, F. J.; Wisham, W.; and Giedt, F. H. "A Report on the Validity of the Rorschach Prognostic Rating Scale," *J. Proj. Tech.*, 1953, 17, no. 4.

3. ——, and Wisham, W. "A preliminary Report on the Predictability of the Rorschach Prognostic Rating Scale," *J. Proj. Tech.*, 1951, 15, 421–422. (Abstract)

4. Klopfer, B. "Introduction: The Development of a Prognostic Rating Scale," *J. Proj. Tech.*, 1951, 15, 421. (Abstract)

5. Mindess, H. "Predicting Patients' Responses to Psychotherapy: A Preliminary Study Designed to Investigate the Validity of the 'Rorschach Prognostic Rating Scale,'" *J. Proj. Tech.*, 1953, 17, 327–334.

6. ——. "Application of the Scale to a Group of Psychiatric Patients," *J. Proj. Tech.*, 1951, 15, 422. (Abstract)

7. Seacat, G. F. "Factors Related to Duration of Psychotherapy," *J. Proj. Tech.*, 1951, 15, 422. (Abstract)

8. Sheehan, J., and Spiegelman, M. "Application of the Scale to a Group of Stutterers," *J. Proj. Tech.*, 1951, 15, 422. (Abstract)

The Freudian and Jungian Approaches
to Development of Ego and Self*

Preliminary Considerations

A source of possible confusion is the use, by Freudians and Jungians alike, of the term *ego.* While this is not the place to discuss the
complicated relationships denoted by this term, certain differences
in the use of this concept by Freudians and Jungians should be
pointed out, even at the price of over-simplification.

When Jungians use the term *ego,* they usually refer to that total
aspect of an individual's personality of which he is aware and with
which he identifies. The system *ego* is mostly conscious, and the
mythological figure of the "hero" is the symbolic expression of the
system *ego-consciousness.* This includes the conscious system of values, the conscience, which, in the Freudian formulation, is part of
the super-ego.

When Freudians employ the term *ego,* they refer to a complex of
functions which mediate between the demands of the drive impulses,

---

* This Appendix was prepared by Jack Fox. As noted on page 565, the Appendix sup-
plements Chapter 16.

The author would like to express his gratitude to Dr. E. Pumpian-Mindlin and
Dr. René A. Spitz for their careful reading of the manuscript and the many valuable
and helpful suggestions they offered. The responsibility for the formulations is, of
course, the author's.

the super-ego, and the external situation. Genetically, this system is developed out of introjected relations between the id and reality * and a series of identifications and is closely bound up with a growing and increasingly differentiated body image. Functionally, the ego-system regulates the gratification, or the postponement of gratification, of drive impulses in concordance with the demands of the super-ego and the requirements of external reality. Another important function is the defense of the system against unacceptable drive impulses, threatening anxiety, overwhelming shame, or severe guilt. Topographically, part of the system *ego* is conscious, part unconscious. Particularly, the defensive functions of the ego are largely unconscious. A large part of the super-ego, especially introjected parental commands and prohibitions, is also unconscious.

In the Jungian system, this unconscious part of the Freudian ego and super-ego is largely included in the complex "shadow." The "shadow" refers to that total aspect of the personality of which the individual is not aware because he cannot accept it and identify with it. He tends to project it upon objects in his environment.

Another concept that needs clarification in its use is represented by the term "archaic." Jungians understand by "archaic" forces a system of unconscious complexes which represent man's inherent instinctual and spiritual forces. When these forces break through into

---

* "It is easy to see that the ego is that part of the id which has been modified by the direct influence of the external world acting through the Pcpt-Cs; in a sense it is an extension of the surface differentiation." [7, page 29]

Pcpt-Cs is an abbreviation standing for "the system Perception-Consciousness."

Recent formulations of ego development by Hartmann, Kris, and Loewenstein [16, 17, 18] emphasize innate factors of ego development. Consequently, they postulate an original undifferentiated state of ego and id.

"In the earliest postnatal stage it is difficult to disentangle the nuclei of functions that will later serve the ego from those that we shall attribute to the id. Also, it is often hard to decide what part of it could already be described in terms of mental functioning. Neither is there at that stage any differentiation of the self from the world outside. That there is no ego in the sense we use the term for later stages, seems clear; what the state of the id is at that level is unknown. This stage we may term the undifferentiated stage. . . . This conception of the earliest postnatal stage seems to be in agreement with Freud's later thoughts. At least once, in the 'Outline' (1939) he speaks of '. . . the id, or rather, the undifferentiated ego-id.' " [10, page 17]

This represents a rapprochement with the Jungian point of view which calls this undifferentiated stage the "uroboros." [14]

consciousness, they do so in pictorial forms. These pictorial representations are characteristically universal and must be considered a symbolic expression of these underlying forces. The pictorial symbols are called "archetypes." This is an over-simplification of the Jungian view, inasmuch as the archetype is not only a symbolic expression of an underlying force, but also an organ of psychic representation, functioning, and regulation.

In the Freudian system, the term "archaic" refers to the developmental and functional level of the primary process in which ideation is pictorial, symbolic, magical, and is primarily regulated by wish-fulfillment, or the pleasure principle. Many symbolic representations in the primary processes of the Freudians are identical with the Jungian archetypes of instinctual impulses. A major difference appears in the interpretation of the phenomenological data. The Freudians place their emphasis upon the genetic aspects and point to their instinctual derivation, while Jungians emphasize the prospective aspects and point out their directional meaning for future development.

While Freudians do not stress the inheritance of spiritual or moral forces as much as Jungians do, Freud himself pointed this out as a strong possibility and includes these among the archaic forces of the super-ego [6].*

---

* "Through the forming of the ideal all the traces left behind in the id by biological developments and by the vicissitudes gone through by the human race are taken over by the ego and lived through again by it in each individual. Owing to the way in which it is formed, the ego-ideal has a great many contacts with the phylogenetic endowment of each individual—his archaic heritage." [7, page 48]

"The experiences undergone by the ego seem at first lost to posterity; but when they have been repeated often enough and with sufficient intensity in the successive individuals of many generations, they transform themselves, so to say, into experiences of the id, the imprint of which is preserved by inheritance. Thus, in the id, which is capable of being inherited, are stored up vestiges of the existences led by countless former egos, and, when the ego forms its super-ego out of the id, it may perhaps only be reviving images of egos that have passed away and be securing them a resurrection." [7, page 52]

It is for this reason that in Jungian analysis the analyst is intent on separating the images of the actual parents from the archetypal parental images which the child projects upon his parents. Likewise, clinicians who deal with children and their parents frequently are aware of the considerable discrepancy between the child's image of his parents, and the impression they (the clinicians) gain of the parents by direct contact.

The "Self" is a distinctly Jungian concept which finds little or no parallel in the Freudian system.

Jung conceives the system ego-consciousness to be in dynamic opposition (in Gegensatzspannung: polarity of tension) to the system of the unconscious. In the first half of a person's life span the system ego-consciousness is the center of self-regulation or homeostasis of the total system. During this period the organism is primarily engaged in the conquest of outer reality for the purpose of the perpetuation of the race and the establishment of security for himself and his descendants and fulfills a natural purpose (Naturzweck). For this struggle with external reality, the system ego-consciousness is able to usurp a major share of the available libido or life energy.

Normally, when a person enters the second half of his life span, his position in the external world is relatively firmly established. His internal reality, which has been neglected in the meanwhile, demands now more attention—presumably, due to the damming up of its demands—and is able to usurp libido from the ego system. The system ego-consciousness which, heretofore, has perceived itself as the *rider* of the horse, begins to realize now that it is merely the *horse's* rider. The individual feels himself at the mercy of forces he does not understand. He must turn inward in order to come to terms with these forces. Thus, a complete change of values must take place. The conquest of external reality becomes relatively unimportant; the understanding of inner reality becomes an imperative of major importance.

In this process of turning inward, the individual becomes aware of the vast store of spiritual and cultural resources within himself and the relative insignificance of the system ego-consciousness. In this process of the development of inner awareness, he catches glimpses of a new center of self-regulation, or homeostasis, the Self. With the ascendancy of the Self as a center of homeostasis, the unconscious and the ego are no longer dynamically opposed, but are related to each other as parts of the large Self; the opposition of the ego and the unconscious is resolved by their synthesis into the Self (a striking parallel to Hegel's philosophy where the opposition of the Absolute Idea and Absolute Nature is resolved by their synthesis into the Absolute Spirit).

With this turning inward, man becomes culturally creative and productive and thereby fulfills the second great purpose of life: the purpose of culture (Kulturzweck).

In recent years, the term "self" has come to be increasingly used by Freudian theoreticians to distinguish the object of perception (the self) from the ego as a complex of functions [16, 17, 18].

The Freudian Approach

In the Freudian view the newborn infant has no ego. Excitation and discharge follow each other closely, with hardly any delay. Excitation is presumably and probably experienced as painful and discharge as satisfying, leading to sleep. This feeling of satisfaction is called the "oceanic feeling." The "oceanic feeling" is the experience of satisfaction obtained from the union with the mother's breast at a time when a difference between self and object does not as yet exist; also, ego and nonego are still one. It is an experience of unity with the universe, a feeling of something unlimited, boundless, like the ocean.

> Originally the ego included everything, later it detaches from itself the external world. The ego-feeling we are aware of now is thus a shrunken vestige of a far more extensive feeling—the feeling which embraced the universe and expressed an inseparable connection of the ego with the external world. [5, page 13]

It is, perhaps, best likened to the feeling the fetus may experience in the womb—in that state which is mythologically represented by the "land of milk and honey," the "Schlaraffenland," and other symbolic expressions, in which gratification follows upon the mere experiencing of a need. The "oceanic feeling" is related to the Jungian concept of the "uroboros," an original state of wholeness from which the polarities "conscious-unconscious," "ego-nonego," will later emerge [14].

In later development, the longing for the oceanic feeling becomes the quest for self-esteem, that is, for narcissistic supplies from the parental figures—and later from the super ego—which re-establish in part the oceanic feeling in the feeling of being loved and cared for (and, ultimately, in being fed milk when the need arises).

As a defense against too much influx of excitation, which tends to produce traumatic states, the infant begins to develop an apparatus of perception by means of which it can shut off the influx of excitation from the outside and return to a state of sleep. Thus, the first function of the perceptive apparatus is not perception but protection against the influx of stimuli. Making use of the property of adaptation of the sensory organs, the infant develops a shield against stimuli, a stimulus barrier [4, pages 32–35].*

However, since the infant cannot shut off excitation from within, but is dependent upon objects in the external world for the reduction of this sort of tension, the first longing for an object emerges. This situation creates also the first basic conflict: the conflict between stimulus hunger (the longing for the object) and the longing for the oceanic feeling, which implies the abolition of the object. Both aspects of this conflict express themselves in the primitive oral way in which the infant deals with the world. The mechanism of introjection satisfies the longing for the object by incorporation; at the same time, this incorporation causes the object to disappear and re-establishes the oceanic feeling. This is the primitive matrix from which the later structures of the personality emerge. The constitution of the first oral object constitutes at the same time the primitive ego, with a primitive reality testing (the longing for the object) and a primitive passive-receptive mastery. Fenichel [1] states:

> In this primary identification, instinctual behavior and ego behavior are not differentiated from each other. It is all one: the first (oral) object love, the first motor reaction to external stimuli, and the first perception. Identifications play a great part in the process of building up the subsequent ego, whose nature therefore depends on the personali-

---

* Later on, when there is a first differentiation of inside and outside, the stimulus barrier is applied also against excessive internal stimuli by treating such stimuli as though they came from the outside. (This is the primary model of projection.) [4, page 35]

ties of the persons around the infant. The imitation of the external world by oral incorporation is also the basis for the primitive mode of thinking, called magic, to be discussed later.*

The origin of the ego and the origin of the sense of reality are but two aspects of one developmental step. This is inherent in the definition of the ego as that part of the mind which handles reality. The concept of reality also creates the concept of the ego. We are individuals inasmuch as we feel ourselves separate and distinct from others.†

The constitution of the first oral object also brings about this separateness and distinctness, as it drives the first wedge between the inner and the outer world (inner versus outer sense organs) and something that senses—later perceives—both. This something is the beginning of the body image which serves as the core for later ego development.

This early separation of the self from the external world and the ego from the id is at once an atomistic process—having at its base the development of a number of ego nuclei, in connection with the various needs of the infant—and yet a vague, global process, since the external world is still largely undifferentiated.

The differences between the perceptions of infants and adults have the consequence that they experience the world differently. Observations made on psychotics, who have regressed to the primitive modes of perception, confirm the fact that they experience the world in a more vague and less differentiated way. Objects are not necessarily sharply distinguished from one another or from the ego or from parts of it. The first images are large in extent, all enveloping, and inexact. They do not consist of elements that are later put together, but rather of units, wholes, which only later are recognized as containing different elements. Not only are perception and motility inseparable, but also the perception of many sense organs overlap. The more primitive senses, especially the kinesthetic senses and the data of depth sensibility (proprioception) prevail.‡

While primary, unlimited omnipotence is associated with the oceanic feeling, the constitution of the first oral object limits this omnipotence and brings about the projection of this omnipotence

---

* O. Fenichel, *The Psychoanalytic Theory of Neurosis,* page 37. Copyright 1945 by W. W. Norton & Company, Inc., and used with their permission.

† *Ibid.,* page 35.

‡ *Ibid.,* page 38.

upon the external object. The omnipotent object is now the one that brings about satisfaction and a return of the oceanic feeling; consequently, this object must be mastered.

> The stage of primary narcissism, in which omnipotence was felt and "mastery" was no problem yet, is thus followed by a period of passive-receptive mastery in which difficulties are overcome by influencing powerful external objects to give what is needed. Whenever the subsequent active types of mastery fail or do not offer any hope of success, a temptation is at hand to fall back to the state of passive-receptive mastery.*

Likewise, the oral mode of incorporation is the matrix—and an archaic model—of love and hate in their later differentiated forms. In its primitive form, it is neither love nor hate; it is merely the taking in of the object which satisfies the stimulus hunger, but which, simultaneously, brings about the disappearance of the object. Differentiation begins when incorporation serves to heighten self-esteem on the one hand, while on the other beginning feelings of aggression accrue to the mode of incorporation and give it the destructive, swallowing aspect.

This early period of beginning ego formation is characterized by the primacy of the "primary process." The mental life of the infant is dominated by pictorial and symbolic representation. This representation is predominantly "autistic"—that is, motivated by drives and therefore wish-fulfilling in character. The first object representation is probably that of the satisfying object. On the other hand, the first judgmental function of the ego is a crude differentiation between that which can be satisfyingly incorporated and that which is unsatisfactory and painful and must be spit out. A fusion of these primitive modes of object representation and judgment results in more effective reality testing. Now, object representations can be judged with respect to their incorporability. Moreover, the fact that wish-fulfilling object representations are often not followed by a decrease in tension, leads to the differentiation between reality and fantasy.

At this early stage, the ego is often threatened by "primal anxiety."

---

* Fenichel, *op. cit.*, page 41. By permission.

This "primal anxiety" is produced by a swamping of the weak ego by an excess of excitation which breaks through the stimulus barrier and which the ego is unable to master. This swamping of the ego with excitation is relieved by emergency vegetative discharges, such as crying and diffuse motor movements. These vegetative discharges are involuntary and therefore beyond mastery by the weak ego. Consequently, excessive excitation and emergency vegetative discharges are experienced by the helpless infant as painful traumatic states. The experience of these painful traumata is referred to as "primal anxiety."

With the development of object representation and the appearance of a primitive ability to judge, the function of anticipation emerges. With the emergence of this function, the ego has at its disposal an instrument by means of which it can avoid "primal anxiety." The ego can now anticipate in fantasy the consequences of certain cues and actions. Some of these consequences it will recognize (judge) as dangerous because they lead to trauma. This recognition is also experienced as anxiety. However, this anxiety is qualitatively and quantitatively different from "primal anxiety." While "primal anxiety" is the painful experience of trauma of which the organism is the victim, anxiety is a signal that trauma is threatening and permits the ego to initiate action—voluntary motor movements—to avoid the traumatic situation. The ego is now the master of the situation instead of the victim. In this way, anxiety (a homeopathic dosage of "primal anxiety") becomes ego-building, in contrast to "primal anxiety," which is ego-destroying.

One must keep in mind that the boundary between ego and non-ego at this early stage is tenuous. Often, much of what is later ego is included in the non-ego, and vice-versa. Moreover, what is at one time ego may at the next moment be non-ego. The characteristics of objects come to be incorporated into the ego by a primitive mode of actual identification and imitation (fascination), while aspects of the ego, such as the pressures of drives, are often projected into the non-ego. In this manner, inner characteristics are ascribed to objects, and object characteristics are perceived as ego characteristics. This gives the primary process the flavor of animism and magic.

Since perception is still more or less global, similarities are often taken for identities and parts for wholes; in this manner a pictorial representation or symbol comes to be over-determined in meaning; it can stand for any number of objects and processes. The animistic and magic mode also impresses upon the infantile fears the character of the talion ("eye for eye, tooth for tooth") principle; for example, the desire to destroy by incorporation becomes the fear of being swallowed.

The maturation of the motor apparatus becomes crucial in the further development and strengthening of the ego. As the child learns to control his limbs and learns to walk, he becomes less helpless and dependent upon his environment when confronted by the threat of anxiety. This furthers the development of the ego in three directions. (1) With the help of his primitive ability to judge, he can now repeat in his fantasy the states in which he was overcome by anxiety and experiment with a variety of pictorial representations of his own actions until he hits upon one by which he can master the situation. This brings about a relief from anxiety and, secondarily, pleasure—functional pleasure. In that manner, mastery becomes invested with libido to the extent to which it is able to overcome threatening anxiety. (2) The child is now able to anticipate in his imagination anxiety-threatening situations and to experiment with a variety of hallucinated motor activity to cope with them. (3) When pressed by his own instinctual drives, he can hallucinate a variety of actions until he finds a mode that is least dangerous and most satisfying. To the extent to which this anticipatory hallucination is interposed between drive impulses and final motor discharge, the child's actions become purposeful. Furthermore, this process builds up frustration tolerance and facilitates the further development of reality testing, since the trial action can be verified or falsified in the action proper.* To quote Fenichel again:

> It is, from a psychological point of view, a gradual substituting of actions for mere discharge reactions. This is achieved through the interposing of a time period between stimulus and reaction, by the ac-

---

* All three of these principles also underlie the child's play activities. The first can also be observed in the repetitive dreams of people suffering from the effects of severe trauma.

quisition of a certain tension tolerance, that is, of an ability to bind primitive reaction impulses by counter-cathexis. The prerequisite for an action is, besides mastery of the bodily apparatus, the development of the function of judgment. This means the ability to anticipate the future in the imagination by "testing" reality, by trying in an active manner and in a small dosage what might happen to one passively and in an unknown dosage. . . . The ability to judge reality and the ability to tolerate tensions are two aspects of one and the same faculty. To direct one's actions according to external necessity means to be able to foresee dangers and to fight or to avoid them.*

Moreover, the development of controlled motility and purposeful action facilitates the development of the child's independence from his environment and, consequently, leads to a further separation of the ego from the non-ego as well as to functional pleasure in this independence, which expresses itself in the form of self-assertion.

The development of language is the most important step in the transition from the primary to the secondary process. The ability to attach word symbols to objects and parts of objects, as well as to their representations, sharpens the perceptual process and greatly facilitates the discrimination of details as well as of differences. Of course, this leads also to a sharpening of reality testing and a facilitation of mastery. It is evident that the transition from the primary process to the secondary process is a gradual one. Many aspects of the primary process function side by side with the developing features of the secondary process and mutually influence each other. The interpenetration of the two processes is best exemplified by the "word-magic," which becomes prevalent at this period. To name an object is to exert control over it. This word-magic is a function of the increased ability for reality testing and mastery which has been brought about by the use of language, as well as a function of the magic identity of the object and its representation which is derived from the primary process.

The faculty of speech changes the anticipating functions of the ego; the establishment of name symbols for things consolidates consciousness and gives the possibility of anticipating events in the models of words.†

---

* Fenichel, *op. cit.*, page 42. Used by permission.
† *Ibid.*, page 43.

The hegemony of the secondary process over the primary process is established when anticipated events, the trial actions, are expressed in words rather than in pictorial representation. It is then only that thinking becomes logical and syntactical, rather than pictorial and syncretistic. While the primary process is primarily governed by the pleasure principle and is characterized by mobile libido cathexes, the secondary process is governed predominantly by the reality principle and is characterized by bound libido cathexes. The process of the establishment of the hegemony of the secondary over the primary process is a gradual one, extending through the latency period, and becomes firmly established only during adolescence. A crucial pre-condition, however, seems to be the successful negotiation of the Oedipus complex.

The resolution of the Oedipus complex is crucial also in the establishment of another aspect of the ego, namely the super-ego. While, however, the ego is governed primarily by the reality principle and by rationality, the super-ego partakes more of the qualities of the id, since it is the psychic instance of the parental dispensations of approval and disapproval and the totality of the parent-child relationships during the affect-charged and danger-fraught Oedipal situation. Thus, while it is a late precipitate of the relations between id and reality, it is governed by imperatives, rather than by rationality, and therefore comes into opposition to the ego as well as the id.

The energies of the ego derive from the id. The aggressive drives, when partially neutralized and employed by the ego, serve the function of discrimination, separation, and negative judgments, or the analytic functions of the ego. On the other hand, the libidinous drives, when harnessed by the ego, are employed in its synthetic functions. This synthetic function expresses itself in the mediation between the claims of the id, the super-ego, and the external reality. It expresses itself also in the relation of various experiences to each other, and in the ability to generalize and to simplify. The "need for causality" is also an expression of this synthetic function, derived in part from the child's curiosity about the reproductive function [15].

The constructive ego functions develop maximally under optimal conditions—that is, when the developing organism is spared exposure to overwhelming anxiety and is free from overprotection which smothers the development of mastery and reality testing. This overwhelming anxiety becomes particularly important when it is connected with the drive impulses. This may arise (1) during the period of passive mastery when the drives mount to an intolerable intensity and produce a severe trauma before external relief is brought about; (2) through reality factors, such as burning oneself severely, or threats and prohibitions; (3) by fears arising from the operation of the talion principle; (4) because of guilt. The intolerable anxiety is avoided and eliminated from consciousness by the development of various defense mechanisms against the drive impulses. While the anxiety is thus eliminated, the drive impulses as well as the ego efforts that keep them in check are thus prevented from further maturation. A fixation has taken place which keeps some energy bound that would otherwise be available to the constructive functions of the ego. Fixation also occurs as a consequence of over-gratification. Over-gratification leads to a reluctance to give up old satisfactions and go on to new ones.*

There seems to be a reciprocal relationship between the constructive functions and ego defensiveness. The more energy is bound in defensive efforts, the less is available to the constructive functions of the ego.

> The purpose of the defense-mechanisms is to avert dangers of various kinds. It cannot be disputed that they are successful; it is doubtful whether the ego can altogether do without them during its development, but it is also certain that they themselves may become dangerous. Not infrequently it turns out that the ego has paid too high a price for the services which these mechanisms render. The expenditure of energy necessary to maintain them and the ego-restrictions which they almost invariably entail prove a heavy burden on the psychic economy. [2, page 392]

While a part of the drive impulses and of the ego are thus split off from the main body of the personality and prevented from further

---

* Fixation is also a function of hereditary factors, such as the strength of various component instincts (partial instincts).

development, the resulting symptom or symptoms, which are an expression of the inadequate elimination of the conflict, are synthesized into the ego. This occurs either by a permanent deformation of the ego, so that the originally ego-alien symptom becomes an ego-syntonic character attitude, or by psychic elaboration of the symptom and its inclusion in the ego economy so that "epinosic" or secondary gain can be derived from it. To quote Nunberg:

It seems, in fact, that a certain degree of hypofunction of the ego in regard to synthesis is an evidence of its weakness and provides a favorable basis for the encroachment of repression or other defense mechanisms. On the other hand, the power of resistance of this function is so great that the ego, having been split by the symptom formation, intensifies its endeavors to assimilate the symptoms, to take it into its organization. The end result is that the entire symptom or an individual striving is now accepted by the ego, although it had been rejected at the onset of the process of illness (secondary gain from illness). [15, pages 191–192]

References

1. Fenichel, O. *The Psychoanalytic Theory of Neurosis.* New York: W. W. Norton & Company, Inc.; 1945.

2. Freud, S. "Analysis Terminable and Interminable," *Collected Papers,* Vol. V. London: Hogarth Press; 1950.

3. ——. *The Basic Writings.* New York: The Modern Library, Inc.; 1938.

4. ——. *Beyond the Pleasure Principle.* New York: Liveright Publishing Corp.; 1950.

5. ——. *Civilization and Its Discontents.* London: Hogarth Press; 1949.

6. ——. *Collected Papers.* London: Hogarth Press; 1953.

7. ——. *The Ego and the Id.* London: Hogarth Press; 1949.

8. ——. *Gesammelte Werke,* Vol. 13. London: Imago Publishing Co.; 1940.

9. ——. *A General Introduction to Psychoanalysis.* New York: Garden City Publishing Co.; 1943.

10. Hartmann, H. "The Mutual Influences in the Development of Ego and Id," *The Psychoanalytic Study of the Child,* Vol. 7. New York: International Universities Press; 1952.

11. Jung, C. G. *The Integration of Personality.* New York: Farrar and Rinehart; 1939.

12. ——. *Psychological Types or the Psychology of Individuation.* New York: Harcourt, Brace & Co., Inc.; 1923.

13. ——. *Ueber Die Psychologie Des Unbewussten.* Zurich: Rascher; 1943.

14. Neumann, E. *Die Ursprungsgeschichte Des Bewusstseins.* Zurich: Rascher; 1949.

15. Nunberg, H. *Practice and Theory of Psychoanalysis,* Nervous and Mental Disease Monographs, No. 74, 1948.

16. *The Psychoanalytic Study of the Child,* Vol. 2. New York: International Universities Press; 1947.

17. ——. Vol. 5, 1950.

18. ——. Vol. 7, 1952.

19. Schilder, P. E. *Mind: Perception and Thought in Their Constructive Aspects.* New York: Columbia University Press; 1942.

Index of Names*

---

* Page numbers in Roman type are text pages. Page numbers in *italics* refer to listings of an author's works in the References at ends of chapters.

Index of Subject Matter

Card	Page on which mentioned
IV	14, 29–30, 31–32, 38, 41, 64, 73, 82, 84–85, 87, 103, 110, 113, 122, 124, 135, 146, 147–148, 148–149, 150–151, 155, 162, 220, 226–227, 228–229, 230, 323, 324, 329, 332, 333, 335, 345, 346, 348, 385, 393–394, 396, 419, 434, 440, 616–617, 624, 628–629, 641, 662–664, 669, 681, 683, 696, 697
V	33–36, 41, 66, 68–69, 74, 101–102, 131–132, 156, 168, 204, 217, 219, 220, 225, 230, 233–234, 323–324, 337, 348, 394–395, 398, 434, 587, 617–618, 624, 629–630, 641, 663, 664–665, 669, 681
VI	14, 53, 61, 62, 65, 67–68, 75, 81, 82, 85, 87–88, 98, 108, 117, 119, 120–121, 125, 129–130, 134–135, 136–138, 139–140, 142, 143, 147, 155–156, 168–169, 204, 213, 219, 220, 230, 234–235, 323, 329, 332, 333, 336, 345, 346, 347, 348, 386, 395–396, 434, 440, 618, 624, 630–631, 641, 663, 665–666, 669, 696
VII	25–26, 41, 54, 55, 62–63, 76, 88–89, 90, 104, 106, 114, 116, 128, 131, 135, 145, 152–153, 158, 159, 161, 169, 209, 210, 212, 230, 325, 333, 345, 386, 396–397, 419, 619–620, 631–632, 641, 666–667, 680, 683
VIII	13, 27–28, 31, 39, 41, 42–43, 51, 57–58, 60, 77, 97, 111, 120, 130–131, 138, 142, 148, 152, 170, 173, 176–178, 182, 183–184, 190, 193, 196–197, 204, 206, 208, 209, 210, 219, 222, 225, 230, 243, 266, 280, 281, 282, 297, 302, 325–326, 336, 338, 340, 345, 384, 397–398, 430, 431, 433, 434, 435, 436, 533, 583, 620–621, 632–635, 641, 668–670
IX	41, 43–44, 50–51, 52, 78, 85, 92, 100, 115–116, 117–118, 123, 125, 135, 141, 150, 154, 157, 159, 172, 178, 181, 183, 190, 193, 194, 197, 198, 208, 209, 213, 214, 216–217, 219, 220, 228, 243, 297, 298, 326–327, 338, 340, 384, 398–399, 430, 431, 433, 434, 435, 622, 635–636, 641, 670–671, 681, 683, 698
X	13, 24, 26–27, 38, 39, 41, 44–46, 55–56, 79, 80, 88, 94, 102–103, 110–111, 123–124, 161, 170, 173, 174, 178, 179, 190, 191–192, 193, 204, 206, 212, 215, 218, 220, 221, 225, 235, 243, 297, 298, 314, 327, 331, 338, 340, 384, 399–400, 419, 430, 431, 433, 434, 584, 623–624, 636–637, 641, 658, 671–672, 683

(VIII, IX, and X) %   297, 374–375, 430, 431, 647